Strategies of Peace

STUDIES IN STRATEGIC PEACEBUILDING

Series Editors

R. Scott Appleby, John Paul Lederach, and Daniel Philpott
The Joan B. Kroc Institute for International Peace Studies
University of Notre Dame

Published in the Series

STRATEGIES OF PEACE
Transforming Conflict in a Violent World
Edited by Daniel Philpott and Gerard F. Powers

Strategies of Peace

Transforming Conflict in a Violent World

Edited by
DANIEL PHILPOTT
and
GERARD F. POWERS

OXFORD
UNIVERSITY PRESS

2010

OXFORD
UNIVERSITY PRESS

Oxford University Press, Inc., publishes works that further
Oxford University's objective of excellence
in research, scholarship, and education.

Oxford   New York
Auckland   Cape Town   Dar es Salaam   Hong Kong   Karachi
Kuala Lumpur   Madrid   Melbourne   Mexico City   Nairobi
New Delhi   Shanghai   Taipei   Toronto

With offices in
Argentina   Austria   Brazil   Chile   Czech Republic   France   Greece
Guatemala   Hungary   Italy   Japan   Poland   Portugal   Singapore
South Korea   Switzerland   Thailand   Turkey   Ukraine   Vietnam

Copyright © 2010 by Oxford University Press, Inc.

Published by Oxford University Press, Inc.
198 Madison Avenue, New York, New York 10016

www.oup.com

Oxford is a registered trademark of Oxford University Press

Library of Congress Cataloging-in-Publication Data
Strategies of peace / edited by Daniel Philpott and Gerard F. Powers.
p. cm.—(Studies in strategic peacebuilding series)
ISBN 978-0-19-539591-4; 978-0-19-539590-7 (pbk.)
1. Peace-building. I. Philpott, Daniel, 1967–
II. Powers, Gerard F.
JZ5538.S7427 2010
303.6′6–dc22   2009013416

Printed in the United States of America
on acid-free paper

*To Fr. Theodore M. Hesburgh, C.S.C., with
undying gratitude*

To Mrs. Joan B. Kroc, in loving memory

*Your vision, magnanimity, and generosity
made the Kroc Institute a living reality*

Acknowledgments

This volume is the result of conversations that have taken place over several years at the Kroc Institute for International Peace Studies at the University of Notre Dame. The papers were initially presented at a conference to celebrate the twentieth anniversary of the Kroc Institute, "Strategic Peacebuilding: The State of the Art," on November 5–7, 2006. The editors thank the Kroc Institute for its financial, logistical, and intellectual support. Colette Sgambati Potts was particularly helpful in arranging the authors' meetings, in which crucial planning took place. For helpful assistance in editing, we thank Cathy Laake, Wing Wong, Alicia Quiros, Caitlin Foster, Andrew Masak, Diana Philpott, Anna Zaros, and John Ashley. We also thank Theo Calderara and Linda Donnelly at Oxford University Press for their invaluable editorial support.

Contents

Contributors

R. SCOTT APPLEBY is Professor of History and John M. Regan Jr. Director of the Kroc Institute for International Peace Studies at the University of Notre Dame.

SIMON CHESTERMAN is Global Professor and Director of the New York University School of Law Singapore Program and Associate Professor of Law at the National University of Singapore.

DAVID CORTRIGHT is Director of Policy Studies at the Kroc Institute for International Peace Studies at the University of Notre Dame.

HAL CULBERTSON is Executive Director of the Kroc Institute for International Peace Studies at the University of Notre Dame.

JEANETTE KNUTSON ENRIGHT is Educational Consultant with the International Forgiveness Institute in Madison, Wisconsin.

ROBERT D. ENRIGHT is Professor in the Department of Educational Psychology at the University of Wisconsin–Madison and a board member of the International Forgiveness Institute in Madison.

LARISSA FAST is Assistant Professor in the Department of Sociology and the Kroc Institute for International Peace Studies at the University of Notre Dame.

ANTHONY C. HOLTER is on the faculty of the Mary Ann Remick Leadership Program in the Alliance for Catholic Education and Concurrent Assistant Professor of Psychology at the University of Notre Dame.

ROBERT C. JOHANSEN is Professor of Political Science and Senior Fellow at the Kroc Institute for International Peace Studies at the University of Notre Dame.

JOHN PAUL LEDERACH is Professor of International Peacebuilding at the Kroc Institute for International Peace Studies at the University of Notre Dame.

GEORGE A. LOPEZ is the Rev. Theodore M. Hesburgh, C.S.C., Professor of Peace Studies at the Kroc Institute for International Peace Studies at the University of Notre Dame.

DANIEL PHILPOTT is Associate Professor in the Department of Political Science and the Kroc Institute for International Peace Studies at the University of Notre Dame.

GERARD F. POWERS is Director of Catholic Peacebuilding Studies at the Kroc Institute for International Peace Studies at the University of Notre Dame and is Coordinator of the Catholic Peacebuilding Network.

OLIVER P. RICHMOND is Professor in the School of International Relations, University of St. Andrews, and Director of the Centre for Peace and Conflict Studies.

NAOMI ROHT-ARRIAZA is Professor of Law at the University of California, Hastings College of the Law.

NICHOLAS SAMBANIS is Professor of Political Science at Yale University.

JACKIE SMITH is Associate Professor in the Department of Sociology and the Kroc Institute for International Peace Studies at the University of Notre Dame.

PETER WALLENSTEEN is the Richard G. Starmann Sr. Research Professor of Peace Studies at the Kroc Institute for International Peace Studies at the University of Notre Dame and the Dag Hammarskjöld Professor of Peace and Conflict Research at Uppsala University, Uppsala, Sweden.

Strategies of Peace

Introduction: Searching for Strategy in an Age of Peacebuilding

Daniel Philpott

The most recent generation in global politics might well be called the "age of peacebuilding." What merits the moniker is an intense, diverse, and global wave of efforts to end the violence and colossal injustices of civil war, genocide, dictatorship, and large-scale poverty and to foster justice and prosperity in their stead. Since 1988, the United Nations (UN) has undertaken peacebuilding operations in revolutionary number and frequency. Since the end of the Cold War, an unprecedented number of civil wars have ended through negotiated settlements. A "third wave of democracy," beginning in 1974, has seen some eighty societies move toward human rights, democracy, and the rule of law.[1] Everyone, it seems—from the UN to the World Bank to the World Social Forum to relief and development agencies—has pursued ambitious quests to end poverty. Transitional justice has become a global pursuit, involving variously national trials, vetting practices, international criminal tribunals, a permanent International Criminal Court, over thirty truth commissions, an outbreak of reparations and public apologies, and sometimes forgiveness in the political realm. Western states have struggled to establish security and the rule of law in sites of violence and anarchy—the United States in Somalia, Afghanistan, and Iraq; Germany in Afghanistan; and the European Union (EU) in Kosovo and the Democratic Republic of Congo. Human rights organizations, religious institutions, tribal elders, and citizens of domestic societies have sought to resolve and transform conflict in innovative ways, too.

But if this montage of energies describes a trend, so too it evokes urgent questions. Are all of these efforts truly ones of peacebuilding? Which have been successful? Under what conditions are they successful? Which are just? By what criteria? Do some of these efforts affect others, positively or negatively? Most of all, are there concepts, doctrines, or paradigms that tell us how peacebuilding ought to be pursued?

The dominant thinking is the "liberal peace"—dominant in that it pervades the most powerful and prestigious institutions and governments who take on the work of peacebuilding.[2] Its aims are simple and familiar: to end armed violence and to establish human rights, democracy, and market economies. Its intellectual provenance is the liberal tradition that arose from the Western Enlightenment. It envisions the UN, outside intervening states, state governments, and oppositional factions, undertaking mediation, military intervention, war settlement, disarmament, election monitoring, refugee resettlement, and the creation of free government institutions, free markets, and a free media. A cardinal virtue is finitude: when will the operation end?

Such an approach is far too narrow, this volume argues. None of the authors herein rejects human rights, democracy, economic growth, or the United Nations. But the building of peace, we propose, is far wider, deeper, and more encompassing and involves a far greater array of actors, activities, levels of society, links between societies, and time horizons than the dominant thinking recognizes. It involves the United Nations carrying out sanctions against terrorist groups in a way that also promotes good governance, human rights, and economic development in the countries where the sanctions are targeted. It involves coordinating the international prosecution of war criminals with the need to settle a civil war and the efforts of local cultures and leaders to bring peace. It involves educating the children of the next generation so as to transform their hatred into tolerance and even friendship. It involves nongovernmental organizations (NGOs) and civil society. It involves religious actors, who are all but ignored in most current thinking on peacebuilding. It involves combating inequalities that are embedded in global structures of power and wealth. It involves trials, truth commissions, and reparations, and also apology, forgiveness, and rituals of reconciliation. Not only is the broad range of these players, practices, and periods crucial for achieving a sustainable peace, each is linked to others through cause and effect, for better or for worse. Effective peacebuilding, it follows, aims to strengthen these ligatures of interdependence, accenting, deepening, and synchronizing them, and linking them further with the efforts of governments and international institutions and with the broad project of building a just peace in and between societies. Any particular effort at such strengthening may be called a strategy of peace.

What follows in the rest of this introduction is a brief analysis of the liberal peace and its critics—not because strategic peacebuilding merely defines itself against the liberal peace but because the concept becomes clearer when situated in the global conversation about peacebuilding. Prominent criticisms of the liberal peace as well as movements within the liberal peace indeed point in the direction of strategic peacebuilding. Next comes a deeper definition and description of strategic peacebuilding. The introduction closes with a conceptual map of the volume that shows how the chapters both reflect strategic peacebuilding as well as advance it through strategies of peace.

The Liberal Peace and Its Critics

When, in 1989, four decades of worldwide ideological rivalry came to an end, the global consensus on human rights, democracy, and free markets sharply expanded as did possibilities for cooperation in the UN Security Council—a "new world order," U.S. President George H. W. Bush called it. Meanwhile, large-scale ethnic conflicts raged around the world,[3] and a form of violent and impoverishing anarchy known as the "failed state" became prevalent. This was a world that, to paraphrase Voltaire's description of the Holy Roman Empire, seemed neither new nor global nor particularly orderly. These two divergent trends converged as supply and demand to yield what is known as the UN Revolution, an intense spate of efforts by the Security Council and its authorized agents to bring peace and relief to sites of calamity. Between 1987 and 1994, the Security Council increased its resolutions by four times, its peacekeeping operations by three times, its economic sanctions sevenfold, its military forces in the field from 10,000 to more than 70,000, and its budget for peacekeeping from $230 million to $3.6 billion.[4] Of its fifty-five peace operations since 1945, forty-one (75%) began after 1989.[5] Between 1989 and 1999, it sent out thirty-three peace operations, more than double the fifteen missions it had conducted during the previous four decades.[6] Between 1989 and 2005, it conducted twenty-two "post-conflict peacebuilding operations"—the most extensive sort in administrative terms.[7]

Not only the number but just as notably the ambition of these operations swelled. Exceeding the boundaries of traditional peacekeeping operations, which depend on the consent of the parties to a conflict and do not legally constitute intervention, many of these operations involved armed force sanctioned by Chapter VII of the UN Charter and overrode state sovereignty, flouting the will of at least one party to the conflict. Other operations formally remained traditional peacekeeping operations under Chapter VI but mushroomed in their mission, coming to be dubbed "Chapter six and a half." Both sorts pursued aims ranging among humanitarian relief, disarmament of armed factions, election monitoring, refugee resettlement, the construction of government institutions, and at times even running government institutions—the latter a particularly poignant departure from the principle of state sovereignty.

These operations coincided with yet another trend, a marked rise in the frequency of civil wars being settled through negotiations rather than the victory of one side or a petering out. Political scientist Monica Duffy Toft reports that between 1940 and 1989, 75 to 100 percent of civil wars in any one decade ended in military victory, whereas only a handful ended in negotiation. By contrast, during the 1990s, a sharply increased 42 percent of civil wars ended in negotiations, coming to exceed the 40 percent that ended in military victory.[8] In fact, more civil wars ended through negotiations between 1989 and 2004 than in the previous two centuries.[9] It is frequently in conjunction with such negotiations that UN operations have taken root.

The manifesto of the UN revolution was former Secretary General Boutros Boutros-Ghali's *Agenda for Peace* of 1992. Written in the heady days of the new world order, the document both reflects on the ballooning of UN operations and sets a course for its continuation. Four major peace operations were envisioned by Boutros-Ghali: (1) preventive diplomacy; (2) an expanded version of traditional peacekeeping; (3) peacemaking, which brings hostile parties to agreement generally through peaceful means but at times through Chapter VII enforcement; and finally, (4) postconflict peacebuilding, a range of efforts to consolidate peace after a settlement.[10] Subsequent documents written or commissioned by secretary generals have followed up on the proposals of *An Agenda for Peace*. Boutros-Ghali himself issued a supplement in 1995.[11] In 2000, Secretary General Kofi Annan commissioned Algerian diplomat Lakhdar Brahimi to convene a panel on peace operations, which recommended greatly enhanced institutional capacities.[12] That same year, in response to a challenge from Annan, the government of Canada convened an International Commission on Intervention and State Sovereignty to produce *Responsibility to Protect*, a set of principles intended to guide and promote humanitarian intervention.[13] In 2004, a similar panel, this one commissioned directly by Annan, produced *A More Secure World*, recommending UN reforms that included a Peacebuilding Commission to coordinate and strengthen transitions from war to peace.[14]

Here the assumptions of the liberal peace can be found—its stress on human rights, democracy, free markets, and the central role of international institutions and state governments in building peace.[15] In 1996, Boutros-Ghali issued a document called *An Agenda for Democratization*.[16] The same assumptions can be found among those departments and officials in Western governments that most involve themselves in building peace, not least the U.S. government, which has played an integral role in UN-authorized peace operations in Iraq (1990s), Somalia, Haiti, Cambodia, Bosnia, and Afghanistan, and in operations outside UN mandates in Kosovo and Iraq (1999 and 2003). They are found, too, in the Washington Consensus, a doctrine of economic development shared by the World Bank and agencies of the U.S. government stressing reduced trade barriers and public sectors and generally free market economic policies in developing country governments.[17] They are found in much scholarship on UN peace operations.[18]

In 2005, Andrew Mack reported in the *Human Security Report* that contrary to abounding myths, civil wars, genocides, and international crises all declined sharply after the end of the Cold War, and he credited UN peace operations as the primary source of the trend.[19] Have UN operations achieved such success? Scholars differ over the question, and their differences depend on the stringency of their standards.

Representative of a skeptical assessment is political scientist Roland Paris, who, focusing on the effects of postconflict peacebuilding operations in promoting political and market liberalization, finds that only two out of eleven operations between 1989 and 1999—Namibia and Croatia—were successful, measured by amelioration of the conditions that give rise to conflict and a positive impact on "the likelihood of stable and lasting peace within the host country."[20] Political scientists George Downs and Stephen John Stedman take Paris to task for adopting such demanding standards that he cannot distinguish between catastrophic failures and partial successes and hence derives too pessimistic a verdict. To them, UN operations are successful if they bring large-scale violence to an end and do so on a self-enforcing basis that allows them to exit without fear of violence resurging. On this basis, they survey sixteen UN efforts to implement peace accords between 1980 and 1997 and conclude that six were successes, four were partial successes, and six were failures.[21] Reasoning roughly similarly about success is arguably the most sophisticated study of peacebuilding to date, political scientists Michael W. Doyle and Nicholas Sambanis's *Making War and Building Peace*, an analysis, both quantitative and qualitative, of the factors that contribute to peace in the wake of civil wars. They measure success in terms of both sovereign peace, which "requires an end to civil war, undivided sovereignty, no residual violence . . . and no mass human rights abuses by the state," as well as a more robust participatory peace, which includes all of these ends but also a "minimum level of political openness." Doyle and Sambanis discover (among their other conclusions) that UN peace operations have a significant positive effect on participatory peace two years after the end of a war and that UN peace operations are positively correlated with the length of the peace, reducing peace failures by 50 percent.[22]

The debate over criteria for success need not be settled here; it ought only to be noted that even the most favorable evaluations judge the success of UN peace operations to be mixed. Doyle and Sambanis's quantitative analysis is probabilistic and includes cases of both successful and failed peace operations. One of their findings is that in the short run, UN missions have little effect on whether parties resume warfare, though in the long run their pacifying effect is stronger—again, a mixed verdict.[23] Other studies show a large proportion of peace settlements relapsing into violence. The negotiated settlements that have become so characteristic of the post–Cold War period revert to violence three times as often as civil wars that end in the victory of one side.[24] According to Charles T. Call and Elizabeth M. Cousens, most studies show that somewhere between a fifth and a third of all settled conflicts revert back to warfare within five years.[25] Andrew Mack's 2007 study showed that armed conflicts ending with a negotiated settlement experienced a reversion rate of 43 percent within five years.[26] Most arresting are two outbreaks of violence that followed the breakdown of UN peace operations: Angola in 1993, which resulted in 350,000 deaths, and Rwanda in 1994, which left 800,000 dead. Peacebuilding still has a long way to go.

Reacting to this mixed verdict, these and other analysts have proposed improvements. Paris diagnoses the problem as a rush to bring about political and economic liberalization, which undermines stability if it takes place in the absence of stable government institutions. "Institutionalization before liberalization," he counsels.[27] Downs and Stedman claim that good peacebuilding rests on a better understanding of two critical variables—the difficulty of the environment and the willingness of outside parties to intervene—and the factors that shape both. Within operations, Stedman considers demobilizing combatants to be the most important task.[28] Doyle and Sambanis somewhat complexify Downs and Stedman's model by proposing a "peacebuilding triangle" in which international capacities, levels of hostility, and local capacities are the three crucial assets for peacebuilding success.[29] Former Ambassador James Dobbins and his coauthors (who, like Downs and Stedman, think that peacebuilding operations have been a mixed success) stress sizing up the necessary resources—which they calculate with admirable precision—and adopting a multiplicity of practices.[30] Francis Fukuyama's analysis of state-building criticizes the Washington Consensus for devaluing state capacity and argues for measures that strengthen state institutions under the rule of law, but remains broadly skeptical of international efforts at peacebuilding.[31] In her study of civil wars, Toft argues that negotiated settlements, which are far less likely than victories to remain stable, will only last when an outside party offers combatants a combination of harms and benefits for adhering to it; third-party intervention alone is not enough. She particularly stresses the importance of security sector reform.[32] Inquiring into the kinds of domestic institutions and territorial settlements through which civil wars have been settled, political scientists Philip G. Roeder and Donald Rothchild analyze and argue that majoritarian democracy is far more stable than power sharing or partition.[33] All of these analyses, however, work roughly within the assumptions of the liberal peace: stable peace, human rights, democracy, and market economies are the primary ends; intergovernmental institutions, state governments, and warring parties are the primary actors. Generally—with the possible exception of certain aspects of Doyle and Sambanis's model that are stressed in Sambanis's chapter herein—they do not approach the holism of strategic peacebuilding.[34]

Yet in the principle and the practice, in the doctrine and the debate over peacebuilding during the period inaugurated by the UN revolution, one can discern a movement toward holism.[35] Since the early days of no-fly zones in Iraq and intervention in Somalia, peacebuilding operations have taken on an increasingly complex, multifold, and ambitious array of tasks. First in Cambodia and Bosnia, then more extensively in eastern Slavonia, Kosovo, and East Timor, operations took the form of an "international administration" that assumed, at least for a short time, sovereign powers, much like international trusteeships did earlier in the twentieth century.[36] In the doctrine of the UN, strains of holism are perceptible in both *An Agenda for Peace* and in the *Supplement to an Agenda for Peace*, where Boutros-Ghali wrote of the multiple tasks involved in postconflict peacebuilding.[37] They crescendo in the Brahimi Report, which points to the need for peacebuilding strategy, integrating peacebuilding into peacekeeping operations, and incorporating a comprehensive program for national reconciliation into peace operations,[38] and in a 2001 statement of the Security Council recognizing that

> peacebuilding is aimed at preventing the outbreak, the recurrence
> or the continuation of armed conflict and therefore encompasses
> a wide range of political, development, humanitarian, and human
> rights programmes [sic] and mechanisms. This requires short- and
> long-term action tailored to address the particular needs of societies
> sliding into conflict or emerging from it. These actions should focus

on fostering sustainable development, the eradication of poverty and inequalities, transparent and accountable governance, the promotion of democracy, respect for human rights and the rule of law, and the promotion of a culture of peace and non-violence.[39]

Then, the report, *A More Secure World*, proposed a UN Peacebuilding Commission whose mission would include coordinating the efforts of the UN Security Council, the Economic and Social Council, the International Monetary Fund, the World Bank, and representatives of principal donor countries, the country where the intervention is taking place, and regional and subregional organizations—also a thrust toward holism.[40] In December 2005, the Peacebuilding Commission was created. For its part, the World Bank took a step toward holism in a 2006 report proclaiming and documenting the role of civil society in peacebuilding.[41] But for all of their thrusts, strides, and movements toward holism, these landmark statements of the liberal peace stop short of directly and forthrightly conceptualizing an approach to peacebuilding that integrates diverse and interdependent actors, activities, and time horizons.[42]

A Proposal for Strategic Peacebuilding

The authors in this volume take up from where these trajectories have led the business of peacebuilding. A lasting and even reasonably just peace, we claim, depends on a wide array of actors and activities, at all levels of society and between societies, oriented toward the past, the present, and the future. These sectors are interdependent, and in taking them into its range of vision, strategic peacebuilding evinces holism—its most quintessential characteristic. It is the mission of advocates and practitioners of strategic peacebuilding to exploit this interdependence and holism, synergetically linking sectors that would otherwise remain isolated or in conflict. The intentionality of such efforts is what gives force to the adjective *strategic*. Strategic peacebuilders are like doctors who understand that the body is composed of interconnected systems and then specialize in certain regions of connection with the conviction that these subsystems crucially sustain the entire anatomy. A feature of this medicine is its interest not only in laws, institutions, and policies but in emotions, attitudes, beliefs, legitimacy, and, broadly speaking, the wide range of relationships among citizens. In pursuing this interest, it draws wisdom not only from the liberal tradition of human rights, democracy, free markets, and international law and institutions but also from cultural, religious, and tribal traditions.

"Get real!" exclaimed one interlocutor at the November 2006 conference at the University of Notre Dame where the essays for this volume were first presented. How can a holistic approach be anything other than utopian in the face of large-scale violence like the wars in Yugoslavia or Rwanda? Realists might also ask how, given the strains that peacebuilding operations already face, a still more ambitious set of undertakings can be envisioned. Call and Cousens caution that in the context of the UN, calls for integrated strategy "tended to lose out to 'laundry lists' and what could be called a 'no agency left behind' notion of peacebuilding."[43] In advocating greater attention to interdependence, holism, and integration, none of the authors herein has in mind a Peacebuilding Panopticon or a World Office of Strategic Peacebuilding that will direct and command the efforts of all who are involved. Even the Peacebuilding Commission does not have such ambitions, and at the time of this writing has not yet realized the coordinating functions that it was mandated to perform. Nor do the chapters herein call for an abolition of internationally sanctioned military intervention or international policing.[44] Rather, particular nodes of interdependence, instances of overlap between activities, actors, and other kinds of sectors are what the authors identify and propose ways to develop. Through many such efforts, which may begin to be coordinated once they occur, a more holistic approach to peacebuilding can emerge. Our proposal is not to throw in the kitchen sink but to mix together carefully heretofore unmixed ingredients. Far from placing more strain on the UN and other institutions, such an approach ought to lessen the pressure that they face by spreading the work of peacebuilding over a far greater array of actors endowed with variegated expertise and assets.

That strategic peacebuilding can be successful is evinced through examples in the chapters that follow. John Paul Lederach and R. Scott Appleby's contribution details the fruits of strategic peacebuilding in Mozambique, Colombia, and the Philippines. Gerard Powers points to the successful efforts of religious mediators in Guatemala, northern Uganda, and elsewhere. Naomi Roht-Arriaza touts transitional justice efforts in Guatemala for their success in bridging national and local levels to be healing for victims of human rights abuses. Many other success stories emerge. The chapters likewise contain examples of operations that were mixed or lacking in success because of an arguable dearth of strategic peacebuilding. Simon Chesterman, for instance, evaluates several UN missions, among them Kosovo, Somalia, Cambodia, and East Timor, and concludes that their limitations were due in good part to insufficiently strategic aims, inadequate coordination among actors, and poor standards for evaluating success. To be sure, he cautions that modest expectations are in order, but he still believes that progress in all of these areas would improve UN operations—and would, in fact, involve strategic peacebuilding.

Each of the essays asserts some way in which sectors, practices, policies, or time horizons can be linked fruitfully—that is, a strategy of peace. The strategies take a wide variety of forms and involve a wide variety of sectors and activities, reflecting the diverse disciplines and methods of the authors, who include sociologists, legal scholars, peace scholars, political scientists, psychologists, and a historian. By and large, these differences are complementary, reflecting the very character of strategic peacebuilding. At times, they involve creative tensions. Nicholas Sambanis and Jackie Smith each call for a greater integration of economic development into peacebuilding but differ over the wisdom of economic liberalization and the role of international financial institutions. In his concluding essay, Oliver Richmond applauds George Lopez and David Cortright for linking fighting terror with building peace on the ground through

UN policy but still worries that UN counterterrorism policies risk radicalizing extremists and undermining peace processes. Such disagreements are constructive because they offer readers a wider portfolio of strategies of peace to explore and evaluate.

Generally, the book's chapters are arrayed in three broad clusters that each makes the case for strategic peacebuilding in a different way. Chapters 1 through 4 set forth strategic peacebuilding at a general, conceptual level: the theory of strategic peacebuilding. Chapters 5 through 8 make up a second cluster, one that presents peacebuilding "from above," that is, with a central stress on international institutions, especially the United Nations and the International Criminal Court. Chapters 9 through 13 form the third and final grouping, presenting peacebuilding "from below," emphasizing the role of civil society, economic, religious, educational, and other nongovernmental actors. That these divisions are not perfect is entirely to be expected: linkages between levels are a leitmotif in strategic peacebuilding. The essays in the second cluster call for international institutions to be linked to the work of national and nongovernmental actors, and several of those in the third cluster advocate the same sort of links in the other direction. The clusters are a matter of emphasis.

John Paul Lederach and Scott Appleby's chapter orients the whole volume by laying out a foundational theory of strategic peacebuilding, one to which subsequent chapters refer. Lederach is a prominent scholar and practitioner who has pursued what he calls the "art of peacebuilding" in locales as diverse as Nicaragua, Colombia, Nepal, Spain, and Kazakhstan; he is credited with pioneering a paradigm shift from conflict resolution to conflict transformation.[45] His writings have developed many of the intellectual planks of strategic peacebuilding: relationships, reconciliation, transformation, the importance of multiple social levels and a wide time horizon that involves healing the past as well as envisioning the future, and an "elicitive" method that taps local cultures for their peacebuilding codes.[46] He teams up with Scott Appleby, a historian and scholar of religion whose book *The Ambivalence of the Sacred* was one of the first to give conceptual depth to the idea of religious peacebuilding. Appleby founded the Catholic Peacebuilding Network, a worldwide association of activists and scholars who seek to advance the study and practice of peacebuilding in the Philippines, Burundi, Colombia, and many other locales.[47] Lederach and Appleby extend and develop the ideas behind these pursuits, weaving into a new synthesis the concepts of interdependence; holism; transparency; communication; coordination between levels, actors, and practices; and the idea of a comprehensive *justpeace*.

Then, a chapter by Peter Wallensteen, a long-standing leading peace researcher, gives historical and conceptual specificity to the concepts that Lederach and Appleby develop. After laying out the precedents for peacebuilding in both political practice and peace scholarship, Wallensteen unveils an approach to peacebuilding that, echoing the metaphor of a body composed of multiple systems, describes the construction of peace as combining state-building, democracy-building, security-building, nation-building, and market-building. He closes by probing four contextual questions that must be answered for effective peacebuilding to take place: how the previous war ended, how the previous war started, who is conducting peacebuilding, and the nature of the neighborhood where peacebuilding is taking place. Through developing and applying answers to these questions, effective strategic peacebuilding takes place.

How should peacebuilding initiatives, particularly those of multilateral agencies and NGOs, be evaluated? This is the question that Hal Culbertson, a practitioner and analyst of peacebuilding in both NGO and university settings, poses. His answer is far more than a technical one. A central criterion for assessment, consistent with the vector of this volume, is the NGO's or civil society organization's strategic adaptation to the other actors and sectors of the society in which peacebuilding is taking place. He cites the finding of the remarkable Joint Utstein Study of Peacebuilding that of 336 peacebuilding projects funded by foreign and development ministries in Germany, the Netherlands, Norway, and the United Kingdom, 55 percent showed no commitment to a "wider country strategy of peace." Joining this insight with several others based on a holistic understanding of peacebuilding, Culbertson's essay offers a useful framework for monitoring and evaluating peacebuilding programs.

Peacebuilding can also be evaluated through moral reasoning. What is just peacebuilding? By what criteria should it be assessed? These are the questions for which my own chapter offers a framework, a set of standards analogous to those that the just war theory poses for war. Its orienting idea is reconciliation, a concept of justice as "restoration of right relationship" that is derived from the Abrahamic religious traditions and whose meaning is much like Lederach and Appleby's notion of justpeace. Animating the ethic of political reconciliation is a set of practices that aim to repair one or more wounds to human flourishing that political injustices leave behind and transform hostile emotions and judgments to ones of assent to just political orders. Reflecting the volume's axial notions, the practices are interdependent and collectively holistic.

The ensuing nine chapters explore strategic peacebuilding in particular contexts. In them can be found the range of actors, activities, and time horizons, the stress on holism and interdependence, and the proposals for linking sectors together—the strategies of peace—that characterize strategic peacebuilding. Legal scholar Simon Chesterman and Nicholas Sambanis both look at UN peacebuilding operations, stressing the need for their integration with certain other practices. Drawing from his experience observing the UN's most ambitious operations—East Timor and Kosovo—Chesterman concludes that "states cannot be made to work from the outside." International assistance can be successful, but only when it complements the creation of local institutions, policies, and practices and the efforts of local actors. The Peacebuilding Commission, he believes, carries potential for enriching such complementarity, but it is too early to judge its success.

Sambanis focuses on that aspect of UN peace operations that he and Doyle believe is most lacking: economic development. He advocates a commitment to economic reconstruction and to integrating such reconstruction into the project of peacebuilding that is far more capacious than the Washington

Consensus approach of creating free market institutions and reducing public sectors. Sambanis describes what this reconstruction consists of, how his and Doyle's peacebuilding triangle reveals the need for it, and who carries it out in his chapter.

The UN is also the focus of George A. Lopez and David Cortright's chapter—not its peace operations but its policies for countering terrorism. Widely recognized experts on sanctions, Lopez and Cortright outline a policy that vividly exemplifies strategic peacebuilding's interdependence of activity. Recognizing the connection between terrorism and good governance, economic development, and human rights, they offer informed recommendations for sanctions and other enforcement measures that enhance (not detract from) these ends. In so doing, they propose ways to combat violence while also improving the environments that incubate this violence in the first place.

Robert C. Johansen's chapter also strongly illustrates strategic peacebuilding's interdependence by exploring two pursuits whose clash begets vociferous controversy today in countries like Uganda—the prosecution of war criminals through the International Criminal Court and achieving a negotiated settlement to civil war, which some argue requires amnesty or at least forgoing trials. His approach is precisely a strategy for peace: a presumption for prosecution, but one that is pursued so as best to promote long-term peace in war-ridden societies and is potentially overridden in cases where it prevents such peace. With sophistication, he addresses the dilemmas to which his approach gives rise and proposes concrete solutions.

Legal scholar Naomi Roht-Arriaza makes the case for strategic interdependence and complementarity in another realm that is integral to building a just peace—transitional justice. As she describes, it is a realm with a trajectory toward holism all of its own, beginning with debates over whether to prosecute in Latin America in the 1980s, proceeding to the rise of robust truth commissions in Chile and South Africa in the 1990s, and now coming to involve rich "hybrids" of both trials and truth commissions, often combined with practices of vetting, reparations, and commemorations. Roht-Arriaza's piece partners with Johansen's essay on trials, then, in plumbing the other institutions involved in this complementarity. She argues that practitioners of transitional justice need to recognize another sort of holism—a linking of international, regional, national, and local transitional justice mechanisms, each of which complements the others in its strengths and weaknesses.

Like Johansen, peace scholar Larissa Fast takes up the tension between two activities that often come into conflict in the field: humanitarian relief and other dimensions of peacebuilding, like mediating an end to wars. Her response to the problem seems at first to be a dissonant one for the volume: the two activities should not be linked, she avers, lest humanitarian relief become diverted and compromised. But respecting other sectors' autonomy can be construed as a strategy for peace. Amid war, anarchy, and chaos, such respect requires intentionality, awareness, and coordination. In arguing for such a severance, Fast takes on a rival position that would link humanitarianism and politics. She explains why the case for separation is more persuasive.

Sociologist Jackie Smith challenges the liberal peace head on, especially its optimism about market economies. Like Roland Paris, she believes that a rapid push for free markets, free trade, and minimal government in the wake of armed conflict can actually destabilize societies rather than build lasting peace. Both her diagnosis and her solution to the problem exceed Paris's call for sequencing. For her, the chief obstacle to peace is local structures of inequality that are in turn embedded in global structures of inequality, which, if not addressed, will only lead to further war. What sort of strategy can combat these inequalities and hence offer hope for a sustainable peace? Her bold and surprising answer leads us far beyond the corridors of international financial institutions.

What of strategic peacebuilding's concern with changing hearts and minds? What of its emphasis on the long run? Both factors receive play in the chapter by psychologists Robert D. Enright, Jeannette Knutson Enright, and Anthony C. Holter, who draw conclusions from the curriculum for teaching forgiveness to children that they have established in the school system of Belfast, Ireland. Forgiveness contributes to peace by encouraging a new generation to turn away from communal hatred and toward civic friendship, a virtue that resembles Lederach and Appleby's notion of right relationship as well as my own concept of reconciliation. Forgiveness, civil society, affective change, the educational sector, and the long run: all of these features add new hues to strategic peacebuilding's palette.

One sort of actor in particular, one also associated with hearts, minds, and the long run, has been virtually neglected by the liberal peace: the religious. The chapter by Gerard F. Powers, an expert on international affairs in the Catholic Church, is a strong corrective. Behind the neglect of religion, he explains, is the secularization paradigm, which views religion as an irrational, violent, and intolerant force that is destined for extinction. The religious can be violent, he acknowledges, but they have also proven to be powerful, passionate, and effective agents of social and political transformation, their efforts ranging from high-level mediation to interreligious dialogue to grassroots and civil society efforts. What lies behind their influence? Under what conditions are they most successful? What can the answers to these questions teach religious peacebuilders as well as secular Western governments? These issues are at the heart of Powers's inquiry.

Finally, political scientist Oliver Richmond concludes with a chapter that synthesizes and comments on the entire volume. A prolific scholar of peacebuilding and commentator on the liberal peace, Richmond evaluates the essays and the collective argument of the project from the perspective of an engaged intellectual, employing both the tools of international relations theory and his wide experience observing peacebuilding efforts on the ground around the world.

This is strategic peacebuilding—an approach that takes up and seeks to extend the movement toward holism that peacebuilding has traveled over the past two decades. Insofar as it is sound, it is an approach that ought to be of interest to a wide variety of parties, including officials in the United Nations, the World Bank, and other international organizations, religious leaders, NGO leaders and staff, educators, economists, activists, tribal and village leaders, international lawyers and judges, state officials in countries struggling to escape war and poverty, civil society leaders, and people living and working at the grass roots wherever peacebuilding does or should take place. But strategic peace-building might prove to be of interest to Western governments as well. Since the end of the Cold War, the U.S. and European governments have experienced their most difficult foreign policy dilemmas in locales where creating a sustain-able peace in the aftermath of formal war proved far more difficult than military victory itself—as noted at the beginning of this introduction, this includes the U.S. experience in Somalia, Afghanistan, and Iraq; Germany's in Afghanistan; and the European Union's in Kosovo and the Democratic Republic of Congo. To recommend a strategic, holistic approach to peacebuilding in these cases is not necessarily to approve of the wars that begat these challenges in the first place. It is only to say that aims like fighting terrorism, promoting democracy, and creating stability in sundered societies might well be pursued more profit-ably through adopting into policy the insights in the chapters that follow. At the time of this writing, a new president has taken office in the United States, one who promises to conduct America's foreign policy with greater sensitivity to the character of its footprint on countries around the world. Might strategic peacebuilding prove an asset?

Apart from who is building the peace, much is at stake. The lives of thou-sands (even hundreds of thousands) of people, government based on human rights and accountability, the prospect of escaping abject poverty, the protec-tion of local villages and their cultures, justice for war criminals, the healing of hatred and revenge, stability between countries and within regions, and the avoidance and alleviation of AIDS, famine, and other calamities—all depend on whether societies widen and deepen their peace or collapse back into war. Just as suffering itself is multiple and interdependent, one form begetting another, so must peacebuilding be capacious, multivalent, and strategic.

NOTES

The author thanks Gerard Powers and Scott Appleby for helpful comments and suggestions.

1. The exact number of countries that have become democracies since the "third wave" began in 1974 is not clear. In his *The Third Wave: Democratization in the Late Twentieth Century* (Norman: University of Oklahoma Press, 1991), Samuel P. Huntington documents thirty transitions between 1974 and 1989. Freedom House reports that the number of "free" countries increased by thirteen from 1989 to 2004. See Freedom House Press Release, *Russia Downgraded to "Not Free"* (Washington, D.C.: Freedom House, 2004); and Freedom House, *Freedom in the World 2005: The Annual Survey of Political Rights and Civil Liberties* (Washington, D.C.: Freedom House, 2005). Democracy theorist Larry Diamond estimates that from 1974 to 1996, between thirty-six and seventy-seven states became democracies, depending on how one counts democratization exactly. See his "Is the Third Wave of Democratization Over? An Empirical Assessment," Working Paper no. 236, Kellogg Institute, University of Notre

Dame, March 1997. Here, I adopt an estimate from the high end of the spectrum by writing of societies that have "moved toward" democracy.

2. For descriptions of the liberal peace, see Roland Paris, *At War's End: Building Peace after Civil Conflict* (Cambridge: Cambridge University Press, 2004), 40–51; Oliver Richmond, "Patterns of Peace," *Global Society* 20, no. 4 (2006); Oliver P. Richmond, "The Problem of Peace: Understanding the 'Liberal Peace'," *Conflict, Security, & Development* 6, no. 3 (2006).

3. This is not to say that a wave of ethnic conflicts broke out just after the Cold War—a prevailing myth. Ethnic conflict had been increasing for several decades during the Cold War and continued to remain at a high level just after the Cold War ended. The *Human Security Report* of 1995 shows that after a high point for the entire Cold War period in 1991, struggles for self-determination (most of them ethnic or communal in nature) declined sharply up through 2004. See James D. Fearon and David D. Laitin, "Ethnicity, Insurgency, and Civil War," *American Political Science Review* 97, no. 1 (2003); Ted Robert Gurr and Barbara Harff, *Ethnic Conflict in World Politics* (Boulder, Colo.: Westview Press, 1994), xiii, 11; *The Human Security Report: War and Peace in the 21st Century* (Oxford: Human Security Centre, 2005).

4. Michael W. Doyle and Nicholas Sambanis, *Making War and Building Peace* (Princeton, N.J.: Princeton University Press, 2006), 6–7.

5. James Dobbins et al., *America's Role in Nation-Building: From Germany to Iraq* (Santa Monica, Calif.: RAND Corporation, 2003), xiv–xv.

6. Paris, *At War's End*, 17.

7. Roland Paris, "Bringing the Leviathan Back In: Classical versus Contemporary Studies of the Liberal Peace," *International Studies Review* 8 (2006): 433.

8. Monica Duffy Toft, *Securing the Peace: The Durable Settlement of Civil Wars*, (Princeton, N.J.: Princeton University Press, 2010), 6–7. Different figures, but ones yielding the same conclusion, come from Elizabeth M. Cousens and Charles T. Call. "The trend toward negotiated settlements after the Cold War also created entry points for international peacekeeping: between 1946 and 1990, twice as many conflicts ended through victory than through negotiations, whereas between 1995 and 2004, negotiated settlements were three times as likely to end war as outright victory," they write. They add in a note that "between 1994 and 2004, out of 48 wars ended, 36 concluded with negotiation compared to victory." See Charles T. Call and Elizabeth M. Cousens, "Ending Wars and Building Peace: International Responses to War-Torn Societies," *International Studies Quarterly* 9 (2008): 5.

9. *A More Secure World: Our Shared Responsibility: Report of the High-Level Panel on Threats, Challenges, and Change* (New York: United Nations, 2004), 33–34.

10. Boutros Boutros-Ghali, *An Agenda for Peace*, 2nd ed. (New York: United Nations Publications, 1995).

11. Ibid.; contains the supplement.

12. *Report of the Panel on United Nations Peace Operations* (New York: United Nations, 2000).

13. *Responsibility to Protect: Report of the International Commission on Intervention and State Sovereignty* (Ottawa: International Development Research Centre, 2001).

14. *A More Secure World*.

15. Paris, *At War's End*, 40–51.

16. Boutros Boutros-Ghali, *An Agenda for Democratization* (New York: United Nations, 1996).

17. For a description, see Francis Fukuyama, *State Building: Governance and World Order in the Twenty-First Century* (Surrey, U.K.: Profile Books, 2004), 20–23.

18. See, for instance, Richard Caplan, *The International Governance of War-Torn Territories: Rule and Reconstruction* (Oxford: Oxford University Press, 2006); Noah Feldman, *What We Owe Iraq: War and the Ethics of Nation-Building* (Princeton, N.J.: Princeton University Press, 2006); Virginia Page Fortna, *Peace Time* (Princeton, N.J.: Princeton University Press, 2004); Michael Ignatieff, *Empire Lite: Nation Building in Bosnia, Kosovo, and Afghanistan* (Toronto: Penguin Books, 2003); Stephen John Stedman, ed., *Ending Civil Wars* (Boulder, Colo.: Lynne Rienner, 2002); Barbara F. Walter, *Committing to Peace* (Princeton, N.J.: Princeton University Press, 2002).

19. *Human Security Report 2005*, 1–9.

20. Paris, *At War's End*, 55–58.

21. George Downs and Stephen John Stedman, "Evaluation Issues in Peace Implementation," in *Ending Civil Wars: The Implementation of Peace Accords*, ed. Stephen John Stedman, Donald Rothchild, and Elizabeth Cousens (Boulder, Colo.: Lynne Rienner, 2002), 50, 59. Call and Cousens share Downs and Stedman's criticism of Paris and advocate a "moderate standard" of "no renewed warfare plus decent governance." See Call and Cousens, "Ending Wars and Building Peace," 7.

22. Doyle and Sambanis, *Making War and Building Peace*, 73, and Nicholas Sambanis's chapter in this volume. The broad verdict of "mixed success" is shared by other systematic analyses, including Caplan, *International Governance*; James Dobbins, *The Beginner's Guide to Nation-Building* (Santa Monica, Calif.: RAND Corporation, 2007).

23. Doyle and Sambanis, *Making War and Building Peace*, 110.

24. Call and Cousens, "Ending Wars and Building Peace," 2.

25. Ibid., 5.

26. Andrew Mack, *Global Patterns of Political Violence* (New York: International Peace Academy, 2007); cited in Call and Cousens, "Ending Wars and Building Peace," 5.

27. Paris, *At War's End*, 179–211. See also Jack Snyder, *From Voting to Violence: Democratization and Nationalist Conflict* (New York: Norton, 2000).

28. Stedman, *Ending Civil Wars*, 3.

29. Doyle and Sambanis, *Making War and Building Peace*, 64.

30. Dobbins, *The Beginner's Guide to Nation-Building*.

31. Fukuyama, *State Building*, 1–57.

32. Toft, *Securing the Peace*, 2–6.

33. Donald Rothchild and Philip G. Roeder, "Power Sharing as an Impediment to Peace and Democracy," in *Sustainable Peace: Power and Democracy after Civil Wars*, ed. Philip G. Roeder and Donald Rothchild (Ithaca, N.Y.: Cornell University Press, 2005).

34. Even Paris, for his sharp criticism of the liberal peace, does not contest its goals. His dispute is about sequencing more than it is about what ends ought to be pursued. He even grounds his case in Enlightenment political thought, arguing that the same thinkers who generated the liberal peace also understood the importance of establishing stable government institutions. See Paris, *At War's End*, 46–51.

35. For one account of a holistic approach to peacebuilding involving the UN, see Thomas M. Franck, "A Holistic Approach to Building Peace," in *Peacemaking and Peacekeeping for the New Century*, ed. Olara A. Otunnu and Michael W. Doyle (Lanham, Md.: Rowman and Littlefield, 1998).

36. See William Bain, *Between Anarchy and Society: Trusteeship and the Obligations of Power* (Oxford: Oxford University Press, 2003); Caplan, *International Governance*; and Dominik Zaum, *The Sovereignty Paradox: The Norms and Politics of International Statebuilding* (Oxford: Oxford University Press, 2007).

37. Boutros-Ghali, *Agenda for Peace*, 19, 61.

38. *Report of the Panel on UN Peace Operations*, 1, 6, 7.

39. Statement by the president of the Security Council, quoted in Call and Cousens, "Ending Wars and Building Peace," 6.

40. *A More Secure World*, 83, 84.

41. Social Development Department Sustainable Development Network, "Civil Society and Peacebuilding: Potential, Limitations and Critical Factors," World Bank, 2006.

42. It is important to note that alongside the present work are other analyses in which the UN, Western governments, and international institutions are not the only or even the primary actors but are situated in a world of grassroots initiatives and civil society activities, of NGOs and religious leaders, of globalized markets and their local merchants, of truth commissions and tribal rituals, of villages and metropolises, of immediate crises and long-term transformations—efforts and analyses that have initiated the idea of strategic peacebuilding. For these, see citations in John Paul Lederach and R. Scott Appleby's chapter. See also Mary B. Anderson and Lara Olson, *Confronting War: Critical Lessons for Peace Practitioners* (Cambridge, Mass.: Collaborative for Development Action, 2003); Johannes Botes, "Conflict Transformation: A Debate over Semantics of a Crucial Shift in the Theory and Practice of Peace and Conflict Studies?" *International Journal of Peace Studies* 8, no. 2 (2003); Necla Tschirgi, *Peacebuilding as the Link between Peace and Security: Is the Window of Opportunity Closing?* (New York: International Peace Academy, 2004).

43. Call and Cousens, "Ending Wars and Building Peace," 3.

44. It should be noted that some of the authors do place a strong stress on nonviolence in the larger corpus of their writings. There is no general agreement on the issue among the present authors.

45. Botes, "Conflict Transformation."

46. See especially John Paul Lederach, *Building Peace: Sustainable Reconciliation in Divided Societies* (Washington, D.C.: U.S. Institute of Peace, 1997); John Paul Lederach, *The Little Book of Conflict Transformation* (Intercourse, Penn.: Good Books, 2003); John Paul Lederach, *The Moral Imagination: The Art and Soul of Building Peace* (Oxford: Oxford University Press, 2005); John Paul Lederach, *Preparing for Peace: Conflict Transformation across Cultures* (Syracuse: Syracuse University Press, 1995).

47. R. Scott Appleby, *The Ambivalence of the Sacred: Religion, Violence, and Reconciliation* (Lanham, Md.: Rowman and Littlefield, 2000).

I

Strategic Peacebuilding: An Overview

John Paul Lederach and R. Scott Appleby

As faculty members of a peace institute, we study worldwide efforts to reduce violence, resolve conflict, and build peace, and we regularly receive inquiries and requests from people confronting a variety of challenges posed by intense conflict. Consider the following examples, drawn from well-known cases and from our own experiences, keeping in mind the following question: what are the "strategic" dimensions of building peace in this context?

Following a decade of struggle, the African nation of Mozambique gained its independence from Portugal in June 1975. Twice the size of California, the new nation was plagued by poverty, a 90 percent illiteracy rate, and periodic, devastating droughts. The 230,000 Portuguese settlers who fled in the mid-1970s left the country bereft of most skilled, professional, and business people; they also took working capital and sabotaged equipment as they departed. Therefore, the economy at independence was in a shambles. Samora Machel, the military leader of the independence movement known as FRELIMO (the Front for the Liberation of Mozambique), became the new nation's first president. FRELIMO's Marxist-Leninist ideology inspired opposition in the form of the Mozambique National Resistance, or RENAMO, which was composed of former Portuguese soldiers, disgruntled FRELIMO deserters, and common criminals. RENAMO launched a guerrilla war in the early 1980s directed at destabilizing FRELIMO. By 1992, the RENAMO insurgency had left over a million Mozambicans dead and had displaced 6 to 8 million others.

    Throughout the civil war, the religious communities of Mozambique constituted the nation's civil society. The Catholic Church, which had maintained close ties with the colonial government well into the 1960s, grew more diversified politically, with many priests supporting the Marxist FRELIMO leadership. The relationship between the mission-educated President Machel and the Catholic Church nonetheless deteriorated rapidly after independence. From the late 1970s until 1982, FRELIMO attempted to suppress the evangelistic, publishing, and educational activities of the churches in Mozambique. It appropriated the churches' considerable rural assets in particular and hounded religious actors across the country. State persecution served to galvanize the religious, however, prompting them to renewed efforts of ministry. During this period, the churches came to represent the single largest and most influential alternative voice and institution in the country. Repression, furthermore, triggered the emergence of nonviolent liberationist elements in the churches.

The larger Mozambican religious community was divided, however. Muslims were generally hostile toward FRELIMO. Evangelical and Pentecostal organizations such as the Shekinah, Christ for the Nations, the End-Time Handmaidens, and Frontline Fellowship recognized and supported RENAMO; these groups conducted fund-raising and lobbying operations on behalf of the insurgents in Washington, London, and elsewhere. On the other hand, the Protestant ecumenical association—the Mozambican Council of Churches—supported FRELIMO and condemned RENAMO, as did the United Methodist Church in the United States. The Catholic bishops issued pastoral letters condemning atrocities committed by both sides and calling for negotiations.

Relations between the government and the religious groups and churches improved markedly between 1981 and 1988, the period when the United States provided $240 million in primarily humanitarian aid to the FRELIMO government. This policy had its intended effect: in 1983, Mozambique began to allow nongovernmental organizations (NGOs), such as the private relief agency CARE, to operate in the nation, and in the late 1980s Mozambique moved toward a less centralized economy. The government could no longer deny that the churches were providing essential social services—such as the distribution of food and clothing, education, and health care—which the state itself was unable to supply during the war with RENAMO.

The Mozambique churches were able to draw on an international religious network of social services, channel desperately needed assets into the country, and thus relieve some of the pressing economic needs. In addition, the churches maintained their infrastructure in the rural areas despite the ravages of the civil war. State officials often had to rely on religious groups for information about rebel-controlled areas. In time, the horrendous condition of the economy and the depredations of the civil war itself forced FRELIMO to reconsider its own policies and seek the cooperation of any groups willing to help bring the conflict to an end. In this context, the Community of Sant'Egidio took on a major role in hosting and mediating the complex negotiations that eventually led to the end of the civil war.

What element of strategic peacebuilding did this transnational organization of lay Catholic professionals bring to the setting?

In 2006, following the election of Álvaro Uribe as president of Colombia, representatives of the government opened a process to demobilize the paramilitary structure in the war-torn nation. In the long history of government–insurgent negotiations, different administrations had asked the Catholic bishops and their support staff to provide oversight, good offices and guarantees of safety and integrity, and occasional facilitation. As the new initiative took shape, Church leadership faced questions regarding how it would respond to the new requests and what role it would play in the process. Specifically, the role of paramilitaries in human rights abuses in Colombia and their proximity to government actors generated concerns, as did the prospect of an end-game scenario which, hidden under the umbrella of a "peace process" and "reconciliation," would fail to address the need for truth, justice, and reparations.

In this context the ethics of peacebuilding came into stark contrast with the pragmatics of negotiation and the dismantling of an armed organization. Victim communities affected by paramilitarism—communities that the Church had accompanied in some regions—expressed anxiety about the process. They feared renewed violence and worried whether they would receive the acknowledgment and reparations they deserved. Not least, the victimized communities felt pressure to engage in reconciliation—but what, they asked, does reconciliation mean in this context?

The situation became even more complex in light of the fact that the Church was also engaged in on-again, off-again negotiations with armed insurgencies on the left. In addition, local parishes were supporting communities of internally displaced persons and helping maintain fledgling peace zones that had been declared at grassroots levels in at least three different regions.

What did a "strategic peacebuilding" perspective offer to the Catholic Church as it attempted to balance these competing claims and build peace in the context of a fifty-year insurgency?

In August 2008, a historic peace accord in Mindanao between the Moro Islamic Liberation Front (MILF) and the government of the Philippines nearly reached fruition. The result of seven years of negotiation facilitated by the Malaysian government, the Memorandum of Agreement on Ancestral Domain (MOA-AD) had survived numerous iterations and stages of consensus building. In the last push, following the initialing of this yet-to-be signed negotiating document, a divided Supreme Court declared it unconstitutional.

Immediately a variety of international, civil society, and local actors lodged protests and encouraged the negotiators to salvage the historic opportunity to end a conflict that traces its roots across centuries in this largest southernmost island of the archipelago. The negotiators asked: How might the resources and methods provided by a strategic peacebuilding approach sustain the negotiation process at a time of crisis?

Several groups working in Nogales—where half the city is located on the Arizona side of the border, and the other half in Mexico—identify the need for help from someone who can view the situation comprehensively, see the big picture, identify a path forward, and facilitate a common approach to local issues. They recruit peacebuilders to the scene.

These groups are not alone. Borders in many countries create interdependent communities living in close proximity, while the policies that regulate immigration are formulated thousands of miles away in national capitals. The economic globalization that creates flows of capital and workforces underscores the artificiality of maps and mocks pretensions to sovereignty. Workers and their families are buffeted about by the economic and social hurricane. "We are not in open war, but we have got a mess on our hands," they say.

Does strategic peacebuilding offer relevant analysis, diagnosis, and paths to constructive change to people caught in the crossfire of immigration and the globalization of economies?

At its core, peacebuilding nurtures constructive human relationships. To be relevant, it must do so strategically, at every level of society and across the potentially polarizing lines of ethnicity, class, religion, and race. This book proposes the need for *strategic* peacebuilding—the capacity to develop strategies to maximize the impact of initiatives for constructive change within this complexity. It focuses on transforming inhumane social patterns, flawed structural conditions, and open violent conflict that weaken the conditions necessary for a flourishing human community. We are, in the words of Oliver Wendell Holmes, "seeking the simplicity on the other side of complexity"—a simplicity that makes a real difference. Strategic peacebuilders must embrace complexity and find within any given situation or issue practical approaches that stitch together key people and initiatives to reduce violence, change destructive patterns, and build healthy relationships and structures.

Strategic peacebuilding therefore denotes an approach to reducing violence, resolving conflict and building peace that is marked by a heightened awareness of and skillful adaptation to the complex and shifting material, geopolitical, economic, and cultural realities of our increasingly globalized and interdependent world. Accordingly, peacebuilding that is strategic draws intentionally and shrewdly on the overlapping and imperfectly coordinated presences, activities, and resources of various international, transnational, national, regional, and local institutions, agencies, and movements that influence the causes, expressions, and outcomes of conflict. Strategic peacebuilders take advantage of emerging and established patterns of collaboration and interdependence for the purposes of reducing violence and alleviating the root causes of deadly conflict. They encourage the deeper and more frequent convergence of mission, resources, expertise, insight, and benevolent self-interest that characterizes the most fruitful multilateral collaborations in the cause of peace.

There are certain hallmarks of the constructive relationships that strategic peacebuilders seek to foster among conflicted peoples. These include the cultivation of interdependence as a social and political context for the effective pursuit of human rights, good governance, and economic prosperity; the promotion of transparent communication across sectors and levels of society in the service of including as many voices and actors as possible in the reform of institutions and the repair or creation of partnerships conducive to the common good; and the increasing coordination and (where possible) integration of resources, programs, practices, and processes. These hallmarks characterize the reflexive practice of peacebuilders themselves who think and act strategically.

Elements of these definitions of strategic peacebuilding require unpacking and elaboration.

Peacebuilding: Comprehensive and Sustainable

In this chapter we explore peacebuilding in its most capacious meaning by conceptualizing it as an ideal type—which is to acknowledge that peacebuilding in this "ultra" mode may exist only in our imaginations and on paper, rather than in the real world of practice. We take this ideal-type approach for at least three reasons.

First, many if not all elements in the definition and description of peacebuilding that we present in this chapter do, in fact, appear in actual peacebuilding activities and operations; all of them appear in peacebuilding activities and operations, collectively considered; and all of them are central to the successful building of peace.[1] In short, we add nothing to the array of activities and aspirations already associated with the building of peace.

Second, a comprehensive definition and description of peacebuilding is necessary if the peace being built is to be sustained over time. A sustainable peace, the historical record shows, requires long-term, ongoing activities and operations that may be initiated and supported for a time by outsiders but must eventually become the ordinary practices of the citizens and institutions of the society in question. We believe, furthermore, that peacebuilding occurs in its fully realized mode when it addresses every stage of the conflict cycle and involves all members of a society in the nonviolent transformation of conflict, the pursuit of social justice, and the creation of cultures of sustainable peace. Properly understood, the building and sustaining of a culture of peace and its supporting institutions requires a range of relationship-building activities encompassing the entire conflict cycle, rather than merely the postaccord, coming-out-of-violence period. Accordingly, activities that constitute peacebuilding run the gamut of conflict transformation, including violence prevention and early warning, conflict management, mediation and resolution, social reconstruction and healing in the aftermath of armed conflict, and the long, complex work of reconciliation throughout the process.[2]

In addition, peacebuilding theory articulates the end goal of these disparate but interrelated phases of conflict transformation. The end goal is perhaps best expressed by the idea of a *justpeace*, a dynamic state of affairs in which the reduction and management of violence and the achievement of social and economic justice are undertaken as mutual, reinforcing dimensions of constructive change.[3] Sustainable transformation of conflict requires more than the (necessary) problem solving associated with mediation, negotiated settlements, and other elements of conflict resolution; it requires the redress of legitimate grievances and the establishment of new relations characterized by equality and fairness according to the dictates of human dignity and the common good.

To say that a *justpeace* is the end goal of peacebuilding is not to suggest that peacebuilding ends when the fundamental requirements of a *justpeace* are established; rather, the practices of peacebuilding that help bring about this desired state of affairs must become routinized in the society. For example, effective institutions for participatory government, once established, require continual oversight, nurturing, and renewal.

Part of the rationale for conceptualizing peacebuilding in this comprehensive sense is a recognition that conflict does occur in a cycle, that each phase of the cycle is related to the others, and that efforts toward a sustainable peace must address each phase of the cycle in the context of the overall conflict. Accordingly, efforts toward "prevention," for example, should not be confined to one temporal period—that is, "before the conflict occurs" (in most societies, some level of violence has already occurred among the belligerents). Rather, systematic efforts toward the prevention of further violence should be prominent in every stage of conflict, including the peace process and the post-settlement implementation period.

Each of the tools available to a peacebuilder must be applied in situ, of course. For example, efforts to prevent the recurrence of violence after a period of state oppression, genocide, or civil war, which often occur while a negotiated settlement is being implemented, will require a particular and somewhat different set of skills than efforts undertaken to prevent an unprecedented outbreak of deadly violence in a society simmering with ethnic, religious, or political tensions but not yet plunged into war.[4] Nonetheless, prevention must unfold at every stage of conflict. The building of constructive personal, group, and political relationships, in short, is perpetual, occurring as a constitutive part of prevention, negotiation, transitional justice, and problem resolution.

Third, an ideal-type definition offers the advantage of identifying the distance between the current scope, scale, and transformative impact of efforts to end violence and build peace, on one hand, and the fullest possible realization of peacebuilding potential, on the other. Our definition therefore includes a prescriptive dimension; we believe that the greater potential can be realized by envisioning peacebuilding as a holistic enterprise, a comprehensive and coherent set of actions and operations, that can be improved by greater levels of collaboration, complementarity, coordination, and, where possible, integration across levels of society.

In short, a comprehensive definition of sustainable peacebuilding, if widely adopted, would stimulate the further realization of the comprehensive *reality* of sustainable peacebuilding. Accordingly, we urge a more consistent incorporation of the myriad elements of peacebuilding practice in peacebuilding initiatives, as appropriate to the context, and a more realistic assessment of the time frame necessary for integrating them into a coherent program for sustainable peace.

Time has been the stumbling block of several otherwise savvy or at least well-intended interventions. The robust definition of peacebuilding we advocate incorporates the often bitter lessons of experience, learned from interventions (or noninterventions) such as Rwanda, Cambodia, Iraq, and Afghanistan, regarding the critical importance of getting both the timing and the duration of interventions right.

As various chapters in the present volume illustrate, a lack of clarity about the end goal of such interventions clouds planners' thinking about timing and duration. Professional peacebuilders, well aware that a comprehensive and sustainable approach to ending violence in deeply divided societies takes significantly more time and commitment than governments and intergovernmental agencies typically allot, might subscribe to a modified form of Colin Powell's dictum: "If it's broke," they might say, "who cares who broke it? We are going to try to fix it." "Fixing it," they realize, requires strategic thinking about how to forge the collaborative local-national-transnational alliances and partnerships and movement-to-movement, person-to-person relationships that will be needed to build a *justpeace*. Consider the experience-based counsel of peacebuilders who have observed and consulted in settings of sustained violence across millions of miles and dozens of years: the period of time it takes to accompany a society out of a protracted period of deadly violence, achieve stability, and move toward a *justpeace*, will be at least as long as it took the conflict to gestate, turn violent, and run its course.[5]

Such sobering considerations might give pause to politicians and policy makers, potential donors, intergovernmental organizations, and other critical contributors to any peacebuilding operation that would be planned according to the requirements of our comprehensive definition. Presumably, no one wants to sink (much less dive) into what looks like a quagmire—which is how long-term interventions within "bloody borders" far from home can readily be depicted. How does one go about building the political will necessary to compel governments and other players to expand the time horizon of their commitment?[6]

Two partial responses begin the discussion of this crucial question. First, one cannot object to the fact that states and intergovernmental agencies act in their own interests. Yet we are encouraged by the growing realization by powerful actors, ranging from major foundations to the European Union, that smart investment in carefully planned and coordinated peacebuilding operations is "in their own interests," given the increasingly interdependent environment. This interdependence can be seen most vividly in the current debates, in places like Nogales, Colombia, and Mozambique, about immigration, displaced populations, and the strain put on both the international and local communities as people seek survival from the hotbeds of conflict. This is only predicted to increase when we consider the impact of environmentally driven conflicts, particularly over issues like the access to and use of water and land, as the case of Mindanao's indigenous peoples suggests.[7]

That awareness of the utility of "carefully planned and coordinated peacebuilding operations" brings us to a second and fuller response, which is the burden of this chapter. How do we best attempt to ensure that peacebuilding operations fulfill their potential by leading societies to the threshold of a *just-peace*? Our answer, in a word, is that we do our best to ensure that "strategic" planning and performance inform peacebuilding operations.

Strategic Peacebuilding: Interdependent and Integrated

Peacebuilders, like other professionals working on the international stage, encountered a new set of circumstances in the aftermath of the Cold War, as regional conflicts, civil wars, genocides, and ethnic cleansings, and the so-called war on terror unfolded within the context of the technology-driven expansion of world markets, mass communication, and the rapid transfer of social and intellectual capital that marks the current phase of globalization.[8] This new world brings with it a new horizon of possibilities and challenges peacebuilders to respond with an ever-greater capacity for strategic thinking and action.

Our answer to two related questions stands behind this claim. First, one might ask: why is it necessary today to challenge the conventional understanding of peacebuilding by calling on its practitioners to be more *strategic*—what has changed? Second, how is strategic peacebuilding different than peacebuilding as previously understood?

What has changed? The end of the Cold War superpower standoff between the United States and the Soviet Union opened the field, not only for the explosion of various kinds of regional and local wars but also for the interventions of a dizzying array of international and transnational, governmental and nongovernmental actors. The problems facing twenty-first-century societies are no longer (if ever they were) contained within national boundaries or susceptible to solutions based on one way of knowing and assessing the world.

As scholar-practitioners reflecting on the new global reality, we can identify four insights about the nature of contemporary conflicts and their possible solutions that help us rethink peacebuilding and fashion it as a strategic enterprise.

First, the players have multiplied. In the post–Cold War era a wider range of actors and institutions mattered. Recalling our opening vignettes, for example, consider the variety of religious, civil, nongovernmental, academic, legal, and other actors that were necessary to negotiate the end of Mozambique's civil war, advance the peace process in Mindanao, and mediate between the military, the paramilitaries, the victimized groups and the rebels in Colombia. Although most of them had already been on the scene in various capacities, the changing nature of the conflicts suddenly required new kinds of participation by a wide range of nonofficial and nongovernmental actors; no longer was peacemaking the exclusive purview of governments.

In short, a traditional peace studies approach to conflict resolution, in contemplating root causes and structural change, tended to take the nation-state as the primary unit of analysis. In the aftermath of the Cold War, the framing question became: how do we adjust the scope, scale, and priorities of peacebuilding to incorporate a much wider range of actors?[9]

In addition, practitioners of on-the-ground peacebuilding began to realize that deadly conflicts, if they are to be transformed, require multiple points of analysis and intervention to create sustainable change. Accordingly, peacebuilders began to seek strategic alliances and coordination over the longer term, rather than "merely" a negotiated solution. In this regard, a second framing question for the inchoate practice of strategic peacebuilding emerged: how do we design processes that envision conflict as the opportunity for wider constructive social change?[10]

Third, the field of play was enlarged to encompass and link two previously unlikely spheres of action: the local and the global. At the local level, the capacity and need for communities to activate and mobilize resources to face the realities of internal conflicts rose sharply. It was impossible to think about peace without engaging, including, and respecting the local community.

Practitioners specialize in the dynamics of peacebuilding within the boundaries and on the terms set by local communities, but they recognize that local communities today always already exist within national and global contexts. Accordingly, peacebuilders, especially during the course of the past two decades, have become experienced in cultivating and applying human and material resources both within and beyond the local community. Peacebuilding practice is thus an interdisciplinary, local-global, expertise-driven approach to building sustainable peace.

Striking the right balance is a delicate and difficult business. The relationship between the three distinct transformative processes at the heart of peacebuilding—striving for social justice, ending violent conflict, and building healthy cooperative relationships in conflict-ridden societies—is complex. These processes of transformation are interrelated most fundamentally at the local level; even when violence originates and occurs at the national or regional level, its impact is felt most keenly and directly in neighborhoods, towns, villages, cities—in local communities. To violate the principle of subsidiarity by moving too quickly beyond the most immediate community of concern and agency, to national or regional actors as agents of conflict management, is to undermine any hope of genuine resolution and transformation of most conflicts. Bringing representatives of warring sides to peace talks typically requires concerted effort by those wielding high levels of political and social authority. But they cannot replace cultural agents who, operating on the local level, interpret agreements and prepare the society for their implementation and the transitions called for by the agreements.[11]

On the other hand, the proliferation of transnational social movements for global-local justice influenced peace studies scholar-practitioners to think beyond borders, to locate both the causes of conflict and potential change agents both within and beyond nation-states. The nation-state, meanwhile, came under increasing pressure—from "above" (the international and transnational community of nations and intergovernmental and nongovernmental organizations, institutions, and foundations), from "below" (local communities and grassroots movements for change), and from "across" (demands for forms of autonomy at regional levels).

The principle of indigenous empowerment suggests that conflict transformation must actively envision, include, respect, and promote the human and cultural resources from within a given setting. The setting and the people cannot be seen as the problem and the outsider as the answer. Rather, the longterm goal of transformation demands that external agents of change take as the primary task of accompaniment the validation of the people and the expansion of resources within the setting.

In this regard the framing question posed by and for would-be strategic peacebuilders was: how do we build the global movement for justice while at the same time empowering the voice and capacity of local communities?[12]

Fourth, a paradigm shift came with the understanding that peacebuilding requires more than management of the conflict, reduction of violence, or agreement on political issues. Peacebuilding must address the healing of peoples scarred and alienated by the lived experience of sustained violence in their communities and nations. Healing increasingly is understood not as a postconflict form of therapy but as a precondition for the prevention of renewed conflict and the transformation of destructive social and structural patterns.

Promoting reconciliation and healing as the sine qua non of peacebuilding is predicated on a hard-won awareness that violent conflict creates deep disruption in relationships that then need radical healing—the kind of healing that restores the soul, the psyche, and the moral imagination. Such healing, it is recognized, draws on profound rational, psychological, and transrational resources, especially the spiritual dimension of humanity. Its preferred modalities are therefore symbolic, cultural, and religious—the deepest personal and social spheres, which directly and indirectly shape the national and political spheres.

In this respect, the framing question for strategic peacebuilding seems to be: how do we heal broken humanity?[13]

The builders of a comprehensive and sustainable peace, we suggest, engage each of these four fundamental questions, which together reflect the particular challenges of the contemporary global condition. To illustrate these challenges and the response offered by peacebuilding that is strategic, we consider again our opening vignettes.

How do we adjust the scope, scale and priorities of peacebuilding in order to incorporate a much wider range of actors?[14] The timely and crucial role of the transnational Community of Sant'Egidio in the resolution of Mozambique's civil war is by now a classic example of "track-two" diplomacy blossoming into "track one"; of an outsider (who was also a partial insider) providing the good offices, international resources, and connections conducive to moving the negotiations from phase to phase; and of the coordinating and empowering function of peacebuilding that is strategic.[15]

No stranger to the setting, Sant'Egidio had been involved with the Christian churches in Mozambique since 1976, when a young Mozambican priest studying in Rome, Don Jaime Goncalves, joined the community. The new freedom of movement in Mozambique in the 1980s allowed the community to demonstrate its neutrality, social concern, and dedication to rigorous dialogue. Sant'Egidio representatives became personally familiar with leaders of both warring parties and established ties to missionaries serving in the war zones controlled by RENAMO. In 1981, Goncalves, now the archbishop of Beira, met with Enrico Berlinguer, the secretary general of Italy's Communist Party, who opened a channel of dialogue between FRELIMO and Sant'Egidio. In 1982, representatives of the community negotiated the release of missionaries REN-AMO had taken captive; the occasion provided the opportunity for Sant'Egidio to build a relationship of trust and credibility with the insurgents that proved invaluable in the subsequent peace talks. In 1985, Sant'Egidio arranged a critical meeting between President Machel and Pope John Paul II.

The growing perception of Sant'Egidio as an impartial moderator and facilitator of constructive dialogue was reinforced by the way the community used its influence with governments and churches. The community established networks in Italy to obtain funds and material for Mozambique and to spread information in Europe on Mozambique's crisis. A parallel network soon appeared inside Mozambique itself, where Sant'Egidio members made overtures to the Islamic as well as the Christian communities, extending its social services and educational network across denominational and traditional lines. In addition, community leaders went to Maputo, Mozambique's capital, in 1984 to discuss humanitarian needs with government ministers. The meeting led to the establishment of a program, supported by the Italian government at Sant'Egidio's request, to deliver massive shipments of food and medicine to the war-torn nation.

In 1986, President Machel was killed in an airplane accident and replaced by Joaquim Chissano. Chissano recognized that there was no military solution to the civil war; it would have to be settled through political and diplomatic means. He also confronted a staggering debt and a worsening economic situation that the nation's Eastern-bloc allies, preoccupied with their own economic difficulties, were unable to assuage. Western aid was contingent on specific reforms in social, economic, and political policies. FRELIMO responded with the Structural Adjustment Program to move Mozambique toward a free-market economy. Prompted by the U.S. government, it also took steps to draw up a new constitution, inviting a variety of interest groups and churches to participate in the process.

FRELIMO moved to consolidate support from the religious community in Mozambique with a number of concrete concessions. The state began returning confiscated church properties, granted the churches permission to erect new buildings, and opened positions within the party to religious believers. In 1987, Sant'Egidio arranged for the pope to visit Mozambique during his African tour. Pope John Paul II met with President Chissano on September 16, 1988, in Maputo. The pope emphasized the solidarity of the Church with the aspirations of the Mozambican people for economic, social, cultural, and spiritual development, and he stressed that the role of the Church in the country was not a form of foreign intervention but a response to the desires and intentions of the people.

At this point Sant'Egidio and the Mozambican Christian Council (CCM), which represented seventeen of the nation's Protestant denominations, were able to initiate peace talks to end the civil war. Late in 1987, Chissano approved a proposal that permitted CCM to establish contact with a RENAMO delegate in Washington, D.C. In February 1988, the CCM invited Alexandre dos Santos, the Roman Catholic archbishop of Maputo, to join the peace delegation as an equal member. Goncalves, the archbishop of Beira, also joined the group. Although RENAMO consistently denied any responsibility for the continuing atrocities in Mozambique, the delegation, known as the Peace and Reconciliation Commission, became convinced that RENAMO was serious in pursuing a resolution to the conflict. In 1989, peace talks were held between these Protestant and Catholic leaders and RENAMO in Nairobi, Kenya. Although the church-mediated talks in Nairobi did not produce a concrete outcome, they created a new dynamic for peace by legitimating a forum in which both sides could formulate their demands.

At this juncture, Sant'Egidio in effect became the forum for the face-to-face talks. The first direct contact between RENAMO leadership and the FRELIMO government took place at Sant'Egidio headquarters in Rome on July 8, 1990. Joining Archbishop Goncalves on the mediation team were two Sant'Egidio representatives, Andrea Riccardi and Don Mateo Zuppi. A fourth team member, Mario Raffaelli, represented the Italian government. In concert with the Italian government, U.S. advisors, the United Nations, and several other governmental and nongovernmental organizations, the representatives of Sant'Egidio were able to maintain a momentum for peace among the two parties over the course of ten rounds of talks, which were held from 1990 to 1992 in the sixteenth-century Carmelite convent in Rome that serves as the international headquarters for Sant'Egidio. Following two closing summits, the General Peace Accord was signed on October 4, 1992.

Clearly, Sant'Egidio's contributions were indeed strategic. We refer here not only to its impartial stance but especially to its networking ability; its range of governmental and nongovernmental partners across Europe, the United States, and Africa; its cultural and religious literacy and sophistication; and above all, its capacity to mobilize resources in a timely fashion at critical junctures in the march toward an agreement. It seems fair to conclude that the expansion of actors in Mozambique's evolution toward peace, which included not only Sant'Egidio but also the churches and other religious communities native to the country, was essential to effective conflict resolution.

The link between this concern, for expanding the range of actors building peace, and the next two questions, relating to ways of effecting larger social change and pursuing justice—is embedded in the vignette describing the decision of civic leaders and officials in the city of Nogales to invite extralocal peacebuilders to assist in the conceptualization of the region's challenges and solutions. As readers will recall, the leaders of Nogales recognized that the "local" issues confronting them—including the patterns of migration as they affect the composition of the workforce, the health of the local economy, the respective rights and obligations of immigrants and citizens, cultural and ethnic tensions, and violence—are also inevitably regional, national, and indeed global issues. This is a complicated pattern that is being replicated in thousands of "borderland" communities around the world not unlike Nogales.

The strategic peacebuilder in such cases is not only a coordinator and network builder but a comparativist. She draws on knowledge of national and international law, contacts in a variety of professional fields, and the experiences of other communities in similar contexts. Yet she also depends heavily, of course, on the local wisdom and experience of the people of Nogales.

The skills needed for strategic peacebuilding are increasingly honed, and named as such, by a range of professionals trained in one or more of a variety of disciplines and areas of expertise. For example, we have peace studies colleagues at Notre Dame, Uppsala, Nairobi, Chiang Mai, Bogota, and elsewhere who advise the United Nations and specific governments on counterterrorism initiatives that favor nonviolent measures as alternatives to military operations. These scholars and faculty experts no longer rely exclusively on intelligence reports, aggregate data, and statistical analyses. They now depend on instantaneous communications and insight from the fields of conflict to stay abreast of the constantly changing dynamics on the ground and integrate into their recommendations and analysis the specific social and economic contexts, victims' experiences, human rights concerns, and justice claims of local communities. This is peacebuilding in a globalized world, where those previously voiceless now have the capacity to be heard and measured in the decision-making processes of so-called international elites.

How do we design processes that envision conflict as the opportunity for wider constructive social change?[16] How do we build the global movement for justice while at the same time empowering the voice and capacity of local communities?[17] To answer these interrelated questions by way of illustration, we consider the example of Mindanao. In that case, as in most, the prominently visible aspect of peacebuilding is the high-level negotiations that took place. Equally crucial, however, is a wider context of activities, roles, and initiatives that provided an infrastructure for constructive change in Mindanao. A short list would necessarily include the following:

1. A decade of grassroots initiatives that built relationships in local communities across the important divisions among Muslim, Christian, and indigenous Lumad groups;

2. Education and training programs in conflict transformation and peacebuilding undertaken during this same period that reached a wide range of civil society actors and created important links between local peacebuilders and the representatives of both the Philippine national army and the MILF, who on numerous occasions participated in the workshops;

3. The careful nurturing and development of ever-widening civil society networks dedicated to peacebuilding and human rights (e.g., the Peaceweavers coalition, with an active constituency of more than twenty organizations);

4. The commitment on the part of the government to create a national office to sustain and coordinate its peace efforts beyond a particular administration;
5. The commitment on the part of religious leaders to develop the Bishop-Ulama Conference that has met on a regular basis for more than a decade;
6. Sustained and long-term funding by a range of international donors to build the local capacity and institutional platforms of the local and regional organizations;
7. The commitment on the part of Malaysia, the MILF, and the Philippine government to slowly but surely negotiate the basis of the document over the course of seven years.

At the point of the collapse in negotiations, violence rose sharply and trust decreased among the players in the formal process. At the same time, however, the web of relationships mobilized within and around Mindanao. Sets of relationships between a variety of different actors that had not existed ten years ago—for example, those between civil society actors, militaries on both sides, negotiators, and the concerned international community—began to coordinate a response to the emergency needs of the communities affected by the renewed violence. These unofficial but critical actors mobilized conferences within and outside Mindanao that put forward numerous proposals for reinitiating the negotiations and the beginnings of wider consultations that moved from local to higher levels. At the time of this writing, the outcome regarding the final formal agreement is unknown, but the infrastructure of a multiplicity of actors engaged in a common concern, functioned in ways unthinkable a decade earlier. What is clear is that the final, most visible aspect of the process—the formal negotiations—rests on the courage and creativity of not only the negotiators but also the wider set of relationships, activities, and initiatives that will be needed to sustain the peaceful transformation of a social, religious, economic, and political conflict that traces its roots across centuries. This commitment to a web of activity, the development of capacity for creative response, and the high level of coordination among improbable actors represent a striking example of strategic peacebuilding.

"How do we help heal broken humanity?" is a question that cannot be dismissed as a luxury or as the work of ex post facto humanitarian actors; it is central to the heart of conflict transformation—if the conflict is actually to be transformed and the transformation sustained over time. The question and its answers are also organically connected to the questions posed previously, for, as we shall see, "healing broken humanity" necessarily involves the strategic peacebuilder in efforts to enlarge the circle of participants in peace negotiations, connect the resolution of local conflicts to larger processes of social change, and address fundamental questions of justice.

The dilemmas posed in the example of Colombia are instructive in demonstrating this inherent link between healing broken humanity and the pursuit of a *justpeace* that is, by definition, socially inclusive and transformative.

Although the Colombian government's goal of ending paramilitarism through negotiation is laudable, strategic peacebuilding requires that we place those negotiations in a context of wider transformation. The guidepost necessarily begins with and returns to the people most affected by decades of extreme abuses of human rights and the destruction of anything approximating human security at the community level. Transformation asks the hard questions of what kind of change is sought, for whom, and by whom? Processes that purport to improve the lives of local communities without sufficient engagement of their experience, without the provision of spaces to acknowledge their voice and concerns will, in the end, create political compromises and other outcomes that replicate new forms of structural violence and social exclusion. Strategic peacebuilding requires approaches that enable people who must live with the outcomes and decisions of negotiations to have adequate and secure mechanisms to participate and influence the process and the decisions.

It is no longer sufficient, that is, to fall back on the exclusive politics of old in settings of protracted conflict that suggest the common good can be assured by a small number of elite negotiators without meaningful participation of those most affected. Strategic peacebuilding requires a capacity to envision and creatively develop the mechanisms of public participation to which negotiators are accountable. The most significant weakness of far too many peace processes has been the gap between elite levels of decision making and the communities that are the recipients and inheritors of those outcomes. To build participation and voice that forges constructive change requires a far more strategic approach, with peacebuilders striving to ensure that peace is established via a reconstituted public space and new social contract.

With respect to the example of the Catholic Church in Colombia, consider the variety and specificity of roles Church officials and members have been asked to play. The key to their success as strategic peacebuilders lies in how effectively these actors mobilize their innate and extraordinary vertical and horizontal relationships across Colombian society to help forge new spaces of participation, engagement, and support for those most excluded and affected by the violence and to ensure public accountability for high-level decision makers. The healing central to peacebuilding in our era is often the restoration of voice and presence, and it depends on the creation of spaces that redefine relationships—spaces configured by the key principles of participation and voice for those most affected by the violence and accountability for those on all sides who perpetrated the violence for decades.

Justice at the Core of Strategic Peacebuilding

In most settings, the effort to validate and empower local actors, even while calling the global community to become a transparent and robust force for peace, requires that strategic peacebuilders pay close and careful attention to the demands of justice. Specifically, this often means considering the evidence on the links between inequalities and violence and paying attention to the ways inequalities are produced and reproduced within a given society.

Conflicts are more likely to escalate into violence when inequalities exist. When access to political and economic power is not at least somewhat equally available and distributed within a given society, conflicts are more likely to remain latent, generating hostilities as well as more complex problems with wider ramifications. Therefore, any attempt to end or prevent violent forms of conflict must address power sharing and transparency of decision making directly, including the vertical as well as horizontal power dimensions of intractable conflicts.

Jackie Smith's chapter in this volume raises the issue of power dynamics in the context of the debate about the relationship between free markets, economic growth, economic inequality, and violent conflict. Conflict transformation, she contends, entails reorganizing power relations, empowering some groups and reigning in others. Such reorganization of power relations can happen peacefully through processes such as the creation of mechanisms for the rule of law and fostering a human rights culture. "As global integration expands and becomes more institutionalized through trade relationships, political and economic institutions, and global communications and exchanges of all kinds, it is increasingly problematic to view a particular conflict without accounting for how it is embedded in broader regional and global sets of power relations," Smith has argued.

Similarly, the strategic peacebuilder will work to ensure the human rights foundation of a range of peacebuilding activities that may not explicitly advocate for or use the discourse of human rights, including formal peace negotiations, reconciliation work on the ground, international institution-building, and social justice movements. Numerous analyses of truth commissions, for instance, point to the need for strengthening civil society and extensive human rights education to help postconflict societies rebuild and reconcile.

"Fostering human rights is a crucial part of any attempt to overcome the inequities that divide societies," Smith writes. "And human rights education is also an antidote to the escalation of conflicts into violence, and so the lessons of truth commissions might be fruitfully extended to societies that are not currently experiencing such violence." Indeed, a strategic peacebuilding approach should encourage these sorts of connections, "not least because conflicting parties are embedded within broader networks of economic, political, and/or cultural relations that may be fueling or mitigating violent tendencies."[18]

Smith's recommendations for expanding the scope of analysis is typical of the new awareness of scholars and practitioners that an array of competencies is required if peacebuilding is to be comprehensive and sustainable. To succeed in fostering a *justpeace*, peacebuilders must nurture sustainable human relationships at every level of society—between local ethnic and religious groups, political parties and governments, faith-based groups and NGOs, state and international offices or agencies dedicated to conflict transformation, and so on. In this context peacebuilding therefore requires, inter alia, various kinds of expertise, including knowledge of international norms and institutions, global politics, economic development, the requirements of vibrant civil societies, the religious and cultural dynamics of deadly conflict, and religiously and culturally nuanced methods of conflict transformation. Accordingly, any comprehensive effort to build sustainable peace must draw on the experiences and writings of reflective practitioners and scholars working in the fields of conflict resolution, security studies, human rights advocacy, international law, and economic development, as well as psychological studies, trauma healing, ethnic and cultural studies, and religion and spirituality. These disciplines are not often marshaled together in the same enterprise, but, as we argue, strategic peacebuilding thrives on such unlikely alliances.

This confluence of actors, competencies, and resources underscores our definition of peacebuilding as a set of complementary practices aimed at transforming a society riddled by violent conflict, inequality, and other systemic forms of injustice into a society oriented toward forging a *justpeace*. Strategic peacebuilding encompasses practices of mediation and conflict resolution that bring a stop to open warfare, as well as measures to perpetuate peace agreements (monitoring, enforcing, and the like), demobilization of armed parties, accountability for human rights violators, economic development, reconciliation efforts, and the resettlement of displaced peoples. It also involves a multiplicity of institutions, including international nongovernmental and civil society organizations and religious groups.

Taking all these factors into account and attempting to discern a path forward is a formidable task. If peacebuilding begins and ends with the local, even while calling the national and international communities to reform; is attuned to culture and cultural particularity; envisions and unfolds within a long-term, even multigenerational horizon of change; draws consistently on a array of competencies; and requires the art of healing and reconciliation of victimized peoples, it is indeed a vast undertaking!

We come then to the key framing question: out of this vastness, how does the word *strategic* enhance the art of peacebuilding?

The Art of Strategic Peacebuilding

As we have seen, a multiplicity of actors, originating from and working at all levels of society, with different capacities and areas of expertise, constitutes the reality of peacebuilding today. None of these actors, considered in isolation from the others, has provided the conditions for a sustainable and comprehensive peace in societies divided or threatened by violence. Their collective efficacy increases, however, when they work together—that is, when their operations are interdependent and coordinated to some degree.

That, at least, is the conclusion of the *Human Security Report* (HSR), the most extensive, comprehensive, and conclusive study of peacebuilding to date. In accounting for the gradual reduction in wars and other forms of deadly violence in recent years, HSR author Andrew Mack writes: "Not one of the peacebuilding and conflict prevention programs on its own had much of an impact on global security in this period. Taken together, however, their effect has been profound."[19]

Both the extant literature on peacebuilding and the direct experience of observing and mediating conflict on the ground compels us to take Mack's dictum one step further: the effectiveness of peacebuilding operations in stimulating the kind of constructive social change that promotes a *justpeace* increases dramatically when the efforts of the many relevant actors, aware of their unique contributions, find points of coordination—and, where possible, integrate their efforts—around a vision of systemic change that depends on dynamic interdependencies. Peacebuilding becomes strategic when initiatives, whether from below, above, inside, or out, begin to link and coordinate with differentiated spaces and processes to effect the wider desired change. In a word, constructive transformation unfolds in relational spaces. Strategic peacebuilding requires the capacity to envision and encourage the intentional confluence—the flowing together—of improbably related processes and people toward constructive change.

Indeed, this focused definition of *strategic* features an improbable, atypical, unconventional element. The honorable and effective work of peacebuilding can and does occur in the absence of what we call strategic conceptualizing and planning by scholars, policy makers, nongovernmental officials, and the like. But bringing together, say, religious leaders and trauma therapists to pursue the healing of memories, World Bank analysts and subsistence farmers to fashion local development projects, government housing officials and slum dwellers to negotiate urban reform measures—bringing such disparate actors together under the right circumstances and with a strategy in hand for dynamic coordination and collaboration—requires the kind of creative and innovative thinking called for by the current world context. Such exercises in relationship building are precisely the kind of improbable alliances to be fashioned by the moral imagination and technical expertise of the strategic peacebuilder. Indeed, what makes the operation strategic is precisely the flowing together of people and processes who would not normally come together or head in the same direction, who now collaborate to realize a horizon of possible measures to reduce violence and advance justice.[20]

The phrase "strategic peacebuilding" requires clarity and precision about the change goals sought in a given context. In pursuit of those goals, relational spaces are then explored. The practice of strategic peacebuilding develops around the critical question of "who" and "what types of processes" will be needed to initiate, develop, and sustain the desired transformation. Our assumption is simple: in settings of deep-rooted conflict, pursuing transformation requires an alliance of key people and processes that converge in a more precise and coordinated way on the overall desired change. It requires us, no matter our expertise or access within the wider system, to recognize that the quality of the change process we seek depends on bringing together key relationships and influence that would not naturally converge.

Strategic peacebuilders therefore are intentional in thinking carefully about a range of resources and relationships that go beyond their natural niche, their most immediate circle of influence, access, and exchange. This does not mean that any specific activity, research, or approach is not important on its own; it simply means that "strategic peacebuilding" must build toward a common, coordinated set of goals. These common goals are configured within the specific connotations of "strategic."

To put it negatively, under what conditions would the word *strategic* not apply? First, thinking and acting is not strategic when the time horizon is too narrow or constricted. Let us imagine the plight of a U.S. artillery colonel in Baghdad tasked with discerning a path to "reconciliation" (as called for in the Iraq Study Group Report of November 2006). Were he to approach the situation solely by considering the immediate goals to be accomplished for U.S. forces to withdraw from Iraq—such as ensuring security for the Iraqi people, training the Iraqi police force, stabilizing key neighborhoods, and so on—the colonel's recommendations might have been considered prudent or even "tactical" in service of short-term political purposes. But by failing to comprehend the bigger picture, especially what would serve the long-term interests of stability, security, and peace in the region, such calculations would fall dreadfully short of the standards of strategic peacebuilding.[21]

Second, research or practice that focuses narrowly on one aspect of change within the larger historic cycles of violence or structural injustice is hardly strategic. In the service of postviolence reconciliation, for example, offers of amnesty or forgiveness made in the effort to prevent the recurrence of violence can be considered strategic only if they are coordinated or integrated with a commitment to retributive and restorative measures designed to uphold and strengthen the rule of law.[22]

To illustrate this point, we return to our opening example regarding the Catholic Church in Colombia. Although the Church may fulfill a short-term role by monitoring the process of demobilization of paramilitaries, that role defined in the narrow sense does not constitute strategic peacebuilding. Given the Church's accompaniment of local displaced communities, access to government officials, and direct relationships with armed groups, the key to acting strategically is found in how processes and roles are integrated toward a wider transformation of the historic patterns of conflict and violence. Strategic action requires considering how the process of demobilization sparks and sustains acknowledgment of past harms and processes of increased transparency and appropriate forms of reparation for those most harmed. These requirements imply that government programs move beyond rote application of narrowly defined negotiations toward initiatives that bring forward into the public arena processes that embrace the challenge of looking truthfully at human rights abuses and responsibilities. Such processes are engaged with local communities affected by the waves of violence and seeking reparation. In other words, the narrow role of monitoring cannot be isolated from the wider potential of transformation that involves and links national government, local communities, and the transition of militias away from violence—all spaces of relationships that the Church can mobilize and encourage through an ethical and moral imagination that requires dialogue, advocacy, and public leadership.

Third, approaches that are issue-dependent must take cognizance of their "echo effect" in related areas of the conflict. Research or practices that seek to forge solutions or end disputes—such as alternative dispute resolution practices—must take strategic measure of their implications for other official and unofficial mediation practices, police reform, and the like.[23]

Fourth, peacebuilding initiatives that are focused exclusively on a particular social sector or level must be integrated with initiatives at other levels. To be considered duly strategic, for example, grassroots/community-level peacebuilding measures must proceed with an informed awareness of the dynamics and intended outcomes of elite-based negotiations. Similarly, attempted political change based on a worldview in which the nation-state is the primary or exclusive actor has repeatedly failed, not least because the worldview was not sufficiently inclusive and comprehensive.[24]

To illustrate the point, we consider the virtual impossibility of a breakthrough occurring in Mindanao in the absence of an innovative approach that resists confining the circle of participants to the government and "the opposition." In fact, the situation is complicated by many players, both within and beyond state borders. Strategic mediation must consider the potential for the outbreak of conflict on any or all of these levels, and the interests of key players at each one.

To make peacebuilding strategic, in short, requires that research and practice employ a comprehensive perspective that does not restrict the inquiry/ practice to the immediate presenting concern but embeds it in a systemic, encompassing analysis. All of the areas mentioned become more strategic if they are time expansive (e.g., they take account of historic patterns, dynamics of exclusion and oppression, historic experiences of trauma, and so on); systemically oriented (i.e., they embed understanding within a multifaceted structural view of change); and multidependent (i.e., linking people, movements, levels, phenomena in a process that includes interdependence but strains for something greater, such as principled collaboration for the common good).

To repeat: we are not arguing that research and practices that engage particular timeframes of action or levels of work are not important on their own. We are suggesting that if they do not include a robust inquiry into the "wider and deeper," then they are aspects of peacebuilding without the qualifier "strategic."

Five Suggestions for Practitioners

What practical suggestions can we make for those currently working to build peace within their particular niche, area of expertise or issue, and who seek to become strategic? Speaking directly to the practitioners, we can identify five.

First, the cornerstone of strategic practice is the act of locating oneself within the wider system of conflict and change. Without a comprehensive vision of the landscape, it is impossible to see clearly your particular contribution, the importance of other sectors and initiatives, or the points of coordination and convergence that must be forged. To do otherwise is like arguing that what matters most for the sound performance of a boat is a good rudder, sail, or hull. Systemically, they are all needed and need each other. The least strategic approach is to believe that you and your particular contribution are the only ones that exist, matter, or should be given priority.

Second, learn to think about your goals in reference to change processes that build and transform constructively those things that most concern you. When you develop a capacity to envision peacebuilding as change processes that lead to desired transformation, you will naturally notice and identify much more clearly the key relational spaces, alliances, and influences that are needed and mutually interdependent for achieving those goals.

Third, focus on clusters of influence and contribution around the change goals. Cluster thinking requires you to reflect on sets of people and platforms that would need to align to affect a more robust change process. The most effective change processes are those that integrate unusual sets of people in a common direction. For example, when key businessmen in South Africa began to align with social change activists, apartheid cracked. This was by no means the only thing that created the change, but this clustering of influence contributed a unique and what we would call strategic impact on the overall situation.

Retain the idea of contribution as opposed to attribution. Too often, peacebuilders worry about getting credit or laying claim to the outcome of a particular process. System change happens when sets of influences align, each contributing and affecting their sector and the whole. Attribution, within a systems view, is senseless and potentially counterproductive because it requires one to locate a single cause and effect. Strategic thinking understands that transformation flows through multiple causes and effects.

Fourth, identify system change facilitators or existing spaces where system change converges. A system change facilitator, as we call it, refers to a role (not necessarily found in a single person or institution) within the system that pays attention to the multiple changes processes happening simultaneously. This role consists of identifying the needs of the change processes in the system, imagining creative ways to support those changes process, and how and when they may converge toward wider, sustained change. In a complex system like peacebuilding, we have too few spaces that notice and create points of coordination for strategic impact. Specific activities include identifying and prioritizing strategic change processes, naming the gaps and needs in promoting and sustaining those change processes and supporting them with corresponding resources, creating and encouraging a strategic convergence of processes, and staying vigilant about the bigger picture.

Fifth, develop a capacity to think simultaneously rather than sequentially. Most peacebuilding programs and initiatives develop around some form of sequential thinking, that is, we first do A, then B, then eventually C. The logic of this approach is its capacity to provide phases and deliverable programs. The dynamic of change and social transformation is rarely if ever logical or linear, however. Thus the weakness inherent in sequential planning is its limited capacity to see emerging and unexpected interdependencies related to change within the wider system. The capacity to notice simultaneity—the attentiveness to the ways in which A, B, and C are happening at the same time—increases one's ability to identify the various aspects of change that eventually will be needed, nurture their development along the way even though they are not currently connected, and watch for opportune moments where they may converge.

Conclusion: Five Principles of Strategic Peacebuilding

To summarize our argument, we conclude by reviewing five principles underlying the peacebuilding conceptual framework we have presented in this chapter. These principles animate the basic philosophy of peacebuilding at its most robust and provide a guideline for assessing the strategic weight of specific initiatives.

First, strategic peacebuilding is *comprehensive*. This principle commits us to develop the lenses that permit us to see the overall picture of needs, actions, vision, and design—the architecture of peacebuilding. We must be able to step back from the day-to-day swirl of crises and reactions to situate ourselves, as well as events, in the broader flow of the vision and purpose of our efforts.

Second, strategic peacebuilding is *interdependent*. This principle proposes that peacebuilding is connected to the nature and quality of relationships. It is a *system* of interconnected people, roles, and activities: no one person, activity, or level is capable of designing and delivering peace on its own. All things are linked and mutually affect one another. Interdependence seeks to build the relationships necessary for pursuing and sustaining desired change. In specific terms, this often means that we must develop processes that link and relate dissimilar concerns and activities and that forge relationships between people who are not like-minded.

Third, strategic peacebuilding is *architectonic*, that is, it pays attention to design and infrastructure. This principle demands that we provide the social spaces, logistical mechanisms, and institutions necessary for supporting the processes of change engendered to pursue a *justpeace*. Peacebuilding infrastructure can be likened to the foundation and pillars that hold up a house. In this instance the foundations are people, their relationships, and the social spaces needed to support the processes of change from division and violence to increased ownership and responsibility for the building of peace. Infrastructure creates the platform that enables processes to weather the immediate intensity of permanently emerging crises while pursuing with patience the slow, long-term desired change.

Fourth, strategic peacebuilding is *sustainable*. This principle emphasizes the long-term concern for where our activity and energy is leading. Rather than thinking only in terms of immediate effective responses to issues and crises, sustainability requires that we think in terms of what creates ongoing capacity within the setting for responding to and transforming recurring cycles of conflict and crisis. Drawing inspiration from appropriate technology, sustainable peacebuilding seeks to discover and strengthen the resources rooted in the context of the protracted conflict.

Fifth, strategic peacebuilding is *integrative*. This principle pushes us beyond the visible aspects of any given activity and requires that we situate the design and assessment of peacebuilding action in terms of how it links immediate need with the desired vision of change. To seek integration means to gauge how to respond proactively to emerging, dynamic social situations such that we are responsive to immediate concerns and needs, while at the same time reinforcing the platform supportive of change processes. We are crisis-responsive, not crisis-driven. Striving for integration of people and resources raises analytic inquiries to the level of the strategic who, what, where, and how of any activity. It requires of peacebuilders a more comprehensive view of the situation in terms of levels, timeframes, processes, and their respective roles/activities.

Achieving a minimal consensus on a comprehensive definition of strategic peacebuilding, we believe, is a first step toward deepening the transformative agency of peacebuilding and establishing it as a guiding concept for practitioners, policy makers, and scholars.

Thus we find it appropriate and heartening that the chapters in this volume address a wide range of topics, themes, and activities not always included in the same conversation—including debates about the relationship between economic growth, democratization, and violence reduction; the role of religious actors in transforming conflict; the relationship between counterterrorism, sanctions, and peacebuilding; and the ways of strengthening the peacebuilding agency of the United Nations. All of these are part of peacebuilding in its most comprehensive and sustainable form—the mode of peacebuilding, that is, which we indicate by the adjective *strategic*. That the authors collectively illustrate the convergences of these various themes and topics within the parameters of one coherent conversation and, furthermore, take steps toward imagining their possible confluences, is—how shall we put it?—improbable.

Thus, we begin.

NOTES

1. What is peace? is a question asked continually, not least by people working actively for it in their personal and professional lives, including the authors in this volume. The question is complicated but hardly impossible to answer. One can discern something approaching a consensus among mainstream secular and religious thinkers, which identifies the conditions for the elimination of deadly violence and the development of local and national communities that respect the dignity of each individual and promote authentic human flourishing. These conditions include the absence of war and other forms of deadly violence, such as violations of human dignity by state or nonstate actors (i.e., negative peace) and extends to basic human security, access to food and clean drinking water, housing, justly compensated employment, education, and other

expressions of positive peace. See, inter alia, Chester A. Crocker, Fen Osler Hampson, and Pamela Aall, eds., *Turbulent Peace: The Challenges of Managing International Conflict* (Washington, D.C.: U.S. Institute of Peace Press, 2001); Louis Kriesberg, *Constructive Conflicts: From Escalation to Resolution* (Lanham, Md.: Rowman & Littlefield, 1998); John Paul Lederach, *Building Peace: Sustainable Reconciliation in Divided Societies* (Washington, D.C.: U.S. Institute of Peace Press, 1997); and Oliver Ramsbotham, Tom Woodhouse, and Hugh Miall, *Contemporary Conflict Resolution: The Prevention, Management and Transformation of Deadly Conflicts,* 2nd ed. (Cambridge, UK: Polity, 2005).

2. See, inter alia, Elizabeth Cousens, *Peacebuilding as Politics: Cultivating Peace in Fragile Societies* (Boulder, Colo.: Lynne Rienner, 2001); Michael Pugh, *Regeneration of War Torn Societies* (Houndmills, Basingstoke, Hampshire: Macmillan; New York: St. Martin's Press, 2000).

3. John Paul Lederach, "Justpeace: The Challenge of the 21st Century," in *People Building Peace* (Utrecht: European Centre for Conflict Prevention, 1999). See also Pierre Allan and Alexis Keller, eds., *What Is a Just Peace?* (Oxford: Oxford University Press, 2006); and Chadwick Alger and Michael Stohl, eds., *A Just Peace through Transformation: Cultural, Economic, and Political Foundations for Change* (Proceedings of the International Peace Research Association, Eleventh General Conference, University of Sussex, 1986). The idea that peaceful change must address both root causes and transform violent expressions of conflict has been present for many years in peace studies literature and beyond. Roman Catholic Social Teaching, especially sections of the encyclicals of Pope John XXIII, Pope Paul VI, and Pope John Paul II, can be read as commentaries on Paul VI's admonition: "If you want peace, work for justice." The literature of peace studies, including the titles cited previously in these notes, with its focus on root causes of conflict, has consistently expressed a concern that peace not be understood as a static concept of tranquility on the surface but must address root causes requiring a rigorous inquiry into the interplay of justice and peace. See, for example, Johan Galtung, "A Structural Theory of Imperialism," *Journal of Peace Research* 8: 81–117; and Adam Curle, *True Justice: Quaker Peace Makers and Peace Making* (London: Invicta Press, 1981). Glen Stassen coined the phrase "just peacemaking" as the overarching nomenclature that articulated the multifaceted nature of peacebuilding that must include elements that both advocate for needed change while reducing reliance on violence as the only way to produce the change or respond to conflict. See Glen Stassen, *Just Peacemaking* (Louisville, Ky.: Westminster/John Knox Press, 1992). Within the conflict transformation field, John Paul Lederach initiated a framework for peacebuilding that explicitly argued for the convergence of *nonviolent activism,* often framed as efforts to raise awareness and escalate conflict from out of a latent state of passivity as part of the necessary work for justice, and *mediation,* often seen as a mechanism to deescalate acute conflict and violence. He referred to this convergent space as a transformational approach to conflict and peacebuilding. Lederach proposed the use of a single word, *justpeace,* to highlight the significant need to focus more carefully on the gap, particularly within the practice of peacebuilding, that the professional field of conflict resolution has evolved greater capacity through negotiation and mediation to lower violence but has not equally evolved a capacity to increase justice in human relationships, structures, and institutions. See John Paul Lederach, *Preparing for Peace* (Syracuse, N.Y.: Syracuse University Press, 1995). Lisa Schirch links the goal of *justpeace* with strategic peacebuilding in a comprehensive overview that brings together a much wider array of approaches and specialty areas in the field. See Lisa Schirch, *The Little Book of Strategic Peacebuilding* (Intercourse, Penn.: Good Books, 2004).

4. John Darby, ed., *Violence and Reconstruction* (Notre Dame, Ind.: University of Notre Dame Press, 2005); John Darby, *The Effects of Violence on Peace Processes* (Washington, D.C.: U.S. Institute of Peace Press, 2001).

5. John Paul Lederach, *The Moral Imagination: The Art and Soul of Building Peace* (New York: Oxford University Press, 2005).

6. For trenchant criticism of the UN peacekeeping operations in the 1990s, see William Shawcross, *Deliver Us from Evil: Peacekeepers, Warlords and a World of Endless Conflict* (New York: Simon & Schuster, 2000).

7. See "The Water and Conflict Bibliography" funded by the Carnegie Foundation and hosted by the Pacific Institute (http://biblio.pacinst.org/conflict).

8. Martin Wolf, *Why Globalization Works* (New Haven, Conn.: Yale University Press, 2004).

9. See, inter alia, Morton Deutsch and Peter T. Coleman, eds., *The Handbook of Conflict Resolution: Theory and Practice* (San Francisco, Calif.: Jossey-Bass, 2000); Edward Newman and Albrecht Schnabel, eds., *Recovering from Civil Conflict: Reconciliation, Peace, and Development* (Portland, Ore.: F. Cass, 2002).

10. Schirch, *The Little Book of Strategic Peacebuilding*; I. William Zartman, ed., *Peacemaking in International Conflict: Methods and Techniques* (Washington, D.C.: U.S. Institute of Peace, 2007); Lederach, *The Moral Imagination*.

11. Caritas Internationalis, the worldwide Catholic relief and development organization, has developed significant expertise in conflict transformation and peacebuilding. Its how-to manual and conceptual guide to the topic, *Working for Reconciliation: A Caritas Handbook 1999*, makes explicit the centrality of grassroots agency: "As we look back on the history of peacemaking and peace processes we see that they have traditionally centered on diplomacy, mediation, the cessation of hostilities and the achievement of peace agreements. These things we are all familiar with. Once a peace agreement is signed the diplomats and mediators go home and parties to the conflict get on with life under the terms of the peace agreement. *This is not sufficient any more.*" What must be developed, the handbook continues, are cohorts of indigenous peacebuilders—agents for nonviolent change who, as members of the society experiencing strife, have a vested and long-term interest in applying their irreplaceable local knowledge to the tasks of social transformation and hoped-for reconciliation. Such local and regional conciliators have become essential actors "because peace settlements do not bring about the required change of heart, which is the crux of peace, particularly in complex internal conflicts." Brian Starken, ed., *Working for Reconciliation: A Caritas Handbook* (Vatican City: Caritas Internationalis, 1999), 4.

12. John Paul Lederach, *The Little Book of Conflict Transformation* (Intercourse, Pa.: Good Books, 2004).

13. Barry Hart, ed., *Peacebuilding in Traumatized Societies* (New York: University Press of America, 2008); Carolyn Yoder, *The Little Book of Trauma Healing* (Intercourse, Pa.: Good Books, 2006).

14. See, inter alia, Deutsch and Coleman, *Handbook of Conflict Resolution*; Newman and Schnabel, *Recovering from Civil Conflict*.

15. This account of Sant'Egidio's role in ending the civil war in Mozambique is adapted from R. Scott Appleby, *The Ambivalence of the Sacred: Religion, Violence, and Reconciliation* (Lanham, Md.: Rowman & Littlefield, 2000), 158–164.

16. Schirch, *The Little Book of Strategic Peacebuilding*; Zartman, *Peacemaking in International Conflict*; Lederach, *The Moral Imagination*.

17. Lederach, *The Little Book of Conflict Transformation*.

18. Jackie Smith, personal communication.

19. Andrew Mack, ed., *Human Security Report 2005: War and Peace in the 21st Century* (New York: Oxford University Press, 2005).

20. Lederach, *Building Peace.*

21. See, for example, Gerard F. Powers, "Our Moral Duty: How Would U.S. Withdrawal Affect the Iraqi People," *America, 198,* no. 5 (February 18, 2008).

22. For the basic themes of the debate, see, inter alia, C. Dale White, *Making a Just Peace: Human Rights and Domination Systems* (Nashville, Tenn.: Abingdon Press, 1998); Priscilla Hayner, *Unspeakable Truths: Confronting State Terror and Atrocity* (New York and London: Routledge, 2001); Neil J. Kritz, ed., *Transitional Justice: How Emerging Democracies Reckon with Former Regimes* (Washington, D.C.: U.S. Institute of Peace Press, 1995); and A. James McAdams, ed., *Transitional Justice and the Rule of Law in New Democracies* (Notre Dame, Ind.: University of Notre Dame Press, 1997).

23. Among the key recommendations that emerge from this view is the importance for state- and national-level actors to engage the basic premises of strategic peacebuilding, requiring that they more fully embrace the paradox of their agency. Strategic peacebuilding requires the practicality of the interest-based pragmatists in reference to programmatic response to core challenges while at the same time nurturing the moral imagination necessary to envision constructive change as spaces of interaction that encourage and sustain a wider participation of improbable people and processes. This is particularly true of high-level negotiations whose primary weakness has been the lack of imagination for how a wider public can be informed, be engaged, and have points of access into the framing and delivery of processes that so affect their lives. Typically, this is seen only as a literal afterthought of peace accords. Strategic peacebuilding forges the kind of imagination that envisions the nature of change and locates key constituencies that will need to be included and supported early and often in the process. In practical terms, it requires innovation in how state-level processes make visible and include multilevel and multisector connections.

24. Analyses of peacebuilding operations from various perspectives and levels of sympathy include Michael Doyle and Nicholas Sambanis, *Making War and Building Peace: United Nations' Peace Operations* (Princeton, N.J.: Princeton University Press, 2006); Elizabeth M. Cousens and Chetan Kumar, *Peacebuilding as Politics: Cultivating Peace in Fragile Societies* (Boulder, Colo.: Lynne Rienner, 2001); Oliver Richmond and Henry Carey, *Subcontracting Peace: The Challenges of the NGO Peacebuilding* (Aldershot, Hampshire, U.K.: Ashgate, 2005); Roland Paris, *At War's End: Building Peace after Civil Conflict* (Cambridge: Cambridge University Press, 2004); Fen Osler Hampson, *Nurturing Peace: Why Peace Settlements Succeed or Fail* (Washington, D.C.: U.S. Institute of Peace Press, 1996).

2

Strategic Peacebuilding: Concepts and Challenges

Peter Wallensteen

Peacebuilding is one of the novel terms in political discourse that actually has a longer history, for instance, in the early work of Galtung.[1] It is parallel to concepts such as security community, which also stem from an academic concern.[2] When conditions require, such terms take on a political dimension and become operational in ways often not anticipated by the original inventor of the concept. Peacebuilding today is one such urgent concern. It is not difficult to explain why. The Uppsala Conflict Data Program has identified 121 armed conflicts, that is, small or large wars, since 1989; and 231 since the end of World War II. By historical standards this is a staggering amount. At its peak, in the early 1990s, there were 51 armed conflicts waged around the planet at the same time. In 2005 the number was "down" to 31. Since the end of the Cold War, a majority of UN member states have had a war on their territory or have had their nationals in a war. Including member states' engagement in international peacekeeping efforts, dealing with war today is a universally shared concern.[3]

Wars in seemingly distant places affect the entire planet. The major refugee flows come from wars, the largest one at the end of 2006 being the exodus from Iraq into neighboring countries but also into the European Union.[4] Furthermore, refugees from wars may face greater difficulties in returning after the triggering event than would be the case for those displaced because of natural disasters. Politics, economic conditions, and social demands all enter into their situation. They may become permanent diasporas that play a political role in their host country's relations to their home state. This is only one example of how such events have major repercussions. Thus, peace is a benefit to all and as a consequence, peacebuilding is a global issue.

Research into the conditions of peacebuilding still is fairly limited. The events of the 1990s have sparked renewed concern on the conditions of peacebuilding as well as strategies that could be potentially useful for international, regional, and local actors. In the policy debate as well as in the scholarly community there have emerged numerous concepts of peacebuilding and appropriate strategies. In this chapter, a selected set of concepts of peacebuilding are discussed to contribute to increased consistency. Also, thoughts on policy strategies will be presented together with ideas on urgent research needs.

An example of the need for research concerns the issue of the actual reduction of armed conflicts since the early 1990s. This has been attributed to the involvement of the international community. These conflicts have not been ended by themselves or even by the parties. International efforts have been central for the creation of peace, through mediation, negotiations, peace agreements, and peace arrangements. This seems to demonstrate that international efforts can succeed in reducing the incidence of war. The *Human Security Report* 2005 (HSR) presented these arguments.[5] They have gained considerable acceptance, and parallel, for instance, the results of the high-level panel of the UN secretary general, which suggested the formation of the UN Peacebuilding Commission on the basis of similar findings. This commission is now in operation.[6] Still, conclusive, scholarly based proof of the connection is lacking. HSR demonstrates a reverse covariation: as international peacemaking activities go up, the number of conflicts goes down. It also shows that other plausible explanations, such as increased economic wealth and growth in the number of democratically ruled states, do not follow the same patterns. These finding are made on a global and macro level of analysis. The literature on actual interventions tells a more rugged history with less straightforward successes. Thus, further study is warranted on the correlation of global, regional, and local levels to validate the role of the international community, but the conclusion of the HSR is the most authoritative for the time being.[7]

Peacebuilding and the Conflict Typology

The understanding of peacebuilding has become a major challenge to the international community. Peacekeeping missions have been supplemented with peacebuilding functions. Clearly, this refers to postwar situations. This is drawn from one of the earlier definitions, the one by UN Secretary General Boutros Boutros-Ghali in 1992, when the phrase actually was "postconflict peacebuilding" and concerned "action to identify and support structures which will tend to strengthen and solidify peace in order to avoid a relapse into conflict."[8] In principle, this implies that there are preconflict peacebuilding efforts as well. Possibly these could be defined as preventive measures, actions by the international community to contain the emergence of new wars. In later usage the word *postconflict* has been incorporated into the delimitation of peacebuilding. It makes sense to refer only to postwar actions, although they, of course, also have a long-term ambition to prevent the emergence of renewed conflict by the same parties over the same issues. The international efforts and much of scholarly understanding have come to concentrate on postwar situations. Thus, it is important to scrutinize such war situations first to then be able to encircle and define peacebuilding as a general concept.

There are differences in the type of conflict that have an impact on how actors and scholars can conduct a discussion on peacebuilding strategies. A typology of conflicts will assist in categorizing different peacebuilding efforts before we can settle for a general definition.[9]

The post–Cold War conflicts over Liberia, Burundi, Haiti, and Sierra Leone are often given as typical examples of challenging situations for peacebuilding tasks. These cases all share the need for the reconstruction of a society *after a protracted internal war*. Peacebuilding in this case entails the reforming of state structures, and also bringing together factions that have been fighting for a long time. Issues of war crimes, reconciliation, as well as economic reconstruction are high on the agenda. The list of activities is long. These are situations where we also find peacekeeping missions (by the UN or by regional organizations) engaged in multidimensional tasks. Internal conflicts have become a major concern for peacebuilding theorizing. This category definitely deserves attention. In much writing, however, it seems to be the only category that is referred to.

However, there are other situations as well, one of which is *the creation of entirely new states* as a result of conflict. An example of an unsolved conflict is the Israel–Palestine conflict, but this category also includes the separation of Eritrea from Ethiopia after a long war inside the then-existing Ethiopian state seemingly ended that conflict. Other, not terminated situations that concern the status of particular territories and where state boundaries might be affected are, for instance, those over Northern Ireland; the conflict between Sri Lanka and the Liberation Tigers of Tamil Eelam; the conflict over the Basque provinces and their status in Spain; and the one over Abkhazia in Georgia. A question to ask is whether the task of peacebuilding in this type of conflict would be the same as the one of reconstructing a country torn by civil conflict. In reality, a potential or agreed territorial separation actually involves the reconstruction of the former central state as well as the construction of an entirely new unit. There is a dual state-building activity, and peacebuilding would then rather refer to the management of the relations between the two new entities. The renewed war between Ethiopia and Eritrea less than seven years after the agreed separation testifies to the significance of this. It also illustrates the lack of effective peacebuilding action. Very little attention was paid to this relationship internationally following the dissolution of Ethiopia and the ending of the war in 1991.

Then, there are the *classical interstate wars*. They are not that many today, but the category remains very important, as exemplified by a most recent one: the 2003 war between the United States and its allies on the one hand and Iraq under Saddam Hussein on the other. This conflict has then transformed itself into an internationalized civil war and also contains features of a potential break-up of the state. This is an exceptional situation. In this category of conflicts more typical are territorial conflicts, for instance, over border issues. There are also cases that involve internal affairs, such as the removal of an entire government. This provides for a set of different challenges to peacebuilding efforts that require further elaboration. Even if the removal of a dictator may be immediately applauded, the long-term presence and dependence on external actors may create resentment and color internal dynamics.

Obviously, the tasks are many following a war. The proliferation of concepts tells us that. Many of them center on the functions of the state. The state is central to many wars, whether they concern the control of government or a particular piece of territory.[10] Thus, peacebuilding will have to deal with the state. This means that when confronting a case of peacebuilding, an important first question to ask is whether this involves a significant state-building component. As already observed, most references today are to peacebuilding within states, which often means exactly this: there is an important element of state reconstruction involved. Thus, we have to consider the issue of the state when developing a terminology for peacebuilding.

Peacebuilding and the State

There are good reasons to concentrate on the state, as it has a set of unique functions that are relevant for postwar conditions. These concern such matters as maintaining a monopoly of violence, generation of tax revenue, exerting territorial authority, and providing legitimacy of decision making. There are different peacebuilding dimension for each of these elements of the state. Thus, peacebuilding has to be understood as an activity covering many sectors, and, in theory and practice, making them interact in reinforcing dynamics.

A common conception found in leading literature points to one of the key elements, that is, *state-building*, but as a more limited task, for instance, of reforming state structures, establishing noncorrupt practices, and fairness and transparency in governmental transactions. There is also a separate concern aimed at *democracy-building*: creating specific political structures and a political culture in line with predominant thinking in the world today. Democracy-building could be said to cover the input factor into a state's policy making, responding to such issues as how policies are made, the degree of popular representation, whether equal access is guaranteed, how and when elections are conducted, and so on. The concept of state-building could then be limited to the output side of policies, giving answers to questions about how decisions are made, how they are implemented, and by whom. The rule of law is an obvious element in this, actually relevant both for the input and output sides, but it also relates to the next aspect.[11]

Highly related are the issues of the security sector and its reforming, what could be called *security-building*. It is a matter of reconstructing a state after a war and considering its territorial authority. Will the postwar regime actually exert control over the territory under its formal control, with what means, and how are those means checked? In any war, the security services (be they the military, the police, the intelligence operations, paramilitary activities, or revolutionary armies) have national priority. During the war, they are the ones with the first access to resources, decision making, and privileges. The postwar conditions challenge many of these advantages and thus make such sectors problematic to deal with. There is a civilian–military relationship that has to be established, which will affect the state structures that are created and the scope for democracy-building. There are also other priorities in society, making the demobilization of the armed forces a necessity. Military leadership as well as ordinary soldiers may find this difficult, and they also believe that the civil economy has little to offer.

These concerns are different from what is customarily referred to as *nation-building*, which deals with the creation of a common attitude of belonging together, possibly healing the divides and wounds that the war left behind, a more "soft" aspect than the "hard" ones of (re)creating state structures and dealing with postwar security. This ambition could be said to focus on the legitimacy of the new postwar arrangement. Reconciliation includes the recognition of past wrongdoings and an incorporation of the perspectives of the other side.[12] The expectation is that a unifying nation-building effort will improve relations in a society in the long run, and thus make the new conditions more acceptable to all. This is a tall order, of course, and it is likely to be the more complex the more there is of ethnic diversity and experience of recent ethnically defined conflict.

Nation-building is likely to be more possible if the state formation conflict has a colonial nature, where the polarization is between a distant center (colonial metropolis) and a local liberation movement, than when it has to do with a nearby center with more interspersed populations. There is a difference between the decolonization movements of the 1950s and 1960s in Africa and the separation movements of Biafra, Bangladesh, or the Tamil Tigers during the following decades. These have often not been accepted by the original anticolonial movements as equally legitimate. Eritrea and East Timor are interesting cases where the liberation movement was waged as an anticolonial struggle (having had different colonial masters than the central government at the time, i.e., Ethiopia and Indonesia) and thus had more popular legitimacy. Internationally, these two movements and the following creation of new states were not accepted until after the end of the Cold War, when the national center changed its mind (after the fall of the Mengistu and Suharto regimes, respectively). The conflict with the former center, however, has continued to be significant in the building of a postwar identity and has resulted in renewed conflict.

In addition to these tasks, there is the need to reconstruct the economy and, as it were, shape market conditions. This could be referred to as *market-building* of the internal economy and establishing its relationship to external economic activities. This is necessary for the postwar government: the economy has to move on, generating the revenue the state needs and giving jobs to the unemployed (not the least the ex-combatants), thus reducing the pressure on the state to provide such services. However, experience is that international support is short-lived, international aid is temporary, and international trade is unpredictable. There is a need to import goods and services but also to develop export products, which require competitiveness and capital. Investment may be forthcoming in sectors that are attractive to the international market (i.e., oil, mining) but not necessarily conducive for job creation or policies against corruption.

All of these peacebuilding ambitions have their own names and can be seen as independent tasks, but they also relate to one another. Arriving at the appropriate mix and spacing such activities in a reinforcing way is a major political task. This is where different peacebuilding strategies become important. In total, this is what will be judged when evaluating the postwar policies. Together, however, these aspects would tentatively define a broad concept of *peacebuilding*: to provide the postconflict conditions that make the inhabitants of a society secure in life and dignity now and for the foreseeable future.[13] Only with this sense of basic security are people interested in investing money, time, and energy in doing all these other tasks. If a society or a relationship is likely to collapse again, within some few years, what is the point in making long-term commitments? This also means that the different elements of peacebuilding have to be clearly identified and related to one another. A task of a strategy of peacebuilding is to arrive at an interaction among these factors, creating the sustainable conditions that yield the basic security needed.

This first definition works for all the types of conflicts that have entered into a postwar phase. For internal conflicts this should be fairly obvious, as governance is likely to be what was disputed and possibly regulated by the victor or in a mutual peace agreement. In state-formation conflicts that have resulted in two separate states, there is a need for internal peacebuilding, particularly in the novel entity: bureaucracies have to be built (state-building), procedures have to be developed for popular influence (if democracy-building is the priority), borders have to be surveyed and controlled (part of security-building), taxes have to be collected, an economy has to be stimulated (efforts of market-building). The pressure for nation-building is likely to be particularly strong: the new national identity has to be cemented to justify all the sacrifices that the conflict involved. Here, there is a strong difference between those situations where states were created fairly peacefully (such as Slovakia and the Czech Republic breaking up their common union in 1993, or the dissolution of the Soviet Union) and the violent situations in former Yugoslavia or between Ethiopia and Eritrea. It can be postulated that the emphasis on national identity is likely to be higher the more violence there has been in the process of the break-up.

The way state formation conflicts end will affect international relations in the postconflict situation. The dissolution of the British Empire in India resulted in a peacefully agreed separation, but its implementation led to the deaths of millions of people and left the subcontinent divided ever since. For each population security has been sought within its own state, rather than with the former adversary. Interstate security dilemmas rise under these conditions. For instance, the Eritrean decision to make its own currency (to get its own economy going, that is, a market-building effort) is said to have soured the relations to Ethiopia (which was not informed beforehand and whose economy depended on Eritrean ports for trade and transactions, immediately affecting its own market-building plans). When a minor border dispute occurred in the following year, it immediately escalated into a war (the war thus was fought over a piece of territory deemed at least symbolically important to both, a failure in mutual security-building). There was no confidence and, in effect, no peacebuilding between the two countries. Thus, even though security was built internally, the international dimension had been neglected. This suggests that what takes place inside one of the formerly united units will affect that other. Independence is not absolute, and a border, however solid, is not enough as a guarantee against the other.

State-formation conflicts after a war that has resulted in the creation of two internationally recognized states constitute a subcategory of interstate wars. The classical interstate wars are fought between neighbors that have had both cooperative and conflictual relations through history. Peacebuilding in these cases involves the creation of regional security arrangements, as covered in the term *security community*.[14] In such a community, there is some degree of integration, but the key issue is that the parties actually do not expect conflicts to be solved by violent means. An attitudinal change has taken place cementing the relations. This may sometimes appear utopian, but in fact such transitions have taken place throughout history, even among major powers. Britain and France were rivals during the 1800s, whereas during the 1900s they were on the same side in all major wars.

The case of Franco-German relations after 1945 is seminal, however, and illustrates all the dimensions of peacebuilding we have identified. It involved a state reconstruction effort (of defeated Germany, developing a decentralized federal structure); democracy-building (democratizing German society, civilian control over the armed forces, even including a right for soldiers to refuse certain orders); national redefinition (war crimes pursued and Germany defining itself as a democratic, peaceful and European country); and market integration (the Marshall Plan, the German currency reform). It was a successful transformation of the inner operations of a society. Important is that this was combined with integration into the rest of Europe (what today is the European Union, EU). It is a unique example of peacebuilding that has left a lasting imprint on world history.

In many other interstate conflicts similar strategies have been less successful or even avoided. Many divides have instead been strengthened, rather than reduced, as time passes and interaction occurs. The two Koreas remain divided, having fought a war in the early 1950s and that war continued to be an important marker for the separated identities of the two sides. The most recent interstate war, the United States versus Iraq, has not included a successful peacebuilding strategy.

To analyze peacebuilding there is, consequently, a need to keep in mind the difference in the type of conflict (internal, state formation, interstate conflicts) as well as the focus of ambitions (e.g. the building of state structures, democracy, security, identities, legitimacy, markets, all at the same time, in a sequence, or only concentrating on some of the tasks). The different elements of peacebuilding mean that we have to be concerned about the strategy for peacebuilding. What are the elements that are normally given priority in post-war society? With this in mind and with a tentative, overarching general definition where peacebuilding is defined as the provision of present and future conditions of security in life and dignity, the achievements in research with implications for strategic considerations can now be reviewed.

Researching Peacebuilding

Peacebuilding in this way is clearly a major undertaking. I have isolated four key dimension and three different types of postconflict situation. This makes twelve different challenging situations to peacebuilding efforts. Recent research has seldom made such detailed specifications but tends to treat internal and state formation conflicts as one and the same and not say much at all on interstate conflict. Furthermore, the four dimensions are seldom separated in research and, thus, not completely covered. There have been more case studies of, for instance, security-building strategies (particularly on ex-combatants), but few very systematic projects (dealing with a large number of cases). The field, in other words, finds itself in an early stage. Furthermore, there is a strong focus on individual cases, rather than on regional aspects, and fairly little on workable strategies undertaken by international, national, or local actors. Still, there are some important debates and insights, which have to be presented. The following section deals with studies that include at least a comparative approach.

A first observation is that peacebuilding is a novel activity, and thus it is difficult to determine the appropriate time frames. Some studies measure the achievements after two or five years.[15] At best, this is a first period that shows that a society has overcome the immediate postwar conditions. But it is not enough to say that a country or a relationship is beyond the risk of relapse after such a short period. Even under the best of circumstances, peacebuilding is likely to be a concerted process for ten or fifteen years. Frequently used examples in literature and public discussions include Germany and Japan, which began to return to pre–World War II economic levels fifteen years after their defeat.[16] Lebanon was beginning to appear "normal" in 2005, fifteen years after the end of the war: the center of Beirut was reconstructed, the Syrian forces were moved out, and democracy was taking root. However, many of these efforts were undone by the renewed destruction in 2006, again increasing the tensions among the different groups in the society. Uganda's major war ceased in 1986 and by the late 1990s the country was on an economic upturn, although still challenged by rebels in the north of the country.

The number of years that have passed without a return to war is only a crude indicator of whether a country has successfully managed the transition from war to peace. Return to war, of course, is a sign that something failed in peacebuilding, particularly if it is a war with the same actors that fought the previous war. However, conflicts in new constellations may in fact say that peacebuilding worked in one relationship, but that no efforts were taken in another relationship. The definition provided here suggests that it should be for the society as a whole, rather than an arrangement with a particular former enemy. Any war would be a sign of failure.

Thus, I ask what recent research provides in terms of explaining the continuation of comprehensive peace after a devastating war. There seems to be a clustering of explanations emerging from four separate, general questions, cutting across the dimensions and types I have introduced. First, studies point to the ending of the (previous or last) war: which types of ending? Second, there can also be factors relating to how the last war started: what were the causes and have they been removed or handled? Third, is there the postwar capacity for peacebuilding? Fourth, what is the neighborhood in which a society finds itself—is it supportive or not?

First, there is the point of beginning postwar peacebuilding: *how did the last/latest war end?* There is a strong correlation between earlier war experiences and relapse into renewed war. A crucial factor is the type of ending. That may be highly significant for what is to follow in a particular relationship or society as a whole. There are two typical ways of ending a war and thus starting a new era of peacebuilding. One is that the warring parties sign a peace agreement; another is that one of them defeats the other and imposes its own "peace," that is, victory.

It is easy to be sarcastic about peace processes and resulting peace agreements: peace negotiations appear cumbersome; they are full of setbacks, political maneuvers, and concerns with seemingly insignificant details. This is not novel. All negotiations have this character; ending a civil war by negotiations is a particularly difficult task. What matters is whether the negotiators deal with the appropriate issues, whether they find an agreement that has sustainable qualities, and whether the agreement includes all parties. These are issues and actors that have to be dealt with.

As noted, there have been 121 wars since 1989, but there are also 144 peace agreements. In forty-six cases, a peace agreement helped end the conflict.[17] In general terms, one-third of all conflicts end through a negotiated settlement or through a cease-fire, another third ends in victory, and a third simply goes on. This record of negotiated endings is historically novel, particularly for civil wars. The histories of Europe and North America provide few historical lessons in civil war peacemaking. Most civil wars in these areas have ended through victories rather than through peace agreements. Typical examples are the U.S. Civil War and the various revolutions in France, England, and Russia that are often associated with civil wars. In history, peace has exclusively been something negotiated *between* states, not within states. This means that, for instance, Europe also finds itself in an era of working out how to deal with the problem of internal peace (peace within the state). That can be seen, from Belfast (Northern Ireland) to the Balkans, from the Basque country to Baku (Azerbaijan). The Western world cannot claim that it has an advantage in this area; it is learning at the same time as all others.

It is also important to ask who makes the agreements. Normally and immediately researchers and practitioners tend to think of the warring parties. Indeed, they are important, but that might not be enough. A recent study by

Desirée Nilsson suggests that the inclusion of nonwarring parties in agreements increases their durability.[18] This is the first work along this line, but it is suggestive. The inclusion of more stakeholders may make negotiations more complex, but the result may be more lasting. An interpretation is that this means that more actors have an interest in the agreement. In particular, nonarmed actors—the civil society—gain access and have a role, and thus an interest in the implementation of agreements. It goes without saying that this also means giving a more prominent role to women in the peace process as such. The results are likely to improve the quality of postwar society.

Wars may also end in victories. Victories can have a lasting quality. However, a major study of civil wars and peacebuilding since 1944 concludes that peacebuilding after a peace agreement (rather than after a victory) has a greater chance of keeping the peace.[19] The peace agreements clearly are important for the outcomes. There have been very few studies of different types of victories, however. The examples that are used often stem from interstate conflict, rather than the other categories. In the present discussion on the interstate war in Iraq, the experiences of Germany and Japan are often referenced. A most significant point is constantly overlooked. The leadership of Germany and Japan formally and symbolically capitulated, that is, they admitted defeat and instructed their troops to surrender. They became prisoners of war and were treated according to international law of the time, that is, with respect. In contrast, the Iraq war of 2003 did not include such an act of capitulation by the losing side, although there were many acts of victory by the winner. There is an important legal and psychological difference, which probably has a significant effect for peacebuilding after victory.[20]

Second, *the way the previous war started* provides lessons for the appropriate strategies of peacebuilding to prevent a recurrence of war. There is an increasing body of literature on the general causes of civil war. Largely, research has gone into factors associated with greed, need, and creed: actors fighting for their own gain, for the basic needs of a large segment of the population, or for the creation of a new society.[21]

There has been considerable attention to economic questions, thus potentially relating to postconflict market-building ambitions. Paul Collier and associates argue that "lootable" raw materials, such as diamonds, are likely to increase the likelihood of war because they serve to finance wars as well as enrich the actors themselves.[22] Interestingly, this observation has also been made by policy makers and led to action. Take, for instance, the UN use of sanctions on the sale of particular resources, as part of a new form of measure. Targeted sanctions stem from an analysis of the significance of such resources for power and warfare.[23] Diamonds were among the first resources pointed to: easy to transport, high unit value, and little weight. Recent studies by Macartan Humphreys and work by Joseph Bamidele compare different types of resource dependencies to point out which ones are more prone to conflict or more optimal for lasting peace.[24] Bamidele argues that for Africa resources with a large labor absorption capacity are more conducive for peace. That means that agricultural production creates more employment.

The peacebuilding strategy that follows from this analysis of economic causes is not obvious. To diversify a country's economy certainly is a logical conclusion, but to do this immediately after a war is a tremendous task. To return to the illustrative cases of Germany and Japan, both went back to previous industrial production as part of their postwar recovery (excluding armaments, which were banned). This seems also to be the pattern in internal conflicts. For instance, Lebanon focused after 1990 again on becoming a tourist attraction, with the use of international capital (particularly from other Arab countries). The success in this approach became visible during the 2006 war: there were thousands of international tourists in the country, dramatically evacuated during the first weeks of the renewed conflict. Another case is Uganda, which invited the old Asian entrepreneurs back to the country after the war endings in the mid-1980s. For new states emerging as a result of a state formation conflicts, this is likely to be acute. How can an independent economy be created? As we have seen, Eritrea came into a renewed war with Ethiopia, whereas East Timor (now Timor-Leste) hoped for incomes from a new source: oil discoveries. Changing the economy is likely to be a difficult proposition running counter to the needs of immediate postwar reconstruction. What one already knows will be the first priority in reconstruction, followed by easily mobilized skills that can be brought back to the country. Only in some instances will there be a chance of immediately developing something entirely different.

This brings in the different concern of finding ways in which resources can be shared within the state. It is also more possible to do in the postconflict environment. There are many ways of doing this. This is the significance of a functioning taxation system, tariffs on produce crossing the borders, as well as the creation of funds for long-term investment. A situation where few control all the wealth and the rest are marginalized is clearly an unlikely scenario for peacebuilding. The poorer the conditions, the more contention there is likely to be for scarce revenue, threatening to result in authoritarian regimes or state failure.

Collier and colleagues and other studies point to the significance of unemployment, which Marx once described as a "reserve army." In Marxist thinking, it was a way for capitalism to depress wages. Keynesian thinking differs on this point.[25] What we see today is a much more literal meaning. If war is the only "employment" around and somebody is paying, then why not take on this as any other occupation? It is an option that is referred to in stories of unemployed in the Middle East and in Afghanistan, as well as among young people in the favelas of Rio de Janeiro or in the run-down areas of Los Angeles. Joining the drug lords may pay better than finishing school. The "reserve army" becomes an "active army." Thus, to think about employment creation as part of peacebuilding makes a lot of sense. After war, there are needs that have to be met, but are there enough resources? Many war endings include the provision of international support, particularly in cases of negotiated settlement. A focus for such efforts might be the meeting of basic needs that also involve hiring a lot of labor.

Increasingly, issues of governance and leadership are getting attention as causes of conflict and thus become a key consideration for peacebuilding in internal postconflict situations. The phrase "state failure" has been used to describe this.[26] In the appendix to this chapter, an overview is provided of different types of state failure to assist in gaining the full picture. Clearly the state as such needs to be singled out, and that is also done in most concepts of peacebuilding. The focus may not necessarily and exclusively be on institutional capacity, however. There are other initiatives and institutions that may need encouragement, on a national level. Courts, agencies, and bureaucracies all have a role to play. A "good" state would be one that can constitute a national capacity to deal with conflict and be an exponent of the "conflict carrying capacity" of society.[27] The decline of a broad set of state and national institutions in this fundamental way suggests that such institutions not merely provide law and order but also bestow an element of redress, even "justice." If that ability is not there, the result could become chaotic. Thus, in the fear of creating too strong a state, some prefer no state at all; in the fear of having no state, others prefer an authoritarian order. A task is to find intelligent constructions in between these extremes. However, here is an important lacuna. There are, for instance, no global measures on efficacy and integrity of state institutions that can be used to compare states or follow developments over time.[28]

This points to a future challenge for peacebuilding: what type of state is sufficiently strong to distribute the costs and benefits of society in a legitimate way, but not so strong that it can overrun the economy or suppress groups in society? This is the direction in which the debate on peacebuilding may be moving, for instance, from the works of Roland Paris.[29] Paris and others, be they practitioners or academics, criticize the early imposition of democratic institutions such as national elections. They express a preference for postponing this political measure in favor of institution-building (or, what here has been termed state-building, in contrast to democracy-building). This is an important critique of prevalent strategies for peacebuilding. In reality, it is often more a discussion of timing. When are the conditions ripe for democracy? Too early after a war may mean that the "warlords" have a heroic status and are the only ones with access to resources, making it likely that they can get democratic recognition. Too late in the process, however, may give room for the same warlords to criticize the transitory arrangements and undermine democracy-building. Clearly, early after a war, civil society and other actors are likely to be weak and economic development varied. Only later are civil society actors likely to gain strength and contribute to a broader representation in the elections. Larry Diamond, analyzing the situation in Iraq in 2004, pointed to the possibility of first calling local elections, as a way around the problem of timing the introduction of democracy.[30]

A discussion in democracy-building cannot be pursued only in theory. In reality, some authority has to rule, even during a transition. Who is it likely to be, and what will be its role in the following democratization? The international support for long-term commitment cannot be taken for granted, although huge resources have gone into such situations as those found in Timor-Leste (primarily 1999–2002), Afghanistan (since 2001), Kosovo (since 1999), and

Bosnia-Herzegovina (since 1995). International authority took over some of the functions that would normally belong to the state, but state-building was part of the international mandate. The record of success can be debated: there has been a return to war in only one case (Afghanistan) but considerable sporadic conflict in two others (Timor-Leste, Kosovo) and tensions in all. Paradoxically, the long international presence is an indication of a failure in providing the conditions that confidently can be regarded as peacebuilding where the national and local levels regain control.

This brings us straight to the third question: *who is doing peacebuilding?* Clearly, this is something that has been taken over by the international community. Some reduction in armed conflict has been observed. But as a long-term strategy, this is not sustainable. There is also increasing evidence to underline the significance of peacebuilding based on local capacity. When studying the early development of conflicts, one can observe that the internal mediators and the local third parties, what is sometimes called "moderates," or the groups that are in between the warring factions, are also those targeted by belligerents and militants. This means that the "center," the political space where much of the population is often located (politically speaking), may be without spokespersons. The extreme sides may manage to polarize the situation. When this results in civil wars, international efforts at peacebuilding enter as a replacement for local capacity. This may be necessary, but it is also a major problem. There is a danger that a heavy international presence may further reduce local conflict resolution capacity, contribute to the erosion of traditional authority, and with that, undermine bodies that might be able to competently deal with conflicts on a local level.[31] There are now studies emerging of recent experiences of international peacebuilding efforts. Roland Kostic's work on Bosnia-Herzegovina is one example; John Heathershaw's work on Tajikistan is another.[32] Both seem to bring out the same message, albeit with different emphases and meaning. The international efforts may lead to a stifling of local initiative or delay or prevent the emergence of local capacity to deal with the situation. Louise Olsson has analyzed UN engagement in Namibia from the perspective of the role of women in the war-ending and early peacebuilding processes.[33]

An important conclusion is that international peacebuilding strategies have to primarily enhance local capacity and interact with such actors; thus, peacebuilding will have to be differently shaped in different situations. There is a danger of unproductive tension between local and international capacity.[34] There are different mandates driving these two efforts. Often international peacebuilding will have more access to resources, comparatively speaking, but will also be less committed to a particular situation. The experts and managers will move on within a short period of time, but the locals will remain in the situation. Finding ways these two levels can connect and support each other is highly significant.

In interstate peacebuilding, however, international efforts are much more rare. We have already alluded to the postconflict experiences in Ethiopia–Eritrea and India–Pakistan relations. These actors have been strong enough to block international involvement, except for limited tasks of peacekeeping or observation teams. The strategies of peacebuilding need different forms. The example of the Franco-German relations suggests that a regional approach may be more practical.

This leads us to a fourth issue that affects all three types of conflict and concerns: *the neighborhood in which peacebuilding takes place.* Neighboring countries may contribute to a war directly (by supplying their own troops, allowing bases for warring parties, expressing political support, etc.) or indirectly (e.g., by not being capable to control their own borders). Clearly, what happens in one country is to some extent dependent on what happens with its neighbor(s).[35] There are interconnections—the closer to the scene, the closer the interconnections. There are concepts such as "regional conflict complexes" and "regional security communities" expressing exactly this.[36] Regional spill-over effects can be seen in some of the conflictual African regions.

There is a debate, however, over whether the neighborhood itself is the problem or whether internal conflicts are triggered from internal causes. Michael E. Brown has argued that the proximate causes of internal conflicts are mostly internal (thirty-two out of thirty-six cases, in his overview, 1996: 582). The typical cases of externally driven conflicts were the conflicts in Georgia, Moldova, Afghanistan, and Sierra Leone. However, he as well as others would agree that there are a number of regional dimensions of internal conflicts, for instance, regional instability, arms trade, refugee flows, and disruption of trade and transportation. Harbom and Wallensteen (2005) report that there is much international engagement in a large majority of all armed internal conflict over a period of time. Clearly there are close connections, and they have become even more obvious since Brown presented his findings. Entire regions have been dramatically affected by war and disputes, weakening not only one state but several: the Mano River region is one (Liberia, Sierra Leone, Guinea, Côte d'Ivoire). The African Great Lakes region is another (Congo, Rwanda, Burundi, Uganda); the Horn of Africa a third; the connections between Darfur (Sudan), Chad, and the Central African Republic have also received attention and appear to lead to a spread of armed conflict. These are areas where links are close, the borders fragile, and the states weak—all contributing to new opportunities for those who see potential gains in armed options. Thus, there are not only state failures, as mentioned before, but also regional failures.

This affects peacebuilding in a number of ways. It may make it difficult to build peace in one country if the neighboring state is war-torn and collapsing. There are, however, also elements of a reversal. Peace in one country may assist peace efforts in another: Liberia and Sierra Leone may interact supportively in peacebuilding in the middle of the first decade of the 2000s, compared to the dynamics five or ten years earlier. The same may apply to developments in Burundi, the Democratic Republic of Congo, and southern Sudan. Certainly the picture is not complete, but there has been a discernible trend of slowly but systematically unfolding peacebuilding activities in many

African states over the past half-decade. It is also clear that regional initiatives play a role in this reversal. Neighbors shift from exploitative to supportive stances, and that may contribute to peacebuilding. Regional settings for peacebuilding have to be taken into consideration. Remarkably little research has gone into this.

The account given for Africa is in stark contrast to the Middle East, where fighting and conflict strategies have been dominating the agenda of the main actors, particularly since the collapse of the Oslo Process by late 2000 and after the events of September 11, 2001. In other parts of the world, different patterns dominate: the critique of peacebuilding seen in the Balkans does not emerge from the need to undo the security that has been built, but aims at finding ways to turn peacebuilding into a more effective and locally informed approach. Similarly, the relative peace of East Asia suggests again different ways of managing conflict. In the disputes around North Korea, for instance, the neighboring countries have been heavily involved in diplomacy and economic pressure, but have not resorted to militarily undermining the regime or initiating armed action.

The regional approach to peacebuilding has received little attention. Peace agreements contain fewer such aspects and after a victory, neighbors mostly seem to adapt to the new conditions. Regional peacebuilding in interstate conflict has been almost completely lacking, and—possibly as a consequence—so is research. This suggests an important agenda, where not only knowledge of security but also broader expertise is brought to bear. It may also have an effect on negotiations for ending wars or implementing peace.

Conclusion

The field of peacebuilding studies is in its early phases. It has largely concentrated on internal conflicts and thus developed conclusions relevant for peacebuilding after such wars. For instance, there is a common observation that countries with dependence on one commodity for export are at risk of renewed war and that unemployment provides an additional risk for conflict. Peacebuilding policies clearly need to address issues of sharing resources, finding investment, and creating jobs. This relates largely to the needs of one particular aspect: the market-building dimension of peacebuilding. The tasks are likely to be the same, whether we discuss the formation of a new government after a war or a new state as a separate entity.

However, an emerging conclusion is also emphasizing weak local capability to deal with conflict through a functioning state or another locally legitimate framework. This is a challenge to peacebuilding that points to the representativeness of the state and the space it allows for local capacity (an aspect of statebuilding). The importance of democracy-building is discussed as to appropriate timing and sequencing, although it is seldom questioned as a goal.

Security-building is an obviously important matter. The international efforts of peacekeeping have this as a central task, and other matters are seen as auxiliary. However, strategies for long-term security-building require considerable study for all three types of conflict. In the interstate postwar situation, there is a tradition of analysis in terms of a security dilemma. This concept is also useful for describing internal conditions, something that has not been done much so far.

Nation-building in terms of finding common identities in postconflict situations is a challenge that seems to have paralyzed researchers as well as practitioners. There are few ideas on systemic approaches, but there is much awareness of the significance of this factor. It seems to provide a particular challenge to peacebuilding research.

Finally, this chapter has pointed to the lack of regional studies, particularly how the regional dimension may systematically support or undermine peacebuilding efforts of individual countries or actors. Such interaction seems particularly pertinent for future studies.

Peacebuilding is a strategic topic in itself. It is located in the crossroads of academic research and practical application. The urgency of such research is clear as practice evolves, whether or not there is research. Research needs to incorporate such experiences and also develop solid insights that can contribute to improving present strategies.

Appendix: A Typology of State Failure

	Ability of Internationally Recognized Government to Provide Services to the Population	
	Services Maintained	Services Reduced or Ceasing
Services within the internationally recognized territory	1. *Minimized state* (thinning out of state operations, e.g. due to its international finances)	7. *Partial nonperformance state* (e.g. Iraq and armaments, or govt not in control of finances)
are /to be/ provided by recognized Govt	2. *Discriminatory state* (services not equal for all groups in the society)	8. *Full Non-Performance State* (Somalia, Afghanistan)
in between situation	3. *Transitory state* (devolution, phase of break-up) 4. *De facto divided state* (e.g. Somalia, Somaliland)	9. *Mandate state* (functions taken over—temporarily– by international authority) 10. *Contested state* (no actors provide services, block each other)
are challenged by other actors	5. *"Liberated zones"* (e.g. territories nominally under central control, in practice under rebels setting up "model state") 6. *Organized crime state* (Mafia administers official services)	

Note: The point of departure is an internationally recognized state, with its own government and its own territory. The functions of the state may be impaired prior to or as part of conflict.

NOTES

This chapter is a substantial elaboration of my inaugural speech as the Richard G. Starmann Sr. Research Professor of Peace Studies, Joan B. Kroc Institute for International Peace Studies, November 5, 2006. This chapter has benefited from many commentators, notably Roland Kostic, for which I am grateful, while I remain solely responsible for the analysis presented.

1. Galtung, Johan, 1976. "Three Approaches to Peace: Peacekeeping, Peacemaking and Peacebuilding," in Galtung, Johan, *Peace, War and Defence. Essays in Peace Research vol. 2*, Copenhagen: Christian Ejlers, pp. 282–304.

2. Deutsch, Karl W., et al., 1957. *Political Community and the North Atlantic Area*, Princeton, N.J.: Princeton University Press.

3. Harbom, Lotta, Stina Högbladh, and Peter Wallensteen, 2006. "Armed Conflict and Peace Agreements," *Journal of Peace Research* 43(5): 617–631.

4. Refugee flows are constantly monitored by UNHCR, Human Rights Watch, and Refugees International. The link to armed conflicts is obvious even from a visual inspection of the Web sites of these organizations.

5. *Human Security Report 2005. War and Peace in the 21st Century*, Human Security Centre, University of British Columbia, Vancouver, BC, Canada, www.humansecurityreport.info.

6. The proposal is found in United Nations, 2004, *A More Secure World: Our Shared Responsibility*, Report of the Secretary General's High-Level Panel on Threats, Challenges and Change. The new commission was established in June 2006 by the UN General Assembly and selected Burundi and Sierra Leone as the first countries to work with.

7. The recent work of Manuel Fröhlich et al. (2006) studying the contributions of the UN Special Representatives confirms the observations from HSR. An obvious indicator would be global military expenditures, but they show a sharp rise since 2000, at a time when the conflict patterns are neither declining nor rising. See *SIPRI Yearbook 2006*, New York: Oxford University Press, chapter 8.

8. Boutros-Ghali, Boutros, 1992. *An Agenda for Peace*, New York: United Nations.

9. This trichotomy of conflict is presented in Wallensteen, Peter, 2007. *Understanding Conflict Resolution*, 2nd ed., London: Sage, chapter 4.

10. The distinction of government and territory as the chief incompatibilities in armed conflicts is central to the Uppsala Conflict Data Program, see www.ucdp.uu.se.

11. The dilemmas in postwar democracy-building are penetrated in Jarstad, Anna, and Sisk, Tim, eds., 2008. *From War to Democracy*, Cambridge: Cambridge University Press.

12. Brounéus, Karen, 2003. *Reconciliation—Theory and Practice for Development Cooperation. A Report for the Swedish International Development Cooperation Agency.* Stockholm: Sida.

13. There is a proliferation of definitions for this concept from its contemporary launching by former UN Secretary General Boutros Boutros-Ghali in his report *An Agenda for Peace*. As noted, the concept was used by Johan Galtung already in 1976. For an overview, see Gawerc, Michelle I., 2006. "Peace-Building: Theoretical and Concrete Perspectives," *Peace & Change* 31(4): 435–478, and Fetherston, A. B., 2000. "Peacekeeping, Conflict Resolution and Peacebuilding: A Reconsideration of Theoretical Frameworks," *International Peacekeeping* 7(1): 190–218.

14. Deutsch, et al., 1957.

15. An example of what can be achieved with short time periods is Doyle, Michael W., and Sambanis, Nicholas, 2000. "International Peacebuilding: A Theoretical and Quantitative Analysis," *American Political Science Review* 94(4): 779–801.

16. Valuable insights are provided by Dobbins, James F., 2003–2004. "America's Role in Nation-Building: From Germany to Iraq," *Survival* 45(4): 87–110. A classic treatment is Organski, A.F. K., and Kugler, Jacek, 1980. *The War Ledger*, Chicago: University of Chicago Press, which used the expression "the Phoenix factor" for these two cases.

17. Harbom et al., 2006, and www.pcr.uu.se/database.

18. Nilsson, Desirée, 2006. *In the Shadow of Settlement. Multiple Rebel Groups and Precarious Peace*, Uppsala University: Department of Peace and Conflict Research.

19. Doyle and Sambanis, 2000, p. 789.

20. Woodward asserts that President Bush in 2003 wanted to end the war on Iraq on an aircraft carrier to remind the public of Japan's capitulation in 1945 (Woodward, Bob, 2006. *State of Denial. Bush at War, Part III*, New York: Simon & Schuster, p. 186). A difference that escapes Woodward is that in 1945, Japanese officers signed the act of surrender on instructions from the emperor, whereas in 2003 there were no Iraqis onboard the ship. As part of this, the Japanese authorities had to save and protect civil and military property. In the same vein, the capture of Saddam Hussein in December 2003 was only seen as a way of militarily defeating the insurgency (ibid., p. 275), and the issue of capitulation does not seem to have been on the mind of the American leadership.

21. Zartman, I. William, 2000. "Mediating Conflicts of Need, Greed and Creed," *Orbis* 44(2): 255–266.

22. The argument is more nuanced than what is presented here. Among numerous studies see, for instance, Collier, Paul, et al., 2003. *Breaking the Conflict Trap. Civil War and Development Policy*, New York: World Bank and Oxford University Press.

23. For an overview and evaluation of this development see, for instance, Wallensteen, Peter, and Staibano, Carina, eds., 2005. *International Sanctions: Between Words and Wars in the Global System*, London and New York: Frank Cass.

24. Humphreys, Macartan, 2005. "Natural Resources, Conflict and Conflict Resolution," *Journal of Conflict Resolution* 49(4): 508–537. Bamidele, Joseph, 2006. *Natural Resource Dependence and the Political Economy of Civil Conflict in Sub-Saharan Africa*. PhD dissertation, University of London.

25. Peter Skott finds that theoretically one explanation does not exclude the other; see "Effective Demand, Class Struggle and Cyclical Growth," *International Economic Review* 30(1989:1): 231–247. Also, women and the elderly have been analyzed from the perspective of being "reserve armies" for a capitalist economy.

26. Chesterman, Simon, Ignatieff, Michael, and Thakur, Ramesh, eds., 2005. *Making States Work: State Failure and the Crisis of Governance*, Tokyo, New York, Paris: UN University Press.

27. This concept has been elaborated particularly by Jenkins, J. Craig, and Bond, Doug, 2001. "Conflict Carrying Capacity, Political Crisis and Reconstruction," *Journal of Conflict Resolution* 45(1): 3–31.

28. This has been apparent, for instance, when one wants to see how states implement UN-decided sanctions initiatives. Daniel Strandow, Uppsala, has made this observation as part of a sanctions project.

29. Paris, Roland, 2002. "International Peacebuilding and 'Mission Civilisatrice,'" *Review of International Studies*, 28: 637–656; and Paris, Roland, 2004. *At War's End. Building Peace after Civil Conflict*, Cambridge: Cambridge University Press.

30. Diamond, Larry, 2005. "Building Democracy after Conflict. Lessons from Iraq," *Journal of Democracy* 16(1): 9–23.

31. Chesterman, Simon, 2004. *You, the People: The United Nations, Transitional Administration, and State-Building*, Oxford: Oxford University Press.

32. Kostic, Roland, 2008. "Nation-building as an Instrument of Peace? Exploring Local Attitudes towards International Nation-Building and Reconciliation in Bosnia and Herzegovina," *Civil Wars* 10(4): 384–412; Heathershaw, John, 2007. "Peacebuilding as Practice: Discourses from Post-Conflict Tajikistan," *International Peacekeeping* 14(2): 219–236.

33. Olsson, Louise, 2001. "Gender Mainstreaming in Practice: The United Nations Transitional Assistance Group in Namibia," *International Peacekeeping* 8(2): 97–110. Olsson's latest work deals with East Timor.

34. On this score, recent case studies point in the same direction as the statistical work by Doyle and Sambanis, 2000.

35. Harbom, Lotta, and Wallensteen, Peter, 2005. "Armed Conflict and Its International Dimensions, 1946–2004," *Journal of Peace Research* 42(5): 623–635 report on this.

36. See for instance, Deutsch et al., 1957; Buzan, Barry, 1991. *People, States and Fear*, Boulder, Colo.: Lynne Rienner; and Wallensteen, 2007.

REFERENCES

Bamidele, Joseph. 2006. *Natural Resource Dependence and the Political Economy of Civil Conflict in Sub-Saharan Africa*. PhD Dissertation, submitted to the University of London, United Kingdom.

Boutros-Ghali, Boutros. 1992. *An Agenda for Peace*. New York: United Nations.

Brown, Michael E. (ed.). 1996. *The International Dimensions of Internal Conflict*. Cambridge, Mass.: MIT Press.

Brounéus, Karen. 2003. *Reconciliation—Theory and Practice for Development Cooperation. A Report for the Swedish International Development Cooperation Agency*. Stockholm: Sida.

Buzan, Barry. 1991. *People, States and Fear*. Boulder, Colo.: Lynne Rienner.

Chesterman, Simon. 2004. *You, the People: The United Nations, Transitional Administration, and State-Building*. Oxford: Oxford University Press.

Chesterman, Simon, Michael Ignatieff, and Ramesh Thakur (eds.). 2005. *Making States Work: State Failure and the Crisis of Governance*. Tokyo, New York, Paris: UN University Press.

Collier, Paul, et al., 2003. *Breaking the Conflict Trap. Civil War and Development Policy*. New York: World Bank and Oxford University Press.

Deutsch, Karl W., et al., 1957. *Political Community and the North Atlantic Area*. Princeton, N.J.: Princeton University Press.

Diamond, Larry. 2005. "Building Democracy After Conflict. Lessons from Iraq." *Journal of Democracy* 16(1): 9–23.

Dobbins, James F. 2003–2004. "America's Role in Nation-Building: From Germany to Iraq," *Survival* 45(4): 87–110.

Doyle, Michael W., and Sambanis, Nicholas. 2000. "International Peacebuilding: A Theoretical and Quantitative Analysis," *American Political Science Review* 94(4): 779–801.

Fetherston, A. B. 2000. "Peacekeeping, Conflict Resolution and Peacebuilding: A Reconsideration of Theoretical Frameworks." *International Peacekeeping* 7(4): 190–218.

Fröhlich, Manuel, Bütof, Maria, and Lemanski, Jan. 2006. "Mapping UN Presence. A Follow-up on the Human Security Report," *Die Friedens-Warte. Journal of International Peace and Organization* 81(2): 13–23.

Galtung, Johan. 1976. "Three Approaches to Peace: Peacekeeping, Peacemaking and Peacebuilding," in *Peace, War and Defence. Essays in Peace Research Vol. 2.* Copenhagen: Christian Ejlers, pp 282–304.

Gawerc, Michelle I. 2006. "Peace-Building: Theoretical and Concrete Perspectives," *Peace & Change* 31(4): 435–478.

Harbom, Lotta, and Wallensteen, Peter. 2005. "Armed Conflict and Its International Dimensions, 1946–2004," *Journal of Peace Research* 42(5): 623–635.

Harbom, Lotta, Högbladh, Stina and Wallensteen, Peter. 2006. "Armed Conflict and Peace Agreements," *Journal of Peace Research* 43(5): 617–631.

Heathershaw, John. 2007. "Peacebuilding as Practice: Discourses from Post-Conflict Tajikistan," *International Peacekeeping* 14(2): 219–236.

Human Security Report 2005. War and Peace in the 21st Century. Human Security Centre, University of British Columbia, Vancouver, BC, Canada.

Humphreys, Macartan. 2005. "Natural Resources, Conflict and Conflict Resolution," *Journal of Conflict Resolution* 49(4): 508–537.

Jarstad, Anna, and Sisk, Tim (eds.). 2008. *From War to Democracy.* Cambridge: Cambridge University Press.

Jenkins, J. Craig, and Bond, Doug. 2001. "Conflict Carrying Capacity, Political Crisis and Reconstruction," *Journal of Conflict Resolution* 45(1): 3–31.

Kostic, Roland. 2008. "Nation-Building as an Instrument of Peace? Exploring Local Attitudes towards International Nation-Building and Reconciliation in Bosnia and Herzegovina," *Civil Wars* 10(4): 384–412.

Nilsson, Desirée. 2006. *In the Shadow of Settlement. Multiple Rebel Groups and Precarious Peace.* Uppsala: Uppsala University Department of Peace and Conflict Research.

Olsson, Louise. 2001. "Gender Mainstreaming in Practice: The United Nations Transitional Assistance Group in Namibia," *International Peacekeeping* 8(2): 97–110.

Organski, A. F. K., and Kugler, Jacek. 1980. *The War Ledger.* Chicago: University of Chicago Press.

Paris, Roland. 2002. "International Peacebuilding and 'Mission Civilisatrice,'" *Review of International Studies* 28: 637–656.

Paris, Roland. *At War's End. Building Peace after Civil Conflict.* Cambridge: Cambridge University Press, 2004.

SIPRI Yearbook 2006. New York: Oxford University Press.

Skott, Peter. 1989. "Effective Demand, Class Struggle and Cyclical Growth," *International Economic Review* 30(1): 231–247.

United Nations. 2004. *A More Secure World: Our Shared Responsibility.* Report of the Secretary-General's High-Level Panel on Threats, Challenges and Change, United Nations, 2004.

Wallensteen, Peter. 2007. *Understanding Conflict Resolution,* 2nd ed. London: Sage.

Wallensteen, Peter, and Staibano, Carina (eds.). 2005. *International Sanctions: Between Words and Wars in the Global System.* London and New York: Frank Cass.

Woodward, Bob. 2006. *State of Denial. Bush at War, Part III.* New York: Simon & Schuster.

Zartman, I. William. 2000. "Mediating Conflicts of Need, Greed and Creed," *Orbis* 44(2): 255–266.

3

The Evaluation of Peacebuilding Initiatives

Putting Learning into Practice

Hal Culbertson

The peacebuilding enterprise is at a critical point in its development as a field of practice. Peacebuilding emerged in the early to mid-1990s as a distinct focus of interventions by multilateral agencies and nongovernmental actors. Much of the impetus for peacebuilding stemmed from concrete needs on the ground. As the number of civil conflicts increased after the end of the Cold War, it became apparent that international peacekeeping forces were only able to address the immediate security needs and that other kinds of intervention that focused on rebuilding societal structures and institutions were needed to prevent a relapse into conflict.[1] In addition, the peacebuilding enterprise quickly expanded to include efforts at conflict prevention.[2]

Proponents of peacebuilding in the relief and development community argued for a greater focus on peace in development agendas based on research that documented shortcomings of humanitarian and development efforts in conflict settings.[3] This analysis challenged the assumption that aid can be apolitical and proposed new models of postconflict assistance that are more sensitive to conflict impact and seek to address underlying causes of conflict.

The initial arguments for peacebuilding were largely deductive in character, given the paucity of peacebuilding experience previously.[4] Now that the field has had over a decade of experience, however, calls are increasing for more inductive evidence of the value and impact of peacebuilding.[5] Although it has established a foothold in the international community and donor agendas, both as a new dimension of other fields of practice (such as development) and as a distinct kind of intervention, peacebuilding still must compete for resources and attention with relief and development activities as well as health, education, and other areas of intervention.

As this suggests, the legitimacy of the field as a whole, and not just individual initiatives or approaches, is at stake. Tschirgi underscores the urgency of the situation: "Unless there is growing evidence that changes in programming, institutional reform, and more effective collaboration and coordination among different actors serve to promote conflict prevention, conflict management and post-conflict reconstruction, the peacebuilding agenda will not be sustainable politically or in terms of deploying the necessary resources."[6]

The new challenges posed by the post-9/11 world create additional pressure to show the relevance and effectiveness of peacebuilding. As Lund observes, "Whether the anti-terrorist agenda will now skew or subvert the decade-long process of formulating a multi-dimensional concept of peacebuilding and nation-building, or instead it will be tempered by them, is a crucial question that needs to be tracked, not pre-empted."[7]

Although some in the peacebuilding community have resisted evaluation, arguing that peace work will not show results in the short run or cannot be measured, the mood seems to be changing.[8] The peacebuilding community is increasingly recognizing that evaluation can be an important tool for improving and legitimating the field. Significantly, efforts to develop better evaluation systems and processes are coming as much from peacebuilding practitioners themselves as from the donor community.[9]

This chapter explores how evaluation can be used to improve the peacebuilding field as a whole. It focuses on civil society peacebuilding efforts; however, it also draws on literature on peacebuilding initiatives by the international community, and many of the observations and conclusions are relevant to the evaluation of these wider peacebuilding efforts. As emphasized in the definition of peacebuilding elaborated by Appleby and Lederach in chapter 1, the analysis of peacebuilding is grounded in an understanding of the field that emphasizes the multisectoral and multilevel nature of the peacebuilding enterprise and the challenges these pose for evaluation efforts. It identifies a set of issues in the field that would benefit from more systematic evaluation. It then concludes by exploring how evaluation processes could be improved to foster greater learning about these issues.

Paradigms of Evaluation

Evaluation processes can be understood in terms of two broad paradigms: accountability and learning. The fundamental difference between these orientations concerns who is viewed as the intended "user" of the evaluation findings. A user is someone who has a stake in an initiative or program, such as program staff, beneficiaries, staff from related organizations, and, in many cases, the public. Although accountability perspectives give significant weight to the interests and perspectives of donors or other external users who authorize organizational activities, learning approaches give greater weight to the interests of organizational staff, practitioners in the field, and even the broader public.

Accountability Models

The end result of an accountability evaluation is typically a judgment about the worth, merit, or value of an initiative.[10] Donors frequently need to make such assessments as they decide whether to continue to fund an initiative or replicate it in other areas. Organizations may also make such assessments internally and may use evaluations to inform those decisions. A key element in such an evaluation is the establishment of standards against which program performance will be measured, and then the measurement of how successful the program was in meeting those standards.

Historically, the practice of evaluation in nongovernmental organizations (NGOs) has been shaped largely by accountability concerns. In the 1980s and 1990s, the number of NGOs increased dramatically, and their share of international aid grew, as donors turned away from government-led development initiatives.[11] This growth, together with several highly publicized scandals, led to demands for greater scrutiny of NGO activities.[12]

Evaluation became a prominent tool for donors to maintain accountability among recipients of their funds. Evaluation processes tended to focus on two dimensions of accountability, which Edwards and Hulme called functional and strategic accountability.[13] First, donors sought to assess whether resources were used as planned, much like an external financial audit. Second, donors sought to assess the success of the project in achieving its stated goals and objectives.

A set of standard practices and procedures for managing projects and conducting evaluations was developed that facilitated these assessments. Planning processes were used, particularly the logical framework planning matrix,[14] that required recipients to specify high-level goals, mid-level objectives, and immediate outputs of every project. In addition, project planners were required to specify indicators of success against which their project would be measured in the evaluation.

Because development assistance was the predominant form of international aid at the time, many of the models and tools developed were particularly aimed at development interventions. A standard set of evaluation criteria was developed by the Organisation for Economic Co-operation and Development (OECD) Development Assistance Committee (DAC) and is widely used as the basic framework for evaluations by aid agencies.[15] This includes consideration of relevance (whether the project is suited to local needs and priorities, as well as donor policies), effectiveness (whether the project achieves its objectives), efficiency (whether the project is cost-effective), impact (the positive and negative changes produced by the project, directly or indirectly, intended or unintended), and sustainability (whether the benefits of the project will continue after donor funding has ceased). These criteria were closely tied to the logframe planning system, which specified the outputs, objectives, and goals for the project and the indicators that would be used to measure success at each level.

In reaction to the dominant role of donor perspectives in evaluation processes, alternative approaches which stress accountability to beneficiaries have also been developed. As Kaldor has observed, the very structure of NGOs as nonprofit, voluntary organizations creates a separation between donors and beneficiaries that weakens the accountability of the organization to the beneficiaries, whose interests are easily overlooked in program decision making.[16] In response, participatory approaches to evaluation have been developed that foster high levels of involvement by local community members in planning and implementing the evaluation and responding to the results. Such an evaluation may be an extension of the participatory nature of a project itself, with participants setting standards and then evaluating the initiative's success in achieving them.[17]

Learning Models

Whereas the accountability paradigm focuses on assessing past performance, learning approaches are oriented toward improving future actions of the organization that undertook the initiative or other related constituencies. As Patton observes, "Using evaluation results to improve a program turns out, in practice, to be fundamentally different from rendering judgment about overall effectiveness, merit, or worth."[18] Evaluation oriented toward learning is more open and inductive in its methodology and results in recommendations for improvements rather than mere assessments of past performance quality. In practice, this means that organizational leadership and staff play a larger role in shaping the objectives of the evaluation, determining its timing, framing questions or criteria to be evaluated, and responding to the findings.

As Church and Rogers indicate, this approach to evaluation in some cases has led to an expanded role for the evaluator.[19] Unlike accountability evaluations, where the evaluator is usually an external expert who collects and analyzes information for an external donor, evaluators using a learning approach might spend significant time working with organizational leadership and staff after the evaluation to discuss the findings and implement the recommended changes in policy or procedures. This has sometimes raised concerns about the objectivity and neutrality of the evaluator, which was the prime concern in accountability models; however, in learning models, this expanded role may be seen as essential to create effective feedback loops that can facilitate organizational change.

This approach to evaluation has close connections with the growing interest in organizational learning. Organizational learning first emerged in the corporate sector as a field of study and practice focusing on how organizations incorporate various kinds of feedback from their experiences into their planning and decision making.[20] More recently, many NGOs have made it part of their overall mission to become "learning organizations."[21] In these organizations, evaluation is often understood as a critical tool for fostering learning.[22]

Evaluation can also be used to foster learning more generally. This approach, often referred to as "conceptual" use, emphasizes the role evaluation can play in educating a wider community about the issues under evaluation.[23] As Weiss observed, insights from evaluation sometimes do not have an immediate effect on specific actions, but nonetheless play a role in bringing about change by percolating into the public discourse and subtly shaping views and attitudes toward programs and policies. For example, evaluations of prison rehabilitation programs that indicated they did not decrease recidivism did not have any discernible impact on prison policy for many years. However, over time, these evaluations shaped debates about prison reform that led to significant changes in policy, such as the California legislature's removal of rehabilitation as a primary goal of incarceration.[24]

Sometimes, evaluations designed to increase knowledge are targeted at a specific community or group, rather than the public at large. For example, evaluations are sometimes designed to identify best practices and lessons learned that will improve future activity by similar agencies or help establish professional standards in the field. Such evaluations might compare a range of organizational efforts in a certain field of activity to derive general principles that successful or good programs follow in designing and implementing activities.

For example, Child Friendly Cities (www.childfriendlycities.org) has intentionally adopted a best practices approach to evaluating various efforts that support children's rights in urban areas around the globe. Based on a broad range of experiences of members of its network, the organization's secretariat has created a data bank of these best practices under the UN Convention on the Rights of the Child and synthesized these into general principles that can guide future projects.

Evaluations can also contribute to the development of a field of practice by critically examining the broader theory of change behind a program initiative. A theory of change is an explanation of how and why a set of activities will bring about the broader changes it seeks to achieve.[25] Theories of change often operate implicitly. They may be gut instincts or commonsense assumptions, such as the belief that increasing interaction between members of conflicting groups will reduce stereotypes or prejudice. Of course, they also may be informed by social science theories as well as cultural perspectives.

In a theory of change evaluation, the evaluation team seeks to make the underlying theory of change explicit and then establishes evaluation goals and priorities to test the theory of change. For example, if a program's underlying theory of change is that interaction between members of conflicting groups will reduce prejudice against the opposing group more generally, the evaluation might seek to measure the extent to which participants have developed positive perceptions of project participants from the other group as a result of interacting. Given the project's theory of change, the evaluation would also consider the extent to which these positive perceptions are transferred to members of the opposing group who did not participate in the project or to the group as a whole. By designing the evaluation around the program's theory of change, the evaluation results can inform other efforts that are based on similar theories and contribute to the accumulated wisdom about how best to implement this kind of project.

Paradigm Choices

Accountability and learning orientations toward evaluation are not mutually exclusive. Evaluations done primarily for the purposes of accountability have increasingly considered lessons learned and areas for improvement. Furthermore, donors, who are often seen as primarily interested in accountability, are increasingly recognizing the role evaluation can play in promoting wider learning and are actively developing evaluation models to promote this.[26]

However, tensions can arise between the accountability and learning paradigms. As Ebrahim points out, evaluations undertaken with accountability as the primary motivation tend to focus on penalizing organizations for not meeting expectations or not complying with accepted norms rather than helping them improve their performance or the performance of the field in general.[27] In some cases, the evaluation becomes primarily a symbolic act of legitimating or delegitimating an organizational effort, rather than one intended to improve it. Even if legitimated through an evaluation, the organization may receive additional funding or support, but not significant feedback on how to improve its programs or effectiveness. Moreover, organizational staff or beneficiaries who understand evaluation in terms of accountability may skew or avoid disclosing information that could be important for learning. In this way, the accountability focus can inhibit the learning potential of evaluation.

As a result, one must consider the strengths and weaknesses of each approach in determining which type of evaluation is most appropriate for a given situation. As Carlsson notes, where the mechanism that links the activities undertaken with the overall objectives of the effort is well understood and agreed on, an accountability orientation will likely be the most appropriate.[28] Accountability approaches are well suited to determining whether the activities were implemented as planned and the quality of the implementation. For example, a project focusing on reducing malaria by providing low-cost mosquito nets could be evaluated by measuring the number of nets distributed, the recipients' use of the nets, and the reduction in the rate of malarial infection in the area. Because both the cause of malaria and the impact of using a mosquito net properly are fairly well understood, evaluating key aspects of implementation is a good indicator that the project had its intended impact.

However, when projects test new methodologies or pursue complex social goals through approaches that are not well understood, evaluating whether the program was implemented in accordance with preestablished criteria may not be the most appropriate focus for evaluation. As Riddell observes about evaluations aimed at assessing the impact of development interventions, "Donor funds would probably be better spent in helping NGOs develop and experiment with different methods of assessment than in undertaking a large number of impact studies based on methods used to date."[29] In such cases, an evaluative approach that probes the underlying theory of change and results in suggestions for improving the effort is better suited to the needs of the initiative.

The Peacebuilding Enterprise

Understanding the evaluation issues facing the peacebuilding community requires an understanding of the nature of the enterprise in which it is engaged. To this end, this section sketches the contours of the peacebuilding enterprise through an analysis of its overall goals, particularly noting several ways these goals create dilemmas that the peacebuilding community must grapple with in evaluating its efforts. As will be seen, the complexity of the enterprise shapes both the issues that deserve attention through evaluation and the kind of evaluation approaches that need to be used.

Goals

At the risk of sounding tautological, I begin by observing that the enterprise of peacebuilding is best understood as any activity or initiative that is intended to promote peace. This approach does not begin with a specific set of activities, such as conflict resolution, mediation, or the development of democratic political institutions; instead, it begins with an orientation toward a broad goal—peace—and considers any person or entity that is intentionally designing programs and initiatives toward that end to be part of the peacebuilding enterprise.

As Ken Bush argues, if peacebuilding is understood as a specific set of activities, this limits the concept in ways that may be detrimental to the development of the field.[30] To overcome this problem, he proposes to define peacebuilding as an impact, so that any activity undertaken to achieve that impact would be considered a peacebuilding activity. In this way, relief and development programs that seek to make a community less conflict-prone through carefully directed economic development activities but do not directly engage partners in dialogue about conflict or conflict resolution workshops would still be considered part of the enterprise. The key element is not the particular kind of activity undertaken but the broader intent that the initiative will have a positive impact on the conflict.

This understanding of the peacebuilding community is highly inclusive, but not all-inclusive. As Larissa Fast notes in chapter 11, relief organizations sometimes seek to keep their efforts separate from peacebuilding initiatives, as a way of preserving their neutrality or credibility. In such cases, these efforts would not be considered part of the peacebuilding enterprise and should not be evaluated in terms of their impact on peace.

Viewed from this perspective, peacebuilding is an extraordinarily complex and multifaceted endeavor. Those who have attempted to approach the concept of peace systematically find a dichotomy at its core. Johan Galtung's famous distinction between positive and negative peace is often understood as delineating two fundamental dimensions of the concept of peace. *Negative peace* refers to the absence of violent conflict, whereas *positive peace* refers to the presence of just relations in society.

Though initially developed as a conceptual tool, the distinction between positive and negative peace has come to reflect more practical distinctions in the field of peacebuilding. This can be seen in the overall goals that practitioners articulate for their activities. Interestingly, the Reflecting on Peace Practices project, which involved listening to a broad spectrum of "peace practitioners" from a wide range of contexts, arrived at a similar distinction between two fundamental goals actually operating within the field: stopping violence and destructive conflict, and addressing political, economic, and social grievances that drive conflict.[31]

Evaluation Dilemmas

The relationship between these two overarching goals generates significant dilemmas for the evaluation of peacebuilding efforts. Although it is common to view the two as closely intertwined—even as two sides of the same coin—the nature of their mutual interaction is unclear when viewed in the context of evaluation. These dilemmas stem from several factors.

First, NGOs and other civil society actors typically articulate their peacebuilding goals in terms of positive (rather than negative) peace. Directly contributing to ceasefires is usually beyond the capacity of most NGOs, although there are a few notable exceptions, such as the contribution of Sant'Egidio to peace negotiations in Mozambique.[32] Of course, NGOs are sensitive to the impact of their activities on negative peace. Many have adopted "do no harm" principles and processes to ensure that their initiatives do not unintentionally fuel conflict. However, this is not typically understood as the organization's primary contribution to peacebuilding. This contribution is usually expressed in language about reconciling broken relationships, changing attitudes toward the other, and contributing to equitable development and just social institutions.

To what extent should such efforts to build positive peace, such as an effort to rebuild an interethnic marketplace in a war-torn region, be evaluated by their impact on the level of armed conflict? On the one hand, because such an effort is intended to build better relationships between ethnic communities, and in turn reduce tensions between them, one might expect that the effort would have some impact on the level of violence. On the other hand, it might be too ambitious to expect such a project, even a broad based and widely supported one, to contribute to a discernible reduction in armed violence. Furthermore, tying the success of this project to reductions in the level of violence might make it susceptible to criticism if violence continues, even if the project is achieving its immediate objectives. As a result, project designers might seek to frame the project as a purely positive peacebuilding effort and delink it from negative peace concerns.

Second, the evaluation problem is complicated by the fact that hard data on negative peace are often more easily assembled and analyzed than data on positive peace. Databases like the Conflict Data Project at Uppsala University provide a good basis for assessments of changes in negative peace in a given locality. However, similar data on changes in positive peace are more elusive. One can rely on indices such as the Freedom House index or human rights reports to assess movements toward positive peace, but these may not reflect the kinds of changes that are targeted by a given project.

Third, the evaluation dilemma is further magnified when one unpacks the operative concept of positive peace. As discussed in more detail in chapter 1, positive peace is a comprehensive, all-encompassing goal that may require changes in virtually all sectors of society—economic, social, and political. As such, conceptions of positive peace are shaped in significant ways by local factors, including historical, cultural, and religious understandings of justice and the common good. Thus, a deep understanding of local perspectives on peace would be needed to assess the impact of peacebuilding initiatives.

However, as Roland Paris argues, virtually all peacebuilding operations undertaken by the international community have reflected a liberal internationalist perspective by attempting to introduce a market economy and liberal democracy, sometimes with disastrous consequences.[33] If positive peace is defined by this agenda, then the criteria selected for evaluating the success of peace initiatives may measure adherence to this agenda more than progress toward peace in the eyes of local people.

As a result, NGOs and other civil society actors who seek to contribute to peacebuilding may find themselves negotiating between conflicting conceptions of positive peace as they develop criteria for evaluation. For example, a local community may think that giving more freedom to the media will only empower voices that seek to divide the community, whereas members of the international community may see this as a prerequisite for a peaceful society. Or these roles may be reversed. For example, after the Dayton Accords, several international donors in Bosnia and Herzegovina provided funding to develop an unbiased media there and to counteract its use to fan ethnic tensions. However, some donors effectively censored programming that they thought could inflame ethnic tensions, undermining their stated goal of developing a free media and alienating local media owners.[34]

In addition to illustrating the political contentiousness that can surround peacebuilding projects, this case also highlights the more general uncertainty and disagreement regarding whether and how a particular effort will contribute to positive peace in a given locality. Is a truly free media in a postconflict context an institution that strengthens peace, or is it a potential tool for those who would reignite the conflict? How does the use, or abuse, of the media during conflict affect its capacity to serve as a source of peacebuilding? When are international efforts to strengthen local media in postconflict situations most (and least) effective?

An accountability evaluation that focused on whether the project was implemented according to plan and the quality of the implementation can easily fail to address important and useful questions such as these. As Church and Shouldice observe, "Current evaluation generally explores whether a project has met its stated goals but does not question whether the beliefs about how to instigate change on which the project is based are accurate."[35] An evaluation-focused on learning, on the other hand, would treat this situation as an opportunity for gaining greater insights into how media efforts can better contribute to peacebuilding. In such situations, there is certainly a need for accountability to make sure that funds are spent properly and projects are implemented appropriately. However, there is also a need for learning that is too often left unexplored.

Peacebuilding Strategies: Where Can We Improve?

Given comprehensive, multifaceted goals and a highly complex working environment, one of the key issues facing the peacebuilding community is its strategy for achieving its goals, particularly its strategy for contributing to positive peace. Indeed, peacebuilding practitioners often cite strategic issues, such as the linkages between grassroots involvement and wider peace processes or the relationship between context and strategy development, as among the most central to their work.[36] However, these kinds of issues are often neglected in the evaluation of peacebuilding initiatives.[37]

Organizational strategy is notoriously difficult to define, in part because the term is used to refer to a variety of distinct but overlapping concepts.[38] For our present purposes, strategy is understood as involving an organization's choices about how to deploy its varied resources to meet its overall goals. This approach to organizational strategy emphasizes the alignment of internal resources with external realities. Although goals are sometimes viewed simply as broad statements of organizational vision or as rallying points for staff, they also reflect strategic choices about the organization's positioning in the wider environment relevant to other actors and initiatives as well as decision making about the effectiveness of intervention approaches adopted in the situation. Strategic decision making thus involves an alignment of organizational resources, including its expertise, reputation, and material resources, with the external environment to achieve organizational goals.

The Strategic Environment

A key component in organizational strategy is the organization's position within the wider context or environment. In the context of a business's activities, this may involve an analysis of the competition for a good or service and the definition of a unique niche for the organization's products or services. Although similar issues also affect the nonprofit sector, especially as the number of NGOs continues to grow, increasing the competition for scarce resources, NGOs also have a strategic interest in coordinating activities and services with other agencies and initiatives to achieve their broader objectives.[39]

In the context of peacebuilding, the need for coordination with other actors takes on particular significance. In many cases, coordination is not just a means to an end; instead, it may be an end in itself to get certain actors to work together. As such, coordination is not just about tactical concerns, such as making sure that efforts are not overlapping or redundant with other agencies. It is a key element of an overall strategy for bringing about wider change or impact.

Yet few organizations evaluate their strategies for achieving wider impact in the surrounding environment.[40] Even when the wider strategy is that of the funding agency supporting a project, peacebuilding initiatives often fail to consider links with donor strategies. In one of the largest reviews of peacebuilding evaluations undertaken to date, Smith analyzed evaluations of over 336 projects funded by foreign and development ministries in Germany, the Netherlands, Norway, and the United Kingdom.[41] One of the most significant findings of the study was that more than 55 percent of the projects made no reference to a wider country strategy for peacebuilding. In some cases this was because the donor agency did not have a wider strategy for peacebuilding; in other cases, however, such a strategy existed, but the project was not linked to it. Smith argued that such a high rate constituted a "strategic deficit" in peacebuilding practice.

One reason for the neglect of this aspect of strategy in evaluation is the inherent difficulty of measuring peacebuilding impact. Fast and Neufeldt identify several challenges that bedevil attempts to evaluate this impact.[42] These include the inherent long-term nature of peacebuilding efforts, the difficulty of measuring changes in intangible dimensions such as relationships and attitudes, and the vast political, economic, and social contexts in which peacebuilding occurs.

Unlike some other types of intervention, peacebuilding impact cannot be determined through aggregation methods. In assessing the impact of microfinance initiatives, for example, impact studies typically focus on the changes in the lives of recipients of microloans and draw conclusions based on the kind of changes observed across a large pool.[43] Although peacebuilding initiatives do work with individuals, and their changes of attitude and behavior can to some extent be measured and aggregated, many of the changes desired in these initiatives are broader changes in structures, policies, and relationships between communities, which cannot be readily assessed through aggregation approaches.

Another reason wider impact is neglected may be fear of accountability for matters over which the organization has no control. Given current approaches to evaluation, which focus on measuring results, it is no surprise that impact strategies are neglected. NGO peacebuilding initiatives are often a small piece of a much larger and more complex peacebuilding endeavor, and NGOs do not want to be (and should not be) held accountable if the wider project fails.[44]

NGOs sometimes assume that the only way to contribute on a wider scale is to expand their programs, perhaps by replicating them in other villages or cities, or for chance events to put them in the spotlight or carry their efforts beyond their local community. However, contributions can also happen through strategic engagement with other actors, including UN agencies, other NGOs and NGO networks, local governmental agencies, social movements, governmental policies and programs, donor initiatives, or complex interventions by the international community to secure implementation of a peace agreement.

Of course, these issues are complicated by the fact that peacebuilding efforts do not have a natural institutional home on the national or international levels.[45] Unlike health initiatives, which are usually spearheaded by a ministry of health or other public or international health institution, or rule-of-law initiatives that revolve around the development of legal and judicial institutions, peacebuilding initiatives cut across and involve the work of highly diverse institutional actors. As discussed by Simon Chesterman in chapter 5, the UN has taken steps to create coordinating agencies, including the new Peacebuilding Commission, but its capacity to provide an institutional home is still untested.

As a result, coordination takes a wide range of forms in peacebuilding initiatives. It may involve simply taking cognizance of other actors and their strategies in program planning and implementation and could also extend to actively engaging with others in joint efforts and everything in between. Coordination also needs to happen across a broad array of differences, including coordination between insiders and outsiders (most often the local community and international actors), between actors in different societal sectors (government, military, civil society, business communities), and between actors in different professional fields and disciplines (including health, education, security, agriculture, the judiciary, and many others). In addition, each institution or sector may be affected somewhat differently by conflict, making the coordination challenges in any given situation unique.

Evaluation efforts should provide feedback to peacebuilders on how engagement with other actors and initiatives can enhance (or inhibit) program reach and impact. The purpose of such an inquiry is not to establish that the organization's efforts led to peace writ large, which is unlikely to be the case, or even to show the exact level of its contribution to certain outcomes through some kind of attribution analysis. Rather, what is important to learn is how such engagement strengthened (or weakened) the overall capacity for peacebuilding in the society.

Useful areas for exploration might include the organization's choice of wider initiatives to engage in, the quality of its engagement, and the impact of the engagement on the wider initiative and the organization—issues rarely discussed in evaluations focused on accountability. If a local peacebuilding initiative chooses to participate in a national social movement for peace, for example, is this the kind of link that could foster greater impact in society at large, or does this do little to expand the reach of the initiative? What costs and benefits does this create for the organization and the social movement? Or if a Catholic NGO engages with a Muslim NGO to promote interreligious dialogue in an area marked by violence between their members, how does the joint nature of the initiative affect its legitimacy and impact, and how is it viewed in the wider community? Similar questions could be asked regarding engagement with UN coordinating agencies or local officials.

Of course, positioning strategies do not necessarily have to involve align-ment with a wider peacebuilding initiative; they may also involve criticism or advocacy for alternative approaches. NGOs are highly independent actors, and this approach to evaluating impact strategies does not seek to remove that inde-pendence. The key question is not whether the NGO joined a wider initiative, but whether it engaged it constructively.

Strategy Formulation

Strategy formulation is often understood solely as the making of strategic plans. However, as Mintzberg and Waters observe, although strategic plans are an important point of reference, they are only one end of a continuum that consti-tutes organizational strategy formation.[46] They distinguish between "deliberate strategies," which take the form of plans, and "emergent strategies," which are formed through patterns of decisions and actions by organizational personnel that occur despite or in the absence of strategic plans.

For example, an NGO that states in its strategic plan that it seeks to reduce intercommunal violence at a local university by training students in nonvio-lent approaches to conflict would be following a deliberate strategy in organ-izing trainings for students. If the NGO learns through its engagement with students that the university administration's mismanagement of conflicts is a major contributing factor in the violence, and the NGO then works with univer-sity administrators to develop their conflict management system, the strategy guiding this effort would be emergent rather than deliberate. As Mintzberg and Waters argue, emergent strategies are not necessarily a sign that organizational leaders are out of control; instead, they may be reacting to opportunities or changes in the environment in wholly appropriate ways.[47] Indeed, emergent strategies may later become deliberate strategies as part of a subsequent stra-tegic planning process.

Strategy formulation in any organizational context can be understood as the interaction of deliberate and emergent strategies. Based on a wide range of case studies, Mintzberg and Waters delineate several amalgams of deliberate and emergent strategies, including planned strategies that are based largely on goals articulated in a strategic plan, entrepreneurial strategies where there is a highly individual vision that is elaborated in subsequent actions, umbrella strategies where organizational leaders provide broad boundaries but leave decisions within those boundaries, and consensus strategies where all organi-zational personnel converge on a pattern of mutual adjustment of goals. The key factors determining the mix of deliberate and emergent strategies are the degree of control needed or desired by organizational leaders and the volatility of the external environment.

The evaluation of peacebuilding strategies needs to give appropriate weight to each aspect of strategy formulation. The deliberative dimension of peace-building has received much greater attention than emergent strategies. This is due in large part to the fact that standard NGO evaluation systems focus almost exclusively on strategic plans as the point of reference for evaluation.

Recent assessments of the planning of peacebuilding projects indicate a need for more appropriate tools for designing peacebuilding interventions. As Smith observes, "It is striking that project documentation frequently offers no clear analysis of the problem that is to be addressed by the project. When present, the analysis often gets no further than acknowledging that there is a conflict and therefore conflict resolution activities are appropriate."[48]

To assist in formulating deliberate strategies, peacebuilders need planning tools that help them better articulate their understanding of the conflict(s) they confront and the kinds of changes that are needed to foster sustainable peace. This understanding can be articulated through a variety of methods, including conflict maps or implementation frameworks that delineate changes needed across various sectors, such as the demobilization of militants, the removal of discriminatory laws, and equitable economic development.

In creating such a framework, those developing an intervention strategy must consider whether to emphasize prioritization or integration. While focusing primarily on high-level peacebuilding operations by the international community instead of civil society initiatives, Stedman et al.'s work on ending civil wars provides a good illustration of the prioritization approach.[49] They divide peacebuilding into several subgoals, including the demobilization and reintegration of combatants, disarmament, elections, human rights, and refugee repatriation. Based on an analysis of sixteen cases, they conclude that while other sectors should not be neglected, the demobilization of soldiers and the demilitarization of politics should be given the highest priority in peacebuilding operations, given the central role they play in relation to needs in other sectors.

Lederach's approach, on the other hand, emphasizes the need for integrating multiple dimensions and even multiple time frames in responding to deep-rooted conflict.[50] Like Stedman, Lederach posits that sustainable peace requires changes in a range of arenas, which he describes as the personal, relational, structural, and cultural spheres. However, Lederach's arenas are not seen as distinct sectors but as concentric circles with each embedded in the subsequent arena. Given the complex interconnections between these dimensions, particularly at the local level, he encourages peacebuilders to consider all of these dimensions as they develop peacebuilding projects and to be particularly sensitive to opportunities to develop activities that integrate multiple dimensions.

Likewise, Anderson and Olson suggest that integrative strategies are a prerequisite for effective peacebuilding.[51] They note that peacebuilding efforts aimed at changing public attitudes and building interpersonal relationships are much more likely to succeed if they are linked with processes that seek to change social and political structures. Of course, as they recognize, this does not mean that each organization or initiative must itself be multisector and integrated. If a project is well coordinated with other peacebuilding efforts in other sectors or working on other issues, the organization itself may not need to diversify its program. Thus, a key strategic choice, and one that deserves greater attention in evaluation, concerns whether an organization develops an integrated program itself or seeks stronger coordination with efforts by other actors.

In cases where an organization does develop a highly integrated initiative, evaluating such an initiative poses some unique challenges. As Bush observes, an educational initiative that also seeks to improve relationships between members of different ethnic groups can be understood as having both an educational and a peacebuilding goal.[52] Such a project might succeed in improving relations between students but fail in improving test scores. Or it might lead to improved test scores but fail in improving relationships. In either case, the effectiveness and value of pursuing the project as an integrated initiative is brought into question. Peacebuilding efforts which integrate multiple dimensions, such as combining local refugee resettlement with involvement in national-level reconciliation efforts, may pose similar dilemmas.

To meet these challenges, peacebuilders will need to better articulate the underlying rationale for pursuing integrated programming and then evaluate the validity of that rationale in practice. An examination of initiatives that integrated peacebuilding with health programs provides a useful model of how to evaluate initiatives with two simultaneous goals. MacQueen and Santa-Barbara identify five mechanisms or stratagems through which health initiatives can play a role in peacebuilding.[53] For example, one stratagem posits that certain health needs of the population may form superordinate goals that transcend the interests of the conflicting parties and provide opportunities to promote cooperation between them. They note that in El Salvador in the mid-1980s, UNICEF, the Catholic Church, and other organizations negotiated three days of tranquility each year for seven years that allowed immunization of children against common diseases. Evidence suggests that the common interest in child health on both sides of the conflict played an important role in gaining agreement to these temporary cease-fires. In addition, this appears to have strengthened the standing of the Church as it participated in the peace accord process. A similar evaluation of the particular stratagems behind integrated efforts would be useful in many other areas.

Whereas deliberate strategies are often the focus of evaluation, emergent strategies are rarely examined. The implications of this neglect for the evaluation and improvement of peacebuilding endeavors are far-reaching. Given the volatility of their working environment, peacebuilders frequently need to adjust plans in light of a changed environment. If evaluation efforts do not consider these adaptations of strategy, an important opportunity for learning is lost.

In reflecting on his years of experience in peacebuilding practice, Lederach underscores the pivotal role that unplanned occurrences or serendipitous decisions play in bringing about wider change:

My greatest contributions to peacebuilding did not seem to be those that emerged from my "accumulated skill" or "intentional purpose." They were those that happened unexpectedly. At a certain point, I came to call this "divine naiveté", which originally I defined as the practitioner's dilemma of learning more from mistakes than successes. The reality was that these were not mistakes in the proper sense of the word; they were important things that happened along the way that were not planned.[54]

The evaluation of serendipity may seem to be a futile undertaking. Yet models have been developed to explore how emergent and deliberative strategies interact. A recent study of nonprofit governance examined how a board chairperson and organizational CEO blended deliberate and emergent strategies in guiding a new organization committed to developing stronger nonprofit boards.[55] The study used an ethnographic method to probe how decisions made in response to opportunities or concerns of stakeholders are woven into more deliberative strategic planning. Although such an evaluation is difficult to conduct and will require the development of new evaluation tools and approaches, it could provide significant insights into the practice of peacebuilding.

Implications for Evaluation Processes

If improving the strategic dimensions of peacebuilding initiatives is a priority for the field, what practical steps can be taken to make evaluation more effective in addressing issues of strategy?

Designing Projects

Giving greater emphasis to learning about strategy begins at the project design phase, when plans for evaluation approaches and criteria are often determined and funding for evaluation is allocated. As currently implemented, program planning systems often do not promote the consideration and articulation of specific strategies for achieving wider impact.[56] Although wider goals may be stated and indicators that these goals are being achieved may even be included in the plan, the particular strategy through which the program will contribute to these wider goals is often left implicit. To evaluate a strategy, evaluators must know what strategic choices were made during the design phase (and during project implementation) and why they were made.

One approach to encouraging greater attention to strategy issues in planning is the development of a theory of change. Theories of change were first developed as an approach to evaluation, as already discussed. Over time, however, theories of change have increasingly been used as project planning tools.

Although theories of change are not usually discussed in conjunction with strategies, the links between them deserve attention. Articulating the underlying beliefs and assumptions about how the project is intended to work can sharpen program goals and strategies, help identify relevant indicators, and promote learning from program activities. Reflection on a project's theory of change can also generate questions that will be relevant to peacebuilding practitioners in other contexts. For example, if a dialogue among community religious leaders is intended to have an impact on local members of these religious communities, one key link between the activity and goal is the communication systems within each religious community that report on and discuss the dialogues. Given the key role they play in the project strategy, these communications systems deserve close attention in the project's monitoring and evaluation system. An evaluation that explored the role of these systems in the project and reflected on how these systems can be effectively used to broaden the project's impact could be useful to practitioners in many other contexts.

Scope of Evaluations

Evaluations based on an accountability paradigm often focus on the project or program level. Donors typically provide funds to specific projects or programs, and thus their interest in accountability most naturally requires an evaluation of the recipient of the funds. In the case of the U4 (Germany, Great Britain, Norway, and the Netherlands), for example, individual project evaluation was the norm, and over 40 percent of peacebuilding projects funded by U4 countries were evaluated.[57] However, "despite this considerable effort in evaluating peacebuilding activities, and though many of the evaluations draw useful conclusions about individual projects, there is no basis for drawing wider conclusions about, for example, what works and what does not work in U4 peacebuilding."[58]

When viewed from the perspective of the peacebuilding community, evaluations that are wider in scope may provide more useful feedback that fosters learning by the community. Such an evaluation can compare efforts of different actors as well as observe how different actors coordinated their efforts. These could include evaluations of the overall response to a specific conflict by a particular funding agency, the evaluation of all efforts of a particular type or in a particular sector, systemwide evaluations of how all sectors responded to a given conflict, or international comparisons of peacebuilding initiatives.[59]

An evaluation of ten years of grant making in the area of conflict resolution by the Mott Foundation provides an instructive example of the value of wider scope for learning. In addition to evaluations of several specific initiatives, the report derives a number of lessons from a diverse range of experiences. For example, it notes the critical importance of the point of entry into a conflict situation and observes how "skilled, committed and publicly known university faculty and students proved to be appropriate partners and project participants in several programs."[60]

Evaluation Methods

If the promotion of learning by the peacebuilding community is the goal of an evaluation, then the participation of peacebuilding practitioners in evaluations is critical. As Church and Shouldice note, external evaluators may not understand the local environment or may miss important local factors affecting the project.[61] Practitioners bring questions and perspectives that complement those of professional evaluators or academics, who typically make up evaluation teams. Including practitioners, both local and those from other contexts, would give the peacebuilding community an important stake in and link to evaluation.

Of course, making learning a priority will also require changes in the way that evaluations are conducted. Although the OECD/DAC guidelines provide a useful point of reference, they do not focus attention directly on strategic issues. Analysis of the "effectiveness" of a project is akin to operational strategy; however, the practice of assessing effectiveness looks primarily at whether the program met the established targets for its objectives laid out in its plan. Thus, evaluation of issues such as the merits of an integrated programming strategy might fall outside the scope of this criterion.

These guidelines need revision to more adequately meet the current needs of the peacebuilding community. Interestingly, the OECD/DAC has recognized that its criteria would need adjustments if they were used to evaluate interventions other than development. In providing guidelines for the evaluation of humanitarian efforts in complex emergencies, the OECD/DAC recommended adding several criteria, including coverage (whether the effort reaches major groups facing life-threatening suffering wherever they are and is devoid of extraneous political agendas), coherence (whether humanitarian actors are acting coherently with military, security, trade, and development policies and with the policies of other humanitarian actors), and coordination (whether humanitarian actors are working effectively with other actors in the situation). The OECD/DAC has begun a similar process to adapt its general guidelines to the needs of conflict prevention and peacebuilding initiatives, and preliminary reports have been published.[62] Issuing guidelines that focused evaluations on the strategic challenges facing the peacebuilding community would be a welcome step.

Dissemination and Use of Evaluations

If evaluations are to promote learning by the practitioner community, they must be available to the practitioner community. Of course, the dissemination of evaluation findings raises a number of delicate ethical and political issues. Confidentiality may sometimes be necessary to protect the disclosure of sensitive information. In addition, the public release of evaluation reports, positive or negative, can create dilemmas for both funders and the organizations they support. As a result, evaluators have found it necessary to determine from the outset who will be entitled to see the final product.[63]

Nonetheless, organizations should make every effort to disseminate relevant evaluations to the wider community. The Internet has made it possible to disseminate written reports cheaply and widely. In recent years, a number of Web sites have begun to post evaluations of peacebuilding projects.[64] These evaluations not only provide insights into the achievements of peacebuilding projects in a wide range of settings but also suggest models for new projects and innovative approaches to evaluation. Wider dissemination could increase use of evaluations in the development of new peacebuilding programs.

Conclusion

The current challenges facing the peacebuilding community would benefit from evaluations that seek to promote learning. In the complex and volatile environments where peacebuilding efforts are implemented, program impact beyond immediate results is subject to myriad external factors beyond the control of the implementing organization or agency. In such a situation, many of the primary questions facing peacebuilding practitioners are strategic in nature: Are we working with the right people or groups to bring about wider change in the situation? Are the activities appropriate for bringing about those changes? Did we build appropriate linkages with other efforts that reinforce and multiply impact?

An approach to evaluation rooted in accountability is unlikely to provide the feedback needed to improve the practice of peacebuilding. Although setting goals and performance indicators as part of project design and then evaluating success in achieving these intended outcomes is useful, this approach to evaluation can easily neglect emergent strategies or underlying theories of change that effectively guide program efforts. Given the fundamental nature of peacebuilding as a multidimensional and multilevel enterprise, evaluating the advantages and disadvantages of alternative strategies is critical to the further advancement of the field.

In addition, organizations or efforts resist being held accountable for outcomes they have little control over, even as they hope to contribute to these outcomes. As a result, organizations that perceive they will be held in some sense accountable for wider impact are likely to narrowly circumscribe their program goals and may neglect integration with wider efforts. Recent research on donor evaluations[65] and practitioner attitudes[66] suggests that this is happening.

Peacebuilding practitioners should be encouraged to think deeply about the role their initiatives play in wider peace efforts. Peacebuilders cannot deliver peace on their own. However, they can deliver outcomes that help move peace processes or efforts forward if their initiatives are linked with others. A learning approach to evaluation processes can encourage reflection and action that will improve these critical links.

NOTES

I thank John Darby for his useful comments on earlier versions of this chapter.

1. Tschirgi, Necla. 2004. "Peacebuilding as the Link between Peace and Security: Is the Window of Opportunity Closing?" In *International Peace Academic Studies in Security and Development*. New York: International Peace Academy, p. 2.

2. Lund, Michael. 2003. "What Kind of Peace Is Being Built? Taking Stock of Post-Conflict Peacebuilding and Charting Future Directions. A Discussion Paper." International Development Research Centre, p. 6.

3. Anderson, Mary B. 1999. *Do No Harm: How Aid Can Support Peace—or War*. Boulder, Colo.: Lynne Rienner. Uvin, Peter. 1998. *Aiding Violence. The Development Enterprise in Rwanda*. West Hartford, Conn.: Kumarian Press. Menkhaus, Ken. 2003.

"Measuring Impact: Issues and Dilemmas. A Discussion Paper." War-Torn Societies Project (WSP), p. 3.

4. Ibid.

5. Lund, 2003, p. 16.

6. Tschirgi, 2004, p. 15.

7. Lund, 2003, p. 20.

8. Anderson, Mary B., and Lara Olson. 2003. *Confronting War: Critical Lessons for Peace Practitioners.* Cambridge, Mass.: Collaborative for Development Action, pp. 8–9. Church, Cheyanne, and Julie Shouldice. 2003. *The Evaluation of Conflict Resolution Interventions, Part II: Emerging Practice and Theory.* Derry/Londonderry, Northern Ireland: INCORE, pp. 6–7.

9. Lederach, John Paul, Reina C. Neufeldt, and Hal Culbertson. 2007. *Reflective Peacebuilding: A Planning, Monitoring, and Learning Toolkit.* Mindanao, Philippines: Joan B. Kroc Institute for International Peace Studies, University of Notre Dame and Catholic Relief Services Southeast, East Asia Regional Office. Church, Cheyanne, and Mark Rogers. 2006. *Designing for Results: Integrating Monitoring and Evaluation in Conflict Transformation Programs: Search for Common Ground.* Available at http://www. sfcg.org/programmes/ilr/ilt_manualpage.html (accessed October 26, 2006). Anderson, Mary B., and Lara Olson. 2003. *Confronting War: Critical Lessons for Peace Practitioners.* Cambridge, Mass.: Collaborative for Development Action. *Conflict Sensitive Approaches to Development, Humanitarian Assistance, and Peacebuilding: Tools for Peace and Conflict Impact Assessment.* 2003. FEWER, International Alert, Saferworld. *Strategic and Responsive Evaluation of Peacebuilding: Toward a Learning Model.* 2001. Naivasha, Kenya: NPI-Africa and the NCCK-CPBD Project.

10. Patton, Michael Quinn. 1997. *Utilization-Focused Evaluation: The New Century Text,* 3rd ed. Thousand Oaks, Calif.: Sage, p. 65.

11. Smillie, Ian. 1997. "NGOs and Development Assistance: A Change in Mind-Set?" *Third World Quarterly* 18 (3): 563–577.

12. Ebrahim, Alnoor. 2003. "Accountability in Practice: Mechanisms for NGOs." *World Development* 31 (5): 813.

13. Edwards, Michael, and David Hulme. 1995. "NGO Performance and Accountability: Introduction and Overview." In *NGOs—Performance and Accountability: Beyond the Magic Bullet,* edited by M. Edwards and D. Hulme. London: Earthscan Publications.

14. A logical framework, or "logframe," is a project design and management tool. The framework is usually presented in the form of a matrix. The rows in the matrix describe the logical link between a project's activities, outputs, purposes, and overall goal. The columns specify indicators that will be used to measure project success at various levels, the means that will be used to verify the indicators, and underlying assumption about the project design.

15. OECD/DAC. 1999. "Evaluation and Aid Effectiveness: Guidance for Evaluating Humanitarian Assistance in Complex Emergencies." Organisation for Economic Co-operation and Development, Development Assistance Committee.

16. Kaldor, Mary. 2003. "Civil Society and Accountability." *Journal of Human Development* 4 (1): 5–27.

17. Ross, Marc. 2001. "Action Evaluation in the Theory and Practice of Conflict Resolution." *Peace and Conflict Studies* 8 (1).

18. Patton, 1997, p. 68.

19. Church and Rogers, 2006.

20. Argyris, Chris, and Donald Schön. 1978. *Organizational Learning: A Theory of Action Perspective.* Reading, Mass.: Addison-Wesley.

21. Roper, Laura, and Jethro Pettit. 2003. "Development and the Learning Organisation: an introduction." In *Development and the Learning Organization*, edited by L. Roper, J. Pettit, and D. Eade. Oxford: Oxfam GB, p. 1.

22. Riddell, Roger C. 1999. "Evaluating NGO Development Interventions." In *International Perspective on Voluntary Action: Reshaping the Third Sector*, edited by D. Lewis. London: Earthscan, p. 234. Carlsson, Charlotte, and Paul G. H. Engel. 2002. "Enhancing Learning through Evaluation: Approaches, Dilemmas and Some Possible Ways Forward" (Background Papers). Maastricht: ECDPM.

23. Weiss, Carol Hirschon. 1982. "Policy Research in the Context of Diffuse Decision Making." *Journal of Higher Education* 52 (6).

24. Ibid.

25. Weiss, Carol Hirschon. 1995. "Nothing as Practical as Good Theory: Exploring Theory-Based Evaluation for Comprehensive Community Initiatives for Children and Families." In *New Approaches to Evaluating Community Initiatives: Concepts, Methods, and Contexts*, edited by J. Connell and others. Washington, D.C.: Aspen Institute.

26. McGarvey, Craig. 2004, 2006. "Learning Together: Collaborative Inquiry among Grantors and Grantees." Kellogg Foundation. 1998. *Evaluation Handbook*.

27. Ebrahim, Alnoor. 2005. "Accountability Myopia: Losing Sight of Organizational Learning." *Nonprofit and Voluntary Sector Quarterly* 34 (1): 56–87.

28. Carlsson and Engel, 2002, p. 10.

29. Riddell, 1999, p. 237.

30. Bush, Kenneth. 1998. *A Measure of Peace: Peace and Conflict Impact Assessment (PCIA) of Development Projects in Conflict Zones.* The Peacebuilding and Reconstruction Program Initiative & The Evaluation Unit, International Research and Development Centre, pp. 33–34.

31. Anderson and Olson, 2003, p. 12.

32. Ross, Marc Howard, and Jay Rothman. 1999. "Issues of Theory and Practice in Ethnic Conflict Management." In *Theory and Practice of Ethnic Conflict Management*, edited by M. H. Ross and J. Rothman. London/New York: Macmillan/ St. Martin's Press, p. 2. Aall, Pamela. 2001. "What Do NGOs Bring to Peacemaking?" In *Turbulent Peace: The Challenges of Managing International Conflict*, edited by C. A. Crocker, F. O. Hampton, and P. Aall. Washington, D.C.: U.S. Institute of Peace, p. 374.

33. Paris, Roland. 2004. *At War's End: Building Peace after Civil Conflict.* New York: Cambridge University Press.

34. Kumar, Krishna. 1999. *Promoting Social Reconciliation in Postconflict Societies: Selected Lessons from USAID's Experience.* Center for Development Information and Evaluation. U.S. Agency for International Development.

35. Church and Shouldice, 2003, p. 23.

36. Anderson and Olson,. 2003, p. 2.

37. Church and Shouldice, 2003, p. 23.

38. Mintzberg, Henry. 1987. "The Strategy Concept I: Five P's for Strategy." *California Management Review* 30 (3).

39. Cooley, Alexander, and James Ron. 2002. "The NGO Scramble: Organizational Insecurity and the Political Economy of Transnational Action." *International Security* 27 (1): 5–39.

40. Anderson and Olson, 2003, p. 14.

41. Smith, Dan. 2004. "Towards a Strategic Framework for Peacebuilding: Getting Their Act Together." In *Overview Report of the Joint Utstein Study of Peacebuilding.* Bratvaag: Royal Norwegian Ministry of Foreign Affairs.

42. Fast, Larissa A., and Reina C. Neufeldt. 2005. "Envisioning Success: Building Blocks for Strategic and Comprehensive Peacebuilding Impact Evaluation." *Journal of Peacebuilding and Development* 2 (2): 24–41, p. 25.

43. Microfinance Gateway Impact Assessment Center. 2006. Available at http://microfinancegateway.com/section/resourcecenters/impactassessment.

44. Prendergast, John, and Emily Plumb. 2002. "Building Local Capacity: From Implementation to Peacebuilding." In *Ending Civil Wars: The Implementation of Peace Agreements*, edited by S. J. Stedman, D. Rothchild, and E. M. Cousens. Boulder, Colo.: Lynne Rienner, p. 328.

45. Tschirgi, 2004, p. 5.

46. Mintzberg, Henry, and James A. Waters. 1985. "Of Strategies, Deliberate and Emergent." *Strategic Management Journal* 6 (3): 257–272.

47. Ibid., p. 271.

48. Smith, 2004, p. 45.

49. Stedman, Stephen John. 2001. "International Implementation of Peace Agreements in Civil Wars: Findings of a Study of Sixteen Cases." In *Turbulent Peace: The Challenges of Managing International Conflict*. Edited by Chester A. Crocker, Fen Osler Hampson, and Pamela Aall. Washington, D.C.: U.S. Institute of Peace, pp. 737–752.

50. Lederach, John Paul. 2003. *The Little Book of Conflict Transformation*. Good Books.

51. Anderson and Olson, 2003.

52. Bush, 2001, p. 4.

53. MacQueen, Graeme, and Joanna Santa-Barbara. 2000. "Conflict and Health: Peacebuilding through Health Initiatives." *British Medical Journal* 321: 293–296.

54. Lederach, John Paul. 2005. *The Moral Imagination: The Art and Soul of Peacebuilding*. Oxford: Oxford University Press, p. 115.

55. Morrison, J. Bart, and Paul Salipante. 2007. "Governance for Broadened Accountability: Blending Deliberate and Emergent Strategizing," *Nonprofit and Voluntary Sector Quarterly* 36 (2): 195–217.

56. Smith, 2004, p. 46.

57. Ibid., p. 50.

58. Ibid., p. 51.

59. OECD/DAC, 1999.

60. Mott Foundation. 1999. *Reaching for Peace: Lessons Learned from Mott Foundation's Conflict Resolution Grantmaking, 1989–1998*. Charles Stewart Mott Foundation. Available at: http://www.mott.org/publications/pdf/SPECIALreachingforpeace.pdf (accessed October 26, 2003), p. 26.

61. Church and Shouldice, 2003, p. 13.

62. OECD/DAC, 2007. "Encouraging Effective Evaluation of Conflict Prevention and Peacebuilding Activities: Toward DAC Guidance." *OECD Journal of Development* 8 (3): 7–106.

63. Ibid., p. 23.

64. These include the ALNAP Evaluation Reports Database (http://www.alnap.org), the CR Info—Completed Evaluations (http://www.crinfo.org/action/recommended.jsp?list_id=882), the DAC Evaluation Resource Center (http://www.oecd.org/dac/evaluationnetwork/derec), and Search for Common Ground Evaluations (http://www.sfcg.org/sfcg/sfcg_evaluations.html).

65. Smith, 2004, p. 53.

66. Anderson and Olson, 2003.

REFERENCES

Aall, Pamela. 2001. "What Do NGOs Bring to Peacemaking?" In *Turbulent Peace: The Challenges of Managing International Conflict*. Edited by Chester A. Crocker, Fen Osler Hampson, and Pamela Aall. Washington, D.C.: U.S. Institute of Peace.

Anderson, Mary B. 1999. *Do No Harm: How Aid Can Support Peace—or War*. Boulder, Colo.: Lynne Rienner.

Anderson, Mary B., and Lara Olson. 2003. *Confronting War: Critical Lessons for Peace Practitioners*. Cambridge, Mass.: Collaborative for Development Action. Available at: http://www.cdainc.com/publications/rpp/confronting_war_critical_lessons_for_peace_practitioners.php (accessed October 7, 2006).

Argyris, Chris, and Donald Schön. 1978. *Organizational Learning: A Theory of Action Perspective*. Reading, Mass.: Addison-Wesley.

Bush, Kenneth. 1998. *A Measure of Peace: Peace and Conflict Impact Assessment (PCIA) of Development Projects in Conflict Zones*. Working Paper No. 1. The Peacebuilding and Reconstruction Program Initiative and The Evaluation Unit. International Research and Development Centre.

Bush, Kenneth. 2001. *Peace and Conflict Impact Assessment (PCIA) of Swedish Development Cooperation with Sri Lanka*. Swedish International Development Cooperation Agency (SIDA).

Carlsson, Charlotte, and Paul G. H. Engel. 2002. "Enhancing Learning through Evaluation: Approaches, Dilemmas and Some Possible Ways Forward." Background Papers. Maastricht: ECDPM.

Church, Cheyanne, and Mark Rogers. 2006. *Designing for Results: Integrating Monitoring and Evaluation in Conflict Transformation Programs*. Search for Common Ground. Available at: http://www.sfcg.org/programmes/ilr/ilt_manualpage.html (accessed October 26, 2006).

Church, Cheyanne, and Julie Shouldice. 2003. *The Evaluation of Conflict Resolution Interventions, Part II: Emerging Practice and Theory*. Derry/Londonderry, Northern Ireland: INCORE.

Conflict Sensitive Approaches to Development, Humanitarian Assistance, and Peacebuilding: Tools for Peace and Conflict Impact Assessment. 2003. *FEWER, International Alert, and Saferworld*. Available at: http://www.international-alert.org/conflict_sensitivity/resource_pack.html (accessed May 30, 2007).

Cooley, Alexander, and James Ron. 2002. "The NGO Scramble: Organizational Insecurity and the Political Economy of Transnational Action." *International Security*. 27(1): 5–39.

Ebrahim, Alnoor. 2003. "Accountability in Practice: Mechanisms for NGOs." *World Development* 31(5).

Ebrahim, Alnoor. 2005. "Accountability Myopia: Losing Sight of Organizational Learning." *Nonprofit and Voluntary Sector Quarterly* 34(1): 56–87.

Edwards, Michael, and David Hulme. 1995. "NGO Performance and Accountability: Introduction and Overview." In *NGOs—Performance and Accountability: Beyond the Magic Bullet*. Edited by Michael Edwards and David Hulme. London: Earthscan Publications.

Fast, Larissa A., and Reina C. Neufeldt. 2005. "Envisioning Success: Building Blocks for Strategic and Comprehensive Peacebuilding Impact Evaluation." *Journal of Peacebuilding and Development* 2(2): 24–41.

Kaldor, Mary. 2003. "Civil Society and Accountability." *Journal of Human Development* 4(1): 5–27.

Kellogg Foundation. 1998. *Evaluation Handbook*. Available at: http://www.wkkf.org/Pubs/Tools/Evaluation/Pub770.pdf (accessed October 26, 2006).

Kumar, Krishna. 1999. *Promoting Social Reconciliation in Postconflict Societies: Selected Lessons from USAID's Experience*. Center for Development Information and Evaluation. U.S. Agency for International Development.

Lederach, John Paul. 2003. *The Little Book of Conflict Transformation*. Good Books.

Lederach, John Paul. 2005. *The Moral Imagination: The Art and Soul of Peacebuilding*. Oxford: Oxford University Press.

Lederach, John Paul, Reina Neufeldt, and Hal Culbertson. 2007. *Reflective Peacebuilding: A Planning, Monitoring, and Learning Toolkit*. Mindanao, Philippines: Joan B. Kroc Institute for International Peace Studies, University of Notre Dame and Catholic Relief Services Southeast, East Asia Regional Office.

Lund, Michael. 2003. "What Kind of Peace Is Being Built? Taking Stock of Post-Conflict Peacebuilding and Charting Future Directions. A Discussion Paper." International Development Research Centre. Available at: http://www.idrc.ca/uploads/user-S/10527469720lund_final_mar_20.pdf (accessed October 7, 2006).

MacQueen, Graeme, and Joanna Santa-Barbara. 2000. "Conflict and Health: Peacebuilding through Health Initiatives." *British Medical Journal* 321: 293–296.

McGarvey, Craig. 2004, 2006. "Learning Together: Collaborative Inquiry among Grantors and Grantees." Available at: http://www.grantcraft.org/index.cfm?fuseaction=Page.viewPage&pageID=619 (accessed October 7, 2006).

Menkhaus, Ken. 2003. "Measuring Impact: Issues and Dilemmas. A Discussion Paper." War-Torn Societies Project (WSP). Available at: http://www.interpeace.org/jset/servlet/JsServlet?svc=IO&cmd=load&path=files%2FUsers%2Fwsp%2FDocuments%2FMeasuring%20Impact.pdf (accessed October 17, 2006).

Microfinance Gateway Impact Assessment Center (Web site). 2006. Available at: http://microfinancegateway.com/section/resourcecenters/impactassessment (accessed October 27, 2006).

Mintzberg, Henry. 1987. "The Strategy Concept I: Five P's for Strategy." *California Management Review* 30(1).

Mintzberg, Henry, and James A. Waters. 1985. "Of Strategies, Deliberate and Emergent," *Strategic Management Journal* 6(3): 257–272.

Morrison, J. Bart, and Paul Salipante. 2007. "Governance for Broadened Accountability: Blending Deliberate and Emergent Strategizing," *Nonprofit and Voluntary Sector Quarterly* 36(2): 195–217.

Mott Foundation. 1999. *Reaching for Peace: Lessons Learned from Mott Foundation's Conflict Resolution Grantmaking, 1989–1998*. Charles Stewart Mott Foundation. Available at: http://www.mott.org/publications/pdf/SPECIALreachingforpeace.pdf (accessed October 26, 2003).

OECD/DAC. 1999. "Evaluation and Aid Effectiveness: Guidance for Evaluating Humanitarian Assistance in Complex Emergencies." Organisation for Economic Co-operation and Development, Development Assistance Committee.

OECD/DAC. 2007. "Encouraging Effective Evaluation of Conflict Prevention and Peacebuilding Activities: Toward DAC Guidance." *OECD Journal of Development* 8(3): 7–106.

Paris, Roland. 2004. *At War's End: Building Peace after Civil Conflict*. New York: Cambridge University Press.

Patton, Michael Quinn. 1997. *Utilization-Focused Evaluation: The New Century Text*. 3rd ed. Thousand Oaks, Calif.: Sage Publications.

Prendergast, John, and Emily Plumb. 2002. "Building Local Capacity: From Implementation to Peacebuilding." In *Ending Civil Wars: The Implementation of Peace Agreements*. Edited by Stephen John Stedman, Donald Rothchild, and Elizabeth M. Cousens. Boulder, Colo.: Lynne Rienner.

Riddell, Roger C. 1999. "Evaluating NGO Development Interventions." In *International Perspective on Voluntary Action: Reshaping the Third Sector*. Edited by David Lewis. London: Earthscan.

Roper, Laura, and Jethro Pettit. 2003. "Development and the Learning Organisation: an introduction." In *Development and the Learning Organization*. Edited by Laura Roper, Jethro Pettit, and Deborah Eade. Oxford: Oxfam GB.

Ross, Marc. 2001. "Action Evaluation in the Theory and Practice of Conflict Resolution." *Peace and Conflict Studies* 8(1).

Ross, Marc Howard, and Jay Rothman. 1999. "Issues of Theory and Practice in Ethnic Conflict Management." In *Theory and Practice of Ethnic Conflict Management*. Edited by Marc Howard Ross and Jay Rothman. London/New York: Macmillan/St. Martin's Press.

Smillie, Ian. 1997. "NGOs and Development Assistance: A Change in Mind-Set?" *Third World Quarterly* 18(3): 563–577.

Smith, Dan. 2004. *Towards a Strategic Framework for Peacebuilding: Getting Their Act Together*. Overview Report of the Joint Utstein Study of Peacebuilding. Bratvaag: Royal Norwegian Ministry of Foreign Affairs.

Stedman, Stephen. 2001. "International Implementation of Peace Agreements in Civil Wars: Findings of a Study of Sixteen Cases." In *Turbulent Peace: The Challenges of Managing International Conflict*. Edited by Chester A. Crocker, Fen Osler Hampson, and Pamela Aall. Washington, D.C.: U.S. Institute of Peace.

Strategic and Responsive Evaluation of Peacebuilding: Toward a Learning Model. 2001. Naivasha, Kenya: NPI-Africa and the NCCK-CPBD Project.

Tschirgi, Necla. 2004. *Peacebuilding as the Link between Peace and Security: Is the Window of Opportunity Closing?* International Peace Academic Studies in Security and Development. New York: International Peace Academy. Available at: http://www.ipacademy.org/Publications/Publications.htm (accessed October 15, 2006).

Uvin, Peter. 1998. *Aiding Violence. The Development Enterprise in Rwanda*. West Hartford, Conn.: Kumarian Press.

Weiss, Carol Hirschon. 1982. "Policy Research in the Context of Diffuse Decision Making." *Journal of Higher Education* 52(6).

Weiss, Carol Hirschon. 1995. "Nothing as Practical as Good Theory: Exploring Theory-Based Evaluation for Comprehensive Community Initiatives for Children and Families." In *New Approaches to Evaluating Community Initiatives: Concepts, Methods, and Contexts*. Edited by James Connell et al. Washington, D.C.: Aspen Institute.

4

Reconciliation: An Ethic for Peacebuilding

Daniel Philpott

A genocide in Rwanda that killed 800,000 people; a civil war in
Sudan that took over 2 million lives; wars in Northern Ireland and
the Middle East that have taken far fewer lives but have convulsed
societies and regions; the thousands of injustices committed by communist dictatorships in East Germany and Poland. In all of these settings—ones where human rights violations number in commas and
zeros—is situated the central theme of this volume: the multiplicity
and interdependence of practices that constitute strategic peacebuilding. Where injustice and suffering is colossal, systemic, and splayed
into manifold dimensions, the building of peace involves a range of
actors, activities, time horizons, and modes of analysis. Multiplicity
and interdependence attend even the concept of peace itself: peace
scholars commonly make a distinction between a negative peace,
involving the cessation of armed hostilities, and positive peace, which
realizes a degree of justice. Understanding the many dimensions
of peacebuilding in turn involves multiplicity and interdependence
among modes of analysis: empirical, policy prescriptive, and legal—
and also ethical. The latter sort is pursued in this essay: what constitutes justice in the wake of its massive despoliation?[1]

Justice in fact embodies the multiple dimensions of peacebuilding, all of which are shot through with ethical questions. Should
negotiators forgo the prosecution of war criminals to secure their
assent to a peace settlement? Are conditional amnesties justifiable? If
so, under what conditions? What are the respective roles of international and domestic actors in prosecuting war criminals? May leaders
apologize on behalf of entire nations? Are reparations owed to representatives of past generations? Who owes them, and how much? Can

states practice forgiveness? Or does forgiveness unjustifiably sacrifice retributive justice? Might outside states or international organizations exercise the prerogatives of sovereignty in helping societies rebuild? Many of these questions, many of these several dimensions of peacebuilding's ethical multiplicity have been taken up by political philosophers, legal theorists, theologians, and other scholars. Many overlap with other chapters in this volume—prosecution versus peace in Robert Johansen's chapter, the several dilemmas of transitional justice that arise in Naomi Roht-Arriaza's chapter, the prerogatives of outside states and institutions in Simon Chesterman's piece, and forgiveness in Robert Enright, Jeannette Knutson Enright, and Anthony Holter's chapter. What only a few scholars have addressed, though, is peacebuilding's ethical interdependence. Might a just response in one area be related to a just response in another area? Might an ethical approach to one dimension of peacebuilding be incomplete if it is not accompanied by a similar engagement of other dimensions? Is there a common concept that links together the ethics that govern peacebuilding's several dimensions? What is needed is a holistic ethics of peacebuilding, developing the moral logic of its several component activities, identifying their complementarities, and resolving tensions between them.

A model of success for such a project is the ethic produced by the just war tradition. Developed over centuries in the West and resonating in several cultural traditions, the just war ethic ingeniously derives from philosophical roots a set of integrated ethical guidelines that governs a wide range of questions of war and that has succeeded in becoming institutionalized in international law, taught in military academies, invoked in trials and truth commissions, and appealed to in political debates, even if its standards are still seldom heeded in practice.[2] Although notions of justice for dealing with past political evil also have ancient pedigrees, a similarly integrated ethic for contemporary recovering states remains at a comparatively early stage. Whether one will ever succeed in commanding the consensus and influence of the just war ethic is an open question, one whose answer surely depends on the long-term conversation of a community of scholars.

This chapter joins that conversation. It outlines a general approach to the justice of dealing with the past in political settings where colossal evil has taken place. Its orienting concept has arisen from debates about justice in recovering societies all across the globe: reconciliation. The term is eponymous for truth commissions in Chile, South Africa, Sierra Leone, Liberia, East Timor, and Peru and often appears in the discourse of scholars, analysts, and political actors elsewhere. True to peacebuilding, reconciliation is an ethic of multiplicity and interdependence. The ethic begins by recognizing a multiplicity of wounds that political injustices leave behind. It is then constructed from a multiplicity of traditions that it brings into dialogue, also a kind of interdependence. It draws its core concepts from religious traditions—Judaism, Christianity, Islam—where reconciliation finds its richest and most ancient expression, but then seeks to synthesize these concepts with the best insights of the liberal tradition—human rights, democracy, and law—to form an ethic for modern politics. The result of the synthesis is an ethic of restorative justice whose central virtue is mercy, understood in its classical sense. From this center, the ethic then derives six practices that give reconciliation political expression: building just institutions, acknowledgment, reparations, accountability, apology, and forgiveness. Manifesting multiplicity, each practice addresses different wounds of political injustice in different ways. Interdependently, the practices relate to one another through synergies and tensions. This chapter seeks to depict this multiplicity and interdependence by presenting a conceptual map of an ethic of reconciliation. Of necessity, it will touch briefly on many issues whose justification, explanation, and application require far more attention than can be offered here.[3] It is rather the holistic, interwoven character of the ethic—reflecting the same characteristics of peacebuilding—that is conveyed.

The Wounds of Political Injustice

In its most ancient meanings, reconciliation connotes a comprehensive restoration of right relationship. The Jewish concept of shalom, for instance, describes a state of peace where everyone is living in right relationship with God and with everyone else, in every respect. Advocated here is a more limited concept of political reconciliation. It draws on holistic religious conceptions of restoration and aspires to a subset of what they envision—right relationship in the political order. In modern political orders, at least reasonably just ones, right relationship is realized through the rule of law, which the state lives under and promotes and which citizens uphold when they respect and recognize the rights and dignity of other citizens. The kind of rupture in right relationship relevant to political reconciliation, then, is political injustices—deeds through which agents of the state or opposition forces violate the rule of law in the name of political ends or simply unjust laws and structures. In contemporary contexts of peacebuilding, political injustices have typically occurred on a colossal and systemic scale—in commas and zeroes. They depict the fundamental condition that an ethic of peacebuilding must address.

Exactly which sorts of actions and structures are political injustices? According to whose rule of law? The institutions and political processes through which societies have dealt with the past over the past generation—truth commissions, trials, reparations schemes, and the like—have almost uniformly adopted as their governing standards the norms of human rights and the laws of war that can be found in the United Nations Charter, the Universal Declaration of Human Rights, and sundry international legal instruments. Most prominent are the three crimes with which the Nuremberg Trials charged Nazi war criminals in 1945 and 1946, including military aggression, war crimes, and crimes against humanity, in which a body of people is violently persecuted. Genocide and torture are also strongly embedded in international law and appear often in procedures for transitional justice. More recently, rape has joined the company of crimes in many of these procedures—an important victory for the rights of women. Injustices that do not involve mass atrocity, like deep economic inequalities or the violation of civil rights, are often taken up as well in transitional justice and the debates that surround it.

Human rights and the laws of war define what political injustices are, but not the wide extent to which they wound their victims. What are the ways they break right relationship and diminish human flourishing? Here arises the first important form of multiplicity in the ethic: there are at least six forms of wounds that political injustices leave behind, six respects in which political injustices diminish the human flourishing of those who are involved in them. This array of wounds depicts the complex social affliction that the ethic must confront.

Human rights and the laws of war not only define what political injustices are but depict the first and most fundamental respect in which these injustices wound their victims. Because the status of a citizen as a subject of the rule and a bearer of human rights is a fundamental dimension of right relationship in the political order and, indeed, of human flourishing, the violation of this status does egregious harm to the victim's dignity.

Political injustices do far more than strip victims of their guaranteed rights. A second dimension of woundedness is their harm to the victim's very person, her body and her soul. This dimension includes a whole range of harms, including death; the loss of family and friends; permanent bodily impairment; sexual violation; ongoing trauma and grief; humiliation; the loss of economic livelihood; disrespect for one's race, ethnicity, nationality, or gender; the taking of the land of one's community; and many other harms.

Compounding these harms themselves is victims' frequent ignorance of the source and circumstances of the political injustices inflicted on them—a third dimension of woundedness. Relatives of the missing or the dead express this injury most poignantly. "If they can just show us the bones of my child, where did they leave the bones of my child?" the mother of a missing political activist in South Africa exclaimed.[4]

The wound of ignorance is deepened further by a fourth dimension of woundedness—the failure of fellow citizens to acknowledge victims' suffering, either through ignorance or indifference. South African political philosopher André Du Toit wrote that "for the victims, this actually is a redoubling of the basic violation: the literal violation consists of the actual pain, suffering and trauma visited on them; the political violation consists in the refusal (publicly) to acknowledge it."[5]

A fifth dimension of woundedness pertains to the perpetrator. It may be thought of as the "standing victory" of the message of injustice that the perpetrator communicated through his act. In addition to the material, psychological, and spiritual harms that a perpetrator of political injustice leaves behind is the undefeated triumph of the disregard for the victim's dignity that defines the act. This standing victory is itself a harm to the victim as well as an attack on the shared values of a just political community.

The sixth dimension, also pertaining to the perpetrator, is the wound that a political injustice inflicts on the perpetrator himself. That evil objectively diminishes the soul of the wrongdoer, dissevering his acting self from his true moral self, is an insight as old as Plato's *Gorgias* and several religious traditions. Perpetrators psychologically and spiritually wounded in this way often go on to commit further political injustices and contribute to undermining just and stable political orders.

Each of these six dimensions of woundedness entails harms to human flourishing that result directly from acts of political injustice. They may, then, be called "primary wounds." But wounds harm persons and relationships in a further sense: by leading victims, perpetrators, and citizens at large to form emotions—revenge, hatred, resentment, and the like—that in turn lead them to make hostile judgments toward political orders and other members of them, which then lead them to participate in and commit more war crimes, massacres, torture, and acts of international aggression or simply refuse their assent to nascent peace agreements or constitutional orders, thus depriving them of much-needed legitimacy. These further deeds may be thought of as "secondary wounds." Instances of them can be found anywhere that injustices of one period have resulted in recurrent injustices or at least lasting enmity within or between countries: Rwanda, Northern Ireland, Bosnia, Kosovo, the Basque Country, Iraq, Israel and Palestine, Kashmir, Nanking, post-Versailles Germany, and many others.[6]

Reconciliation as a Concept of Justice

Landscapes of woundedness have given rise to a range of ethical approaches to redressing the past, among which reconciliation has as many critics as it does proponents, who differ as much over its meaning as they do over its merits. These divide broadly into advocates and nonadvocates, with each group having its own variants.

Reconciliation, For and Against

Nonadvocates include both outright critics and simple avoiders of reconciliation. Virtually all of them take as the central task in dealing with the past the construction of constitutional liberal democracy: the rule of law, civil and political rights, democratic institutions and elections, and stable, uncorrupted courts. Some would add, variously, punishing criminals of the past regime or the war and establishing popular legitimacy for the new regime, civic trust, a healthy pattern of democratic deliberation, or some form of economic justice. Generally, they reason much along the lines of the liberal peace described in the introduction to this volume. Nonadvocates either ignore or criticize reconciliation because they believe that it calls for something different than or directly compromises constitutional liberal democracy. Among those who discuss reconciliation, some acknowledge it as a concept of justice, say, restorative justice, but consider it the wrong concept. Others consider it not to be justice at all but a set of healing practices that ought not to stand in the way of justice.

Critics of reconciliation offer several more specific objections. Some perceive that reconciliation's emphasis on harmony sacrifices some crucial element of justice. Most often, they have in mind retributive justice, which they believe to be sacrificed by forgiveness or by amnesties that are justified by arguments for healing. For others, what is sacrificed is structural economic justice, the reduction of gross inequalities that feed conflict.[7] Critics also take reconciliation to task for its soulcraft—its efforts to bring about changes in the heart in ways that cross the line between what is properly public and private. In a similar spirit, some question the religious basis of reconciliation, doubting its place within the liberal democratic institutions that are being constructed in so many settings of peacebuilding.[8] Others simply regard reconciliation as unrealistic, setting forth utopian goals amidst the rubble of colossal social fracture.

Reconciliation's advocates also make a great variety of arguments, differing mainly over reconciliation's status as a concept of justice. One sort agrees with those nonadvocates who argue that reconciliation is not a concept of justice but a set of healing practices, including forgiveness, trauma recovery, and the embrace of friendship. For them, these practices are to be favored, either as a complement to justice or as a second-best substitute when prosecution is too costly. Some advocates of South Africa's Truth and Reconciliation Commission (TRC), for instance, took this second-best approach in arguing that ideally apartheid officials would be prosecuted, but given the need for healing and stability, an amnesty that was conditional on a restorative public truth telling could be allowed.[9] Such arguments can be heard from a variety of quarters, sometimes taking a pragmatic form, sometimes smacking of exoneration of the status quo. In 1992, for instance, President Alfredo Cristiani of El Salvador offered amnesty to military generals and death squad leaders during the country's civil war with the argument that the moment was one for reconciliation; after World War II, some conservative Germans used the language of reconciliation in advocating a halt in the prosecution of Nazis.

Other advocates of reconciliation see it not as a complement to justice, an alternative to justice, or as something to be balanced against justice, but as itself a concept of justice. What some of these advocates mean by reconciliation turns out to be almost identical to the justice that nonadvocates seek. David Crocker, for instance, advocates a "thin" form of reconciliation that reaches beyond "nonlethal coexistence" to a "democratic reciprocity" involving mutually recognized rights and responsibilities within constitutional liberal democracy.[10] Others, though, view reconciliation as a fuller, more distinct concept of justice. Probably the most prominent of these views it as restorative justice, a concept that calls for the restoration of relationships among the many dimensions in which injustice severs them and among the many parties who were involved in the severance. Archbishop Desmond Tutu, for instance, argued for restorative justice in South Africa, placing special emphasis on forgiveness.[11]

An Ethic of Restorative Justice

The ethic of reconciliation defended here is one of restorative justice. To many modern Western ears, it will seem strange to call reconciliation a concept of justice at all. Justice is rather what the liberal tradition of John Locke, Immanuel

Kant, and their legatees thought it was, involving human rights, democracy, constitutional government, and some notion of just punishment, either along retributivist or consequentialist lines, or else what the utilitarian tradition of Jeremy Bentham, John Stuart Mill, and their progeny thought it was, entailing those institutions that maximize happiness, usually thought to be liberal and democratic.[12] But restorative justice is indeed justice. As will be explained further, it can be found in the Jewish, Christian, and Islamic traditions, though it has contemporary secular proponents as well. At least if it is interpreted broadly enough, it fulfills the Roman jurist Ulpian's classical definition of justice: the will to render everyone his or her due. To modern Western ears, *due* may connote only desert or entitlement—punishment for crimes, restitution for harm, and rights for all. But restorative justice conceives due more widely as that which restores people to human fulfillment and right relationship in the political order following political injustices.

The concept of restorative justice first gained currency in the thought and practice of criminal justice in New Zealand and the United States, particularly at the level of local communities. Intellectuals associated with Chile's truth commission and then, far more famously, Archbishop Tutu of South Africa's TRC, applied the concept to whole political orders. Though its proponents, like reconciliation's proponents, do not all agree on what it means, they generally converge on some common themes: crime is primarily a rupture of relationship between offender and victim and between victim and community; response to crime ought to be oriented toward repairing these relationships and the dimensions of injury and harm they leave behind; and such repair ought to involve the active participation of victims, offenders, and members of the community through dialogue, narrative, and negotiation.[13]

As an expression of an ethic of political reconciliation, restorative justice invokes peacebuilding's multiplicity: responding to the many wounds and ruptures, primary and secondary, that political injustice causes, it proposes a matching multiplicity of practices. Each of the practices—and again, there are six, including building just institutions, acknowledgment, reparations, accountability, apology, and forgiveness—in a unique way aims to transform the wounds that political injustices have inflicted to a state of comparatively greater human flourishing.

The first justification of the six practices is simply the intrinsic value of these restorations. Because they aim to restore the primary wounds that the political injustices caused, they may be called "primary restorations." When a prime minister or president issues an apology to victims on behalf of an entire political community, he confers recognition on these victims, helps defeat the standing victory of the injustices that agents of the state committed on behalf of the political order, and beckons the members of his state to join their own voices to further these ends. When a truth commission confers acknowledgment on victims, it also provides them with recognition, publicly proclaims their restored citizenship, perhaps reveals information about the circumstances of their suffering, and at times encourages or pressures perpetrators to express public contrition for their crimes. The other practices—accountability, reparations, forgiveness, and building just institutions—help restore victims and their wounds in other unique ways.

Just as acts of violence also produce secondary wounds—emotions, then judgments, then further acts of injustice—so the practices of reconciliation can also bring about "secondary restorations," that is, transformations of judgments about the character of the political community. These take the form of assent to a peace settlement or a new regime as legitimate, a renewed identification with the national community, an increase in trust toward fellow citizens, and willingness to engage in democratic deliberation. The acknowledgment conferred by truth commissions, the restoration of basic rights entailed in the creation of reasonably just institutions, the defeat of the message of injustice conferred by apology of punishment—all of these actions help bring about secondary restorations.

Summed up and defined, the ethic of reconciliation is as follows. As a concept of justice, political reconciliation entails the will to restore the spectrum of six wounds that political injustices cause and the full array of parties that political injustices involve—victims, offenders, members of the community, and the state—to a state of right relationship in the political order. It comprises six practices that aim to restore each party in the distinct respect in which the injustice wounded it. Cumulatively, political reconciliation seeks to restore an entire political community or a relationship between political communities to a condition of respected citizenship, rule of law, legitimacy, and trust.

The central virtue of an ethic of reconciliation is mercy. This also may seem strange in modern Western parlance, where mercy most often means "to let someone off the hook" by canceling the punishment that he or she justly deserves, and is thus in deep tension with justice. But an ethic of reconciliation draws on an older understanding of mercy, which is something much wider. In his *Dependent Rational Animals*, philosopher Alasdair MacIntyre draws from Thomas Aquinas in defining mercy, or *misericordia*, as the virtue by which one feels grief or sorrow over someone else's distress.[14] Here, mercy is similar, though it might also include sympathy toward a person who is suffering in any way, including a way that arises from his or her own fault.[15] The practices of political reconciliation are all ones of mercy, the good that is internal to them being restoration of persons and relationships. Perhaps surprisingly, this is true even for accountability and punishment. The concept of restorative punishment for which I argue can indeed be understood as a manifestation of reconciliation, informed by mercy. Mercy, in this understanding, then, is closely convergent with justice—the justice that restores people and relationships.

The Role of Religion

These foundational concepts for an ethic of reconciliation find some of their strongest articulations in religious faiths. For adherents of these faiths, this fact is of straightforward importance: reconciliation finds support in their own deepest convictions. It is important, too, for peacebuilding processes around the world, to which religious leaders and communities have served as strong contributors through their unique moral authority and influence.[16] They have been instrumental in the downfall of authoritarian regimes in numerous locales, including Poland, Lithuania, Ukraine, the Philippines, Indonesia, Turkey, Kenya, South Africa, Chile, and Brazil. They have mediated settlements of civil war in El Salvador, Nicaragua, Guatemala, East Timor, Uganda, Liberia, and Mozambique, and the departure of dictatorships or occupations in East Germany and East Timor. Religious leaders and communities were instrumental in forming and conducting truth commissions in Guatemala, Brazil, Chile, South Africa, Sierra Leone, East Timor, Peru, and East Germany.[17] To be sure, in other cases, religious communities exercised little influence or were counterproductive in peacebuilding. In Argentina, in contrast to Brazil and Chile, the Catholic Church supported a military dictatorship and its crimes during the civil war from 1976 to 1983. In Sri Lanka, Czechoslovakia, Hungary, Bulgaria, Greece, Romania, Russia, Cameroon, Burma, and elsewhere, religious actors did little to oppose authoritarianism. In Rwanda, churches were even acquiescent and sometimes supportive of the 1994 genocide, though in its aftermath some of them have carried out reconciliation work within civil society. Generally, those religious communities that contributed to peacebuilding most effectively, whether through mediation, nonviolent opposition to dictatorship, transitional justice institutions, or civil society efforts were those that practiced the highest degree of institutional autonomy from dictatorships and carried liberal democratic doctrines of justice and, often, a concept of reconciliation.[18]

Some religious traditions also bring to peacebuilding the foundations for an ethic of reconciliation—especially its core ideas of restorative justice and mercy—rooted in their scriptures, rituals, and, most of all, theology. Familiarity and space constraints confine the present analysis to Judaism, Christianity, and Islam. This is not to deny the resources for reconciliation that other traditions offer. Rich resources can be found in certain tribal traditions in North America, New Zealand, Australia, and Africa, for instance. Conversely, even in the Abrahamic traditions, not all theologians conceive of reconciliation as a concept of justice for political orders. Indeed, such an understanding has only emerged in any of these faiths in the past few decades. Still, these three faiths offer a grounding for restorative justice and mercy that at least some of their proponents see as the basis for an ethic of political reconciliation.

In the Jewish scriptures, the Hebrew words that translate to justice in English are the same words that translate into righteousness (*sedeq* and *mishpat*), the condition of the people of Israel living in comprehensive right relationship according to the covenant God made with them. This state of right relationship is also closely related to shalom, the Jewish concept of peace, a thoroughgoing condition of right relationship. Lederach and Appleby's concept of *justpeace* is indeed much like shalom. Following their disobedience to the covenant, God is willing to restore the people of Israel on their repentance and true conversion. This willingness flows from *hesed,* or covenant love, the Hebrew word that is translated to "mercy." Generally, mercy amounts to God's help for the distressed, those who suffer from both misfortune and sin. The Jewish scriptures also recount God's punishment for sin and call for punishment of crime on the civil level. It is in God's generations-long relationship with the corporate people of Israel, whom he continues to restore and whom he refrains from punishing measure for measure, that mercy is most salient. Between people, reconciliation's logic of restoration and mercy is manifested in the Jewish tradition through *teshuva*, a set of practices involving restitution, remorse, confession, and a commitment to change.[19]

In the New Testament, God's merciful covenant love is extended through his self-revelation and atoning work in Jesus Christ. Over the centuries, theologians have understood atonement through a variety of metaphors and emphases, most of which stress restoration in one way or another: victory over sin, release from captivity, solidarity with victims. Only "penal substitution" theories of certain strands of the Protestant Reformation tend to view atonement as a payment of debt that involves no transformation. In the New Testament, particularly the letters of Paul, justice is also understood as living in right relationship. Atonement restores right relationship for wrongdoers, victims, and, indeed, all of creation. Here, too, this will to restore is the meaning of mercy. Like the Old Testament, the New Testament affirms the possibility of divine punishment as well as the justice of civil punishment. But it places comparatively more central emphasis on forgiveness as an ethic for relationships between people.

In the New Testament, the Greek words translated to "reconciliation" are found—*katallage* and *katallosso*—appearing there fifteen times, twelve of these in the letters of Paul. Its meaning is either the process of restoration of right relationship or the condition of right relationship that results from this restoration.[20] Because right relationship, or comprehensive righteousness, is the meaning of justice in the Scriptures, it follows that reconciliation can just as well mean the restoration of justice or a resulting state of justice. In this sense, it can be said that reconciliation is a concept of justice.

Although the meanings of justice, peace, reconciliation, and mercy in Islam are not precisely equivalent to those in the Jewish scriptures or the New Testament, they converge closely with their meanings in the present ethic of reconciliation. The Qur'an's words for justice, *'adl* and *qist*, with some interpretive effort, can be understood as comprehensive right relationship.[21] As for reconciliation, the Arabic *sulh* refers to a restoration of right relationship between two or more parties who have been at odds, whereas a related word, *musalaha*, translates more directly to reconciliation and connotes comprehensiveness. The Arabic word for peace, *salam*, is closely related, both linguistically and in meaning, to the Jewish shalom, and describes a broad state of harmony. The Arabic words for mercy, *rahma, rahim,* and *rahamin*, denote a wide notion of compassion, a general will to restore.[22] Mercy is indeed the first of ninety-nine names accorded to Allah. Although the Qur'an contains no concept of original sin or divine atonement, it repeatedly describes Allah as forgiving the repentant and calls for forgiveness between people, always with restoration of relationship as the goal.[23] A notion of restorative justice can be found in at least some portions of Islamic criminal law as well.[24] Like the Jewish and Christian scriptures, the Qur'an also depicts God as exercising punishment and allows (but does not always require) retribution in human affairs. Traditional Arab Islamic cultures have developed elaborate rituals of *sulh* (settlement) and *musalaha* (reconciliation) that bring about reconciliation between estranged peoples through apology, confession, remorse, restitution, and forgiveness.[25]

Such brief characterizations can hardly plumb the depth, subtlety, similarities, and differences of these traditions. Some scholars have argued, for instance, that Judaism and Islam call for restitution, punishment, apology, and justice before forgiveness can take place, whereas Christianity envisions forgiveness taking place initially or unilaterally. Theologians within each tradition in fact disagree among themselves over these relative emphases, many of them arguing so as to minimize the differences. One problem, attendant on the relatively recent entry of theologies of reconciliation in the political realm, is yet unsolved in all three traditions: the relationship between forgiveness and punishment in politics. Still, the notions of justice, peace, mercy, and reconciliation and the depiction of God's response to evil and injustice in the three traditions yield the building blocks of an ethic of political reconciliation.

To some skeptics, though, theological concepts and language ought not to be involved in politics at all. Their argument comes from the tradition of liberal political philosophy, though even there it is quite recent, voiced most prominently by John Rawls, who argues for a concept of "public reason" that requires political discourse to be secular.[26] Liberal commentators, for instance, criticized Archbishop Tutu for his overt use of Christian language and ritual in chairing South Africa's TRC.[27] Reconciliation, though, is not always practiced in settings of constitutional liberal democracy. Truth commissions have now taken place in Morocco, a predominantly Islamic state, as well as in Sierra Leone, which is 60 percent Islam, and have been proposed in both Afghanistan and Iraq. Here, the Western concept of separation between religion and politics is untenable. It is important to remember that even Western European societies, situated at secularization's supposed ground zero, have established churches or officially recognize certain religious bodies. The United States, where most advocates of public reason live and write, in fact practices the highest degree of constitutional separation of religion and state in the world.[28] Numerous critics of an argument for "religious restraint" have offered strong arguments for why, even in liberal settings, religion ought not to be excluded from public debate. Most centrally, the placing of epistemological or other substantive limits on language, religious or secular, is incompatible with liberalism's own commitments to open debate, tolerance, free expression, and the benefits of argument.[29]

If religious language is not to be excluded in principle, there is still a good reason that in certain settings—namely, in societies where practices for dealing with the past take place among populations who are of different faiths or are divided between religious and secular perspective—holders of religious concepts ought to seek common terms with proponents of other religions and of secular concepts. The reason lies in the benefits of consensus for the practice of reconciliation. Especially when peacebuilding deals with fundamental matters of law, punishment, and constitutionalism, widespread popular assent and legitimacy is crucial. This is not to be achieved through religious believers setting aside their commitments but by entering into dialogue with people of other religious traditions as well as secular perspectives with the goal of finding an "overlapping consensus" on basic principles of justice that can guide the practices. The fact that the ethic here can be expressed in secular language assists greatly in finding this consensus. For religious believers, this language will not carry the full meaning and basis for the ethic, which they may still want to articulate publicly. For the purpose of forging consensus, they are willing to agree to use secular justifications as well.

A Political Ethic

Arguing also in the spirit of contemporary liberal political philosophy, some skeptics will object that certain other elements of an ethic of reconciliation—restoration, transformation of judgment, forgiveness, a virtue of mercy—cross the boundary between what is properly public and private and that the state is not competent to pursue them. True, the state need not be the only agent of political reconciliation. Civil society actors, including religious communities and nongovernmental organizations (NGOs), bear unique restorative assets. But the state has plenty of warrant to be involved. By definition, political injustices are caused by agents acting in the name of the political order. What they violate is the most fundamental rights of citizenship, those that any state has the obligation to uphold. Because states speak in the name of the political order, uphold the law, and promote justice, they are not only warranted but obligated to repair (insofar as they can) the range of wounds that result from political injustices. There is a further basis for the state's role: insofar as wounds result in political judgments that erode citizens' faith in institutions and can lead them to armed opposition, constitutional liberal democratic states have an interest in the practices that transform these judgments into ones that create legitimacy, trust, and assent.

Political reconciliation, though, is also bounded. To be sure, it commingles the thick and the thin, the political and the personal, but in several important respects it honors the boundaries of the political. In liberal polities, these boundaries will include the full range of liberal freedoms. Of course, political reconciliation is not only to be practiced in liberal democracies but might take place in a traditional Muslim society, for instance—though the ethic here always insists on basic human rights and respect for the laws of war as articulated in international law. Wherever it is practiced, though, political reconciliation ought to respect limits of three sorts, I argue.

First, the state that practices political reconciliation deals only with those wounds that result from political injustices. Although it may deal with these in their several dimensions, it does not seek to restore those relationships, whether they exist between family members, neighbors, or townspeople, that have been fractured by some other event, even one that is somehow related to the war or the injustices of the regime. It does not seek to restore relationships in respects other than mutual citizenship. Behind these limits lie the intrinsic connection between the state and the law. All political injustices violate some sort of law—if not always the explicit laws of a regime, at least the international law that governs war and human rights. Because laws are those norms that the state expresses as the community's morality and backs up with its sanctioning power, the state has a unique mandate to deal with their violation—but no mandate to deal with ruptures other than their violation.

A second set of limits also involves the law. They are the constraints posed by the entire body of laws, rights, and procedures embodied in the constitution of the state where political reconciliation is being practiced. The practice of accountability, for instance, whether it involves trials, vetting, or other forms of public censure, must always respect the due process rights of alleged perpetrators. All practices of political reconciliation also ought to respect the complete rights of citizens as well as the boundaries between religion and state as a given constitution prescribes these. Political reconciliation respects laws both because the rule of law is one of its background commitments and because one of its key goals is to restore and strengthen the rule of law to communities where it is lacking or weak. So, then, it must respect those laws where they exist.

A third, distinct (but closely related) set of limits pertains to the competence of the state given the sort of organization it is—large, collective, and public. Not only should the state respect the spheres of protection that its constitution establishes, it should refrain from attempting to perform transformations it cannot competently effect. Constraints, then, arise to govern each of the practices. The state may significantly restore victims' dignity by publicly acknowledging their suffering, but it cannot provide them with long-term therapy (though it might well provide the resources for it as reparations). It may commend to its people practices that seek emotional transformation like acknowledgment, apology, and forgiveness and even carry them out collectively in the people's name, but it should always leave them as voluntary for individuals themselves to practice. It cannot begin to understand the range of inner influences, for instance, that lead a person to determine whether, when, or how to forgive, and so must respect one's freedom to decide this. None of these constraints emerge from a strong separation between the public and the private but from reflection on what sort of actions the state does and does not perform well.

Such borders, boundaries, lines, and spheres demarcate the contours of where an ethic of political reconciliation may be practiced. It respects the rule of law, basic human rights, and the just constitutional provisions of the country in which it operates, as well as spheres where individual freedom ought to be respected. None of these boundaries choke off the practices. Even within its proper contours, each may exert significant political sway.

One other form of limit to political reconciliation is worth stressing, also in response to an important criticism: its typical partial fulfillment. Some of the six practices will take place in some places but not others. In any given country, some of the practices (but not others) will take place. Sometimes this selectivity will create skewed justice, as when acknowledgment and forgiveness occur without accountability for wrongdoers. Often, this selectivity arises from power differentials among parties in the negotiations of transitions. When perpetrators of political injustices continue to hold power after peace settlements, for instance, they prevent their own prosecution.[30] Sometimes the practices occur but are flawed: lustration procedures, for instance, may occur without fairness or due process. For all of this partiality, though, all six practices do occur, some of them on a global scale. The fact that they are partial does not rob them of their moral validity; rather, it means that they fall short of their full moral potential. Indeed, it is the combination of their occurrence, their inner moral logic, and their flawed practice that beg the need for an ethic of reconciliation.

The Six Practices

Reconciliation as a conception of justice is enacted in the political order through the six practices. The practices are a bridge from the abstract to the particular; they are the concrete activities that bring reconciliation about.[31] Each practice in some way moves some set of parties from one or another dimension of woundedness to a condition where they are more restored than they were before. Cumulatively, they may help an entire society be more restored than it was before. Each is a particular kind of activity—acknowledging, forgiving, and so on—that achieves this good in a different respect, corresponding to the parties involved and the forms of wounds it seeks to repair. Each is then subject to a corresponding set of ethical standards that explain how, by whom, and under what circumstances the activity may be conducted justly.

Like the wounds of injustice, the practices are multiple and interdependent. Though they virtually always remain partially fulfilled and are frequently subject to political compromises, they are complementary to one another and together model the holism of strategic peacebuilding. Each of them restores relationships in some irreplaceable way. The interdependent character of the practices also gives rise to ethical dilemmas. If political realities force a society to choose one against the other, which one ought to be dropped? Here, these dilemmas cannot be addressed in detail. What is offered is rather a broad outline of the practices, showing the institutions and procedures through which they are enacted, how they purport to restore wounds of injustice, and the kinds of moral criteria that pertain to them.

Building Just Institutions

Recall that human rights and the laws of war perform a double duty in the ethic. They both define a political injustice as well as describe the good whose absence is the first form of woundedness that political injustices inflict. Among the practices, building just institutions plays a similar role. Political societies based on human rights, democracy, the rule of law, and just economic institutions; relationships between political societies that are based on international law and the laws of war; and finally, the legitimacy of these laws and institutions—meaning assent to them through the judgments of those who live under them[32]—are the very goals of political reconciliation. These same laws, institutions, and judgments also perform a restorative act insofar as the lack of legal guarantee for human rights, rights under the laws of war, and the like is a form of woundedness, a failure of human flourishing. Though building just institutions may not come readily to mind as a practice that seeks to remedy past injustices—reparations, forgiveness, and trials do so more obviously—in fact, they transform injustice by supplying something that was egregiously absent. Because the practice of building just and legitimate institutions is also the fundamental goal of reconciliation, it is the most basic of the six practices and a practice against which the other practices ought not to be compromised or traded off.

This has an important implication for political reconciliation—namely, that reconciliation is not true reconciliation if it is not based on justice and should not be mistaken for the irenicism of a peace agreement that fails to ensure fundamental elements of justice like basic human rights, including those of minorities. Dictators must be defeated; shalom, *sedeq*, positive peace, *justpeace* must be established. In some settings, reconciliation has indeed come under heavy fire for short-circuiting justice. One example comes from the struggle against apartheid in South Africa. Noting the prevalence of reconciliation in the language of fellow church leaders and activists, in 1986 a group of black theologians penned what is known as the Kairos Document, where they stressed that reconciliation and recognition of the enemy's humanity must not mean compromise in the struggle for justice: apartheid must end. Militant liberationists in Kashmir criticize reconciliation as the Indian government's rhetorical strategy for defending the status quo. Similar examples can be adduced from all over the world. The present ethic accordingly permits a just war, whether it takes the form of a defense against outside aggression, humanitarian intervention, a revolution, or a self-determination movement. But resorting to the use of force must itself be just. The criteria embedded in the just war tradition supply the ethic of reconciliation with a compelling framework for assessing this justice, although there is not space here to defend these criteria philosophically, resolve internal disputes within the tradition, or apply it to new problems.[33] There is also an important sense in which nonviolent resistance movements, when they have a "reasonable chance of success," to borrow one criterion of the just war tradition, offer a mode of struggle against injustice that embodies the spirit of reconciliation. As articulated by theorists and practitioners like Martin Luther King Jr. and Mahatma Gandhi, such movements actively oppose injustice even while inviting enemies to turn away from injustice (apology) and bringing attention to the injustices of oppressive rule (acknowledgment), thus modeling the holistic character of the ethic. The efficacy of such movements should not be underestimated. A recent report from Freedom House describes some sixty successful "people power" movements for democratization in the past generation.[34]

Another controversy arising from the practice of building just institutions is the place of economic justice in reconciliation. Again, reconciliation has been criticized for going without it: The South African TRC may have been a model of forbearance toward enemies, runs the argument, but it did nothing to address the economic injustices underpinning apartheid. Truth and reconciliation in El Salvador and Guatemala did nothing to bring about land reform. An important truth lies behind the criticisms. The economic dimension to justice is essential both in an intrinsic sense and because of its importance for legitimacy. But putting economic justice into practice runs into two problems. First, exactly what "economic justice" means is subject to far more dispute in the world than what "human rights" means. Even in the liberal tradition, of which human rights are a cornerstone, disagreements over the content of a just distribution are legion. Certain economic rights like subsistence and minimal standards of labor may be widely agreed on as basic, but the broader question of distribution remains open. Second, even if agreement on a just distribution could be attained, the best policies for bringing it about are also hotly disputed. The role and strategy of international financial institutions is notoriously controversial. Unclear, too, is what degree of effective economic reform can be demanded within the time frame of a peace agreement. Such reform may rather be a long-term proposition. None of this is to dismiss the importance of economic justice, but only to underline the need for further reasoning about its meaning and its pursuit.

Of all the practices in the ethic, building just institutions is the one that most converges with the commitments of the liberal tradition. Human rights, the rule of law, and the components of a just war are also endorsed widely in contemporary Christianity, Judaism, and Islam. Each tradition contains disputes over the justification, content, and extent of rights as well as opponents of rights altogether. Especially the most basic human rights and laws of war enjoy an impressive global overlapping consensus.

Acknowledgment

Restoring the wounds of injustice involves far more than restoring rights or even administering just punishment. The failure of the political community—the state and the citizens for whom it speaks—to recognize victims' suffering and victims' own ignorance of the circumstances that brought it about must be addressed as well, for not only are these direct forms of woundedness but also sources of secondary wounds—alienation from and hostility to new political orders and peace agreements. Through the practice of acknowledgment, communities recognize victims' suffering, the intrinsic injustice in this suffering, and the victims' rights of citizenship; they confer on victims empathy and knowledge of the circumstances of the injustice; and by calling an injustice an injustice they help defeat the standing victory of the perpetrator's message. Acknowledgment is more than knowledge: it confers a public recognition of injustice that was committed in the name of the political order.[35] Alone, it rarely brings about the long-term healing of the victim, but it performs the important public, political dimension of it.

Several kinds of public forums have performed acknowledgment in the past generation. The most prominent and thorough is the truth commission, over thirty of which have occurred around the world. Appointed by a government, the purpose of a truth commission is to bring to light a reliable record of human rights violations during a particular period. Though virtually all commissions produce an official report at the end of their labors, they vary in the method through which they discover the truth about the past: some involve public hearings, some of which are televised; some involve extensive subpoena powers; some offer amnesties; and others vary with respect to these and other features. Public acknowledgment can take other forms as well, including museums, monuments, rewriting school textbooks, and other forms of commemoration.

True to the interdependent character of an ethic of political reconciliation, acknowledgment often yields fruit for other practices as well as secondary restorations—changes in judgments regarding the political order. Descriptions of truth commissions from South Africa to El Salvador have recounted stories of victims forgoing demands for revenge and retribution after being publicly acknowledged at a hearing. Through telling the truth about past injustices publicly, acknowledgment helps delegitimate these injustices and establish the legitimacy of new regimes. Sometimes, the information that a truth commission discovers then aids in both trials and determinations of reparations. Truth commissions have also elicited contrition and apology from perpetrators.

Criticisms and controversies surround all forms of public acknowledgment. They are taken to task for lacking balance, focusing on the misdeeds of one side disproportionately to another, or imposing a version of the truth that suits one side. Museums and monuments rarely escape criticism from those discontented with their portrayal of victims and perpetrators. Then, does acknowledgment truly restore? Or does it just open the wounds and reinflame agonistic emotions? Some critics have taken truth commissions to task for meddling in matters of the heart rather than sticking to gathering information.

Again, space is too limited here to cover all such controversies. But one virtue of acknowledgment can be noted: personalism. Acknowledgment restores best when the recognition that it confers is most direct, personal, and empathetic. Guatemala's Recovery of Historical Memory Project (REMHI), a truth commission created and carried out by the Catholic Church, manifested personalism in its effort to send trained volunteers, or *animadores*, to rural villages where they took the testimony of victims in a manner that was psychologically, emotionally, and spiritually supportive, not merely effective in eliciting information.[36] Personalism is also increased when the work of a truth commission is conducted in local forums that allow direct citizen participation. The community panels of East Timor's Commission on Reception, Truth, and Reconciliation took place in villages, for instance. Here, the restorative work that acknowledgment accomplishes can be done best.

Reparations

Like acknowledgment, reparations confer public recognition on victims. Unlike acknowledgment, they take a material form: cash payments, health services, and the like, which are geared toward alleviating or compensating victims for the harm they have suffered, both physical and mental. This harm, of course, can never be reversed, particularly when it takes the form of the death of relatives or long-term injury. But it can be addressed through public measures. Reparations are usually conferred by a national court or a special body appointed by a national government, but sometimes also by an international court. Like truth commissions, reparations have become more common in the past generation.

Some view reparations as fulfilling a straightforward obligation on the part of the political community to compensate property and goods that were lost due to political injustices. Though sometimes such compensation can be determined easily, claims can also be bewilderingly complex, especially when properties have changed hands since the original seizure, as in postcommunist Eastern Europe or postgenocide Rwanda, or still more when claims are made by descendants of victims long dead. Here, as Jeremy Waldron has argued, compensation is virtually impossible to assess.[37] Still worse, it is also notoriously difficult to place a monetary value on forms of harms like the loss of relatives.

A different way of viewing the argument for reparations, though, can avoid becoming immersed, at least to some extent, in complex determinations of amounts. In what can be called the symbolic expression argument, reparations perform much the same communication as acknowledgment does, with their material dimension giving this communication all the more force. A soft proportionalism, by which greater harms result in greater reparations, still applies, but the question of exact compensation is not as important.

Reparations may well depend for their success on other practices complementing them, again evoking the ethic's holism. Some common objections to reparations are that they amount to "blood money," money that appears to pay off victims so that they drop further demands; that they equate the injustice victims suffered with financial goods; or even that they buy victims' silence. Reparations best overcome these objections and attain their greatest legitimacy when acknowledgment or apologies accompany them, expressing public recognition and remorse for the political injustices. A crucial factor in achieving a deal on reparations between the German government and survivors of forced labor during the Holocaust, for instance, was a public apology in 2000 from German President Johannes Rau to living victims and the German government's agreement to implement a school curriculum that would sustain memory of the Holocaust well into the future.[38] The complementarity of other practices enable the moral success of reparations.

Punishment

A practice of punishment in an ethic of reconciliation? It will seem a strange fixture to followers of global debates over transitional justice that so often pit reconciliation, mercy, forgiveness, and restorative justice against punishment, retribution, and imprisonment. Often, those who share the core commitments of the liberal peace take the side of punishment in these disputes, with advocates of reconciliation responding with comparative leniency. Prosecuting human rights violators and war criminals is at the center of transitional justice for members of the human rights community, who generally articulate either one or a combination of two justifications of punishment that have pervaded the liberal tradition since the Enlightenment. Retributivists hold—broadly speaking, with variations[39]—that criminals ought to be punished simply because they deserve it. Consequentialists focus on the effects of punishment, arguing in this context that accountability is necessary for the legitimacy of a new regime based on human rights and democracy.

A contrasting ethic of reconciliation need not reject punishment. A rationale for punishment exists that is quite compatible with the logic of the ethic and affirms some elements of both retributivism and consequentialism, but also differs importantly from both. Its logic can be articulated through the Abrahamic religious traditions and is found in certain contemporary philosophers. Theologian Christopher B. Marshall has called it "restorative punishment."[40] Desert, proportionality, due process of law—restorative punishment shares all of these elements of retributivism. But its central rationale for punishment is different—the restoration of persons, relationships, political communities, and relationships between political communities. Punishment, like the other practices in the ethic, is a political community's communication: one that expresses censure to the wrongdoer for violating the values of a just political community; that delegitimates the message of injustice entailed in his crimes; that invites him to repent, express contrition, and join the community again; and that recognizes the dignity of the victim. Hardship, including imprisonment, is not forgone. It is part and parcel of communicating the gravity of the offense and can serve as a material expression of penance on the part of the criminal. Punishment might also deter future crimes, contribute to a new regime's legitimacy, and immobilize dangerous criminals—restorative punishment shares these aims with consequentialism. The validity of punishment does not depend on such outcomes, nor on the perpetrator's reform. It is sufficient that it is a communication of censure that strengthens the community's values, invites perpetrators to contrition and reform, and honors the dignity of the victim. Such a logic of restorative justice, Marshall explains, can be discovered through an interpretation of the Jewish and Christian scriptures. Other scholars have made the case for a similar rationale in the Qur'an.[41]

What does restorative punishment mean for political orders addressing past injustices? At the level of states and relationships between them, restorative punishment favors those measures that accomplish a range of restorations, including reintegrating perpetrators into the community and bringing victims and citizens into the process, and that act complementarily to the other practices in an ethic of political reconciliation. For the masterminds of major atrocities and even the willful murderer, torturer, or rapist, whose culpability is not diminished on account of his own duress or some other factor, arguably only long-term imprisonment can communicate the gravity of the offense. If justified restoratively, the verdicts of the International Criminal Court can be compatible with an ethic of political reconciliation. For a wide range of lesser crimes and criminals, other forms of punishment (or some combination of them) can restore a broader spectrum of wounds. Public forums like truth commissions have a punitive function insofar as they bring public shame and censure onto a perpetrator; they also, at least when these forums take a certain form, play a restorative function in that they allow victims to confront perpetrators with their stories of suffering and allow perpetrators, should they choose, to show remorse directly. Such an event is not unheard of. The South African TRC saw several cases of hardened human rights violators coming to show remorse for their deeds in the context of commission hearings. Truth commissions at the village level, like those that took place in East Timor, increase the local and personalist character of the meeting between victims and perpetrators while administering integrative punishments like community service. Still other countries have turned to schemes of vetting, or "lustration," as it was called in the Czech Republic, that bar human rights violators from holding public office. Combinations of punishments are possible, too. East Timor, Sierra Leone, and Germany, for instance, staged hybrids of trials and truth commissions.

Blanket amnesties are incompatible with restorative punishment. When political realities force them, amnesties may be necessary, but they are always less than just. The South African TRC offered perpetrators, even of atrocities, amnesty in exchange for public testimony, a deal that created space for other practices like acknowledgment and sometimes apology and forgiveness to occur. But unequivocally, justice—the justice that restorative punishment enacts—was sacrificed. Generally, a presumption for accountability ought to apply. A peace agreement or a regime transition may demand forgoing prosecution at the moment, but it need not prevent it from ever occurring. In both Chile and Argentina, for instance, amnesties granted or upheld amidst a transition from dictatorship to democracy were later chipped away by human rights lawyers.

Other issues are relevant to restorative punishment as well—due process, questions of culpability, the problem of prosecuting human rights violations that were not illegal under the law of the regime where they were committed, and the challenges of carrying out punishment in countries where judicial institutions are rudimentary or broken down. All must be incorporated into a full-blown theory of restorative punishment.

Apology

Public apologies, like reparations and truth commissions, are another practice that has become more common over the past generation. Sometimes individual perpetrators express it; sometimes heads of states or other political leaders express it in the name of the collectivity that they lead. Political scientist Barry O'Neill assembled a database of 121 apology incidents occurring between 1980 and 1995 in the setting of relations between states.[42]

An apology is a restorative communication in several respects. Through it, perpetrators express contrition and assume responsibility for their deeds.

In doing so, they rejects the message of injustice and domination communicated through their act of political violence and will the restoration both of their own soul and of the victims, who continue to be diminished by their message of injustice. Apology does not nullify deserved punishment; when expressed in conjunction with punishment, it effectively answers the community's censure and bolsters its just values. Apology also invites the victim to forgive, thus begetting a separate restorative practice. In all of the Abrahamic faiths, contrition on the part of the sinner is a vital step in being restored and forgiven by God.

When apology is practiced by the head of a collectivity, it raises further ethical issues. For instance, can a group like a state, a nation, or a military unit commit evil? Or can only individuals do so? If groups cannot precisely commit evil, people acting in the name of the group—wearing its uniform, acting in the capacity of an employee or otherwise an agent—whether they are leaders or subordinates, certainly can. When they do, the responsibility for the evil becomes in part collective, even while the individual's responsibility remains intact. So, too, leaders can apologize for the evil committed in the name of their group, or at least the collective dimension of that evil. Because that collective dimension lives on beyond the individual perpetrators, a subsequent leader can apologize for past evil as well. What leaders cannot do, though, is supplant the perpetrators' obligation to apologize for their own role in the deed or the prerogative of citizens or other group members to endorse or refuse that apology. These individuals, after all, may have refused to cooperate with the evil, avoided it, or may simply refuse contrition for one reason or another. There are proper roles, then, for both leaders and individual group members in apologizing.[43]

Forgiveness

The practice of forgiveness in political settings has also become more common in the past generation, though its recorded instances are far rarer than the other practices. South African President Nelson Mandela is perhaps the only head of state to have practiced it.[44] Other presidents and prime ministers—President Patricio Aylwin of Chile, for instance—have commended forgiveness to their citizens. Civil society leaders, especially religious leaders, have encouraged citizens to practice forgiveness far more often. It is difficult to say just how often victims themselves have practiced forgiveness. The best available indicator is a proxy—a discourse of forgiveness, as was present in South Africa, Northern Ireland, Poland, East Timor, Chile, El Salvador, Guatemala, Rwanda, Sierra Leone, Bosnia, and Germany.

Of the six practices, forgiveness is the one that most falls outside the liberal peace paradigm and is most distinctively characteristic of religious traditions. Even in these traditions, though, its pedigree in politics is not very long. Only in the past generation or so has political forgiveness gained entrance into the social teachings of the Abrahamic faiths.[45]

Forgiveness is also the most harshly criticized of the six practices, often at the hands of Western liberals, who charge it with disrespecting victims, robbing victims of their autonomy, risking wounding victims further, condoning evil, nullifying just retribution, failing to take seriously the value of resentment, imposing a value that is essentially religious, and being inappropriately promoted through politics.[46] Some of these criticisms, though, are properly ones of bad forgiveness rather than forgiveness per se. Forgiveness does not condone evil; it is unintelligible apart from naming an evil as such. Nor is it intelligible as a forgetting of evil; rather, it begins with a recall of it. To forgive is not to cease to oppose unjust structures or acts of violence, even through force when force is just. It does not nullify the right to self-defense or require that victims return to a condition of vulnerability to violence or other serious mistreatment. While heads of states and other leaders may commend forgiveness, the freedom of victims to decide whether, when, and how to forgive must always be respected. Because it requires an inward decision and is often most difficult, it must never be forced or pressured.

What exactly is forgiveness? Some define it as a victim's relinquishment of justified anger, resentment, and all claims that a perpetrator owes him something for the deed. Forgiveness, especially as the religious traditions explain it, does not just cancel; it also constructs. It imitates God's will not only to free the wrongdoer of punishment but also to restore him and the surrounding community, as described in the scriptures of the Abrahamic faiths. Along with relinquishing anger and claims, the forgiving victim wills new relationships in a host of ways. In naming the evil and seeking to overcome it, he asserts that the perpetrator's message of injustice no longer diminishes him. He looks at the perpetrator as someone who is no longer a perpetrator but is now "in good standing." His memory of the perpetrator's deed may not disappear but is overcome through a subsequent act of mercy. If the perpetrator has not apologized, he invites this apology and, indeed, the restoration of his soul. In traveling from being a victim of violence to an active constructer of peace, the victim regains agency and takes on a kind of strength. Victims can also experience a healing of the debilitating, corrosive effects of anger and resentment. Inasmuch as the forgiver wills right relationship and achieves some degree of restoration, he brings about reconciliation, though not the whole of it. Forgiveness may or may not be accompanied by apology and contrition on the part of perpetrators. A victim may also decline to reestablish full relationship with a perpetrator, too, perhaps to protect himself or his property.

Political forgiveness does all of these things in response to a political injustice in particular. It invites right relationship in the political order, where victims and perpetrators come to respect one another's citizenship. Sometimes forgiveness can bring about the secondary restoration of legitimacy and stability in the political community. When victims and perpetrators of political injustices are no longer hostile to each other, they may well offer more assent to their political order. Mandela's magnanimous choice to forgive, for instance, doubtless led South African whites to be less hostile toward the post-apartheid government than they would have been had he prosecuted their leaders or even remained hostile in his rhetoric; many blacks were inspired to follow his example. Because all of these restorations make up the justice of reconciliation, forgiveness can be said to be an act of justice—again, a surprising and disso-nant claim in the liberal tradition.[47] Of course, it is at the same time an act of mercy, reconciliation's chief virtue.

Like the five other practices, forgiveness complements the other practices of reconciliation. It begets apology if apology has not already occurred, just as apology invites forgiveness in the case that apology occurs first. Nothing about forgiveness negates the justice of reparations or requires relinquishing a strug-gle against social injustice. But what about punishment? Are forgiveness and punishment reconcilable in an ethic of reconciliation? Or are debates around the globe correct in seeing them as being at odds? In the present ethic, forgive-ness and punishment are compatible. Both forgiveness and punishment enact a division of labor in which each one restores in different respects. A victim could in fact will both forgiveness and punishment at the same time. Forgive-ness wills the restoration of the perpetrator and the political order in all the ways already described. A call for punishment is a call for the communication from the community that also defeats the message of the perpetrator, calls him to remorse, honors the value of the community, and so on. In its own way, each practice wills restoration. The compatibility of punishment and forgiveness is furthered still by the fact that the state carries out the punishment. The state can best communicate on behalf of the community. The state, of course, also performs other important dimensions of punishment like police work, trials, and imprisonment, all of which have their own sets of ethical norms attached to them. Such a division of labor, where many parties participate in justice in many ways, is indeed the logic of restorative justice.

Things become a little more complicated when a head of state is the for-giver. If heads of state can apologize on behalf of groups, why can they not for-give on behalf of groups? The state also has the duty to enforce law and punish criminals. Maintaining the compatibility of punishment and forgiveness at this level requires seeing the state as playing two roles. When a leader of a state for-gives—as Mandela did—he forgoes anger, resentment, and hostility toward a wrongdoer or even another collective people who committed injustices against himself or members of his group. But individual perpetrators must still face the punishment through which the community communicates its censure, a punishment whose implementation is the duty of the state. Of course, in the case of South Africa, few apartheid leaders were prosecuted, in part because of the amnesty provisions of the agreement that ended apartheid. But in princi-ple, a head of state could both prosecute and forgive.

Conclusion

All of the practices interact, sometimes in tension, sometimes complementarily. Each is in its own way restorative, seeking to heal one or another dimension of woundedness caused by political injustice. That is the chief moral accomplish-ment of an ethic of reconciliation—to increase human flourishing by restoring right relationships in a political order. The participants in the practices have, in some respect, to some degree, traveled from a condition of one or more forms of woundedness to a condition where they are restored to some degree. Each practice performs the virtue of mercy, understood in its classical sense. In like spirit, the chief justification for an ethic of reconciliation is that it restores human flourishing more fully than efforts to address injustices that do not involve the several distinct practices. Were a society's dealings with its past to lack any one of the practices, were reconciliation in any of these respects to be peeled back, stripped down, or shorn of a layer, then it would leave an important moral dimension of restoration unfulfilled. Both together and in isolation, though, each practice yields moral dilemmas. The descriptions of the practices here only allude to or briefly explore these dilemmas. Other dilemmas are not addressed at all. The purpose of the chapter, rather, is to show how each of the practices is restorative in nature, applicable to politics, and constitutive of a holistic, interwoven ethic of political reconciliation.

NOTES

1. Scholars and other analysts have come to call this question "transitional justice," referring to initiatives to address injustices of the past during the transitional period in which a peace agreement is implemented or an authoritarian regime has just left the stage. Such a usage is too narrow. The term can be retained, but only with caveats and widenings. One sort pertains to the adjective *transitional*. Transitions are often uncertain. As mentioned in the introduction to this volume and in Jackie Smith's chapter, peace agreements frequently do not last, nor do movements toward democratization. Furthermore, trials, truth commissions, reparations, and other activities that are much the same as those that occur in transitional periods sometimes occur long after (sometimes a generation or more after) the actual transition. Other emendations of transitional justice pertain to its noun, *justice*. The term transitional justice arose amid debates over the prosecution of human rights violators. Justice, especially as defined in this chapter, involves a far wider range of questions and efforts. Transitional justice, then, can be redefined as "the sum total of activities that states and citizens undertake to redress past political injustices in order to restore political orders both shortly after peace agreements or regime transitions have taken place as well as long into the future."

2. Michael Walzer, *Just and Unjust Wars: A Moral Argument with Historical Illustrations* (New York: Basic Books, 1977), arguably remains the most widely cited contemporary text of the just war tradition. My own approach to this ethic resonates strongest with John Finnis, "The Ethics of War and Peace in the Catholic Natural Law Tradition," in *The Ethics of War and Peace: Religious and Secular Perspectives*, ed. Terry Nardin (Princeton, N.J.: Princeton University Press, 1996).

3. This chapter is part of a larger work in progress, *Just and Unjust Peace: An Ethic of Political Reconciliation*.

4. Brandon Hamber and Richard A. Wilson, "Symbolic Closure through Memory, Reparation and Revenge in Post-Conflict Societies," *Journal of Human Rights* 1, no. 1 (March 2002): 40.

5. André Du Toit, "The Moral Foundations of the South African TRC: Truth as Acknowledgment and Justice as Recognition," in *Truth v. Justice: The Morality of Truth Commissions*, ed. Robert I. Rotberg and Dennis Thompson (Princeton, N.J.: Princeton University Press, 2000), 133.

6. Here I do not mean to adopt a simple "ancient hatreds" explanation for communal conflict. Such conflict has complex causes, long-term, intermediate-term, and immediate, and range from the manipulations of elites, the media, economic inequalities and changes, demographic changes, state failure, and culture. I do make the more modest claim that the emotions arising from one set of injustices can be an important cause, among others, of further injustices. Making this case well, in my view, are Stathis Kalyvas, *The Logic of Violence in Civil War* (Cambridge: Cambridge University Press, 2006); Stuart Kaufman, *Modern Hatreds: The Symbolic Politics of Ethnic War* (Ithaca, N.Y.: Cornell University Press, 2001); Roger D. Peterson, *Understanding Ethnic Violence: Fear, Hatred, and Resentment in Twentieth-Century Eastern Europe* (Cambridge: Cambridge University Press, 2002). On the role of emotions in politics, see John Mercer, "Rationality and Psychology in International Relations," *International Organization* 59 (2005); Robert C. Roberts, *Emotions: An Essay in Aid of Moral Psychology* (Cambridge: Cambridge University Press, 2003).

7. See, for instance, Mahmood Mamdani, "Reconciliation without Justice," *South African Review of Books* 46 (1996).

8. For arguments falling along these lines, see Timothy Garton Ash, "True Confessions," *New York Review of Books* 44 (1997); Rajeev Bhargava, "Restoring Decency to Barbaric Societies," in *Truth v. Justice: The Morality of Truth Commissions*, ed. Robert I. Rotberg and Dennis Thompson (Princeton, N.J.: Princeton University Press, 2000); David A. Crocker, "Retribution and Reconciliation," *Philosophy and Public Policy* 20, no. 1 (2000), David A. Crocker, "Truth Commissions, Transitional Justice, and Civil Society," in *Truth v. Justice: The Morality of Truth Commissions*, ed. Robert I. Rotberg and Dennis Thompson (Princeton, N.J.: Princeton University Press, 2000); Kent Greenawalt, "Amnesty's Justice," in *Truth v. Justice: The Morality of Truth Commissions*, ed. Robert I. Rotberg and Dennis Thompson (Princeton, N.J.: Princeton University Press, 2000); Amy Gutmann and Dennis Thompson, "The Moral Foundations of Truth Commissions," in *Truth v. Justice: The Morality of Truth Commissions*, ed. Robert I. Rotberg and Dennis Thompson (Princeton, N.J.: Princeton University Press, 2000). For the economically based criticism, see, among others, Mamdani, "Reconciliation without Justice."

9. See Peter Digeser, *Political Forgiveness* (Ithaca, N.Y.: Cornell University Press, 2001); Greenawalt, "Amnesty's Justice."

10. Crocker, "Retribution and Reconciliation."

11. John W. De Gruchy, *Reconciliation: Restoring Justice* (Minneapolis, Minn.: Fortress Press, 2003); Desmond Tutu, *No Future without Forgiveness* (New York: Doubleday, 1999).

12. For an excellent survey of concepts of justice, see D. D. Raphael, *Concepts of Justice* (Oxford: Oxford University Press, 2001).

13. John Braithwaite, *Crime, Shame, and Reintegration* (Cambridge: Cambridge University Press, 1989); John Braithwaite and Philip Pettit, *Not Just Deserts: A Republican Theory of Criminal Justice* (Oxford: Oxford University Press, 1990); Michael L. Hadley, ed., *The Spiritual Roots of Restorative Justice* (Albany: State University of New York Press, 2001); Paul McCold, "Restorative Justice and the Role of the Community," in *Restorative Justice: International Perspectives*, ed. Burt Galaway and Joe Hudson (Monsey: Criminal Justice Press, 1996); Eugene McLaughlin et al., eds., *Restorative Justice* (Thousand Oaks, Calif.: Sage Publications, 2003); Heather Strang and John Braithwaite, eds., *Restorative Justice and Civil Society* (Cambridge: Cambridge University Press, 2001); Daniel W. Van Ness and Karen Heetderks Strong, *Restoring*

Justice: An Introduction to Restorative Justice (Atlanta: Anderson Press, 2006); Howard Zehr, *Changing Lenses* (Scottdale, Penn.: Herald Press, 1990).

14. Alasdair C. MacIntyre, *Dependent Rational Animals: Why Human Beings Need the Virtues* (Chicago: Open Court, 1999), 124–25.

15. My understanding of mercy is informed most by Pope John Paul II, "Dives in Misericordia," 1984.

16. See Douglas Johnston and Brian Cox, "Faith-Based Diplomacy and Preventive Engagement," in *Faith-Based Diplomacy: Trumping Realpolitik*, ed. Douglas Johnston (Oxford: Oxford University Press, 2003).

17. I argue this claim in Daniel Philpott, "When Faith Meets History: The Influence of Religion on Transitional Justice," in *The Religious in Response to Mass Atrocity: Interdisciplinary Perspectives*, ed. Thomas Brudholm and Thomas Cushman (Cambridge: Cambridge University Press, 2009).

18. See ibid.

19. Irving Greenberg, "Religion as a Force for Reconciliation and Peace: A Jewish Analysis," in *Beyond Violence: Religious Sources of Social Transformation in Judaism, Christianity, and Islam*, ed. James L. Heft (New York: Fordham University Press, 2004); Sol Schimmel, "Joseph and His Brothers: A Paradigm for Repentance," *Judaism, Quarterly Journal of Jewish Life and Thought* 37, no. 1 (1988); Solomon Schimmel, *Wounds Not Healed by Time: The Power of Repentance and Forgiveness* (Oxford: Oxford University Press, 2002); Moshe Weinfeld, *Social Justice in Ancient Israel* (Minneapolis, Minn.: Augsburg Fortress Publishers, 1995); Perry Yoder, *Shalom: The Bible's Word for Salvation, Justice, and Peace* (Newton, Kan.: Faith and Life Press, 1987).

20. De Gruchy, *Reconciliation*, 46, 51.

21. Majid Khadduri, *The Islamic Conception of Justice* (New York: Johns Hopkins University Press, 1984), 3–12.

22. Mohammed Abu-Nimer, *Nonviolence and Peace Building in Islam* (Gainesville: University Press of Florida, 2003), 60; Khadduri, *The Islamic Conception of Justice*, 3–12; Carol Schersten LaHurd, "'So That the Sinner Will Repent': Forgiveness in Islam and Christianity," *Dialog* 35, no. 4 (1996): 288; A. Rashied Omar, "Between Compassion and Justice: Locating an Islamic Definition of Peace," *Peace Colloquy* (Spring 2005): 9.

23. Abdulaziz Abdulhussein Sachedina, *The Islamic Roots of Democratic Pluralism* (New York: Oxford University Press, 2001), 106.

24. Nawal H. Ammar, "Restorative Justice in Islam: Theory and Practice," in *The Spiritual Roots of Restorative Justice*, ed. Michael L. Hadley (Albany: State University of New York Press, 2001), 169–73. See also Sachedina, *Islamic Roots of Democratic Pluralism*.

25. Abu-Nimer, *Nonviolence and Peace Building in Islam*; George E. Irani and Nathan C. Funk, "Rituals of Reconciliation: Arab-Islamic Perspectives," *Arab Studies Quarterly* 20, no. 4 (1998).

26. Robert Audi and Nicholas Wolterstorff, *Religion in the Public Square: The Place of Religious Convictions in Political Debate* (Lanham, Md.: Rowman and Littlefield, 1997); John Rawls, "The Idea of Public Reason Revisited," in *The Law of Peoples* (Cambridge, Mass.: Harvard University Press, 1999); Lawrence Solum, "Constructing an Ideal of Public Reason," *San Diego Law Review* 30 (1993).

27. See Gutmann and Thompson, "The Moral Foundations of Truth Commissions."

28. Jonathan Fox and Shmuel Sandler, "Separation of Religion and State in the Twenty-First Century: Comparing the Middle East and Western Democracies," *Comparative Politics* (2005).

29. See the arguments of Nicholas Wolterstoff in Audi and Wolterstorff, *Religion in the Public Square*, Christopher J. Eberle, *Religious Conviction in Liberal Politics* (Cambridge: Cambridge University Press, 2002), Jeffrey Stout, *Democracy and Tradition* (Princeton, N.J.: Princeton University Press, 2004).

30. Samuel P. Huntington, *The Third Wave: Democratization in the Late Twentieth Century* (Norman: University of Oklahoma Press, 1991), 211–31.

31. Again, MacIntyre comes to our aid. A practice, he explains in *After Virtue*, is: "any coherent and complex form of socially established cooperative human activity through which goods internal to that form of activity are realized in the course of trying to achieve those standards of excellence which are appropriate to, and partially definitive of, that form of activity, with the result that human powers to achieve excellence, and human conceptions of the ends and goods involved are systematically extended." His definition identifies crucial components of practices. The good of reconciliation, the excellence that it achieves, is restoration of relationships in the political order. Alasdair MacIntyre, *After Virtue: A Study in Moral Theory*, 2nd ed. (Notre Dame, Ind.: University of Notre Dame Press, 1984), 187.

32. I understand legitimacy to have two primary meanings. One is normative, pertaining to the intrinsic rightness of laws and institutions. The other is descriptive, pertaining to the degree to which laws and institutions enjoy assent in the judgments of those who live under them. I deploy the latter meaning presently.

33. The version of the just war theory that I find most compelling is Finnis, "The Ethics of War and Peace." For a prominent attempt to extend the just war framework to humanitarian intervention, see *Responsibility to Protect: Report of the International Commission on Intervention and State Sovereignty* (Ottawa, Ont.: International Development Research Centre, 2001). For a variety of perspectives on the justice of self-determination movements, see Margaret Moore, ed., *National Self-Determination and Secession* (Oxford: Oxford University Press, 1998).

34. Adrian Karatnycky and Peter Ackerman, *How Freedom Is Won: From Civic Resistance to Durable Democracy* (New York: Freedom House, 2005).

35. On knowledge versus acknowledgment, see Du Toit, "The Moral Foundations."

36. Michael Hayes and David Tombs, eds., *Truth and Memory: The Church and Human Rights in El Salvador and Guatemala* (Leominster, U.K.: Gracewing, 2001); 34, 107, 25, Paul Jeffrey, *Recovering Memory: Guatemalan Churches and the Challenge of Peacemaking* (Uppsala, Sweden: Life & Peace Institute, 1998), 51; Recovery of Historical Memory Project, *Guatemala: Never Again!* (Maryknoll, N.Y.: Orbis Books, 1999), xxiii–xxix.

37. Jeremy Waldron, "Superseding Historical Injustice," *Ethics* 103, no. 6 (1992).

38. See J. D. Bindenagel, "Justice, Apology, Reconciliation and the German Foundation: Remembrance, Responsibility, and the Future," in *Taking Wrongs Seriously: Apologies and Reconciliation*, ed. Elazar Barkan and Alexander Karn (Stanford, Calif.: Stanford University Press, 2006).

39. See Ted Hondereich, *Punishment: The Supposed Justifications* (Harmondsworth, U.K.: Penguin, 1971).

40. See Christopher D. Marshall, *Beyond Retribution: A New Testament Vision for Justice, Crime and Punishment* (Grand Rapids, Mich.: Eerdmans, 2001); For other philosophers who reason along similar lines, see R. A. Duff, *Punishment, Communication, and Community* (New York: Oxford University Press, 2001); Jean Hampton, "The Moral Education Theory of Punishment," *Philosophy and Public Affairs* (1984); Marshall, *Beyond Retribution*, Elizabeth Moberly, *Suffering, Innocent, and*

Guilty (London: SPCK, 1978), Herbert Morris, "Persons and Punishment," *Monist* 52 (1968).

41. Ammar, "Restorative Justice in Islam." This is not to elide disputed issues of interpretation. Obviously, some scriptures in the texts of each of the Abrahamic faiths seem on their face to run against a restorative logic of punishment. The full case for biblical and Qur'anic restorative punishment lies in sources like those that I have cited here.

42. Barry O'Neill, *Honor, Symbols, and War* (Ann Arbor: University of Michigan Press, 1999), 178–82.

43. For a good sociological account of apology, see Nicholas Tavuchis, *Mea Culpa: A Sociology of Apology and Reconciliation* (Stanford, Calif.: Stanford University Press, 1991). For a work on apology in international politics, see Jennifer Lind, *Sorry States: Apologies in International Politics* (Ithaca, N.Y.: Cornell University Press, 2008).

44. See Trudy Govier, *Forgiveness and Revenge* (London: Routledge, 2002), 68–72.

45. See, for instance, Abu-Nimer, *Nonviolence and Peace Building in Islam*; William Bole, Drew Christiansen, and Robert T. Hennemeyer, *Forgiveness in International Politics: An Alternative Road to Peace* (Washington, D.C.: U.S. Conference of Catholic Bishops, 2004); Marc Gopin, *Between Eden and Armageddon: The Future of World Religions, Violence, and Peacemaking* (Oxford: Oxford University Press, 2000); Alan Torrance, "The Theological Grounds for Advocating Forgiveness and Reconciliation in the Sociopolitical Realm," in *The Politics of Past Evil* (Notre Dame, Ind.: University of Notre Dame Press, 2006); Miroslav Volf, *Exclusion and Embrace: A Theological Exploration of Identity, Otherness, and Reconciliation* (Nashville, Tenn.: Abingdon Press, 1996).

46. For a piece that contains both thoughtful criticism of forgiveness as well as a survey of criticisms, see Thomas Brudholm, "On the Advocacy of Forgiveness after Mass Atrocities," in *The Religious in Response to Mass Atrocity: Interdisciplinary Perspectives*, ed. Thomas Brudholm and Thomas Cushman (Cambridge: Cambridge University Press, 2009), 124–156.

47. Christopher D. Marshall also argues that forgiveness is an act of justice. See Marshall, *Beyond Retribution*.

5

Whose Strategy, Whose Peace?

The Role of International Institutions in Strategic Peacebuilding

Simon Chesterman

Tolstoy wrote that all happy families are happy alike, while every unhappy family is unhappy in its own way. It is tempting to say the same thing of states, as successful states enter an increasingly homogenous globalized economy and weaker states slip into individualized chaos. That would be only partly true. The peacebuilding efforts considered in this volume demonstrate the importance of local context—history, culture, individual actors—but they also suggest more general lessons as to how external actors may help states emerging from crisis. This chapter critically examines the lessons applicable to efforts by international institutions—prominently, but not only, the United Nations—to support or impose transitions from conflict to durable peace.

In early 1995, chastened by the failed operation in Somalia, the failing operation in Bosnia and Herzegovina, and inaction in the face of genocide in Rwanda, UN Secretary General Boutros Boutros-Ghali issued a conservative supplement to his more optimistic 1992 *Agenda for Peace*. The *Supplement* noted that a new breed of intrastate conflicts presented the United Nations with challenges not encountered since the Congo operation of the early 1960s. A feature of these conflicts was the collapse of state institutions, especially the police and judiciary, meaning that international intervention had to extend beyond military and humanitarian tasks to include the "promotion of national reconciliation and the re-establishment of effective government." Nevertheless, he expressed caution against the United Nations assuming responsibility for law and order or attempting to impose state institutions on unwilling combatants.[1] General Sir Michael Rose, then commander of the UN Protection Force in

Bosnia (UNPROFOR), called this form of mission creep crossing "the Mogadishu line."[2]

Despite such cautious words, by the end of 1995 the United Nations had assumed responsibility for policing in Bosnia under the Dayton Agreement. The following January, a mission was established with temporary civil governance functions over the last Serb-held region of Croatia in eastern Slavonia. In June 1999, the Security Council authorized an interim administration in Kosovo to govern part of what remained technically Serbian territory for an indefinite period; four months later, a transitional administration was created with effective sovereignty over East Timor until independence. These expanding mandates continued a trend that began with the operations in Namibia in 1989 and Cambodia in 1993, where the United Nations exercised varying degrees of civilian authority in addition to supervising elections.

Efforts to construct or reconstruct institutions of the state from the outside are hardly new: decolonization and military occupation are the estranged ancestors of more recent activities in this area. What was novel about the missions undertaken in Kosovo and East Timor was the amount of executive authority assumed by the United Nations itself, placing it in the position of an occupying power. Though this power was presumably understood to be exercised in a benevolent fashion, problems associated with foreign rule repeated themselves with some predictable results in the cases examined here.

Postconflict reconstruction through the 1990s thus saw an increasing trend toward rebuilding governance structures through assuming some or all governmental powers on a temporary basis. Such transitional administration operations can be divided into two broad classes: where state institutions are divided and where they have collapsed. The first class encompasses situations in which governance structures were the subject of dispute with different groups claiming power (as in Cambodia or Bosnia and Herzegovina) or ethnic tensions within the structures themselves (such as Kosovo). The second class comprises circumstances in which such structures simply did not exist (as in Namibia, East Timor, and Afghanistan). A possible third class is suggested by recent experiences in Iraq, where regime change took place in a territory with far greater human, institutional, and economic resources than any comparable situation in which the United Nations or other actor had exercised civilian administration functions since World War II.[3]

The term *nation-building*, sometimes used in this context, is broad, vague, and often pejorative. In the course of the 2000 U.S. presidential campaign, Governor George W. Bush used it as a dismissive reference to the application of U.S. military resources beyond traditional mandates. The word was also used to conflate the circumstances in which U.S. forces found themselves in conflict with the local population—most notably in Somalia—with complex and time-consuming operations, such as those under way in Bosnia, Kosovo, and East Timor. Although it continues to be used in this context, notably within the United States, *nation-building* also has a more specific meaning in the postcolonial context, referring to efforts by new leaders to rally a population within sometimes arbitrary territorial frontiers. The focus here is on the *state* (that is, the highest institutions of governance in a territory) rather than the *nation* (a people who share common customs, origins, history, and frequently language) as such.[4]

Within the United Nations, the word *peacebuilding* is generally preferred. This has been taken to mean, among other things, "reforming or strengthening governmental institutions,"[5] or "the creation of structures for the institutionalization of peace."[6] It tends, however, to embrace a far broader range of activities than those particular operations under consideration here—at times being used to describe virtually all forms of international assistance to countries that have experienced or are at risk of armed conflict.[7]

Strategic peacebuilding, in the sense used in this volume, is a little—but only a little—more specific. It embraces the set of complementary practices intended to transform a society from a state of violence or deep injustice to long-term sustainable peace and justice. Key questions to be answered, of course, are who determines the strategy for a given crisis and who evaluates the sustainability and justice of the peace that may emerge. One of the strengths of this volume is that it recognizes that the answers to these "who" questions will typically not be confined to a single actor, and the answer may change over time.

It is frequently assumed that the collapse of state structures, whether through defeat by an external power or as a result of internal chaos, leads to a vacuum of political power. This is rarely the case. The mechanisms through which political power are exercised may be less formalized or consistent, but basic questions of how best to ensure the physical and economic security of oneself and one's dependents do not simply disappear when the institutions of the state break down. Nonstate actors in such situations may exercise varying degrees of political power over local populations, at times providing basic social services from education to medical care. Even where nonstate actors exist as parasites on local populations, political life goes on. How to engage in such an environment is a particular problem for policy makers in intergovernmental organizations and donor governments. But it poses far greater difficulties for the embattled state institutions and the populations of such territories.

International actors, the focus in this chapter, may play a critical role—if only in creating the opportunity for local actors to establish legitimate and sustainable governance. This relationship between the international and the local is a central theme in the editors' conception of strategic peacebuilding. Sometimes creating such opportunities means holding back. Humanitarian and, to some extent, development assistance flows most freely in response to crisis, but it rarely addresses the underlying causes of either poverty or conflict, as Larissa Fast shows in her chapter. As Jackie Smith argues, such assistance, if not well managed, may in fact undermine more sustainable recovery by establishing relationships of dependence and distorting the economy with unsustainable allocations of resources.

Until recently, there was little strategy in how international actors approached such problems. Indeed, reflecting Boutros-Ghali's earlier objections, there was no agreement that postconflict reconstruction was something in which the United Nations should become involved. The fact that such operations continue to be managed by the UN Department of Peacekeeping Operations is suggestive of the ad hoc approach that characterized transitional administration. This was evident in the 2000 Report of the Panel on UN Peace Operations, known as the Brahimi Report, which noted the likely demand for such operations as well as the "evident ambivalence" within governments and the UN Secretariat itself concerning the development of an institutional capacity to undertake them. Because of this ambivalence, it was impossible to achieve any consensus on recommendations, so the Department of Peacekeeping Operations continued to play the dominant supporting role.[8]

The creation in December 2005 of a Peacebuilding Commission, then, was a significant development—even if only as belated recognition that this was an important function of the United Nations. Established by the General Assembly to (among other things) "propose integrated strategies for post-conflict peacebuilding,"[9] it remains a work in progress. In theory, this could be the vehicle that develops and oversees policies embracing the interdependence of issues demonstrated in this volume. As we will see, however, theory has rarely led practice in the UN experience of peacebuilding.

This chapter evaluates strategic peacebuilding by the United Nations. The section that follows highlights some of the difficulties inherent in the political project of seeking to lay the foundations of peace from the outside; the next section explores the prospects for improvement, with particular reference to the Peacebuilding Commission. A survey of the practice shows significant improvement in technical areas such as staging elections; the Peacebuilding Commission may remedy some of the coordination problems and funding gaps that plague postconflict operations. It is far from clear, however, that the political contradictions inherent in such operations are being adequately understood, let alone addressed. There has been a good deal of improvement in the tools and the tactics available, but not much sign of strategy.

Problems

Is it even possible to establish the necessary political and economic conditions for legitimate and sustainable national governance through a period of benevolent foreign autocracy under UN auspices? This contradiction between ends and means has plagued recent efforts to govern postconflict territories in the Balkans, East Timor, Afghanistan, and Iraq. Such state-building operations combine an unusual mix of idealism and realism: the idealist project that a people can be saved from themselves through education, economic incentives, and the space to develop mature political institutions; the realist basis for that project in what is ultimately military occupation.

Much research has focused on the doctrinal and operational difficulties experienced by such operations.[10] This is a valuable area of research, but it may obscure three sets of contradictions between means and ends that undermined such operations: the means are inconsistent with the ends, they are frequently inadequate for those ends, and in many situations they are inappropriate for the ends.

Inconsistent

Benevolent autocracy is an uncertain foundation for legitimate and sustainable national governance. It is inaccurate and often counterproductive to assert that transitional administration depends on the consent or "ownership" of the local population.[11] It is inaccurate because if genuine local control were possible, then a transitional administration would not be necessary. It is counterproductive because insincere claims of local ownership lead to frustration and suspicion on the part of local actors. *Clarity* is therefore required in recognizing (1) the strategic objectives, (2) the relationship between international and local actors and how this will change over time, and (3) the commitment required of international actors to achieve objectives that warrant the temporary assumption of autocratic powers under a benevolent international administration.

In a case like East Timor, the strategic objective—independence—was both clear and uncontroversial. Frustration with the slow pace of reconstruction or the inefficiencies of the UN presence could generally be tempered by reference to the uncontested aim of independence and a timetable within which this was to be achieved. In Kosovo, failure to articulate a position on its final status inhibits the development of a mature political elite and deters foreign investment. The present ambiguity derives from a compromise that was brokered between the United States and Russia at the end of the NATO campaign against the Federal Republic of Yugoslavia in 1999, formalized in Security Council resolution 1244 (1999). Nevertheless, the United Nations is now blamed for frustrating the aspirations of Kosovars for self-determination. Many national and international observers blamed lack of progress in resolving the issue of final status as a key factor in fueling the violence that erupted in the province in March 2004. Martti Ahtisaari's ongoing efforts to broker a final status agreement continue to be frustrated by the attachment of each side to positions—independence or integration—that are both unambiguous and irreconcilable.[12]

Obfuscation of strategic political objectives leads to ambiguity in the mandate. Niche mandate implementation by a proliferation of postconflict actors may further complicate the transition to durable peace. More than five years after the Dayton Agreement, a "recalibration" exercise required the various international agencies present in Bosnia and Herzegovina to perform an institutional audit to determine what, exactly, each of them did.[13] Such dysfunction strongly suggests the need for the strategic approach called for in this volume and also points to the practical barriers to implementing it. Subsidiary bodies and specialized agencies of the United Nations should in principle place their material and human resources at the direct disposal of the transitional administration: all activities should be oriented toward an agreed political goal, which should normally be legitimate and sustainable government. Ideally, the unity of civilian authority should also embrace command of the military. In reality, the reluctance of the United States and other industrialized countries to put their troops under UN command makes this highly improbable. Coordination thus becomes more important to avoid some of the difficulties encountered in civil–military relations, for example, in Afghanistan.

Clarity in the relationship between international and local actors raises the question of ownership. This term is often used disingenuously—either to mask the assertion of potentially dictatorial powers by international actors or to carry a psychological rather than political meaning in the area of reconstruction. Ownership in this context is usually not intended to mean control and often does not even imply a direct input into political questions.[14] This is not to suggest that local control is a substitute for international administration. As the operation in Afghanistan demonstrates, a "light footprint" makes the success of an operation more than usually dependent on the political dynamic of local actors. Because the malevolence or collapse of that political dynamic is precisely the reason that power is arrogated to an international presence, the light footprint is unsustainable as a model for general application. How much power should be transferred and for how long depends on the political transition that is required; this in turn is a function of the root causes of the conflict, the local capacity for change, and the degree of international commitment available to assist in bringing about that change.[15]

Local ownership, then, must be the end of a transitional administration, but it is not the means. Openness about the trustee-like relationship between international and local actors would help locals by ensuring transparency about the powers that they will exercise at various stages of the transition. Openness would also help the states that mandate and fund such operations by forcing acknowledgment of their true nature and the level of commitment required to effect the transition.

Clarifying the commitment necessary to bring about fundamental change in a conflict-prone territory is, however, a double-edged sword. It would ensure that political will exists prior to authorizing a transitional administration, but perhaps at the expense of other operations that would not be authorized at all. The mission in Bosnia was always expected to last beyond its nominal twelve-month deadline but might not have been established if it had been envisaged that troops would remain on the ground for a full decade or more. Donors contemplating Afghanistan in November 2001 balked at early estimates that called for a ten-year, $25 billion commitment to the country. In the lead-up to the war with Iraq, the chief of staff of the U.S. Army was similarly pooh-poohed—and later forced into retirement—by the leadership of the Defense Department when he testified to the Senate that several hundred thousand soldiers would be required for postwar duties.[16] Political considerations already limit the choice of missions, of course: not for lack of opportunity, no major transitional administration has been established in Africa, where the demands are probably greatest. The primary barrier to establishing transitional administration–type operations in areas such as Western Sahara, Somalia, and the Democratic Republic of the Congo has less to do with the difficulty of such operations than with the absence of political will to commit the resources necessary to undertake them.[17]

Resolving the inconsistency between the means and the ends of transitional administration requires a clear-eyed recognition of the role of power. The collapse of formal state structures does not necessarily create a power vacuum; as indicated earlier, political life does not simply cease. Constructive engagement with power on this local level requires both an understanding of culture and history as well as respect for the political aspirations of the population. Clarity will also help here: the international presence either exercises quasi-sovereign powers on a temporary basis, or it does not. This clarity must exist at the formal level, but it leaves much room for nuance in implementation.

Most obviously, assertion of executive authority should be on a diminishing basis, with power devolved as appropriate to local institutions. The transfer of power must be of more than symbolic value: once power is transferred to local hands, whether at the municipal or national level, local actors should be able to exercise that power meaningfully, constrained only by the rule of law. Unless and until genuine transfer is possible, consultation is appropriate but without the pretense that this is the same as control. Where international actors do not exercise sovereign power—because of the size of the territory, the complexity of the conflict, or a simple lack of political will—this is not the same as exercising no power at all. Certain functions may be delegated to the international presence, as they were in Cambodia and Afghanistan, and international actors will continue to exercise considerable behind-the-scenes influence either because of ongoing responsibilities in a peace process or as gatekeepers to development assistance. In either case, the abiding need is for clarity as to who is in charge and, equally important, who is *going* to be in charge.

Inadequate

International interest in postconflict operations tends to be ephemeral, with availability of funds linked to the prominence of a foreign crisis on the domestic agenda of the states that contribute funds and troops. Both have tended to be insufficient. Funds for postconflict reconstruction are notoriously supply- rather than demand-driven. This leads to multiplication of bureaucracy in the recipient country, inconsistency in disbursement procedures, and a focus on projects that may be more popular with donors than they are necessary in the recipient country. Reluctance to commit funds is surpassed only by reluctance to commit troops: in the absence of security, however, meaningful political change is impossible. This was confirmed in the most brutal way possible with the attacks on UN personnel in Baghdad on August 19, 2003.

The ephemeral nature of international interest in postconflict operations is, unfortunately, a cliché. When the United States overthrew the Taliban regime in Afghanistan, President Bush likened the commitment to rebuild the devastated country to the Marshall Plan. Just over twelve months later, in February 2003, the White House apparently forgot to include *any* money for reconstruction in the 2004 budget that it submitted to Congress. Legislators reallocated $300 million in aid to cover the oversight.[18] Such oversights are disturbingly common: much of the aid that is pledged arrives either late or not at all. This demands a measure of artificiality in drafting budgets for reconstruction, which in turn leads to suspicion on the part of donors—sometimes further delaying the disbursement of funds. For example, $880 million was pledged at the Conference on Rehabilitation and Reconstruction of Cambodia in June 1992. By the time the new government was formed in September 1993, only $200 million had been disbursed, rising to only $460 million by the end of 1995. The problem is not simply one of volume: Bosnia has received more per capita assistance than Europe did under the Marshall Plan, but the incoherence of funding programs, the lack of a regional approach, and the inadequacy of state and entity institutions have contributed to the country remaining in financial crisis.[19]

Many of these problems would be reduced if donors replaced the system of voluntary funding for relief and reconstruction for transitional administrations with assessed contributions, which presently fund peacekeeping operations. The distinction between funds supporting a peacekeeping operation and those providing assistance to a government makes sense when there is some form of indigenous government, but it is arbitrary in situations where the peacekeeping operation *is* the government. Given existing strains on the peacekeeping budget, however, such a change is unlikely. A more realistic proposal would be to pool voluntary contributions through a trust fund, ideally coordinated by local actors or a mixed body of local and international personnel, perhaps also drawing on private sector expertise. At the very least, a monitoring mechanism to track aid flows would help ensure that money promised at the high point of international attention to a crisis is in fact delivered and spent. The experience of Afghanistan suggests that there is perhaps some learning taking place in this area, though even during one of the greatest outpouring of emergency relief fund in recent history—in response to the tsunami that struck the Indian Ocean region on December 26, 2004—Secretary General Kofi Annan felt compelled to remind donor governments, "We have often had gaps in the past [between pledges and actual donations] and I hope it is not going to happen in this case."[20] The use of PricewaterhouseCoopers to track aid flows also points to a new flexibility in using private sector expertise to avoid wastage and corruption.

Parsimony of treasure is surpassed by the reluctance to expend blood in policing postconflict territories. In the absence of security, however, meaningful political change in a postconflict territory is next to impossible. Unless and until the United Nations develops a rapidly deployable civilian police capacity, either military tasks in a postconflict environment will include basic law and order functions or these functions will not be performed at all. The military—especially the U.S. military—is understandably reluctant to embrace duties that are outside its field of expertise, but this is symptomatic of an anachronistic view of UN peace operations. The dichotomy between peacekeeping and enforcement actions was always artificial, and in the context of internal armed conflict where large numbers of civilians are at risk, it becomes untenable. Moreover, as most transitional administrations have followed conflicts initiated under the auspices or in the name of the United Nations, inaction is not the same as noninterference. Once military operations commence, external actors have already begun a process of political transformation on the ground. As the Independent Inquiry on Rwanda concluded, whether or not a peace operation has a mandate or the will to protect civilians, its very presence creates an expectation that it will do so.[21]

A key argument in the Brahimi Report was that missions with uncertain mandates or inadequate resources should not be created at all:

> Although presenting and justifying planning estimates according to high operational standards might reduce the likelihood of an operation going forward, Member States must not be led to believe that they are doing something useful for countries in trouble when—by under-resourcing missions—they are more likely agreeing to a waste of human resources, time and money.[22]

This view finds some support in the report of the International Commission on Intervention and State Sovereignty, *The Responsibility to Protect*, which called for the "responsibility to rebuild" to be seen as an integral part of any intervention. When an intervention is contemplated, a postintervention strategy is both an operational necessity and an ethical imperative.[23] There is some evidence of this principle now achieving at least rhetorical acceptance—despite his aversion to nation-building, President Bush stressed before and during operations in Afghanistan and Iraq that the United States would help in reconstructing the territories in which it had intervened.

More than rhetoric is required. Success in state-building, in addition to clarity of purpose, requires time and money. A lengthy international presence will not ensure success, but an early departure guarantees failure. Similarly, an abundance of resources will not make up for the lack of a coherent strategy—though the fact that Kosovo has been the recipient of twenty-five times more money and fifty times more troops on a per capita basis compared with Afghanistan, goes some way toward explaining the modest achievements in developing democratic institutions and the economy.[24]

Inappropriate

The inappropriateness of available means to desired ends presents the opposite problem to that of the inadequacy of resources. Although the question of limited resources—money, personnel, and international attention—depresses the standards against which a postconflict operation can be judged, artificially high international expectations may nevertheless be imposed in certain areas of governance. Particularly when the United Nations itself assumes a governing role, there is a temptation to demand the highest standards of democracy, human rights, the rule of law, and the provision of services.

Balancing these against the need for locally sustainable goals presents difficult problems. A computerized electoral registration system may be manifestly ill-suited to a country with a low level of literacy and intermittent electricity, but should an international nongovernmental organization refrain from opening a world-class medical clinic if such levels of care are unsustainable? An abrupt drop from high levels of care once the crisis and international interest passes would be disruptive, but lowering standards early implies acceptance that people who might otherwise have been treated will suffer. This was the dilemma faced by the International Committee of the Red Cross, which transferred control of the Dili National Hospital to national authorities in East Timor almost a year before independence.

Although most acute in areas such as health, the issue arises in many aspects of transitional administration. In the best tradition of autocracies, the international missions in Bosnia and Kosovo subscribed to the vast majority of human rights treaties and then discovered raisons d'état that required them to be abrogated. Efforts to promote the rule of law tend to focus more on the prosecution of the highest profile crimes of the recent past than on developing institutions to manage criminal law in the near future. Humanitarian and development assistance are notorious for being driven more by supply than demand, with the result that projects that are funded tend to represent the interests—and, frequently, the products and personnel—of donors rather than recipients.[25] Finally, staging elections in conflict zones has become something of an art form, though more than half a dozen elections in Bosnia have yet to produce a workable government.

Different issues arise in the area of human resources. Staffing such operations always takes place in an atmosphere of crisis, but personnel tend to be selected from a limited pool of applicants (most of them internal) whose skills may be irrelevant to the tasks at hand. In East Timor, for example, it would have made sense to approach Portuguese-speaking governments to request that staff with experience in public administration be seconded to the UN mission. Instead, it was not even possible to require Portuguese, Tetum, or Bahasa Indonesia because they were not official UN working languages. Positions are often awarded for political reasons or simply to ensure that staff lists are full; once in place, there is no effective mechanism to assess an individual's suitability or remove him or her quickly if warranted. A separate problem is the assumption that international staff who do possess relevant skills are also able to train others in the same field. This is an entirely different skill, however, and simply pairing international and local staff tends to provide less on-the-job training than extended opportunities to stand around and watch—a problem exacerbated by the fact that English tends to be used as the working language. One element of the light footprint approach adopted in Afghanistan that is certainly of general application is the need to justify every post occupied by international staff rather than a local. Cultivating relations with diaspora communities may help address this problem, serving the dual function of recruiting culturally aware staff and encouraging the return of skilled expatriates more generally.

The "can-do" attitude of many people within the UN system is one of the most positive qualities that staff bring to a mission. If the problem is getting 100 tons of rice to 10,000 starving refugees, niceties of procedure are less important than getting the job done. When the problem is governing a territory, however, procedure is more important. In such circumstances, the can-do attitude may become a cavalier disregard for local sensibilities. Moreover, many staff in such situations are not used to criticism from the population that they are "helping," with some regarding it as a form of ingratitude. Where the United Nations assumes the role of government, it should expect and welcome criticism appropriate to that of the sort of political environment it hopes to foster. Security issues may require limits on this, but a central element in the development of local political capacity is encouraging discussion among local actors about these matters—apart from anything else, it enhances the legitimacy of the conclusions drawn. International staff sometimes bemoan the prospect of endless consultation getting in the way of their work, but in many ways that conversation is precisely the point of their presence in the territory.

Just as generals are sometimes accused of planning to refight their last war, so the United Nations experiments in transitional administration have reflected only gradual learning. Senior UN officials now acknowledge that to varying degrees, Kosovo got the operation that should have been planned for Bosnia four years earlier, and East Timor got what should have been sent to Kosovo. Afghanistan's very different light footprint approach draws, in turn, on the outlines of what Lakhdar Brahimi argued would have been appropriate for East Timor in 1999.

The United Nations may never again be called on to repeat operations comparable to Kosovo and East Timor, where it exercised sovereign powers on a temporary basis. Even so, it is certain that the circumstances that demanded such interventions will recur. Lessons derived from past experiences of transitional administration will be applicable whenever the United Nations or other international actors engage in complex peace operations that include a policing function, civilian administration, development of the rule of law, establishment of a national economy, staging of elections, or all of the above. Learning from such lessons has not, however, been one of the strengths of the United Nations.

Prospects

If there is a single generalizable lesson to be learned from the recent experience of state-building, whether as transitional administration or preventing state failure, it is modesty. The challenges before the United Nations now are not, therefore, to develop grand theories or a revivified trusteeship capacity. Rather, what is required are workable strategies and tactics with which to support institutions of the state before, during, and after conflict. As indicated earlier, doing this effectively requires clarity in three areas: (1) the strategic aims of the action; (2) the necessary institutional coordination to put all actors—especially security and development actors—on the same page; and (3) a realistic basis for evaluating the success or failure of the action. Clarity in these three areas, if embraced as policy and implemented as practice, would represent a key move toward something one might call strategic peacebuilding.

Strategy

The accepted wisdom within the UN community, articulated most recently in the Brahimi Report, is that a successful UN peace operation should ideally consist of three sequential stages. First, the political basis for peace must be determined. Then a suitable mandate for a UN mission should be formulated. Finally, that mission should be given all the resources necessary to complete the mandate.[26] The accepted reality is that this usually happens in the reverse order: member states determine what resources they are prepared to commit to a problem, and a mandate is cobbled together around those resources—often in the hope that a political solution will be forthcoming at some later date.

Strategic failure may affect all levels of an operation. The most common types of failures are at the level of overall mandate, in the interaction between different international actors with competing or inconsistent mandates, and in the relationship between international and national actors on the ground.

Kosovo's uncertain final status, for example, has severely undermined the ongoing peace operation there, contrasting starkly with the simplicity of East Timor's transition to independence. Clarity concerning the political trajectory of a territory under transitional administration is essential, but lack of strategy also undermines efforts to prevent the collapse of state institutions. In Afghanistan, prioritizing the military strategy at times undermined the professed political aims—most prominently in decisions to support warlords for tactical reasons in the hunt for al Qaeda even as they undermined Hamid Karzai's embryonic government in Kabul.

A second level at which strategic failure may take place is when different actors have competing or inconsistent mandates. Security actors are a notorious example of this—with the independence of the NATO-led Kosovo Force (KFOR) and the International Security Assistance Force (ISAF) in Afghanistan at times undermining the authority of the international civilian presence. Ensuring a single chain of command would be desirable, but it runs against the received wisdom that the United Nations is incapable of waging war. A more achievable goal would be bringing the political process into line with development assistance. The United Nations has done this rhetorically in the term *peacebuilding*,[27] but without creating any capacity to focus political attention, design policy and strategy, and oversee operations in this area. (The Peacebuilding Commission is considered in the next subsection.)

As indicated by the discussion on political trajectory and ownership, international actors have sometimes been less than effective at managing expectations and relationships with national actors. Clarity about respective roles—and about the final authority of the population in question to determine its own future once a territory is stabilized and no longer regarded as a threat to international peace and security—would help. Where there is no existing legitimate governance structure in place, or if there are competing structures, the concept of "shadow alignment" may be helpful. This requires an assessment of available formal and informal policies and systems that can be built on, adapted, and reformed. The aim is to avoid a legacy of diverted institutions that may undermine the development of legitimate and accountable structures.[28]

Reference to strategy should not be misunderstood as suggesting that there is some template for governance that can be applied across cases. Instead, clarity about the purposes of engagement and the respective responsibilities of international and national actors provides a framework for developing a coherent strategy that takes the state itself as the starting point.

Coordination and the Peacebuilding Commission

The High-Level Panel on Threats, Challenges, and Change rightly criticized the UN experience of postconflict operations as characterized by "countless ill-coordinated and overlapping bilateral and United Nations programs, with inter-agency competition preventing the best use of scarce resources."[29] Its key recommendation to remedy this situation was the call for a Peacebuilding Commission to be established as a subsidiary organ of the UN Security Council under Article 29 of the UN Charter.[30]

This new body was to have four functions. First, it would identify countries that are under stress and risk sliding toward state collapse. Second, it would organize, "in partnership with the national Government, proactive assistance in preventing that process from developing further." Third, it would assist in the planning for transitions between conflict and postconflict peacebuilding. Fourth, it would marshal and sustain the efforts of the international community in postconflict peacebuilding over whatever period may be necessary. Other guidelines mapped out institutional and procedural considerations, including the need for the body to be small and flexible, considering both general policy issues and country-by-country strategies. It was to include representatives of the Security Council, the Economic and Social Council (ECOSOC), the International Monetary Fund and the World Bank, donor countries, troop contributors, and regional organizations, as well as national representatives of the country under consideration.[31] A Peacebuilding Support Office would integrate system-wide policies and strategies, develop best practices, and provide support to field operations. Among other functions, the office would submit twice-yearly early warning analyses to the Peacebuilding Commission to help it in organizing its work.[32]

The commission was generally considered to be one of the more positive ideas to come from the High-Level Panel and appeared likely to be adopted by the membership of the United Nations. When the secretary general drew on this to present his own vision of the Peacebuilding Commission in his "In Larger Freedom" report of March 2005, he specifically removed any suggestion of an early warning function—anticipating pressure from governments wary that they might be precisely the ones under scrutiny.[33] This essentially dropped the first two of the High-Level Panel's four functions, but the secretary general elaborated on how the other two might work in practice:

> A Peacebuilding Commission could perform the following functions: in the immediate aftermath of war, improve United Nations planning for sustained recovery, focusing on early efforts to establish the necessary institutions; help to ensure predictable financing for early recovery activities, in part by providing an overview of assessed, voluntary and standing funding mechanisms; improve the coordination of the many post-conflict activities of the United Nations funds, programs and agencies; provide a forum in which the United Nations, major bilateral donors, troop contributors, relevant regional actors and organizations, the international financial institutions and the national or transitional Government of the country concerned can share information about their respective post-conflict recovery strategies, in the interests of greater coherence; periodically review progress towards medium-term recovery goals; and extend the period of political attention to post-conflict recovery.[34]

Two essential aspects of how the commission would function were left unresolved: what its membership would be, and to whom it would report—the Security Council or the ECOSOC. These issues ended up paralyzing debate on the commission in the lead-up to the September 2005 World Summit and were deferred for later consideration. The World Summit Outcome document broadly endorsed the secretary general's view of the Peacebuilding Commission as essentially limited to mobilizing resources for postconflict reconstruction:

> The main purpose of the Peacebuilding Commission is to bring together all relevant actors to marshal resources and to advise on and propose integrated strategies for post-conflict peacebuilding and recovery. The Commission should focus attention on the reconstruction and institution-building efforts necessary for recovery from conflict and support the development of integrated strategies in order to lay the foundation for sustainable development. In addition, it should provide recommendations and information to improve the coordination of all relevant actors within and outside the United Nations, develop best practices, help to ensure predictable financing for early recovery activities and extend the period of attention by the international community to post-conflict recovery.[35]

In one sense, the evolution of the Peacebuilding Commission is a fairly typical example of ideas and norms being diluted as they move through the policy and intergovernmental waters. Early warning died a fairly quick death even before reaching the summit. A second attempt by the High-Level Panel to strengthen early warning by creating a deputy secretary general for Peace and Security was dropped entirely.[36] The outcome document of the 2005 summit did resolve to develop early warning systems for natural disasters, particularly tsunamis, but early warning of manmade disasters was the subject for a more tepid call for the international community to support the United Nations in developing such a capability at some point in the unspecified future.[37]

On the postconflict responsibilities of the Peacebuilding Commission, its role in planning and formulating strategy was more subtly undermined. The High-Level Panel had seen it as assisting in the "planning" for the transition from conflict to postconflict.[38] The secretary general limited it to improving "United Nations planning for sustained recovery."[39] By the summit, it was limited to "advis[ing] on and propos[ing] integrated strategies."[40] The Peacebuilding Support Office, meanwhile, did not receive the requested twenty new staff members or any new responsibilities beyond assisting and supporting the commission by drawing on existing resources within the Secretariat.[41]

The General Assembly formally established the Peacebuilding Commission on December 30, 2005. Described as an "intergovernmental advisory body," its standing members comprise seven members of the Security Council (ambiguously described as "including permanent members"), seven members of ECOSOC, five of the top providers of assessed and voluntary contributions, five of the top troop contributors, and a further seven elected by the General Assembly for regional balance.[42] Selection of these members was predictably politicized: in particular, the permanent members of the Security Council ensured their membership, joined by Denmark and Tanzania. The seven ECOSOC members were Angola, Belgium, Brazil, Guinea-Bissau, Indonesia, Poland, and Sri Lanka; those from the top financial contributors to the United Nations were Germany, Italy, Japan, the Netherlands, and Norway; those from the top military contributors were Bangladesh, Ghana, India, Nigeria, and Pakistan. The seven members elected by the General Assembly were Burundi (which soon became a focus of the commission's attention, together with Sierra Leone), Chile, Croatia, Egypt, El Salvador, Fiji, and Jamaica.

Far from being a new Trusteeship Council, then, the Peacebuilding Commission began to look more like a standing pledging conference, one of the most important forms of coordination for donors that currently exists.[43] If it can succeed in sustaining attention on a postconflict situation beyond the current limits of foreign policy attention deficit disorder, the commission will have achieved a great deal. It is less clear that this additional layer of coordination will assist in how these new resources are spent.[44]

Problems of coordination tend to arise at three levels: (1) the strategic level (for example, the final status of Kosovo), (2) the operational level (for example, competing donor agencies in Bosnia), and (3) the national level (for example, getting international actors to sign onto a national development framework in Afghanistan). The problem with the Peacebuilding Commission proposal is that its establishment under the Security Council (or the ECOSOC) may see it fall somewhere between (1) and (2)—lacking the authority to challenge the Security Council in New York and lacking a field presence to ensure operational cohesion on the ground. Much will, of course, depend on how the commission functions. If it acts as an operational body that can bring key stakeholders—importantly, including the international financial institutions, troop contributors, donor governments, and national representatives—onto the same page in terms of the security, humanitarian, political, and economic priorities and sequencing for a territory, it may avoid the wasted resources seen in previous operations. At the very least, if it can force the United Nations to speak with one voice on postconflict reconstruction—rather than being represented variously by the departments and specialized agencies—it will have achieved a significant improvement. The key component is some body that is able to speak truth to power: unless the commission (or the Peacebuilding Support Office) is able to advise the Security Council against dysfunctional mandates or unrealistic strategies, it will not fulfill its lofty aspirations.

If it is to be successful, two additional coordination dynamics need to be addressed. The first is the problem of coordination across time. This embraces both the conflicting timetables of internationals (diminishing interest and thus reduced resources after eighteen to twenty-four months) and locals (increasing absorptive capacity and the ability to use resources most productively only after the crisis period has passed), as well as the tension between demands for quick impact and gap-filling projects versus the development of sustainable institutions. The second coordination dynamic is the emergence of local actors as an independent political force. Consultation through an instrument such as the Peacebuilding Commission may be helpful, but not if it complicates the more important consultative mechanisms on the ground that manage day-to-day political life in the postconflict territory. The most important aspect of this second dynamic is, once again, clarity: clarity about who is in charge at any given time, and also clarity about who will be in charge once the attention of the international community moves on. This points to the importance of a strategic framework within which both international and national actors see their responsibilities as complementary rather than sequential.

Evaluation and Exit Strategies

In his April 2001 report on the closure or transition of complex peacekeeping operations, UN Secretary General Kofi Annan warned that the embarrassing withdrawal of peacekeepers from Somalia should not be repeated in future operations. The report was called "No Exit without a Strategy."[45] For the UN Transitional Administration in East Timor, elections provided the basis for transfer of power to local authorities; they also set in place political processes that would last well beyond the mission and the development assistance that followed. In Kosovo, where the UN operation was determinedly called an interim administration, the absence of an agreed end-state has left the territory in political limbo. Reflection on the absence of an exit strategy from Kosovo, following on the apparently endless operation in Bosnia and Herzegovina, led some ambassadors to the Security Council to turn the secretary general's phrase on its head: "no strategy," the rallying cry went, "without an exit."

East Timor presents two contradictory stories in the history of UN peace operations. On one hand, it is presented as an outstanding success. In two and a half years, a territory that had been reduced to ashes after the 1999 referendum on independence held peaceful elections and celebrated independence. On the other hand, however, East Timor can be seen as a series of missed opportunities and waste. Of the UN Transitional Administration's annual budget of over $500 million, around one-tenth actually reached the East Timorese. At one point, $27 million was spent annually on bottled water for the international staff—approximately half the budget of the embryonic Timorese government, and money that might have paid for water purification plants to serve both international staff and locals well beyond the life of the mission. More could have been done or done earlier to reconstruct public facilities. This did not happen in part because of budgetary restrictions on UN peacekeeping operations that, to the Timorese, were not just absurd but insulting. Such problems were compounded by coordination failures, the displacement of local initiatives by bilateral donor activities, and the lack of any significant private sector investment. When East Timor (now Timor-Leste) became independent, it did so with the dubious honor of becoming the poorest country in Asia.[46] The outbreak of fighting in May 2006 proved to many that warnings of an unduly abrupt withdrawal were well founded.[47]

Evaluations of the UN operation in Cambodia (1992–1993) varied considerably in the course of the mission and have continued to do so with the benefit of hindsight. Prior to the 1993 election, prophecies of doom were widespread, with questions raised about the capacity of the United Nations to complete a large military and administrative operation.[48] Immediately after the election was held with minimal violence, Cambodia was embraced as a success and a model for such future tasks.[49] Subsequent events suggested that these initially positive evaluations were premature. Many commentators outside the United Nations now regard the UN Transitional Authority in Cambodia (UNTAC) as a partial failure, pointing to the departure from democratic norms in the 1997 coup. Within the United Nations, UNTAC continues to be regarded as a partial success. The important variable is how one views the political context within which UNTAC operated. If the purpose of the mission was to transform Cambodia into a multiparty liberal democracy in eighteen months, it clearly did not succeed. If, however, one takes the view that Hun Sen—who had led Cambodia from 1979 and later seized power from his coalition partners in a coup four years after the 1993 elections—was always going to be the dominant political force in Cambodia, and that the purpose of the mission was to mollify the exercise of that power by introducing the language of human rights to Cambodian civil society, fostering the establishment of a relatively free press, and taking steps in the direction of a democratic basis for legitimate government, the mission was indeed a partial success.

Two lessons were (or should have been) learned in Cambodia. The first was to underscore the fragility of complex peace operations. Even though UNTAC was, at the time, the largest and most expensive operation in UN history, it still faced enormous difficulties in bringing about a fundamental change in the psyche of the country. Without peace and security, and without the rule of law, democratic processes may be unsustainable in themselves. Providing these foundations, if it was possible at all, would have required a more sustained commitment to remaining in Cambodia after the elections. The counterfactual is speculative because there was no willingness before or after the vote for UNTAC to remain beyond the completion of its mandate.

Second, the aftermath of the UN engagement in Cambodia—the 1997 coup, the flawed elections in 1998—began to raise questions about the relative importance of democracy. Though it may not be directly traceable to Cambodia, a shift began to occur in the rhetoric that saw "good governance" sometimes replace democracy in the peacebuilding and development jargon.[50]

Clarity about the objectives of an operation, then, may be helpful—even if it requires a retreat from the rhetoric that justifies the expenditure of resources for a peace effort. Often it will not be possible (even if it were desirable) to transform a country over the course of eighteen months into, say, Canada. Instead, perhaps the most that can be hoped for is to create the conditions in which a vulnerable population can start a conversation about what kind of country they want theirs to be.

Conclusion

In his book *In My Father's House,* Kwame Anthony Appiah notes that the apparent ease of colonial administration generated in some of the inheritors of postcolonial nations an illusion that control of the state would allow them to pursue as easily their much more ambitious objectives. Once the state was turned to the tasks of massive developments in infrastructure, however, it was shown wanting: "When the postcolonial rulers inherited the apparatus of the colonial state, they inherited the reins of power; few noticed, at first, that they were not attached to a bit."[51]

Given the fraught history of so many of the world's states, it is not remarkable that some states suffer basic crises in their capacity to protect and provide services for a population—on the contrary, it is remarkable that more do not. As indicated in the introduction, discussion of such institutional crises frequently suggests that, when a state "fails," power is no longer exercised within the territory. In fact, the control of power becomes more important than ever—even though it may be exercised in an incoherent fashion.

Engagement with such states requires, first and foremost, understanding the local dynamics of power. The much-cited Weberian definition of the state as claimant to a monopoly of the legitimate use of force is less a definition of what the state *is* than what it *does.* The legitimacy and sustainability of local power structures depends, ultimately, on local actors. Certain policies can help—channeling political power through institutions rather than individuals, and through civilians rather than the military; imposing term limits on heads of state and government; encouraging and regulating political parties—but their implementation depends on the capacity of local leaders to submit themselves to the rule of law and local populations to hold their leaders to that standard.

For international actors, a troubling analogy is to compare engagement with weak states to previous models of trusteeship and empire. Current efforts at state-building attempt—at least in part—to reproduce the better effects of empire (inward investment, pacification, and impartial administration) with-out reproducing its worst features (repression, corruption, and confiscation of local capacity). This is not to suggest nostalgia for empire or that such poli-cies should be resurrected. Only two generations ago, one-third of the world's population lived in territory considered non–self-governing; the end of colo-nialism was one of the most significant transformations in the international order since the emergence of sovereign states. The analogy may be helpful if it suggests that a realistic assessment of power is necessary to formulate effective policies rather than effective rhetoric.

States cannot be made to work from the outside. International assistance may be necessary, but it is never sufficient to establish institutions that are legitimate and sustainable. This is not an excuse for inaction, if only to mini-mize the humanitarian consequences of a state's incapacity to care for its vul-nerable population. Beyond that, however, international action should be seen as part of a process complementary to the creation of local processes, providing resources and creating the space for local actors to start a conversation that will define and consolidate their polity by mediating their vision of a good life into responsive, robust, and resilient institutions. Strategic peacebuilding, if it means anything, recognizes this complementarity and the need for policies and practices that see national and international processes not as competing and sequential but as interdependent and overlapping.

NOTES

This work draws on material discussed at greater length in Simon Chesterman, *You, The People: The United Nations, Transitional Administration, and State-Building* (Oxford: Oxford University Press, 2004) and Simon Chesterman, Michael Ignatieff, and Ramesh Thakur, eds., *Making States Work: State Failure and the Crisis of Governance* (Tokyo: United Nations University Press, 2005). Many of the examples cited draw on confidential interviews conducted in Dili, Kabul, New York, Phnom Penh, Pristina, and Sarajevo between 1999 and 2006.

1. "Supplement to An Agenda for Peace: Position Paper of the Secretary-General on the Occasion of the Fiftieth Anniversary of the United Nations," UN Doc A/50/60-S/1995/1, 3 January 1995, available at http://www.un.org/Docs/SG/agsupp.html, paras. 13–14.

2. Michael Rose, "The Bosnia Experience," in *Past Imperfect, Future Uncertain: The United Nations at Fifty*, ed. Ramesh Thakur (New York: St. Martin's Press, 1998).

3. See generally Chesterman, *You, the People.*

4. Massimo D'Azeglio famously expressed the difference in the context of post-Risorgimento Italy: "We have made Italy," he declared. "Now we must make Italians." On the creation of states generally, see James Crawford, *The Creation of States in International Law* (Oxford: Clarendon Press, 1979). On nation-building, see, e.g., Benedict Anderson, *Imagined Communities: Reflections on the Origin and Spread of Nationalism* (London: Verso, 1983); Ranajit Guha, ed., *A Subaltern Studies Reader, 1986–1995* (Minneapolis: University of Minnesota Press, 1997); Jim MacLaughlin, *Reimagining the Nation-State: The Contested Terrains of Nation-Building* (London: Pluto Press, 2001).

5. "An Agenda for Peace: Preventive Diplomacy, Peacemaking, and Peace-keeping," Report of the Secretary-General pursuant to the statement adopted by the Summit

Meeting of the Security Council on January 31, 1992, UN Doc A/47/277-S/24111, June 17, 1992, available at http://www.un.org/Docs/SG/agpeace.html, para. 55.

6. "Supplement to An Agenda for Peace," para. 49. From a UN development perspective, peacebuilding aims "to build and enable durable peace and sustainable development in post-conflict situations." See, e.g., "Role of UNDP in Crisis and Post-Conflict Situations," Policy Paper Distributed to the Executive Board of the United Nations Development Programme and of the United Nations Population Fund, DP/2001/4, UNDP, New York, November 27, 2000, available at http://www.undp.org, para. 51. The Development Assistance Committee of the Organisation for Economic Co-operation and Development (OECD) maintains that peacebuilding and reconciliation focuses "on long-term support to, and establishment of, viable political and socio-economic and cultural institutions capable of addressing the root causes of conflicts, as well as other initiatives aimed at creating the necessary conditions for sustained peace and stability": OECD, *Helping Prevent Violent Conflict, Development Assistance Committee Guidelines* (Paris: OECD, 2001), available at http://www.oecd.org, 86.

7. Elizabeth M. Cousens, "Introduction," in *Peacebuilding as Politics*, eds. Elizabeth M. Cousens and Chetan Kumar, A Project of the International Peace Academy (Boulder, Colo.: Lynne Rienner, 2001), 5–10.

8. See "Strengthening of the United Nations: An Agenda for Further Change," UN Doc A/57/150, September 9, 2002, para. 126: "To strengthen further the Secretariat's work in international peace and security, there is a need to bring a sharper definition to the existing lead department policy, which sets out the relationship between the Department of Political Affairs and the Department of Peacekeeping Operations. The Department of Political Affairs will increase its focus in the fields of preventive diplomacy, conflict prevention and peacemaking. The Department will also intensify its engagement in policy formulation across the full spectrum of the Secretariat's tasks in the domain of international peace and security. It will continue to be the lead department for political and peace-building offices in the field. The Department of Peacekeeping Operations will be the lead department for the planning and management of all peace and security operations in the field, including those in which the majority of personnel are civilians."

9. GA Res 60/180 (2005), para. 2(a).

10. See, e.g., Richard Caplan, *International Governance of War-Torn Territories: Rule and Reconstruction* (Oxford: Oxford University Press, 2005); Roland Paris, *At War's End: Building Peace after Civil Conflict* (Cambridge: Cambridge University Press, 2004).

11. See further Simon Chesterman, "Ownership in Theory and in Practice: Transfer of Authority in UN State-Building Operations," *Journal of Intervention and State-Building* 1, no. 1 (2007).

12. Nicholas Wood, "Serbs Criticize UN Mediator, Further Bogging Down Kosovo Talks," *New York Times*, September 2, 2006.

13. International Crisis Group, "Bosnia: Reshaping the International Machinery" (Sarajevo/Brussels, November 29, 2001), available at http://www.crisisgroup.org,13.

14. See further Chesterman, "Ownership."

15. Michael W. Doyle, "War-Making and Peace-Making: The United Nations' Post-Cold War Record," in *Turbulent Peace: The Challenges of Managing International Conflict*, eds. Chester A. Crocker, Fen Osler Hampson, and Pamela Aall (Washington, D.C.: U.S. Institute of Peace Press, 2001), 546.

16. Eric Schmitt, "Pentagon Contradicts General on Iraq Occupation Force's Size," *New York Times*, February 28, 2003.

17. UN envoy James Baker is said to have been asked once by Polisario representatives why the United Nations was treating Western Sahara differently from East Timor. He replied to the effect that if the Sahrawis wanted to be treated like the Timorese, they had best go find themselves an Australia to lead a military action on their behalf.

18. Paul Krugman, "The Martial Plan," *New York Times*, February 21, 2003; James G. Lakely, "Levin Criticizes Budget for Afghanistan; Says White House Isn't Devoting Enough to Rebuilding," *Washington Times*, February 26, 2003. Aid was later increased further: David Rohde, "US Said to Plan Bigger Afghan Effort, Stepping Up Aid," *New York Times*, August 25, 2003.

19. See, e.g., International Crisis Group, "Bosnia's Precarious Economy: Still Not Open for Business" (Sarajevo/Brussels, August 7, 2001), available at http://www.crisisgroup.org.

20. Scott Shane and Raymond Bonner, "Annan Nudges Donors to Make Good on Full Pledges," *New York Times*, January 7, 2005.

21. "Report of the Independent Inquiry into the Actions of the United Nations during the 1994 Genocide in Rwanda," UN Doc S/1999/1257, December 15, 1999, available at http://www.un.org/Docs/journal/asp/ws.asp?m=S/1999/1257, 51; "Report of the Panel on United Nations Peace Operations" (Brahimi Report), UN Doc A/55/3-05-S/2000/809, August 21, 2000, available at http://www.un.org/peace/reports/peace_operations, para. 62.

22. Brahimi Report, para. 59.

23. International Commission on Intervention and State Sovereignty, *The Responsibility to Protect* (Ottawa: International Development Research Centre, December 2001), available at http://www.iciss.ca, paras. 2.32, 5.1–5.6.

24. See James Dobbins et al., *America's Role in Nation-Building: From Germany to Iraq* (Santa Monica, Calif.: RAND, 2003), 160–166.

25. See generally Shepard Forman and Stewart Patrick, eds., *Good Intentions: Pledges of Aid for Postconflict Recovery* (Boulder, Colo.: Lynne Rienner, 2000).

26. Brahimi Report, paras. 9–83.

27. See note 5.

28. "Achieving the Health Millennium Development Goals in Fragile States," High-Level Forum on the Health MDGs, Abuja December 2004, available at http://www.hlfhealthmdgs.org/Documents/FragileStates.pdf, 21.

29. "A More Secure World: Our Shared Responsibility," Report of the High-Level Panel on Threats, Challenges, and Change, UN Doc A/59/565, December 1, 2004, available at http://www.un.org/secureworld, para. 38.

30. Ibid., paras. 261–265.

31. Ibid., paras. 264–265.

32. Ibid., paras. 266–267.

33. "In Larger Freedom: Towards Development, Security, and Human Rights for All," UN Doc A/59/2005, March 21, 2005, available at http://www.un.org/largerfreedom, para. 115.

34. Ibid., para. 115.

35. "2005 World Summit Outcome Document," UN Doc A/RES/60/1, September 16, 2005, available at http://www.un.org/summit2005, para. 98.

36. "High-Level Panel Report," paras. 98, 293–294.

37. "World Summit Outcome Document," paras. 56(f), 138.

38. "High-Level Panel Report," para. 264.

39. "In Larger Freedom," para. 115.

40. "World Summit Outcome Document," para. 98.

41. Ibid., para. 104.

42. GA Res 60/180 (December 30, 2005), paras. 1, 4.

43. Stewart Patrick, "The Donor Community and the Challenge of Postconflict Recovery," in *Good Intentions: Pledges of Aid for Postconflict Recovery*, eds. Shepard Forman and Stewart Patrick (Boulder, Colo.: Lynne Rienner, 2000), 40–41. In the absence of funds that can be disbursed quickly to a recovery process, significant external resources typically arrive only after such a conference, which brings donor states, UN agencies, and the international financial institutions together with local representatives to evaluate proposed reconstruction plans. The relative transparency of these meetings reduces the temptation of donors to free ride on the efforts of others. More subtly, by involving disparate actors in providing support for postconflict recovery as a form of public good, the pledging conference encourages the notion of a "donor community," bound by certain ethical obligations toward the recovering state. Pledging conferences also enable donors to shape and publicize recovery plans jointly, which may increase domestic support for foreign assistance as part of an international effort. For recipients, pledging conferences offer the opportunity to focus the minds of donors on a crisis and gain public assurances that some of their needs will be met. While these aspects are positive, pledging conferences often bear the trappings of political theater. Donors may make grand gestures that in reality double-count resources previously committed to a country or that cannot be delivered promptly. In addition, mediating different donor interests through a conference does not remove the problems caused by the inconsistency of those interests. Donors continue to avoid controversial areas like security sector reform, preferring to fund items that will gain recognition and prestige. Finally, despite the public nature of the pledges made, there is no consistent monitoring process to ensure that pledges are realistic and transparent.

44. See further Simon Chesterman, "From State Failure to State Building: Problems and Prospects of a United Nations Peacebuilding Commission," *Journal of International Law and International Relations* 2 (2006).

45. "No Exit Without Strategy: Security Council Decision-Making and the Closure or Transition of United Nations Peacekeeping Operations," Report of the Secretary General, UN Doc S/2001/394, April 20, 2001.

46. "Getting Ready for Statehood," *Economist* (London), April 13, 2002.

47. "UN Prepares to Start a New Peacekeeping Mission in East Timor," *New York Times*, June 14, 2006.

48. See, e.g., William Branigin, "UN Performance at Issue as Cambodian Vote Nears," *Washington Post*, May 20, 1993.

49. "A UN Success in Cambodia," *Washington Post*, June 18, 1993.

50. "Good governance" was an intentionally vague term that spoke less to the formal structures of government than how a state is governed. The term *governance* itself emerged within the development discourse in the 1990s as a means of expanding the prescriptions of donors to embrace not only projects and structural adjustment but government policies. Though intergovernmental organizations like the World Bank and the International Monetary Fund are technically constrained from referring to political processes as such, "governance" provides a convenient euphemism for precisely that. See, e.g., Goran Hyden, "Governance and the Reconstitution of Political Order," in *State, Conflict and Democracy in Africa*, ed. Richard Joseph (Boulder, Colo.: Lynne Rienner, 1999).

51. Kwame Anthony Appiah, *In My Father's House: Africa in the Philosophy of Culture* (New York: Oxford University Press, 1992), 266.

6

How Strategic Is UN Peacebuilding?

Nicholas Sambanis

Today United Nations peacekeeping is the multidimensional management of a complex peace operation, usually following the termination of a civil war, designed to provide interim security and assist parties to make those institutional, material, and ideational transformations that are essential to make peace sustainable. That is a new role for the UN. UN peace operations during the Cold War were more limited and focused on monitoring or policing the adherence to a truce by hostile parties.

This new, expanded role for the UN represents an effort to respond to complex new challenges to international security that emerged since the end of the Cold War. An explosion of new internal armed conflicts led to a similar explosion in UN peacekeeping missions in the mid-1990s. The new perspective on how to build sustainable peace after civil war is embodied in two landmark reports—the Brahimi and "No Exit without Strategy" Reports of 2000 and 2001, which built on Secretary General Boutros Boutros-Ghali's 1992 report *Agenda for Peace* and its 1995 *Supplement*. Although the UN has been generally effective in its new role, important and highly publicized failures have generated policy debates on how to improve their peacebuilding capacity.

This chapter engages with those policy debates by considering whether the UN peace missions are sufficiently strategic. Strategic peacebuilding is a concept best described by a set of complementary practices that are all aimed at achieving self-sustaining peace. Strategy is necessary because the desired goals of multidimensional peace operations are complex and extend beyond achieving the absence of armed conflict. Strategic peacebuilding involves a blend of several intervention practices, including mediation, observation, policing, tactical enforcement, conflict resolution, humanitarian assistance, reconstruction, and institutional transformation—all helping create sustainable peace.

Much criticism of UN peace missions is based on a claim that peacebuilding goals are not sufficiently adaptive to local contexts and interventions by different actors sometimes have conflicting effects. Strategic peacebuilding should address those issues. Different intervention practices are interdependent in complex ways. Whereas one form of intervention may help shore up the foundations for another intervention strategy, the two together may work better, or in some cases, they may work well only if they are properly sequenced. Appropriate standards of peacebuilding success may also vary by context and the proximity to the war. If the goal of peacebuilding intervention is social justice and political inclusion, then best practices will be different than in cases where the goal of peacebuilding intervention is simply the absence of war.

For any conflict situation, "sustainable peace" is the best measure of successful peacekeeping. Successful and unsuccessful efforts to achieve that measure are influenced by three key factors that characterize the environment of the postwar civil peace: the degree of hostility of the factions, the extent of local capacities remaining after the war, and the amount of international assistance provided. Together, these three constitute the interdependent logic of a "peacebuilding triangle": the deeper the hostility, the more the destruction of local capacities, the more you need international assistance to succeed in establishing a stable peace. This chapter explains how each of those dimensions affects the nature of the postwar challenge and highlights the need to foster fast return to economic growth in postconflict societies to generate private incentives for peace.

The UN is not good at fighting wars, and the effects of UN peace missions are felt more with respect to what we might call participatory peace—a peace that includes not only the absence of war but also restoration of the state's sovereignty over all of its territory and some degree of political openness. Resolving problems of divided sovereignty is an essential part of state-building that the UN or other peacebuilding actors cannot afford to ignore. UN missions can have positive and lasting effects by keeping the peace in the early stages of the peace process, when risks of a return to war are greatest. They can also have lasting effects if they help set the foundations for political institutions that sustain the peace in the long run. Over time, however, economic growth and development are the critical determinants of a low risk of return to civil war. The peacebuilding literature has not yet identified lessons or best practices to facilitate a closer connection between UN peacekeeping and strategies for postwar economic reconstruction and development. I address this issue by establishing the importance of postwar economic growth for sustainable peace and by considering some of the complexities that arise in trying to coordinate peacebuilding strategies.

Evolving Standards of Peace Interventions

In the early 1990s with the end of the Cold War, the UN agenda for peace and security rapidly expanded. At the request of the Security Council Summit of

January 1992, Secretary General Boutros-Ghali prepared the conceptual foundations of an ambitious UN role in peace and security in his seminal report, *An
Agenda for Peace*.[1] In addition to preventive diplomacy designed to head off conflicts before they became violent, the secretary general outlined the four interconnected roles that he hoped the UN would play in the post–Cold War international
politics: peace enforcement, peacemaking, peacekeeping, and postconflict reconstruction.[2] Together, these strategies would offer the muscle, diplomacy, and
technical expertise necessary for rebuilding peace after civil war.

An *Agenda for Peace* was the culmination of an evolution of UN doctrine and
suggests a role for the organization that is very different from the one initially
envisaged in first-generation peacekeeping, where blue helmets would simply
be interposed between forces after a truce had been reached and the UN's role
was designed more to contain conflicts from spreading to other countries than
to transform societies so that new conflicts within those societies would be less
likely to occur.[3]

The best peacekeeping practices of impartiality and neutrality were developed with the old model in mind, and new, more flexible ways of interacting
with the parties became necessary as peacebuilding roles evolved. *Impartiality*
and *neutrality* are frequently used interchangeably. Scholars and practitioners
often speak of peacekeepers as "neutral," "disinterested," "impartial," or "unbiased"; they tend to mistake the need for impartiality with a policy of "strict
neutrality" and a disposition of passivity. *Neutrality* should instead be defined
as a synonym for noninterference with respect to peacekeeping outcomes
and *impartiality* as equal enforcement of unbiased rules. It is as important for
peacekeepers to be impartial concerning, for example, which party in a freely
conducted democratic election wins the election as it is for them to be nonneu-
tral (i.e., not passive) with respect to violations of the peace and obstructions to
their ability to implement their mandate.

This is closely related to the interpretation of another key principle of UN
peacekeeping—the nonuse of force. Peacekeeping uses soldiers not to win
wars but to preserve the peace. Peacekeepers must also be able to protect their
right to discharge their functions, in accordance with the spirit of the parties'
initial consent. Emphatic avoidance of the use of force can only limit the peacekeepers' impact on the ground. But use of force must be limited to protect a
mandate authorized by a peace treaty or ceasefire (as happened in Cyprus in
1974, or Namibia in 1989). If peacekeepers find that their role is turning to
war-fighting, then the limits of UN involvement have likely been reached, and
the peacekeepers must withdraw.

Beyond monitoring and interposition of forces, the key strategy of UN missions today is to foster economic and social cooperation with the purpose of
building confidence among previously warring parties. The UN can do this by
helping develop the social, political, and economic infrastructure that is necessary to prevent future violence. This multidimensional peacekeeping is aimed
at capacities expansion (mainly through economic reconstruction) and institutional transformation (for example, reform of the police, army, and judicial
system, elections, civil society rebuilding).

The UN has a commendable record of success, ranging from mixed to transformative, in multidimensional peace operations as diverse as those in Namibia, El Salvador, Cambodia, Mozambique, and Eastern Slavonia.[4] The UN role in helping settle those conflicts has been fourfold. It served as a peacemaker, facilitating a peace treaty among the parties; as a peacekeeper, monitoring the cantonment and demobilization of military forces, resettling refugees, and supervising transitional civilian authorities; as a peacebuilder, monitoring and in some cases organizing the implementation of human rights, national democratic elections, and economic rehabilitation; and in a very limited way as peace enforcer when the agreements came unstuck.

The rationale behind these operations is that the roots of the conflict must be addressed to build foundations for stable, legitimate government. This is not the only way to peace, however. A lesson learned—or at least suggested— by recent literature on civil war is that large-scale armed conflict can be prevented effectively by boosting the government's counterinsurgency capacity.[5] If rebellion is not feasible, then peace can be achieved. Possibly the cost to such a strategy is the perpetuation of repressive regimes, and this understanding of peace is antithetical to the standards currently used by the United Nations and other international agencies involved in peacebuilding.

What Constitutes a Peacebuilding Success?

Peace can be thought of as a continuum, ranging from no peace (war) to negative peace (absence of war) to social harmony.[6] Social harmony is an elusive goal for most societies. What standard of peace should be the goal for societies emerging from civil war? Michael Doyle and I in our joint work have argued that negative peace does not reflect what is needed for peace to be self-sustaining in troubled societies. Rather, we propose a standard of participatory peace that combines the absence of war with an end to lower level violence and mass human rights violations, restoration of sovereignty of the state, and a modest standard of political openness.[7]

By this definition, peacebuilding success is not very common. In the post-1945 period, there have been eighty-four failures and thirty-seven successes of *participatory peace* two years after the end of a civil war.

Participatory peace is meaningful if it can be sustained after the peacekeepers leave. This corresponds with extensive discussions in the United Nations Security Council in which "sustainable peace" was proposed as the ultimate purpose of all peace operations, and *sustainability* was defined as the capacity for a sovereign state to resolve the natural conflicts to which all societies are prone by means other than war (S/2001/394). "Peacebuilding," the report noted, "is an attempt, after a peace has been negotiated or imposed, to address the sources of present hostility and build local capacities for conflict resolution." Thus, for example, few observers think that peace has been successfully built in Kosovo today, even though Kosovo is not at war. NATO forces militarily separate the resident Kosovars and

Serbs and deter both a potential attack from Belgrade to reunify the breakaway province and a potential declaration of formal independence by the Kosovars.

How Can Participatory Peace Be Achieved?

In *Making War and Building Peace,* Michael Doyle and I evaluate the conditions under which participatory peace can be attained in the short term—two to five years after the end of a civil war. We propose a simple model in which peacebuilding outcomes are shaped by three dimensions—local capacities, postwar hostility, and international capacities. The deeper the hostility and the lower the local capacities for peace, the easier it is for war to resume and the more extensive the need for international capacities for peace. To test our model empirically, we use a number of measures for these three dimensions, drawing on common sense and the literature on civil war for possible measures.

Hostility is measured by the number of deaths and displacements, the number of factions, the signing of a peace treaty, the type of war (distinguishing ethnoreligious wars from all others), the level of ethnic fractionalization, and war duration.[8] Ethnoreligious wars, high ethnic fractionalization, absence of a peace treaty, many factions, long wars, and high numbers of deaths and displacements should all make peacebuilding harder.

We measure local capacities with country-level indicators of socioeconomic development, such as electricity consumption per capita, real per capita income, and the annual rate of change in real per capita income.[9] Higher levels of economic development should increase the likelihood of peacebuilding success because they provide private incentives for people to keep the peace. We also measure the degree of an economy's dependence on natural resources. Heavy reliance on natural resources reduces the likelihood of peacebuilding success because it makes the economy more susceptible to external price shocks and because resource-rich economies have been associated with corrupt political institutions.[10] Local capacities are measures of institutional quality and of the economic opportunity costs of returning to war: higher capacities imply higher opportunity costs and better institutions, hence, a better chance of building peace.

The most important measure of international capacities for our study is the presence and mandate of UN peace operations. Mandates measure the mission's strength, its technical and military capabilities, and the level of international commitment. Mandates are classified into observer missions (in which civilian officials or military officers monitor a truce or treaty), traditional peacekeeping (in which formed military units monitor a truce or treaty), multidimensional peacekeeping (in which a peace treaty authorizes international civilian officials and military units to help build or rebuild political, economic, and social institutions), and enforcement missions with or without transitional administration (in which, in the absence of consent, international military forces intervene to impose peace). We can also capture all UN missions with a binary variable denoting any UN intervention and also separate facilitative missions that basically offer monitoring and reporting (observer and traditional peacekeeping operations [PKOs]) from transformational UN missions that have a more intrusive mandate (multidimensional and enforcement). Another distinction could be between consent-based missions authorized under Chapter VI of the UN Charter and enforcement missions.

Another obvious measure of international capacities is foreign economic assistance. Measuring the amount of economic assistance available to all countries from all sources (bilateral, nongovernmental organization [NGO], multilateral) is too difficult, so we use instead the amount of net current transfers per capita to the balance of payments of the country.

The results for the short-term participatory peace model are presented in detail elsewhere (see Doyle and Sambanis, 2006). Briefly, the data lend support to the model, and we find evidence for the expected relationships between participatory peace and the explanatory variables mentioned, though not all results are equally robust. Table 6.1 summarizes those results by presenting estimates of changes to the probability of success in participatory peace in the short run as a result of changes in each of the explanatory variables in the model. Table 6.1 gives a sense of the relative importance of each explanatory variable. The one result we found to be very robust is that UN missions are extremely important for participatory peacebuilding in the short run.

The importance of the UN diminishes as we turn to narrower concepts of peacebuilding, such as the absence of war. I present some of these results in a later section, where I also turn to the longer term effects of UN missions. First, I return to the question of whether UN missions are sufficiently strategic.

TABLE 6.1. Estimates of Changes to the Probability of Peacebuilding Success Two Years after the End of the War in the Doyle-Sambanis Model of Participatory Peace as a Result of Changes to the Explanatory Variables

Mean change in the probability of success	95% Confidence interval	As a result of the following change
−0.364	−0.563 to −0.157	*War type* (from nonethnic to ethnic)
−0.074	−0.151 to −0.013	*Deaths amd displacements* (from 40th to 60th percentile)
−0.103	−0.212 to −0.024	*Number of factions* (from 3 to 4)
0.0066	0.0023 to 0.0121	*Net current transfers* (from 40th to 60th percentile)
0.359	0.093 to 0.554	*UN mandate* (from facilitative to transformational)
0.324	0.03 to 0.61	*Treaty* (from 0 to 1)
0.012	−0.002 to 0.028	*Development level* (from 40th to 60th percentile)
−0.05	−0.083 to −0.018	*Primary commodity dependence* (from 40th to 60th percentile)

Strategic Peacekeeping

The extent to which root causes can be addressed adequately depends on available resources and on the design of an appropriate mandate. Does the UN have the capacity, internal coherence, and resources needed to field sufficiently strategic peacekeeping missions?

The first concern of strategic peacekeeping is to properly identify the type of conflict underlying the civil war so as to design appropriate intervention strategies. Political scientists have explored a wide range of theories about why and how parties enter into and resolve various kinds of conflicts. At the more abstract level, "neoliberal" theories explore conflicts among rational actors over absolute goods valued for their own sakes. "Neorealists" examine conflicts among rational actors that raise issues of security and relative gains, based on the assumption that relative power (dominance) alone provides security and therefore the gains that truly matter. "Constructivists" relax the assumption that perceived identities and interests are fixed and explore the circumstances in which conflicts and social relations more generally constitute and then reshape identities and interests.[11] Aspects of each of these factors can be found in the peacekeeping record that Doyle and I examined in our joint research. Factions and their leaders seek absolute advantages as well as relative advantages. Sometimes, international actors assist the peace process by eliminating old actors (war criminals, factional armies), introducing new actors (domestic voters, political parties, international monitors, NGOs), fostering changes of identity (reconciliation), or by all three methods together. A more informative analytic lens portrays the peace process through two classic game situations, coordination and cooperation, each of which incorporates neoliberal, neorealist and constructivist dynamics.

Thus, to simplify, conflicts can be over coordination or cooperation, depending on the structure of the parties' preferences over possible outcomes of the negotiations. Each preference structure characterizes a specific type of conflict, and different intervention strategies are optimal for different conflict types. Some conflicts are mixed, reflecting elements of both, and conflicts do change over time, evolving from one to the other and sometimes back again.[12] Well-chosen strategies can maximize the available space for peace, whereas strategies that are poorly matched to the conflict at a particular time can reduce the space for peace.

Basic game theory has clearly established that coordination problems have a payoff structure that gives the parties no incentives to violate agreements.[13] The best strategy to resolve coordination problems is information provision and improvement of the level of communication between the parties.[14] Communication gives the parties the ability to form common conjectures about the likely outcomes of their actions.[15] By contrast, cooperation problems create incentives to renege on agreements, particularly if the parties discount the benefits of long-term cooperation in favor of short-run gain. In one-shot games of cooperation (of which the prisoner's dilemma is a well-known example), the parties will try to trick their adversaries into cooperating while they renege on their promises. These structural differences between cooperation and coordination problems imply that different peacekeeping strategies should be used in each case.

Figure 6.1 suggests that different strategies are needed to resolve different types of problems. Transformational peacekeeping or enforcement with considerable international authority are needed to resolve cooperation problems, whereas facilitative peacekeeping, such as monitoring and interposition of troops are sufficient to resolve coordination problems. Facilitative peacekeeping has no enforcement or deterrence function. Transformational peacekeeping can increase the costs of noncooperation for the parties and provide positive inducements by helping rebuild the country and restructure institutions so that they can support the peace. Enforcement may be necessary to resolve the toughest cooperation problems.[16] Not all civil war transitions are plagued by cooperation problems. Some wars resemble coordination issues, whereas frequently, we find both types of problems, in which case intervention strategies must be carefully combined or sequenced.

How can peacekeeping have an impact? The literature suggests that peacekeepers can change the costs and benefits of cooperation by virtue of the legitimacy of their UN mandate, which induces the parties to cooperate; by their ability to focus international attention on noncooperative parties and condemn transgressions; by monitoring and reporting on the parties' compliance with agreements; and by their function as a trip-wire that would force aggressors to go through the UN troops to change the military status quo.

Ultimate success, however, may depend less on changing incentives for existing parties within their preferences and more on transforming preferences —and even the parties themselves—and thus turning a cooperation problem into a coordination problem. The institution-building aspects of peacekeeping are therefore a revolutionary transformation in which voters and politicians replace soldiers and generals; armies become parties; war economies become peace economies. Reconciliation, when achieved, is a label for these changed preferences and capacities.[17]

| | Peacekeeping Strategy | |
	Facilitation	Transformation
Cooperation Problems	Ineffective/ Counterproductive	Best
Coordination Problems	Best	Inefficient

FIGURE 6.1. Matching Problem Type and Strategy Type.

To be sure, the difficulty of a transformative strategy cannot be overestimated. Most societies even after war look a great deal like they did prewar. But, for example, if those that have committed the worst war crimes can be prosecuted, locked up, and thus removed from power, the prospects of peace rise. The various factions can begin to individualize rather than collectivize their distrust and hostility, and at the minimum, the worst individuals are no longer in control.[18] Here, initiatives that foster hybrid (local-national-international) institutions can have an important effect by engaging local actors in the peacebuilding process and ensuring that reforms are not imposed top-down.[19]

Even where enforcement is used at the outset, the peace must eventually become self-sustaining. Consensual peace agreements can rapidly erode, forcing all the parties to adjust to the strategies of "spoilers." Their success or lack of success of doing so tends to be decisive in whether a sustainable peace follows.

How can the peacekeepers know what type of conflict they are facing? A first clue is the peace treaty. If a treaty has been signed that outlines a postwar settlement, then the parties' preferences have been revealed to some extent (though the fact that some peace treaties are quickly undermined also means that only by observing the parties' compliance with the treaty can we be more certain about their true preferences). Patterns of compliance with the treaty can help distinguish moderates from extremists. In other cases, such knowledge cannot be attained until the first (or several) encounters with the parties. Where a treaty is not in place, all parties can be assumed to be spoilers, and strong peacekeeping must be used. Subsequent cooperation or conflict with the peacekeepers can help distinguish those parties who respond to inducements from those who are committed to a strategy of war. This also means that UN missions must be flexible to adjust their mandate given observations of cooperation or conflict on the ground and based on the peacekeepers' changing assessments about the nature of the conflict.

A treaty is usually the outcome of a "mutually hurting stalemate," which is a necessary (but not sufficient) condition for successful peace.[20] Such a stalemate exists when the status quo is not the preferred option for any faction, while overturning the status quo through military action is unlikely to be successful. This condition pushes parties to the negotiating table, and their declared preferences for peace are more credible as a result of their inability to forcibly achieve a better outcome.[21]

However, the parties will not negotiate a settlement unless peace is likely to generate higher rewards than continued fighting. This condition becomes unattainable if "spoilers" are present. Spoilers are leaders or parties whose vital interests are threatened by peace implementation.[22] These parties will undermine the agreement and reduce the expected utility of a negotiated settlement for all parties. In terms of our previous arguments, the presence of spoilers implies the "payoff structure" of a prisoner's dilemma or assurance game because spoilers will not coordinate their strategies with moderates. Thus, if spoilers are present in a peace process, peacekeepers can only keep the peace if they can exercise some degree of enforcement by targeting the spoilers and preventing them from undermining the negotiations. The dynamics of spoiler problems deserve a closer look.

Spoiler problems were first systematically analyzed by Stephen Stedman, who identified three types—total, greedy, and limited—according to their strategies and likely impact on the peace implementation process. These are behavioral types, and Stedman defines them in terms of their preferences over the strategies they use to undermine the peace. However, all parties can act as total spoilers if conditions deteriorate markedly. Parties whose ultimate goals over the outcomes of the peace are more moderate will have incentives not to spoil the peace process if they can get a reasonable outcome. The difficulty facing the peacekeepers is to distinguish moderates from extremists, or total spoilers, when conditions are such as to encourage all parties to defect from agreements.

The principal gain of good UN peacekeeping will be to allow moderates—limited spoilers with specific stakes—and greedy opportunists to act like peace-makers in the peace process without fearing reprisals from total spoilers, who are unalterably opposed to the peace settlement. Effective strategies must combine consent from those willing to coordinate and cooperate with coercive carrots and sticks directed at those who are not. The empirical record suggests that strategically combining peacemaking, peacekeeping, reconstruction, and enforcement is a valuable way the UN and other international organizations can help shore up the foundations of a lasting peace.

To have such a positive effect, getting the mandate right is critically important for any UN mission. It is not sufficient for the UN to send large numbers of troops to the field, if those troops are not given the rules of engagement and mandate to make peace. The number of peacekeeping troops alone is not a good predictor of peacebuilding success.[23] We show in our supplement that there is no statistically significant difference in the number of peacekeeping troops per square kilometer in transformational missions compared with facilitative missions. Thus, it is not the case that transformational peacekeeping works better because there is more concentrated force.[24] This also indicates that the Security Council often underfunds and underresources transformational missions because they should, on average, have more troops to deal with more difficult peacebuilding ecologies.

Moreover, the effects of peacekeeping troops per square kilometer on the probability of participatory peace success are negative (though nonsignificant).[25] This might seem jarring, but it is actually consistent with our theory. A large troop deployment with a weak mandate is a sure sign of lack of commitment by the Security Council and creates an impediment for effective intervention. This result is influenced by one observation—Rwanda—where there was a large troop deployment (in per capita terms) with no authority to intervene to stop the violence. Large numbers of troops per capita in monitoring missions (observer missions and traditional PKOs) actually *reduce* the chance of peace-building success (examples are Cyprus, Lebanon, Rwanda). Such deployments are inefficient and potentially counterproductive. The large troop deployment with a narrow mandate in monitoring operations indicates, on one hand, that the Security Council recognizes the severity of the conflict and, on the other hand, that it is unwilling or unable to give those troops an adequate mandate to resolve the conflict. Thus, there is often a mismatch between the problem and the treatment—better targeted mandates should improve the effectiveness of UN missions. There is room for improvement in the design of strategic missions in the UN.

Related to this discussion is the empirical result, reported in Doyle and Sambanis (2006), that observer missions have been more effective than traditional peacekeeping. Traditional peacekeeping is used in cases that are not as ripe for resolution as those where the UN dispatches monitors to verify the implementation of a peace agreement. But the effectiveness of observer missions is not enough to suggest that the UN is good at detecting a "coordination type" of problem. Many of the cases where traditional peacekeeping is used are too complex and the conflict remains unresolved. The mismatch between the underlying peacebuilding ecology and the type of treatment in the cases where traditional peacekeeping is used might suggest an inability to fully assess the factions' preferences, or it might indicate that in many cases there is just not sufficient political will to address difficult peacebuilding challenges.

Indeed, if we look at the average levels of the explanatory variables in Doyle and Sambanis that have a negative effect on the probability of peacebuilding success (ethnic war, deaths and displacements, primary commodity exports), we see that they are higher in cases where traditional peacekeeping was used as compared to cases where observer missions were used. By contrast, the averages of variables that have a positive influence on peacebuilding (transfers and development level) are lower. Hence, the cases where traditional peacekeeping was used were harder to resolve, but the type of UN "treatment" was not much different. This could help explain the higher failure rate of traditional peacekeeping.

At the same time, there is no clear evidence that the peacebuilding ecology is harder in cases where transformational UN peacekeeping is used. On the one hand, transformational UN missions are sent less frequently to ethnic wars, more frequently to cases where there is a peace treaty, and more frequently to countries where primary commodity exports are a smaller percentage of the economy. This might explain the higher success rate of those missions. On the other hand, transformational UN peacekeeping is used more in cases with higher levels of deaths and displacements, more factions, and much lower levels of economic development levels and net current transfers, all of which should lower the probability of peacebuilding success. Thus, what we see is that the peacebuilding ecology does not differ markedly in cases where facilitative as opposed to transformational peacekeeping is used, which points to an absence of clear strategy in the design of UN peace missions.[26]

UN responses are not always well calibrated to peacebuilding challenges. The UN seems to respond with the right mandate in those cases where it dispatches monitors and where it sends transformational UN peacekeeping missions, but in some of the cases where it may be using the wrong mix of resources and mandate, it dispatches traditional peacekeeping missions. Or, more plausibly, traditional peacekeeping in the context of civil wars is a stop-gap measure, sent to help contain or moderate but not cure a conflict. When the great powers and the Security Council are not prepared to confront the true dimensions of a conflict and send an enforcement mission, lightly armed peacekeepers are too often sent to places such as the former Yugoslavia where, in the words of one UN official, "there is no peace to keep."[27]

How Can the UN Be More Strategic?

Effective transitional strategy must take into account levels of hostility and factional capacities. Whether it in fact does so depends on strategic design and international commitment. Designs for transitions incorporate a mix of legal and bureaucratic capacities that integrate in a variety of ways domestic and international commitments.

Important lessons can already be drawn from efforts to establish effective transitional authority.[28] First, a holistic approach is necessary to deal with the character of factional conflicts and civil wars. Successful exercises of authority require a coordinated approach that draws in elements of "peacemaking" (negotiations), peacekeeping (monitoring), peacebuilding, reconstruction, and discrete acts of enforcement, when needed, to create a holistic strategy of reconciliation.[29]

Transitional strategies should first address the local causes of continuing conflict and, second, the local capacities for change. Effective transitional authority is the residual dimension that compensates for local deficiencies and the continuing hostility of the factions—the (net) specific degree of international commitment available to assist change.

Local root causes, domestic capacity, and effective transitional authority are three dimensions of a triangle whose area is the "political space"—or effective capacity—for building peace. This metaphor suggests that some quantum of positive support is needed along each dimension but that the dimensions also substitute for each other—more of one substitutes for less of another, less deeply rooted causes of war substitute for weak local capacity or minor international commitment. In a world where each dimension is finite, we can expect, first, that compromises will be necessary to achieve peacekeeping; second, that the international role must be designed to fit each case; and, third, that self-sustaining peace is not only the right aim, it is the practically necessary aim of building peace when the international community is not prepared to commit to long-term assistance.

International peace operation mandates must take into account the characteristics of the factions and whether the parties are prepared to coordinate or must be persuaded or coerced into cooperation. These mandates operate not on stable states but, instead, on unstable factions. These factions (to simplify) come in various dimensions of hostility. Hostility, in turn, is shaped by the number of factions, including the recognized state as one (if there is one). Numerous factions make it difficult for them to cooperate and engender suspicion. In addition, few or many factions complicate both coordination and cooperation. In addition, harm done—casualties and refugees generated—creates the resentment that makes jointly beneficial solutions to coordination and cooperation more difficult to envisage. The more hostile and numerous the factions, the more difficult the peace process will be, and the more international assistance/authority will be needed if peace is to be established.

In less hostile circumstances (with few factions, a hurting stalemate, or less harm done), international monitoring and facilitation might be sufficient to establish transparent trust and self-enforcing peace. Monitoring helps create transparency among partners lacking trust but having compatible incentives favoring peace. Traditional peacekeeping assistance can also reduce trade-offs (for example, helping fund and certify the cantonment, demobilization, and reintegration of former combatants). In these circumstances—with few players, some reconciliation, less damage—international coordination and assistance can be sufficient to overcome hostility and solve implementation problems. An international peacekeeping presence itself can deter defections from the peace treaty, because of the possible costs of violating international agreements and triggering further international involvement in an otherwise domestic conflict. International capacity-building—such as foreign aid, demobilization of military forces, institutional reform—will assist parties that favor the peace to meet their commitments.

In more hostile circumstances, international enforcement can help solve commitment and cooperation problems by directly implementing or raising the costs of defection from peace agreements. International enforcement and long-term trusteeship will be required to overcome deep sources of distrust and powerful incentives to defect from agreed provisions of the peace. As in other conflict-cooperation situations, such as prisoner's dilemma and mixed motive games,[30] the existence of deeply hostile or many factions (or factions that lack coherent leadership) complicate the problem of achieving self-enforcing cooperative peace. Instead, conscious direction and enforcement by an impartial international agent to guarantee the functions of effective sovereignty become necessary, and peacekeepers must include activities such as conducting free and fair elections, arresting war criminals, and policing and administering a collapsed state. The more difficult it is for the factions to cooperate, the greater the international authority and capacity the international peacekeepers must wield. In addition to substantial bodies of troops, extensive budgets for political reconstruction and substantial international authority need to be brought to bear because the parties are unlikely to trust each other and cooperate. International mandates may need to run from monitoring to administration to executive authority and full sovereign trusteeship like supervision if peace is going to be maintained and become eventually self-sustaining.

War-torn countries also vary in economic and social capacity. Some started out with considerable economic development (the former Yugoslavia) and retain levels of social capacity in an educated population. Others began poor and the war impoverished them further (Angola, Sudan, Cambodia). For both types of cases, reconstruction is vital; the more the social and economic devastation, the larger the multidimensional international role must become, whether consent-based multidimensional peacekeeping or nonconsent enforcement followed by and including multidimensional peacekeeping. International economic relief and productive jobs are the first signs of peace that can persuade rival factions to truly disarm and take a chance on peaceful politics. Institutions need to be rebuilt, including a unified army and police force and the even more challenging development of a school system that can assist the reconciliation of future generations. In countries with low levels of local capacities, competition over resources will be intense at the early stages of the peace process, and this can further intensify the coordination and collaboration problems that the peacekeepers will be asked to resolve.

There should therefore be a relation between the depth of hostility (harm and factions) and local capacities (institutional and economic collapse), on one hand, and the extent of international assistance and effective authority, from monitoring to enforcing, needed to build peace on the other hand. In a world where each dimension is finite, we can expect, first, that compromises will be necessary to achieve peacekeeping success and, second, that the international role will be significant in general and successful when it is designed to fit the case. The extent of transitional authority that needs to be delegated to the international community will be a function of the level of postwar hostility and local capacities.

The relations among the three dimensions of this peacebuilding triangle are complicated. The availability and prospect of international assistance and the existence of extensive local capacities, for example, can, if poorly managed, both raise the gains from victory (spoils of war and rebuilding assistance) and reduce the costs of fighting (as the assistance serves to sustain the fighting). Deep war-related hostilities can also have dual effects. They increase rational incentives to end the conflict but make peace harder to achieve.

Two Important Problems with Current Approaches to Peacebuilding

Recent policy debates on UN peacebuilding have highlighted two possible weaknesses in current approaches. The first weakness has to do with the UN's promotion of democratic solutions to conflicts. Multiparty democracy may work well in some contexts and poorly in others. The second weakness is less about the goals and more about the operational implementation of peacebuilding interventions, which are often poorly coordinated with other peacebuilding activities occurring alongside UN intervention. I take up these issues briefly but do not resolve the debates, as there is inadequate evidence for an adjudication of the different perspectives.

Too Much Emphasis on Democratization?

In recent years, the UN's capacity to organize and hold elections in post–civil war states has increased dramatically, and political liberalization has been a component of most multidimensional missions. There is a lot of criticism of that approach in the literature, with most opposition concentrating on the question of the timing of elections, arguing that elections should be held only after political institutions have matured. There are several cases that illustrate the risks associated with moving to multiparty democracy in countries with weak political institutions. Bruce Jones makes a convincing argument that pressure to transition to multiparty democracy in Rwanda was one of the key reasons behind conflict escalation and contributed to the genocide. Jack Snyder argues similarly that multiparty transition in Burundi had negative effects by encouraging conflict among warlords.[31] Roland Paris argues along the same lines that liberalization—economic or political—may be too ambitious a standard for most states emerging from civil war and, if we were to use such an ambitious standard, most UN peace missions would be judged to be failures.[32]

Although the dangers highlighted by these studies seem well founded, there are few (if any) alternatives that seem clearly more viable and less conflict-inducing than a strategy of promoting elections. Most casual observers of the news from Iraq will remember the strong local opposition to the delays in handing over sovereignty of that country to Iraqis after the U.S. invasion in 2003. Getting the people to vote peacefully and express their political voice is a peacebuilding goal and sign of progress in its own right.[33] Simply waiting will not necessarily create the political and civil structures that critics of elections argue are necessary to avoid a hijacking of the political system by warlords and spoilers. The same dangers that can undermine elections can also undermine any other interim arrangement short of outright military occupation or the imposition of a repressive regime that can quell opposition. Elections are clearly better at offering more legitimate local solutions than interim governments that are controlled by outsiders.

Because democracy is usually seen as a relatively good long-term outcome in most cases, the question then becomes how might a society ruled by decree transition smoothly to democracy, how long will such a transition take, and at what cost? As far as I know, there are no satisfactory answers to these questions in the literature. No empirical study to date has shown unequivocally that elections have a negative *causal* effect on peace processes and that other political strategies that do not involve elections have a clearly superior outcome. One theoretically interesting alternative articulated by Michael Barnett—encouraging deliberation to build what he calls a "republican peace"—seems to suffer from the same problems as any democratization strategy because it assumes the willingness of local actors to cooperate.[34] One lesson that seems to be emerging from the literature is that democratization is more likely to succeed if countries are integrated quickly in the international system by, for example, becoming members of other multilateral and regional organizations that have a high concentration of other democracies.[35] Democratic norms and networks can flourish more easily in such an environment.

Lack of Coordination of Peacebuilding Activities?

An argument frequently seen in the literature is that fragmented approaches to peacebuilding interventions by the international community create obstacles to successful peace transitions.[36] UN missions have not had the best record of strategic coordination with other actors.

There can be a number of causes of coordination failure: different parties are engaged in the mediation and the implementation phase of a peace agreement,[37] many actors with overlapping mandates or conflicting agendas are involved in the process,[38] diffuse intervention efforts generate spoiler problems. Bruce Jones's thoughtful assessment of these issues suggests that effective missions will be characterized by a continuity of actors, the use of the "friends mechanism" (i.e., the UN will be assisted by important regional actors interested in a positive outcome), and by coordination of international operations that avoids conflict or duplication of effort.

Creating an integrated mission is often easier said than done. Most studies on the topic seem to conclude that what is needed is an actor to take the lead and coordinate a committee of interested actors, each offering different expertise. The key challenge, therefore, would be to determine who that lead coordinator should be. One recommendation might be to assign that role to the party undertaking the most difficult task—the provision of security. Another recommendation might be to have the international financial institutions follow (rather than lead) in civil war transitions, with the World Bank and the International Monetary Fund pledging resources to countries that invite UN peacekeepers to create mutually reinforcing incentives for peacebuilding. The creation of the Peacebuilding Commission is a step in the right direction toward creating the capacity to better integrate UN missions. The General Assembly established the commission as an intergovernmental advisory body, and its membership reflects current debates about the need to include the largest contributors (of funds and troops) in decision making while also achieving a regional balance that is not always easy to achieve in the Security Council after several failed efforts at reform.

A related and even more difficult question is how different interventions should be sequenced: does security come first and everything else second? Does the economy come first? Or should all reforms be tried simultaneously? Although opinions on sequencing in the policy literature abound, there is to date no useful guide to answer these questions if we look for strong empirical evidence in support of a specific sequencing plan. Several rules of thumb exist, and some times they are conflicting because they are generalizations that derive from the experience of a single or a few cases. The generalizations run into problems when applied to different contexts. In light of the fact that the literature is not yet mature enough to provide definitive answers and the necessary data for such assessments are not available, I argue that a rule of thumb that seems commonsensical is that sequencing patterns should be different in difficult as opposed to easy peacebuilding ecologies. Where the factions are few, coherent, and reconciled, then extensive interventions that combine political reforms with reconstruction and development assistance can be implemented on the basis of a settlement while security is being provided by lightly armed peacekeepers. In harder ecologies, harder choices must be made, and political liberalization may have to be delayed to avoid sparking new conflict over the design of political institutions. In such cases, however, it is hard to see how progress can be made without a heavy footprint—security provision that is not limited to peacekeeping.

UN Missions' Impact on Long-Term War Avoidance

Much of the discussion up to this point has focused on a broad standard of peacebuilding success that does not privilege the absence of war over other considerations. This definition of peacebuilding is not uncontroversial. In some cases, this standard may be too high for what can reasonably be expected within a short period. In the long term, the effects of UN missions or other peacebuilding interventions may best be measured against a more modest standard—war avoidance.

How have UN missions fared against such a standard? We can get a sense of this by looking at a statistical analysis of the effects of the UN on peace duration. For such an analysis, I use a survival model, which estimates the "hazard" (or risk) of peace failure at time t given that the peace has not failed until that point. These models can account for what is called "right-censoring" in the statistical literature (the fact that a peace that has not failed up to the end of analysis time can fail in a subsequent period).[39] The dependent variable is peace duration, and I code it by measuring months at peace from the end of the war until either the peace fails or up to a censoring point, which in this case is the end of December 1999. Peace failure implies that a new civil war starts in the country and that that war is connected to the previous one.[40]

In the single-record, single-failure data set used previously, we have seventy-three peace failures with mean peace duration of fifty-three months. Failures cannot occur at time $t = 0$, but there are several failures of the peace in the first month. The model used earlier to study short-term peacebuilding can now be estimated differently to study long-term peacebuilding. Given its greater versatility, the Cox model is a better initial choice than the more frequently used Weibull model or other parametric hazard models.[41]

Model 1 in table 6.2 is the core model with controls added for real per capita income, the rate of growth of real per capita income at the end of the war, and the level of ethnic fractionalization. These three variables did not have a significant association to participatory peace in the short run, so they were excluded from table 6.2. Because I am now using a different concept of peacebuilding and there are several arguments in the literature that link those variables to civil war, I add them to the model.

TABLE 6.2. Duration Models of the Hazard of War Recurrence

	Model 1	Model 2	Model 3	Model 4
Ethnic war	1.14	0.996	0.95	1.12
	(0.31)	(0.27)	(0.29)	(0.31)
Dead and displaced (log)	1.14	*1.12*	1.13	**1.20**
	(0.065)	(0.070)	(0.077)	(0.08)
Number of Factions	1.04	1.06	1.06	1.01
	(0.099)	(0.08)	(0.085)	(0.07)
Net current transfers	0.999	0.999	0.999	0.999
	(9.18e-07)	(1.13e-06)	(1.22e-06)	(1.01e-06)
Ethnic fractionalization	**3.78**	**3.81**	**3.94**	**4.32**
	(1.88)	(1.98)	(2.11)	(2.32)
Electricity consumption	0.999	—	—	—
	(0.0002)	—	—	—
Real GDP growth	**0.96**	**0.96**	**0.96**	**0.96**
	(0.012)	(0.014)	(0.015)	(0.014)
Real GDP (log)	—	0.78	0.79	0.74
	—	(0.10)	(0.11)	(0.13)
Primary commodity exports/GDP	**3.52**	3.29	2.92	2.38
	(1.90)	(2.00)	(1.79)	(1.42)
Any UN intervention	**0.54**	—	—	—
	(0.16)	—	—	—
UN Chapter VI missions	—	**0.48**	**0.47**	**0.41**
	—	(0.17)	(0.18)	(0.16)
Negotiated settlement	—	**0.43**	**0.37**	**0.33**
	—	(0.17)	(0.14)	(0.13)
Military outcome	—	**0.54**	**0.50**	**0.38**
	—	(0.18)	(0.16)	(0.12)
40s peace start	—	—	—	0.22
	—	—	—	(0.197)
50s peace start	—	—	—	**3.37**
	—	—	—	(1.80)
60s peace start	—	—	—	1.30
	—	—	—	(0.50)
70s peace start	—	—	—	0.80
	—	—	—	(0.33)
80s peace start	—	—	—	0.57
	—	—	—	(0.33)
Time dependence (p)	—	—	0.62	—
	—	—	(0.055)	—
Observations	129	131	131	131
Number of failures	69	70	70	70
Log pseudo-likelihood	−267.95	−268.91	−182.74	−260.32
Wald χ^2 (d.f.)	73.73	102.88	108.93	154.32
	(9 d.f.)	(11 d.f.)	(11 d.f.)	(16 d.f.)

Note: Reported are hazard ratios and coefficient robust standard errors; bold indicates significance at the 0.05 level; italics indicate significance at the 0.05 level with one-tailed test.

UN intervention is significant ($p = 0.039$) and reduces the risk of peace failure by about 50 percent.[42] But the strongest result in this analysis, consistent with much of the literature on civil war onset, is that local capacities are critical in determining proneness to a new war outbreak. Local capacity variables now take away some of the effect of the hostility variables (only deaths and displacements is significant, and this is not very robust). Countries with higher levels of income, fast-growing postwar economies, and lower dependence on natural resource exports are far more likely to experience longer peace durations despite the negative effects of postwar hostility. The effects of variables like the number of factions or the nature of the war (was it ethnic or not?) are nonsignificant as we might expect any impact that they have to be limited to the immediate postwar period. High fractionalization has a significant ($p =$ 0.007) negative effect on peace duration, which lends support to the hypothesis about the difficulties of achieving long-lasting peace in fractionalized countries after civil war.

The results on local capacities are quite robust to small specification changes. By contrast, the effects of UN intervention are less robust. One problem is that UN enforcement missions seem to have negative effects on peace duration, probably due to the very challenging circumstances in which they are employed and because they are designed to end wars and not build long-lasting peace. Thus, in model 2, I use a variable that identifies only consent-based UN missions (I drop enforcement missions) and find that they are significant ($p = 0.044$) and have a positive effect on peace duration (the odds ratio in model 2 for Chapter VI missions is under 1, reducing the risk of peace failure by about 50 percent). This effect is not mitigated when I control for other variables, such as war outcomes (both negotiated settlements and military victories lead to longer peace durations than less decisive outcomes, such as truces or military stalemates). In model 2, I have also measured local capacities with the log of per capita real income measured before the start of the war to avoid confounding with other variables that measure wartime damage, such as deaths and displacements. Income is positively associated with longer peace durations ($p = 0.054$) and this is consistent with the results from the larger literature on civil war onset. A test of the proportional hazard (PH) assumption now shows that it is not satisfied in model 2. Reestimating the model using Weibull regression (model 3) produces substantively similar results and showed that the risk of war recurrence has negative duration dependence (i.e., peace becomes more stable as time passes). To account for the fact that exposure to the risk of peace failure is higher in countries where the war ended early in the analysis period, I added controls for the decade during which the peace process started (model 4). This marginally satisfied the PH assumption underlying the Cox model and improved some of the results and made deaths and displacements highly significant ($p = 0.008$).

These results highlight the importance of including economic rehabilitation in a peacebuilding mandate and dovetail with recent findings in the literature on civil war that demonstrate the power of these variables in influencing the risk of war onset. Scholars of civil war use income per capita as a measure of state strength, and it has been shown that heavy dependence on oil results in authoritarian state structures. Thus, the results may suggest that postwar authoritarianism and state weakness increase the risk of war recurrence. Consent-based UN missions have a positive impact, but this is overshadowed by local capacity variables. Thus, a war-prevention strategy for the UN in countries that are emerging from civil war should be to help build institutions that resist the corrupting pressures of resource-dependent economies and allow fast economic growth. The UN's impact in rebuilding institutions will be particularly important in ethnically divided societies that are at higher risk of a return to civil war.

This analysis is corroborated by a survival analysis using time-series cross-section data. I do not present that analysis here but summarize the results.[43] The presence of any UN mission increases the chances of long-lasting peace, and this is particularly true if we split the sample in a way that allows us to drop some of the early peace processes, when the UN had not yet developed sufficiently multidimensional approaches to peacebuilding. I find evidence that the UN has actually become better at peacekeeping over time, because by dropping cases with peace durations longer than ten years, I find that the significance of the UN variable improves.

To explore further the lasting influence of UN operations, I used several time lags and coded another version of the UN variable that allows me to study the effect of only those missions that have departed. Using Weibull regression due to an identified positive time-dependence of peace, I found that UN interventions are weakly significant over time, but that their effect dissipates after a few years. The effect of local capacities remains strong, but sorting out the long-term effects of UN missions in this case is harder because the presence of the UN in the early days of a mission may facilitate a return to growth, so some of the effects of missions will be captured by the local capacity variables. What that analysis suggests, however, is that a strategy of multidimensional peacekeeping combined with interventions that foster economic growth represents the best chance of post–civil war societies to achieve lasting peace.

The Importance of Economic Growth in Peace Transitions

The results reported here on the importance of economic growth for sustainable peace are consistent with other studies that have looked at the link between economic development and civil war onset. Several empirical studies have established that civil wars have high economic costs.[44] These costs are incurred through several channels. For example, Ghobarah, Huth, and Russet argue that health standards decline in a civil war country and neighboring countries, and this reduces available human capital for economic production and creates high health costs for the state.[45] Montalvo and Reynal-Querol show empirically that refugee flows, which are often caused by civil wars, increase the prevalence of certain diseases in neighboring countries.[46]

How can fast growth resume after civil war? Some authors have argued that economic growth actually rebounds quickly after wars and that there are no negative long-term effects of war on economic growth.[47] Chen, Loayza, and Reynal-Querol argue that although civil war has a negative impact on countries' levels of political development, health, and educational achievement, once peace is established, economic recovery is possible.[48] Their analysis shows that progress in social development indicators occurs as per capita income rises and public spending shifts away from military expenditures. They find that economic growth, mortality rates, and education levels in civil war countries improve significantly postwar relative to the prewar period, and these gains are actually greater than those made in comparable periods in countries not affected by civil war.[49] The reasons for these increases are likely to be connected to the economic and humanitarian assistance that most civil war countries receive during their transition to peace. But "control group" countries—that is, countries not affected by civil war—have greater gains in political openness relative to post–civil war countries. Thus, available evidence points to a useful role that UN peace missions can play by filling in the institutional and democratic deficit in post–civil war countries. Such a role is likely to enhance the prospects of economic recovery.

Although there is not much contestation of the idea that faster growth improves the prospects for peace, several authors have criticized the economic strategies used by the UN and other agencies and organizations involved in peacebuilding. Economic liberalization policies are seen as imposing unreasonable strain on countries emerging from civil war. As a more prudent strategy, authors have proposed a more gradual pace of economic reform and greater protections for war-affected groups. These arguments are summarized well in Roland Paris's book, which effectively points to the need for greater "institutionalization before liberalization."[50]

Paris argues that peacebuilding missions promote Western liberal democracy as a cookie-cutter solution along with principles of economic liberalism that are not always compatible with local norms and traditions in the war-affected countries.[51] He does not reject the idea that liberal institutionalism is a good way to promote "positive peace," but advocates for a gradual introduction of liberal principles to avoid social conflict.

In a similar vein, Smith (see chapter 10 in this volume) makes the argument that peacekeeping has an "economic imperialist" dimension because peace missions are "designed to protect the interests of Northern states." The goal of economic liberalization is often to integrate post–civil war countries to the world economy, but Kaldor and Luckham, among others, argue that economic globalization delegitimates state authority and this is one of the causes of "new wars."[52] The argument here is that the "standard" economic policy package in peacebuilding operations that is supported by funds from the international financial institutions undermines the state in ways that make it more vulnerable to future conflict.

It is hard to see, however, how the task of rebuilding the political economy of a state where the population is divided into hostile factions can involve measures that do not temporarily reduce the governments' regulatory and policy-making capacity. This is needed to create assurances that there is external oversight of government policies. Though there is little doubt that "local ownership" is necessary for sustainable peace, in some transitions this is a goal that should be postponed. Where the risks of renewed warfare are great and transitional administration is necessary, there cannot be local owner-ship because locals cannot be trusted to work out an equitable, sustainable solution.[53] In the economic sphere, policies to attract foreign investment are, in fact, critical for a return to fast economic growth, because in large wars local financial capital will have migrated to safe havens overseas, and some incentive and assurance is necessary for that capital to come back.

There is now a growing understanding in the relevant international organ-izations that standard policies of structural adjustment and economic liberali-zation like reductions in public spending, privatization of public assets, and elimination of wage and price controls and subsidies are not applicable to the first stages of post–civil war recovery. Yet critics of international economic involvement must go beyond these simple arguments that are now less contro-versial than they were ten or twenty years ago and propose alternative pathways for a quick return to economic growth. Basic things like provision of services to the population can be quickly achieved and are important as confidence-building measures.[54] An equitable division of the "peace dividend" is also a reasonable goal, despite the fact that there is no clear evidence linking eco-nomic inequalities (between individuals or groups) to the onset of large-scale internal armed conflict. In many peace transitions, land redistribution or provi-sion of basic services like education to large segments of the population were important components of successful peacebuilding, according to many careful observers.

The legitimation of property rights, needed to transform a war economy into a peace economy, will require some form of political liberalization, despite the risks of such reforms highlighted by Paris and others. Revitaliz-ing the export industries of the country and redirecting government expendi-tures toward productive investment and away from military expenditures are also reasonable economic goals in a peace transition. In such an economic transition, lessons learned from the past ten years suggest that there is a need for separate humanitarian assistance and economic development assist-ance.[55] Humanitarian assistance targets affected individuals and groups with no necessary link to the economic reconstruction policy. Other emergency grants and assistance will also be necessary to rebuild the civilian adminis-tration, demobilize ex-combatants and reintegrate them in society, and find employment for all war-affected populations. But the criticisms of interna-tional financial institutions' "rigidity" and their proclivity toward financial restraint must also be informed by the risk that humanitarian assistance and development aid can easily become prizes over which the factions can fight in societies that are politically unstable.

Although rapid immersion into the wild world of economic globalization will undoubtedly create strain in post–civil war societies just as it does in every society, are there any viable, practical, and clear economic alternatives beyond vague calls for a better "global systemic framework" for peacebuilding? Smith (this volume) seems to argue that the problem is that the UN is subordinate to the international financial institutions and that a better approach would be to promote a "global culture of solidarity and human rights."[56] Direct espousal of such a goal would undoubtedly be difficult for the international financial institutions, whose articles of agreement impose a doctrine of economic neutrality with respect to political agendas. Everyone appreciates, of course, that economic targets have political consequences, and there can be several ways to improve the coordination of activities of the international financial institutions with agencies such as the Department of Peacekeeping Operations, which have an explicitly political mandate. My proposal earlier in this chapter is for the international financial institutions to commit resources where the UN is willing to commit peacekeeping troops and technical expertise in institutional rebuilding.

Conclusion

Participatory peace that lasts depends on heavy international involvement in the immediate postwar period and a rapid return to a growing economy. The more we move away from a negative definition of peace and toward an understanding of peace that has an element of participation, the more we will need extensive and often muscular third-party intervention to deter spoilers, build transformative political institutions, and provide guarantees that the peace will not collapse soon after the peacekeepers leave.

Rebuilding local capacities in ways that allow countries to grow economically reduces the risk of a new war, as do economic reforms that lower countries' dependence on natural resources. Over time, the positive effect of UN peace missions only works in indirect ways, if it helps countries build the institutions needed for self-sustaining peace.

The UN has had a good record in its peacebuilding interventions, but there is room for improvement. The empirical record shows that UN missions are not always sufficiently strategic. Better matching between the underlying peacebuilding ecology and the UN mandate and resources is likely to improve the prospects for peacebuilding success. What is also missing from current missions is a clear plan on how to integrate economic development as a key goal of the transition process.

Integrated mission strategies are now a necessity, given the wide range of policy objectives that peacebuilders are asked to achieve. The difficult—and still unanswered—question is who should be in charge of coordination of an integrated, multidimensional peace mission. Should it be whoever provides security? Should military agencies be subordinated to civilian agencies? Should local leaders take control of the process, or should the transition be governed by external actors?

The areas of policy intervention are multiplying: demobilization, disarmament, and reintegration of ex-combatants; refugee repatriation; elections; economic reconstruction; humanitarian assistance; security provision—these are all areas of policy intervention that are important, and different agencies have expertise and resources that they can bring to bear on each one. Beyond the fairly obvious calls for better integration of operational strategies from these agencies, there is no clear sense of how to achieve all these objectives of postwar peacebuilding in ways that create no new social tensions and waste the least amount of financial resources. This is because we do not yet know how much each of those objectives contributes to peace (or even what the *right* definition of peace should be) or what the best practices to achieve each of those objectives are. Part of the problem is that outcomes we can study are so highly case-specific that it is hard to generalize about best practices of peacebuilding. Another part of the problem is that there are inherent tensions in peacebuilding processes: restoring state sovereignty may (in some cases) undermine minority rights; promoting human rights and reconciliation as a peacebuilding standard may make it harder for parties to reach a peace settlement in the first place; fostering growth of local or informal institutions may be impossible in situations where a heavy international presence and an enforcement mandate are needed to impose a peace; and creating the conditions for a return to economic growth may require political liberalizations that, in some societies, may trigger new social conflicts. Though there is no clear or easy answer on how to address these complex challenges, the UN has shown that it is best suited to take the lead in future peacebuilding initiatives. UN missions must take advantage of the formative role that they can play in the early stages of peace transitions and set the stage for self-sustaining peace by creating incentives for the transformation of war economies into peace economies. They can do this more effectively if they assume the role of coordinator of integrated peace missions that involve the World Bank and other donors as well as bilateral actors who can provide security in the most difficult situations.

NOTES

This chapter draws on Michael W. Doyle and Nicholas Sambanis, *Making War and Building Peace: United Nations Peace Operations* (Princeton, N.J.: Princeton University Press, 2006).

1. Boutros Boutros-Ghali, *Agenda for Peace: Report of the Secretary-General*, UN document A/47/277-S/24111, June 17, 1992. Quotes are from paras. 20–21 and 55–99.

2. For a discussion of each of these strategies see, among others, Michael Doyle and Nicholas Sambanis, "Peacekeeping Operations," in *The Oxford Handbook on the United Nations*, edited by Thomas G. Weiss and Sam Daws (Oxford: Oxford University Press, 2007).

3. For a relevant discussion of the evolution of standards of peacebuilding, see Simon Chesterman's contribution to this volume (chapter 5).

4. Success is, of course, an ambiguous and contested term. We discuss its various meanings and how to measure it in *Making War and Building Peace* in both the data analysis and case studies.

5. See James D. Fearon and David D. Laitin, "Ethnicity, Insurgency, and Civil War," *American Political Science Review* 97, no. 1 (2003): 75–90.

6. See Kenneth Boulding, "Toward a Theory of Peace," in *International Conflict and Behavioral Science*, edited by Roger Fisher (New York: Basic Books, 1964), 70–87.

7. This is consistent with (though possibly less expansive than) the definition of peacebuilding proposed by John Paul Lederach and Scott Appleby in this volume (chapter 1): "Peacebuilding that is strategic draws intentionally and shrewdly on the overlapping and imperfectly coordinated presences, activities, and resources of various international, transnational, national, regional, and local institutions, agencies, and movements that influence the causes, expressions, and outcomes of conflict. Strategic peacebuilders take advantage of emerging and established patterns of collaboration and interdependence for the purposes of reducing violence and alleviating the root causes of deadly conflict. They encourage the deeper and more frequent convergence of mission, resources, expertise, insight, and benevolent self-interest that characterizes the most fruitful multilateral collaborations in the cause of peace."

8. Details on the measurement of all the variables included in the model can be found online at http://pantheon.yale.edu/~ns237/index/research/SupplementforDS2006.pdf.

9. We measure electricity consumption and real income the year before the war started because the hostility variables would have a direct effect on these measures after the war. Real income growth may have the same problem, but it has tremendous variability in post–civil war countries, and it seems much more responsive as a measure of postwar developments.

10. We use two measures: primary commodity exports as a percent of GDP and oil export dependence, a binary variable coded 1 if a country's fuel exports make up more than 33 percent of its total merchandise exports. For results using the oil variable, see our supplements.

11. The literature expounding the three is vast, but for central differences see Robert Keohane, *After Hegemony* (Princeton, N.J.: Princeton University Press, 1984); Joseph Grieco, "Anarchy and the Limits of Cooperation: A Realist Critique of the Newest Liberal Institutionalism," *International Organization* 42, no. 3 (1988): 485–507; and Martha Finnemore and Kathryn Sikkink, "Taking Stock: The Constructivist Research Program in International Relations and Comparative Politics," *Annual Review of Political Science* 4 (2001): 391–416.

12. For a theoretical discussion of the problem of providing assurance and building trust in conflicts that combine elements of both coordination and cooperation games, see Andrew Kydd, "Trust, Reassurance, and Cooperation," *International Organization* 54, no. 2 (2000): 325–357.

13. For a precise game-theoretic definition of coordination and collaboration games, refer to James Morrow, *Game Theory for Political Scientists* (Princeton, N.J.: Princeton University Press, 1994); and David M. Kreps, *Game Theory and Economic Modeling* (Oxford: Clarendon Press, 1990).

14. A useful summary of the literature is Robert Axelrod and Robert Keohane, "Introduction" and "Conclusion," in *Cooperation under Anarchy*, edited by Kenneth Oye (Princeton, N.J.: Princeton University Press, 1986).

15. Morrow, *Game Theory*, 222.

16. Transformative peacekeeping is different from peace enforcement. The former can only deter or punish occasional violations. If the violations are systematic and large-scale, a no-consent enforcement operation might be necessary.

17. On the role of reconciliation in peacebuilding process, see chapter 4 in this volume.

18. See Gary Bass, *Stay the Hand of Vengeance* (Princeton, N.J.: Princeton University Press, 2000); for the difficulties, see Jack Snyder and Leslie Vinjamuri, "Trials and Errors: Principle and Pragmatism in Strategies of International Justice," *International Security* 28, no. 3 (2003/2004): 5–44; and Chandra Sriram, *Confronting Past Human Rights Violators* (Oxford: Hart, 2004). See also chapter 9 in this volume on the importance of human rights and justice in peacebuilding processes.

19. Roht-Arriaza (see chapter 9) discusses the Truth Commissions in Haiti and Guatemala as good examples of such hybrid institutions.

20. The mutually hurting stalemate is from I. William Zartman, *Ripe for Resolution* (Oxford: Oxford University Press, 1985), where he discusses "ripe" conflicts. Additional conditions for conflict ripeness in Zartman's theory are a sense of crisis, a deadline for negotiations, a reversal in the parties' relative strength, a leveraged external mediation, and a feasible settlement that can address all the parties' basic needs.

21. The settlement of El Salvador's civil war is a good example of a hurting stalemate.

22. Stephen John Stedman, "Spoiler Problems in Peace Processes," *International Security* 22, no. 2 (1997): 7.

23. The statistical analysis that supports the discussion in this section is presented in the online supplements of *Making War and Building Peace*.

24. A comparison of the means cannot reject the null hypothesis of no difference ($p = 0.94$).

25. These results are reported in the supplements.

26. UN missions, however, do go to cases that are overall harder to resolve than cases without UN intervention. These selection effects and the issues that they generate for estimating the effects of UN missions on peacebuilding are discussed in the supplement to *Making War and Building Peace* and in Nicholas Sambanis, "Short-Term and Long-Term Effects of United Nations Peace Operations," *World Bank Economic Review* (forthcoming).

27. See Shashi Tharoor, "Should UN Peacekeeping 'Go Back to Basics'?" *Survival* 37, no. 4 (1995–1996): 52–64.

28. See Thomas Franck, "A Holistic Approach to Peace-building," in *Peacemaking and Peacekeeping for the New Century*, edited by Olara Otunnu and Michael W. Doyle (Lanham, Md.: Rowman and Littlefield, 1998), 275–295; and Elizabeth Cousens, Chetan Kumar, and Karin Wermester, eds., *Peacebuilding as Politics* (Boulder, Colo.: Lynne Rienner, 2000).

29. See Alvaro DeSoto and Graciana del Castillo, "Obstacles to Peacebuilding in El Salvador," *Foreign Policy* 94 (1994): 69–83. This is the coordinating role that Japan, for example, played in Cambodia in organizing the Tokyo conference and the International Committee on the Reconstruction of Cambodia.

30. Axelrod and Keohane, "Introduction" and "Conclusion"; Kenneth Oye, "Explaining Cooperation under Anarchy," *World Politics* 38, no. 1 (1985): 1–24.

31. Bruce D. Jones, *Peacemaking in Rwanda: The Dynamics of Failure* (Boulder, Colo.: Lynne Rienner, 2001). Jack Snyder, *From Voting to Violence* (New York: Norton, 2000).

32. Roland Paris, *At War's End: Building Peace after Conflict* (New York: Cambridge University Press, 2004).

33. This point is made well by Terence Lyons, "The Role of Postsettlement Elections," in *Ending Civil Wars*, edited by Stephen Stedman et al. (Boulder, Colo.: Lynne Rienner, 2002), 215–235.

34. Michael Barnett, "Building a Republican Peace: Stabilizing States After War," *International Security* 30, no. 4 (2006): 87–112.

35. For an empirical analysis of this issue, see Jon Pevehouse, "Democracy from Outside? International Organizations and Democratization," *International Organization* 56, no. 3 (2002): 515–549.

36. Good examples of this argument are Bruce Jones, "The Challenges of Strategic Coordination," in *Ending Civil Wars* edited by Stephen Stedman et al. (Boulder, Colo.: Lynne Rienner, 2002), 89–116; and Barnett R. Rubin, "Constructing Sovereignty for Security," *Survival* 47, no. 4 (2005): 93–106.

37. See Jones, "The Challenges of Strategic Coordination."

38. For a view that interagency competition contributes to poor coordination of UN missions, see "A More Secure World: Our Shared Responsibility," Report of the High-Level Panel on Threats, Challenges, and Change, UN Doc A/59/565, December 1, 2004, http:/www.un.org/secureworld.

39. For a methodological discussion, see Janet M. Box-Steffensmeier and Bradford S. Jones, *Timing and Political Change: Event History Modeling in Political Science* (Ann Arbor: University of Michigan Press, 2003).

40. It is not straightforward to have a similar long-term analysis of the more ambitious participatory peace standard. There are a number of problems with coding the dependent variable: there are no reliable data on levels of residual violence over time; levels of political openness can vary over time, so it is possible that some cases would "fail" one year, then "succeed" years later if they become more democratic; and a deadline is needed to code undivided sovereignty because peace processes are often designed to resolve problems of divided sovereignty gradually, and we must have a uniform standard on how long it should take for a peace mission to succeed in resolving problems of divided sovereignty.

41. In each model, I test the proportional hazard assumption and, if it is not satisfied, I use a Weibull model, which is appropriate if the hazard rate is monotonically increasing or decreasing.

42. This effect is robust to controlling for non-UN missions. Hazard ratios under 1 indicate a negative coefficient (i.e., a negative effect). Ratios above 1 indicate a positive effect.

43. For results and discussion, see Sambanis (forthcoming).

44. See James C. Murdoch and Todd Sandler, "Economic Growth, Civil Wars, and Spatial Spillovers," *Journal of Conflict Resolution* 46 (2002): 91–110, for a cross-country study of the economic growth spillover effects of civil war; and R. Soares, "The Welfare Cost of Violence across Countries," *Journal of Health Economics* 25, no. 5 (2006): 821–846, for country-specific analyses of the economic effects of political violence.

45. P. Ghobarah Hazem, Paul Huth, and Bruce Russett, "Civil Wars Kill and Maim People, Long after the Fighting Stops," *American Political Science Review* 97, no. 2 (2003): 189–202.

46. Jose G. Montalvo and Marta Reynal-Querol, "Fighting against Malaria: Prevent Wars while Waiting for the 'Miraculous' Vaccine," *Review of Economics and Statistics* (forthcoming).

47. See Adam Przeworski, Michael E. Alvarez, Jose Antonio Cheibub, and Fernando Limongi, *Democracy and Development: Political Institutions and Wellbeing in the World 1950–1990* (Cambridge: Cambridge University Press, 2000). For an analysis of the economic effects of the world wars, see A. F. K Organski and Jacek Kugler, "The Costs of Major Wars: The Phoenix Factor," *American Political Science Review* 71, no. 14 (1977): 1347–1366. For an analysis of the effects of the war in Vietnam, see Edward Miguel and Gerard Roland, "The Long Run Impact of Bombing Vietnam," NBER Working Paper No. W11954, January 2006.

48. This conclusion is reached through an event-study methodology that compares prewar and postwar levels of economic and political variables of interest in forty-one countries. See Siyan Chen, Norman Loayza, and Marta Reynal-Querol, "The Aftermath of Civil War," World Bank Working Paper (2007).

49. There can be several mechanisms for fast growth recovery after war. One is the growth that results from international aid. Another is that war affects some production factors more than others, increasing rates of return for relatively less affected factors, thereby propelling forward the mechanism of economic convergence that leads to higher growth. For a discussion of the latter mechanism, see Robert Barro and Xavier Sala-I-Martin, *Economic Growth* (New York: McGraw-Hill, 1995), cited in Chen, Loayza, and Reynal-Querol (2007).

50. Paris, *At War's End*.

51. A similar argument with reference to Nicaragua and Haiti is made by William Robinson, *Promoting Polyarchy: Globalization, U.S. Intervention and Hegemony* (Cambridge: Cambridge University Press, 1996).

52. Mary Kaldor and Robin Luckham, "Global Transformations and New Conflicts," *IDS Bulletin* 32 (2001).

53. For a discussion of this point, see Simon Chesterman's contribution to this volume (chapter 5).

54. See Susan L. Woodward, "Economic Priorities for Successful Peace Implementation," in *Ending Civil Wars*, edited by Stephen Stedman et al. (Boulder, Colo.: Lynne Rienner, 2002), 183–213.

55. Ibid.; see also chapter 11 in this volume.

56. This paradigm derives from Benhabib Seyla, "On the Alleged Conflict between Democracy and International Law," *Ethics and International Affairs* 19 (2005): 85–100.

7

Targeted Sanctions, Counterterrorism, and Strategic Peacebuilding

George A. Lopez and David Cortright

With the imposition of comprehensive trade sanctions on Iraq in August 1990 through resolution 661, the United Nations Security Council (UNSC) ushered in a new era in the use of collective coercive economic measures as a means of fulfilling its mandate under Chapter VII of the UN Charter to protect international peace and security.[1] The next seventeen years witnessed an active phase of UNSC-imposed sanctions, with dozens of resolutions levied against nearly twenty distinct targets, including myriad national and subnational actors who would disturb attempts to build peace in war-torn nations and the new brand of transnational terrorism that has arisen in al Qaeda. As documented in this volume, alongside these unfolding global actions and realities, modern peace researchers and practitioners were developing the cases and the conceptual contours necessary for a deeper meaning of protecting international peace and security through strategic peacebuilding.

To some analysts and practitioners, United Nations–mandated and –enforced sanctions, including the more narrowly targeted smart sanctions that are the subject of much of this chapter, epitomize a top-down, unequal, violent, and ineffective tool for enhancing peace and security.[2] Our own study, research, and experience, however, teaches us that the evidence of sanctions' development, implementation, and reform—as well as their versatility in restraining war, curbing norm violations and constricting terrorism—qualifies them to be an integral part of peacebuilding, both conceptually and strategically. This is not to suggest that the UN sanctions policy is flawless or to deny their many impacts, sometimes adverse, in various aspects of local and global life. Rather, on balance, and especially if we employ the Lederach-Appleby framework for strategic peacebuilding outlined in this volume (see chapter 1), we believe a reasonable case can be made for the use and scrutiny of sanctions as a significant component of strategic peacebuilding. A number of reasons support our claim.

First, sanctions pressure a target by altering the costs and benefits for continuing to pursue the behavior labeled unacceptable by the international community. At their best, sanctions establish a new bargaining dynamic between target and imposers. Thus, sanctions contribute to the transformation of a conflict to a new state of affairs; when successful, new and sustained dialogue toward conflict resolution will emerge, even if it is forced by sanctions' coercion. Sanctions research details that this occurs outright in at least one-third of sanctions cases, and our own work illustrates how even partial compliance with sanctions by targets can lead to positive endings of disputes.[3]

Because UN sanctions are strongly coercive, some would claim they do economic violence to nations, targets, and the innocents. Yet because economic sanctions offer a middle course "between war and words,"[4] they fit with much of the nonviolent social change criteria crucial to strategic peacebuilding. Sanctions are meant to avoid the costs of military action, yet they provide a more forceful option beyond diplomatic remonstrance. When employed effectively, they can exert significant pressure on those targeted. When designed and applied astutely, sanctions can serve as the basis for a bargaining dynamic in which the promise of lifting sanctions becomes an incentive to encourage political concessions and cooperation.[5] In this sense, they also reinforce the conflict transformational aspect of strategic peacebuilding.

Finally, Lederach and Appleby highlight the need for peacebuilding to include transnational phenomena and movements, as well as aim toward institutional change to contribute to greater peace and justice. Although economic sanctions have an imperfect record in some aspects of these criteria, the process of sanctions reform, particularly constricting trade in blood diamonds or denying travel and banking access to human rights violators, emerged from the research and praxis work of various transnational actors, such as Human Rights Watch, International Alert, and International Crisis Group. Moreover, in increasing the institutional capacity of various actors to close borders during arms embargoes or capture terrorists' assets, the UN and member states have forged coalitions of nongovernmental organizations (NGOs) and various national institutions, as well as governments and regional intergovernmental organizations (IGOs). In some cases, these developments have spawned new arrangements for how local and global political actors work together in creating peace and justice.

To understand in some detail the contribution of United Nations–imposed economic sanctions to strategic peacebuilding involves a number of critical themes, which this chapter addresses. The first theme regards how the often contentious development of sanctions, specifically their reform from a reinvigorated peace and security technique of the early 1990s to a major component of the global struggle against terrorism, contributes to vigorous and sustainable peace "on the ground" in situations of violence. The second theme includes the manner in which sanctions policy formed at the highest levels of international authority works its way through the multiple layers of international actors and across time to insert itself—sometimes successfully and other times less so—into the strategic peacebuilding equation. Finally, the recent evolution of the UN institutional network, which has employed targeted sanctions as its central coercive tool in counterterrorism policy, illustrates how complex the challenges are for ensuring that UN Security Council action can be a positive component of strategic peacebuilding in this most difficult peace and security dynamic.

Sanctions, Smart Sanctions Reform, and Strategic Peacebuilding

The record of Security Council sanctions since 1990 and their relationship to aspects of strategic peacebuilding reveals a pattern of institutional learning, adaptation, and occasionally, innovation. Not surprisingly, the early phase of the UNSC's use of sanctions as a means for advancing the UN mandate to preserve peace and security (1990–1994) was dominated by the influence of the five permanent members of the council. Although sanctions provided the major powers with a powerful tool for collective action within the UNSC, the wide-ranging social impacts of these measures resulted in declining consensus on Iraq and disagreements on the appropriateness of sanctions for attaining council goals of peace and security.

The devastation caused by sanctions to the social and economic infrastructure of Iraq, as well as further concerns about adverse humanitarian impacts of sanctions there and in Haiti, meant that various nongovernmental actors joined numerous UN member governments to condemn sanctions for undermining the second pillar of the UN core mandate: to enhance the human condition. Herein lay the important bridge between the post-1990 emergence of the sanctions tool and sanctions reform toward strategic peacebuilding. Although UN sanctions initially reflected a top-down approach, most members and especially the Secretariat quickly recognized that unless sanctions were formulated with human rights and humanitarian concerns in mind, they would be short-lived and ineffective. Furthermore, unless sanctions implementation involved a plethora of global, regional, and national actors committed to uphold international norms and the development of authentic peace with security (what authors in this volume would call strategic peacebuilding) sanctions would quickly fall out of favor in the international community.

As we have documented extensively in our prior research work, by 1994 the UNSC had learned numerous lessons from these early, flawed sanctions episodes. The council moved to adapt its measures to mitigate unanticipated consequences and explored prospects for improving sanctions implementation, monitoring, and evaluation.[6] An era of sanctions reform then ensued as the council shifted its focus from comprehensive to more selective measures. Much of that process, and its smart sanctions products, are significant for strategic peacebuilding because they broadened the number of global actors involved in sanctions and, more directly, related sanctions goals and means to peacebuilding.

Aided by a series of international expert processes chaired by Switzerland (financial sanctions), Germany (arms embargoes and travel bans), and Sweden (the implementation of smart sanctions) the UNSC abandoned the use of general trade sanctions and relied instead on targeted measures. These so-called smart sanctions included financial assets freezes, travel bans, aviation sanctions, commodity boycotts, and arms embargoes. As the UN counterterrorism program developed after September 2001, the council mandated the application of these more precise tools to disable terrorist networks.[7]

In conjunction with the move to smart sanctions, efforts to assess the humanitarian impact of particular sanctions cases became a regular feature of UN sanctions policy. In 1995, the Department of Humanitarian Affairs (DHA) commissioned a report on the impact of sanctions on humanitarian assistance efforts.[8] Two years later, the DHA developed a methodology and series of specific indicators for assessing humanitarian impacts.[9] Many of the recommendations in these studies became the basis for an ongoing humanitarian assessment methodology developed by DHA's successor, the Office for the Coordination of Humanitarian Affairs (OCHA). In 2003, OCHA updated its indicators and methodology in light of recent cases and based on the success of the earlier venture.[10] Assessment reports and missions to examine the impact of sanctions are now a routine feature of sanctions cases, and they are complemented by the work of the NGO humanitarian community, which monitors sanctions cases and issues reports designed to prevent potential humanitarian problems.

In each of the categories of targeted sanctions—finance, travel, arms, and commodities—the Security Council introduced important innovations that increased the prospects for the UN to help set better conditions in a crisis for stable peace by crafting more focused and more humane sanctions. In the area of financial sanctions, the council moved beyond freezing the assets of governments alone. In the early cases of Iraq, Libya, and Yugoslavia, it imposed financial sanctions only on government assets. Beginning in 1994, with action against the military junta in Haiti, the Security Council applied financial sanctions against designated individuals and entities as well. This pattern continued through the Angola and Afghanistan cases in the latter part of the decade. In the cases of the Democratic Republic of the Congo (DRC) and Côte d'Ivoire, the UNSC was authorized to apply targeted measures on designated individuals.

As the Security Council shifted toward imposing targeted sanctions in cooperation with member states, it developed the capacity to develop and publish lists of designated sanctions targets. The entities and individuals on these designation lists were subjected to asset freezes and travel bans. This technique was used extensively and seemingly effectively, with financial sanctions and visa bans imposed on lists of designated targets in the cases of Angola, Sierra Leone, Afghanistan, Liberia, DRC, Sudan, and Côte d'Ivoire. After the terrorist attacks of September 11, 2001, this practice was expanded and improved in significant ways as the council attempted to constrain the activities of terrorists.

Less successfully, but rather important to the prospects for peacebuilding, the council also attempted to make improvements in the design and implementation of arms embargoes. In the four instances where arms embargoes were imposed as stand-alone measures—Somalia, Rwanda, Ethiopia/Eritrea, and Yugoslavia 1998–2001—the impact of these measures was minimal. Only in the case of Iraq, where the United States and other countries made a major commitment to enforcement, did the continuing restrictions on the supply of arms and dual-use technologies have a significant military-political impact.[11]

To overcome the problems resulting from inadequate implementation of arms embargoes, the Security Council adopted a number of policy innovations. Arms embargo resolutions included prohibitions against not only the supply of arms and ammunition but also training, military cooperation, and various support services, including air transportation. More vigorous efforts also were made to monitor compliance with arms embargoes. The most extensive effort, involving a wide array of regional, transnational, and private actors, occurred during the 1991–1995 UNSC sanctions imposed on the Belgrade government. A network of sanctions assistance missions (SAMs) was organized by the Conference on Security and Co-operation in Europe (predecessor of the Organization for Security and Co-operation in Europe) and the European Community (EC).

In no other UNSC sanctions episode has the extensive involvement of transnational actors occurred to this degree. In October 1992, customs officials (primarily from France) were dispatched to Bulgaria, Hungary, and Romania to form the first SAMs. SAMs were also established in Albania, Croatia, the Former Yugoslav Republic of Macedonia, and Ukraine. The EC established a Sanctions Assistance Missions Communications Center (SAMCOMM) at its headquarters in Brussels and created the post of sanctions coordinator. By March 1995, the SAMCOMM staff had grown to twenty-six people.[12] These measures established a substantial institutional capacity for monitoring and enforcing sanctions. It was the first time major regional organizations stepped in to assist the United Nations in providing staff and financial resources for the implementation of UN sanctions. Because little detailed analysis has been done of the SAMs' successes and shortcomings, such border control mechanisms constitute a ripe area for further analysis for those interested in the way peacebuilding can benefit from the power of regional and international organizations.

Efforts have also been made to encourage member states to criminalize violations of UN arms embargoes and strengthen export control laws and regulations. These initiatives helped create a firmer foundation in the domestic law of member states for penalizing companies and individuals who supply arms and military related goods in violation of UN arms embargoes. In 2004, the UNSC directed UN peacekeeping forces in the DRC and Côte d'Ivoire to assist with monitoring arms embargoes in these countries. This added significant new responsibilities to the mission of UN peacekeepers in these countries. It brought into direct, strategic interaction the UN role in resource constriction via sanctions and traditional peacekeeping. Recent studies confirm that even modest attention by peacekeepers to issues of arms restrictions can enhance both the peacekeeping mission and the embargo itself.[13]

Another important innovation for strengthening the peacebuilding role of sanctions was the creation of special investigative and expert panels, which helped the UNSC overcome its lack of monitoring capacity for assessing sanctions cases.[14] The first panel was established in conjunction with the arms embargo against Rwandan Hutu rebels by Resolution 1013 in 1995. The Council created the United Nations Independent Commission of Inquiry (UNICOI), which issued six reports from 1996 through 1998 documenting the illegal supply of arms to the rebel groups in eastern Zaire. UNICOI reports provided voluminous evidence of wholesale violations of the arms embargo and contained numerous recommendations for cracking down on arms smuggling in the region. A breakthrough toward more effective monitoring came in the case of Angola. In 1999, the Angola sanctions committee became more active in monitoring sanctions violations and encouraging greater implementation efforts. The UNSC also appointed a panel of experts and a subsequent monitoring mechanism to improve compliance with the Angola sanctions. The panel of experts and monitoring mechanism issued a series of reports that focused continuing attention on sanctions implementation efforts.[15]

The Angola panel of experts and the monitoring mechanism were followed by similar investigative panels for Sierra Leone, Afghanistan, and Liberia. An investigative panel was also created to examine the exploitation of mineral wealth and natural resources in DRC and to monitor compliance with sanctions after 2003. Panel reports were also commissioned in 2003 for Somalia and in 2004 for Sudan and Côte d'Ivoire. In each of these settings, the investigative panels produced detailed reports on sanctions violations and smuggling activities. The Sierra Leone panel of experts focused on the link between arms trafficking and diamond smuggling and found a pattern of widespread violations of UN sanctions. The panel issued numerous policy recommendations, the most important of which was that sanctions be imposed on the government of Liberia for its role in undermining sanctions implementation and providing support for the rebels in Sierra Leone.[16] Sanctions on the Charles Taylor regime soon followed.

The UNSC created a monitoring mechanism for Afghanistan in July 2001, through Resolution 1363, and established an associated Sanctions Enforcement Support Team to strengthen the implementation of the arms embargo, travel sanctions, and targeted financial sanctions imposed against the Taliban regime. After the overthrow of the Taliban, in 2002 the UNSC altered the mission of the monitoring group through Resolution 1390. It later created a new Analytic Support and Sanctions Monitoring Team to investigate and provide support for the continued financial, travel, and arms sanctions on former Taliban leaders and members of al Qaeda. The Liberia panel of experts report confirmed allegations of the Monrovia government's extensive involvement with and support for the armed rebellion of the Revolutionary United Front (RUF) in Sierra Leone. The panel recommended a series of measures for strengthening the enforcement of the arms embargo, diamond embargo, and travel sanctions against Liberia.[17]

What may prove to be the most noteworthy development of the 1990s was the emergence of commodity-specific sanctions. Oil embargoes were imposed as part of the comprehensive sanctions against Iraq. Oil was also named specifically in sanctions imposed on governments in Yugoslavia, Haiti, the National

Union for the Total Independence of Angola (UNITA) group in Angola, and the military junta in Sierra Leone. An embargo on the export of logs was imposed against the government of Liberia. Diamond embargoes were introduced in 1998 with the case of Angola. The latter two commodities had taken on labels, "the logs of war" and "blood diamonds," respectively, as appropriate indicators of how detrimental the illicit trade in each has become for disrupting the prospects for stable peace in a war-torn area.

As nongovernmental agencies and human rights groups documented the role of diamond smuggling in financing the armed rebellions in Angola and Sierra Leone, the UNSC took action to interdict the trade in blood diamonds. The council imposed diamond embargoes against UNITA in 1998 through Resolution 1173, the RUF areas of Sierra Leone in 2000 through Resolution 1306, and the government of Liberia in 2001 through Resolution 1343.

As a means of enforcing these measures, the UN worked with diamond-exporting countries, the diamond industry, and NGOs to establish the Kimberley Process, an international agreement among dozens of countries to combat the trade in conflict-related diamonds. Governments created certificate-of-origin systems designed to protect the legitimate diamond trade by screening out blood diamonds. Targeted diamond sanctions became a tool for the UNSC to shrink the financial base sustaining armed conflict in Africa, and they became a model for commodity-focused embargoes of the future.[18]

This survey of expanded UN sanctions policy through smart sanctions demonstrates that multilateral economic sanctions have matured significantly since 1990, as UN diplomats, expert investigators, academic scholars, nongovernmental analysts, and many others have contributed to a process of learning, adaptation, and reform. The result has been a substantial transformation of sanctions policy making and increased likelihood that sanctions will be humane and effective and will contribute to greater prospects for strategic peacebuilding.

The targeted, more selective sanctions of recent years, supported by humanitarian assessment missions and expert panel reports, bear little resemblance to the poorly monitored, often blunt measures imposed in the early 1990s. Although many problems remain in the implementation of UNSC sanctions, the substantial progress of this period has evolved sanctions into a more viable means of reinforcing other efforts made by the UN or more directly in local communities to engage in strategic peacebuilding.

Smart Sanctions, Counterterrorism, and Strategic Peacebuilding

There are many ways in which terrorism has been an integral part of international and internal wars for decades. Whether in resolved conflicts, as in Northern Ireland or South Africa, or in any of the fourteen ongoing violent conflicts in which at least one of the contending parties has been labeled a terrorist group, dealing with terrorists past and present poses a complex and challenging issue for strategic peacebuilding. The deadly and changing parameters of this age of "new" terrorism are becoming more starkly defined. So are questions about the appropriateness and effectiveness of current strategies of counterterrorism.

At the core of this debate, and a central factor that makes counterterrorism related to peacebuilding, are concerns regarding the utility of military force and the need for a level of cooperation that spans from the local to the global in the elimination of terrorism. Various reports indicate that despite relative successes in the global campaign against terrorism, more attacks from al Qaeda and related groups have occurred since September 11, 2001, than in the years prior to that date.[19] Doubts have been raised about Western strategy, particularly U.S. action in Afghanistan and Iraq, and its overreliance on military solutions (and undervaluation of nonmilitary mechanisms) for counterterrorism.

Military force can be useful, and may well be necessary for some counter-terrorism missions. But in the medium to long-term time period, heavily armed troops are rarely able to penetrate terrorist networks, and their continued occupation of areas where terrorism exists is likely to breed more resentment and terrorism. When military force is used excessively, it galvanizes support for the jihadists and has the direct opposite effects from those intended. A growing number of analysts agree that defeating al Qaeda and related networks will require a multifaceted strategy encompassing a wide range of policy tools and forms of international cooperation.[20]

Countering this multifaceted and complex terrorist threat requires many of the same structural arrangements for international cooperation and engagement in specific substantive issues that are required in strategic peacebuilding. Organizationally, both counterterrorism and strategic peacebuilding succeed if they entail a broadly cooperative effort involving legal, economic, political, and social cooperation from virtually every nation in the world, and from civil society sectors, both internal and transnational. For each, actions taken and policies that are prioritized should focus on concerns for good governance, economic development, and the protection of human rights.

The United Nations is particularly relevant and important to this counterterrorism effort as it is the primary source of international political legitimacy and legal authority for many nations. Although the recent history of the United Nations taking up this responsibility reveals how it frequently lacks resources and operational capacity, it is indispensable in developing political consensus for the international cooperation required to counter the terrorist threat. Examining the successes and shortcomings of the UN role in counterterrorism since 9/11 can help determine the prospects of strategic peacebuilding taking root in particular war-torn locales.[21]

The modern era of UN involvement against terrorism began in the 1990s, when the UNSC adopted Resolution 748 (1992) calling on Libya to cease its support of terrorism and turn over suspects wanted in connection with the bombings of Pan Am flight 103 and French UTA flight 772. Targeted UN sanctions against Libya, in combination with more comprehensive measures by the United States, were successful in dissuading the country from further support for terrorism and eventually led to the extradition of the bombing suspects for trial at The Hague. UN sanctions against Libya were accompanied by extensive diplomatic dialogue and the promise of economic benefit to encourage Libyan reengagement with the world community. This led to Tripoli's agreement, in 2003, to dismantle its programs for the development of weapons of mass destruction.

UNSC sanctions to counter terrorism were also employed against Sudan (Resolution 1054 in 1996) for harboring Osama bin Laden and what later evolved into al Qaeda. In 1999, Afghanistan (Resolution 1267) was also a target for sanctions as the United Nations became more active in applying pressure on regimes that supported or harbored terrorist operations. These UNSC sanctions efforts were closely integrated with intelligence and diplomatic efforts by the United States and other countries and played an important (if little noticed) role in mobilizing international pressure against state support of terrorism.[22]

In the wake of the September 2001 attacks, the United Nations launched a second, more expansive phase of its campaign against international terrorism. Targeting the diverse and widely dispersed transnational networks of al Qaeda and other related nonstate actors, the Security Council adopted resolution 1373 (2001) mandating a worldwide campaign by all 191 UN member states to deny finances, travel, or assistance of any kind to terrorists and those who support them. Resolution 1373 created the Counter-Terrorism Committee (CTC), and three years later the council adopted SCR1535 (2004) to strengthen the CTC through the creation of an unprecedented Counter-Terrorism Executive Directorate (CTED). To complete its cluster of constraints on terrorism operations, the UNSC also adopted resolutions 1540 and 1566 (both in 2004), prohibiting the transfer of weapons of mass destruction or related materials to nonstate actors and calling on UN member states to strengthen their cooperation with UN counterterrorism mandates.

These efforts have produced an unprecedented expansion of UN counterterrorism activities and a parallel increase in counterterrorism committees and professional staffing. They stimulated significant international action to build counterterrorism capacity, particularly in the former Soviet bloc and in the global South. The UN counterterrorism program has also sparked greater international cooperation and coordination among regional and subregional organizations, along with specialized international agencies. These UN counterterrorism efforts face numerous challenges and contradictions, as we examine shortly, but they have been partially effective in establishing global legal requirements and building international cooperation in the fight against terrorism.

As was the case in the increased resort to sanctions in the UNSC after 1990, after the adoption of Resolution 1373, and when faced with the kind of national security challenge that terrorism poses, there has been a natural tendency for large and powerful states to want to "go it alone" in countering the danger or to overmanage whatever cooperation institution they use to counter terror. The result has been that the multifaceted strategies needed to actually succeed in counterterrorism have been slow to develop, especially regarding the effective use of regional and international organizations among other actors. In fact, there have been some significant differences among the powerful democratic states that have retarded the possibilities for effective peacebuilding via counterterrorism.

In the days following the 9/11 attacks, and again at the G8 summits in 2005 and 2006, European and U.S. leaders acknowledged their shared vulnerability and vowed to work together in the global fight against terrorism. Over time, however, the underlying counterterrorism strategies of the United States and Europe diverged. Most notably, the European community has adopted a more institutionalized, rule-based approach, as opposed to the ad hoc and extralegal efforts employed by the United States. On the continent, information sharing and cooperation among a wide range of agencies are the norm. Europe's open society and removal of border controls make it easier for extremists to operate, but the high degree of law enforcement cooperation among dozens of countries is more easily facilitated by the same openness, and it provides important protections. Many terrorist operations have been disrupted and militant suspects arrested through the cooperative efforts of European law enforcement agencies.[23]

Another major difference between the United States and Europe—indeed, between the United States and most of the world—is the degree of importance accorded the United Nations as a principal actor. In Europe and most other regions of the world, the legal authorization and political leadership of the United Nations are indispensable for cooperative international action against terrorism. UNSC Resolution 1373 (2001) and other counterterrorism measures provided the essential legal and political authorization permitting nations and regions to act. In the United States, by contrast, there is greater disdain for international legal agreements and a more critical view of the United Nations. The significant institutional mechanisms of the CTC and CTED in particular warrant more detailed analysis because their effectiveness and relationship to strategic peacebuilding can be more readily assessed than was possible earlier.[24]

Advancing the Shared Tasks: Good Governance, Development, and Human Rights

As the international community has gained more experience in the strengths and shortcomings of varied approaches to counterterrorism, especially those measures that rely heavily on the integration of global mandates with local implementation, it has become increasingly clear that capacity-building and institutional development of civil society organizations and of good government itself are critical to success. Moreover, counterterrorism in its best form correlates directly to strategic peacebuilding in that the most significant CTC and UN successes in the former have been efforts to increase the capacity of national elites and institutions, as well as sectors of civil society, to improve their contribution to good governance. In addition, the development of successful counterterrorism, especially when the concerns of the global South and transnational civil society are heard, addresses issues of economic development and considers the enhancement of human rights, not their compromise, as both a means and a goal. This integrates many of the ends and means of sanctions and incentives-based counterterrorism with those of strategic peacebuilding.

Many of the measures required by UNSC Resolution 1373—creating more effective law enforcement capabilities; improving border, immigration, and customs controls; regulating banks and financial institutions; enhancing security at ports and border crossings—parallel the steps needed to strengthen good governance. These steps are increasingly recognized as essential to economic development and the expansion of social and economic opportunity. Trade and investment depend on stable government and the rule of law. Thus, technical assistance programs that build governance capacity also advance the prospects for economic development. There are ways diverse multilateral agencies have engaged in counterterrorism, and the CTC/CTED as facilitating organizations, have learned important lessons in these areas.

This linkage between technical assistance and economic development indicates that multilateral aid strategies need to be focused on both integrated economic development and the provision of technical assistance to meet counterterrorism requirements and long-term peacebuilding needs. Recent policy papers from the Organisation for Economic Co-operation and Development/ Development Assistance Committee (OECD/DAC) have highlighted the links between development cooperation and terrorism prevention.[25] The DAC has argued that the fundamental goal of poverty reduction shared by all development agencies can help prevent an environment hospitable to terrorism. Certainly the legitimacy of development objectives should not be threatened, but it is evident that development funders can do much to contribute to the basic goal of enhancing counterterrorism capacity and the potential of strategic peacebuilding. Moreover, greater development assistance can help address the root causes of terrorism. Many of the adverse social conditions in which terrorists thrive fall within the realm of primary concerns for development cooperation.

To realize these goals, greater direct dialogue is needed between security officials and the staff of development agencies, with the goal of identifying where counterterrorism and good governance agendas overlap and are mutually reinforcing.[26] Counterterrorism activities are traditionally viewed very differently by the security and development communities, paralleling similar tensions between the security and the peacebuilding communities. As it often unfolds, the former tend to be mainly concerned with enforcement and protection, whereas the latter have a focus on more fundamental structural issues. The close relationship between security and development is increasingly acknowledged as the development community aims to support the optimum functioning of civil society institutions.[27] Conversely, there is also recognition among security sector actors that short-term operations related to counterterrorism will not bring sustainable benefit without corresponding attention to underlying longer term development work.

The brief history of global counterterrorist efforts underscores the imperative that various actors must reinforce development and good governance goals as well as security capacity in government in a mutually beneficial cycle. These aims are interdependent and rely on the same factors for success, including participatory processes, transparency, and accountability. Technical aid and advice have become significant aspects of development assistance for many nations, particularly those with low levels of state capacity to meet the requirements of global counterterrorism mandates. The prospect of increased development aid and capacity-building assistance could be an inducement for many states to implement more completely UN mandates. A program of providing increased development assistance in combination with security-related capacity-building efforts could be highly attractive to many developing nations.

The CTC has been tasked with facilitating the provision of technical assistance to help nations of goodwill comply with UN counterterrorism requirements. What the CTC has learned in this process has been both enlightening and discouraging regarding the depth of the need for linking good governance with development aid. These lessons include the following.

- Relatively few countries have the extensive legal, administrative, and regulatory capacities needed to freeze financial assets, prevent the travel of designated individuals, deny safe haven to terrorists and their supporters, and suppress the recruitment and military supply of terrorist groups.[28]
- Many states face deep deficiencies in their operational and administrative capacity to implement UNSC counterterrorism mandates. Moreover, many states lack expertise even to determine their deficiencies in implementation capacity. These nations need improvements in legislation and legal authority, as well as better administrative machinery and equipment to implement legislative mandates. Their bureaucrats need training and performance guidance in meeting the standards.
- A significant number of states need help improving policing and law enforcement systems and creating financial regulatory mechanisms and financial intelligence units. Assistance may also be needed for the development of computerized links among security-related units, improved systems for identifying fraudulent travel documents, better mechanisms for controlling customs and immigration, and computerized equipment to screen passengers and cargo at border entry points.
- The demand for this kind of assistance far outpaces supply. Nearly 100 countries have expressed an interest in technical assistance from the CTC,[29] although the actual number of states needing assistance is greater.

Acting as a global switchboard of sorts, the CTC made some headway in connecting needy national bureaucracies with states, institutions, and professional groups that might assist them. The primary international organizations providing various types of assistance have been the United Nations Office on Drugs and Crime/Terrorism Prevention Branch, the Commonwealth

Secretariat, and the International Monetary Fund (IMF). Member countries of the OECD have also provided legislative drafting assistance on a bilateral basis. The IMF has been the main source of assistance for drafting legislation to counter the financing of terrorism.[30]

In the last area of concern for peacebuilding and counterterrorism—humanitarianism and human rights—the experience of the recent past reveals deep divisions among various actors. In some cases, including UNSC permanent members Russia, the United States, and China, national government officials have used the fight against terrorism as a justification for limiting democratic freedoms and suppressing dissident and minority groups or targeting specific individuals. The human rights NGO community has been aggressively defending human rights, often by condemning counterterrorism strategies and actions. IGOs, especially the UN, have attempted to articulate not only a defense of human rights in a time of terrorism but the argument that these two policy goals—enhanced human rights and effective counterterrorism—are not in a zero-sum relationship. Thus, Secretary General Kofi Annan stated in 2003:

> There is no trade-off to be made between human rights and terrorism. Upholding human rights is not at odds with battling terrorism: on the contrary, the moral vision of human rights—the deep respect for the dignity of each person—is among our most powerful weapons against it. To compromise on the protection of human rights would hand terrorists a victory they cannot achieve on their own. The promotion and protection of human rights . . . should, therefore, be at the centre of anti-terrorism strategies.[31]

Two years later, in his address at the Madrid summit in March 2005, Annan expressed regret that "many measures which States are currently adopting to counter terrorism are infringing on human rights and fundamental freedoms."[32] This theme was echoed in the UN High-Level Panel, which cautioned that "approaches to terror focusing wholly on military, police and intelligence measures risk undermining efforts to promote good governance and human rights."[33] Annan included the defense of human rights as one of the five pillars of global counterterrorism strategy.[34] UNSC Resolution 1456 stated: "States must ensure that any measure taken to combat terrorism comply with all their obligations under international law, and should adopt such measures in accordance with international law, in particular international human rights, refugee, and humanitarian law."[35]

A strong case can be made that protecting human rights and strengthening democracy are essential over the long run to the fight against terrorism. Protecting human rights and guaranteeing the freedom to voice dissenting views without government interference can help prevent the rise of political extremism.[36] This claim is not a political preference as much as an empirical trend worth noting. For example, a National Academy of Sciences study in 2002 noted, "terrorism and its supporting audiences appear to be fostered by

policies of extreme political repression and discouraged by policies of incorporating both dissident and moderate groups into civil society and the political process."[37] The 2002 UN Policy Working Group observed that "a lack of
hope for justice provides breeding grounds for terrorism."[38] People without
an opportunity to voice their opinions and organize politically often turn to
violence as the only way of expressing grievances. As Alan Krueger observed in
the *New York Times*, "the freedom to assemble and protest peacefully without
interference from the government goes a long way to providing an alternative
to terrorism."[39]

Human rights organizations have lobbied for greater UN efforts to uphold
these standards, arguing in 2006 that the CTC has "an obligation to ensure
respect for human rights in counter terrorism efforts by member states."[40]
In April 2005, the Office of the UN High Commissioner on Human Rights
decided to appoint "a special rapporteur on the promotion and protection of
human rights and fundamental freedoms while countering terrorism."[41] The
first report of the rapporteur, in December 2005, stated that "States are not
receiving a clear enough message from the [Counter-Terrorism] Committee
concerning their duty to respect human rights while countering terrorism."[42]
The report also expressed a desire to continue "dialogue with the Committee
and the Counter-Terrorism Executive Directorate including, in particular, the
joint identification and compilation of 'best practices' in the field of effective
and human rights compatible responses to terrorism." As a result, the CTED
now includes an expert on human rights on its staff, which will enhance the
ability of the CTC to ensure that counterterrorism best practices are compatible with respect for human rights. Many observers believe that this progress
would not have occurred if the transnational human rights community had not
mobilized so strongly, and for so long, to attain this objective.[43]

Coordination, Redundancy, and the New Reform Process in the
UN Counterterrorism System

We began this chapter by describing the evolution of United Nations sanctions
as more humane, "smarter" policy tools to complement strategic peacebuilding. We then discussed how the UNSC decided to employ such smart sanctions techniques in the battle against global terrorism and discussed the new
procedures and institutional actors the UN created for that task. As these processes unfolded, what became clear was that effective counterterrorism, whether
via smart sanctions or through the work of special agencies, needed to include
strategic assistance provided by the UN and related actors. This work aimed
to support the emergence and sustenance of good governance, increased economic development, and the enhancement of human rights. Coming full circle, these very policy goals for counterterrorism strategy have historically been
associated with the creation of sustainable peace and, thus, are central to strategic peacebuilding. In the previous section, we further explicated how these
goals relate mostly to positive developments that unfolded under the auspices

of the work of the CTC and CTED, as well as the organizations they drew into their cooperative orbit.

The achievements we have noted, although authentic, are short-lived. If the UN system is to play a lead role in the type of counterterrorism that fosters good governance, economic development, and human rights, substantial additional adaptation and innovation must be forthcoming.[44] Next we outline the problems that have developed that stifle effective counterterrorism action and provide a series of recommendations for improvement. As with the earlier discussion, we note how such changes enhance or restrict the prospects for successful strategic peacebuilding.

The range of regional and international organizations with actual or potential involvement in the UN counterterrorism mission is vast. Thus far, the CTC has made important strides in encouraging regional organizations to strengthen their counterterrorism capacity. Some regional organizations have created their own counterterrorism units, which share information with the CTC and attend semiannual regional coordination meetings. The Organization of American States (OAS) has played a leading role and has established a counterterrorism secretariat within the Inter-American Committee against Terrorism (CICTE). During 2002, the secretariat designed and deployed the CICTE online antiterrorism database. CICTE also participated in the drafting of model regulations for the prevention of terrorist financing and in meetings of the Caribbean Financial Action Task Force. The OAS Convention against Terrorism entered into effect in July 2003 and, as of February 2004, was signed by thirty-three of thirty-four member states.

After the Madrid bombings of March 2004, the European Council adopted the Declaration on Combating Terrorism and created the position of European coordinator for counterterrorism.[45] The Asia-Pacific Economic Cooperation forum had already established a Counter-Terrorism Task Force in February 2003. Similar regional bodies exist within the Commonwealth of Independent States and the Association of Southeast Asian Nations. The CTC has worked with these and other regional bodies to enhance overall international coordination in the campaign against terrorism.

Other geographic regions continue to lag behind. Much of South Asia and large parts of Africa have not adequately developed the necessary regionally coordinated mechanisms to facilitate local state implementation of counterterrorism resolutions mandated by the UNSC. Progress has been made among fourteen Arab states with the creation of a Middle East and North Africa FATF-style regional body, which was formally established in November 2004. Similar efforts are needed in North Africa and other regions to more effectively address other key issue areas covered in Resolution 1373, including border control, law enforcement, and judicial practice. Convening regional and subregional workshops to develop best practices, facilitated by the CTC and coordinated by local bodies, would be an important step toward achieving this task.[46]

Coordination among international and regional organizations has lost ground during the past few years, and the CTC has not been able to play as effective a coordinating role among states and organizations as it did at the outset of its tenure. Its declining ability to fulfill that function is partly due to administrative and other limitations imposed by operating within the UN headquarters in New York, which gravitates toward bureaucratic procedural approaches to the issues it faces to avoid potential political disagreements. As primarily a set of political bodies (or purely a political body in the case of the UNSC), the UN in its grand form is less well suited over time to the task of implementing many of the technical aspects of the resolutions it adopts. More effective might be the development of a narrowly defined, specialized agency, rather than a committee of the council, located in Vienna or Geneva with like-minded agencies, rather than in New York.[47]

Coordination and cooperation within the UN system also needs improvement. Of special concern is the relationship between the CTC and the UNSC committee and monitoring team established to enforce sanctions against al Qaeda and the Taliban. The monitoring team established by Resolution 1526 consists of eight staff members, yet it was tasked with the job of investigating and reporting on member state efforts to implement the sanctions measures. Coordination between the monitoring team and the CTED has been strained at times.

Inadequate cooperation between the monitoring team and CTED is part of a larger problem of overlap and poor coordination among the dozens of UN bodies addressing terrorism-related issues. There are now four special UNSC bodies working on counterterrorism issues, each with its own staff of experts: the CTC and the CTED, the al Qaeda and Taliban committee and monitoring team, the Resolution 1540 committee and staff experts, and the Resolution 1566 committee and working group. These bodies have a combined staff of forty professional experts. Although the mandates of the various committees are separate, they have many overlapping purposes and responsibilities. UN member states have obligations with respect to all four committees. The potential for the duplication of efforts and bureaucratic inefficiency under these circumstances is considerable. Reforming these inefficiencies and tackling the future challenges —as we outline shortly—are critical to the long-term viability of a counterterrorism policy that would actually contribute to peace and peacebuilding.

A long-term consideration for the future of the UN counterterrorism program—and for linking it more demonstrably to the UN purpose of building peace—is the prospect of creating a new international agency to combat terrorism. Monitoring the implementation of states' counterterrorism obligations requires a long-term and unwavering commitment—one that will not diminish as the memories of the most recent horrific terrorist attack fade or if the UNSC is seized with specific threats to international peace and security that require its urgent attention. Some states may take decades to develop their infrastructure to fully implement the counterterrorism obligations imposed by the UNSC and international treaties. Given the importance and long-term nature of the task, and the above-mentioned political and institutional limitations of working within the UN, serious consideration should be given to studying alternative models to the current approach, including the establishment of a dedicated counterterrorism organization outside of New York.

Creating a new agency would also be a means of giving greater priority and more permanence to the global fight against terrorism. Counterterrorism—one of the key security tasks of our era—is one of the few issues for which there is not a dedicated international agency. Human rights, refugees, chemical weapons, children's rights, and many other issues all—quite appropriately—have specialized agencies that are reasonably well resourced and operate within the UN system. It seems appropriate that a similar agency be created in the field of counterterrorism.[48]

It is conceivable that the CTED might create a precedent for and eventually evolve into a larger counterterrorism agency. Combining CTED with the staffs of the sanctions monitoring team and the two other counterterrorism expert groups would immediately create a sizable agency, one that then could be expanded on as nations determine the need. Ideally, such an agency should function within the UN system and operate under the authority of the UNSC, as is the case with the International Atomic Energy Agency. This would enable the proposed agency to bring matters to the attention of the council. It would give greater political weight to its operations and link it to potential enforcement authority.

Whether other UN member states will support an expansion of CTC/CTED capacity or the creation of a new international organization remains uncertain. The debate on these issues has yet to be joined. What has been agreed by many, as illustrated by this chapter, is that the structure and function of global counterterrorism efforts need to be dynamically integrated. As is the case in strategic peacebuilding, the structural underpinning that authoritatively administers a set of policies must do so in a manner that is inclusive of all relevant actors affected by policy. In addition, the form and the function of this inclusivity should produce greater peace and justice in dealing with difficult conflict situations. These are but a few of the critical issues that need to be addressed as the UNSC considers future options for creating greater organizational capacity in the struggle against international terrorism.

Achieving these ambitious objectives will be a difficult and long-term process. Preventive strategies pose enormous challenges for the United Nations and for the world's leading countries. A comprehensive approach includes not only coercive measures but also persuasive policies that seek to win hearts and minds. Like the other dimensions of successful counterterrorism strategy and strategic peacebuilding, this longer term preventive effort depends on a greater commitment to cooperation, multilateral action, the rule of law within good governance, and, particularly, a deep respect for human rights.

NOTES

Research for this chapter was supported by generous grants from the Royal Danish Ministry for International Affairs and the U.S. Institute of Peace. The authors also acknowledge the research assistance provided by Benjamin Rooney and Oldrich Bures, as well as students in the spring 2004 Counter-Terrorism Research Seminar at the University of Notre Dame. This chapter closely parallels portions of a policy document titled *An Action Agenda for Enhancing the United Nations Program on Counter-Terrorism* (Goshen, Ind.: Fourth Freedom Forum, 2004).

1. Though some observers view the active use of Security Council sanctions as a fulfillment of functions envisioned by the founding members of the UN, skepticism regarding the legal basis of comprehensive UN sanctions and controversies regarding the reach of Chapter VII authorization have been a concern to a number of analysts. See Paul Conlon, *United Nations Sanctions Management: A Case Study of the Iraq Sanctions Committee, 1990–1994*, Procedural Aspects of International Law Series (Ardsley, N.Y.: Transnational Publishers, 2000); and Vera Growlland-Debbas, ed., *United Nations Sanctions and International Law. The Graduate Institute of International Studies*, vol. 1 (The Hague: Kluwer Law International, 2001).

2. The most articulate and consistent of these analysts is Joy Gordon, "Sanctions as Siege Warfare," *The Nation*, March 1999; and "Cool War: Economic Sanctions as a Weapon of Mass Destruction," *Harper's*, August 2, 2002.

3. David Cortright and George A. Lopez, *The Sanctions Decade: Assessing UN Security Council Sanctions in the 1990s* (Boulder, Colo.: Lynne Rienner, 2000), pp. 14–32.

4. Peter Wallensteen and Carina Staibano, eds., *International Sanctions: Between Words and Wars in the Global System* (New York: Frank Cass, 2005).

5. Our past research confirms this mix of coercion and the promise of its release as a bargaining tool that increases the likelihood of sanctions success. See David Cortright and George A. Lopez, *The Sanctions Decade*, especially chapter 2.

6. We provide a more detailed account of this history in David Cortright, George A. Lopez, and Linda Gerber-Stellingwerf, "Sanctions," in Thomas G. Weiss and Sam Daws, eds., *The Oxford Handbook on the United Nations* (New York: Oxford University Press, 2007), pp. 349–369.

7. For an overview of these targeted sanctions see, David Cortright and George A. Lopez, eds., *Smart Sanctions: Targeting Economic Statecraft* (Lanham, Md.: Rowman & Littlefield, 2002); and Wallensteen and Staibano, *International Sanctions*.

8. Claudia Von Braunmühl and Manfred Kulessa, *The Impact of UN Sanctions on Humanitarian Assistance Activities, Report on a Study Commissioned by the United Nations Department of Humanitarian Affairs* (Berlin: Gesellschaft für Communication Management Interkultur Training, December 1995).

9. Larry Minear et al., *Toward More Humane and Effective Sanctions Management: Enhancing the Capacity of the United Nations System*, Occasional Paper 31 (Providence, R.I.: Thomas J. Watson Jr. Institute for International Studies, Brown University, 1998).

10. Manuel Bessler, Richard Garfield, and Gerard McHugh, *Sanctions Assessment Handbook: Assessing the Humanitarian Implications of Sanctions* (New York: United Nations Inter-Agency Standing Committee, 2004).

11. For more detailed analysis of arms embargoes, see Andy Knight, *The United Nations and Arms Embargoes Verification* (Lewiston, N.Y.: Edwin Mellen Press, 1998); and Michael Brzoska and George A. Lopez, eds., *Putting Teeth in the Tiger* (forthcoming).

12. United Nations Security Council, *Letter Dated 24 September 1996 from the Chairman of the Security Council Committee Established Pursuant to Resolution 724 (1991) Concerning Yugoslavia Addressed to the President of the Security Council, Report of the Copenhagen Roundtable on United Nations Sanctions in the Case of the Former Yugoslavia, Held at Copenhagen on 24 and 25 June 1996*, S/1996/776, New York, September 24, 1996, paras. 33 and 34.

13. See Damien Fruchart et al., *United Nations Arms Embargoes*, SIPRI and SPITS of Uppsala University, November 2007.

14. Much of the analysis that follows is drawn from our earlier work, especially Cortright et al., "Sanctions", and Cortright and Lopez, *Sanctions and the Search for Security*, pp. 204–217.

15. United Nations Security Council, *Report of the Panel of Experts on Violations of Security Council Sanctions against UNITA* (UN document S/2000/203), March 10, 2000; *Interim Report of the Monitoring Mechanism on Angola Sanctions Established by the Security Council in Resolution 1295 (2000) of April 2000* (UN document S/2000/1026), October 25, 2000; *Final Report of the Monitoring Mechanism on Angola Sanctions* (UN document S/2000/1225), December 21, 2000; *Addendum to the Final Report of the Monitoring Mechanism on Sanctions against UNITA* (UN document S/2001/363), April 11, 2001; *Supplementary Report of the Monitoring Mechanism on Sanctions against UNITA* (UN document S/2001/966), October 12, 2001; *Additional Report of the Monitoring Mechanism on Sanctions against UNITA* (UN document S/2002/486), April 26, 2002; and *Additional Report of the Monitoring Mechanism on Sanctions against UNITA* (UN document S/2002/1119), October 16, 2002.

16. United Nations Security Council, *Report of the Panel of Experts Appointed Pursuant to Security Resolution 1306 (2000), Paragraph 19, in Relation to Sierra Leone,* (UN document S/2000/1195), December 20, 2000.

17. United Nations Security Council, *Report of the Panel of Experts Pursuant to Security Council Resolution 1343 (2001), Paragraph 19, Concerning Liberia* (UN document S/2001/1015), October 26, 2001.

18. David Cortright, George A. Lopez, and Linda Gerber, "The Viability of Commodity Sanctions: The Case of Diamonds," in Cortright and A. Lopez, *Sanctions and the Search for Security*, pp. 181–200.

19. Richard A. Clarke et al., *Defeating the Jihadists: A Blueprint for Action* (Washington, D.C.: Century Foundation Press, 2004).

20. See, for example, Paul Wilkinson, *Terrorism versus Democracy: The Liberal State Response* (London: Frank Cass, 2003).

21. Much of the discussion that follows relies heavily on David Cortright and George A. Lopez, eds. *Uniting against Terror* (Cambridge, Mass.: MIT Press, 2007), pp. 3–12.

22. The history and details of these cases are chronicled in Cortright and Lopez, *The Sanctions Decade* and Cortright and Lopez, *Sanctions and the Search for Security*.

23. Karen Greenberg, *From the Editor: European Counterterrorism and Its Implications for the U.S. War on Terror,* Special Edition, *NYU Review of Law and Security* 2 (Summer 2005): 2–3.

24. Our own policy work in this area led us to write a series of interim reports on the CTC and CTED. Some of the material in the sections that follow are drawn from those reports as well as from David Cortright et al., "Global Cooperation against Terrorism," in Cortright and Lopez, eds., *Uniting against Terror*, pp. 23–46.

25. Organisation for Economic Co-operation and Development, *A Development Co-operation Lens on Terrorism Prevention: Key Entry Points for Action. DAC Guidelines and Reference Series* (Paris: OECD, 2003).

26. Steven Monblatt, Executive Secretary, Inter-American Committee against Terrorism, Organization of American States, "Developing Regional Cooperation" (statement at the CTC special meeting, Almaty, Kazakhstan, January 26–27, 2005).

27. A recent example is DAC/GOVNET, *The Challenge of Capacity Development: Working towards Good Practice*, February 1, 2006.

28. United Nations Security Council, *Security Council Resolution 1377 (2001),* S/RES/1377, New York, November 12, 2001.

29. Curtis Ward, personal communication with authors, June 16, 2004.

30. Curtis A. Ward, "Purposes and Scope: Technical Assistance Activities in the Counter-Terrorism Committee" (unpublished paper, 2004), p. 16.

31. Kofi Annan, "Conference Report" (keynote address, conference on "Fighting Terrorism for Humanity," International Peace Academy, New York, September 22, 2003), p. 10.

32. United Nations, "Secretary General Offers Global Strategy for Fighting Terrorism, in Address to Madrid Summit," SG/SM/9757, press release, Madrid, Spain, March 10, 2005.

33. United Nations, *A More Secure World: Our Shared Responsibility: Report of the Secretary-General's High-Level Panel on Threats, Challenges and Change*, A/59/565, para. 147.

34. Report of the Secretary-General, Uniting against terrorism: recommendations for a global counter-terrorism strategy, A/60/825. New York, United Nations General Assembly, April 27, 2006, http://www.un.org/unitingagainstterrorism/sg-terrorism-2may06.pdf (accessed May 18, 2006), section VI, paras. 110–118.

35. United Nations Security Council, Security Council Resolution 1456 (2003), S/RES/1456, New York, January 20, 2003, para. 6.

36. Alan Krueger, "Economic Scene," *New York Times*, May 29, 2002.

37. John Gershman, "A Secure America in a Secure World," Foreign Policy in Focus Special Report, FPI Task Force on Terrorism, September, 2004.

38. United Nations General Assembly, Security Council, *Report of the Policy Working Group on the United Nations and Terrorism*, A/57/273-S/2002/875, New York, August 6, 2002, para. 16.

39. Krueger, "Economic Scene."

40. See, for example, Human Rights Watch, "Open Letter to the United Nations Counter-Terrorism Committee," January 25, 2005, http://hrw.org/english/docs/2005/01/25/uzbeki10074_txt.htm (accessed May 9, 2006).

41. Human Rights Resolution 2005/80, "Protection of Human Rights and Fundamental Freedoms While Countering Terrorism," http://ap.ohchr.org/documents/E/CHR/resolutions/E-CN_4-RES-2005–80.doc (accessed June 21, 2006).

42. Report of the Special Rapporteur on the promotion and protection of human rights and fundamental freedoms while countering terrorism, E/CN.4/2006/98. December 28, 2005, http://daccessdds.un.org/doc/UNDOC/GEN/G05/168/84/PDF/G0516884.pdf?OpenElement (accessed June 21, 2006)

43. Rosemary Foot, "The United Nations, Counterterrorism, and Human Rights: Institutional Adaptation and Embedded Ideas," *Human Rights Quaterly* 29 (2007): 489–514.

44. For a full explication of these reforms, see Cortright and Lopez, *Uniting against Terror*, pp. 237–272; and Eric Rosand, "Global Terrorism: Multilateral Responses to an Extraordinary Threat," Coping with Crisis Working Paper Series (New York: International Peace Academy, April 2007).

45. The text of the declaration is available online at the *European Union*, http://www.eu2004.ie/templates/document_file.asp?id=10707 (accessed August 20, 2004).

46. Reports received by the CTC show deficiencies in regions with less developed regional organizational capacity to assist states in implementing Resolution 1373. More information on the Eastern and Southern African Anti-Money Laundering Group is available online at the OECD, http://www1.oecd.org/fatf/Ctry-orgpages/org-esaamlg_en.htm (accessed June 15, 2004).

47. This recommendation also appears in Rosand, "Global Terrorism."

48. See Eric Rosand, "The UN Security Council's Counter-Terrorism Efforts," in Roy S. Lee, ed., *Swords into Plowshares: Building Peace through the United Nations* (Leiden: Nijhoff, 2006), pp. 73–83.

8

Peace *and* Justice?

The Contribution of International Judicial Processes to Peacebuilding

Robert C. Johansen

In discussions about how to end armed conflicts and nurture peacebuilding, some observers argue that pursuing justice by trying to bring political leaders accused of horrible crimes to trial often interferes with achieving a cease-fire agreement and sustaining peace thereafter.[1] On the other hand, human rights advocates claim there can be no lasting peace without justice and no deterrence of crimes without judicial action against perpetrators. Yet in Michael P. Scharf's words, "history appears to be replete with many instances of peace based on injustice, as well as situations where pursuing justice has thwarted the quest for peace, and where justice has been successfully traded for peace."[2] Investigations of mass murder and prosecutions of those responsible for it may increase instability and deepen hostility among adversarial groups in one society but contribute to a sense of political catharsis that relaxes tensions, enables social healing, and opens the door to restorative justice in another. Context matters.

The establishment of the International Criminal Court (ICC) has brought the possible trade-off between justice and peace more directly to the forefront because of the increased possibility that political leaders may be indicted for war crimes or crimes against humanity, thereby motivating them to resist a peace agreement unless and until it offers them amnesty from future prosecution. On one hand, arguments for seeking justice and disallowing impunity for wrongdoers are compelling, not only because justice, impartially pursued, is desirable in itself and may deter future crimes, but also because the truth-revealing function of trials and the public act of assigning moral responsibility for crimes may contribute to sustainable peace and reconciliation in the long run. On the other hand, arguments for achieving an immediate peace in a society being torn apart by ongoing war and for providing incentives to stop fighting are also compelling. If at times it seems that trade-offs between the two values are necessary, what should be done?[3]

In this chapter I argue that to maximize both peace and justice, international judicial institutions, the United Nations, national governments, and human rights organizations should adopt a rule-based utilitarian ethic in which lessons learned from past judicial proceedings to enforce human rights law and prudential political bargaining for peace should be synthesized to achieve the lowest possible (estimated) loss of life, considering both the short and the long term.[4] Although this thesis is necessarily imprecise because it is impossible to predict accurately the future of conflict, especially in strife-ridden societies, it offers a clear guideline that can be helpful in decision making, for judicial officers and political negotiators as well as the public at large. Moreover, this thesis encourages a more creative synthesis of lessons learned from both judicial proceedings and political negotiations for cease-fires than has been developed up to now.

The central question of this analysis is: to what extent and in what ways do international judicial processes contribute to peace and peacebuilding? The discussion begins with a look at the meaning of peacebuilding, followed by some cautionary comments about the difficulties of drawing causal connections between judicial proceedings and peacebuilding. Second, the discussion explores common consequences of judicial activism—that is, arguments for and against investigating and prosecuting those who are accused of genocide, crimes against humanity, and war crimes. Third, I suggest guidelines for designing and conditionally employing judicial proceedings to encourage an end to ongoing violent conflict and discourage the resumption of violence after a cease-fire. These are based on lessons drawn from recent conflicts and international judicial practice. Fourth, the analysis closes with a discussion of how to maximize both peace and justice in peacebuilding strategies.

This analysis confirms the idea that international judicial practices are most conducive to peacebuilding when they are understood to be only one of many factors in strategic peacebuilding and when they are deliberately employed as part of an overall strategy thoughtfully orchestrating a wide range of related legal, political, economic, and public education practices—a central theme advanced by John Paul Lederach and Scott Appleby in their Overview, by Daniel Philpott in the Introduction, and by the contributors to this book more generally. For instance, judicial practices can easily be discredited and thought to be divisive if they are viewed in isolation and expected to do much more than they are able to do. But they can do well in establishing accountability for wrong-doing and in reaffirming socially constructive norms for conduct, while receiving approval from local people for these contributions, *if* other initiatives, perhaps from a truth commission, a legislature, educational media, religious organizations, or well-trained police and national judicial processes take up other tasks that international judicial institutions cannot manage but which do need to occur for healing to result.

Definitions, Causality, and Assumptions

Definitions

It is useful to note at the outset that the two concepts of peacebuilding and justice-seeking share several goals: to prevent future violations of fundamental human rights norms, strengthen the rule of international and national law, address the consequences and injustices of past abuses, promote understanding and reconciliation in a violence-ridden society, and reshape the international system in ways that will increase compliance with norms of peace and human rights in the long run.

One's definition of *peacebuilding* heavily influences one's calculus of the "contribution of international judicial proceedings to peacebuilding." Within this chapter, *peacebuilding* means "social integration." Within "social" I include political, economic, legal, and other dimensions of social life. "Social integration" can occur in a tiny village community, a city, a state, or the international community. If social integration can occur in international society, as I think it can, then peacebuilding can also occur in the international community among national societies, as well as among different groups inside a state. The latter locus for peacebuilding is widely accepted; the former is often ignored. A concept of peacebuilding that includes the former takes account of cross-border interactions and international norms and institutions that promise to increase the willingness and ability of states to prevent violence among themselves and within their societies.

"Globalization" may bring either social integration or disintegration. It may increase transnational cross-cutting social cleavages—an integrative function of social conflicts—or decrease them, in which case it could eventually build a global apartheid system. The peacebuilding (social integration) discussed in this chapter includes both horizontal and vertical dimensions of integration. "Strategic peacebuilding" includes all dimensions of social integration from the local to the global. At their best, international judicial proceedings contribute to peacebuilding at every level, from the smallest village that suffered an atrocity to the system of global order. Peacebuilding as processes of social integration includes efforts "to establish effective governance institutions, strengthen the rule of law, encourage sustainable development, and build trust between citizens and the state, as well as among citizens themselves."[5] Thus, all the main issues in the choices over how to make peace and whether to pursue justice through judicial proceedings are relevant to the peacebuilding strategist.

As suggested, for purposes of careful analysis, peacebuilding needs to be defined to include not only its impact within a state but also its impact on interstate relations, and its possible impact on the nature of the global order itself. If international judicial processes contribute to intrastate peacebuilding by deterring crimes in a particular society, for example, these processes may indirectly affect other societies as well. In addition, these processes may influence military conduct *between* countries by reinforcing, for example, the expectation that violations of the Geneva Conventions will receive international attention if a national government does not honor the conventions or if alleged violations are not handled in an appropriate way by domestic judicial institutions. There is some evidence, for example, that the number and scope of atrocities in Darfur declined, although they were not totally halted, after word spread that the ICC would attempt to prosecute crimes there.[6] In the long run, recurring expectations among countries that international legal procedures are an ever-present reality can modify state conduct and eventually the structure of international relations. Constructivist studies of the role of international norms have also shown that norms may influence people's identities, because the internalization of norms constitutes identities as well as shapes the legitimacy of major political institutions.[7] In a genuine sense, expanding the rule of law among nations through international judicial proceedings can help "domesticate" the international system.[8] The domestication process can be viewed as (global) systemic peacebuilding, transforming the global order into a more effective rule-of-law society.

Because the boundary between domestic and international politics is increasingly porous, and because relevant actors are not limited to states, either in terms of upholding human rights or violating them, we ought not to take a primarily state-centric perspective in studying peacebuilding. Transnational political and economic relations may affect peacebuilding as much as international political and economic relations, as this examination of the role of international judicial processes will demonstrate.

When I speak of the rule of law or of a "rule-of-law society," I mean to invoke a society in which a broad range of democratic values and time-honored judicial practices are present, including fair elections; freedom of speech, press, and assembly; robust guarantees for minority rights that limit majority rule to ensure respect for nonderogable human rights; checks and balances; widespread support for the belief that law should be impartially implemented and adjudicated, with due process protections, and that law should be no respecter of persons. This kind of a rule-of-law society is certainly conducive to realizing the values of human dignity and is a primary manifestation of peacebuilding. As defining the rule of law can be controversial, my description is intended to be fully consistent with the UN Secretary General's definition of the concept as "a principle of governance in which all persons, institutions and entities, public and private, including the state itself, are accountable to laws that are publicly promulgated, equally enforced and independently adjudicated, and which are consistent with international human rights norms and standards."[9] It includes "measures to ensure adherence to the principles of supremacy of law, equality before the law, accountability to the law, fairness in the application of the law, separation of powers, participation in decision-making, legal certainty, avoidance of arbitrariness and procedural and legal transparency."[10]

Causal Connections

The purpose of this analysis of international judicial processes and peacebuilding arises from a desire to identify ways that judicial proceedings focused on assessing the responsibility for gross violations of human rights may contribute to social integration or sustainable peace. Implementing justice through judicial proceedings, of course, may be desirable in itself, without regard for whether it contributes to peacebuilding in the short run. Yet it does not make sense to pursue justice without some regard for its impact on peacebuilding, because a failure to contribute to the latter could undermine justice as well as peace further down the road. Thus, we are interested in how the two interact. In the long run, justice pursued through exemplary judicial processes normally contributes to peacebuilding.

Of course, the ways that judicial processes may contribute to peacebuilding are extremely complex and influenced by the consequences of other peacebuilding measures. This study begins with three explicit assumptions. First is the relatively uncontroversial assumption that enforcing the law discourages illegal conduct. This is widely assumed to be true in domestic legal systems and no doubt has an analogue in the international legal system, despite the latter's highly decentralized nature. Of course it is difficult to *prove* that law enforcement increases legal conduct because it is difficult to know how many people would have broken the law in the absence of enforcement. Thus, it is difficult to know how many lives might be saved by international enforcement of human rights law, particularly if one attempts to consider the long-term life-saving benefits of weaving a stronger fabric of international law. But we can conjecture how many lives might have been saved by international enforcement of human rights law. Political leaders orchestrated the killing of more than 2 million people in Cambodia. Hutu leaders massacred an estimated 800,000 Rwandans in a few weeks. Effective enforcement of agreed-on international law could have saved most of these lives in what are only two of many examples where law enforcement could make dramatic differences.

A second, related assumption is that reducing illegal conduct in the form of gross violations of human rights contributes to peacebuilding. If many laws in a society are rights affirming, then legal, predictable conduct dignifies human life in a rule-of-law society and enhances social integration (peacebuilding).

A third assumption is that exemplary law enforcement processes contribute more to peacebuilding than deeply flawed processes. Not all law enforcement is the same. Obviously, some judicial processes come much closer to ideal expectations than others. Flawed processes do not "teach" the desired rule-of-law message. Bad laws or bad legal practice can even undermine respect for the law. Apartheid, for example, had an elaborate legal framework in South Africa, yet enforcing its laws did not contribute to peacebuilding. Dictators and leaders in authoritarian political systems may use judicial prosecutions to eliminate their opponents and ensure their own power. Although authoritarian legal systems in China and Vietnam, for example, stabilized those societies, prevented their fragmentation, and organized effective economic development programs, these exceptions to the assumption advanced here do not negate the general principle that the more legal processes appear to be unfair, partisan, manipulative, truth-denying, one-sided, and corrupt, the less likely they are to contribute to peacebuilding.

To consider another example, if a revolutionary process is brewing in a society, law enforcement by a hated government may contribute to violence and social disintegration, not peacebuilding. Of course even deeply flawed, draconian legal processes may increase people's *compliance* with the law (if not respect for it) because they are intimidated. To illustrate the complexities, it seems that Saddam Hussein's totalitarian political system prevented Kurds, Shiites, and Sunnis from civil war, but such a system did not contribute much to peacebuilding in a comprehensive sense. In the present analysis, peacebuilding should not be construed as merely synonymous with maintenance of order among potentially adversarial groups, although peaceable relations among all are essential. Here the concept also includes steps toward genuine social integration in a democratizing society.

A fourth assumption is that to assess the overall impact of judicial practices on peacebuilding, it is necessary to examine peacebuilding over one or preferably several decades of time. Good judicial processes not only render a verdict on a specific case, they also teach the society to respect law and to support a culture of respect for human rights.

To complicate assessment further, we might ask about the timing of initiatives: does peacebuilding begin with efforts to arrange a cease-fire among warring parties, or does it begin only after achieving peace? Some of the same factors that contribute to peacebuilding before a cease-fire in phase one may not contribute to peacebuilding after a cease-fire in phase two. To illustrate, two warring groups in intrastate conflict may advance a cease-fire arrangement by agreeing that there shall be an amnesty for all belligerents. Subsequently, having no investigations or prosecutions may cause resentment and social unrest, especially if a large number of persons in the society were victimized by criminal conduct of one or both parties before the cease-fire. We must acknowledge that what advances peacebuilding may vary from time$_1$ to time$_2$, and so on.

Because the prospects for peace are sometimes affected by anticipations of judicial processes begun before a cease-fire is arranged, it is necessary to examine (1) conditions under which the prospect of investigations and prosecutions of crimes apparently help end war and (2) other conditions under which they appear to prolong the fighting. Some ways of ending a war contribute far more to peacebuilding than others. Even if we focus on the same time period in a conflict cycle to compare two conflicts, peacebuilding in one society may be helped by truth telling (postapartheid South Africa) or by prosecutions (post–World War II Germany), whereas these do not help or are not needed in another society (post-Franco Spain).

Indeed, "postconflict peacebuilding" can be advanced or undermined by conduct before a war ends, so a focus on postconflict events alone is too limited. As experience in the former Yugoslavia demonstrates, certain conduct during fighting, such as "ethnic cleansing," can irretrievably embitter relations among people who previously lived amicably together and frequently intermarried. Insufficient attention has been given to such "peace-unbuilding" or "peace-dismantling," perhaps because those elites who exercise military power do not like to acknowledge that the application of violent means often makes matters worse, even if one achieves military victory. There are many reasons why violent conduct today, which usually kills more civilians than soldiers and rips time-honored social fabrics quickly to shreds, might be considered uncivilized: it can easily destroy civility among human groups. In so doing, it forces peacebuilding to start at a far more difficult, disadvantageous point than before the collective violence began.

Arguments For and Against Judicial Activism

The Rome Statute proclaims a purpose that provides perhaps the best argument for using international judicial processes: "to guarantee lasting respect for and the enforcement of international justice."[11] Insofar as international judicial processes contribute to "lasting respect for . . . justice" they also contribute to peacebuilding because citizens will begin to trust the capacity of judicial institutions, and the willingness of others, to protect them through legal means, thereby rendering resort to armed conflict undesirable. Especially in societies with effectively functioning legal and political institutions, progress in justice-seeking contributes to progress in peacebuilding and vice versa.

Assessing the contributions of international judicial proceedings to peacebuilding requires answers to the following seven questions.

1. Do international judicial proceedings help reduce atrocities or establish cease-fires?
2. Do international judicial proceedings curtail impunity and help deter future crimes?
3. Do international judicial proceedings bring out the truth and discourage collective guilt?
4. Do international judicial proceedings provide due process for defendants, reduce the power of perpetrators, and limit their future political roles?
5. Do international judicial processes aid domestic legal processes and bring nonpartisanship and desirable external expertise and support into peacebuilding efforts to establish a rule-of-law society?
6. Do international judicial proceedings encourage reconciliation?
7. Do international judicial proceedings help domesticate the international system and move it toward a global rule-of-law society?

Because of the limited scope of this chapter and the short time periods that have passed since international tribunals have been used following the end of the cold war, final answers to these questions cannot be provided, but the discussion illustrates preliminary findings and how detailed case studies could explore the ways that judicial action influences peacebuilding.

Do International Judicial Proceedings Help Reduce Atrocities or
Establish Cease-Fires?

ICC indictments may encourage both reductions in atrocities during ongoing
fighting and the willingness of leaders to enter negotiations for cease-fires. In
the ICC's first case, involving the Lord's Resistance Army (LRA), which has
been fighting the Ugandan government for two decades, available evidence
indicates that the indictments of five leaders of the LRA added significantly to
the psychological, legal, and political pressure on LRA leaders, pushing them
toward fewer abductions of children, a reduction of their violent attacks, and
willingness to enter cease-fire negotiations.[12] Prior to the indictments, the LRA
had continued bloody atrocities for nearly twenty years. The conflict in northern Uganda received very little international attention until the ICC became
involved. The court's indictments of LRA leaders raised the international community's awareness of the conflict and focused the spotlight of public opinion
on the leaders' atrocities.

The indictments seemed to discourage the leaders from continuing the
war, because continuation of their way of fighting, which included widespread
abduction of children for soldiers and sex slaves, would have provided additional and fresh evidence of their atrocities. This evidence would, of course,
be consequential if they ever faced a prosecutor. The Court's activities drew
"greater international and regional attention to the conflict and put pressure on
both sides to resolve it."[13] Soon after the indictments, the LRA began to seek a
cease-fire agreement. The LRA leaders' insistence that amnesty for themselves
must be included in a peace accord reveals the importance of indictments.

In another major case for the ICC, Osman Hummaida, the former director of the Sudanese Organization Against Torture, has noted that following the
United Nations's referral of atrocities in Darfur to the ICC in March 2005, "for
the very first time, there was a decline in aerial bombardment and Janjaweed
attacks on civilians. Those committing the crimes took the ICC investigation
seriously."[14] Salih Mahmoud Osman, a member of the Sudanese Parliament, further indicated that accountability has been an "important element" in "providing
protection to survivors in Darfur and preventing further depopulation and ethnic cleansing. . . . Soon after the situation was referred to the ICC there were no
attacks for three months."[15] Although the impact seemed to decline somewhat
as progress slowed in prosecuting the accused, the impact might have deepened
if judicial processes would have been more effectively carried forward.

Although these cases demonstrate a peacebuilding benefit from ICC action,
the Ugandan case suggests that the first phase of judicial influence provided
an incentive for LRA leaders to decide to seek a cease-fire agreement, but in a
second phase, the indictments slowed progress in finding terms for an agreement that would be accepted by all. The ICC was not ready to quash the indictments, and the LRA indictees would not accept a cease-fire without amnesty.
They feared prosecution if the war ended without first having amnesty in place.
As the UN Secretary General's Special Adviser on the Prevention of Genocide,

Juan Méndez, acknowledged, "the threat of prosecution can be a clear disincentive for actors in an armed conflict to give up their resort to violence."[16] The Catholic Archdiocese's Justice and Peace Commission of Gulu in the northern district of Uganda issued a strong criticism of the ICC for accepting the Ugandan government's referral of LRA atrocities: "To start war crimes investigations for the sake of justice at a time when the war is not yet over, risks having, in the end, neither justice nor peace delivered."[17] Some Ugandan church leaders saw the ICC's investigation and indictments as "disruptive" to peace processes. They claimed that judicial prosecution "discourages LRA members from seeking amnesty pursuant to a Ugandan law passed in 2000."[18] The archdiocese also said the ICC initiative "potentially undermines traditional mechanisms of reconciliation and reintegration. The threat of prosecution may serve as a stick, but the carrot of amnesty and reconciliation must be retained in order to reinforce the peace process."[19]

In the face of criticism, Yves Sorokobi, an ICC spokesman, stated that "if it is in the interest of justice to proceed with a peace agreement, the ICC is ready to suspend its investigation." In addition, the ICC prosecutor, Luis Moreno-Ocampo, "was reported by international media as saying if a solution to end the violence was found, and continuing the investigation did not serve the interests of justice, then the ICC would stop the probe."[20]

Those policy makers and observers who seem to prefer amnesty to indictments as an inducement to a cease-fire should recall that for more than fifteen years the LRA showed no interest in a cease-fire. The Ugandan government had tried an amnesty program before the ICC indictments, but without any success in bringing the war toward an end. Not one commanding officer sought amnesty. It appeared that, in the words of one close observer, "nothing short of effective military action against the LRA would drive its leaders to opt for negotiation."[21] It was in the face of persistent international indifference to the war and the exhaustion of other alternatives that focus turned to calling on the ICC. For the Ugandan government to refer the LRA atrocities to the ICC "was . . . a strategy for engaging the international community by committing . . . ICC proponents to the arrest and prosecution of top LRA leaders, just as the United Nations had earlier proposed."[22] By excluding top leaders from amnesty, those most responsible might be brought to justice.

International cooperation was also necessary to press Sudanese leaders to quit giving sanctuary to the LRA in camps in Sudan. According to Payam Akhaven, empirical evidence shows that the Ugandan government's referral of atrocities to the ICC "has contributed to the LRA's incapacitation." In addition, Sudan "has been persuaded to end its support of the LRA."[23] These developments "weakened the LRA's military capability, encouraged significant defections among LRA commanders, and forced otherwise defiant leaders to the negotiating table."[24] These results were "in sharp contrast to the period preceding the referral, during which LRA atrocities reached a new peak." New willingness to negotiate "is linked to the LRA's political isolation and military containment—both of which are linked to the new context created by the ICC referral. In this respect at least, it would not be unreasonable to suggest that even without a single prosecution, the LRA referral has already been a suc-cess."[25] Yet many observers downplayed the ICC's initial peacebuilding ben-efits as time passed and the LRA leaders continued to resist a cease-fire without the lifting of their indictments.

Given the possibility that ICC indictments and arrest warrants might contribute to saving lives one day but impede achieving a signed cease-fire agreement the next, it is useful to look more closely at the Ugandan case and what the people most affected by LRA atrocities have thought about how to proceed. When the evidence is ambiguous regarding humanitarian benefits that might flow from prosecution in a peacebuilding strategy, the preferences of the people most affected should be given additional weight, as long as those preferences are within the law and not aimed at revenge. Usually it is difficult to know their preferences because their opinions are inaccessible. In this case, a highly professional survey of Ugandan opinion at the village level is available for examination. This opinion study shows some pluralism among those liv-ing in the four districts of northern Uganda most affected by the war, and also some substantial agreement by sizable majorities of the population.

The opinion study was prepared against the backdrop of knowledge that some, both within Uganda and in humanitarian and governmental agencies outside, argued that the ICC's involvement might "prolong the conflict and undermine peace talks between the LRA and the government's mediator, Betty Bigomge, as well as other local initiatives, such as the work of the Ugandan government's Amnesty Commission and the exploration of using traditional tribal methods to deal with past crimes."[26] On the other hand, proponents of international judicial processes said that "pursuing peace at the expense of jus-tice is not a viable long-term option."[27]

In the four northern districts, 45 percent of all people had witnessed the killing of one of their own family members.[28] In the face of such general trauma, their top priorities were clear: food and peace. Yet most people "viewed peace and justice as a complex relationship that was not necessarily mutually exclusive."[29] Most sought both, including reparations for victims.

Three-fourths (76 percent) said those responsible for abuses "should be held accountable for their actions." Even when asked whether "they would accept amnesty if it were the only road to peace," 29 percent still said "no."[30] A majority gave high priority to accountability for crimes committed by all sides. Sixty-six percent favored trials and punishment for the LRA; an even higher per-centage (76 percent) said the Ugandan (government) Defense Forces should be held accountable for atrocities they committed.[31] Even in regions where people were assumed to prefer traditional justice measures, most respondents (66 percent) believed that "LRA members should face punitive and/or formal legal processes and that community-oriented options for dealing with perpetrators would only be appropriate for low-level LRA members."[32] These preferences are quite understandable. Many of the LRA fighters were children, abducted and taken away to be used as child soldiers to commit atrocities. Many people wanted their children to return to their villages and were ready to forgive them if they returned. But many believed that the leaders, more culpable for heinous crimes, should face some accountability proceedings and should acknowledge the crimes they committed. Up to now, the LRA leaders have denied any wrong-doing, despite their refusal to stand trial and their insistence on amnesty.

Although 65 percent of the people supported some amnesty processes for the LRA, only 4 percent said amnesties should be granted uncondition-ally. Most said that the government's blanket amnesty "should be reformed" and that "some form of acknowledgement [of misconduct] and/or retribution should be required of all those granted amnesty."[33]

Although 84 percent believed that the international community "should be involved in holding accountable those responsible for human rights viola-tions,"[34] 73 percent knew "nothing or very little about the ICC's existence and work." Of the people who had heard of the court, "a majority attached high expectations to it, believing that the ICC would contribute both to peace (91 percent) and justice (89 percent)."[35] Of those who knew about the court, 94 percent supported its involvement in response to atrocities.[36]

The authors of the opinion survey concluded that "peace and justice will be achieved in Northern Uganda only through an inclusive process that involves a wide range of stakeholders, including victims, bystanders, and perpetrators."[37] Clearly, those who have been most affected by the violence should have a voice in determining the processes for moving beyond it, not only in deference to the democratic principle but also because meeting the people's desires and expectations, insofar as they are humane, contributes to peacebuilding and reconciliation. It seems that an effort aimed at providing some justice without delaying peace too long could attempt to prosecute the top leaders and offer amnesty, with some conditions, such as acknowledgment of wrongdoing, for all the rest. (The ICC indicted only five of the LRA's top leaders and promised not to indict others to enable the amnesty program to encourage a stop to the fighting.)

This approach is confirmed by a subsequent study conducted by the UN Office of the High Commissioner for Human Rights in Acholiland, Lango, and Teso subregions of northern Uganda: "The population broadly believes that both the LRA and the Government, and specifically their leaders, should be held accountable for the harms they have caused during the conflict."[38]

Do International Judicial Proceedings Curtail Impunity and Help Deter Future Crimes?

States' widely shared determination to eradicate impunity for heinous crimes finds explicit expression in the Rome Statute's provision "to put an end to impu-nity for perpetrators and to contribute to the prevention of [genocide, crimes against humanity, and war crimes]."[39] In a more general UN context, all fifteen members of the Security Council have committed themselves to ending impu-nity and establishing accountability for such crimes.[40] In a recent assessment of the genocide in Sudan, Osman Hummaida said that "ending the culture of impunity is key to protection of civilians."[41]

Most international legal experts believe that the ICC's existence and future work will reduce impunity, a peacebuilding achievement in itself, and also increase the deterrence of future crimes. However, there is little agreement about the degree to which these consequences will occur. Clearly, the possibility that international legal proceedings might be mounted against violators of international humanitarian and human rights law, especially the law against genocide, arises now as never before, in the minds of political leaders everywhere.[42] Exponents of retributive justice have a strong argument that international judicial proceedings to punish war crimes, crimes against humanity, and genocide do indeed contribute to the pursuit of justice and the saving of lives.

The creation and continued backing of the ad hoc tribunals for Yugoslavia and Rwanda and the establishment of the ICC, all of which draw on the concept of extraterritorial jurisdiction (including universal jurisdiction), plus the establishment of the Special Court for Sierra Leone and other mixed tribunals for Cambodia, Kosovo, and Timor-Leste, together produce a new international reality: a general presumption against impunity.[43] Of course such a presumption does not mean there will be perfect compliance.

To buttress compliance, the United Nations has helped establish all of the mixed tribunals, and the secretary general has said that UN-endorsed peace agreements cannot give amnesty for genocide, war crimes, crimes against humanity, or other gross violations of human rights. Moreover, amnesties given by other actors cannot, in his view, prevent prosecutions by UN-created or -assisted courts.[44] The UN Human Rights Committee also has said "that blanket amnesty laws and pardons are inconsistent with the Covenant [on Civil and Political Rights] because they create 'a climate of impunity' and deny the victims this 'right to a remedy.'"[45] Of course, the Genocide Convention, which is nearly universally endorsed, *obligates* states to punish wrongdoers.[46]

General principles of international law obligate states to carry out these tasks in response to crimes against humanity:

1. to investigate, prosecute, and punish the perpetrators;
2. to disclose to the victims, their families, and society all that can be reliably established about those events;
3. to offer the victims adequate reparations; and
4. to separate known perpetrators from law enforcement bodies and other positions of authority.[47]

Corresponding to these state obligations are an emerging set of rights that make impunity unacceptable, including "a right to know the truth" and a "right of the victim to see justice done."[48] Indeed, the right to know the truth "has achieved the status of a customary international law norm."[49]

Leila Nadya Sadat challenges "conventional wisdom that 'swapping justice for peace,' is morally and practically acceptable." Several longitudinal studies, she notes, indicate that in the long run "amnesty deals" "foster a culture of impunity in which violence becomes the norm, rather than the exception."[50] She cautions against letting the South African success with conditional amnesty confuse the picture. This exception to the general rule, she concludes, should not be substituted for the rule: "both state and international practice now suggest that exile and amnesty is a largely unacceptable response to the commission of *jus cogens* crimes."[51] The law against impunity seems clear and the culture of support for the law is rising.

Deterrence

The extent to which reducing impunity and prosecuting gross violations of human rights will deter future crimes is widely debated and no doubt influenced by many factors,[52] including the extent to which would-be criminals expect that they might be prosecuted. Before the creation of the two temporary international tribunals in the 1990s (the International Criminal Tribunal for the former Yugoslavia and the International Criminal Tribunal for Rwanda), the permanent ICC, and more recently the hybrid tribunals, most perpetrators could reasonably expect that they would never face a trial or any form of accountability. From that low point of accountability, the creation of the permanent ICC is a major step forward in establishing conditions conducive to peacebuilding. The ICC ensures that the international community will give increased attention to gross violations of human rights. The Court clearly increases the possibility that law-breakers will be held accountable, particularly in weak states. As Patrick Hayden has written, because the ICC is a permanent criminal court, it "will serve as a greater deterrent to those who might otherwise be tempted to commit war crimes and other egregious human rights abuses." Knowledge that the ICC is always on watch "may deter individuals from acting with a sense of impunity and thereby decrease the occurrence of future atrocities."[53] M. Cherif Bassiouni concludes that "fair trials affirm that atrocities are wrong and unacceptable—drawing a clear line for all to see—and incarceration prevents the guilty from repeat offenses and potentially serves as a deterrent to others."[54]

A court indictment affirms the international community's interest in upholding fundamental human rights norms and publicizes both the norms and major alleged violations of them. This helps educate people about the importance of the norms and of compliance with them even if there are not immediate arrests or trials. Because people do not want to be indicted, they are more likely to conduct themselves in ways that a court would not find objectionable, thus demonstrating benefits of international judicial processes in publicizing and applying existing norms, building new norms, and setting legal precedents.

In addition, an indictment might be viewed as a de facto "smart sanction."[55] An indictment has an admirable specificity that economic sanctions seldom have achieved. The indictment identifies the law that may have been violated and the individual person who is accused of wrongdoing. The indictment applies only to that person. Although the accused should be considered innocent until proven guilty, if the person refuses to stand trail, his or her ability to travel is greatly reduced after an arrest warrant is issued. The person must limit travel to places in the world where the ruling authorities are willing to shield the accused. Significantly, the top LRA leadership indicted by the ICC chose not to travel to Juba, Sudan, in 2006, where peace talks were being held, because of fear that someone might arrest them. As a result, others needed to play an enhanced leadership role, perhaps opening the door eventually to displacement of the indictees. Thus indictment may limit freedom of movement and possibly the power of the accused because of their need to maintain low visibility to avoid arrest.

More generally, deterrence is enhanced by the extent to which international judicial proceedings can gather evidence promptly, archive it, and identify and protect witnesses. As an aid to peacebuilding, the ICC strengthens accountability, transparency, and legal compliance. It reinforces the legal duty imposed on all states to address atrocities like genocide, mass murder, and rape.[56] Even potential law-breakers who reside in states that have not ratified the Rome Statute might be deterred by knowledge that they could be investigated by the ICC if the Security Council decided to refer their case to the court.[57] Only the five permanent members of the Security Council have the direct opportunity to stop a possible UN referral of crimes to the ICC for review of their own nationals' conduct. As a consequence, the ICC and the UN together can contribute significantly to the rule of law internationally and thereby to the deterrence of gross violations in the areas under court jurisdiction.

Numerous international experts support this conclusion: Catherine Lu has noted that the work of the ICC promotes deterrence of future crimes because it punishes perpetrators.[58] Steven R. Ratner and Jason S. Abrams emphasize that "accountability . . . serves a preventive purpose. It can signal to future violators of human rights that their actions will not simply be forgotten in some political compromise."[59] Bruce Shapiro's work demonstrates that "establishing the facts of atrocity and accurately laying out lines of accountability aid in democratic transition [and] help dampen cycles of generalized revenge."[60] Sadat reports "evidence that the credible threat of punishment may in time affect the behavior of perpetrators, making international criminal justice an important component of constraining inter- and intra-state violence and the commission of atrocities."[61] Many other legal experts emphasize the existing global responsibility to ensure that crimes are properly punished and wrongdoing is carefully examined to identify abuses when they occur and to uphold the norms for appropriate conduct.[62]

International judicial proceedings are more likely than national proceedings to have a spill-over effect in deterring people's illegal conduct in other states.[63] However, where criminal prosecution is not feasible in the foreseeable future, investigatory or truth commissions can provide a method of accountability. Reports can be detailed, authoritative, and unbiased, including identification of perpetrators and victims. Their work can foster social and spiritual healing, encourage legislation for reparations, support future trials or nonpenal sanctions (such as disqualification from public office), provide a record for future generations, and recommend reforms and compensation or other corrective measures.[64] Truth commissions also usually require fewer resources than domestic or international trials meeting full due process standards.[65]

Do International Judicial Proceedings Help Bring out the Truth and Discourage Collective Guilt?

Whenever someone grossly violates human rights, the victims, their families, and the society at large are all entitled to learn the truth about what happened and have a recognized authority acknowledge what occurred and who was responsible. International judicial proceedings usually do help establish an authoritative picture of what happened in the commission of a particular crime. Sentencing may also include some reparations for injuries. Insofar as they help provide facts for informing a society's memory of conflict and a basis for "settling human rights accounts," they "can be part of the formula for a lasting peace, as opposed to a lull in the fighting."[66] But trials are insufficient to provide a full picture of events. For strategic peacebuilding, they need to be supplemented with truth commissions or other instruments of accountability, especially where atrocities are widespread.

If a trial is poorly conducted or designed to cover up the truth and allow impunity for political leaders, it may in fact do so.[67] Such an outcome may be worse than no trial at all, particularly if it is a national tribunal whose proceedings preclude, delay, or complicate action by the ICC, limited by the principle of complementarity, even though the national proceeding may be less than satisfactory.

In addition to the truth-disclosing benefit of international judicial processes, they also demonstrate that although some people are guilty of horrendous crimes, not all people of a particular ethnicity, religion, or nationality are guilty of such misdeeds. Guilt can be "denationalized" so that individuals, rather than an entire group, bear its burden. This ability not to condemn or express hostility toward an entire group is obviously helpful in peacebuilding strategies, where relationships need to be transformed and past prejudices overcome.

The secretary general's Special Representative for the Prevention of Genocide, Juan Méndez, argues that judicial processes "are the most effective means of separating collective guilt from individual guilt, and thus to remove the stigma of historic misdeeds from the innocent members of communities that are collectively blamed for the atrocities committed on other communities."[68] This is especially important for peacebuilding strategies that need "to break the cycle of ethnic violence, because trials would allow the victimized communities to distinguish between ordinary members of rival ethnic groups and those who manipulate their fears for political ends."[69]

Do International Judicial Proceedings Provide Due Process for Defendants, Reduce the Power of Perpetrators, and Limit Their Future Political Role?

If international judicial proceedings provide due process protections equivalent to those that are now widely expected of and generally practiced by international jurisprudence, the rights of the accused are likely to be better protected in international tribunals than in many national judicial processes. The high international standards are likely to have a salutary influence on national and local judicial processes as well, although at times national public opinion seems vengeful and likely to favor less impartiality, less due process, and more harsh punishments than provided by international proceedings. Yet in the long run, even in societies where criticism of the international tribunals runs strong, the positive influence of such tribunals is likely. All international tribunals from Nuremberg to the present appear to have met high standards of due process for defendants. This conclusion applies to penal systems, prosecution, defense, court processes, and, since the Nuremberg and Tokyo tribunals, punishment. Exemplary legal procedures affirm the values and demonstrate the practices that provide a solid basis for peacebuilding and nurturing a rule-of-law society.[70]

If, following due process, those accused of major crimes are indicted and can be arrested and tried, and if they are convicted, then those officials obviously will have been removed by international judicial processes from positions of political or military power, at least during the time they serve their sentences. International judicial processes are better able to achieve such results than either diplomacy or truth commissions. In addition, the conviction of the guilty is likely to reduce the prospects that they will ever return to public office or be empowered to commit more violations of human rights. These are clear benefits for peacebuilding strategies.

Of course, major hurdles include finding sufficient evidence and witnesses to indict and convict, and being able to make arrests and hold international trials, even if evidence is uncovered. The fact that President Slobodan Milosevic was indicted while head of government and later brought to trial, despite the difficulties and idiosyncrasies of his situation, indicates that international judicial processes can aid in discrediting and removing perpetrators from power.

Even if an arrest is not imminent and a trial cannot be held, an indictment by the ICC may handicap indictees who refuse to stand trial, thereby increasing pressure on them to stop gross violations, discrediting them in office, emboldening possible critics, and preventing them from traveling or representing their government abroad. The indictments by the International Criminal Tribunal for the former Yugoslavia (ICTY), for example, demonstrate some peacebuilding benefits even when no one was willing to arrest Ratko Mladic and Radovan Karadzic. They were barred from holding further public office because the Dayton Accords explicitly said that no one who was indicted and refused trial could hold public office. To be sure, political and diplomatic leverage, not a judicial proceeding shaped the relevant provisions, but they were made possible and influential by the indictment of the ICTY.

Plausibly, an indictment by an external court could *increase* domestic political support for an indictee, stimulated by a rally-around-the-flag response from local supporters, particularly if the court is seen as prejudiced against their society. Yet these counterproductive consequences are not normal nor are they likely to be long-lived if the ICC enjoys a good reputation throughout the world.

Do International Judicial Processes Aid Domestic Legal Processes
and Bring International Nonpartisanship and Desirable External
Expertise and Support into Peacebuilding Efforts?

International judicial processes usually set a positive example for domestic
judicial institutions and the local legal culture, although the extent to which
the example actually changes local practice may vary enormously from place
to place. When a proceeding occurs in The Hague and little is communicated
about what may seem to most people to be a process far removed from local
realities, it may have little impact. In the best of circumstances, international
judicial processes potentially can inform domestic legal practice while high-
lighting the importance of the international norms that should guide conduct
and domestic judicial practice. International tribunals can conduct trials that
national judicial institutions often lack the capacity to carry out, either because
of local biases, potentially disruptive political tensions, security threats to witnesses and the families and legal counsels of the litigants, or limited jurisprudential expertise and independence. The ICC can spare national judicial
institutions from excessive political strain during a postwar transition, while
offering exemplary experience in legal processes. International judges have
provided important "balance, independence and expertise" in Bosnia and other
countries in proceedings that otherwise would have "test[ed] local judges' dis-
interestedness and ability to resist political and tribal pressures."[71]

International trials help bring international law into the domestic political
arena and offer a plumb line useful for protecting minorities and upholding
fundamental human rights in domestic politics. If the ICC maintains a reputation for integrity and impartiality, people who want to be good citizens of the
world community as well as of their national society will be able to stand with
the Court's verdicts against criminal conduct by citizens of their own society in
the face of possible criticism by fellow nationals who are more committed to
the accused than to impartial application of the law. This clarification of values
and the law may enable reconciliation to arise more successfully than if trials
were imposed by an occupying government or domestic institutions if those
were dominated by a revenge-seeking hostile party.

Yet when considering an overall strategy of peacebuilding aimed at nurturing a rule-of-law society, "no single mechanism or approach can satisfy the
many . . . goals of justice, truth, prevention and deterrence, reconciliation, and
domestic capacity-building in the aftermath of severe atrocities."[72] Multiple
means are needed to achieve multiple goals. Trials can coexist with truth commissions, international trials can coexist with national judicial processes, and
these both with political processes and economic policies aimed at reconciliation. The more deeply rooted the atrocities, the more likely the need for external help to withstand pressures on the accountability processes and to give the
appearance (as well as the reality) of impartial proceedings. In sum, the presence of some international legal proceedings in a weak state provides invaluable opportunity for capacity-building with local litigators and judges.

In many ways, hybrid courts may have a more extensive positive influence on local legal processes than a distant ICC, particularly in building local judicial capacities, because the hybrids are less distant, psychologically and politically, from the society in question than is The Hague. A hybrid court may be better able to communicate both the importance of accountability and the fairness of a proceeding.[73] It can include local judicial officials in the proceedings and, after its work is completed, leave behind people and institutions that gradually move more fully into local processes. Its proceedings occur in the geographic vicinity of the crimes and the locus where social healing may begin.

The hybrid courts in East Timor, Sierra Leone, and Cambodia help bring justice to the people that the ICC seeks to serve but has had difficulty reaching, because the hybrids are linked to their respective countries and offer more physical and linguistic accessibility to the local media, population, and professional elites.[74] They may be better at communicating effectively, although this function is one in which the ICC can presumably improve. A hybrid court usually will have an easier opportunity to convince indigenous populations of the merit of their mission and gain access to local media. They foster a sense of local ownership, which can mobilize popular support and in turn can give rise to a sense of legitimacy within the society and the court itself. In a sense, the population is better able to participate and feel a stake in the trials, yet the international personnel and accountability provide safeguards against judicial improprieties or inappropriate governmental interference.

This is well illustrated in the hybrid court in Timor-Leste and its ability to provide international expertise and opportunity to absorb fundamental international human rights values. In contrast, in Uganda, many local people do not feel that a tribunal in The Hague is "their court. The Court in the Netherlands may be benevolent, but it seems to some to be a neo-colonial interference that is poorly informed about local customs when it comes to accountability, forgiveness, and reconciliation."[75]

Because of the advantages of having a judicial proceeding close to the locus of the crime, particularly when it comes to building domestic legal capacities and popular support for the judicial proceeding and the law, where possible the ICC should consider holding sessions nearer to where the violations occurred.[76] It might also experiment with establishing judicial panels that include local as well as international jurists. In addition, the court should expand its capacity and budget for communicating with people in the society most directly affected by a particular trial.

If a state asks for international support for its efforts to investigate and prosecute gross violations of human rights, the global community should offer assistance. It can do so quickly and at relatively low cost (compared to violent conflict) by providing help with international judges, law enforcement officials, forensic experts, legal advisors, and other specialists.

To the extent that international judicial processes are able to render impartial verdicts and communicate their processes and verdicts well, they will aid peacebuilding in the long run, not only because they assign legal responsibility to individuals for illegal conduct but also because they uphold the rights of all others, regardless of ethnicity, race, class, or religion, and they do this by employing legal processes rather than military instruments. Moreover, shining a globally authoritative international spotlight on heinous crimes and the universal norms prohibiting them will strengthen the norms over time, gradually expand people's willingness to comply with them, and teach national citizens that an impartial global rendering of justice is possible.

Do International Judicial Proceedings Encourage Reconciliation?

The issue of whether international judicial processes encourage reconciliation is a vexing and difficult question to answer, perhaps equal in importance to the question of whether they encourage cease-fires. International trials, if well conducted and accurately perceived by the people affected, help resolve questions of innocence and guilt, provide some redress for injuries, and encourage some closure to social disruption, thereby enabling societies to heal and reconcile.[77] In some cases, international proceedings may even lay the groundwork for encouraging restorative justice and forgiveness. Rwanda may be a case in point. Despite the difficulties, criticisms, and mixed results of the International Criminal Tribunal in Rwanda (ICTR), it focused on a few high-level officials, enabling or forcing domestic actors to focus on the rest and on restorative justice and reconciliation rooted in traditional culture. In South Africa, of course, there were no international trials, yet an alternative instrument of accountability, the Truth and Reconciliation Commission, laid the groundwork for some reconciliation and even occasional forgiveness.

On the other hand, international trials that are unfair or that are widely perceived to produce one-sided consequences, even if reasonably fair, may keep a society divided or antagonize hostile opponents. In the case of East Timor, the healing process is impeded because many of those accused of crimes are now living in Indonesia and are beyond the reach of the UN-supported hybrid court that was established. A wall of Indonesian sovereignty is protecting some of the allegedly biggest culprits.

Political realists and advocates of a rights-based approach strongly disagree on the political utility of amnesties for those accused of gross violations of human rights. But the normative inutility of amnesties for leaders who have ordered or acquiesced in serious offenses can hardly be denied. Strategic peacebuilding should take into account both political and normative utilities. As indicated, even those Ugandan villagers eager to have peace and the return of their child soldiers did not want the leaders of the LRA to avoid some truth telling and accountability. Moreover, when the leaders of the Northern Alliance in Afghanistan proposed amnesty that would include its adversaries, such provisions were not included in the Bonn Agreement because "a majority of Afghans surveyed oppose[d] amnesties for serious offenses."[78] UN Secretary General Kofi Annan has said that "United Nations–endorsed peace agreements can never promise amnesties for genocide, war crimes, crimes against humanity or gross violations of human rights."[79] A report of the UN

High Commissioner for Human Rights stated that "a blanket amnesty, particularly where war crimes and crimes against humanity have been committed, promotes a culture of impunity and is not in conformity with international standards and practice."[80]

In any case, to devise amnesty arrangements that will "effectively remove spoilers and genuinely help to create conditions for strengthening the rule of law—rather than just permitting impunity—is enormously difficult in practice."[81] Clearly, the consequences of amnesties or international trials may vary from case to case and should be assessed accordingly. Generally speaking, an unconditional amnesty, which excuses people from breaking universally agreed-on laws, is an unlikely way to lay the foundation for building a rule-of-law society. Although an international trial at The Hague may do little to strengthen the domestic rule of law in a postconflict society with weak political institutions,[82] when trials are compared to national amnesties, a trial will at the least advance international standards of justice, whereas amnesty will undermine it and often make reconciliation more difficult.

Because reconciliation must ultimately rely for progress on a rule-of-law society and because international judicial processes usually nurture the rule of law, they play a key role in national peacebuilding and reconciliation. They also influence *global* peacebuilding, which brings us to our final question.

Do International Judicial Proceedings Help Domesticate the International System and Move It toward a Global Rule-of-Law Society?

International judicial processes are likely to have a profound impact on the global order, albeit one that is difficult to quantify or even to detect over a short period of time.[83] In the short run, recent actions by international tribunals "have assisted in bringing some criminals to justice, promoted the development and acceptability of both substantive and procedural international criminal law, and at least sustained, if not reinforced, the general international notion of the unacceptability of serious violations of human rights."[84] In the longer run, every time that the international community emphasizes accountability, it nurtures the rule of law in global society. It helps "build a culture of respect for human rights and [to] highlight the dangers of individuals and groups espousing philosophies of hatred."[85] Accountability not only addresses wrongdoing in a particular case with a particular perpetrator and victim, it also "serves goals for the international community as whole." It is of fundamental importance to recall that the crimes discussed in this chapter "violate the most central norms of humanity, and all states have a moral and political interest in seeing an effective remedy."[86] On the moral and political interests of states lies the promise for actions that will turn legal norms into lived realities through successful global peacebuilding.

For two reasons, the judgments of the ICC and other international judicial processes are of such fundamental significance that they are likely to change the structure and functioning of the international system in the long run.[87] To begin with, for the first time in human history, a permanent criminal court, whose basic constitution has been ratified by 108 states, exists to hold individuals *personally* responsible for international human rights crimes, even if they are government officials. Second, defendants may not use as a defense argument a claim that they are acting on behalf of their state, their national government, or simply following superior orders (that are illegal).[88] The value of holding individuals accountable, which the International Military Tribunal at Nuremburg first officially recognized in affirming that individuals do have obligations that extend "beyond those owed to the state,"[89] appears to be so momentous[90] as to override most negative criticisms of international judicial processes, such as the failure of an indictment to lead to an immediate arrest or the failure of the court to deter crimes in the short run. A court established to render decisions about individual legal responsibility of persons acting as government officials "suggests a reduction in state sovereignty" because in these proceedings "individuals . . . have obligations not only to domestic law but also to a 'higher' international law, and because they can no longer hide behind the shield of immunity of state agencies."[91] In international judicial processes, universal humanitarian norms in international law are, in some cases, beginning to take primacy over domestic law.[92]

Guidelines for Researchers and Policy Makers

Reducing Loss of Life

The overall goal of saving as many lives as possible should be the fundamental guideline in deciding if and when to employ international judicial processes in the service of peacebuilding. This life-saving guideline is rooted both in internationally endorsed human rights norms and the morality of most religious and ethical traditions.[93] It postulates a simple goal, yet it is not simple to calculate how many lives may be lost or saved from a particular course of action, particularly if one considers both the long and the short run, as well as the future benefits from nurturing a global culture of compliance with international humanitarian and human rights law. Nor is it simple to implement life-saving policies once they are chosen. Nonetheless, this is a reasonable place to begin in formulating proposals for political decision making and future research. With this guideline in mind, the international community should proceed with as many warranted international judicial processes as a society coming out of gross violations is able to tolerate without increasing loss of human life.

Table 8.1 indicates the need to calibrate the use of judicial proceedings with the strength and cohesiveness of the society where its impact will be primarily felt. Of course Table 8.1 includes the possibility that judicial proceedings might be pursued in national courts or in a hybrid of national and international judicial processes. One hopes that ICC proceedings would always be of high quality and function at the level of "highly professional judicial proceedings." For national tribunals to succeed, a country's judicial culture needs what Ratner and Abrams consider the "four critical prerequisites for the administration of justice." These include "a legal framework of criminal law and procedure; a trained cadre of judges, lawyers, and other experts; adequate infrastructure; and a culture of respect for the fairness and impartiality of the process."[94] Without these, certainly some international participation is required to ensure that trials do not simply facilitate revenge or vendettas that will impede peacebuilding.

Table 8.1 assesses only the domestic component of peacebuilding impact from judicial proceedings. No attempt is made to include the global peacebuilding impact. From the vantage point of international society, there is a presumption for trials: in most cases it would be desirable to prosecute those accused of heinous crimes. Impunity undermines the rule of law in global society. But in looking, for the moment, through national lenses, one might conclude that where political institutions are as uncertain as those described in the two right-hand columns of Table 8.1, any prosecutions should be attempted by the ICC or hybrid courts, not by national courts.

Because judicial practices are sometimes deeply flawed and attempted where institutions and local culture are not prepared to sustain the rule of law, they will fail to achieve most of the desired ends of legal enforcement. From these flawed procedures, it is easy to conclude that law enforcement fails to contribute to peace, justice, and the deterrence of future crimes. Drawing such conclusions from a partial picture of practice should be guarded against because to do so is not a fair test of what international enforcement can achieve under more favorable conditions, nor does it include the benefits of global (as differentiated from national) peacebuilding. International diplomacy should focus on how to create those more favorable conditions rather than quickly dismiss possible benefits of international legal enforcement.[95] Nonetheless, under the anticipated outcomes specified in the lower right-hand part of the table, it would be inadvisable to hold trials until conditions have improved.

One particularly troubling feature of international judicial proceedings is that those who are investigated, indicted, and tried often feel that they are treated unfairly because not all states are subject to the same standards. The United States, Russia, and China, for example, are not parties to the Rome

TABLE 8.1. Prospects for Judicial Success in Peacebuilding

Nature of anticipated judicial processes	Nature of Society		
	Strong social and political institutions; some cross-cutting groups engaged in national processes	Weak social and political institutions; few cross-cutting groups	Fragmented social and political institutions; society divided into hostile groups; some want partition
Highly professional	Very high	High	Moderate
Flawed yet somewhat professional	High	Moderate	Low
Unprofessional and unfair	Low	Very low	Very low

Statute and can prevent their nationals from being brought before the ICC by a UN Security Council decision because of their veto power there. Sudanese officials claim that they are being subjected to ICC proceedings without their consent and are being treated unequally before the law because they are politically weak. The ability of international judicial processes to contribute positively to peacebuilding is limited by both the perception and the reality that some societies are being "bullied" into accepting international enforcement while others evade the same standard. As former U.S. Supreme Court Justice Robert Jackson, who was the U.S. chief prosecutor at the Nuremberg War Crimes Tribunal, acknowledged, "unless those who sat in judgment accepted for themselves the same standards of accountability as were imposed on the German defendants, the Nuremberg Judgment would be deeply discredited from both a legal and political point of view."[96]

Because politically selective, inequitable enforcement can never contribute to domestic or global peacebuilding as effectively as would equitable legal obligations for enforcement, one way to increase the peacebuilding contribution of the ICC would be to expand its jurisdiction to cover more countries, including the United States, Russia, and China.

Advancing Peace, Justice and Reconciliation through Judicial Processes

One benefit of the ICC is that it is always in place and able to gather evidence promptly and authoritatively, although as presently constituted it lacks sufficient personnel to perform this task in all the places where it is needed. Fresh evidence gathered as soon as possible after massive crimes is the most useful evidence for documenting crimes and identifying and protecting witnesses. Such evidence is essential for stopping crimes, even if it subsequently might be used by a truth commission instead of a court.

The precise mechanisms that can be useful in promoting reconciliation cannot be determined in the abstract. Ratner and Abrams say that "any mechanism can only work with the support of the people of the particular state."[97] This conditional judgment is instructive in most circumstances. Yet it seems to overlook instances where an initially unpopular judicial process, even when imposed from the outside, did in fact contribute to peacebuilding in the long run, so this judgment may undervalue international judicial processes. The benefits of the Nuremberg and Tokyo war crimes tribunals imposed on German and Japanese officials come to mind.[98] Nonetheless, it is clear that widespread public support for international judicial processes will enhance prospects for reconciliation, especially if the support is drawn from across a spectrum of diverse groups in the immediately concerned society.

Ratner and Abrams also conclude that if a society has a democratically elected government, then that government's voice should determine how to proceed: "If that government adopts a course that rejects accountability in favor of a compromise with former abusers, amnesty, or other forms of impunity, almost any effort at accountability seems crippled, if not still-born."[99] Again, this formulation may overstate the merit of local control if it appears likely to justify impunity. Because international judicial institutions are sometimes capable over time of increasing public sentiment in favor of denying impunity, they should be used where warranted. The deciding factor should be the professionalism and impartiality of the proceedings, particularly where they are likely to garner respect.

Advancing Peace, Justice, and Reconciliation with Peacebuilding Strategies that May Suspend Judicial Prosecution

Although judicial processes can contribute enormously to finding justice, sustaining peace, and opening a door to reconciliation, there are times when, like it or not, formal judicial processes simply will not be used. In some contexts they even may be undesirable, for a time, because they would be destabilizing or because political impediments would prevent their effective functioning. The following guidelines, informed by recent experiences in Uganda and elsewhere, can be useful in developing peacebuilding strategies even if trials do not occur.

1. Peacebuilding should encourage truth telling even if formal prosecutions are not possible. This is a minimum requirement of respect for surviving victims. Truth telling by both victims and perpetrators in most cases provides a reasonable foundation for reconciliation. If truth telling could benefit from the help of external law enforcement personnel, forensic experts, legal advisors, or by moving proceedings entirely outside the country in which crimes occurred, the international community should consider helping do this as a duty required of it by its commitment to international humanitarian and human rights law.[100]

2. Local, national, and international stakeholders should be brought together to discuss and "develop an integrated and comprehensive strategy for peace and justice."[101] Without coordination in the overall peacebuilding strategy, energies among various actors will be divided. They may oppose one another in trying to find the right balance between accountability and forgiveness.

3. Peacebuilding strategies should try to ensure that any amnesty provisions will not prevent victims or families from seeking justice and redress for injury, or deny people the possibility of learning the truth about the circumstances in which they were victimized.[102] Those receiving amnesty for serious crimes should not be allowed to retain public office after civil strife ends. The international community is unlikely to respect an unconditional amnesty, blanket amnesty, or self-amnesty. If amnesty procedures are desirable, they should provide amnesty only on an individualized and conditional basis.[103]

The somewhat reflexive, self-serving amnesty process set in motion by the Ugandan government does not meet the needs of the surviving victims. It needs to be reformed so it "is more inclusive and better meets victims' expectations,"[104] and clearly differentiates between the top five LRA leaders, whom the ICC indicted, and the rest. Acknowledgments of wrongdoing, commemoration of victims, apologizing to surviving victims, imposing penalties or punishment, and paying reparations should be considered and possibly required of those to be granted amnesty, especially those most culpable. Such elements "are key to successfully reintegrating former LRA members into the community."[105]

4. If prosecution and trials seem inadvisable because of fears that they would risk generating serious increases in intersocietal tensions and destabilize a society, then peacebuilding strategies should exercise special care to ensure that efforts to reconcile hostile groups do not attempt to quiet victims for the purpose of allowing impunity for criminal conduct. Legitimate reconciliation is never "a substitute for justice."[106]

5. Peacebuilding strategies should also guard against "inequities in the distribution of the burdens of reconciliation." Care must be taken to avoid transferring "responsibilities for dealing with past injustice from the perpetrators to the victims."[107]

6. Peacebuilding strategies should not allow a degeneration of reconciliation efforts to the point of allowing them to become merely a state of mind in which people are asked simply to get over their grief and grievances.[108] Reconciliation efforts should not become "forced amnesia" regarding victims and perpetrators. Peacebuilding should "openly confront the past,"[109] even if judicial prosecutions are not possible or desirable. In Uganda, local political leaders should consult with their constituents to see how traditional justice ceremonies might deal with violations committed by members of the LRA, although these usually do not seem to apply to gross, systematic crimes of the severity the LRA has committed.[110] To succeed, peacebuilding normally will include some social, political, and economic transformations.

7. In pluralistic communities, peacebuilding strategies are likely to be most successful when they are articulated "in terms that do not depend entirely on a particular set of religious beliefs."[111]

8. Once accountability mechanisms have been chosen, international and national leaders must make every effort to ensure that they do "not turn into a free-for-all or excuse for vengeance against political enemies."[112]

9. Where criminal prosecution is not feasible, an official investigatory commission of some sort is necessary to provide a degree of accountability. Its work can be detailed, authoritative, and unbiased in identifying both perpetrators and victims. It can foster healing and spiritual reparation, support future trials (if they become viable) or nonpenal sanctions such as disqualification from public office, and establish a clear record for future generations. It also can recommend reforms, compensation, and other corrective measures. Moreover, such a commission would require fewer resources than are usually required for international trials.[113] It could provide a basis for restorative justice in some situations.

10. Regardless of whether international judicial processes are used or another accountability mechanism is employed, it is of vital importance to strengthen the culture of legal compliance with additional measures in a peacebuilding strategy. These should include human rights education, public

information about the possible work of international or domestic courts, the content of the law, the meaning of ratification of treaties specifying crimes and extradition procedures, and ways to upgrade domestic laws so that they criminalize internal war crimes and crimes against humanity. When relevant, states should be encouraged to prosecute crimes that may take place outside their territory, as well as within, if they have the accused on their territory or can extradite them.[114] No matter how successful international judicial processes become, they can never substitute for human rights education and consensus-building to encourage compliance with fundamental norms.

Peace, Justice, and Peacebuilding

Because unnecessary losses of human life may often occur if armed conflicts are prolonged by negotiations over the use of international judicial processes, these may need to be suspended if violence can more speedily be brought to an end. In the ICC's first case, the Ugandan parties faced this dilemma. The foremost desire of people directly affected at the village level is to end the fighting and abductions as soon as possible, regardless of what an immediate cease-fire may mean for law enforcement. Nonetheless, as the interviews with Ugandans also indicate, after the killing stops, more needs to be done in truth telling[115] and addressing the justice needs of those who have survived victimization. Here legal procedures—often aided by international personnel and authority—are essential. Peacemaking, followed by truth telling and justice seeking to the fullest degree they can be realized, will greatly reduce the likelihood of future atrocities. So the basic peacebuilding strategy should never be viewed as a choice between peace *or* justice, or as a choice between expedient bargaining for peace or inexpedient legal protection of human rights. *The most prudent and effective peacebuilding strategy will always include both building peace and protecting human rights.*

Moreover, to be most effective, international judicial processes should always be seen as one part of a much larger, holistic process of peacebuilding. They complement and supplement other essential practices. In isolation, they can be perceived as divisive and inflammatory. Together with other constructive legal, political, economic, and educational efforts, they provide truth-filled accountability for past injustices and clarity about standards that all should follow in the future. To conclude that many influences work together to achieve peacebuilding is not to diminish the importance of international judicial practices. Indeed, the ICC or an excellent hybrid court can perform functions that are essential for effective peacebuilding that no other institutions can provide. These functions include establishing authoritatively what crimes have been committed (and have not been committed), who committed them, and who was injured. In addition, international courts can clarify, publicize, and uphold precise standards for what is acceptable conduct.

These standards gain credibility precisely because they are international and have been endorsed by national governments throughout the world. Lederach and Appleby correctly emphasize that peacebuilding is *local* because it is in local communities that people need to experience security, tranquility, and justice.[116] Nonetheless, local respect for a rule against genocide can often be enhanced by an international legal process because it transcends local prejudices and implements a norm that gains credibility by its universal endorsement. Genocide may be practiced locally, but the norm against it is strongest when it is supported universally. In no society can it be considered legal or morally acceptable to rape or kill a Jew because she is a Jew—or a Muslim or a Christian or a Hindu or a Buddhist.

International judicial processes, if of high professional standards, help establish what Lederach and Appleby aptly list as essential elements of peacebuilding: the rule of law and protection of human rights.[117] International judicial processes at their best also avoid the peacebuilding pitfall of "moving too quickly beyond the most immediate community of concern and agency."[118] Although international courts apply universal laws, they deal with real-world cases that are unavoidably local, giving them opportunities to encourage the building of some local judicial expertise and public understanding of the rule of law. Rather than simply leave the scene when the trials are over, they can at least leave behind more experienced people with a better understanding of the rule of law. To be sure, the ICC and hybrid courts need to give more thought to this latter dimension and how their work can "include, respect, and promote the human and cultural resources . . . within a given setting."[119] This can be done well only with more deliberate intention and strategic planning.

Trading Prosecution for a Cease-Fire?

As the foregoing analysis indicates, it is plausible that in some instances lives can be saved by agreeing to suspend a judicial investigation or prosecution already under way. In such instances, what should the court do? There are many constraints on what the ICC *can* do (regardless of what it would like to do) in stopping a proceeding once it has reached the stage of formal investigation, indictment, or prosecution. To obtain a cease-fire in return for not prosecuting alleged war criminals might not be simple to arrange, even if court officials would decide to do so. Certainly the court is not well positioned to arrange cease-fires. The ICC has expertise in achieving justice, but it is not equipped to make judgments about when or how to negotiate peace. In the Ugandan case, the Security Council, which is charged by the international community with maintaining world peace and security, is in a better position to elicit a peace agreement from the belligerents than is the court. If the Security Council is able to negotiate a cease-fire, it could, acting in accord with the Rome Statute, decide that the ICC should stop all proceedings for one year. It could renew that request indefinitely if it chose to do so.[120] The Security Council is the best situated and most legitimate body to adjust judicial enforcement to the attainment of peace.

At times, it might be possible for the ICC to arrange the equivalent of what might be considered a plea bargain in domestic legal practice. Yet the seriousness of the crimes that the court prosecutes would frequently diminish a desire to offer a lesser charge in return for any benefit that the accused may deliver to the court. The presumption of accountability and a disinclination to accept impunity has grown over the past two decades, making it unlikely the ICC would or should offer perpetrators of serious crimes total immunity from prosecution, even in exchange for an end to violent conflict,[121] except in rare cases. Sometimes questionable amnesties may, after time passes, be reversed through changes in public opinion and new judicial processes.[122] The Rome Statute does authorize the prosecutor to halt proceedings if he or she determines, subject to the approval of a Pre-Trial Chamber of judges,[123] that "a prosecution is not in the interests of justice, taking into account all the circumstances."[124] The meaning of "justice" might be stretched to include "peace" if one understands that war inevitably violates justice for many people. But the court is not equipped to obtain a cease-fire agreement or to enforce it once signed.

For the future, the ICC could explore ways to make its indictments conditional to avoid the political quandary of being blamed for interfering with the achievement of a cease-fire when indictments of top leaders appear to make them reluctant to stop fighting. Again, the proposed guiding principle of maximizing the preservation of human life is useful. Of course, it is always preferable for individual moral responsibility to be assigned for hideous crimes and for those who have wrongfully taken human life to face penalties for this unlawful conduct. Still, if efforts to prosecute perpetrators postpone an end to their killing others, then prosecution might reasonably be postponed or given up altogether. But the bargain to be struck with the accused should be made *conditional* to prevent unwarranted concessions to the accused. Even if the international community should decide to give up prosecutions it should not give up truth telling.

To begin, it must always be made clear that the ICC is not responsible for the accused persons' continued fighting and killing. The court is not asking any indicted person to admit guilt; it is only asking the accused to face a fair trial. This is a reasonable request, if indictments are fairly drawn up. The accused persons' claims that they are entitled to continue fighting or committing atrocities because they do not want to answer to charges against themselves are not reasonable or (quite possibly) legal. The responsibility for continued killing must always be placed on the killers, not on the court.

The ICC might agree to postpone prosecution of charges contained in an indictment (but not the prosecution of future wrongdoing should additional unlawful conduct occur) for as long as the following conditions would exist: the indictees agree to a cease-fire; they implement the cease-fire within their organization; and they maintain the cease-fire, insofar as it depends on the conduct of the accused. In addition, the indicted persons might be required to give a public accounting of their conduct related to the indictment and agree not to hold public office or military rank in the future.[125] These provisions do not impose any severe penalties on the accused, but they do require some truth telling, which is the very least to which the victims and their families are entitled, as well as the least that public trust and the commonweal require.

Identifying International Judicial Processes and Peacebuilding Strategies that Support Each Other

An examination of recent cases of armed conflict and international judicial proceedings demonstrates that successful strategies for making peace and achieving justice always intersect and often inextricably mingle, suggesting that pitting peace against justice or justice against peace is a misleading and destructive oversimplification. As Faisal Al Bagir of the Sudanese Organization Against Torture and the Khartoum Centre for Human Rights and Educational Development explained: "Accountability, political peace processes and civilian protection must all be part of one package for Darfur. There is no contradiction between peace and justice."[126] Although the strategic emphasis to be placed on the different components of the package will vary from case to case and time to time, the package as a whole, and each of three components—peace, accountability, and justice—must always inform peacebuilding strategies.[127] Until there is more understanding of the precise conditions under which international judicial instruments contribute to social integration, the preferred peacebuilding strategy should be to identify, nurture, and employ the qualities of judicial processes and the accompanying social conditions that will build a democratic rule-of-law society. Such a society will contribute to both justice and peace in the long run.

In designing the best peacebuilding strategy, all parties should remember that the ICC or other international judicial processes are only a small part of the peacebuilding picture. Many influences will shape the prospects for peacebuilding. Moreover, the *domestic* peacebuilding picture is only one part of the total peacebuilding picture, which includes the ICC's or other international actors' contributions to upholding norms and reforming structures to curtail gross violations of human rights around the world. Even an estimate that a particular ICC prosecution may not contribute much to domestic peacebuilding is not a sufficient reason to stop it (unless its continuance would violate the life-saving principle). The ICC might still contribute to peacebuilding within the larger global society. Courts in all venues usually face the prospect that one litigant and his or her supporters will not like an outcome of the court's proceedings; yet the court renders a decision for the good of society, even if one subgroup of society becomes somewhat alienated from the judicial processes as a result of that unpopular decision. Similarly, from the perspective of global society, a widely recognized international norm should not go unenforced just because a self-interested subgroup of global society might be unhappy with its enforcement.

We should also remember that the ICC is not well positioned to orchestrate reconciliation in the society where one or more of its elites has committed crimes, even though some expect the court to achieve reconciliation. In Uganda, many criticized the court for not being more adept at promoting reconciliation between the LRA and the people of northern Uganda, from whom many child soldiers were abducted and on whom many crimes were inflicted. Of course the ICC is happy when its work promotes reconciliation and social healing, but its function is primarily focused on trying to uphold law impartially. It is not as well equipped to engineer social integration as are many other governmental, intergovernmental, and nongovernmental agencies. Moreover, its law enforcement function is usually limited to trying the main, high-level wrongdoers, while leaving to national courts and international truth commissions the long-term, arduous tasks of restorative justice and social reconciliation.

With these reflections in mind, the present analysis leads to four general conclusions. First, to provide highly professional, yet locally sensitive investigations of gross violations of human rights, international judicial prosecutions should be the default setting for peacebuilding strategies, unless domestic institutions and agencies working for retributive and restorative justice can carry these out impartially. Whether judicial processes engage national or international institutions, or both, they can provide an improved climate for reconciliation and resumption of normal life. Often the political stresses and social, economic, and ethnic divisions may be sufficiently strong to overwhelm the potential peacebuilding benefits from domestic institutions acting alone. In such cases, they should be buttressed by international participation in hybrid arrangements that aim to glean the best of both worlds. In cases where few credible domestic judicial institutions exist and the ICC is called on to do the job, it can contribute legitimacy, experience, and legal precedents. There are many good reasons to establish a standard procedure whereby the strengths of the ICC can be directly utilized, through collaborative efforts, even when a hybrid court is the chosen instrument. When neither domestic nor international trials are possible, other mechanisms of accountability should be employed.

To a significant extent, existing studies demonstrate that the conditions enabling international judicial contributions to succeed in peacebuilding are similar to the conditions enabling UN peace operations to succeed in the aftermath of violent conflict within a society.[128]

Second, if perpetrators can be brought to trial in exemplary judicial processes, the court decisions can remove many of them from positions of power and signal a fresh start with meaningful moral regeneration in a formerly strife-ridden, poorly governed society. These are *essential* steps for successful peacebuilding and reestablishing trust within society.[129] A society haunted by numerous atrocities is unlikely to succeed at the "perilous task of moral regeneration." This task means "establishing a new order of political, legal, and social relationships that affirms certain moral truths or principles denied by previous modes and orders, and which aims at preventing a recurrence of violations of those moral truths or principles."[130] The ICC is "a legal, moral, and political institution that aims to serve the project of moral regeneration by affirming the rule of law . . . in domestic and international societies; by focusing on individual accountability. . . ; and by promoting deterrence through the punishment of perpetrators, and social reconciliation through reparations for victims."[131] If the ICC is able to perform its duties, it can contribute significantly to moral regeneration after communal violence and internal war, as claimed by many scholars, Amnesty International, Human Rights Watch, and most other human rights organizations, as well as by the UN Secretary General and many governmental leaders.[132]

Lu wisely cautions that the limits of judicial punishment "for advancing the project of moral regeneration," a project that animates peacebuilding, should be kept in mind by peacebuilding strategists. "The moral utility of such measures as punishment, amnesty, and reparation depends on their contribution to the project of moral regeneration." She notes that "punishment, amnesty, and reparation make moral sense only if they do not undermine, but are consonant with, the *positive* promotion of respect for the humanitarian principles underlying the ICC's mandate."[133] This important moral assessment cannot be made in the abstract; it depends on how much evidence is found, how a case is argued, how judges perform and explain their verdicts, how the media portray the issues to the public, and how well the public understands its own moral life.

Third, the overall peacebuilding benefit from international judicial proceedings depends on the extent to which the proceedings demonstrate, and are perceived to demonstrate, that they are fair in upholding the most fundamental human rights. For accountability efforts to have a strong, positive impact, Jane Stromseth, David Wippman, and Rosa Brooks found that "the accountability proceedings . . . [must] demonstrate credibly that previous patterns of abuse and impunity are rejected and that justice can be fair."[134] Without this demonstrative effect, domestic peacebuilding will not be helped by judicial processes. In Uganda, some observers believe that the peacebuilding potential of the ICC wasjeopardized when the court seemed to work too closely with the Ugandan government, one of the two belligerents in the armed conflict. The latter referred its adversary, the LRA, to the court while retaining jurisdiction over its own military officials who had also been accused of war crimes.[135]

Fourth, peacebuilding strategies will succeed in the long run by the extent to which they increase domestic and global legal capacities and nurture a culture of legal compliance and social integration aimed at building just rule-of-law societies nationally and globally.[136] Such strategies should include nurturing structural change that holds individuals accountable to international law. Yet of course, the ICC alone "is insufficient to legitimize or stabilize international order."[137] Although essential, it would also be a mistake to expect too much from international accountability processes (whether trials or truth commissions). There must be a much larger peacebuilding effort to strengthen people's understanding of and commitment to fundamental human rights norms and institutionalizing structures of accountability, using both local and international instruments, rather than acquiescing in existing international structures that allow impunity.

If international society, Lu aptly cautions, "is quick to punish through the ICC, but slow to help empower the destitute and the marginalized, [it] would constitute a perversion rather than a fulfillment of the universalist humanitarian ideals underlying the ICC's mandate." The ICC's ability "to support the project of moral regeneration" in formerly war-torn societies "may depend on . . . transformations in the international economic and political context. . . . The quest for moral regeneration in domestic societies may be inextricably linked to the moral regeneration of international society itself."[138] This is a healthy reminder that we should be ever conscious of ends and focus on *strategic* peacebuilding as part of a holistic enterprise of interconnected measures, not on a particular technique or a legal or institutional fix. As the populations of northern Uganda themselves expressed, "a multi-faceted transitional justice response, combining several processes and institutions to address different types of harm caused by different levels of perpetrators, is required."[139] More important than holding a trial are the purposes and values that it serves, and how it is organically related to other peacebuilding initiatives. International judicial processes will have more positive influences in some contexts and at some stages in a conflict's life cycle than others. They may deter plans for war or ethnic cleansing. They may deter crimes during the waging of violence. They may promote cease-fires by indicting officials accused of illegal conduct and thereby helping international society isolate them, discredit them, and mount effective measures to constrain them. They may aid negotiations of peace agreements by enabling negotiators to say a new government may not include any indicted persons, as happened in the Dayton Accords. Of course, they would directly aid in prosecutions, trials, truth seeking, and reparations. They can expand and legitimate the information for memory. They can protect against gender crimes in a world where gender sensitivity is still far from the norm. Their decisions, even if leaving the immediate litigants unhappy, can contribute to broader social reconciliation.[140] At their best, international judicial processes are a lynchpin in replacing genocide, crimes against humanity, and war crimes with rule-of-law societies, nationally and globally, and respect for human life and dignity throughout the world. Universalizing respect for human life is peacebuilding par excellence.

NOTES

The author thanks Hao Phen for research assistance and substantive suggestions in preparing this chapter.

1. See, for example, Jack Snyder and Leslie Vinjamuri, "Trials and Errors: Principle and Pragmatism in Strategies of International Justice," *International Security* 28, no. 3 (2003/2004): 5–44.

2. Michael P. Scharf, "The ICC's Jurisdiction over the Nationals of Non-Party States: A Critique of the U.S. Position," *Law and Contemporary Problems* 67 (2001): 152.

3. "The question of whether and how accountability proceedings can contribute to strengthening domestic justice systems and to building the rule of law in post-conflict societies is surprisingly under analyzed." Jane Stromseth, David Wippman, and Rosa Brooks, *Can Might Make Rights? Building the Rule of Law after Military Interventions* (Cambridge: Cambridge University Press, 2006), 253. For an excellent, thoroughly documented discussion of accountability issues, see chapters 7, 8, and 9.

4. In addition to suggesting a rule-utilitarian ethic, I give significant weight to the consent of the population immediately affected by atrocities. The rationale for this is that the "default setting" for policy preferences should be to prosecute the accused to assign specific moral responsibility for criminal conduct, reaffirm the norms that all should follow, and provide some modicum of justice for the victims and their

families. But if a situation arises in which it is unclear what to do because proceeding with prosecutions may delay a cease-fire agreement and result in further loss of human life, the ambiguity of the decision should be influenced by what the people who are most directly affected want to do. What one should do to maximize the protection of human life, after all, should be influenced by what the persons whose lives are on the line calculate is the preferred course of action.

5. International Center for Transitional Justice and Human Rights Center at the University of California (Berkeley), "A Voice for Victims" (New York: International Center for Transitional Justice, 2005), 5.

6. See Osman Hummaida, former director of the Sudanese Organization Against Torture, quoted by Deirdre Clancy, "Prosecutor's Announcement Sends Ripples through Sudan," *Monitor: Journal of the Coalition for the International Criminal Court* 34 (May–October 2007): 13.

7. Amitav Acharya, "How Ideas Spread: Whose Norms Matter? Norm Localization and Institution Change in Asian Regionalism." *International Organization* 58 (2004): 239–275.

8. On "domesticating" foreign policies in the international system, see Robert C. Johansen, "The Future of United Nations Peacekeeping and Enforcement: A Framework for Policymaking," *Global Governance* 2 (1996): 301; Robert C. Johansen, *The National Interest and the Human Interest: An Analysis of U.S. Foreign Policy* (Princeton, N.J.: Princeton University Press, 1980), 14–37.

9. United Nations Secretary General, Report of the Secretary General on the Rule of Law and Transitional Justice in Conflict and Post-conflict Societies, UN Doc. S/2004/616 (August 23, 2004), para. 6, p. 4, accessed at http://daccessdds.un.org/doc/UNDOC/GEN/N04/395/29/PDF/N0439529.pdf?OpenElement.

10. Ibid.

11. Preamble to the Rome Statute.

12. See Payam Akhavan, "The Lord's Resistance Army Case: Uganda's Submission of the First State Referral to the International Criminal Court," *American Journal of International Law* 99, no. 2 (2005).

13. International Center for Transitional Justice and Human Rights Center at the University of California (Berkeley), "Forgotten Voices: A Population-Based Survey on Attitudes About Peace and Justice in Northern Uganda" (New York: International Center for Transitional Justice, 2005), 3.

14. Coalition for the International Criminal Court, "Peace and Justice: The Importance of Accountability to Civilian Protection," *CICC Monitor* 34 (May–October 2007): 13.

15. Ibid.

16. Juan E. Mendez, "Accountability for Past Abuses," *Human Rights Quarterly* 19 (1997): 273.

17. Mahnoush H. Arsanjani and W. Michael Riesman, "The Law-in-Action of the International Criminal Court," *American Journal of International Law* 99, no. 2 (2005): 385. Quoted from "Uganda: ICC Could Suspend Northern Investigations," *Spokesman, IRIN News* (April 18, 2005), at http://www.irinnews.org.

18. Arsanjani and Riesman, "The Law-in-Action of the International Criminal Court," 385.

19. Ibid. Also see Katherine Southwick, "North Ugandan Conflict, Forgotten but still Deadly," *YaleGlobal* (March 9, 2005), at http://yaleglobal.yale.edu.

20. Arsanjani and Riesman, "The Law-in-Action of the International Criminal Court," 385.

21. Akhavan, "The Lord's Resistance Army Case," 403.

22. Ibid.

23. Ibid., 404. Perhaps this came about in part because Sudanese leaders themselves were coming under ICC scrutiny for their alleged crimes.

24. Ibid.

25. Ibid., 404–405.

26. International Center for Transitional Justice and Human Rights Center at the University of California (Berkeley), "Forgotten Voices," 3.

27. Ibid.

28. Ibid., 4.

29. Ibid.

30. Ibid.

31. Ibid., 5.

32. International Center for Transitional Justice and Human Rights Center at the University of California (Berkeley), "A Voice for Victims," 7.

33. International Center for Transitional Justice and Human Rights Center at the University of California (Berkeley), "Forgotten Voices," 5.

34. International Center for Transitional Justice and Human Rights Center at the University of California (Berkeley), "A Voice for Victims," 7.

35. International Center for Transitional Justice and Human Rights Center at the University of California (Berkeley), "Forgotten Voices," 5.

36. International Center for Transitional Justice and Human Rights Center at the University of California (Berkeley), "A Voice for Victims," 7.

37. International Center for Transitional Justice and Human Rights Center at the University of California (Berkeley), "Forgotten Voices," 5.

38. Office of the High Commissioner on Human Rights, *Making Peace Our Own: Victims' Perceptions of Accountability, Reconciliation, and Transitional Justice in Northern Uganda*, August 14, 2007, accessed at http://www.reliefweb.int/rw/rwb.nsf/db900SID/AMMF-763G7T.

39. Preamble to the Rome Statute.

40. Paul Seils and Marieke Wierda, "The International Criminal Court and Conflict Mediation" (New York: International Center for Transitional Justice, 2005), 2.

41. Coalition for the International Criminal Court, "Peace and Justice."

42. Of course, this is true primarily in weak states, where international intervention is a possibility, or in other states where human rights norms are already internalized. One wonders how U.S. officials may have thought about their obligation to honor international law when they designed U.S. policies resulting in abusive treatment of detainees during and following military operations in Afghanistan and Iraq. See the discussion of the Alberto Gonzales memorandum, which claimed that U.S. prisoners were not subject to protection by the Geneva Conventions, in Robert C. Johansen, "The Impact of U.S. Policy toward the International Criminal Court on the Prevention of Genocide, War Crimes, and Crimes against Humanity," *Human Rights Quarterly* 28, no. 2 (2006).

43. Seils and Wierda, "The International Criminal Court and Conflict Mediation," 2.

44. See the Report of the Secretary-General, "The Rule of Law and Transitional Justice in Conflict and Post-conflict Societies," UN Doc. S/2004/616, August 3, 2004, para. 21. Quoted in Seils and Wierda, "The International Criminal Court and Conflict Mediation," 2.

45. See Comments of the Human Rights Committee, Consideration of Reports Submitted by State Parties under Article 40 of the Covenant, para 10, U.N. Doc. CCPR/C/79/Add.46 (1955), quoted in Mendez, "Accountability for Past Abuses," 259.

46. Convention on the Prevention and Punishment of the Crime of Genocide, December 9, 1948, 78 U.N.T.S., 277; Mendez, "Accountability for Past Abuses," 260.

47. Mendez, "Accountability for Past Abuses," 261. "For 'grave breaches' of the laws of war . . . there is a clear obligation to punish." See Geneva IV, art. 146. Mendez, "Accountability for Past Abuses," 273.

48. Mendez, "Accountability for Past Abuses," 261.

49. Ibid., 262. See eighth annual report, Leonardo Duspouy, Special Rapporteur appointed pursuant to Economic Social Council resolution 1985/37 U.N. Doc. E/CN.4/Sub.2/1995/20/Corr.1 (1955). Cited also by Mendez, "Accountability for Past Abuses," 259.

50. Leila Nadya Sadat, "Exile, Amnesty and International Law," *Notre Dame Law Review* 81, no. 3 (2006): 955.

51. Ibid., 1034.

52. See Snyder and Vinjamuri, "Trials and Errors"; Dominic McGoldrick, "The Legal and Political Significance of a Permanent International Criminal Court," in *The Permanent International Criminal Court: Legal and Policy Issues*, edited by Dominic McGoldrick, Peter Rowe, and Eric Donnelly (Oxford: Hart, 2004), 556–559.

53. Patrick Hayden, *Cosmopolitan Global Politics* (Aldershot: Ashgate, 2005), 113.

54. On the question of deterrence, see M. Cherif Bassiouni, "Accountability for Violations of International Humanitarian Law and Other Serious Violations of Human Rights," in *Post-Conflict Justice*, edited by M. Cherif Bassiouni (Netherlands: Hotei, 2003), 3–4, 54.

55. Even if arresting the accused is not possible because he or she is shielded by a government, issuing a warrant can effectively prevent the accused person's travel and possibly restrict or freeze the international movement of assets. Steven R. Ratner and Jason S. Abrams, *Accountability for Human Rights Atrocities in International Law: Beyond the Nuremberg Legacy* (Oxford: Clarendon Press, 2001), 301.

56. See ibid.

57. This happened to Sudanese officials, even though Sudan chose, as did the United States, not to become a member of the court.

58. Catherine Lu, "The International Criminal Court as an Institution of Moral Regeneration: Problems and Prospects," in *Bringing Power to Justice? The Prospects of the International Criminal Court*, edited by Joanna Harrington, Michael Milde, and Richard Vernon (London: McGill-Queen's University Press, 2006), 206.

59. Ratner and Abrams, *Accountability for Human Rights Atrocities*, 295–296. The particular instrument chosen for clarifying accountability, whether an investigatory committee, a truth commission, or an international judicial procedure, "is less important than the existence of some process for stigmatizing the offender and ensuring that political settlements and transitions take account of human rights abuses" (296).

60. He speaks here of truth commissions as well as trials. Bruce Shapiro, "The Saddam Spectacle," *Nation* 284, no. 3 (2006): 4.

61. Sadat, "Exile, Amnesty and International Law," 1035.

62. Juan Mendez notes: "For 'grave breaches' of the laws of war . . . there is a clear obligation to punish." Mendez, "Accountability for Past Abuses," 273. See also the Geneva Convention Relative to the Protection of Civilian Persons in Time of War, art. 146.

63. An exception to this generalization might be when exemplary national judicial proceedings are conducted on grounds of universal jurisdiction. In such cases, national proceedings would also have a salutary impact in other countries. I am indebted to Hao Phen for this point.

64. For an excellent analysis of the role of truth commissions, see Priscilla B. Hayner, *Unspeakable Truths: Confronting State Terror and Atrocity* (New York: Routledge, 2001).

65. Ratner and Abrams, *Accountability for Human Rights Atrocities*, 300.

66. Mendez, "Accountability for Past Abuses," 257.

67. The hybrid tribunal investigating crimes in East Timor, for example, has no jurisdiction over persons in Indonesia, even though many of the worst crimes allegedly were carried out by Indonesians, often on the payroll of the Indonesian government.

68. Mendez, "Accountability for Past Abuses," 277.

69. Ibid.

70. Time appears to be on the side of exemplary practice, although the dismissive attitude of U.S. officials in the George W. Bush administration toward honoring the Geneva Conventions protecting the rights of the accused is an alarming step away from exemplary jurisprudential standards by a country long associated with support for human rights.

71. International Crisis Group, "Courting Disaster: The Misrule of Law in Bosnia & Herzegovina," Balkans Report no. 127 (March 25, 2002): 54. Quoted also by Stromseth, Wippman, and Brooks, *Can Might Make Rights?* 239.

72. Stromseth, Wippman, and Brooks, *Can Might Make Rights?* 256.

73. See ibid., 254; and Laura A. Dickinson, "The Promise of Hybrid Courts," *American Journal of International Law* (2003): 295.

74. There have been numerous reports that the populations in Rwanda and Uganda are unaware of or poorly informed about the work of the ICTR and the ICC, respectively. Their citizens feel distant from the judicial processes, the local press does not pay much attention to proceedings to inform the populace, and the families of victims do not feel connected to the processes. International Center for Transitional Justice and Human Rights Center at the University of California (Berkeley), "Forgotten Voices" and "A Voice for Victims."

75. International Center for Transitional Justice and Human Rights Center at the University of California (Berkeley), "A Voice for Victims."

76. The Rome Statute allows for in situ proceedings in Article 3.3. The ICC, aware of its need to communicate more effectively in situations where it is at work, has begun to consider in situ hearings and opening field offices where they would aid fulfillment of the court's mission. See Human Rights Watch, *Courting History: The Landmark International Criminal Court's First Years*, http://www.hrw.org/en/node/62135/section/1, 100–115.

77. "Trials can . . . give victims a sense of justice that helps them move forward without a need to seek personal vengeance," thereby assisting peacebuilding. Stromseth, Wippman, and Brooks, *Can Might Make Rights?* 250.

78. See the Afghan Independent Human Rights Commission, *A Call for Justice: A National Consultation on Past Human Rights Violations in Afghanistan*, p. 21, available at http://www.aihrc.org.af/rep_Eng_29_01_05.htm. For analysis, see Stromseth, Wippman, and Brooks, *Can Might Make Rights?* 252.

79. UN Secretary General, Report of the Secretary General on the Rule of Law and Transitional Justice in Conflict and Post-Conflict Societies, para. 10, delivered to the Security Council, U.N. Doc. S/2004/616 (August 3, 2004).

80. UN High Commissioner for Human Rights, Report on the Mission Undertaken by Her Office, Pursuant to Commission Resolution 200/60, to Assess the Situation on the Ground with Regard to the Abduction of Children from Northern Uganda, paras. 12–13, UN Doc. E/CN.4/2002/86 (2001), available at http://www.ohchr.org/english. Quoted by Akhavan, "The Lord's Resistance Army Case," 410.

81. Stromseth, Wippman, and Brooks, *Can Might Make Rights?* 253.

82. See ibid.

83. On the domestication of the international system, see Johansen, "The Future of United Nations Peacekeeping and Enforcement," 301; Johansen, *The National Interest and the Human Interest*, 14–37.

84. Arsanjani and Riesman, "The Law-in-Action of the International Criminal Court," 402–403.

85. Ratner and Abrams, *Accountability for Human Rights Atrocities*, 295.

86. Ibid.

87. Patrick Hayden concludes that "the move toward individual responsibility (accompanied by the emergence of human rights and humanitarian law) represents a change in focus that is a sign of global transformation towards a more cosmopolitan conception of world law." Hayden, *Cosmopolitan Global Politics*, 114. See also David Held, *Democracy and the Global Order: From the Modern State to Cosmopolitan Governance* (Cambridge: Polity Press, 1995), 101–103.

88. The argument of necessity to follow superior orders may be used to mitigate a punishment, but it cannot be used to justify illegal conduct.

89. Hayden, *Cosmopolitan Global Politics*, 114.

90. See Quincy Wright, *The Role of International Law in the Elimination of War* (New York: Oceana, 1961).

91. Hayden, *Cosmopolitan Global Politics*, 114.

92. See ibid.

93. Paul Gordon Lauren, *The Evolution of International Human Rights: Visions Seen* (Philadelphia: University of Pennsylvania Press, 2003); Brian D. Lepard, *Rethinking Humanitarian Intervention* (University Park: Pennsylvania State University Press, 2002).

94. Ratner and Abrams, *Accountability for Human Rights Atrocities*, 299.

95. A tendency to understate the benefits of international judicial proceedings is found in Snyder and Vinjamuri, "Trials and Errors."

96. Richard Falk, "Criminal Accountability in Transitional Justice," *Peace Review* 12, no. 1 (2000): 82.

97. Ratner and Abrams, *Accountability for Human Rights Atrocities*, 301.

98. These benefits included establishing as virtually indisputable that heinous crimes did occur, so they could not later be credibly denied. In addition, trials established that certain Germans and Japanese did commit the crimes. Both Germans and non-Germans, Japanese and non-Japanese could see some authoritative attribution of responsibility, thereby differentiating those who did behave criminally from those who did not. Impartial trials prepare the ground for peacebuilding because they discourage collective guilt by establishing individual guilt. This is desirable for both those living in the society where the crimes occurred and for those living elsewhere who might form negative stereotypes of the entire nation where crimes occurred.

99. Ratner and Abrams, *Accountability for Human Rights Atrocities*, 301.

100. See ibid., 301–302.

101. International Center for Transitional Justice and Human Rights Center at the University of California (Berkeley), "Forgotten Voices," 5.

102. See Garth Meintjes and Juan E. Mendez, "Reconciling Amnesties with Universal Jurisdiction," *Internatinal Law Forum* 2 (2000): 76–77. Amnesty laws lost constructive peacebuilding influence "when they became shameful tools for perpetuating the impunity enjoyed by violators of human rights, rather than opportunities for

reconciliation among warring parties." Meintjes and Mendez, "Reconciling Amnesties with Universal Jurisdiction," 76–77.

103. Ibid., 97.

104. International Center for Transitional Justice and Human Rights Center at the University of California (Berkeley), "Forgotten Voices," 6.

105. Ibid.

106. International Center for Transitional Justice and Human Rights Center at the University of California (Berkeley), "A Voice for Victims," 18.

107. Ibid.

108. Many observers have felt that President Alfredo Cristiani in El Salvador used reconciliation to mean "get over it," as did some generals in Argentina. Such misuse of reconciliation, of course, does not contribute to peacebuilding.

109. International Center for Transitional Justice and Human Rights Center at the University of California (Berkeley), "A Voice for Victims," 18.

110. International Center for Transitional Justice and Human Rights Center at the University of California (Berkeley), "Forgotten Voices," 6.

111. International Center for Transitional Justice and Human Rights Center at the University of California (Berkeley), "A Voice for Victims," 18.

112. Ratner and Abrams, *Accountability for Human Rights Atrocities*, 301.

113. See ibid., 300.

114. See ibid., 302.

115. In his analysis of recent armed conflicts, Christopher Hedges concludes that reconciliation is not possible without widespread acceptance of "the most precious and elusive of all human narratives—truth." *War Is a Force That Gives Us Meaning* (New York: Anchor, 2003), 82.

116. As they say, "peacebuilding begins and ends with the local." See "Strategic Peacebuilding: An Overview," chapter 1, 35.

117. Ibid., 34.

118. Ibid., 27.

119. Ibid., 28.

120. Article 16. Of course there is no inherent conflict between international judicial proceedings and the work of the Security Council in exercising its primary responsibility for maintaining peace and security. Indeed, when facing the war in the former Yugoslavia, the Security Council decided in Resolution 827 to establish an international criminal tribunal "as a contribution to the restoration of peace." See Dan Sarooshi, "The Peace and Justice Paradox: The International Criminal Court and the UN Security Council," in *The Permanent International Court: Legal and Policy Issues*, edited by Dominic McGoldrick, Peter Rowe, and Eric Donnelly (Oxford: Hart, 2004), 105.

121. The presumption against impunity has been reinforced by the creation and continued support for the ad hoc tribunals for the former Yugoslavia and Rwanda, the exercise of the concept of extraterritorial jurisdiction, including universal jurisdiction, the establishment of the permanent International Criminal Court specifically to prosecute individuals accused of criminal conduct, and the establishment of the Special Court for Sierra Leone and other mixed tribunals for Cambodia, Kosovo, and Timor-Leste. The United Nations has participated in efforts to create all of these mixed tribunals, thereby adding to their legal standing. In addition, all fifteen members of the Security Council have explicitly expressed their commitment to accountability. See Seils and Wierda, "The International Criminal Court and Conflict Mediation," 2. The UN Secretary General has strongly stated that UN-endorsed peace

agreements cannot give amnesty for genocide, war crimes, crimes against humanity, or gross violations of human rights, although it has supported amnesties for less serious crimes. Amnesties given by others are not a bar to prosecution in UN-created or -assisted courts. See Report of the Secretary-General, "The Rule of Law and Transitional Justice in Conflict and Post-conflict Societies," UN Doc. S/2004/616, August 3, 2004, para. 21.

122. This happened in eventually bringing legal charges against former President Augusto Pinochet of Chile, despite his lifetime immunity.

123. Article 53.3.

124. Article 53.1(c).

125. The ban on holding future public office could be considered a penalty for some, but it is not too much to ask of those who are indicted but refuse to stand trial.

126. Coalition for the International Criminal Court, "Peace and Justice."

127. Some of the debate between advocates of justice and advocates of peace may arise from the strong preference of peacebuilders and justice seekers for one more than the other, rather than from careful analysis of how peace and justice can nurture one another.

128. On what enables UN peacekeeping and enforcement to succeed, see these excellent complementary analyses: Michael Doyle, "War Making and Peace Making: The United Nations' Post–Cold War Record," in *Turbulent Peace: The Challenges of Managing International Conflict*, edited by Chester A. Crocker, Fen Osler Hampson, and Pamela Aall (Washington, D.C.: U.S. Institute of Peace Press, 2001); Stephen John Stedman, "International Implementation of Peace Agreements in Civil Wars: Findings from a Study of Sixteen Cases," in *Turbulent Peace: The Challenges of Managing International Conflict*, edited by Chester A. Crocker, Fen Osler Hampson, and Pamela Aall (Washington, D.C.: U.S. Institute of Peace Press, 2001).

129. This conclusion parallels one of the findings of Stromseth, Wippman, and Brooks in their more narrowly focused examination of the "long term impact of accountability proceedings on the rule of law." They conclude that "the effective disempowerment of key perpetrators who threaten stability and undermine public confidence in the rule of law" is necessary to nurture a rule-of-law society. See Stromseth, Wippman, and Brooks, *Can Might Make Rights?* 254.

130. Lu, "The International Criminal Court as an Institution of Moral Regeneration," 191.

131. Ibid., 206. Lu also notes that "as a mechanism of moral accounting that focuses on individual agency and responsibility, the ICC will not be nearly sufficient by itself to address the institutional and structural roots of political violence and atrocity. The verdicts of the ICC therefore should not exhaust the search for moral and especially causal responsibility, which is crucial to the ultimate objective of prevention."

132. See ibid., 191.

133. Ibid., 206.

134. Stromseth, Wippman, and Brooks, *Can Might Make Rights?* 254.

135. Arsanjani and Riesman, "The Law-in-Action of the International Criminal Court," 385.

136. Stromseth, Whippman, and Brooks concluded that the impact of accountability proceedings depends on "the extent to which systematic and meaningful efforts at domestic capacity-building are included as part of the accountability process." See Stromseth, Wippman, and Brooks, *Can Might Make Rights?* 254.

137. Lu, "The International Criminal Court as an Institution of Moral Regeneration," 206.

138. Ibid., 207.

139. Office of the High Commissioner on Human Rights, *Making Peace Our Own: Victims' Perceptions of Accountability, Reconciliation, and Transitional Justice in Northern Uganda*, August 14, 2007, accessed at hhtp://www.reliefweb.int/rw/rwb.nsf/db900SID/AMMF-763G7T.

140. Juan E. Mendez, "A Voice for Victims," in *Annual Report 2004/2005* (New York: International Center for Transitional Justice, 2006), 207.

REFERENCES

Acharya, Amitav. "How Ideas Spread: Whose Norms Matter? Norm Localization and Institution Change in Asian Regionalism." *International Organization* 58 (2004): 239–275.

Akhavan, Payam. "The Lord's Resistance Army Case: Uganda's Submission of the First State Referral to the International Criminal Court." *American Journal of International Law* 99, no. 2 (2005): 403–421.

Arsanjani, Mahnoush H., and W. Michael Riesman. "The Law-in-Action of the International Criminal Court." *American Journal of International Law* 99, no. 2 (2005): 385–403.

Bassiouni, M. Cherif. "Accountability for Violations of International Humanitarian Law and Other Serious Violations of Human Rights." In *Post-Conflict Justice*, edited by M. Cherif Bassiouni. Netherlands: Hotei, 2003, 3–54.

Clancey, Deirdre. "Prosecutor's Announcement Sends Ripples through Sudan." *Monitor: Journal of the Coalition for the International Criminal Court* 34 (May–October 2007): 13.

Coalition for the International Criminal Court. "Peace and Justice: The Importance of Accountability to Civilian Protection." *CICC Monitor*, no. 34 (2007): 13.

Dickinson, Laura A. "The Promise of Hybrid Courts." *American Journal of International Law* (2003): 295.

Doyle, Michael. "War Making and Peace Making: The United Nations' Post–Cold War Record." In *Turbulent Peace: The Challenges of Managing International Conflict*, edited by Chester A. Crocker, Fen Osler Hampson, and Pamela Aall, 529–560. Washington, D.C.: U.S. Institute of Peace Press, 2001.

Falk, Richard. "Criminal Accountability in Transitional Justice." *Peace Review* 12, no. 1 (2000): 81–86.

Hayden, Patrick. *Cosmopolitan Global Politics*. Aldershot: Ashgate, 2005.

Hayner, Priscilla B. *Unspeakable Truths: Confronting State Terror and Atrocity*. New York: Routeledge, 2001.

Hedges, Christopher. *War Is a Force That Gives Us Meaning*. New York: Anchor, 2003.

Held, David. *Democracy and the Global Order: From the Modern State to Cosmopolitan Governance*. Cambridge: Polity Press, 1995.

International Center for Transitional Justice, and Human Rights Center at the University of California (Berkeley). "Forgotten Voices: A Population-Based Survey on Attitudes about Peace and Justice in Northern Uganda." New York: International Center for Transitional Justice, 2005.

———. "A Voice for Victims." 1–40. New York: International Center for Transitional Justice, 2005.

International Crisis Group. "Courting Disaster: The Misrule of Law in Bosnia & Herzegovina." Balkans Report no. 127 (March 25, 2002): 54.

Johansen, Robert C. "The Future of United Nations Peacekeeping and Enforcement: A Framework for Policymaking." *Global Governance* 2 (1996): 299–333.

———. "The Impact of U.S. Policy toward the International Criminal Court on the Prevention of Genocide, War Crimes, and Crimes against Humanity." *Human Rights Quarterly* 28, no. 2 (2006): 301–331.

———. *The National Interest and the Human Interest: An Analysis of U.S. Foreign Policy.* Princeton, N.J.: Princeton University Press, 1980.

Lauren, Paul Gordon. *The Evolution of International Human Rights: Visions Seen.* Philadelphia: University of Pennsylvania Press, 2003.

Lepard, Brian D. *Rethinking Humanitarian Intervention.* University Park: Pennsylvania State University Press, 2002.

Lu, Catherine. "The International Criminal Court as an Institution of Moral Regeneration: Problems and Prospects." In *Bringing Power to Justice? The Prospects of the International Criminal Court,* edited by Joanna Harrington, Michael Milde, and Richard Vernon, 191–209. London: McGill-Queen's University Press, 2006.

McGoldrick, Dominic. "The Legal and Political Significance of a Permanent International Criminal Court." In *The Permanent International Criminal Court: Legal and Policy Issues,* edited by Dominic McGoldrick, Peter Rowe, and Eric Donnelly, 453–478. Oxford: Hart, 2004.

Meintjes, Garth, and Juan E. Mendez. "Reconciling Amnesties with Universal Jurisdiction." *International Law Forum* 2 (2000): 76–97.

Mendez, Juan E. "Accountability for Past Abuses." *Human Rights Quarterly* 19 (1997): 255–282.

———. "A Voice for Victims." In *Annual Report 2004/2005.* New York: International Center for Transitional Justice, 2006.

Ratner, Steven R., and Jason S. Abrams. *Accountability for Human Rights Atrocities in International Law: Beyond the Nuremberg Legacy.* Oxford: Clarendon Press, 2001.

Sadat, Leila Nadya. "Exile, Amnesty and International Law." *Notre Dame Law Review* 81, no. 3 (2006): 955–1036.

Sarooshi, Dan. "The Peace and Justice Paradox: The International Criminal Court and the UN Security Council." In *The Permanent International Court: Legal and Policy Issues,* edited by Dominic McGoldrick, Peter Rowe, and Eric Donnelly, 95–122. Oxford: Hart, 2004.

Scharf, Michael P. "The ICC's Jurisdiction over the Nationals of Non-Party States: A Critique of the U.S. Position." *Law and Contemporary Problems* 67 (2001): 152.

Seils, Paul, and Marieke Wierda. "The International Criminal Court and Conflict Mediation." 1–20. New York: International Center for Transitional Justice, 2005.

Shapiro, Bruce. "The Saddam Spectacle." *Nation* 284, no. 3 (2006): 4–5.

Snyder, Jack, and Leslie Vinjamuri. "Trials and Errors: Principle and Pragmatism in Strategies of International Justice." *International Security* 28, no. 3 (2003/2004): 5–44.

Southwick, Katherine. "North Ugandan Conflict, Forgotten but Still Deadly." *YaleGlobal* (March 9, 2005), http://yaleglobal.yale.edu.

Stedman, Stephen John. "International Implementation of Peace Agreements in Civil Wars: Findings from a Study of Sixteen Cases." In *Turbulent Peace: The Challenges of Managing International Conflict,* edited by Chester A. Crocker, Fen Osler

Hampson, and Pamela Aall, 737–752. Washington, D.C.: U.S. Institute of Peace Press, 2001.

Stromseth, Jane, David Wippman, and Rosa Brooks. *Can Might Make Rights? Building the Rule of Law after Military Interventions.* Cambridge: Cambridge University Press, 2006.

Wright, Quincy. *The Role of International Law in the Elimination of War.* New York: Oceana, 1961.

9

Human Rights and Strategic Peacebuilding

The Roles of Local, National, and International Actors

Naomi Roht-Arriaza

Human rights as concept and as law plays multiple roles in the cessation of armed conflict and in the (re)construction of a more just and peaceful society. Human rights is the rallying cry of those who feel oppressed; it is the standard by which new government efforts to build rule of law will be judged; it is the rubric under which new domestic institutions like ombudsmen and human rights commissions to safeguard individuals and groups against official arbitrariness will operate. Human rights provisions in peace agreements range from those on refugee return and prisoner release to those on trials, truth commissions, vetting, reparations, and other attempts to repair past violations to efforts to ensure a human rights culture.[1] Adherence to human rights treaties will often be one of the earliest acts of a postconflict government, a move imbued with symbolism. Human rights concerns also engage the supervisory mechanisms available on the international level, from UN procedures to regional courts to conditionalities on reconstruction assistance. International human rights law will set the limits to what governments can do: it will influence the shape of power sharing or other arrangements to protect minorities, it will demand resources and planning for education, health, and other economic, social, and cultural rights; it will insist on a minimum of public participation and free expression.

As countries emerge from periods of armed confrontation or extreme repression, human rights lawyers and activists have paid particular attention to strategic peacebuilding, understanding that dealing with the past is a necessary condition for constructing a lasting, positive peace based on a more just order. Over the past twenty years or so, a varied and complex international practice has grown up around post–armed conflict efforts to deal with past crimes, including trials, truth commissions, reparations programs, psychosocial interventions, vetting and recomposition of security forces and public officials, changes in law, and multiple commemorative efforts. Although initially there were fierce debates about whether, for example, truth commissions were better than trials, by now there is a broad consensus that governments can and may use multiple measures, either simultaneously or sequentially.[2] In other words, we needed to embrace dilemmas and paradoxes,[3] in an "ecological model" of post–armed conflict reconstruction and renewal.[4] In this effort, international human rights and humanitarian law have provided the outer limits within a broad range of options.

However, a state's efforts to address human rights violations in the past depend not only on the actions of the central government but also, crucially, on several types of actors who exert their own influence and affect the actions and role of central governments. These include international, regional, transnational, and local actors. Thus far, their importance and interdependence has been insufficiently recognized. Just as different pieces of a postconflict agenda must be thought about as a whole and much thought must go into which tasks go together and which must be done sequentially, the same is true of different sites of action. This chapter looks at the interplay of these different sites, with a focus on the issues raised by the need to provide justice—in a broad sense—for the victims of armed conflict and repressive dictatorship. It concludes that it is important as part of strategic peacebuilding to engage all these levels from the start and carefully think through both synergies and potential tensions involved among them. In particular, until very recently, insufficient attention was paid to the local, subnational town or village, even though that is where most people live their lives and where they may feel most keenly the impact of impunity or lack of reparation. A human rights framework and an approach based on the complementarity of actions at different scales may be quite useful.

The National State

The national state is the starting place for any discussion of postconflict reconstruction, whether physical or moral. The state will necessarily play a central role in defining the contours of state policy, creating a new or reformed national identity and mythology, and allocating resources. In particular, the national state will be the central player in reform of national institutions, from prisons to police and army to the judiciary and prosecutors' service. States will also, obviously, be central to criminal prosecutions for human rights–related crimes in national courts, national truth commissions or other types of truth-seeking efforts, reparations schemes reliant on government funds, and efforts to end exclusionary practices that affect minorities or other aggrieved groups. Where the state as such has been the principal source of human rights violations and violence has been vertical, running from state agents to citizens (as, for example, in Chile), national actions will be particularly important to establish the bright line between the former and current governments.

In fulfilling this key role, however, the national state is limited by a number of factors. Existing institutions may be discredited due to their complicity or silence in the face of repression or gross human rights violations. They may have been so decimated by the violence, or so incipient to begin with, that they must be (re)built from scratch. Money and human and technical resources will be scarce, and competition for resources fierce given ruined infrastructure, fragile or distorted economies, and a predictable surge in common crime in the postconflict period. There may be a continuing lack of trust between former enemies and lack of a culture of political give-and-take that make compromise and negotiation difficult. Moreover, in many societies emerging from periods of armed conflict, the capital city has long centralized resources and opportunities and may be worlds apart from the hinterland. Formal legal systems, often a colonial inheritance, may seem irredeemably biased toward the rich or simply incomprehensible to most people. Even a national truth commission, especially one with a largely written output, may seem remote.

Thus, to build a lasting peace, national responses are not enough. Strategic peacebuilders must look both up—to the international sphere—and down, to the local, to do what needs to be done.

The International and Transnational Contribution:
Catalysts with Caveats

Most obviously, foreign governments and international organizations are providers of money and technical training for national initiatives. Every truth commission, for example, has relied on outside funding to a greater or lesser degree. International and hybrid tribunals are also dependent on outside funding and expertise; indeed, one of the reasons to set up such institutions is to capitalize on outside resources and expertise and, in the case of hybrid (national-international) tribunals and commissions, to use them as a training ground for nationals. The international sphere also constitutes a source of pressure on national governments and nonstate armed actors to conform to certain norms, including the need to take some action to deal with past human rights or armed conflict–related crimes. Thus, certain types of blanket amnesties, at least for genocide, "grave breaches" of the Geneva Conventions, and torture, are clearly prohibited in international treaty law, whereas increasing evidence in the jurisprudence of international treaty bodies and regional courts, national courts, the United Nations, and regional human rights practice points to strong disapproval (if not the absolute prohibition) of amnesty for crimes against humanity and other serious violations of human rights or humanitarian law.[5]

Beyond this, the 1990s saw the beginning of a new architecture of international justice, which in the current century has diversified and taken on multiple forms even as criticism of the initial efforts has multiplied. Robert

Johansen's chapter in this volume considers, among other examples, the international criminal tribunals for the former Yugoslavia and Rwanda; I do no more than mention them here. Although helping popularize and concretize the idea of international justice, advancing international jurisprudence in a number of fields, and disabling people who would otherwise have had a more pernicious effect on local politics, the tribunals also had drawbacks. They have been criticized for failing to make themselves accessible and relevant to the populations of the target countries, for their remoteness, for lack of sensitivity to victims, for outreach failures, for not creating sustainable local justice systems or adequately training the persons who must carry on once they close down, and for not producing a historical record capable of convincing most people that leaders of their ethnicity had done anything wrong.[6]

One solution has been to assay "hybrid" institutions. Truth commissions in Haiti and Guatemala pioneered the use of both national and international commissioners and staff; the Sierra Leone Truth and Reconciliation Commission followed a variant of that model. Hybrid courts in Sierra Leone, East Timor, Kosovo, Bosnia, Cambodia, and elsewhere combine international and national authority and staffing in various ways. Ideally, such institutions can combine international independence, impartiality, and resources with a grounding in national culture and law, reduced costs, on-site accessibility to victims, and greater continuity and sustainability. They run the risk, however, of creating orphan institutions fully owned by neither their national nor international backers.

Starting in 2002, the International Criminal Court (ICC) has represented another variant on the national/international interface. Unlike the ad hoc tribunals, the ICC's jurisdiction is complementary to national courts. Under its mandate to defer to national processes unless national courts are "unable or unwilling," the ICC does not measure success by how many cases it brings to trial. Rather, if the threat of ICC prosecution prods domestic actors into moving forward with some kind of accountability, that should be counted as a success. Much of the actual work of the ICC, therefore, is to use the threat of international prosecution to push and prod.

In addition, even under the best of circumstances, the ICC will only be able to deal with a handful of the leaders on both sides of the conflict. Most combatants, including those forcibly recruited and forced to attack their own communities will never be brought before either an international or an internationalized court. There is an emerging practice recognizing this differentiation. Thus, the UN Security Council has since at least 2000 supported the idea that the International Criminal Tribunals for the former Yugoslavia and Rwanda should, as part of their completion strategy, "concentrat[e] on the prosecution and trial of the most senior leaders suspected of being most responsible for crimes," while transferring cases involving lesser offenders to the national courts. The prosecutor for the ICC has similarly expressed his office's intention to focus on the leaders who bear most responsibility, such as the leaders of the state or organization, while leaving lesser offenders to national courts or other (unspecified) means. The Sierra Leone Special Court has a mandate to prosecute those bearing the "greatest responsibility," which may include not only leaders but midlevel commanders who encouraged others by their acts.

Unless there is heightened cooperation and coordination with other levels and types of justice, therefore, the focus of international and internationalized criminal tribunals on a small group of leaders will lead to an "impunity gap." That gap will have to be filled with either national trials or some other type of justice-related mechanism. Although focusing on leaders and organizers makes sense from a standpoint of both limited resources and moral culpability, it is often quite unsatisfying for victims. Even though survivors recognize its ultimate responsibility, the army high command may be as much of an abstraction as the state itself from a ground-level perspective.[7] Rather, people are interested in seeing on the docket those they saw and heard giving orders and committing atrocities: only then does justice take on a real face. Moreover, those who participated in and organized terror at the local level and who continue to enjoy impunity are often still "the most powerful local members of the local apparatus of repression."[8] It is galling and disturbing to have to live among such people, see them flaunt their power (and often, wealth), and feel permanently silenced and threatened by their very presence. For citizens to perceive a change in their daily lives, those people need to be removed from the scene.

Like international prosecutions, transnational investigations and prosecutions can catalyze domestic legal actions under certain circumstances. The most often cited example is that of the Chilean prosecution of Augusto Pinochet. In the mid-1990s, Pinochet seemed untouchable in the domestic courts: laws granting blanket amnesty, statutes of limitations, referrals to military courts, Pinochet's parliamentary immunity, and his legislative support all inhibited efforts to investigate his participation in crimes. In 1996, a group of lawyers asked a Spanish judge to look into crimes committed in the 1970s in Argentina, including what they styled as genocide, terrorism, and torture. These crimes came within the jurisdiction of the Spanish courts through a universal jurisdiction statute (Article 23.4 of the Law of Judicial Power) that granted the local courts power to investigate a small group of very heinous international crimes without any necessary tie to the place of their occurrence or to the nationality of suspects or victims, based on every state's interest in suppressing such crimes. Three months later, the courts accepted a second complaint, alleging similar crimes in Chile; the two investigations eventually merged. When Pinochet arrived in London for back surgery, he was arrested on a Spanish warrant. The British House of Lords found (twice) that he had no immunity from extradition and prosecution as a former head of state, and that the crimes—at least some of them—constituted extraditable crimes. Eventually, he was returned to Chile on the grounds of his fragile health.

Once there, however, his legal troubles multiplied. His untouchability had been broken, judges had seen their international peers find the charges against him credible, and the Chilean government had strenuously argued abroad that he should be tried at home, not in a foreign court. It now found itself unable to oppose domestic trials. Domestic factors were also key: Chile had been reforming its judiciary and retiring Pinochet-era judges, and the political winds had clearly shifted against Pinochet. The first complaint against him was filed several months before he left for London, as was the first Chilean Supreme Court decision limiting the applicability of the amnesty laws. After he returned, both trends accelerated: at their height, there were over 400 complaints naming Pinochet, and a series of Supreme Court decisions denying him immunity and reopening investigations into his collaborators left the amnesty and statute of limitations narrowed considerably. Thus, the case provides a good illustration of the use of outside pressure, through transnational criminal complaints, to open up blocked domestic legal systems and make them do their job. Before he died in 2006, Pinochet faced both corruption and human rights–related charges and was awaiting trial, while many of his closest collaborators are in jail.[9]

Similar histories can be told elsewhere. In Argentina, where members of the military junta were tried in the mid-1980s, laws prohibiting further prosecutions were also on the books. Pressures to extradite former military officers to Europe on human rights–related charges helped convince domestic legislators and judges to annul the amnesty laws and reopen long-closed cases. Domestic advocates and human rights groups used international pressure strategically to break domestic logjams, pressure the government into guaranteeing access to the courts, and convince sectors of the military that the choice was between prosecution at home or abroad, not between prosecution and no prosecution.[10] In Chad, the case against Hissène Habré in the Senegalese and later Belgian courts served to pressure the Chadian government into opening its police archives, dismissing many Habré-era officials still in government, and eventually extracting a promise from Senegal to try Habré in its courts. In these cases, transnational prosecution seems to have helped open political and legal space for domestic judicial processes.[11]

However, this is not always the case. A minimum threshold of safety and security for witnesses, judges, and lawyers and a quota of civil society pressure are needed before transnational prosecutions can have any positive effect. In Central America, for example, it is hard to discern advances in domestic prosecutions as a result of civil and criminal proceedings abroad, at least so far. That changed briefly with the 2006 arrest warrants and extradition requests issued by a Spanish judge against former presidents Efraín Ríos Montt and Óscar Humberto Mejía Victores, along with other high-ranking Guatemalan officials. The Guatemalan case, like those of Chile and Argentina, was brought under the universal jurisdiction statute and alleged genocide, terrorism, and torture, especially against Mayan groups. Although the local courts initially approved the extradition request, in December 2007 the Guatemalan Constitutional Court ruled that it would not recognize Spanish jurisdiction over the defendants. However, a Guatemalan judge in April 2008 decided that on the request of the Spanish judge, he would publicly hear witness testimony from genocide survivors—the first time such testimony has been heard in a Guatemalan court. The judge received death threats for his actions, a reminder of the continuing difficulties in bringing any kind of prosecution in Guatemala.

In addition, if the domestic legal system is too closed to outside influences or the government is less susceptible to outside pressure, transnational prosecutions will have no effect or even create a backlash—as in, arguably, the Belgian and German investigations of Ariel Sharon or of U.S. officials' actions in Iraq.[12] Thus, such prosecutions aimed at officials of powerful states may be legally ineffective, although they may, nonetheless, have a political impact.

There is undeniably a tension between national and transnational prosecutions as well: to the extent the transnational prosecution is based explicitly or implicitly on the foreign forum being a "court of last resort," as space is opened for domestic efforts—in part due to this catalytic effect of transnational investigations—it becomes less tenable to argue that trial at home is impossible. Those bringing the cases must also take care to create relations based on cooperation, information sharing, and complementarity (rather than competition for funds or media access) and craft cases that will avoid problems of duplication of effort or lead to a court finding that the case is already being adjudicated elsewhere. In cases of widespread or massive violations, this is not hard to do.

In civil law systems, transnational cases have taken the form of criminal prosecutions, in large part because under many civil law systems victims can participate to one degree or another in the criminal proceedings and can obtain damages in the same proceeding once there has been a finding of criminal guilt. In common law systems like the United States and the United Kingdom, they have largely taken the form of civil suits for damages. In the United States, these suits have been brought under the Alien Tort Claims Act (or Alien Tort Statute) and the Torture Victims Protection Act against individual defendants present in the United States.[13] Seventeen cases between 1982 and 2003 have resulted in multimillion-dollar judgments, which have rarely been collected. Nonetheless, the cases have allowed for official acknowledgment of wrongdoing, discouraged potential defendants from visiting the United States and encouraged others to leave, and helped open conversations at home regarding the need for justice.

Regional human rights commissions and courts constitute another potentially potent source of pressure from above. In the Americas, especially, the Inter-American Commission and Court have played key roles in setting out the parameters of what states can do—and not do—in the areas of truth telling, justice, and reparations.[14] (The African system, which is more recent, has not played a major role in this area, nor has the European Court of Human Rights, which has not until very recently dealt effectively with situations of widespread or systematic crimes in places like Chechnya.) The commission's rulings in the late 1990s finding blanket amnesty laws to contravene the American Convention on Human Rights, along with the court's 2001 *Barrios Altos* case, were widely credited with not only spurring Peru to annul its challenged amnesty law to conform to the court's ruling but with influencing domestic courts and legislatures in several countries to limit or annul their own laws.[15] In cases before the Inter-American Court, the state has been found liable after a hearing and ordered to pay reparations to complainants; in other cases, the commission has negotiated a friendly settlement, with parallel results. In a few such cases, continued pressure from the Inter-American Commission and Court contributed to pushing forward domestic prosecutions, for example, in the Myrna Mack case in Guatemala.[16]

Though undoubtedly a positive force in the Americas, the regional human rights system can also create tensions with national efforts to remedy the aftermath of the same events. The most evident tensions have arisen around reparations. The regional systems award reparations on a compensatory damages tort model, that is, one based on putting the victim back into the position he or she would have been in before the violation. The courts award damages for material losses, lost earnings, moral damages, and damage to the "project of life," as well as costs and fees. In an individual case, damage awards tend to run to the hundreds of thousands of dollars. When this model is applied to massive violations such as massacres, however, it becomes problematic. A clear example comes from the Plan de Sánchez case in Guatemala. In 1982, 268 people in the village of Plan de Sánchez were massacred by army troops and their civilian collaborators. The survivors, after getting nowhere in the domestic legal system, brought their case to the Inter-American Commission, which eventually referred it to the court. The court ordered the government to pay $25,000 for each of 236 victims and survivors, for a total of $7.9 million, in addition to providing services to the community, a public apology, and other acts.

Although it represents a victory for human rights and fulfillment of an obligation to the victims, money can be highly divisive for families and communities. The sheer size of the amounts, and the disparities among similarly situated victims it has engendered, has created problems. Individuals and communities have been woefully unprepared to receive a lump sum of this size: some have been threatened or robbed, and others have spent the compensation money but their living situations have remained precarious. At the same time, the Inter-American reparations created false expectations about the potential scope of national reparations, which are smaller by nearly an order of magnitude, and questions about the equity in similarly situated massacre survivors receiving very different sums. Many of these problems are common to other mass disaster or mass tort scenarios and are insoluble to some degree. Perhaps the best that can be done is to urge both regional commissions and courts, and the local communities they benefit, to plan ahead for both potential difficulties and for the potential for long-term local development engendered by the awards.[17]

These international and transnational processes have enriched and complicated the arsenal of tools available to strategic peacebuilders. Even if national governments decide on a blanket amnesty, for instance, they cannot control the possibility of transnational or international prosecutions that are not bound by their national efforts. Even given the wide range of such tools, they will be insufficient to deal with more than a few cases. Whether these are emblematic (for example, against leaders and organizers) or opportunistic (as when a potential defendant travels abroad), they still will not deal in more than general terms with the circumstances and life experiences of most survivors. Given the physical location and procedural demands of the courts involved, they will suffer from remoteness and be difficult for ordinary people to access. For this reason, national and international, regional or transnational efforts will be most effective if complemented by local-level efforts. I turn now to the shape of those efforts.

Adding in the Local

Until recently, lawyers working in the area of post–armed conflict justice have treated countries as undifferentiated wholes. This has its uses in terms of establishing global norms and creating a national (re)founding mythology;[18] certain kinds of tasks can only be carried out on a uniform basis, by a national state. By themselves, these do not capture the ground-level meaning of the conflict for people living in specific local spaces, whose experiences may vary widely. For many people, local power relations affect their lives, and efforts based in a faraway capital may not penetrate sufficiently to matter, especially given the perennial weakness of the central state.

Thus, strategic peacebuilders should look at independent local initiatives as an integral part of their work, incorporating bottom-up local efforts as well as top-down state or internationally driven ones. Such local efforts often precede formal national programs, and they can also follow on or extend such programs, making them more locally relevant. They are particularly important to begin to change conflict-created local power dynamics and may also more easily allow for ownership by survivors and be less prone to large-scale patronage and corruption. At the very least, national and international initiatives should strive to be aware of (and not to undermine) local processes.

One good example comes from the operation of a truth commission (TC). Such commissions necessarily suffer from a series of limitations: they must choose exemplary and illustrative cases, not everyone's story can be told, and places where patterns are repeated over and over may get especially short shrift. The hardest hit communities may not even have survivors in a position to give testimony. Thus, in cases of massive violations, a TC report, no matter how well researched, will provide only a general, not a personal "truth" to many.

Even at its best, a TC is only a snapshot and cannot capture longer term processes of memory formation over time. TC researchers will also confront widespread distrust and various kinds of "gaming" behavior from people who may have been deeply traumatized or who have learned to be wary of outsiders promising help. A one-time opportunity to give testimony (whether public or private) cannot substitute for long-term work to rehabilitate survivors. For these things, longer term, local processes are needed.

The same is true of both national and international justice systems. Even before the years of armed conflict, most poor, rural, dwellers in post–armed conflict states viewed national justice systems as at best irrelevant and at worst an incarnation of the discrimination and oppression to which they have long been (and are) subject. As a recent report put it:

> In many countries, the law is drafted and administered only in the
> national language, which many poor people may be unable to speak
> or read. . . . Courts may be far away, under-funded, and take years
> to decide cases. Bringing a case to court swiftly may require bribes.
> Judicial procedures may be inaccessible for those who lack legal
> representation, which is generally too expensive for the poor.[19]

It is unrealistic to expect even the best set of anti-impunity and judicial reform measures to reverse the centuries of warranted distrust of formal legal systems.

Moreover, it is hard to see how formal justice systems, either criminal or civil, can adequately grapple with the ambiguities, mixed motives, and shades of gray that characterize most armed conflicts. Criminal law categorizes subjects as perpetrator, accomplice, or innocent witness.[20] It does not deal well with bystanders,[21] and even less well with the kinds of forced complicity that are common to recent conflicts. In many places, forced recruits are forced to commit atrocities, often against their own family and neighbors, in an attempt to loosen them from community bonds. Children are forced to kill their parents; villagers are forced by military or paramilitary forces to kill other villagers or be victims themselves. These events continue to divide and traumatize communities years later. They characterize many recent armed conflicts.[22]

In the postwar period, conflicts within and between communities continue, exacerbated by the newly exalted position of some ex-militia or paramilitary members as compared to the almost uniform destitution of their victims. Demobilization, disarmament, and reintegration programs that provide money and training for victimizers but nothing for those who survived them can exacerbate these differences. In addition, regions vary greatly in composition: in some, people never left, whereas others include returning or resettling refugees whose presence creates tensions with existing residents. Sometimes, returning refugees find others in their homes and lands.[23] In some communities, everyone is a massacre survivor. In others, local power is held by ex-militia members, and in others new political forces have emerged. Fear of continued violence contributes to silence about the past, sometimes even within families, and manifests in myriad types of social dysfunctionality, from lynchings to domestic violence to somatic illnesses. This degree of variation and complexity makes international and national responses inadequate and, to some degree, locally irrelevant, and requires further exploration of local responses.

What could such responses look like? For one thing, they would involve communities directly in truth seeking and memorialization exercises in their own region. The church-supported Recuperation of Historical Memory project in Guatemala pioneered the incorporation of laypersons into testimony taking in their local area.[24] Thus, community mapping of violations and resultant harms, and local museums and memorialization projects, would become a cornerstone of post–armed conflict efforts. Such efforts could easily be linked to national TCs or other truth-seeking exercises; the creation of regional offices or meetings with communities to prepare and present testimony to a TC would then be seen not as the culminating moment but as the beginning of a longer term local process. Such documentation and memorialization exercises could include an accounting of not only the costs and victims of armed conflict but also of local traditions and history—and their disruption and change—creating awareness and pride in the ability to survive rather than a sense of perpetual victimization.

Community-supported exhumations and reburials would be another key response. In most cultures, the link between the living and the dead is important, and it is widely disrupted in situations where people are forcibly disappeared or where they are killed and family members are prohibited or intimidated in recovering and burying the body with appropriate ritual. Exhumations are important to local communities and also nationally for purposes of providing evidence in criminal investigations. It is important that the second of these goals not eclipse the first.[25] Local community participation in supporting forensic anthropology teams, carrying out reburials with the requisite ceremonies and markers, and designing and implementing memorials have proven powerful tools. But they also raise or resurface powerful emotions and memories, and community-based psychosocial interventions are often needed to help communities recover. Because both sides abandoned the civilian population during war, trust is hard to come by among survivors; for psychosocial interventions to work, they must be rooted in a long-term relationship and intimate knowledge of cultural practices, which can vary widely within a single country. These interventions are thus often most fruitful when carried out on a local or regional scale.

The biggest questions arise around the uses and abuses of local justice mechanisms. The availability and applicability of local, informal, or traditional justice systems has become highly contested over the past few years, not least because of a number of actual or proposed uses in the wake of armed conflicts in Africa. These systems are seen as integral to a process of local community rebuilding. They allow for justice practices to resonate with the local culture and be accessible and meaningful to people. They can foster a sense of ownership of the process, and can integrate restorative justice mechanisms including public truth telling, acknowledgment and apology, moral and material reparations, along with, if appropriate, culturally relevant punishment or atonement. They can allow for ex-neighbors to find a way to coexist and can be a first step toward reintegration of families, clans, and all manner of intermediate social structures that mediate between the individual and the national polity.

Thus, the water rituals of Mozambique and Sierra Leone cleansed the child soldiers of their crimes and reincorporated them into their communities with a cool, nonviolent heart.[26] In northern Uganda, the Acholi carry out a ceremony called *mato oput*, or drinking the bitter herb, which involves recognition of a wrong and reconciliation with the victims' family. A separate ceremony, involving stepping on an egg, is used to cleanse those who have been away from home and allow them to return.[27] In East Timor, the Truth, Reception and Reconciliation Commission organized community reconciliation processes that incorporated traditional *adat* dispute resolution, including a public airing of facts, apology and/or reparation, and acceptance of responsibility, in exchange for conditional amnesty for low-level offenders.[28] In Peru, local communities found ways first to dehumanize and then rehumanize those who had joined Sendero Luminoso through public reincorporation ceremonies involving truth telling, apology, and symbolic punishment.[29] In Cambodia, religious as well as local civic authorities staged ceremonies to welcome back Khmer Rouge soldiers who laid down their arms in the 1980s.[30] These techniques involve decision making by respected elders after hearing from community members on both sides of an issue.[31]

The Rwandan experience shows some of the difficulties involved in changing the nature of these mechanisms from bottom-up to centrally organized government efforts. Postgenocide, the Rwandan government, faced with over 130,000 mid- and lower-ranked genocide suspects[32] and a rudimentary justice system, chose to adapt the traditional mechanism by creating local-level open-air hearings at which suspects are accused and defended by their neighbors and sentences, ranging from community service to prison, are imposed by a group of lay judges. In response to criticisms that the procedures violated due process norms regarding the presumption of innocence and privilege against self-incrimination, the government added in legal advisors, appeal procedures, and other features that substantially modified the process but did not fully assuage these concerns.

Despite undeniable potential advantages, it is important not to romanticize traditional justice systems. Such systems were generally designed to deal with property and family-related disputes and not with serious (i.e., homicidal) crime. They thus may not be suitable for complex cases involving issues of command and indirect responsibility and victims from many communities and traditions. They can be patriarchal and exclusionary toward women and minorities, and can be coercive, creating pressures on individuals to subsume their own needs into those of the "community." They may assume a degree of community knowledge and cohesion that, if it ever existed at all, certainly does not exist in dispersed and reshuffled communities from which many original inhabitants have fled to the cities or left the country altogether. Indeed, this has been one of the problems with the modified *gacaca* proceedings in Rwanda, which have suffered from a lack of participation. For this reason, they may be less applicable (if at all) in urban areas or the displaced persons camps where many conflict-affected people now subsist. They generally rely on a high degree of case-by-case discretion that can easily become arbitrary.

Finally, they may not be appropriate where conflicts were more "vertical"—involving state agents attacking civilian populations—and less "horizontal," involving neighbors and people of approximately the same socioeconomic level fighting each other and then having to somehow live together in the post–armed conflict era. They may be seriously lacking in basic protections against cruel and inhuman punishment and in due process protections. They may serve impunity where those who continue to exercise power at the local level are the same people who committed the violations in the first place.

From a human rights perspective, such local proceedings raise two sets of concerns. First, human rights advocates question whether a process that does not involve some kind of punishment is adequate. Here there are differing views within the human rights community, but some commonalities: there must be at a minimum some kind of acknowledgment and truth telling, and some reparation of the victim. Many (but not all) traditional ceremonies and reintegration practices centrally include one or both of these elements. Second, due process issues arise in cases involving in naming and punishing someone as a murderer or *genocidaire* when they have no access to a lawyer and usually no right of appeal. Tim Longman argues that there are functional equivalents in traditional practices like gacaca to many of the techniques by which human rights law guarantees fundamental rights in formal trials, including the ability of all community members to see and hear the discussion, present evidence, and raise questions.[33] Nonetheless, it is not clear whether these are sufficient to garner popular legitimacy.

Largely in response to human rights concerns (and pressure from international human rights nongovernmental organizations), governments in Rwanda and East Timor modified the traditional procedures to formalize them and connect them to the formal justice system. This quelled some of the concern around due process violations but raised the question of whether these kinds of spontaneous, culturally specific local dialogue and reincorporation and commemoration ceremonies lose their value if "programmed" or even encouraged by governments or international actors. After all, part of the strength of such initiatives is that they are insider-driven and a product of local initiative. In other words, the kinds of local initiatives that seem to work best do so without any formalization in Western systems of aid and consultation, much less in legal commitments, and may be so place- and time-specific that the attempt to formalize them may backfire, leaving communities with the worst of both worlds.

Conclusions

Just as the different parts of the transitional or post–armed conflict justice agenda are interdependent, so are the different levels or scales on which they are carried out. Truth telling without justice or reparation leaves victims feeling defrauded; reparations without truth and acknowledgment is liable to be seen as blood money, buying silence. Justice alone, narrowly defined as criminal justice or retributive justice, is similarly partial: without some more fulsome process for those who, because resources or will are lacking or because they were bystanders or coerced, will never be tried, local power will never shift, nor will community reintegration be possible. Nor can an overall historical narrative, tracing patterns and causes of armed conflict and setting out recommendations for the future, arise solely from individual prosecutions or civil trials. Yet without some public, legally sound punishment for at least the leaders and organizers, victims remain unsatisfied and unable to fully participate in the new dispensation,[34] even in cases where reparation has been paid and TCs have been instituted.

A similar set of interdependencies applies to the local, national, and international scales. National efforts at justice may need international aid and financing, and may benefit from the catalytic effect that international or transnational prosecutions may provide. International or internationalized courts may play a constructive role when national court systems are in disrepair or unable to function, but without a clear conduit and plan for engaging and eventually turning over cases to national systems, international courts may have little effect on national audiences or legal cultures and may thus play a limited role in conflict transformation. Formal justice, whether national or international, will always only be concerned with a small number of people. For the rest, including unindicted perpetrators, coerced victim/perpetrators, and bystanders, there is a need for both national truth telling and for local acknowledgment, memorialization, community mapping, reparations, and reincorporation processes. The local by itself is insufficient: state-building and construction of a credible, accessible legal system cannot be simply disaggregated locally, left to disparate and shifting local custom. It plays an important complementary role. Similarly, there is no reason why international prosecutions for the few ringleaders cannot coexist with a much larger, richer effort based at the community level and rooted in customary practices. Indeed, that may, at least in some cultural and political contexts, be the truest meaning of complementarity.

NOTES

1. See International Council on Human Rights Policy, Peace Agreements and Human Rights (2006), available at http://www.ichrp.org/public/projects.php?id_projet=27&lang=AN.

2. See Naomi Roht-Arriaza. 2006. "The New Landscape of Transitional Justice," in *Transitional Justice in the Twenty-First Century,* edited by Naomi Roht-Arriaza and Javier Mariezcurrena. Cambridge: Cambridge University Press, pp. 1–16.

3. John Paul Lederach. 2003. *The Little Book of Conflict Transformation.* New York: Good Books, p. 52.

4. Laurel Fletcher and Harvey Weinstein. 2002. "Violence and Social Repair: Rethinking the Contribution of Justice to Reconciliation." *Human Rights Quarterly* vol. 24 (no. 3): 573–639.

5. On the specific legal requirements regarding amnesties, see my background paper prepared for Peace Agreements and Human Rights, supra note 1. See also Report of Diane Orentlicher, independent expert to update the set of principles to combat impunity—Updated Set of Principles for the Protection and Promotion of Human Rights through Action to Combat Impunity, U.N. Doc. E/CN.4/2005/102/Add.1, Feb. 8, 2005 (Orentlicher Principles) and Basic Principles and Guidelines on the Right to a Remedy and Reparation for Victims of Gross Violations of International Human Rights Law and Serious Violations of Humanitarian Law (Van Boven/Bassiouni Principles), G.A. Res. 60/147 (Dec. 16, 2005).

6. For one careful study of the former Yugoslavia and Rwanda, see Eric Stover and Harvey Weinstein, eds. 2004. *My Neighbor, My Enemy.* Cambridge: Cambridge University Press.

7. This is not to argue that survivors are uninterested in seeing the army high command and others of that ilk brought to justice, simply that doing so may be insufficient for many people. It is also true that prosecution of *only* subordinate officials, even if providing a face to survivors, may result in scapegoating those who are less responsible.

8. Victoria Sanford. 2003. *Buried Secrets: Truth and Human Rights in Guatemala.* New York: Palgrave Macmillan, p. 269.

9. For a full description of this process, see Naomi Roht-Arriaza. 2005. *The Pinochet Effect: Transnational Justice in the Age of Human Rights.* Philadelphia: University of Pennsylvania Press.

10. Kathryn Sikkink, and Carrie Walling. 2006. "Argentina's Contribution to Global Trends in Transitional Justice." In *Transitional Justice in the Twenty-First Century: Beyond Truth vs. Justice*, edited by N. Roht-Arriaza and J. Mariezcurrena. Cambridge: Cambridge University Press.

11. Reed Brody. 2006. "The Prosecution of Hissene Habré: International Accountability, National Impunity." In *Transitional Justice in the Twenty-First Century: Beyond Truth vs. Justice*, edited by N. Roht-Arriaza and J. Mariezcurrena. Cambridge: Cambridge University Press.

12. For a description of the Belgian cases against Ariel Sharon and against U.S. officials, see Naomi Roht-Arriaza. 2005. *The Pinochet Effect: Transnational Justice in the Age of Human Rights.* Philadelphia: University of Pennsylvania Press, ch. 7. For a description of the German case against Donald Rumsfeld et al., see www.ccr-ny.org.

13. Other cases have involved suits against corporations for directly engaging in and/or aiding and abetting others to carry out violations, and suits against U.S. officials for violating international law. See Sandra Coliver, Jennie Green, and Paul Hoffman. 2005. "Holding Human Rights Violators Accountable by Using International Law in U.S. Courts: Advocacy Efforts and Complementary Strategies." *Emory International Law Review* vol. 19 (no. 1): 169–226.

14. The Inter-American Commission on Human Rights is charged with monitoring human rights practice in Organization of American States member states and making recommendations to states for improvement. The Inter-American Court of Human Rights can hear cases arising in states that have accepted its jurisdiction and can issue binding judgments, including injunctions and damage awards.

15. *Chumbipuma Aguirre et al. v. Peru.* 2001. Inter-American Court of Human Rights.

16. *Myrna Mack v. Guatemala.* 2003. Inter-American Court of Human Rights. This case resulted in monetary reparations, a public apology, and other moral reparations awarded by the court; after much pushing from the petitioner and various forms of international pressure, the Supreme Court upheld the domestic courts' conviction of the main intellectual authors of the crime in 2004.

17. On the connection between peacebuilding and economic reconstruction, see Nicholas Sambanis's chapter in this volume.

18. See Richard Wilson. 2001. *The Politics of Truth and Reconciliation in South Africa: Legitimizing the Post-Apartheid State.* Cambridge: Cambridge University Press.

19. Commission on Legal Empowerment of the Poor. 2008. *Making the Law Work for Everyone.* New York: UN Development Programme, p. 33.

20. For a discussion of the way criminal law creates a bright line between victims and wrongdoers, see Mark Osiel. 1997. *Mass Atrocity, Collective Memory and the Law.* Ardsley, N.Y.: Transaction, p. 129. Much of the discussion of the blurred line between victims and perpetrators has taken place in the context of forcibly recruited

child soldiers, who were often forced to commit atrocities against their own family or neighbors. See Diane Amann. 2001. "Calling Children to Account: The Proposal for a Juvenile Chamber in the Special Court for Sierra Leone." *Pepperdine Law Review* vol. 29.

21. See Laurel Fletcher. 2005. "From Indifference to Engagement: Bystanders and International Criminal Justice." *Michigan Journal of International Law* vol. 26.

22. See, e.g., Report of the Truth and Reconciliation Commission of Sierra Leone, or the plight of children kidnapped by the Lord's Resistance Army in northern Uganda.

23. For a description of one such community, see Beatriz Manz. 2004. *Paradise in Ashes: A Guatemalan Journey of Courage, Terror & Hope.* Berkeley: University of California Press.

24. Recuperation of Historical Memory Project, Guatemala Nunca Mas. 1998.

25. See Eric Stover and Rachel Shigekane. 2004. "Exhumation of Mass Graves: Balancing Legal and Humanitarian Needs." In *My Neighbor, My Enemy*, edited by E. Stover and H. Weinstein. Cambridge: Cambridge University Press.

26. Alcinda Honwana. 2004. "Child Soldiers: Community Healing and Rituals in Mozambique and Angola." In *International Perspectives on Youth, Conflict and Development*, edited by C. Daiute, Z. Beykont, C. Higson-Smith, and L. Nucci. New York: Oxford University Press, pp. 225–244. Rosalind Shaw. 2003. "Remembering to Forget: Unmaking War for Child Ex-Comatants in Northern Sierra Leone." Uppsala: Nordic Africa Institute. For an account of similar experiences in Uganda with the reintegration of Lord's Resistance Army fighters, see Marc Lacey. 2005. "Atrocity Victims in Uganda Choose to Forgive." *New York Times*, April 18.

27. Refugee Law Project. 2005. "Peace First, Justice Later: Traditional Justice in Northern Uganda," p. 24, 34.

28. Patrick Burgess. 2006. "East Timor's Community Reconciliation Process: A New Tool for Reconciliation?" In *Transitional Justice in the Twenty-First Century: Beyond Truth vs. Justice*, edited by N. Roht-Arriaza and J. Mariezcurrena. Cambridge: Cambridge University Press.

29. Kimberly Theidon. 2006. "Justice in Transition: The Micropolitics of Reconciliation in Postwar Peru." *Journal of Conflict Resolution* vol. 50: 1.

30. Jens Iverson. 2005. "Center Stage: The Contributions of Non-State Actors to Accountability and Reconciliation in Cambodia (unpublished paper on file with author)."

31. Lars Waldorf. 2006. "Mass Justice for Mass Atrocity: Rethinking Local Justice as Transitional Justice." *Temple Law Review* vol. 79.

32. The International Criminal Tribunal for Rwanda has only tried, and only intends to try, 100 or so of the top leaders of the genocide.

33. Timothy Longman. 2006. "Justice at the Grassroots? Gacaca Trials in Rwanda." In *Transitional Justice in the Twenty-First Century: Beyond Truth vs. Justice*, edited by N. Roht-Arriaza and J. Mariezcurrena. Cambridge: Cambridge University Press, ch. 8.

34. Public opinion studies in several Latin American countries as well as Iraq and Uganda have consistently shown a demand for justice, understood as a trial, to be a central demand of many victims. See International Center for Transitional Justice and U.C. Human Rights Center. 2005. "Forgotten Voices: A Population-Based Survey on Attitudes about Peace and Justice in Northern Uganda." International Center for Transitional Justice and U.C. International Center for Transitional Justice and U.C. Human Rights Center. 2004. "Iraqi Voices."

10

Economic Globalization and Strategic Peacebuilding

Jackie Smith

In numerous countries where peace agreements have held without a relapse into conflict beyond the critical period, the structural factors lying at the source of the original conflict remain unaddressed and continue to fester. From Cambodia and Guatemala to East Timor, serious issues related to land tenure, property rights, rule of law, political participation and transitional justice continue to pose serious challenges to peace consolidation and peacebuilding.

> —Neclâ Tschirgi, "Post-Conflict Peacebuilding Revisited: Achievements, Limitations, Challenges"

The post–Cold War era has been marked by a proliferation of persistent intrastate conflicts, many of which have frustrated international attempts to promote peaceful conflict resolution and the emergence of more peaceful societies. By many measures, international peacebuilding operations have achieved only mixed success or have simply failed, and nearly half of all "postconflict" countries see a return of violent struggle.[1] This chapter argues that an important reason for the failure of multilateral peacebuilding interventions is that these initiatives incorporate a set of assumptions about the benefits of market liberalization that are inaccurate. More effective intervention to end violent conflicts requires efforts to better understand how economic globalization impacts the dynamics of civil wars. Contemporary violent conflicts are not purely localized phenomena but are deeply embedded within a global context of complex political and economic relationships. Strategic peacebuilding cannot occur without greater attention to these relationships and how they reproduce power and inequality in the global political and economic systems.

Recent studies on the impacts of multilateral peacebuilding initiatives have concluded that these interventions have, on the whole, not been terribly successful at helping societies transition from states of civil war to long-term, sustainable peace.[2] Two important recent studies of peacebuilding operations—those by Collier and colleagues and Paris[3]—conclude that future interventions must subordinate market liberalization policies to those that strengthen the capacities of institutions to manage societal conflicts. Paris, for instance, calls his proposed strategy "institutionalization before liberalization." I argue that these studies do not go far enough in their prescriptions because they cling to two important assumptions. First, they treat market liberalization and political liberalization, or "market democracy," as inherently linked and complementary processes, both of which are seen as essential to peacebuilding work. Second, they see *economic* liberalization as a central element of peacebuilding, even while they argue for its more gradual introduction in postconflict settings. Although there may indeed be relationships between economic liberalization and the conditions that foster peace, and open markets might be associated with more open political systems, there is considerable debate among social scientists about the nature of these relationships. Market liberalization can proceed in highly authoritarian contexts, and highly democratic countries may in fact limit their participation in global markets in response to democratic pressures. Moreover, existing analyses show that economic liberalization can in fact undermine efforts to rebuild social institutions and foster political liberalization in war-torn societies.[4] This chapter interrogates some key assumptions behind contemporary peacebuilding operations and the proposals to strengthen them, exploring whether the conventional wisdom about the relationship of market liberalization to peacebuilding processes is consistent with existing evidence.

What becomes apparent in this analysis is that much research in the area of peacebuilding fails to adequately address questions of power and its distribution.[5] Sidelining power questions can often serve on a practical level to expedite cease-fire agreements and on an analytical level to generate more parsimonious models of conflict dynamics. But asymmetries of power can mask structural sources of conflicts that can resurface over time. Therefore, by failing to address power imbalances, conflict analysts and practitioners seeking to reduce violent conflict will fail to identify effective peacebuilding strategies. "Strategic peacebuilding" should imply, therefore, a central focus on questions of how power is distributed among conflicting parties along with intervention strategies that seek to reduce the inequities in power that can lead to violent conflict.

Globalization has meant an increasing concentration of political and economic power at the global level.[6] Because of this, strategic peacebuilding should also adopt a perspective that embeds the local within a broader social and political context. As global integration expands along numerous dimensions, it becomes even more important that conflict analysts adopt a systemic framework. Contemporary states are embedded within complex sets of economic and political relationships, as are an array of other transnational actors, such as transnational corporations and civil society groups. Conflicts within states are often reflections of these broader sets of ties, and indeed these apparently localized conflicts depend on resource flows that extend well beyond national borders.[7] Andrew Hurrell describes a "triple anchorage of states" in the international system of states, the global capitalist economy, and transnational civil society.[8] These webs of interdependence shape conflicts within as well as between states, and effective interventions to end violent conflicts must account for these relationships between local and global contexts.

Peacebuilding missions have been described as "transmission mechanisms" of neoliberal models of the state.[9] Paris argues that far from being technical and neutral exercises in conflict management, multilateral peacebuilding operations advance liberal market democracy as the preferred model for domestic governance, advancing a "world revolution of Western liberalism."[10] They do so by (1) encouraging parties to include political and economic liberalization measures in peace agreements, (2) providing technical assistance in constitution writing and other governance tasks, (3) imposing political and economic conditionalities on parties in exchange for financial and other assistance, and (4) performing governance functions in transitional or failed state contexts.[11]

Significantly, this transfer of governance templates is from the rich, Northern core of the global economy to the comparatively poor, Southern, and postcolonial periphery. Peacebuilding itself reflects a long history of inequality in the world system, and it incorporates various forms of power—including structural, institutional, and symbolic power—that remain largely unexamined in existing literature. Robinson demonstrates, for instance, how peacekeeping operations in Nicaragua and Haiti were used to reorganize government practices to make them conform to the needs of globalizing capitalist interests.[12] Thus, peacekeeping can be seen as one mechanism for the development of what Robinson calls the "neoliberal state," or the transformation of national states into entities that support the trade liberalization agenda of globalized capital.[13] In this sense, peacekeeping operations are a part of the "revolution from above," that helped expand the global economy in recent decades.[14] Strategic peacebuilding approaches, therefore, require a critical analysis of how power is reflected and reproduced in the operation of peace intervention missions. They also demand greater attention to the assumptions behind these missions and their objectives.

A critical look at peacekeeping and peacebuilding operations suggests that they are designed largely to protect if not promote the interests of the Northern core states that enjoy privileged influence in global institutional contexts. Peacebuilding interventions—like other international initiatives, such as global trade agreements and multilateral development lending—have helped reproduce neoliberal economic policies. Unlike global trade and financial institutions, however, peacebuilding missions advocate economic liberalization not as an end in itself but as a (presumed) means of promoting economic growth that will reduce violent conflict. However, relatively little empirical research has been done to critically examine the assumption that economic liberalization will actually contribute to peacebuilding aims.

Also integral to the models of governance favored by market liberalization proponents are policies that reduce state regulatory capacities and expand incentives and opportunities for international investment. By reducing the capacities of states to define and defend public goods and by limiting the policy space available for democratic decision making, such practices may obstruct efforts to build stronger institutions and foster democracy in postwar states. Given these possible tensions between the practices of peacebuilding missions and the needs of societies emerging from violent conflicts, I examine four key assumptions in peacebuilding research and practice: first, that market liberalization leads to economic growth; second, that growth will solve the underlying problem of inequality that gives rise to conflicts; third, that a neoliberal model of the state will be effective at promoting peace; and finally, that multilateral peace and security can be improved without addressing fundamental inequities in the global economic order.

Market Liberalization and Growth

In their important World Bank–sponsored study of contemporary internal conflicts, Collier and colleagues conclude that the "key root cause of conflict is the failure of economic development."[15] Societies plagued with internal violence are very often those mired in poverty. Thus, a key strategy for breaking what Collier et al. call the "conflict trap" is to promote market liberalization, expanding the country's access to world markets as a means of promoting economic growth. But will market liberalization generate the growth needed to transform war-torn societies?

Debates about the effects of trade liberalization and economic growth yield conflicting results, but the bulk of new work that is emerging suggests that initial optimism about trade liberalization's prospects were substantially overstated.[16] For instance, the World Bank recently reduced its projections of global gains from trade liberalization by nearly two-thirds, from $832 billion to $287 billion. The projected benefits to the developing countries were reduced by more than 80 percent, from $539 billion to $90 billion.[17] The UN Development Programme (UNDP) *Human Development Report*, moreover, states that "the evidence to support the proposition that import liberalization is automatically good for growth is weak."[18] The analysis of trade offered in the UNDP report suggests that although trade liberalization might indeed be associated with growth in some countries at some times, there is no *direct* link between economic liberalization and growth. Other variables are important for explaining when liberalization helps generate growth and when it cannot.[19] There is no automatic relationship between the two. Thus, despite two decades of radical economic liberalization policies and a doubling of world exports since the early 1990s, we still see a "persistent pool of non-developing low-income countries" that threatens world peace and stability.[20]

Another pattern that emerges from data on global trends in imports and exports suggests that the benefits of trade for poor countries are not at all

comparable to the benefits experienced by rich countries. This should lead us
to seriously question trade liberalization as an effective prescription for helping poor countries emerge from conflict traps. While developing countries are
devoting substantially more of their national resources and energies to promoting exports, they have not achieved substantial gains in terms of global
market shares.[21] For instance, despite a growth in exports between 40–55 percent, African countries' share of world markets grew by just 0.3 percent in the
1990s. India's share of world trade went up just 0.7 percent despite average
annual growth of 10 percent during the 1990s.[22] This type of economic growth
will only contribute to ever-growing inequalities between countries as well as
within them.[23] If one considers the environmental and social costs associated
with developing countries' increased participation in world markets, there is
little overall benefit from trade in terms of expanding the resources available to
most of the population in these regions.

More disturbing, however, is that the higher income developing countries
are finding that growth from trade is not readily sustained. Weisbrot and Bello
found that economic growth rates in Latin America were markedly higher
before the era of neoliberal reforms than they were after countries opened their
borders.[24] Many successful globalizers are finding their place in the highly
stratified global production system slipping. Thus, countries like Mexico and
Brazil are losing high value-added manufacturing jobs to Korea and China,
and India's high-tech sector is losing ground to lower paying industries, such
as textiles and apparel.[25] The terms of trade for developing countries have
been declining over time, and recent measures place overall developing country declines at 0.74 percent. This pattern holds even for the larger developing
countries, such as India, whose terms of trade declined by 1.62 percent; and
Brazil, which dropped 0.18 percent.[26] This record shows that economic policies designed to encourage foreign investment do not necessarily produce the
economic growth expected by neoliberal policy analysts. Whereas economic
growth—that is, expanding the resource pie for all residents of countries
destroyed by war—is clearly vital to peace, there is sufficient evidence to warrant a search for strategies that do not rely on wealth trickling down to local
communities from foreign investors and through export-based production
and trade (see chapter 6). Because sustained peacebuilding work depends on
a stable and predictable social and economic environment, policies that link
conflict-torn countries to a volatile and uncertain global economy are—as is
becoming increasingly apparent—fraught with trouble.

Critics of neoliberal policies often charge proponents of economic liberalization with engaging in what has been called "NAFTA math"—that is, reporting
the economic gains from trade while neglecting to account for the associated
costs, such as job losses, environmental destruction, and vulnerability to international markets. For instance, Public Citizen pointed out that the U.S. Trade
Representative's (USTR) reports on the job gains from the North American Free
Trade Agreement (NAFTA) showed only those jobs created in export industries.
The USTR forgot to subtract those jobs lost in industries that were eclipsed
by competition from new flows of imports. NAFTA math is rampant in many

official accounts of trade's benefits,[27] and those concerned with finding appropriate policy mechanisms to address the problems of violent conflict and fragile states should be careful to note these inflated assessments of trade benefits. A "responsibility to protect" people in war-torn countries seems to require a far more vigorous search for better strategies to advance economic development and to ensure a more equitable distribution of wealth in war-torn countries.

Wise and Gallagher and Weisbrot and colleagues note how trade proponents overlook important costs that liberalization imposes on poor countries.[28] They examine the costs to developing countries of trade liberalization policies in terms of lost tax revenues from tariffs. They conclude that developing countries would lose more than $60 billion in tariff revenue under the nonagricultural market access agreement within the World Trade Organization, around ten times the projected gains from trade liberalization. In countries where as much as 40 percent of government revenues come from tariffs, this cost is substantial, to say the least. It also will limit the capacities of poor governments to operate in the best of conditions, and thus we might rethink whether such policies are desirable for governments emerging from internal wars.

In sum, the evidence linking trade openness to economic growth are mixed, and there is no direct link between expanding a country's access to world markets and growing the economic pie that can help win over combatants and promote sustainable peace. Moreover, the experiences of the global North countries in the area of trade liberalization are poor predictors of the likely effects of trade on poor countries. The evidence shows consistently that the global South has enjoyed fewer and less consistent benefits from trade liberalization than their richer, early industrializing counterparts. Thus, Collier and colleagues are right to conclude that priority must be given to policies that promote peace over those that promote economic growth through markets. But we might ask whether the World Bank prescriptions are generating the kind of economic growth that can really lead to long-term peace. The mounting evidence that policies for economic liberalization are not generating the intended growth effects might go quite a ways toward explaining the shortcomings of peacebuilding operations.

Globalization's critics—whose ranks are gaining ever-larger numbers of policy elites—have developed elaborate analyses and feasible policy prescriptions aimed at remedying the shortfalls of neoliberal economic models.[29] The essence of these approaches is a focus on production for local needs, local ownership, participation, and control, and attention to environmental and social contexts. These types of strategies can be part of efforts to quickly restore public services and generate economic returns that Sambanis (chapter 6) found so essential to successful peacebuilding. They have an advantage of helping increase the direct stakes all citizens would have in postwar peace agreements. Although growth and service restoration may take a bit longer, the process of engaging local communities and providing even limited resources to encourage local engagement and entrepreneurship helps build confidence and mobilizes local skills and energy in the peacebuilding process.

Economic Liberalization and Inequality

Collier and colleagues found that the countries at greatest risk of civil war also experienced high levels of inequality.[30] However, none of the study's numerous recommendations for improving peacebuilding work addresses this specific problem. Instead, there is an implicit assumption that the problem of inequality will be solved by policies that foster economic growth. This may be a valid assumption, but given that inequality is strongly linked to the escalation of conflicts, it bears greater scrutiny than the Collier study gives it. This section examines the question of whether and how economic liberalization affects patterns of inequality.

Economic orthodoxy links poverty reduction to economic growth. The conventional economic wisdom says that "a rising tide lifts all boats," that a growing economic pie will enrich all of society, and that the benefits of growth will "trickle down" to generate other social benefits such as poverty reduction, environmental improvements, and the like. Thus, if economic liberalization generates growth, and growth helps reduce inequality, then economic liberalization is a good policy prescription for war-torn societies. But if economic liberalization does not generate more equitable distributions of wealth, and especially if it exacerbates inequality, then policy makers and analysts must seriously rethink its role in postwar contexts.

How has global economic liberalization impacted inequality in the world? Although it is difficult to identify the specific causal variables, we have considerable evidence showing that economic globalization has had either no direct effect on inequality or that it may be contributing to rising inequality within and between countries. The UNDP recently reported that *"for a majority of countries* [economic] globalization is a story of divergence and marginalization."[31] Global inequality has grown over recent decades of economic globalization, and now the richest 10 percent of the world population controls more than half the world's income, whereas the bottom 40 percent enjoy just 5 percent of world income.[32] This inequality is even greater when measures of wealth are used in place of income. The UNDP data show that inequality in the global South is on the rise, and in turn, this is slowing economic growth and curbing efforts at poverty reduction. The report argues—along with many social scientists and economists—that inequality is a challenge to the international community, because it not only impedes market efficiency and economic growth but also undermines democracy and social cohesion—the very conditions that are required to reduce the likelihood that social conflicts will escalate into violent confrontations.

The 2005 *Human Development Report* paints a far gloomier picture of economic globalization than had many previous official documents. But the evidence is consistent with findings of scholars and other critics of trade liberalization as a policy panacea. Clearly the problem of persistent poverty and underdevelopment is less a function of scarce resources—indeed, the world is far richer by many material measures than it was in prior decades or centuries—than of the unequal distribution of those resources.[33] In the previous section, I highlighted evidence showing that the benefits of trade were not equally distributed among the world's countries, and that the poorest countries and regions were gaining less than rich ones. This inequality in shares of world trade is reproduced in other measures of economic inequality. For instance, sociologists have found a consistent trend toward rising inequality within countries as well as between them.[34] This growing gap between the rich and poor in the world, moreover, corresponds to the timing of neoliberal policy initiatives, which were first launched in the mid-1980s and disseminated through means such as international trade agreements and structural adjustment lending programs of the World Bank and the International Monetary Fund (IMF). The UNDP (2005) reports a current measure of world inequality, the Gini coefficient, of 0.67.[35] This coefficient reflects a highly unequal global system with levels of inequality higher than those of the most unequal (and unstable) countries of the world.[36]

Although rising inequality is associated with the timing of global economic liberalization, we should not automatically assume a causal relationship, because a wide range of variables clearly affect global economic distributions. What can we say about whether and how economic globalization might be affecting inequality? The New Economics Foundation examined the extent to which the economic growth linked to neoliberal policies benefited the poorest segments of national populations. Their conclusions correspond with the UNDP report, and they go further to argue that the 1980s and 1990s generated "antipoor" growth: a very small and declining percentage of the world's economic growth went to those groups in greatest need. People living on less than $1/day received just around 2 percent of the benefits from economic growth in the 1980s, and this declined to less than 1 percent by 2000. Those people living on $2/day enjoyed about 5.5 percent of the growth in the early 1980s, and this share declined to just 3.1 percent by 2000.[37] Thus, just as the benefits of trade liberalization were reduced for poor countries, the benefits of economic growth are small and diminishing for poor people. The declines come as economic liberalization policies have expanded.

Does this association between economic globalization and rising inequality suggest a causal connection? We need theoretical work to show whether there is reason to think that economic liberalization is implicated in persistent and rising inequality. Sociologists identify labor market dynamics as an important part of this puzzle, and both empirical and theoretical work here shows that global economic integration has been systematically undermining the power of working people relative to the owners of capital.[38] A major reason for this is that the policies pursued by the global financial institutions have pressed for the opening of national borders to flows of goods and services while allowing countries to close their borders to flows of people. This creates market distortions in the supply and demand of labor that artificially suppresses costs while also curtailing the possibilities for working people to benefit from expanding trade relationships. This has meant dramatic declines in rates of unionization around the world and enhanced vulnerability of workers to job losses directly linked to import/export sectors. In the United States, for instance, three-quarters of those workers losing their jobs due to trade-related competition reentered the labor market at lower wages than they previously earned.[39] Workers in the United States are comparatively powerful politically, so these losses are likely to be far greater in countries of the global South.

Weak labor rights mean more than just a reduction in the benefits from economic liberalization that accrue to the poorest segments of the population. They also mean that a disproportionate share of the costs of liberalization is borne by the poorest people in society.[40] Rather than helping benefit the world's poorest people, the policies of economic liberalization tend to exacerbate the hardships faced by those most in need. Do the relatively poor, whose ranks may be growing due to rising global inequality, have a stake in a system that promotes expanded economic liberalization without specific efforts to remedy inequality? This is an important question for peacebuilding proponents to ask, because groups that are excluded from economic rewards can more readily be mobilized into violent opposition movements. Thus, Paris's analysis of postconflict peace agreements concludes that more must be done to prioritize efforts to address the problem of inequality over the implementation of traditional market liberalization policies.[41]

Not only do inequality and the systematic reduction in the political power of working people undermine the prospects for stable peace agreements, but contemporary inequality also helps fuel wars. Collier and his colleagues argue that the ability of combatants in civil wars to field armies is enhanced under conditions of high unemployment. Both theory and empirical studies of the effects of economic liberalization show that unemployment is at least a temporary consequence, as losses in globally "uncompetitive" industries are made up by new growth in exports. But experience to date suggests that the losses in employment outweigh employment gains in newly emerging sectors, at least in the short and medium terms.[42] If societies at peace have trouble adapting their employment sectors to the needs of the global economy, then those plagued with internal conflict will have far greater difficulty developing policies to promote high employment when they must open their markets to compete with foreign imports. The employment disruptions caused by market liberalization may in themselves help prolong (rather than curtail) civil wars.

The persistence and especially the increases of inequality in the global system are serious threats to both localized peacebuilding efforts and global peace.[43] They are threats because they undermine the legitimacy and authority of existing institutions. As Hurrell argues, hierarchical modes of governance cost in terms of both legitimacy and efficiency, and the conflicts we are seeing in the world since the end of the Cold War are likely reflections of this legitimacy crisis. More must be done to address this crisis and tackle the problem of inequality to provide the "political prerequisites for meaningful global moral community."[44]

Thus, it would seem that policies aiming *explicitly* to enlarge the share of world and national income going to poor households would be far more effective at reducing poverty than are growth-oriented policies, which treat poverty reduction as a by-product of growth. This would require that peacebuilding initiatives integrate distribution effects into their policy designs.[45] This is obviously more difficult in the short run, because it requires fundamental transformation of power relations, but it is essential for both the aim of economic development and for sustainable peacebuilding. As the UNDP concludes in regard to Guatemala:

> No export growth strategy in Guatemala is likely to produce substantive benefits for human development without deep structural reforms to reduce inequalities and extend opportunity through the redistribution of land and other productive assets, increased public spending for the poor and targeted programmes aimed at breaking down the barriers facing indigenous people. Such measures will ultimately require a change in the distribution of political power in Guatemala.[46]

Ultimately, strategic peacebuilding must be about the redistribution of power (and resources) in society. Walton and Seddon concluded from their study of protests in global South countries against the austerity measures imposed by global financial institutions that these protests reflected a trend toward growing pressure for democratic reforms against the neoliberal, "'bourgeois' form of democracy [that is] more concerned with free trade than individual freedoms, more attentive to property than human rights, and downright skeptical about the social progress promised by earlier developmental states in contrast to the economic progress now promised by the market."[47] In short, the persistent inequality in today's world means that large numbers of people lack a stake in the current system. The prevention of violence on the part of those denied the benefits of globalization will require either new efforts to include marginalized groups in social and economic life or even higher levels of coercion to repress dissent. There is little evidence that proposals to expand economic liberalization without deliberate and robust efforts to address the unequal distribution of resources and opportunities will generate lasting peace.

Peace and the Neoliberal State

Effective states are seen as crucial to sustaining peace agreements at the local level as well as to maintaining regional and global peace and security.[48] At the same time, peacebuilding prescriptions emphasizing economic liberalization may be undermining the ability of war-torn societies to reestablish capable and effective national states. Economic globalization has encouraged governments to adopt policies to promote international trade and investment. One way they have done this is through attaching conditionalities to international loans issued by the World Bank and IMF requiring policy changes favoring international investment and trade. Many of these policies are also integrated into postwar peacebuilding agreements as well, often as prerequisites for obtaining international assistance.

These conditionalities—known as "structural adjustment policies"[49]—vary, but their key requirements include reductions in public spending, privatization of public assets, government support for export industries, guarantees for international investors, and the elimination of domestic wage and price controls.[50] By "structurally adjusting" borrowing states, the policies effectively help transform national states into what Robinson calls "neoliberal states," whose domestic markets are more fully integrated into the global economy.[51] In practice, what these policies do is reduce the capacities and governing role of the state while expanding the influence of international investors and global markets in the society.[52] They also shift power away from representative institutions, workers, and consumers and toward international investors and export industries.[53]

A growing body of research questions the effectiveness of structural adjustment policies for promoting economic growth and other benefits.[54] Summarizing this research, Paris concludes:

> Twenty years after the advent of structural adjustment, the quarrel over [the influence of these programs on economic growth and levels of distributional inequality] remains largely unresolved; Neither the IMF nor the World Bank has been able to demonstrate convincingly that structural-adjustment programs promote economic growth, and the precise relationship between these programs and levels of poverty and distributional inequality is still hotly contested.[55]

Even more important, the policies promoted by multilateral financial institutions may in fact be contributing to human rights violations, thereby protracting conflicts while also undermining possibilities for economic growth. Abouharb and Cingranelli, for instance, analyzed the effects of international financial policies on human rights practices. They found that the structural adjustment policies advanced by the World Bank were associated with higher levels of violations of physical integrity rights, including freedoms from torture, political imprisonment, extrajudicial killing, and arbitrary disappearances.[56]

Despite this dubious record, structural adjustment policies continue to be integrated into international lending agreements and peace agreements, either through multilateral institutions or through bilateral pressures from the countries that are primary sources of official aid and private investment.[57] These practices are counterproductive to peacebuilding work, because—in addition to their association with increased rights violations—they limit the policy space available to governments that must prioritize building or rebuilding democratic institutions and expanding popular commitments to peace agreements. Rather than emphasizing these important goals, structural adjustment policies prioritize the expansion of foreign investment and market liberalization. The effects of these policies on democratic institution-building are seen as secondary to the aim of expanding market liberalization as a means of enhancing economic growth. A critical look at these policies suggests that effective peacebuilding work may require a fundamentally different approach to structuring national institutions.

Kaldor and Luckham's analysis of post–Cold War conflicts identifies a generalized phenomenon that they argue is "almost the reverse of state and nation-building."[58] They see the practices associated with economic globalization as contributing to the delegitimation of public authority that is fueling the escalation and proliferation of "new wars." They conclude that the only effective way to resist these new wars is to engage in systematic efforts to democratize politics and restore legitimate political authority. Whereas Sambanis (chapter 6) calls for caution in this regard, the point that locals must have a stake in the economic choices that will define postwar development remains valid. International intervention can be designed to maintain a larger range of choice and control for the people in countries recovering from war, thereby creating incentives for locals to engage in peacebuilding processes. This prescription, however, is fundamentally different from that promoted by conventional peacebuilding interventions, which encourage the pursuit of economic growth as the main prerequisite to peace. Neoliberal states that are characterized by very limited policy space, reduced capacity to regulate social actors, and policy programs encouraging profit seeking over other social aims are unlikely to build public authority and reverse this trend.

Typical peacebuilding prescriptions reduce the range of policy choices available in postconflict states, thereby obstructing efforts to build legitimate democratic institutions. Most states in the global South—whether or not they have experienced internal wars—have been forced to negotiate limits to their national sovereignty in return for international financing.[59] Countries that borrow money from the World Bank or IMF and undergo other international interventions (such as internationally enforced peace agreements) are not free to determine what economic programs they pursue. Rather than being subject to democratic mechanisms of deliberation and public accountability, major economic decisions are often left to elites or to technical experts acting outside of public scrutiny.[60] Although such policies may seem logical from the perspective of professional economists, they effectively depoliticize decisions at the heart of most societies—those affecting the fundamental organization of economic life and the distribution and use of societal resources. Thus, some of the most important decisions that govern any society are effectively withdrawn from the public sphere. This constraining of the effective policy space undermines the abilities of postwar societies to win the loyalties and confidence of citizens. This is true even where there are successful steps toward elections and other steps of democratization. A democratic state that lacks authority and capacity to shape decisions that affect people's lives is an oxymoron.

In addition to limited space for economic policy deliberation, neoliberal states are also characterized by reduced capacities for regulating economic and other activities within their borders. Peter Evans refers to this model of the modern state as the "lean, mean state," because it emphasizes coercive capacities necessary for the protection of private property and promotion of social stability over social welfare. This reduction in state capacities comes at a time when we find an unprecedented concentration of wealth and power in the hands of private entities, such as transnational corporations and transnational criminal networks. This latter development necessitates greater capacity for effective state governance on behalf of societal interests.

The studies of Collier and colleagues and Paris, however, show that effective attempts to end civil wars require strong domestic institutions that are capable of pursuing multifaceted policy programs. These states must win the loyalties of diverse and often conflicting social groups, and they must therefore be able to make parties feel they have real stakes in the strengthening and perpetuation of government institutions. At the same time, they must be able to regulate private actors that can disrupt peace or otherwise contribute to the exclusion of social groups. States whose primary purpose is seen to be the promotion of markets and profit-seeking activities are unlikely to be effective at limiting the business activities of groups perpetuating violent conflicts. The reduction of state capacities for affecting the distribution of resources contributes to a concentration of resources in the hands of small numbers of people who remain beyond the control of weakened states. These weaknesses of states contribute to the dynamics of the conflict trap discussed by Collier et al.[61] Lean, mean, neoliberal states are thus unlikely to be able to effectively govern the practices of transnational actors, even when this is vital to the maintenance of peace. Nor are they likely to obtain legitimate authority necessary for reversing the trend seen by Kaldor and Luckham.

Another way that peacebuilding policies constrain possibilities for states in postwar settings to escape from conflict traps is by privileging programs that emphasize profit seeking over other social aims. The key assumption behind neoliberal policies is that markets free of government intervention allow actors to engage in the free pursuit of profit that is expected to enhance overall economic well-being. But Collier et al. associate the pursuit of profit among groups engaged in civil wars with the perpetuation of these conflicts.[62] Although the conflicts themselves may not be grounded in explicit economic ambitions, as warring parties organize themselves to amass the resources needed to wage protracted conflict, they tend to become increasingly committed to profit-seeking activities during the course of armed struggles. These profit-seeking practices themselves often depend on the maintenance of armed conflict or at least the absence of effective governance institutions. Thus, the dynamics of wars interact with the incentive structures encouraged by neoliberal economic policies to reinforce conflict traps.

In sum, most analysts of conflict argue that effective peacebuilding work involves the construction of institutions that enjoy widespread legitimacy. Such institutions must be democratic and effective at implementing popular preferences and curbing abuses of power. But the privileging of neoliberal models of the modern state undermines both the legitimacy and political effectiveness of states. This is particularly problematic in societies emerging from armed conflict, where postwar institutions must expand the stakes of all actors in the new government and high levels of inequality often require strong state capacities for economic regulation and redistribution.

Peacebuilding and Global Governance

A final assumption inherent in predominant models of postconflict peacebuilding is that multilateral peace and security can be improved without addressing fundamental inequities in the global economic order. Whereas analysts have rightly identified the ways local and national armed struggles can threaten regional and global peace, the solutions offered typically fail to confront the ways that inequality in the global political order may be fueling more localized conflicts. Moreover, peacebuilding interventions that force warring parties to adopt market liberalization policies may be helping perpetuate rather than reduce violent conflict.

Peace agreements encourage postwar states to become more integrated into a competitive global capitalist economy. As Paris warns, "capitalism . . . is inherently competitive. It inevitably creates winners and losers, which can fuel social unrest."[63] Both Paris and Collier et al. argue for more cautious liberalization of postwar states, even as they maintain that integration into the global capitalist economy is an effective strategy for societies emerging from civil wars. But if capitalism itself "inevitably creates winners and losers," thereby fueling social unrest, is the promotion of globalized capitalism an effective strategy for promoting local or global peace and security?

Although globalized capitalism has helped promote economic growth and new technological innovations, the ability of capitalist markets to maximize human well-being over the long run has come under growing scrutiny. Indeed, the prescriptions of Paris and Collier et al. demonstrate that *global markets are not sufficient* for generating peace, and I have argued that global markets can undermine the achievement of other conditions that are necessary for peace. Collier and colleagues, for instance, argue that new systems of international governance are needed to manage international trade in natural resources so that warring parties cannot use illicit trade to finance wars. They also argue that poor states need global management of commodity prices to ensure the effective and stable governance of their countries. They see a need for greater global social solidarity to enhance the flows of aid from rich to poor countries. Paris also emphasizes nonmarket policies aimed at fostering democratic cultures and empowering civil society. The policy prescriptions in these studies place primary emphasis on making changes in the governance of countries marred by civil wars, rather than in the international system itself.

A systemwide approach to addressing local and national conflicts, however, would lead us to question the extent to which the predominant, market-oriented approaches to peace agreements are likely to support long-term peace and security. Can the international community impose models of economic governance on societies emerging from violent conflict and expect them to build effective and inclusive democratic institutions? Can peaceful national and global societies exist within a global order that emphasizes economic competition and individual profit maximization?

These questions are vital, I think, for addressing the problem of violence in contemporary societies. Most conventional approaches to international peacebuilding and conflict intervention neglect them. If the global economic and political order is fueling conflicts at local and national levels, then national or local strategies will not, on their own, end the violence. Problems must be addressed at the level at which they originate, and thus strategic peacebuilders must ask the tough questions about how the global system is implicated in more localized struggles.

The UNDP *Human Development Report* argues that policies promoting social inclusion are necessary if we are to see a reduction in violence in contemporary societies.[64] As was stated earlier, the global capitalist system emphasizes economic competition, which necessarily excludes those without access to financial and material resources. Social exclusion is a major effect of the global neoliberal order. Thus, we must ask whether policies that enhance countries' participation in global capitalist markets should be as central a part of the solution to violent conflict as predominant discussions make them.

The privileging of globalized markets in the international policy discourse is also the result of highly unequal arrangements in the global political order. The ideologies guiding global neoliberalism and the dissemination of market liberalization policies emerged from the rich countries of the global North, and they were aided by the support of elites in the global South. But poor countries and people had little role in shaping this policy agenda, and the policies of the World Bank and IMF have served to erode the national sovereignty of borrowing states in favor of donor countries.[65] Thus, the policy agenda of market liberalization is not one that emerges from a democratic foundation of deliberation among sovereign equals; rather, it reflects long-standing patterns of global domination and subordination. It is unlikely, then, that this policy approach can be a foundation for a stable and democratic peace.

The place of market liberalization in the international community's hierarchy of policy priorities also reflects major inequities in the global system that threaten long-term global peace and security. The international system is rife with contradictory policies and practices, and one of the most glaring is the tension between the international financial institutions and the UN Charter. The UN was designed to prevent wars and promote conditions that are conducive to international peace. The World Bank, IMF, and World Trade Organization, in contrast, are part of the Bretton Woods system that aimed to expand global trade and international investment. Although the Bretton Woods system was to fall initially within the jurisdiction of the UN system, in practice the global financial institutions operate independently of the UN. Their policies, moreover, are increasingly seen as being at odds with UN principles of equity, human rights, and environmental sustainability.[66]

Over recent decades, the U.S. government and other key proponents of globalized capitalism have worked to systematically reduce the role of the United Nations in global affairs while making the global financial institutions more influential.[67] The major effect of this policy has been to advance neoliberal agendas through largely coercive measures while subordinating other policy objectives to that of expanding global markets. As a result, a comparison of global policy arenas reveals major contradictions among policy aims, outcomes, and norms. For instance, market-oriented policies encourage economic growth, expanding consumption, and participation based on financial means. In contrast, environmental preservation policies emphasize the limits of the natural environment and the precautionary principle. Human rights policies emphasize equality, human needs, and universal rights of participation based on shared humanity. The subordination of the UN to the global financial institutions has meant a prioritization of markets over sustainability and human rights. These institutional contradictions complicate efforts to promote sustainable peace at local or global levels.

Not only do institutional arrangements make it difficult to guarantee that policies promoting equity and sustainability gain at least equal footing with those promoting economic growth, they also are likely to complicate efforts to build democratic cultures that are conducive to peace. An international system that prioritizes markets and economic growth and places the aim of profit seeking over other social objectives contributes to social exclusion and complicates governance at all levels. Thus, policies that seek to restrain economic competition in favor of political or environmental security face important political hurdles. Global neoliberalism has fostered an ideology of competition and "market fundamentalism" that—despite losing some of its luster in recent years—works against efforts to foster democratic civil society and promote a global culture of solidarity and human rights.[68]

In sum, creating a global economic context that prevents combatants from exploiting natural resources to finance civil wars, provides poor country governments with predictable and stable sources of income, and reduces (rather than exacerbates) inequalities of wealth and income requires fundamentally different approaches to peacebuilding than those emphasized in most mainstream policy discourse. To reverse the escalation of internal conflicts and to foster stable and long-term peace, the international community must confront fundamental inequalities in the global system itself that are contributing to conflicts at local, national, and regional levels.

Conclusion

Strategic peacebuilding requires an analytical framework that considers how local actors are embedded within broader economic and political relationships that extend beyond the national to regional and global levels. Although much intervention must take place at the level where violent conflict is experienced most directly, the analyses of the causes of civil wars and their perpetuation show that work must be done beyond local and national levels to address the causes of violence. A global system that privileges markets and opposes state intervention in economies also provides fertile ground for illicit trade that can help finance civil wars. Policies that contribute to rising inequalities at global and national levels fuel grievances that can be used to mobilize groups against one another. An undemocratic global political order is unlikely to foster the values and cultural practices that will support democracy at other levels.

Major studies of international interventions in civil wars have concluded that market liberalization policies can undermine peace strategies. Nevertheless, these studies continue to support the overall policy of market liberalization. I argue that we need to delink the peacebuilding agenda from the neoliberal "globalization project," which emphasizes economic growth and the globalization of markets at the expense of other policy objectives.[69] Although economic growth can expand resources available for peacebuilding, it is more important for policy makers in postconflict settings to actively work to reduce inequality through redistributive policies. Though market liberalization might encourage economic growth, the privileging of global over local and national markets may not serve the development needs of most postwar societies. States require greater policy-making autonomy and capacity for action than they are typically allowed in most peace agreements, trade agreements, and international financial agreements.[70] There must be greater coordination and coherence in international policy prescriptions across different governance sectors to strengthen state capacities.

The 1980s and 1990s have seen a very rapid expansion of the global economic order, and the global political system needs to catch up if we are to have a global economy that serves the needs of people rather than corporations.[71] Although there is widespread rhetorical support for the idea of democracy, we lack global institutions that can effectively protect democracy at local and national levels. As governments bring more policy concerns to intergovernmental bodies like the United Nations and World Trade Organization, they effectively reduce democracy at the national level.[72] Following the work of Karl Polanyi, we might argue that we need to embed the global economy within a global society that is guided by principles of equity, human rights, and environmental sustainability.[73] Such a society will require major changes to global institutions to provide mechanisms for democratic participation and accountability comparable to those achieved in many national contexts. In short, democracy at the national level will be increasingly reduced without steps to democratize global political and economic institutions.

How might this be accomplished? One way is for peace intervention strategies to be more explicit in actively supporting a "democratic globalization network" that advances a more democratic global order.[74] This network—which is largely centered on civil society actors but also includes prodemocratic governments and international officials—must be empowered to more effectively counter the network of transnational corporations and political elites that have systematically advanced their preferred model of neoliberal globalization. Peace operations should serve to alter the relative balance of power between neoliberal and democratic agents. Currently they are reinforcing the already vastly superior resources of neoliberals at the expense of democrats. The policies and practices that enable democracy to flourish are not the same as—and, in fact, are contradicted by—policies that advance globalized capitalism.[75]

Thus, peacebuilders must prioritize policies that strengthen norms and practices conducive to democracy and human rights, rather than subordinating them to the needs of global markets. This would mean, for instance, that policies aiming to reduce poverty should focus directly on putting resources into the hands of poor people rather than on expanding economic growth in the hopes that some new wealth will trickle down to those most in need. It would also mean promoting policies that level the political playing field among citizens to promote more inclusive debates and policies. By taking steps to organize global society around the values of cooperation and social solidarity rather than economic competition, the global community might help reduce new incidences of violent conflict while helping war-torn societies escape the conflict trap.

Scholars of peace initiatives have long argued for greater inclusion of civil society groups and women into peace processes. These proposals have not been effectively incorporated into existing peacebuilding efforts. I summarize three major strategies that this analysis suggests might enhance the prospects for enhancing civil society's role in multilateral peacebuilding initiatives and the development of more effective and democratic strategies for the resolution of violent conflicts.[76]

First, leaders in movements and international institutions should support the development of more inclusive *peacebuilding networks* of nonstate, governmental, and intergovernmental actors working to promote peace, democracy, and more equitable development.[77] These should be deliberate efforts to build alliances between international agencies and civil society actors committed to core democratic and multilateralist norms, working together to engage both states and private financial actors in the tasks of more democratic global governance. It is the relative imbalance of power between civil society and other actors that contributes to conflict escalation and persistent violence. Thus, activities of these multiactor networks should aim specifically to reduce the inequalities of power between civil society actors, states, and the private sector and promote democratic participation and accountability in governance.

Second, multiactor peacebuilding networks should focus in the near term on efforts to democratize global institutions. An overwhelming majority of UN member states favors a system that better reflects the interests of all its members. Civil society groups would also benefit from a UN system that is more representative of all the world's governments. Finally, these reforms would enhance the commitment to the UN system by countries and civil societies that have been largely disenfranchised from global policy making. These changes require focused efforts to bring together supportive governments and international officials and movement actors around a strategy for promoting UN and especially Security Council reforms, including, for instance, those recommended by the recent UN High Level Panel Report on Threats, Challenges and Change.

Third, peacebuilding networks must be more proactive in their efforts to empower actors who have been marginalized by existing political and economic structures. They must struggle to rein in the power of corporations in the global polity so that states and civil society actors can exert more control over decisions that affect their economic lives as well as their political choices. Serious efforts are also needed to enhance democratic accountability and participation *within* states. The recent report of the Panel of Eminent Persons on UN-Civil Society Relations has some good recommendations around which policy makers and activists can mobilize, such as the call for a new Office of Constituency Engagement and Partnerships with its own Under-Secretary General, a Civil Society Unit, and an Elected Representatives Liaison Unit. The World Social

Forum process provides opportunities to make important connections among civil society actors in different parts of the world as well as between civil society and national and international officials. This process should be supported financially and engaged with more seriously by national and international policy elites as a possible mechanism for advancing a more equitable, democratic, and just global political order. Such a global order is an essential prerequisite to peacebuilding everywhere.

NOTES

1. Paul Collier and others, *Breaking the Conflict Trap: Civil War and Development Policy* (Washington, D.C.: World Bank and Oxford University Press, 2003). See also Michael Doyle and Nicholas Sambanis, *Making War and Building Peace: United Nations Peace Operations* (Princeton, N.J.: Princeton University Press, 2006); Stephen John Stedman, ed., *Ending Civil Wars: The Implementation of Peace Agreements* (Boulder, Colo.: Lynne Rienner, 2002).

2. Roland Paris, *At War's End: Building Peace after Civil Conflict* (New York: Cambridge University Press, 2004); Neclâ Tschirgi, "Post-Conflict Peacebuilding Revisited: Achievements, Limitations, Challenges," International Peace Academy Policy Report (October 2004); Collier et al., *Breaking the Conflict Trap.*

3. Collier et al., *Breaking the Conflict Trap;* Paris, *At War's End.*

4. See, e.g., Amy Chua, *World on Fire: How Exporting Free Market Democracy Breeds Ethnic Hatred and Global Instability* (New York: Anchor Books, 2003); John Markoff, *Transnational Democracy in Critical and Comparative Perspective: Democracy's Range Reconsidered,* ed. B. W. Morrison (London: Ashgate, forthcoming).

5. See, e.g., Michael Barnett and Raymond Duvall, "Power in Global Governance: Introduction," in *Power in Global Governance,* eds. M. Barnett and R. Duvall (New York: Cambridge University Press, 2005), 1–32.

6. See, e.g., Markoff, *Transnational Democracy;* William Robinson, *A Theory of Global Capitalism* (Baltimore, Md.: Johns Hopkins University Press, 2004); Philip McMichael, *Development and Social Change: A Global Perspective,* 3rd ed. (Thousand Oaks, Calif.: Pine Forge, 2003); John Markoff, "Globalization and the Future of Democracy," *Journal of World-Systems Research* 5 (1999): 242–262, http://csf.colorado.edu/wsystems/jwsr.html.

7. See, e.g., Neclâ Tschirgi, "Peacebuilding through Global Peace and Justice," *Development* 48 (2005): 50–56.

8. Andrew Hurrell, "Power, Institutions and the Production of Inequality," in *Power in Global Governance,* eds. M. Barnett and R. Duvall (New York: Cambridge University Press, 2005), 33.

9. Roland Paris, "International Peacebuilding and the 'Mission Civilisatrice,'" *Review of International Studies* 28 (2002): 637–656.

10. Ibid., 638.

11. Ibid., 637–656.

12. William Robinson, *Promoting Polyarchy: Globalization, U.S. Intervention and Hegemony* (Cambridge: Cambridge University Press, 1996).

13. Neoliberalism refers to the idea-system favoring market liberalization and rules for a globalized economy. See Robinson, *A Theory of Global Capitalism.*

14. Ibid.

15. Collier et al., *Breaking the Conflict Trap,* 53.

16. See, e.g., Kevin P. Gallagher, "The Demise of the Doha Round? Unpacking Developing Country Resistance," *Review of International Political Economy* (forthcoming).

17. Timothy A. Wise and Kevin P. Gallagher, "Doha Round and Developing Countries: Will the Doha Deal Do More Harm than Good?" Research and Information System for Developing Countries, New Delhi, 2006.

18. UNDP, *Human Development Report 2005: International Cooperation at a Crossroads* (New York: Oxford University Press, 2005), 119.

19. See, e.g., review in Roberto Patricio Korzeniewicz and William C. Smith, "Protest and Collaboration: Transnational Civil Society Networks and the Politics of Summitry and Free Trade in the Americas," North-South Center, University of Miami, 2001.

20. Collier et al., *Breaking the Conflict Trap*, 6.

21. Indeed, this is why international trade negotiations and the Doha Development Round have stalled or collapsed.

22. UNDP, *Human Development Report 2005*, 117.

23. Roberto Patricio Korzeniewicz and Timothy Patrick Moran, "World Inequality in the Twenty-First Century: Patterns and Tendencies" in *The Blackwell Companion to Globalization*, ed. G. Ritzer (Oxford: Blackwell, 2006).

24. Mark Weisbrot, "Globalization on the Ropes," *Harpers* (May 2000): 6; Walden Bello, *Dark Victory: The United States and Global Poverty* (London: Pluto Press, 1999).

25. UNDP, *Human Development Report 2005*; Wise and Gallagher, "Doha Round and Developing Countries."

26. Wise and Gallagher, "Doha Round and Developing Countries."

27. See, e.g., ibid.; Mark Weisbrot and others, "Poor Numbers: The Impact of Trade Liberalization on World Poverty," Center for Economic Policy Research, Washington, D.C., 2004. See also Robin Broad, "Research, Knowledge & the Art of 'Paradigm Maintenance': The World Bank's Development Economics Vice-Presidency (DEC)," *Review of International Political Economy* 13 (2006): 387–419.

28. Wise and Gallagher, "Doha Round and Developing Countries"; Weisbrot et al., "Poor Numbers."

29. See, for instance, John Cavanagh and Jerry Mander, eds., *Alternatives to Economic Globalization: A Better World is Possible*, 2nd ed. (San Francisco: Berrett-Koehler, 2004); "New Principles and Rules to Build an Economic System that Works for People and the Planet," Civil society statement to the G20 Summit, November 2008, http://www.choike.org/bw2/#english2 (accessed November 22, 2008); David Korten, *The Great Turning: From Empire to Earth Community* (San Francisco: Barrett-Koehler, 2007). Joseph Stiglitz, "Towards a New Paradigm of Development," in *Making Globalization Good: The Moral Challenges of Global Capitalism*, ed. J. H. Dunning (New York: Oxford University Press, 2003), 77–107.

30. Collier et al., *Breaking the Conflict Trap*, 4.

31. UNDP, *Human Development Report 2005*, 116.

32. Ibid., 4.

33. Amartya Sen, *Inequality Reexamined* (New York: Oxford University Press, 1995); Food and Agriculture Organization, *The State of Food Insecurity in the World 2006: Eradicating World Hunger—Taking Stock Ten Years after the World Food Summit* (Rome: Food and Agriculture Organization of the United Nations, 2006), http://www.fao.org/icatalog/inter-e.htm (accessed April 3, 2007).

34. There is some debate as to whether between country inequality is rising or stabilizing, and this emerges from the use of different economic measures. Studies

using exchange rates find rising inequality, while those using purchasing power parity (PPP) find slowed or declining inequality at the world level. I agree with the contention by Korzeniewicz and Moran in "Measuring World Income Inequalities" (*American Journal of Sociology* 106 [2000]: 209–214) that exchange rate studies are more reliable, given the measurement and aggregation errors associated with PPP. Salvatore J. Babones and Jonathan H. Turner, "Global Inequality," in *Handbook of Social Problems*, ed. G. Ritzer (Oxford: Blackwell), 101–121; R. P. Korzeniewicz and Timothy P. Moran, "World Economic Trends in the Distribution of Income, 1965–1992," *American Journal of Sociology* 102 (1997): 1000–1039; Roberto Patricio Korzeniewicz and Timothy Patrick Moran, "World Inequality in the Twenty-First Century: Patterns and Tendencies," in *The Blackwell Companion to Globalization*, ed. G. Ritzer (Oxford: Blackwell, 2006).

35. The Gini coefficient is calculated by measuring the distribution of income across a population. A coefficient of 0 is a perfectly equal society where each proportion of the population controls a comparable proportion of the country's income (or wealth); a coefficient of 1 reflects a perfectly unequal society. The Gini coefficient for one of the most equal societies, Sweden, is 0.25 and for one of the most unequal societies, Brazil, is 0.59. The United States' Gini coefficient is 0.41.

36. The Gini coefficient for Namibia is 0.71; Lesotho, 0.63; Botswana, 0.63; Sierra Leone, 0.63; and the Central African Republic, 0.61. Compare with the United States at 0.41 and Denmark at 0.25 (UNDP, *Human Development Report 2005*).

37. New Economics Foundation, "Growth Isn't Working: The Unbalanced Distribution of Benefits and Costs from Economic Growth," New Economics Foundation, London (2006), http://www.neweconomics.org/gen/uploads/ hrfu5w555mzd3f55m2vqwty502022006112929.pdf (accessed October 20, 2006).

38. Korzeniewicz and Moran, "World Inequality in the Twenty-First Century"; Saskia Sassen, *Globalization and its Discontents* (New York: New Press, 1998).

39. UNDP, *Human Development Report 2005*, 124.

40. See, e.g., Bello, *Dark Victory;* UNDP, *Human Development Report 2005*.

41. Paris, *At War's End*, 200–205.

42. Wise and Gallagher, "Doha Round." The fact that more of the labor force today is comprised of internal or international migrants is also likely to affect the social dislocations that impact prospects for violent mobilizations, because people uprooted from home communities who later become unemployed may be particularly vulnerable to recruitment efforts by militant groups.

43. Collier et al., *Breaking the Conflict Trap*.

44. Hurrell, "Power, Institutions and the Production of Inequality," 55.

45. See, e.g., New Economics Foundation, "Growth Isn't Working," and Weisbrot et al., "Poor Numbers."

46. UNDP, *Human Development Report 2005*, 123.

47. John Walton and David Seddon, *Free Markets and Food Riots: The Politics of Global Adjustment* (Cambridge, Mass.: Blackwell, 1994), 339.

48. Simon Chesterman, Michael Ignatieff, and Ramesh Thakur, *Making States Work: State Failure and the Crisis of Governance* (Tokyo: United Nations University Press, 2005); Collier et al., *Breaking the Conflict Trap*.

49. In response to protests against the global financial institutions, officials have renamed structural adjustment policies to Poverty Reduction Strategy Papers, or PRSPs. The content of the prescriptions in these agreements between borrowing governments and the global financial institutions, however, remains largely unchanged. Walden Bello, *Deglobalization: New Ideas for Running the World Economy* (London: Zed Books, 2003). Also, the World Bank and the IMF have failed

to follow a requirement meant to prevent the problems associated with the earlier structural adjustment programs, namely, that they include civil society groups in the development and implementation of PRSPs. Robert O'Brien, "The International Monetary Fund, The World Bank and Labour in Developing Countries," manuscript, McMaster University, Hamilton, Ontario; Peter Willetts, "Civil Society Networks in Global Governance: Remedying the World Trade Organisation's Deviance from Global Norms," in *Colloquium on International Governance* (Palais des Nations, Geneva, 2002).

50. Robert O'Brien, "Workers and World Order: The Tentative Transformation of the International Union Movement," *Review of International Studies* 26 (2000): 533–555; Paris, *At War's End;* and William Robinson, *A Theory of Global Capitalism* (Baltimore, Md.: Johns Hopkins University Press, 2004).

51. Robinson, *A Theory of Global Capitalism.*

52. Nancy Alexander, "Decentralization and Sovereignty: How Policy Space is Eroded," in *Social Watch Report 2006: Impossible Architecture*, edited by S. Watch (Montevideo, Uruguay: Social Watch, 2006), 20–22.

53. O'Brien, "The International Monetary Fund."

54. Joseph Stiglitz, *Globalization and its Discontents* (New York: Norton, 2003); Weisbrot et al., "Poor Numbers."

55. Paris, *At War's End*, 166.

56. Rodwan M. Abouharb and David Cingranelli, "The Human Rights Effects of World Bank Structural Adjustment," *International Studies Quarterly* 50 (2006): 233–262.

57. Luke Eric Peterson, "Bilateral Investment Treaties and Development Policy-Making." Winnipeg: International Institute for Sustainable Development & Swiss Agency for Development and Cooperation, 2004.

58. Mary Kaldor and Robin Luckham, "Global Transformations and New Conflicts," *IDS Bulletin* 32 (2001).

59. Alexander, "Decentralization and Sovereignty."

60. See William D. Coleman and Tony Porter, "International Institutions, Globalization and Democracy: Assessing the Challenges," *Global Society* 14 (2000): 377–398; Michael Goldman, *Imperial Nature: The World Bank and Struggles for Social Justice in the Age of Globalization* (New Haven, Conn.: Yale University Press, 2005); John Markoff and Veronica Montecinos, "The Ubiquitous Rise of Economists," *Journal of Public Policy* 13 (1993): 37–68; and Stiglitz, *Globalization and its Discontents.*

61. Collier et al., *Breaking the Conflict Trap.*

62. Ibid., 79.

63. Paris, *At War's End*, 167.

64. UNDP, *Human Development Report 2005*, chapter 5.

65. Alexander, "Decentralization and Sovereignty"; Hurrell, "Power, Institutions and the Production of Inequality"; and Celine Tan, "Reclaiming Development: Streamline the Bretton Woods Institutions," in *Social Watch Reports 2006: Impossible Architecture*, ed. S. Watch (Montevideo, Uruguay: Social Watch, 2006), 23–25.

66. Leslie Sklair, *The Transnational Capitalist Class* (Cambridge: Blackwell, 2001); Sigron Skogly, "Structural Adjustment and Development: Human Rights—An Agenda for Change?" *Human Rights Quarterly* 15 (1993): 751; and Tan, "Reclaiming Development."

67. Jackie Smith, *Global Visions, Rival Networks: Social Movements for Global Democracy* (Baltimore, Md.: Johns Hopkins University Press, 2008).

68. Seyla Benhabib, "On the Alleged Conflict between Democracy and International Law," *Ethics and International Affairs* 19 (2005): 85–100; Leslie Sklair, *Globalization and Its Alternatives* (New York: Oxford University Press, 2002).

69. McMichael, *Development and Social Change.*

70. Gallagher, "The Demise of the Doha Round?"

71. Christopher Chase-Dunn, "Social Evolution and the Future of World Society," *Journal of World Systems Research* 11 (2006): 171–192.

72. See Markoff, *Transnational Democracy*; and Charles Tilly, "Globalization Threatens Labor Rights," *International Labor and Working Class History* 47 (1995): 1–23.

73. Korzeniewicz and Smith, "Protest and Collaboration."

74. Smith, *Global Visions, Rival Networks.*

75. Tilly, "Globalization Threatens Labor Rights."

76. For more detail, see Jackie Smith, "Social Movements and Multilateralism: Moving from the 20th to 21st Century," in *Multilateralism under Challenge? Power, International Order, and Structural Change*, ed. E. Newman, S. Tharoor, and J. Tirman (Tokyo: United Nations University Press, 2006), 395–421.

77. Korzeniewicz and Smith make a similar recommendation, referring to such networks as "polycentric development coalitions." (Roberto Patricio Korzeniewicz and William C. Smith, "Poverty, Inequality, and Growth in Latin America: Searching for the High Road to Globalization," *Latin American Research Review* 35 [2000]: 7–54).

II

The Response Imperative

Tensions and Dilemmas of Humanitarian Action and Strategic Peacebuilding

Larissa Fast

A typical scenario goes something like this: violence breaks out between warring factions, people flee from their homes trying to escape the violence, United Nations agencies and nongovernmental organizations (NGOs) bring in personnel and supplies to respond to the civilian suffering that inevitably occurs, and diplomats and others work to broker a cease-fire. Though not attempting to minimize the suffering of the thousands of civilians around the world caught up in atrocities and violence nor the difficulties of providing relief or negotiating cease-fire or peace agreements, the contours of the typical story usually hold. The explosion of civil conflict and violence in the post–Cold War era and more engagement on the part of civil society and international organizations in attempting to prevent, respond to, and transform conflict has led to increasing attention on the roles and actors involved in responding to conflict and violence or building peace.

The concept of strategic peacebuilding assumes a variety of roles and actors to build peace. In chapter 1, Lederach and Appleby define it as follows:

> At its core, peacebuilding nurtures constructive human relationships. To be relevant, it must do so at every level of society and across the potentially polarizing lines of ethnicity, class, religion, and race. . . . It focuses on transforming inhumane social patterns, flawed structural conditions, and open violent conflict that weaken the conditions necessary for a flourishing human community.

They argue that peacebuilding extends across the cycle of conflict, from prevention to transformation. In his earlier work, Lederach proposes three levels of actors—grassroots, mid-range, and top leadership—and suggests that peacebuilding crosses the horizontal boundaries of conflict lines and links the vertical levels of actors. As such, it involves a variety of corresponding roles and activities. Furthermore, he asserts it is necessary to work at multiple levels in the short-term, intermediate, and long-term horizons.[1] Not inconsistently, others define peacebuilding as encompassing poverty reduction, humanitarian relief, disarmament, demobilization and reintegration programs for ex-combatants, economic development projects, human rights monitoring and advocacy, and everything in between.

If we take seriously the notion that strategic peacebuilding as a concept requires multiple roles and actors—a web of individuals and institutions—simultaneously and in a complementary fashion working to build peace in a society, what exactly does this mean? How do we build webs and networks of actors working for peace? What are the costs and opportunities of particular roles? How should and do these various roles and actors work together? This chapter explores several key dilemmas and tensions that arise in thinking about humanitarian action as a smaller part of strategic peacebuilding in particular, and ponders the larger question of the conceptual and practical messiness of peacebuilding roles more generally.

Thinking about the relationship (or lack thereof) between humanitarian action and strategic peacebuilding inevitably raises two linked but conceptually separate debates. The first debate emerges out of the peacebuilding literature, broadly defined, and revolves around third-party roles and functions in conflict situations (e.g., the idea of multiple roles and actors in conflict intervention and how they relate to each other). The second debate occurs within the humanitarian assistance and development literatures and examines the question of integration—to what extent should humanitarian action be integrated into or linked to processes designed in the short or long term to promote peace or social change? These debates have occurred somewhat in isolation from each other, yet both explore the dilemmas, tensions, and consequences inherent in choices regarding roles and relationships.

On first glance, it appears that humanitarian assistance and building peace have much in common. They both attempt to respond to and alleviate the suffering of those caught up in violence. But perhaps this is where the comparison does and should end. These responses are different—humanitarian action is designed as a short-term, emergency response, whereas building peace necessitates a longer time frame. Yet the question of how to intervene when the violence rages and ravages communities caught up in destructive conflict remains particularly vexing. Most who write about and define peacebuilding emphasize that it needs to take place across the conflict cycle of prevention, reaction, and rebuilding. While stocked and full in the prevention and rebuilding phases, the conceptual cupboard is mostly bare when it comes to the reaction phase.

The primary reactions of the international community to ongoing civil strife and violence are to provide humanitarian aid and, where political will is sufficient, intervene militarily. Other actions, such as diplomatic attempts to broker cease-fires, local action to protest or counter violence, or public naming and shaming of human rights violations, also occur and are essential to building peace. Few responses, however, offer the immediate and public rewards of aid workers (usually pictured as white foreigners in the media, even though the vast majority of aid workers are national staff) weighing underweight babies as part of a feeding program, dishing out food and water to refugees from the rear of a large truck emblazoned with an agency logo, or compassionately bandaging wounds in a makeshift clinic. The other public and immediate option is military action, hopefully consistent with the more altruistic protective purposes of the "responsibility to protect."[2] The ongoing violence in Darfur, Sudan, is a case in point: the options have appeared as either providing humanitarian assistance or reinforcing the African Union troops, who have been vastly outnumbered and underequipped, with a more robust military presence. A UN peacekeeping force began deploying in late 2007, but is still not yet fully operational. Humanitarian assistance, all acknowledge, is simply a Band-Aid on an increasingly severe and swelling wound. Its reach and effectiveness is compromised because of targeted violence against and harassment of aid workers, despite the life-saving advances they have made.[3] Other options for responding to the immediate violence are few, although it is yet unclear how a new U.S. president or the International Criminal Court indictment of President Omar al-Bashir will change the situation. Do we want to include humanitarian action within the realm of peacebuilding to be able to claim that we are indeed doing *something* to respond to violence?

Implicit in the conceptualizations of strategic peacebuilding is the notion of linkage and/or coordination of roles. The literature on third-party roles in conflict, with some notable exceptions, outlines separate roles but not how to generate a coherent and linked intervention strategy. Those that do write about integrated peacebuilding paradigms assume an intrinsic value to coordination. This chapter argues, perhaps somewhat provocatively, that humanitarian action should not be included within the broader peacebuilding agenda. Putting aside the more common objections to integration—that peacebuilding is too political an endeavor for humanitarians or that security is compromised when impartiality and neutrality are compromised—this chapter maintains an objection to integration because of the need to maintain a moral response to human suffering; that response is humanitarian assistance. If we really want to build peace, we need to reserve and protect space for humanitarian action, regardless of how these efforts may or may not contribute to peacebuilding. Although humanitarian action should be left outside the peacebuilding agenda, it can instead avoid "doing harm" and contributing to conflict. In other words, humanitarian aid cannot build peace, address the root causes of conflict, or transform the structures that contribute to injustice and inequality, nor should it be held accountable to these standards.

Third-Party Roles in Conflict

The literature about third-party roles in conflict is growing and has evolved from an emphasis on mediation and problem solving to an acknowledgment and a more sophisticated understanding of the variety of roles necessary to build peace. In the early years, much of the conflict intervention literature on roles focused on that of the mediator and his or her corresponding responsibility to maintain neutrality and impartiality in the intervention. Codes of conduct for mediators specified these in more detail. As late as 1994, the Academy of Dispute Resolution "Model Standards of Mediator Conduct" describe mediation as a process in which a "neutral third party" facilitates an agreement. The standards list impartiality as one of the rules for a mediator, stipulating that he or she should disclose bias or prejudice.[4] Likewise, the 1998 Academy of Family Mediators lists both impartiality and neutrality as part of its standards of practice.[5]

In contrast to much of the extant literature at the time, Laue and Cormick suggest five roles for a conflict intervention: those of activist, advocate, mediator, researcher, and enforcer.[6] The role(s) an intervener plays is dependent on the base of support and his or her credibility with one or more parties. Furthermore, they argue that neutrality is not possible in any role, because either the intervener is promoting a (positive) change process or acting on behalf of one of the parties. Nor, they write, is neutrality ethically desirable. Instead, interveners in community disputes must work for empowerment, justice, and freedom. Laue reiterates this assumption in a later article, stating "All intervention alters the power configuration among the parties, thus all conflict intervention is advocacy. There are no neutrals."[7] Advocacy, he posits, may be in terms of the party (e.g., a lawyer advocating for a particular party), outcomes (e.g., for a particular policy), or a process (e.g., the process used to reach an agreement).[8] Similarly, Wehr and Lederach examine neutrality and the foundations of mediator credibility and legitimacy. They challenge the cultural assumptions of the "outsider-neutral" mediator role, which assumes that mediators have no existing or future relationship with or connection to either of the parties. For outsider-neutrals, precisely this lack of association forms the basis for the mediator's role in the conflict. They describe another model, that of an "insider-partial," whose legitimacy derives from existing and ongoing relationships based on trust and connection.[9]

These and other challenges to the value of neutrality in mediation, in particular, paved the way for a more expanded conception of third-party roles in conflict intervention. Mitchell, in analyzing a mediation process in Sudan, proposes a typology of fourteen separate intermediary functions. For example, a "convener" brings together the various stakeholders in a conflict, whereas a "facilitator" assists the parties in communicating during and managing the actual mediation process. In his analysis, he speculates about the need for a "coordinator" that would link the various roles in a mediation process. He concludes that some roles may preclude others because of timing issues or because the functions are mutually exclusive.[10]

Ury similarly expands the notion of who can intervene in conflict, promoting the idea of a "third side" in conflict situations. The third side moves beyond the dichotomy of conflict parties and brings bystanders and other community members into conflict intervention in both formal and informal roles.

He urges ordinary citizen involvement in preventing, resolving, and containing conflict as a "kind of *social immune system* preventing the spread of the virus of violence."[11] In preventing conflict, "third-siders" address latent tensions. In resolving conflict, they tackle overt conflict and violence, and in containing conflict, they deal with the power struggles inherent in conflicts at all levels. His roles range from "providers" and "bridge-builders" in the prevention stage, to "mediators" and "healers" in the resolution phase, and "witnesses," "peace-keepers," and "referees" in the containment phase.[12]

Ury's notion of sequencing roles based on conflict stages builds on Fisher and Keashley's earlier idea of a contingency model of intervention. They propose a sequencing of functions based on the stages of a conflict and the propensity of the role to deescalate conflict. Thus, negotiation and mediation occur early on, whereas arbitration, mediation with muscle, and peacekeeping occur later, once the parties are polarized and the conflict has reached a destructive and violent stage. Development aid, they suggest, serves the function of reducing structural inequalities.[13]

The "Responsibility to Protect" report, which the United Nations endorsed as a concept, outlines a sequential view of intervention and elucidates a more expansive set of actions and actors, ranging from noncoercive to coercive options. The task of the International Commission on Intervention and State Sovereignty (ICISS), which produced the report at the behest of former UN Secretary General Kofi Annan, was to establish a consensus regarding the conditions under which intervention would be warranted and the process by which it would be legitimate. The ICISS returned with the idea of the "responsibility to protect": that the international community has a responsibility to prevent, react, and rebuild when individual states are either unwilling or unable to protect their own citizens. In the prevention stage, actors work to address root causes of possible violence via political and diplomatic, economic, and legal mechanisms. The reaction stage includes a range of less and more coercive measures, from sanctions to international military intervention and involves mostly governmental and intergovernmental actors. In the rebuilding stage, a range of actors, from civil society and NGOs to governments, work to rebuild societies and address the sources that caused the violence.[14]

The range of roles and stages outlined here reflects a recognition of the increasing sophistication of actors and the challenges to building peace. Schirch takes a somewhat different approach and examines the universe of tasks needed to build peace. Instead of matching roles to stages, she defines strategic peacebuilding as a "connecting space or nexus for collaboration"[15] that requires a variety of approaches. Common to all approaches are a set of values (e.g., human needs and human rights, interdependence, partnership), relational skills (e.g., negotiation, problem solving, and active listening), analytical frameworks (e.g., structural violence), and processes for peacebuilding. She divides the processes aimed at building peace into four different types: waging conflict nonviolently, reducing direct violence, building capacity, and transforming relationships. She lists humanitarian assistance as one of the mechanisms under the approach of reducing direct violence. Schirch, like the others, puts forth a multilayered and multipronged approach that assumes a variety of actors in intervention. She acknowledges the need to coordinate and concludes that it "cannot simply be one organization or group directing or delegating tasks to others."[16] Instead, she espouses modeling the approaches and skills that peacebuilding actors expect conflict parties to adopt and the need for accountability among and between peacebuilding actors that reflect the values, skills, and tools that each brings to the endeavor.

This call for coordination has resonated with others, both in the humanitarian and the peacebuilding fields. A number of writers have explored issues of coordination and complementarity from a variety of perspectives. For example, a 2006 issue of *International Negotiation* focused on coordination in conflict prevention, conflict resolution, and peacebuilding. Defining coordination "broadly to include information sharing, collaborative analysis and strategizing, resource sharing, formal partnerships, and other means of synchronizing and/or integrating activities,"[17] the editors of the issue argue for "effective coordination" that not only examines the costs and benefits of coordination within a particular context but also the more expansive goals that coordination is designed to achieve. In their view, these expansive goals are sustainable peace and security, and the relevant actors are intergovernmental, NGO, and international organizations in the conflict resolution, humanitarian, development, and security sectors. Nevertheless, they suggest "coordination for coordination's sake" is not a viable or constructive option.

Ricigliano espouses a more nuanced view, looking at degrees of coordination among actors in peacebuilding. He examines the notion of effective collaboration, proposing that this depends on both timing and depth of involvement. In other words, collaboration can happen at multiple stages (e.g., problem/needs identification, consultation, policy making/decision making, analysis, planning, and implementation) and to different degrees, from information sharing (i.e., exchanging ideas or data) to coordination (e.g., dividing types or location of activity), cooperation (e.g., joint programming or activities) and integration (i.e., merging projects or organizations). Deeper coordination, he argues, is easiest when it begins early.[18]

Within the humanitarian literature, the notion of coordination has also received attention. Based on several decades of experience and research, Minear summarizes three models of coordination that the humanitarian community has used: coordination by command, coordination by consensus, and coordination by default.[19] The first has a defined and authoritative leadership structure, the second operates more by persuasion, whereas in the third model, coordination occurs more informally and without any kind of clear structure or design. Minear concludes that stronger command structures facilitate and enhance coordination.

In principle, although coordination is desirable, it has a number of drawbacks. Those who criticize the push for more coordination among actors, and humanitarian actors in particular, argue it takes too much money and time to coordinate and that the benefits are not clear.[20] Minear highlights several additional obstacles. The desire and need for agency visibility and profile can inhibit cooperation, even when it might occur more organically. Furthermore, the rapid response nature of humanitarian action makes it difficult to implement coordination mechanisms, because the need to respond quickly tends to trump other priorities. Minear acknowledges the roles of donors and individual personalities that can either inhibit or foster coordination.[21] In many instances, personality conflicts can greatly inhibit the ability of agencies to coordinate their activities or share information.[22]

Too much integration or coordination also compromises agency independence. If everyone is "inside the system," there is no room for more radical critiques from "outside the system." For example, if all agencies offering humanitarian assistance operate under the same command or coordination structure, it could stifle criticisms of aid delivery mechanisms. This is especially problematic if and when governments and foreign policy are involved. The statements of two senior U.S. officials raised the ire of the American NGO community in the post-9/11 context. In 2001, Colin Powell, then secretary of State, claimed NGOs were "force-multipliers" for U.S. foreign policy in Iraq.[23] In 2003, Andrew Natsios, then head of the U.S. Agency for International Development, threatened to pull funding for NGOs in Iraq that did not acknowledge their U.S. government funding.[24] These statements made many humanitarian and other actors nervous, because it compromised their independence and impartiality and associated them with controversial U.S. foreign policy objectives. Similarly, close coordination between human rights actors and peace negotiators may compromise the ability of either to effectively perform their roles.

This last point raises a significant and underexplored issue: that of how various actors should and can relate to each other. Ricigliano is one of the few scholar-practitioners who advocates an integrated approach to peacebuilding *and* suggests a mechanism for how to achieve this. He makes a compelling argument for more integration and coordination between sectors of activity in peacebuilding (e.g., political, social, structural) and describes how artificial distinctions between them can actually impede progress toward sustainable peace. These distinctions, he suggests, arise out of the different "theories of action" to which agencies ascribe. Specifically, "theories of action, while essential, can actually inhibit an organization from taking a systemic view and achieving real integration with other actors who have different theories of action."[25] Instead, he proposes a "network of effective action" approach that prioritizes coordination through sharing information and adopting an iterative approach as part of the organizations' theories of action. He refers to this as a "chaordic" approach to peacebuilding.[26]

Several weaknesses of Ricigliano's approach exist in relation to the argument of this chapter. First, he conflates relief with development actors and does not make any kind of distinction between them and their different purposes. He refers to both development and relief actors as structural peacebuilders, leaving no space for purely humanitarian actors. Relatedly, he fails to acknowledge how underlying principles and values might drive some agencies to pursue a particular course of action. For humanitarian actors who emphasize neutrality, impartiality, and independence, empowering war-affected populations to better their lives is not a priority; providing life-saving assistance to those in need takes precedence over other matters. Furthermore, the focus on an integrated approach tends to overlook the ideas of role clarity and integrity and how some roles may preclude actors from playing other roles.

Galant and Parlevliet raise the issue of role clarity and integrity in the context of bringing rights-based approaches into addressing conflict or development programming. They assert:

> Different actors can take responsibility for different aspects and roles, provided there is some communication, collaboration and coordination to ensure that all efforts hang together and that there is synergy. Consequently, an imperative in a rights-based approach to conflict management is ensuring role *clarity* and role *integrity*. Different actors in an intervention process may play different roles, and where one actor is called upon to play various roles, his or her primary role should not be compromised.[27]

In other words, they, like some of the authors already mentioned, recognize that playing some roles in conflict situations precludes playing others.

This manifests in different ways depending on an organization's mandate. A central dilemma for humanitarians, development organizations, and those involved in strategic peacebuilding is the extent to which advocacy becomes a part of the mandate and activities of an organization. For example, the founders of Médécins Sans Frontières (MSF) split from the International Committee of the Red Cross (ICRC) on precisely this issue after the Nigerian-Biafran war in the 1960s, with MSF taking a more public advocacy stance on the war. Terry summarizes the difference between the two approaches as a confidentiality issue, pointing out that "MSF speaks publicly only when its personnel have been direct witnesses, and only if it is likely to help the victims to do so. . . . In such [extreme] cases, MSF considers that aid organizations have only one tool left to them, the freedom of speech, and that it has a responsibility to denounce the violence and oppression, even at the cost of expulsion."[28] The ICRC maintained (and still does) that its ability to effectively provide humanitarian aid is dependent on its principles of impartiality and neutrality. These principles, in turn, compel it to pursue any advocacy strategy behind the scenes, if it does so at all.[29] It is precisely respect for the ICRC and its principles of impartiality, neutrality, and quiet diplomacy that allow it access to prisoners and populations where others have none. Indeed, the ICRC's interpretation of humanitarian principles dictates its actions.

The degree to which advocacy contradicts or supports principles of impartiality and neutrality depends in part on the definition of advocacy. The type of advocacy in which an organization engages can influence its ability to perform other roles. As Laue points out, advocacy can be in terms of process, party, or outcome.[30] Kraybill adds values advocacy to this list.[31] In some situations, it is possible to maintain impartiality while simultaneously advocating on behalf of a particular process or values. In other situations, outcome or party advocacy is an important, indeed crucial role, especially in asymmetric conflicts. Asymmetry in conflict implies the need for power balancing and structural change, a long-term effort that requires public and sometimes forceful advocacy on behalf of particular options or outcomes. Organizations and individuals need to make choices between these types of advocacy that are consistent with their mandate and retains their credibility as interveners and the trust of the conflict parties.

In other situations, trust, developed through long-term relationships, paves the way for a role in negotiating peace agreements but may compromise the fundamental purpose for the actor's original presence. For example, in one country rebels have approached individuals from a development organization to play a role in facilitating a peace agreement with the government. Should development organizations get involved in negotiations between parties, in facilitating contacts? Can individuals, employed by organizations, separate their individual selves from their corporate identity? This is part of peacebuilding, but it raises difficult issues for those faced with the choice. The decision to assist with negotiations or to act as a go-between may compromise the organization's accreditation (i.e., the permission the government grants to the organization to operate in a country) because of a perceived partiality toward the rebel group, and thus its ability to fulfill its development mandate. Again, organizations need to make these choices dependent on their own assessment of their role(s), mandates, and values. Perhaps the organization could step in as a convener[32] but not assist in the actual negotiations.

This discussion of third-party roles raises a number of points related to the underlying principles and values that inform how an agency operates, as well as the dilemmas inherent in coordinating or simply linking roles in conflict and building peace. Strategic peacebuilding requires multiple actors and activities and even the integration of the political, social, and structural elements of peacebuilding.[33] Nevertheless, for reasons described next, it is important to maintain a role and space for humanitarian action that remains outside of a peacebuilding paradigm.

The Integration Debate

A central debate within the humanitarian community is the extent to which humanitarian action and actors should stand alone, apart from the more explicitly political roles of peacebuilding or even development.[34] On the one hand, proponents of integration argue that closer coordination between the various actors and activities would increase the effectiveness of peacebuilding. On the other, those who want to guard their independence from the more "political" goals of peacebuilding resist integration under the umbrella of peacebuilding. The more common arguments against integration are intrinsically linked to the traditional humanitarian principles of neutrality and impartiality: first, that peacebuilding is a political endeavor, and as such runs counter to the core values of neutrality and impartiality; and second, that the loss of neutrality and impartiality is related to a decrease in the physical security of aid workers.

The "integrationists"[35] have argued that to make real progress in preventing violence or reconstructing societies emerging from the ashes of war or intractable conflict, it is necessary to link humanitarian action with other possible responses. A number of commentators have suggested that the provision of humanitarian assistance has become a substitute for decisive political action in response to emerging complex emergencies. Indeed, it is often easier for governments to earmark money for humanitarian relief rather than work to negotiate or implement peace agreements, despite the fact that most of the individual country UN consolidated appeals for humanitarian assistance remain underfunded. Charney maintains it is possible to uphold traditional humanitarian principles while at the same time working for broader social change. In his words, "Integration is about unified international action in support of reconciliation and social inclusion."[36] The United Nations integrated missions, first introduced in the Brahimi Report on UN peacekeeping, represent a step toward a conceptual and practical integration.[37] These integrated missions unite all UN activities and actors, including humanitarian ones, in a given country under one banner. Even outside of integrated missions, the Office for the Coordination of Humanitarian Affairs and the Under-Secretary General for Humanitarian Affairs are located under the Secretary General's office, thus implicitly linking the humanitarian with the political. Indeed, a number of commentators express skepticism that the political and humanitarian can be or are separate. For Weiss, "The assumption that politics and humanitarianism can be entirely separated, as if they were parts of two different and self-contained worlds, is a fiction."[38] Instead, he and other integrationists argue that humanitarians must acknowledge and work within the political world in which they operate.

In contrast, the more "purist" humanitarians have long resisted any connection to or association with other actors working in violent conflict zones, from the military to those agencies carrying out development or peacebuilding programming. Purists emphasize the fundamental principles of independence, impartiality, and neutrality and rightly suggest that a purely humanitarian response to alleviate human suffering is enough in and of itself. To taint humanitarian action with a political agenda, such as "building peace" or aid conditionality, is to destroy a basic and time-tested response to violence and war. In the words of commentator David Rieff:

> The tragedy of humanitarianism may be that for all its failings and all the limitations of its viewpoint, it represents what is decent in an indecent world. Its core assumptions—solidarity, a fundamental sympathy for victims, and an antipathy for oppressors and exploiters—are what we are in those rare moments of grace when we are at our best. . . . Independent humanitarianism does many things well and some things badly, but the things that it is now being called upon to do, such as helping to advance the cause of human rights, contributing to stopping wars, and furthering social justice, are beyond its competence, however much we might wish it otherwise.[39]

For purists, even the linkage to development programming is suspect, for development implies elements of normalcy and legitimacy.[40] In an analysis of Operation Lifeline Sudan and the relief-to-development continuum, the reviewers argue that development implies a measure of political and economic stability that is usually not present in complex political emergencies. As a result, development assistance is neither neutral nor impartial. Humanitarian assistance, in contrast, "is provided by the majority of donors unconditionally. . . . Unlike development aid, relief aid does not imply international recognition, or legitimation of the government or other authorities controlling territory."[41] For others, the critique of integration is based more on moral reasons. De Torrenté is particularly derisive in his critique of the integration agenda: "The implication of the coherence agenda is that meeting lifesaving needs is too limited in scope, and that the principles of impartiality, neutrality, and independence that have typically characterized humanitarian action should be set aside in order to harness aid to the 'higher' goals of peace, security, and development."[42] Essentially he argues on ethical and moral grounds that humanitarian action is a good in and of itself.

A more recent and practical critique of the integration agenda is related to an increase in targeted incidents against aid workers. A number of high-profile attacks on the ICRC, the United Nations, and NGOs have generated statements that the loss of impartiality and neutrality has put aid workers at risk. The bombings of the UN and ICRC headquarters in Iraq in August and October 2003 and the murder of seventeen aid workers wearing T-shirts bearing their agency's logo in Sri Lanka in August 2006 tragically illustrate the dangers of aid work. Although the reasons for these attacks remain unclear, some have pointed out that the United Nations' reputation in Iraq was damaged by years of sanctions.[43] In the case of the seventeen Action Contre la Faim national staff killed in eastern Sri Lanka, all but one were Tamil, suggesting a politically motivated attack.

Evidence on the link between security and the protective value of impartiality and neutrality is mixed. In a study of fatalities of aid workers between 1996 and 2005, Stoddard, Harmer, and Haver found that countries with UN integrated missions suffered no higher a rate of fatalities than those without. The study concludes, "It is safe to say that these variables [military intervention, presence of transnational terrorist groups, presence of armed groups or use of integrated mission approach] are not important determinants of violence against humanitarian aid workers."[44] In other words, political tainting or the loss of impartiality and neutrality does not seem to explain attacks on aid workers. Another study of factors contributing to increased physical insecurity for NGOs suggested working with both sides of a conflict as a risk factor for increased insecurity.[45]

Despite these findings, experience and anecdotal evidence imply that the actions of one organization directly impact others. Security management manuals emphasize the transfer effect of one organization's behavior on others.[46] This risk operates at multiple levels. For instance, in one country a humanitarian convoy injured a civilian in a road accident. Several days later, another convoy was attacked in the same location, ostensibly in retaliation for the previous accident.[47] At an organizational level, in another country a relief and development organization was working closely with a human rights organization. Militias attacked both organizations because they did not agree with their agenda of refugee return.[48] At an international level, the risk relates more to foreign policy and relations between states. In Gaza City in August 2006, Palestinian demonstrators attacked humanitarian offices after the start of the war in Lebanon, protesting the lack of protection for Lebanese children. The perception of a link between agendas is often more important than the reality.

The conceptual lack of association, and its concomitant messiness on literal and metaphorical battlefields, and the desire to remain untainted surfaces in examples on the ground. This is both the burden and incentive of the humanitarian principles of independence, neutrality, and impartiality. In studying the perceptions of local communities of the aid enterprise in Afghanistan, researchers discovered, based on their focus group interviews, that Afghans do not care whether the aid arrives via the military or humanitarian actors. Rather, they care more that they receive it.[49] The Multi-Donor Evaluation of Assistance to Rwanda observed a similar trend in the refugee camps of eastern Zaire in 1996, where refugees did not distinguish between Red Cross and other NGOs or humanitarian actors.[50] Given this reality, are we fooling ourselves into thinking that it actually matters? Perceptions on the ground are important and can dramatically influence the levels of safety and security an organization enjoys. An effective approach to security management for humanitarians (and peacebuilders) takes this into account and works to educate local populations about their purpose, values, and goals.

At a minimum, humanitarian aid should do no harm, meaning that humanitarian action should avoid contributing to or exacerbating conflict.[51] Avoiding contributing to the divisions and fault lines that characterize violent conflict is a more limited and achievable task for humanitarians than contributing to the goals of building peace. Terry reaches a similar conclusion:

> Humanitarian actors should ensure that the essential tasks—such as alleviating life-threatening suffering—are undertaken with minimal harm before considering expanding humanitarian action beyond them. If aid organizations pursue conflict resolution and peace-building activities, they are likely not only to increase the negative consequences of humanitarian action, but to further exonerate states of their responsibilities in these realms.[52]

A Separate Space for Humanitarian Action

The central argument of this chapter is that humanitarian assistance should not be incorporated into the larger peacebuilding agenda. The foregoing discussion on peacebuilding roles and integration has a number of implications.

In terms of relationships between peacebuilding roles, interveners in conflict need to think consequentially about their roles. This manifests in several ways. First, it is important to look at both formal and informal mechanisms of coordination or, in the words of Lederach, "weaving the web of strategic peacebuilding." Perhaps it is more productive to reframe the question and ask not whether humanitarian action should be linked with broader efforts but to examine the ways in which it is already linked. This necessitates a look at the informal mechanisms of networking as opposed to the more formal and institutionalized mechanisms of coordination. These informal mechanisms of coordination are often more effective, efficient, and important. Much of the "business" and creative thinking of conferences, negotiating peace agreements, or providing life-saving assistance happens over the dinner table or at local watering holes and not in formal meetings. Although the downside of informal mechanisms is that coordination then depends on who you know versus what you do, it is incumbent on interveners to expand the range of actors, in particular to include local networks, and to think expansively about what constitutes peacebuilding intervention. Peacebuilding, and humanitarian action, need to better use local capacity,[53] and the peacebuilding field needs to think more creatively about immediate responses to ongoing violence.

In reality, conflict resolvers and/or those involved in facilitating or mediating peace agreements or ceasefires at a local, national, or international level, with their emphasis on impartiality, have much in common with humanitarians espousing neutrality. Both shoulder the burden of not being seen as favoring one side or the other. Being seen as talking too long with one side or providing more assistance to one side, regardless of the reality of the situation, can have deleterious effects and lead to accusations of partiality. Each works for and claims allegiance to a larger goal (e.g., providing assistance to a suffering population or crafting a ceasefire that stops the violence). In other words, the implications and burdens of impartiality within the field of conflict resolution/transformation are analogous to those of neutrality for humanitarian action. Both require associating with, talking to, and negotiating with and between all sides, a fact that evokes the ire of advocates ("talking to the bad guys"). Both involve walking a tightrope between both sides and other members of the web of international actors intervening in various ways in conflict. This highlights the import of thinking proactively, consequentially, and ethically about the inherent limitations of roles. In other words, organizations need to find examples of the consequences of particular actions and be clear about their own niche, capacity, and mandates.

Third, guarding space for humanitarians means narrowing the definitions of what constitutes humanitarian action and mediation.[54] Many of the assumptions of humanitarian assistance, such as the short-term nature of assistance as an intervention, actually end up going against some of the core values of strategic peacebuilding, such as empowerment, building the platform for constructive change,[55] and the idea of longer term interventions. It also defuses the moral power of humanitarian action: that we provide relief solely to assist those who are in need of assistance. Relief/humanitarian assistance is not supposed to address structural injustice, nor is it designed to empower people to change their situations. It is a small bandage, and sometimes these are necessary. If we want to be seen as responding to violence, we need to allow purist humanitarian actors and mediators the conceptual and practical space to do their work. Perhaps there is room for ambiguity in many peacebuilding roles, but certain roles (e.g., humanitarian action and mediators) must remain separate to protect the integrity of the role and the safety of the actors.

This leads to the second element of the argument, that of the extent to which humanitarian assistance should be incorporated into the peacebuilding agenda. The dilemma is that the arguments of both purists and integrationists have merit. On one hand, assuming Laue is correct in asserting that all intervention alters the power balance, all humanitarian assistance is political.[56] On the other hand, the underlying values of humanitarian assistance do have intrinsic value and should not be sacrificed for other values. Integrationists go too far in incorporating humanitarian assistance into broader agendas of building peace, but purists need to acknowledge how humanitarian assistance is manipulated for political gain. This means humanitarian assistance should avoid contributing to conflict but should not aim to build peace.

Human rights advocates would not suggest throwing away the convention against torture or the Universal Declaration of Human Rights and Optional Protocols simply because some individuals and states disregard their obligations under these conventions. Nor would police officers or ordinary citizens advocate removing laws declaring murder a crime simply because not everyone abides by them. By the same token, we should not discard the value of humanitarian assistance as a moral and necessary response to human suffering because it does not (and should not) necessarily contribute to a long-term agenda of building peace. Instead, we need to guard the space for humanitarian actors to do their work and search outside the box for ways of building peace.

NOTES

1. John Paul Lederach, *Building Peace: Sustainable Reconciliation in Divided Societies* (Washington, D.C.: U.S. Institute of Peace Press, 1997), John Paul Lederach, *The Little Book of Conflict Transformation, The Little Books of Justice and Peacebuilding* (Intercourse, Pa.: Good Books, 2003), John Paul Lederach, *The Moral Imagination: The Art and Soul of Building Peace* (New York: Oxford University Press, 2005).

2. ICISS, "The Responsibility to Protect: Report of the International Commission on Intervention and State Sovereignty" (Ottawa, ON: IDRC and DFAIT, 2001).

3. For example, according to various IRIN reports (http://www.irinnews. org), in January 2007, a group of NGO and UN staff and African Mission in Sudan peacekeepers were harassed at a social gathering. Sudanese police arrested and subsequently beat those in detention. In addition, more than 400 aid workers were evacuated from Sudan in December 2006. At least twelve aid workers were killed in Darfur alone between May and December 2006.

4. Academy of Dispute Resolution, "Model Standards of Mediator Conduct," 1994.

5. Academy of Family Mediators, "Standards of Practice for Family and Divorce Mediation," 1998. *Impartiality* is defined as "freedom from favoritism or bias, either

in word or action," while *neutrality* "refers to the relationship that the mediator has with the disputing parties" (1). The more recent (September 2005) "Model Standards of Conduct for Mediators," adopted by the Association for Conflict Resolution, the American Bar Association, and the American Arbitration Association, includes impartiality in its standards but makes no mention of neutrality.

6. James Laue and Gerald Cormick, "The Ethics of Intervention in Community Disputes," in *The Ethics of Social Intervention*, ed. Gordon Bermant, Herbert C. Kelman, and Donald P. Warwick (Washington, D.C.: Hemisphere, 1978).

7. James Laue, "The Emergence and Institutionalization of Third Party Roles in Conflict," in *Conflict Management and Problem-Solving: Interpersonal to International Applications*, ed. Dennis J. D. Sandole and Ingrid Sandole-Staroste (New York: New York University Press, 1987), p. 20.

8. Ibid.

9. Paul Wehr and John Paul Lederach, "Mediating Conflict in Central America," *Journal of Peace Research* 28, no. 1 (1991).

10. Christopher Mitchell, "The Process and Stages of Mediation: Two Sudanese Cases," in *Making War and Waging Peace: Foreign Intervention in Africa*, ed. David R. Smock (Washington, D.C.: U.S. Institute of Peace Press, 1993).

11. William L. Ury, *The Third Side: How We Fight and How We Can Stop* (New York: Penguin, 2000), p. 7.

12. Ibid.

13. Ronald J. Fisher and Loraleigh Keashly, "The Potential Complementarity of Mediation and Consultation within a Contingency Model of Third Party Intervention," *Journal of Peace Research* 28, no. 1 (1991).

14. ICISS, "The Responsibility to Protect."

15. Lisa Schirch, *The Little Book of Strategic Peacebuilding*, The Little Books of Justice and Peacebuilding (Intercourse, Pa.: Good Books, 2004), p. 11.

16. Ibid., p. 83.

17. Susan Allen Nan and Andrea Strimling, "Coordination in Conflict Prevention, Conflict Resolution and Peacebuilding," *International Negotiation* 11, no. 1 (2006): 2.

18. Robert Ricigliano, "Collaboration" (paper presented at the annual meeting of the Alliance for Peacebuilding, Shawnee on Delaware, Pa, October 22–24, 2006).

19. Larry Minear, *The Humanitarian Enterprise: Dilemmas and Discoveries* (Bloomfield, Conn.: Kumarian Press, 2002).

20. Nicholas Stockton, "Humanitarianism Bound: Coherence and Catastrophe in the Congo, 1998–2002," unpublished study for the Centre for Humanitarian Dialogue, 2003.

21. Minear, *The Humanitarian Enterprise*, chapter 2.

22. In a study of humanitarian action in the West Bank and Gaza, personalities played a role in the degree to which various UN agencies coordinated their approaches. See Larissa Fast, "'Aid in a Pressure Cooker': Humanitarian Action in the Occupied Palestinian Territory" (Medford, Mass.: Feinstein International Center, 2006).

23. Colin Powell, "Secretary of State Colin L. Powell Remarks to the National Foreign Policy Conference for Leaders of Non-Governmental Organizations," October 26, 2001, available at http://www.yale.edu/lawweb/avalon/sept_11/powell_brief31.htm.

24. Andrew Natsios, "Remarks at the InterAction Forum, Closing Plenary Session," May 21, 2003, available at http://www.interaction.org/forum2003/panels.html.

25. Robert Ricigliano, "Networks of Effective Action: Implementing an Integrated Approach to Peacebuilding," *Security Dialogue* 34, no. 4 (2003): 449.

26. Ibid.

27. Ghalib Galant and Michelle Parlevliet, "Using Rights to Address Conflict—A Valuable Synergy," in *Reinventing Development? Translating Rights-Based Approaches from Theory into Practice*, ed. Paul Gready and Jonathan Ensor (London: Zed Books, 2006), p. 117 (italics in original).

28. Fiona Terry, *Condemned to Repeat: The Paradox of Humanitarian Action* (Ithaca, N.Y.: Cornell University Press, 2002), p. 21.

29. For more on the ICRC principles, see Denise Plattner, "ICRC Neutrality and Neutrality in Humanitarian Assistance," *International Review of the Red Cross*, no. 311 (1996).

30. Laue, "The Emergence and Institutionalization of Third Party Roles in Conflict."

31. Ronald Kraybill, "The Illusion of Neutrality," *Track Two* (November 1992).

32. Mitchell, "The Process and Stages of Mediation."

33. Ricigliano, "Networks of Effective Action."

34. In this chapter, I refer to this as "integration" or the "coherence" agenda. The literature on humanitarian action also addresses this question in discussions on coordination.

35. For more discussion on the "purist" versus "integrationist" debate described in this section, see Antonio Donini, "Issues Note" (paper presented at The Future of Humanitarian Action: Implications of Iraq and Other Recent Crises, brainstorming workshop, Boston, October 9, 2003). Others refer to "Dunantists" (after Henry Dunant, whose work on the battlefields of Solferino led to the founding of the ICRC) or "classicists" on one hand, and "Wilsonians" (who acknowledge the political dimension and linkages or convergence between foreign policy and humanitarian objectives) or "political humanitarians" on the other. The "solidarists," or those who choose partiality to one side or to the poor and oppressed and tend to reject both impartiality and neutrality, are yet another group in the debate. The solidarists are most often faith-based agencies. See also Thomas G. Weiss, "Principles, Politics, and Humanitarian Action," *Ethics and International Affairs* 13 (1999), and Minear, *The Humanitarian Enterprise*, chapter 5.

36. Joel R. Charney, "Upholding Humanitarian Principles in an Effective Integrated Response," *Ethics and International Affairs* 18, no. 2 (2004): 15.

37. Panel on United Nations Peacekeeping Operations, "Report of the Panel on United Nations Peacekeeping Operations" (New York: United Nations, 2000). Espen Barth Eide et al., "Report on Integrated Missions: Practical Perspectives and Recommendations" (New York: UN Executive Committee on Humanitarian Affairs, 2005).

38. Weiss, "Principles, Politics, and Humanitarian Action", p. 12.

39. David Rieff, *A Bed for the Night: Humanitarianism in Crisis* (New York: Simon & Shuster, 2002), p. 334.

40. Mark Duffield, *Global Governance and the New Wars: The Merging of Development and Security* (London: Zed Books, 2001), Joanna Macrae, "Purity or Political Engagement?: Issues in Food and Health Security Interventions in Complex Political Emergencies," *Journal of Humanitarian Assistance* (1998), available at http://www.jha.ac/articles/a037.htm.

41. Joanna Macrae et al., "Conflict, the Continuum and Chronic Emergencies: A Critical Analysis of the Scope for Linking Relief, Rehabilitation and Development Planning in Sudan" (London: Overseas Development Administration, 1996), p. 2.

42. Nicolas de Torrenté, "Humanitarianism Sacrificed: Integration's False Promise," *Ethics and International Affairs* 18, no. 2 (2004): 3.

43. Independent Panel, "Report of the Independent Panel on the Safety and Security of UN Personnel in Iraq" (New York: United Nations, 2003), Paul Reynolds, "Why the UN Is a Target," *BBC News*, August 19, 2003.

44. Abby Stoddard, Adele Harmer, and Katherine Haver, "Providing Aid in Insecure Environments: Trends in Policy and Operations," HPG Report 23 (London: ODI, 2006), p. 59.

45. Larissa A. Fast, "Characteristics, Context, and Risk: NGO Insecurity in Conflict Zones," *Disasters* 31, no. 2 (2007), Larissa A. Fast, "Context Matters: Identifying Micro- and Macro-Level Factors Contributing to NGO Insecurity" (Ph.D. dissertation, George Mason University, 2002).

46. Koenraad Van Brabant, "Operational Security Management in Violent Environments," *Good Practice Review* 8 (London: Humanitarian Practice Network, 2000).

47. Anonymous personal interview with author, fall 2000.

48. Anonymous personal interview with author, July 2006.

49. See the Afghanistan Case Study in Antonio Donini et al., *Mapping the Security Environment: Understanding the Perceptions of Local Communities, Peace Support Operations, and Assistance Agencies* (Medford, Mass.: Feinstein International Famine Center, Tufts University, June 2005).

50. John Borton, Emery Brusset, and Alistair Hallam, "Humanitarian Aid and Effects," Study 3 (Copenhagen: Steering Committee of the Joint Evaluation of Emergency Assistance to Rwanda, 1996).

51. Mary B. Anderson, *Do No Harm: How Aid Can Support Peace—Or War* (Boulder, Colo.: Lynne Rienner, 1999).

52. Terry, *Condemned to Repeat*, p. 245.

53. Others in both the peacebuilding and humanitarian literatures have made similar recommendations. See, for example, Gil Loescher, "Threatened Are the Peacemakers," *ND Magazine* (2005), Alex de Waal, *Famine Crimes: Politics and the Disaster Relief Industry in Africa* (Oxford: James Currey, 1997), John Paul Lederach and Janice Moomaw Jenner, eds., *A Handbook of International Peacebuilding: Into the Eye of the Storm* (San Francisco: Jossey-Bass, 2002), and Schirch, *The Little Book of Strategic Peacebuilding*.

54. Elsewhere I have argued for defining conflict resolution more narrowly, using impartiality and inclusiveness as the two criteria for conflict resolution interventions. See Larissa A. Fast, "Frayed Edges: Exploring the Boundaries of Conflict Resolution," *Peace and Change* 27, no. 4 (2002).

55. Lederach, *The Little Book of Conflict Transformation*.

56. Laue, "The Emergence and Institutionalization of Third Party Roles in Conflict."

REFERENCES

Anderson, Mary B. *Do No Harm: How Aid Can Support Peace—Or War*. Boulder, Colo.: Lynne Rienner, 1999.
Borton, John, Emery Brusset, and Alistair Hallam. "Humanitarian Aid and Effects," Study 3. Copenhagen: Steering Committee of the Joint Evaluation of Emergency Assistance to Rwanda, 1996.
Charney, Joel R. "Upholding Humanitarian Principles in an Effective Integrated Response." *Ethics and International Affairs* 18, no. 2 (2004): 13–20.
de Torrenté, Nicolas. "Humanitarianism Sacrificed: Integration's False Promise." *Ethics and International Affairs* 18, no. 2 (2004): 3–12.
de Waal, Alex. *Famine Crimes: Politics and the Disaster Relief Industry in Africa*. Oxford: James Currey, 1997.

Donini, Antonio. "Issues Note." Paper presented at The Future of Humanitarian Action: Implications of Iraq and Other Recent Crises. Brainstorming workshop, Boston, October 9, 2003.

Donini, Antonio, Larry Minear, Ian Smillie, Ted van Baarda, and Anthony C. Welch. *Mapping the Security Environment: Understanding the Perceptions of Local Communities, Peace Support Operations, and Assistance Agencies.* Medford, Mass.: Feinstein International Famine Center, Tufts University, June 2005.

Duffield, Mark. *Global Governance and the New Wars: The Merging of Development and Security.* London: Zed Books, 2001.

Eide, Espen Barth, Anja Therese Kaspersen, Randolph Kent, and Karin von Hippel. "Report on Integrated Missions: Practical Perspectives and Recommendations." New York: UN Executive Committee on Humanitarian Affairs, 2005.

Fast, Larissa. "'Aid in a Pressure Cooker': Humanitarian Action in the Occupied Palestinian Territory." Medford, Mass.: Feinstein International Center, 2006.

Fast, Larissa A. "Characteristics, Context, and Risk: NGO Insecurity in Conflict Zones." *Disasters* 31, no. 2 (2007).

———. "Context Matters: Identifying Micro- and Macro-Level Factors Contributing to NGO Insecurity." Ph.D. dissertation, George Mason University, 2002.

———. "Frayed Edges: Exploring the Boundaries of Conflict Resolution." *Peace and Change* 27, no. 4 (2002): 528–545.

Fisher, Ronald J., and Loraleigh Keashly. "The Potential Complementarity of Mediation and Consultation within a Contingency Model of Third Party Intervention." *Journal of Peace Research* 28, no. 1 (1991): 29–42.

Galant, Ghalib, and Michelle Parlevliet. "Using Rights to Address Conflict—A Valuable Synergy." In *Reinventing Development? Translating Rights-Based Approaches from Theory into Practice,* edited by Paul Gready and Jonathan Ensor, 108–130. London: Zed Books, 2006.

ICISS. "The Responsibility to Protect: Report of the International Commission on Intervention and State Sovereignty." Ottawa, ON: IDRC and DFAIT, 2001.

Independent Panel. "Report of the Independent Panel on the Safety and Security of UN Personnel in Iraq." New York: United Nations, 2003.

Kraybill, Ronald. "The Illusion of Neutrality." *Track Two* (November 1992): 13–14.

Laue, James. "The Emergence and Institutionalization of Third Party Roles in Conflict." In *Conflict Management and Problem-Solving: Interpersonal to International Applications,* edited by Dennis J. D. Sandole and Ingrid Sandole-Staroste, 17–29. New York: New York University Press, 1987.

Laue, James, and Gerald Cormick. "The Ethics of Intervention in Community Disputes." In *The Ethics of Social Intervention,* edited by Gordon Bermant, Herbert C. Kelman, and Donald P. Warwick, 205–232. Washington, D.C.: Hemisphere, 1978.

Lederach, John Paul. *Building Peace: Sustainable Reconciliation in Divided Societies.* Washington, D.C.: U.S. Institute of Peace Press, 1997.

———. *The Little Book of Conflict Transformation, The Little Books of Justice and Peacebuilding.* Intercourse, Pa.: Good Books, 2003.

———. *The Moral Imagination: The Art and Soul of Building Peace.* New York: Oxford University Press, 2005.

Lederach, John Paul, and Janice Moomaw Jenner, eds. *A Handbook of International Peacebuilding: Into the Eye of the Storm.* San Francisco: Jossey-Bass, 2002.

Loescher, Gil. "Threatened Are the Peacemakers." *Notre Dame Magazine* (2005).

Macrae, Joanna. 1998. "Purity or Political Engagement?: Issues in Food and Health Security Interventions in Complex Political Emergencies." *Journal of Humanitarian Assistance* (1998), http://www.jha.ac/articles/a037.htm.

Macrae, Joanna, Mark Bradbury, Susanne Jaspars, Douglas Johnson, and Mark Duffield. "Conflict, the Continuum and Chronic Emergencies: A Critical Analysis of the Scope for Linking Relief, Rehabilitation and Development Planning in Sudan." London: Overseas Development Administration, 1996.

Minear, Larry. *The Humanitarian Enterprise: Dilemmas and Discoveries.* Bloomfield, Conn.: Kumarian Press, 2002.

Mitchell, Christopher. "The Process and Stages of Mediation: Two Sudanese Cases." In *Making War and Waging Peace: Foreign Intervention in Africa*, edited by David R. Smock, 139–159. Washington, D.C.: U.S. Institute of Peace Press, 1993.

Nan, Susan Allen, and Andrea Strimling. "Coordination in Conflict Prevention, Conflict Resolution and Peacebuilding." *International Negotiation* 11, no. 1 (2006): 1–6.

Panel on United Nations Peacekeeping Operations. "Report of the Panel on United Nations Peacekeeping Operations." New York: United Nations, 2000.

Plattner, Denise. "ICRC Neutrality and Neutrality in Humanitarian Assistance." *International Review of the Red Cross*, no. 311 (1996): 161–179.

Reynolds, Paul. "Why the UM Is a Target." *BBC News*, August 19, 2003.

Ricigliano, Robert. "Collaboration." In *Alliance for Peacebuilding Annual Meeting.* Shawnee on Delaware, Pa., 2006.

———. "Networks of Effective Action: Implementing an Integrated Approach to Peacebuilding." *Security Dialogue* 34, no. 4 (2003): 445–462.

Rieff, David. *A Bed for the Night: Humanitarianism in Crisis.* New York: Simon & Shuster, 2002.

Schirch, Lisa. *The Little Book of Strategic Peacebuilding, The Little Books of Justice and Peacebuilding.* Intercourse, Pa.: Good Books, 2004.

Stockton, Nicholas. "Humanitarianism Bound: Coherence and Catastrophe in the Congo, 1998–2002." London, Unpublished Study for the Centre for Humanitarian Dialogue, 2003.

Stoddard, Abby, Adele Harmer, and Katherine Haver. "Providing Aid in Insecure Environments: Trends in Policy and Operations," HPG Report 23 London: ODI, 2006.

Terry, Fiona. *Condemned to Repeat: The Paradox of Humanitarian Action.* Ithaca, N.Y.: Cornell University Press, 2002.

Ury, William L. *The Third Side: How We Fight and How We Can Stop.* New York: Penguin, 2000.

Van Brabant, Koenraad. "Operational Security Management in Violent Environments." Good Practice Review 8. London: Humanitarian Practice Network, 2000.

Wehr, Paul, and John Paul Lederach. "Mediating Conflict in Central America." *Journal of Peace Research* 28, no. 1 (1991): 85–98.

Weiss, Thomas G. "Principles, Politics, and Humanitarian Action." *Ethics and International Affairs* 13 (1999): 1–22.

12

Turning from Hatred to Community Friendship

Forgiveness Education as a Resource for Strategic Peacebuilding in Postaccord Belfast

Robert D. Enright, Jeanette Knutson Enright, and Anthony C. Holter

Our contribution to strategic peacebuilding is the concept of civic friendship through forgiveness. Ours is a decidedly long-term strategy for peace in which educational institutions are challenged to rethink their social curricula to make room for a new development: forgiveness education. The latter is a strategy for reducing anger and abiding resentment in children to make room for the possibility of friendship across the divide of groups that have been torn apart by violence and war. Because forgiveness education takes much time to sink deeply into children's minds and hearts, our strategy spans the early elementary school years through the end of high school, with increasingly developmental sophistication regarding what forgiveness is and how to achieve it. Only in the later years of schooling are forgiveness and friendship linked toward groups that have been in conflict with the students' own group.

Unless community members, in the unfortunate situation of conflict and war, understand and deliberately cultivate forgiveness, they are unlikely to foster friendship across divided communities. Unless community members cultivate friendship, we predict that any given community beset by decades or centuries of violence will not recover well in a psychological sense, despite the best efforts of lawmakers and economic reformers. Peace, in other words, centers at least in part within people (not only without) and in the structures of society. This is not to invalidate efforts at political and societal reform; it is only meant as a challenge. Without the psychological change within people, the goal of peace in any permanent way will be harder to realize.

We are not alone in our call for internal, psychological transformation as a way of strategically confronting societal conflict. Roger Peterson makes the compelling case that hatred and resentment in Eastern Europe are barriers to a lasting peace in that region.[1] As we will see, forgiveness is one scientifically supported antidote to resentment. In his analysis of ethnic conflicts, Kaufman makes the case that hatred is one of the major variables that continues to fuel conflict even when economic and political barriers begin to fall.[2] Our contribution, beyond these important works, is to point to actual school curricula for transforming hatred and resentment toward friendship.

Our own focus for the past six years has been on children within Belfast, Northern Ireland, a community that has experienced the Troubles and has been working its way to peace in a postaccord society following the Good Friday Agreement on April 10, 1998. Much needs to be accomplished in the impoverished areas that still have a strong paramilitary presence. Might one necessary but not sufficient accomplishment be the change of heart that must take place within people so that their home/community is in better order? Is it possible to resurrect the ancient notion of friendship, with the vision that those who now see factions might, in a couple of generations, begin to see friendship as a community goal? Is it possible to begin with children and educate them in the value of forgiveness and friendship so that, as adults, they will be deeper forgivers and friendship seekers than might have been the case without that education?

First we offer a brief history of the conflicts in Northern Ireland and some of the peace efforts in that region. This is followed by a sketch of the current anger within and toward children and youth in Belfast. After all, if the children are currently unaffected by the Troubles of recent decades, then why bother with the considerable effort that will be needed to establish curricula that focus on forgiveness and friendship? After this brief discussion, we offer an exposition on friendship based on Aristotle's analysis. We then offer scientific evidence from psychology that a lack of friendship, in the form of abiding anger and hatred, has deleterious effects. We then turn to a solution to anger: forgiveness. After briefly defining forgiveness, we examine its effectiveness in cleaning up the human heart. This is followed by a description of forgiveness education within Belfast in particular because we contend that starting with the children is the best chance of developing communities that cultivate friendship. In the penultimate section, we address skeptical views of forgiveness and its place in strategic peacebuilding. We end the chapter with a challenge to those involved in the processes of strategic peacebuilding.

A Brief History of the Troubles in Northern Ireland and the Subsequent Peace Efforts

The roots of the contemporary conflict in Northern Ireland can be traced back to the sixteenth and seventeenth centuries, a period referred to as the Ulster Plantation, when English citizens were given parcels of land in the north of Ireland that had been previously owned and farmed by Irish citizens.[3] The ensuing discord between these groups was distinguished as "cultural, territorial, as well as religious" and was exacerbated over the next several decades through military campaigns (such as the Battle of the Boyne in 1690) and legislative actions (such as the Act of Union in 1801), which increased English interest and governance in Ireland.[4]

Significant armed and legislative actions continued to shape the landscape of Ireland throughout the twentieth century. One of the most noteworthy armed conflicts occurred when local groups of Irish citizens rebelled against the English in what is known as the 1916 Easter Rising. This armed attack against the English, and the subsequent execution of the Irish leaders of the insurrection, precipitated the Government of Ireland Act of 1920.[5] The act effectively created two separate governments: one in the Irish Free State and another in Northern Ireland. The Irish Free State later seceded from the British Commonwealth and became the Republic of Ireland in 1949.

Territorial, political, and religious divisions escalated along with increased inequality in Northern Ireland over the next half-century. Individuals, groups, and neighborhoods were segregated along distinct political and religious divisions: Nationalists (typically Catholic, desiring a unified Ireland) and Unionists (typically Protestant, desiring a maintained union with England). During the mid-twentieth century, many Catholic Nationalists in Northern Ireland were inspired by the global civil rights movement and organized under the Northern Ireland Civil Rights Association to demand equality. Organized protests were met with hostility that fueled action and retaliation by paramilitary groups throughout the region, such as car bombings, murders, kidnappings, and so on, and frequent clashes with the British military and the Royal Ulster Constabulary. Violence directly connected with paramilitary activity claimed the lives of nearly 2,500 people between 1969 and 1979 alone. This period of intergroup and sectarian violence in Northern Ireland that began in the 1960s and continued through the late 1990s is colloquially referred to as the Troubles.

Great strides have been made in the past decade to diffuse intergroup violence of the Troubles and promote peace. The ratification of the agreement in April 1998 was a historic event that began the process of governmental reform, paramilitary decommissioning, and several other key social and education changes in Northern Ireland.[6] Although the success of a power-sharing government was short lived—direct rule from England was reinstated in 2002—preparations are under way to reinstate a local, home-rule government in Northern Ireland.[7] It should also be noted that significant progress has been made with regard to paramilitary decommissioning and disarmament. In July 2005, the Irish Republican Army called for its members to disarm and cease violent activity, and this has been validated by a recent report of the monitoring commission.[8] Despite these positive steps forward about ten years after the agreement, there remains a "significant and enduring level of violence" within Belfast and other communities throughout Northern Ireland.[9]

Certain sections of Belfast are demarked by flags, painted curbs, political murals, and politically charged parades that effectively divide entire neighborhoods by political affiliation, religious and ethnic identity, and paramilitary association.[10] Some of the more notorious interface areas are physically divided by a large concrete and steel "peace" wall. The persistence of sectarian and community violence continues to have deleterious outcomes for individual members of these communities, especially young children.[11] Therefore, it is of utmost importance that children growing up in this ongoing conflict have access to peace education and a voice in peacemaking processes.[12]

Belfast's Children Today: Are They Angry?

Elsewhere, we have surveyed the extent of anger that is present in six- to seven-year-old children in state and Catholic schools within what the locals call "the interface areas" of Belfast.[13] The interface areas are characterized by Catholic and Protestant housing in close proximity, with occasional sectarian violence erupting within the community. Approximately ninety students representing Irish Catholic and British Protestant culture were administered a well-validated anger inventory.

The results were compared with those from Milwaukee, Wisconsin's central city, where ethnic segregation and violence are also common, and from Madison, Wisconsin, where such segregation and violence are not as prevalent. The results showed that the children in Belfast and Milwaukee were statistically equivalent in terms of anger, and both were significantly higher than the children in Madison. In fact, the average scores in Belfast and Milwaukee were at or near the clinical level of anger, suggesting that the *average* six- to seven-year-old in those communities is in need of professional help for levels of anger.

We have abundant observations from our (to date) five years of work within Belfast's schools. Here are only eight examples (of many more that we have) to illustrate that the interface areas of Belfast are in need of intervention to heal the hearts of the children. Some of the examples show the children's anger, whereas others show anger toward them. We can only surmise the anger that may be developing in the children who are targets of others' anger. First, in one school of 212 students in which we work, 100 of them are being treated by medical and psychological professionals outside of the school for sleeplessness, anxiety, and depression. Second, a prominent paramilitary leader ordered that his adolescent son be knee-capped (crippling by gunshot to the knees at close range). Third, for many months, four-year-old girls were terrorized on their way to school by adults throwing rocks and bags full of urine at them, trying to prevent them from going to a school in which different beliefs from their own were taught and learned. Fourth, a teenage boy was crucified to a block of wood by other youths in what was reported as a sectarian act. Fifth, another teenage boy was murdered by other adolescents wielding baseball bats. Once he was down, they stomped on his head. This, too, was identified by police as a sectarian act. Sixth, a group of courageous students from our own university visited a school to help paint the interior walls. Two weeks after the students finished the rewarding but exhausting job, vandals burned the gymnasium of that school in what police called a sectarian act. Seven, three cars were fire-bombed in the school parking lot during school hours at another school; this was also reported by police as a sectarian act. Finally, when we commented to one principal about the wonderfully disciplined behavior of the children in the school, she humbly remarked, "Oh, yes, they are behaving well for now, but after school, too many of them will be standing on the street corner throwing rocks at the bus from the other school nearby."

Social science, then, with the best psychometric measures available, shows the children to be excessively angry. Taking time to be a part of school life—meeting with teachers and principals, and observing children throughout the school day—shows us that some children are perpetrators of violence and the victims of it. The idea of friendship with the "other side" is so distant from many children's minds as to make our proposed project laughable. Yet anger and violence are no laughing matters, nor is our scientific evidence on the efficacy of forgiveness education to reduce anger and restore emotional well-being. Thus, we proceed to an exposition of the life-saving concept of friendship and the meaning of that term. We then turn to a discussion of anger and its diminution through forgiveness education, as a way of eventually fostering friendship.

An Aristotelian Understanding of Friendship and Its Importance

Civic friendship within communities has been the focus of some scholars' work.[14] Yet the appropriation of this Aristotelian concept for direct intervention within communities is rare. This is unfortunate for at least two reasons: (1) Aristotle remains one of the most popular philosophers in the West, and (2) he held up friendship as the primary quality of a good community, or the City.

In two of his central works, the *Nicomachean Ethics* and *Politics*, Aristotle described two kinds of friendship, one on the individual level and the other on the civic level, a collection of partnerships of partnerships. Either kind of friendship is so important that they are said to transcend justice. To say that anything transcends justice is an attention grabber primarily because Aristotle's mentor, Plato, held justice to be the paragon virtue. Yet for Aristotle, friendship is a form of love, the highest form of love. He refers to friendship on one hand as a virtue because it contains an individual's inclination and practice of love. On the other hand, he clarifies that friendship may not be an actual virtue but instead *involves* virtue, presumably because, unlike true virtues, which can be practiced by themselves when others are practicing vice, friendship requires goodness between two or more people.

Aristotle distinguished three kinds of friendship—those of mutual pleasure, utility, and moral goodness. Only the friendship of good will concerns us here because it is the highest form of friendship centered on mutual love and unconditionality (loving the other as an end and not for the fleeting conditions of pleasure or utility). Civic friendship, as we understand Aristotle, is a deliberate fostering of good will toward others as an end in and of itself. It involves the cultivation of support and the development of bonds. It is the deliberate avoidance of factions because all citizens are capable of offering and receiving love and respect.

Civic friendship is more difficult to understand than individual friendship, as it is considered by some to be "more watery."[15] Civic friendship includes more people, in more complex relations than individual relationships, yet each shares important similarities. Both concern moral good, which implies a mutual caring (a return of affection, in Aristotle's words) between and among people. Both imply a certain kind of equality between and among people, not in an arithmetic sense (all get three apples) but in a moral sense. All people are part of the moral good, all can cultivate and offer respect, and all are concerned about the development of virtue in the other. To enter into civic friendship is to enter into a world in which it is necessary that the citizens grow in virtue.

For Aristotle, a city cannot be a good community unless its citizens are good. If the people of a community do not develop friendship, then it is unlikely that the community will actually be a city in the deepest sense of that word. A collection of people living together is not a city, is not a healthy community, simply because the citizens tolerate each other, have good sanitation facilities, or experience a reasonable level of economic justice. To tolerate is not necessarily to love the other; to have friendship, as we have seen, by definition, is to love the other through exercising moral virtue. Tolerance alone is not a positive moral response but the absence of negative thoughts and actions. Friendship, on the other hand, provides those positive thoughts and actions.

The Aristotelian challenge, that we are to deliberately foster friendship, by mutually loving one another, is a high target indeed. Yet it is perfectly consonant with his definition of virtue. For Aristotle, virtue is the disposition of the mind that is inclined to do good, lying in a mean "relative to us," such that a person of wisdom would say, yes, that truly is excellence and should be pursued.[16] In other words, having a good end point helps us take accurate aim at the target, even if we are not sufficiently developed at present to reach the full excellence of that end point. Thus, the end point of a good community is friendship among the people, even if the attainment of true and enduring friendship is difficult at present. At least, to be inclined to seek and practice that friendship is a good goal.

A word on Aristotle's metaphysics is in order. He believed, as we know, in the underlying essence of the moral virtues. The virtues are objective not subjective, absolute not relative, and universal not situation- or culture-specific. He, of course, is entirely correct here.[17] Has there ever been a society that valued sloth over industriousness, cruelty over compassion, or injustice over justice? Surely certain cultures express industriousness, compassion, and justice differently and may even have differing customs or, in some cases, laws to ensure the proper expression of certain virtues, but their essence is unchanged in that communities everywhere prefer industry, compassion, and justice. This is not a trivial point. If virtues are objective, absolute, and universal, then their applicability in various parts of the world is more likely and more reasonable than we may think. It is not a crime to introduce certain virtues such as friendship or forgiveness to war-torn lands in distant places as long as the peacemakers are sensitively aware of the local, cultural, and religious nuances of the particular virtues of the community. It would seem that the introduction of the concepts of friendship and forgiveness would be compatible with both the British Protestant and the Irish Catholic world-views in Belfast. They may have their nuanced differences, but the basic ideas of these social concepts would surely be compatible with their long-standing faith traditions.

We are aware of the dangers of imposing *particular* views of the virtues on cultures that do not share those particular views. Yet education in virtues need not involve something rigidly impositional.[18] Rather, it is about creating the "fund" of concepts or "social capital" that is needed for peace. This, by the way, is a major reason we advocate for local intervention for virtues development rather than what some might call "expert" intervention by people from other lands. We have confidence that the introduction of virtues education, with an emphasis on forgiveness, is a moral good because all peoples in all lands share the *essence* of friendship and forgiveness and the proper expression of these. The *expression* of them differs across world communities. As we leave the student instruction to the local teachers, we avoid a variety of culturally imposed errors. Now that we have a general understanding of the concept of friendship, let us turn to the next section, a discussion of anger and its psychological effects.

Anger and Its Effects

For Aristotle, virtues exist in a "golden mean" between two extremes.[19] For example, courage exists between the extremes of cowardice and reckless bravado. Friendship, similarly, exists between the extremes of a cloying dependence and separation of people by hatred and anger. The latter extreme is our focus here.

Even anger itself can be seen as existing within a mean of complete sanguinity to rage. Anger's mean, or a short-lived exasperation at the imperfections of the world that can energize a person and motivate a quest for justice, is not our concern here. Instead, the extreme of deep and long-lasting anger is our concern, the kind that can be implicated in psychopathology, destroyed relationships, and war and violence on the social level. In other words, our focus is on toxic anger, the kind that can take root in conditions of societal injustice and contribute back to even more injustice. We see this in Belfast, where the children learn the lessons of prejudice and hatred at early ages, with a consequence of continued violence within the interface areas of the city.

Anger and Children

A thorough examination of anger in children and youth is beyond the scope of this chapter. Our intent is modest: to show how what we call toxic anger is related to a host of undesirable characteristics. We have chosen one well-established psychiatric disorder, oppositional defiant disorder (ODD), to discuss. ODD is a diagnostic category of the American Psychiatric Association that is associated with the following anger-related symptoms: the child or youth often loses temper, argues frequently with adults, frequently defies adult authority, annoys others, blames others for what is one's own fault, and is often spiteful, angry, and resentful. A child must exhibit at least four such symptoms over a six-month period to be diagnosed with ODD.

Research on children and youth who have been diagnosed with ODD shows that the children, compared with those without the diagnosis, have more suicide attempts,[20] greater adjustment problems at home and in school, higher rates of depression and anxiety, and relationships characterized by high conflict,[21] and are at greater risk for drug use in adolescence.[22] A recent study of young adult drivers in the United States showed that those with a pattern of aggressive driving, which can put the driver and innocent victims at risk for injury or death, had a higher prevalence of ODD than those who were not aggressive drivers.[23] It should be noted that aggressive driving, what the locals in Belfast call "joy riding," is a persistent problem on the streets in that city late at night.

If left untreated, ODD can lead to conduct disorder, perhaps the most serious of the childhood disorders because of its symptoms of aggression and violence.[24] Clinicians observe that ODD can emerge as early as ages three or four and should be treated by early elementary school. If left undiagnosed or untreated, the anger and opposition can become exceptionally difficult to reverse by adolescence and adulthood.[25] Our intent is not to suggest that most problems in Belfast are centered on ODD or that ODD is the major pressing problem in need of amelioration. Instead, we have chosen only one of several childhood disorders associated with excessive anger to show its severe and disruptive consequences.[26]

Countering Toxic Anger with Forgiveness Therapy and Education

Whenever we are faced with an extreme expression of a virtue, such as cowardice rather than courage, it would be ideal if there were a corrective to the extreme position. This is where psychology can come into play. Psychotherapists have developed a number of programs to counter a variety of excesses, whether it be excessive worry, drinking, or anger. We discuss forgiveness therapy and education as an antidote to toxic anger and as a contribution to strategic peacebuilding on the social level. Prior to that discussion, let us try to be clear on our meaning of the term *forgiveness*.

What Forgiveness Is and Is Not

Forgiveness as a human action toward another who was unjust has ancient origins. The oldest preserved account of one person forgiving another is in the Book of Genesis (chapters 37–45) in the Hebrew Bible. In that account, Joseph was horribly mistreated by his jealous brother and ten half-brothers. When he rose to political influence in Egypt, all of his half-brothers, not knowing him, requested help with famine relief. After showing considerable anger and ambivalence toward them, he eventually wept, hugged them, and unconditionally forgave them. His forgiveness and subsequent generosity helped found the Hebrew nation. His one act of forgiveness is a striking example of how such mercy can improve the conditions of an entire social group.

A somewhat similar story of forgiveness, that of the prodigal son, occurs in the New Testament (Luke 15:11–32). An ungrateful son asked prematurely for his inheritance from his wealthy father. After squandering the gift on reckless living in a foreign land, he returned repentantly to his father. Before the son could ask for forgiveness, the father ran to him, embraced him, and forgave him. As in the Hebrew story, the forgiveness was loving and unconditional, with the forgiver not asking for an apology or any other recompense prior to forgiving. Somewhat similar stories can be found in Islamic and Buddhist traditions.[27]

Even though the origins of the concept of forgiveness are within ancient religious traditions, that concept and its applications need not follow one particular religious tradition, or any religion for that matter. Are not the origins of justice within ancient religious traditions? Yet people practice justice as they wish, some within religious contexts, others within entirely secular contexts. In our experience, forgiveness is the same. People are free to choose the worldviews that best support a forgiving response. In fact, the exploration and study of forgiveness within the academy has taken a decidedly academic turn lately, as we will see shortly.

In modern philosophy, expositions on person-to-person forgiving are consistent with the ancient conceptions. In Joanna North's well-known essay, she presents three conditions during forgiveness: (1) the offender acted unjustly, (2) the forgiver reduces negative reactions such as resentment, and (3) the forgiver institutes or restores goodness, such as compassion, benevolence, and love (agape), toward the offender.[28] Joanna North and Margaret Holmgren emphasize the unconditional nature of forgiving. While North emphasized the principle of moral love underlying a response of forgiving, Holmgren emphasized respect.[29]

The gist of forgiving is that it is a response of mercy toward someone who acted unfairly. The mercy takes two forms, the reduction or cessation of negative responses and the deliberate (willed) offering of a principled moral stance that might be love and respect.

To forgive is not the same as to condone or excuse. In forgiveness, the one offering mercy knows that the other acted unfairly. In excusing, the one so doing finds a mitigating circumstance to conclude that the act, in fact, was not unfair. If James steals Melissa's car and she eventually realizes that he did so to rush a bleeding child to the hospital, her evaluation of his behavior is likely to change. She would not view James as having done anything that requires forgiveness. Thus, to excuse or condone is not to offer mercy to the other; forgiveness is the deliberate act of offering mercy in the face of the other person's injustice.

To forgive is not the same as to forget. We realize that the expression "forgive and forget" is pervasive, but we have never seen one instance in which someone who forgives develops a sort of moral amnesia. When people forgive, they seem to remember in new ways. Thus, if people are fearful of forgiveness lest they become vulnerable to the other's tricks once again, they should realize that forgetting is not an inherent aspect of forgiveness.

To forgive is not the same as to reconcile. Forgiveness is a virtue that is developed and expressed through the will of one person toward another or others. Reconciliation is an interaction between two or more people. James may want to reconcile with Melissa, but it is not entirely within his will. Melissa must respond to his gestures of forgiveness and learn to trust him, and both must come together in good will if reconciliation is to be realized. Thus, forgiveness is one person's act of mercy toward another, whereas reconciliation requires two or more parties for completion.

To forgive does not mean to ignore justice. A grave mistake is to think of forgiveness and justice as opposed to each other. This is what we call either-or thinking, and it could render forgiveness not only irrelevant but also dangerous. For example, suppose James had a violent temper toward Melissa. If she could not protect herself when she forgives, that would be absurd. We should, instead, use "both-and" thinking. For example, if Melissa deliberately dents James's car, he can forgive her and still present her with the auto body shop's bill. Thus, there is nothing inherent in forgiveness that negates justice. The two can and should be practiced together, depending on the circumstances. In Northern Ireland, as one person forgives someone from "the other side," he or she can and should ask for fairness.

The Cognitive Structure of Unconditionality and Its Connection to Friendship

An early development in our group's construction of a psychological theory of forgiveness was to ascertain the cognitive structure that underlies a forgiveness response. We do not mean to imply that forgiveness is entirely or even primarily a cognitive activity. We wish to imply, from a psychological and educational perspective, that forgiveness may require certain cognitive capacities before a therapist or educator introduces the concept. This is important for the construction of appropriate educational material from a developmental perspective. One central underlying cognitive structure to a forgiveness response is what we call *unconditionality*.[30]

Unconditionality is the understanding that all people are equal, regardless of personal, relational, or environmental characteristics (e.g., personality, social skills, athletic ability, or even social privilege). This understanding is based on the Piagetian concept of identity: the understanding that $A + o = A$, or that something nonessential added to the first value does not alter it. Piaget's well-known experiments with conservation demonstrate this principle. Consider an experimenter who pours water from a short, wide container into a tall, narrow container. The structures of the containers are the "o" component, and the volume of water is the "A" component. In other words, the volume of the water is not in any way altered whether it is in a short or a tall container.

Unconditionality arises from this basic cognitive skill of identity. A person is a person whether in a short, wide house or a tall, narrow house. This insight, which a child can make, then leads to a belief in the *moral principle of inherent worth*, the conviction that people are in essence equal, despite varying psychological characteristics, including behavior that may be unfair. A person is a person of worth whether he or she is poor, struggling intellectually in school, or behaving badly, even to the one doing the thinking with the underlying cognitive structure of unconditionality. Offering forgiveness involves acting on this social-cognitive understanding and the moral principle of inherent worth that develops from it.

Let us now suppose that James and Melissa are sufficiently cognitively developed according to the foregoing descriptions. James can use the cognitive structure of unconditionality and apply it in the moral realm so that he sees Melissa as possessing inherent worth. On seeing her worth, he may wish moral good for her. As Melissa does the same toward James, she will wish his good. When both are willing moral good toward the other and when both are aware of this, they are friends by Aristotle's definition of friendship. Of course, insight is not a sufficient condition for the practice of virtue, but without it, a full expression of a virtue, including one's own part in a relation of friendship, is probably unlikely.

The Effectiveness of Forgiveness Therapy and Education

We present in the list below a summary of a portion of our forgiveness intervention efforts over the years. In every case, we use the gold standard of research design, with randomization to treatment condition, pretesting, posttesting, follow-up testing, and the use of psychometrically sound measures. Across all twelve of the studies listed, we see the following pattern: (1) regardless of the age of the participants, which ranged from as young as six to the elderly years, those who have forgiveness education or therapy generally fare better emotionally than the control group; (2) when anger is incorporated as a dependent measure, it invariably declines in the forgiveness condition relative to the control condition; (3) the decrease in anger, anxiety, and depression is usually clinically important in that the decline is often to normal levels where clinically compromised levels were observed at pretest. In sum, forgiveness education and therapy are effective in reducing anger and related emotions in a statistically significant and a clinically significant way.

EXAMPLES OF EXPERIMENTAL STUDIES

Incest survivors. The forgiveness group became emotionally healthier than the control group after fourteen months. Differences between the groups were observed for depression, anxiety, hope, and self-esteem. The results were maintained in a fourteen-month follow-up. *Study*: Freedman, Suzanne R., and Robert D. Enright. "Forgiveness as an Intervention Goal with Incest Survivors." *Journal of Consulting and Clinical Psychology* 64, no. 5 (1996): 983–992.

Men hurt by the abortion decision of the partner. The forgiveness group became emotionally healthier than the control group, similar to the above study. Differences between the groups were observed for anger, anxiety, grief, and forgiveness. The results were maintained at a twelve-week follow-up. *Study*: Coyle, Catherine T., and Robert D. Enright. "Forgiveness Intervention with Postabortion Men." *Journal of Consulting and Clinical Psychology* 65, no. 6 (1997): 1042–1046.

Drug rehabilitation. The forgiveness group became emotionally healthier than the control group, similar to the above two studies. The experimental participants' need for drugs declined substantially, relative to the control group. Results were maintained at a four-month follow-up. *Study*: Lin, Wei Fen, David Mack, Robert D. Enright, Dean Krahn, and Thomas W. Baskin. "Effects of Forgiveness Therapy on Anger, Mood, and Vulnerability to Substance Use among Inpatient Substance-Dependent Clients." *Journal of Consulting and Clinical Psychology* 72, no. 6 (2004): 1114–1121.

Couples at risk for divorce. The forgiveness group as well as the group following Aaron Beck's cognitive behavioral therapy showed that the couples drew closer to one another with improved relationships following treatment. *Study*: Knutson, J. A. "Strengthening Marriages through the Practice of Forgiveness." Doctoral dissertation, University of Wisconsin–Madison, 2003.

Cardiac patients. Again, the experimental (forgiveness) group became emotionally healthier than the control group. At a four-month follow-up, the experimental group had more efficiently functioning hearts than the control group. *Study*: Waltmann, M. A., D. C. Russell, C. T. Coyle, R. D. Enright, A. C. Holter, and C. M. Swoboda. "The Effects of a Forgiveness Intervention on Patients with Coronary Artery Disease." *Psychology and Health* 24, no. 1 (2009): 11–27.

Emotionally abused women. Results are similar to the above studies in terms of emotional health including decreased anxiety, depression, post-traumatic stress disorder symptoms, and increased self-esteem. *Study*: Reed, Gayle L., and Robert D. Enright. "The Effects of Forgiveness Therapy on Depression, Anxiety, and Posttraumatic Stress for Women after Spousal Emotional Abuse." *Journal of Consulting and Clinical Psychology* 74, no. 5 (2006): 920–929.

Terminally ill, elderly cancer patients. After a four-week intervention, the forgiveness group showed greater improvement in psychological health (less anger, more hopefulness toward the future) than the control group. Physical indicators of both groups showed declines. *Study*: Hanson, Mary, Robert D. Enright, and Thomas W. Baskin. "A Palliative Care Intervention in Forgiveness Therapy for Elderly Terminally Ill Cancer Patients." *Journal of Palliative Care* (forthcoming).

At-risk middle school and high school students in Seoul, Korea. The findings are similar to the above study. *Study*: Park, J. H. "Validating a Forgiveness Education Program for Adolescent Female Aggressive Victims in Korea." Doctoral dissertation, University of Wisconsin–Madison, 2003.

First-grade (Primary 3) children in Belfast. Those in the experimental (forgiveness) group became less angry relative to those in the control group. Randomization is by group; analyses are on each individual. *Study*: Enright, Robert D., Jeanette A. Knutson Enright, Anthony C. Holter, Thomas W. Baskin, and Casey Knutson. "Waging Peace through Forgiveness in Belfast, Northern Ireland II: Educational Programs for Mental Health Improvement of Children." *Journal of Research in Education* 17 (2007): 63–78.

In light of the potential importance of forgiveness for strategic peacebuilding in Northern Ireland and in light of the importance of the concept of agape within forgiveness, we turn next to a challenge to the Aristotelian project.

Developing the Aristotelian Conceptions of Friendship and Love

In the beginning of this chapter, we claimed that Aristotle has a deeper challenge to peace than many contemporary thinkers because of his idea that people should be friends with one another, whereas contemporary accounts rarely go further than a call for tolerance, mutual restraint, or justice. We now would like to claim that Aristotle's end point of mutual respect and love (philia) does not go quite far enough. Three points are needed to move the Aristotelian end point to a more accurately moral conclusion

First, his concept of friendship based on mutual respect is underdeveloped because it is unconditional only to a point. For Aristotle, one is friends with another because that other person is good. Although this may seem like a conditional rather than an unconditional statement, we think that it is more akin to an unconditional concept because, once the other obtains goodness, it is more like a settled disposition (*hexis*), and thus the friend is unlikely to stray from the goodness. Thus, for Aristotle, one offers good will to another because he or she is also the bearer of good will. Kant extended this idea with his claim that we have good will toward another because he or she is *capable* of good will. Forgiveness challenges us to extend good will even further to *unconditionality*, to love those who may be incapable of good will at the present time. Our goal, like Aristotle's, is mutual friendship, but a citizen of the city should consider extending love, in the form of unconditional forgiveness, even to the unlovable. This would include enemies from different communities who have fought one another, as is the case in Belfast. Forgiveness has a way of breaking cycles of resentment, which in turn may break cycles of violence.

Second, friendship itself needs to be redefined in light of our current knowledge of forgiveness and love. Perhaps we should not see friendship as the mutual exchange of philia, a natural form of love because all to whom it is offered are lovable, and instead see love as the univocal gift of agape in the hope of a mutual exchange of that agape. Love, in other words, begets love in return. The love extended in agape is service love, not so natural as philia, *storge*, or eros, and thus more difficult and challenging.

Third, agape, unconditionally expressed by individuals, creates one more problem for the Aristotelian program. He placed the whole (in this case, the city) as more important than the parts (in this case, the citizens). For Aristotle, the parts derive their meaning, their very identity, from the whole. Yet as we have argued, the individual's unconditional expression of agape can give the community its distinctive character in the expression of friendship. Therefore, the individual (the parts) primarily (but not exclusively because we do not wish to engage in either-or thinking) determines the character of the whole (the city) and not the reverse. The primacy of the individual is evident in the free choice of each person to either act lovingly or not, to act in a forgiving way or not. Educating the citizens for goodness takes on even more importance, we think, with this model because without good training, good citizens are not developed. Without good citizens the character of the city is at risk, which further puts the citizens at risk. If the children of Belfast are not exposed to the concept of agape and allowed to choose to appropriate it toward members of the out-group, then what kind of a city will the children build when it is their turn to lead?

This new concept of friendship as agape more than philia seems to be consistent with Aristotle's teaching that we must set the target as high and as truthfully as we can so that we might eventually hit it. We contend that some people at some point in the peace process will have to bear the pain of injustice, that is, exercise agape prior to such an overture from the other side. Such moral action is a way to stop the cycle of revenge and be a conduit of good for subsequent generations.[31] The idea of bearing the pain is a difficult concept because it asks people to suffer on others' behalf with no apparent payoff for the sufferer. The practical question is how many in a given community will deepen their idea of love and friendship to include unconditional suffering for the good of the "enemy." What might happen in Belfast if teachers, parents, and students took this idea of bearing the pain seriously enough to apply it in a practical peacebuilding strategy? The possibility of civic friendship seems much more concrete and attainable if the students can learn and practice bearing the pain through agape.

Interlude

To summarize, the children of Belfast are angry. Friendship in communities needs to be a target, even if seen as a high and difficult target, because without it, societies are at risk for the development of toxic anger, factions, and stereotyping. Social science has convincingly shown the deleterious effects of toxic anger. When such toxic anger rises in individual hearts, forgiveness is a powerful antidote. Social science certainly does suggest this on the individual and small relational level. We know what happens in control groups where participants have not yet had the opportunity to practice forgiveness: anger usually remains or can escalate. Thus, one necessity for correcting the extremes of toxic anger is forgiveness, properly understood and practiced. If anger reduction through forgiveness can be appropriated accurately and over time in Belfast, might this contribute a powerful strategy to the peacebuilding process?

Forgiveness Education with Children in Belfast

If forgiveness therapy with adults is effective in reducing anger and improving emotional and relational health, might it be the case that helping children learn about forgiveness is an effective deterrent to toxic anger at the present time and eventually in adulthood? If many children in a war-torn community such as Belfast learn about forgiveness and learn to practice it well, might this have an impact on the relational health of that community? If children learn at an early age that all people have inherent worth, might this form the basis of reducing negative stereotypes of others who have formed factions in the society? Might such knowledge of others' inherent worth form the basis of an emerging friendship where before there were only factions? And might not such friendships contribute to a sustainable peace settlement?

In 2002, we thought it important to begin answering some of these questions. We operated from the following assumptions.

1. Children should learn forgiveness slowly and in an atmosphere of interest and fun. After all, if a coach wishes to develop, say, soccer skills in children, does he or she drill them until they lose their taste for the sport, or does the coach start slowly with a bit of fun to show to the children the beauty of the sport?

2. We need to create curricula based on developmental psychology principles so that the early grades get a more simplified version and the later grades get an increasingly more subtle and challenging view of the virtue of forgiveness.

3. We need to create a curriculum guide so that the children's classroom teacher can rather easily deliver the lessons in an effective manner.

4. If we can create useful teaching tools from the earliest to the latest grades, then students who have had forgiveness education for many years may more naturally appropriate forgiveness when faced with injustice. Such students may be less likely to confuse forgiveness with condoning or excusing, forgetting, or reconciling.

5. Ours is not a quick fix, thus rendering it instantly unpopular. We suspect that it will take two generations of students going through ten to twelve years of schooling in forgiveness before a community impact is realized from this effort. Yet what is twenty years compared with sectarian strife that can and does last for centuries?

6. As more students implement forgiveness and continue to do so into adulthood, the normative social relations within that community may begin to alter toward more positive interactions. In other words, the

quality of justice sought should shift to a wiser justice with a more satisfying outcome than usually is the case within societies divided by factions hostile toward one another. Of course, we do not expect a utopia, but we are expecting a shift in civility and perhaps even in friendship in some sectors of society.

As a postscript to this section, we are well aware of existing educational and community based programs designed to foster mutual understanding between and among factions in Northern Ireland. One of the most widely used social and peace education programs for children in Northern Ireland is Education for Mutual Understanding (EMU). The Education Reform Order of 1989 promoted programs such as EMU to "encourage respect for self and others, the building of relationships, and understanding of conflict" and other themes associated with peace and reconciliation.[32] However, as early as 1990, the mandatory EMU curriculum had received considerable scrutiny and criticism from teachers and scholars who argued that it lacked a strong conceptual framework, did not address the deeper issues of intergroup conflict, and provided insufficient training for teachers.[33]

Forgiveness education directly addresses several of the criticisms levied against existing educational programs such as EMU. First, without forgiveness being a deliberate and deep part of such endeavors, the curricula are basically attempts to change minds and not primarily change hearts. We do not think it possible to create friendships through the intellect, through understanding primarily. In our case, the exercises of helping children use their cognitive schema of unconditionality to foster the insight of inherent worth of all people are only the starting point for a softened heart. Second, such curricular efforts must be persistent, involving an intensive learning experience in any given academic year. Having children from each side get together a few times a year is wonderful, but not sufficient. Having the children hear about forgiveness for a lesson or two and then galloping off to other concepts is not sufficient. Third, the forgiveness and friendship learning need to take place over time, as we have stated here, over generations.

It is important to also acknowledge the intentional, interdenominational communities throughout Northern Ireland, such as the Corrymeela Community, the Christian Renewal Center, and the Columbanus Community of reconciliation, that continue to espouse forgiveness as a way to promote peace and reconciliation.[34] These communities provide a powerful lived example of intergroup harmony, and their commitment to the political and social aspects of forgiveness is an integral component for sustained peace in Northern Ireland. Current forgiveness education in Northern Ireland extends this important work to young children—the future parents, neighbors, and leaders in the country—and joins these communities in acknowledging that sincere friendship is a powerful outcome of interpersonal forgiveness. Forgiveness education for young children, in tandem with interreligious and cross-community programs, represent a unique response to the challenge "to create a culture of forgiveness."[35]

We now turn to a description of one of the curricula, in this case the second grade curriculum, as an example of what happens within the Belfast schools.

Example of the Second-Grade (Primary 4 in Belfast) Curriculum

A seventeen-lesson curriculum guide for teachers of second-grade children was written by a licensed psychologist and a developmental psychologist.[36] Each lesson takes approximately forty-five minutes or less and occurs approximately once per week for the entire class. Additional activities in the guide are provided if a teacher wishes to extend the learning.

In the early years of the program, the teachers were introduced to the ideas of forgiveness and the curricular materials in a workshop directed by the authors of the curriculum or others associated with the project. We envision other methods as the work expands. Audio recordings of the workshop, for example, may become available for download.

Forgiveness is taught by the classroom teachers primarily through the medium of story. Through stories such as Disney's *The Fox and the Hound*, *Cinderella*, *Dumbo*, and *Snow White*, the children learn that conflicts arise and we have a wide range of options to respond to unfair treatment. The curriculum guide is divided into three parts. First, the teacher introduces central concepts that underlie forgiveness—such as the inherent worth of all people, kindness, respect, generosity, and moral love—without mentioning the word *forgiveness*. In part two, the children hear stories in which characters display instances of inherent worth, kindness, respect, generosity, and moral love—or their opposites, such as unkindness, disrespect, and stinginess—toward another character who was unjust. In part three, the teacher helps the children, if they choose, apply the five principles toward a person who has hurt them.

Throughout the implementation of this program, teachers make the important distinction between *learning* about forgiveness and *choosing to practice* it in certain contexts. The program is careful to emphasize the distinction between forgiveness and reconciliation. A child does not reconcile with someone who is potentially harmful, for example. The teachers impress on the children that the exercises in part three are not necessary but completely optional.

The first-grade curriculum is similar, with the exception of the choice of stories. In first grade, the centerpiece stories are from Dr. Seuss.

The Curriculum in Subsequent Grade Levels

In grade 3 (primary 5) the focus is more deliberately on the concept of agape. By grade 5 (primary 7), the curriculum challenges the students to consider not only the theme of forgiving but also the themes of seeking to be forgiven and receiving forgiveness. By secondary school, the students will be asked to develop a deep understanding of friendship and how forgiveness can play a part in fostering it. By later secondary school, the students will be challenged to bring their learning into their community for the purpose of healing misunderstanding, prejudices, and hatred that have grown and established themselves over centuries. The students, of course, will be taught the virtue of temperance, the golden mean that any one person is limited and can only do so much. It is the addition of others like themselves, those helping foster forgiveness and friendship, who can make an impact on the community.

What Has Been Accomplished in the Belfast Schools

In 2002, we started forgiveness education with thirty-six children in three classrooms on the primary 3 (ages six to seven) level. In 2006–2007, teachers were delivering the forgiveness curriculum to over 1,800 students in seventy-five classrooms in Belfast. The program, in other words, grew very rapidly as we added new schools and new grade levels within schools. The preliminary research with classrooms randomized to the experimental (forgiveness education) or control (no forgiveness education until the next year) groups has shown a statistically significant decrease in anger and psychological depression favoring the students in the experimental groups.[37] The children tend to come into the program with anger that approaches the clinical (psychologically unhealthy) level. After the program, the children's level of anger begins to fall toward more normal levels.

We have the technology in place to train teachers in the art of forgiveness. We have teacher curriculum guides that the teachers find easy to use. We have feedback from teachers that the curriculum is fun for the children, relatively easy to implement, and produces excellent results from the teachers' viewpoint. One important piece of evidence that educators value the forgiveness curriculum is this: no teacher who has begun the program has stopped teaching it in subsequent years. The social scientific findings are consonant with the teachers' reports.

Skepticism toward Our Approach

Throughout our twenty-two years of studying forgiveness, we have found that some people consider the act of forgiving to be useless at the least and quite dangerous at the other extreme. Now that we are linking forgiveness to community peace efforts, we suspect that greater controversy will ensue. Our purpose here is to address three kinds of criticism: (1) that leveled at forgiveness itself, (2) that leveled at friendship as a basis of a good community, and (3) that leveled at the interaction of forgiveness and community friendship. We start with forgiveness itself.

Skeptical Views of the Concept of Forgiveness and Its Education

Perhaps we are in denial, but it is our firm conviction that every criticism we have ever heard against the concept of forgiveness has emanated from a misunderstanding of what forgiveness is or what it accomplishes. We consider five such skeptical views here.

1. *Forgiveness as inappropriate: education in our war-torn community will turn my son into a wimp. He needs to know how to fight.* We received this criticism

from a very concerned father who served in a paramilitary army. We suggested two new ways to consider forgiveness. First, his son will be part of a classroom effort. He will not be the only learner, thus he is not likely to be singled out as a wimp. Second, forgiveness education teaches the quest for justice along with forgiveness, lessening the chance that practicing mercy alone will make his son vulnerable. The father accepted these arguments as reasonable, after a heated two-hour debate, and allowed our entrance into his neighborhood for the purpose of training teachers in the art of forgiveness.

2. *Forgiveness as immoral: forgiveness thwarts justice because of its emphasis on mercy.* Aristotle challenged us all not to practice any virtue in isolation. Mercy needs justice to ensure fairness, and justice needs mercy to temper its demands. If we think of forgiveness as a gift given with good intent to a wrongdoer, we can see that the virtue is not immoral.

3. *Forgiveness as dangerous: if my child forgives, he or she will be vulnerable to the bullies in school.* Forgiveness and reconciliation are not the same. A child can consider forgiving the bully and then watch his or her back (and report the bully to school personnel). In other words, a child is free to offer the gift of forgiveness whenever he or she chooses; reconciliation would come when the injuring party recognizes the wrongdoing and takes steps for genuine change.

4. *Forgiveness as weakness: forgiveness is for those who are inferior and cannot assert their rights in a powerful way.* This is Nietzsche's challenge to those who study and practice forgiveness. We think that this view is flawed because it fails to acknowledge the courage necessary to forgive in the face of deep emotional pain and injustice. When we realize that a forgiving person can and should seek justice, the criticism seems to lose its strength.

5. *Forgiveness education as brain-washing: forgiveness education is a form of indoctrination and should be avoided.* We dissent from this view for three reasons. First, moral education has a history going back thousands of years. It is not moral education per se, but how the teachers convey the knowledge may be central to the criticism. Our programs employ the children's actual classroom teachers, who know well those children's religious beliefs, cultural norms, and ethnic customs, thus avoiding indoctrination. Second, does genuine forgiveness bind a forgiver (and the forgiven) in autocratic slavery or set him or her free? We leave the answer to the reader. Third, if we know that we have something good to impart to children, and try to impart it with good educational approaches, who is the unconstructive one, the teacher or the one discouraging or preventing the teaching?

Our addressing the skeptics of forgiveness is only part of the equation. We now turn to those who criticize friendship as a central basis for good communities.

Skeptical View on Friendship as a Necessary Condition for Good Communities

1. *Politics is the art of the possible. Character building puts a restraint on the possible and therefore a focus on friendship and virtue is not practical.* It was Machiavelli who claimed that politics is the art of the possible, deemphasizing virtue. Here

is one example of how far his philosophy took him from virtue. In his most famous work, *The Prince*, Machiavelli instructs princes not to keep faith with men because they will not keep faith with him. Here is why we should question the assertion: he seemed to pride himself on observing history and contemporary society in a sort of scientifically accurate way. Yet he never showed one instance of a successful society that was based deliberately on mistrust.

2. *The greatest power causes the greatest changes. Virtue, with its emphasis on temperance, or the golden mean, may thwart power.* This argument asserts that virtues, including forgiveness, may get in the way of positive social change. We would like the reader to consider, however, whether power by itself is actually a desirable quality for communities. Power, like wealth, can be used for either moral or immoral ends. Thus, those who possess either power or wealth need virtues, like forgiveness, to temper excessive expressions of power and guide them, lest they degenerate into the immoral.

3. *To define the city as an affiliation of partnerships toward mutual sharing in the good life is too restrictive. People may come together for any number of reasons that please them.* This view confuses a given person's opinion about the city and its ultimate purpose. Even if a person uses the city for personal convenience, it does not follow that this is its ultimate purpose. For example, a scholar may say that her chair is a place on which books should be stacked, even though its ultimate purpose is a place on which to sit. The good life is achieved by friendship within and among partnerships.

4. *Even if the city's ultimate purpose is the good life, it can be the individual pursuit of that life rather than a partnership of friends.* The good life by definition is interactive, including others besides the self. If a community has a history of misunderstanding, it becomes all the more necessary to have an emphasis on peacebuilding, with forgiveness being a bridge between the difficulties of the past and current social reconstruction.

5. *Even if the city's ultimate purpose includes partnerships, it need not follow that a partnership of partnerships is required. After all, we all have partnerships in families, places of employment and worship.* Those partnerships, as Aristotle suggests, may not realize justice unless all work together under the law to achieve that justice. A focus on group-to-group forgiveness may make the quest for and the realization of justice more likely primarily because those who are less angry may see more clearly to the fair solutions.[38]

Skeptical Views of the Interplay of Forgiveness and Friendship

1. *Even if friendship as partnerships is one of a city's endpoints, it does not follow that forgiveness is involved. After all, people can practice restraint and tolerance without forgiveness.* Even if people can get along without forgiveness, they may find it difficult to conquer anger without forgiveness when injustices are deep and long-lasting in a society. Restraint and tolerance may still include anger brewing beneath the surface that can easily surface at the hint of further unfairness. Even if the necessity of forgiveness is not established in communities, it is a powerful resource for fostering restraint and tolerance.

2. *There is no such thing as group forgiveness. Thus, forgiveness as part of a partnership of partnerships is unrealistic.* Philosopher Trudy Govier makes the philosophical argument that societies can seem to be angry and revengeful.[39] They possess a certain negative affective and behaviorally normative quality to them. Why do we presume that societies are only capable of possessing *negative* qualities and not that they can possess *positive* normative qualities such as forgiveness and mercy? For Govier, then, group forgiveness can be a reality. We take a subtly different but related view. In our view, the community norms of forgiveness and mercy may emerge when a significant number of the citizens understand, appreciate, and practice those virtues. Let us be clear. We are not presuming that just as an individual can forgive, a community can forgive. Instead, we are arguing that as more and more people appreciate and practice forgiveness, then forgiveness as a norm is more likely to emerge in that community.

3. *Even if societies can possess merciful qualities, how realistic is this to expect? Most people probably can give examples of revengeful societies, but can any of us describe an actual society that deliberately cultivates friendship, mercy, and forgiveness?* The Truth and Reconciliation Commission in South Africa is one encouraging example of the morally possible being implemented for good.[40] Even though that bold social experiment has not yet led to completely satisfying outcomes, it stands as a pioneering model of what can occur within societies beset by violence.[41]

Our forgiveness education model now has underlying psychological theory to explain why it should work, teacher curriculum manuals, a workshop training program that teachers find useful, scientific evidence that the programs are effective in reducing anger in children, and a technology for offering this approach to teachers within many communities. Forgiveness is an ideal, but it is also a part of practical politics.

4. *Aristotle suggested that friendship is fostered by the virtue of love. His conception of love was of the natural kind, philia.* Forgiveness involves what C. S. Lewis would call a higher form of love, agape.[42] It seems irrational to advocate the cultivation of a higher form (a form perhaps more difficult to attain) to foster a lower form of love. This would be true only if we adhered to Aristotle's conception of love. Yet we have already redefined friendship to incorporate and accommodate agape. Thus, we are advocating the development of agape in individual children so that as adults they can apply that agape to community partnerships.

5. *Even if forgiveness can be a tool for fostering friendship within communities, it seems to be useful only in extreme cases, such as societies at war for years or generations, because of its emphasis on deep anger borne out of severe injustice.* Although it is true that the most recent forgiveness efforts have centered on violent and impoverished communities, why should we expect that a harmonious society will not suffer injustices of an unexpected kind in the future? Forgiveness education for societal friendship may act to prevent the creation of societal factions and as an incentive to perhaps enrich existing friendships. After all, even the best of friends disappoint one another at times.

6.   *Isn't your approach simply a traditionally conservative one that blames the victim, places the burden of recovery on that victim, and ignores social programming?* The accusation seems to be taking the either-or form of thinking rather than the both-and approach that we advocated earlier in the chapter. Just as it would be extreme and unwarranted to focus exclusively on character development of citizens, it is equally extreme and unwarranted to think that social ethics and programming will solve all social ills. Our model is motivated by what we as psychologists can bring and by the rarity of focus on virtue ethics among scholars and practitioners of peacebuilding.

The Final Question

What is the end point for the program described here? The practice of forgiveness and friendship, as Aquinas reminds us in his *Summa*, are not the final ends because virtues are more like the arrows that move toward a target; they are not the target itself. The virtues in this case are means to the end of peaceful relationships, within the realization that this is a fallen world and so peace must be taken in its reasonable, realistic sense. As Aquinas further reminds us, the ultimate end point is not only peaceful relations with others but also happiness with God. Given that both sides of the conflict within Belfast are Christian, then this Thomistic end point is not unreasonable. Perhaps one of our next essays will center on Thomas Merton's wisdom: we are not at peace with others because we are not at peace within ourselves (anger, unforgiveness); we are not at peace within ourselves because we are not at peace with God.

The Final Challenge

We applaud those courageous peace workers who strive for better laws, an equitable distribution of goods, a valid verification of weapons, and all that can make for peace. Our essay here is not meant to foster either-or thinking but to encourage both-and thinking and action. Because our approach is not a sufficient condition for peace, neither are the social ethics and public policy approaches sufficient for a lasting peace if members of communities remain wounded and bitter.

We are not offering a new approach here, but a very old one, as the ideas of community friendship and forgiveness are of ancient origin. What is new is a reawakening to the potential of these two ideas and their association within war-torn communities.

In the *Nicomachean Ethics*, Aristotle states that to be just is not enough. Communities need friendship.[43] If a basis of peace is friendship, then a basis of friendship is the growth in virtue. A central virtue that may foster friendship and therefore community peace is forgiveness, perhaps a necessary but not a sufficient condition for a stable peace. Postaccord societies need forgiveness in particular to counter years of toxic anger and make friendship a reality.

NOTES

1. Petersen, Roger Dale. 2002. *Understanding Ethnic Violence: Fear, Hatred, and Resentment in Twentieth-Century Eastern Europe,* Cambridge Studies in Comparative Politics. Cambridge: Cambridge University Press.

2. Kaufman, Stuart J. 2001. *Modern Hatreds: The Symbolic Politics of Ethnic War,* Cornell Studies in Security Affairs. Ithaca, N.Y.: Cornell University Press.

3. For further information on the history of the Troubles, consult the following sources: Cairns, Ed, and John Darby. 1998. "The Conflict in Northern Ireland: Causes, Consequences, and Controls." *American Psychologist* 53, no. 7: 754–760; Darby, John. "Conflict in Northern Ireland: A Background Essay." In *Facets of the Conflict in Northern Ireland,* edited by Seamus Dunn. New York: St. Martin's Press, 1995; Muldoon, Orla T. 2004. "Children of the Troubles: The Impact of Political Violence in Northern Ireland." *Journal of Social Issues* 60, no. 3: 453–468; and Power, P. C., and S. Duffy. *Timetables of Irish History.* London: Worth Press, 2001.

4. Darby, "Conflict in Northern Ireland: A Background Essay."

5. Fay, Marie-Therese, Mike Morrissey, and Marie Smyth. *Northern Ireland's Troubles: The Human Costs,* Contemporary Irish Studies. London: Pluto Press in association with the Cost of the Troubles Study, 1999.

6. The agreement is also known as the Good Friday Agreement or Belfast Agreement. It may be found at www.nio.gov.uk/the-agreement.

7. The Agreement at St. Andrews may be found at www.standrewsagreement.org.

8. The Thirteenth Report of the Monitoring Commission may be found at www.independentmonitoringcommission.org/documents/uploads/thirteenth%report.pdf.

9. Gallagher, Tony. 2004. "After the War Comes Peace? An Examination of the Impact of the Northern Ireland Conflict on Young People." *Journal of Social Issues* 60, no. 3: 637.

10. Darby, John, and Roger Mac Ginty. *The Management of Peace Processes, Ethnic and Intercommunity Conflict Series.* New York: St. Martin's Press, 2000; Jarman, Neil. 2004 "Demography, Development and Disorder: Changing Patterns of Interface Areas." Belfast: Institute for Conflict Research; and Jarman, Neil. 1999. *Displaying Faith: Orange, Green and Trade Union Banners in Northern Ireland.* Belfast: Institute of Irish Studies Queen's University of Belfast.

11. For a review of the impact of the Troubles on children, consult the following sources: Cairns and Darby, "The Conflict in Northern Ireland"; Connolly, P., A. Smith, and B. Kelly. 2002. *Too Young to Notice: The Cultural and Political Awareness of 3–6 Year Olds in Northern Ireland.* Belfast: Community Relations Council; Conroy, John. *Belfast Diary: War as a Way of Life.* Boston: Beacon Press, 1987; Gallagher, "After the War Comes Peace?"; McClenahan, Carol, Ed Cairns, Seamus Dunn, and Valerie Morgan. 1996. "Intergroup Friendships: Integrated and Desegregated Schools in Northern Ireland." *Journal of Social Psychology* 136, no. 5: 549–558; Muldoon, "Children of the Troubles"; Muldoon, Orla T., Karen Trew, and Rosemary Kilpatrick. 2000. "The Legacy of the Troubles on the Young People's Psychological and Social Development and Their School Life." *Youth & Society* 32, no. 1: 6–28; and Trew, Karen. 2004. "Children and Socio-Cultural Divisions in Northern Ireland." *Journal of Social Issues* 60, no. 3: 507–522.

12. This text provides a contemporary account of youth involvement in peace processes. McEvoy-Levy, Siobhán, Joan B. Kroc Institute for International Peace Studies, RIREC Project on Post-Accord Peace Building, and Research Initiative on the Resolution of Ethnic Conflict. 2006. *Troublemakers or Peacemakers?: Youth and Post-Accord Peace Building.* Notre Dame, Ind.: University of Notre Dame Press.

13. Enright, Robert D., Jeanette A. Knutson Enright, Anthony C. Holter, Thomas W. Baskin, and Casey Knutson. 2007. "Waging Peace through Forgiveness in Belfast, Northern Ireland II: Educational Programs for Mental Health Improvement of Children." *Journal of Research in Education* 17: 63–78; Enright, Robert D., Jeanette A. Knutson Enright, Anthony C. Holter, Thomas W. Baskin, and Casey Knutson. 2008. "Waging Peace through Forgiveness in Belfast, Northern Ireland III: Correcting a Production Error and a Case Study." *Journal of Research in Education* 18: 128–131.

14. For an overview of scholarly work pertaining to civic friendship, consult the following sources: Schollmeier, Paul. 1994. *Other Selves: Aristotle on Personal and Political Friendship*, SUNY Series in Ethical Theory. Albany: State University of New York Press; and Scorza, Jason A. 2004. "Liberal Citizenship and Civic Friendship." *Political Theory* 32, no. 1: 85–108.

15. Budziszewski, J. 1997. *Written on the Heart: The Case for Natural Law*. Downers Grove, Ill.: InterVarsity Press.

16. Quotation marks around "relative to us" emphasize that for Aristotle, the expression of virtue is rarely perfect and that different people demonstrate different degrees of that virtue. See, for example, Simon, Yves René Marie, and Vukan Kuic. 1986. *The Definition of Moral Virtue*. New York: Fordham University Press.

17. We say this with some trepidation, knowing full well that relativist models pervade the academy at present. We consider relativist models to be a passing fancy because of the self-contradictions, which are beyond the purview of this chapter, that exist within them.

18. Galston, William A. 2002. *Liberal Pluralism: The Implications of Value Pluralism for Political Theory and Practice*. Cambridge: Cambridge University Press.

19. The term "golden mean" was not originally Aristotle's term, but is now attributed to him.

20. Foley, Debra L., David B. Goldston, E. Jane Costello, and Adrian Angold. 2006. "Proximal Psychiatric Risk Factors for Suicidality in Youth: The Great Smoky Mountains Study." *Archives of General Psychiatry* 63, no. 9: 1017–1024.

21. Greene, Ross W., and Robert T. Ammerman. 2006. "Oppositional Defiant Disorder." In *Comprehensive Handbook of Personality and Psychopathology*, Vol. 3, 285–298: New York: Wiley.

22. Marshal, Michael P., and Brooke S. G. Molina. 2006. "Antisocial Behaviors Moderate the Deviant Peer Pathway to Substance Use in Children with ADHD." *Journal of Clinical Child and Adolescent Psychology* 35, no. 2: 216–226.

23. Malta, Loretta S., Edward B. Blanchard, and Brian M. Freidenberg. 2005. "Psychiatric and Behavioral Problems in Aggressive Drivers." *Behaviour Research and Therapy* 43, no. 11: 1467–1484.

24. Enright, Robert D., and Richard P. Fitzgibbons. 2000. *Helping Clients Forgive: An Empirical Guide for Resolving Anger and Restoring Hope* Washington, D.C.: American Psychological Association.

25. Barcalow, Kelly. 2006. "Oppositional Defiant Disorder: Information for School Nurses." *Journal of School Nursing* 22, no. 1: 9–16.

26. For a more thorough review of the literature, see Enright and Fitzgibbons, *Helping Clients Forgive*.

27. Ibid.

28. North, Joanna. 1987. "Wrongdoing and Forgiveness." *Philosophy* 62: 499–508.

29. Holmgren, Margaret R. 1993. "Forgiveness and the Intrinsic Value of Persons." *American Philosophical Quarterly* 30, no. 4: 341; and North, "Wrongdoing and Forgiveness."

30. Enright, Robert D. 1994. "Piaget on the Moral Development of Forgiveness: Identity or Reciprocity?" *Human Development* 37, no. 2: 63–80.

31. For more on bearing the pain, see Bergin, Allen E. 1988. "Three Contributions of a Spiritual Perspective to Counseling, Psychotherapy, and Behavior Change." *Counseling and Values* 33, no. 1: 21–31.

32. Arlow, Michael. 2004. "Citizenship Education in a Divided Society: The Case of Northern Ireland." In *Education, Conflict, and Social Cohesion*, edited by Sobhi Tawil and Alexandra Harley, 255–314. Geneva: UNESCO, 280.

33. For a detailed overview and critique of EMU, see Arlow, "Citizenship Education in a Divided Society"; Smith, Alan, and Alan Robinson. 1996. "Education for Mutual Understanding: The Statutory Years." Coleraine: University of Ulster; Smith, Ron. 2002. "Professional Educational Psychology and Community Relations Education in Northern Ireland." *Educational Psychology in Practice* 18, no. 4: 275–295; and Wright, Frank. "Some Problems with Education for Mutual Understanding." In *Finding Ways to Go: A Discussion Paper about Community Relations in Northern Ireland*. Coleraine: University of Ulster.

34. Wells, Ronald. 1999. *People behind the Peace*. Cambridge: Eerdmans.

35. Ibid., 80.

36. Knutson, Jeanette, and Robert D. Enright. 2003. *Discovering Forgiveness: A Guided Curriculum for Children, Ages 6–8*. Madison, Wisc.: International Forgiveness Institute.

37. Enright, Robert D., et al., "Waging Peace through Forgiveness in Belfast, Northern Ireland II."

38. The final three points in this list are from Budziszewski, *Written on the Heart*.

39. Govier, Trudy. 2002. *Forgiveness and Revenge*. London: Routledge.

40. Tutu, Desmond. 1999. *No Future without Forgiveness*. New York: Doubleday.

41. Van der Walt, Clint, V. Franchi, and Garth Stevens. 2003. "The South African Truth and Reconciliation Commission: 'Race', Historical Compromise and Transitional Democracy." *International Journal of Intercultural Relations* 27, no. 2: 251–267.

42. Lewis, C. S. 1960. *The Four Loves*. New York: Harcourt.

43. Aristotle, and H. Rackham. 1926. *The Nicomachean Ethics*, The Loeb Classical Library. New York: Putnam's, 453.

13

Religion and Peacebuilding

Gerard F. Powers

In *The Mighty and the Almighty*, Madeleine Albright acknowledges that, as U.S. ambassador to the United Nations and secretary of State, she held the conventional view of foreign policy specialists—that religion is not an appropriate or relevant subject for analysis or discussion. According to Albright, "I cannot remember any leading American diplomat (even the born-again Christian Jimmy Carter) speaking in depth about the role of religion in shaping the world."[1]

Albright's experience as a diplomat reflects what could be called the secularist paradigm.[2] According to this paradigm, Western notions of secularization are equated with that which is "modern," "democratic," and "pluralistic." The cultural and political arrangements in which religion is much more visible and salient—the arrangements that prevail in much of the world—are equated with that which is "premodern," "undemocratic," and "intolerant."[3] As Zbigniew Brzezinski points out, "the prevailing orthodoxy among intellectuals in the West is that religion is a waning, irrational, and dysfunctional aberration."[4] Religion and morality are not—and, more important, should not be—major factors in foreign policy. Joseph Nye and Stanley Hoffmann have noted that because foreign policy tends to focus on the structure of the international system—notably political, economic, and military power relationships—civil society or mass movements have received relatively little attention. Given this relative lack of attention to the "soft power" of "movements from below," the religious influences, which are strongest at this level, often have been missed or underestimated.[5]

Like a growing number of specialists in international affairs, Albright now admits that this secularist paradigm is no longer adequate; understanding international affairs today requires an understanding of religion. In fact, Samuel Huntington's influential thesis that intercivilizational conflicts reflect the new paradigm in international affairs is based in part on his contention that "in the modern world, religion is a central, perhaps *the* central, force that motivates and mobilizes people."[6]

This heightened attention to the public role of religion does not represent a sharp departure from the prevailing orthodoxies of the secularist world-view in one important sense. Religion, according to many, might not be "waning," but it remains mostly irrational and dysfunctional, a source of conflict and division, and a powerful motive force behind exclusivist world views.[7] Al Qaeda's terrorism is exhibit A. Bosnia-Herzegovina, Kosovo, Iraq, Lebanon, Israel-Palestine, Northern Ireland, Afghanistan, Pakistan, Sudan, Kashmir, and Sri Lanka are also cited. The secularists who have long argued that religion has no place in the public square and especially not the foreign ministry would seem to have firm ground on which to build their case.

Not surprisingly, many who specialize in religion have never accepted the descriptive or normative power of the secularist paradigm, with its almost uniformly negative view of the role of religion. In *The Ambivalence of the Sacred*, Scott Appleby contends that the same kind of unwavering, absolute commitment to one's faith, or "religious militancy," that can be a source of division can also be a powerful force for freedom, justice, and liberation.[8] The peaceful revolutions in Eastern Europe; the human rights movement in Latin America; the antiapartheid struggle in South Africa; the downfall of Marcos in the Philippines; the peace process in Colombia, Mozambique, and Uganda; the struggle for freedom in Tibet; and the campaign for democracy in Myanmar are just a few examples of the power of religion at work in the service of justice and peace.

Though there is a growing literature on the positive role of religion in peacebuilding, it deserves more serious consideration, especially by foreign policy specialists.[9] A short article cannot begin to map and analyze the plethora of peacebuilding being done by innumerable faith-based institutions and faith-filled individuals. My task is more limited: to propose several elements of a strategic approach to religious peacebuilding. I first address the inadequacies of the prevailing secularist paradigm. I then discuss the complexity of religious peacebuilding, especially the need to consider religion on its own terms and appreciate the rich set of religious resources that can be mobilized on behalf of peacebuilding. I then examine more closely three critical dimensions of a strategic approach to religious peacebuilding—its inherently public nature; the relationship between nonviolence, just war, and peacebuilding; and the role of ecumenical and inter-religious peacebuilding. Finally, I suggest several implications of this analysis for policy makers.

I approach religious peacebuilding as an academic and a practitioner who has worked on international affairs for more than two decades for and with the huge, diverse, and complex global institution that is the Catholic Church.

Although my analysis reflects my Catholic perspective and experience, I believe it will find resonance with academics and practitioners concerned with religious peacebuilding more generally.

The Inadequacy of the Prevailing Secularist Paradigm

Before elaborating on elements of strategic religious peacebuilding, it is necessary to address the fundamental difference between the secularist view, which sees religion mostly as an atavistic and irrational cause of conflict that should be marginalized and privatized, and those who believe that religion is an underappreciated force for peace that should have a significant role in society. Appleby calls this "weak religion" versus "strong religion."[10]

The secularist paradigm sees religion as a major factor in causing and intensifying conflicts around the world because religion absolutizes and sacralizes differences over issues, leaving little room for compromise. Where religious differences per se are not at issue, religious identity can be a marker of ethnic or national identities that can exacerbate communal divisions and can be easily manipulated by cynical—and often irreligious—political leaders in service of their extremist forms of nationalism. Henry Kissinger, for example, called the 1990s Balkan conflicts "wars of religion" because, he argued, the only difference between the warring parties was religious identity.[11]

Most quantitative studies of religion and conflict focus on these two dimensions of the negative role of religion. They usually distinguish between two kinds of conflicts. In one kind, *religious incompatibility* is a major factor—that is, religious issues are at stake, such as when the primary parties to the conflict make religious claims for control of the state or territory by a religious tradition. In other conflicts, *religious dissimilarity* is a major factor—that is, religious issues are not at stake, but the parties to the conflict are distinguished in part by different religious identities.[12]

These studies suggest that although religion is a factor in a number of conflicts, it is rarely a primary or exclusive factor. One of the most nuanced studies was done by Uppsala University's Department of Peace and Conflict Research. Isak Svensson reports on the incidence of four types of conflicts from 1989 to 2003: (1) 58 percent were conflicts in which religion played no part in either separating the identities of the belligerents or in the claims of the parties to the conflict (e.g., Burundi, Nepal, El Salvador); (2) 20 percent were conflicts in which the parties were separated by a difference in religious identities but without any religious claims at stake (e.g., IRA–British government in Northern Ireland); (3) 11 percent were conflicts between belligerents that belong to the same religious tradition but in which there are religious claims in the conflict (e.g., conflicts among Muslims in Algeria, Egypt, and Indonesia over the religious or secular nature of the state); (4) 11 percent were conflicts where the parties were separated by their religious identities and at least one party made religious claims (e.g., Sri Lanka, Sudan, and Kashmir).[13] In sum, he found that only 22 percent of conflicts involved religious claims. Others have come to similar conclusions.[14] If one looks specifically at terrorism, one also finds that although it is on the rise, religious terrorists make up 36 percent of terrorist groups in the world.[15]

A partial listing of some of the world's bloodiest conflicts of the past century is consistent with these studies. The twentieth century was by far history's bloodiest. The architects of the slaughter of so many millions were men like Adolf Hitler, Joseph Stalin, Pol Pot, Mao Zedong, and Saddam Hussein, none of whom killed in the name of religion; in fact, they were mostly openly hostile toward it. The same could be said of more recent examples—the Democratic Republic of Congo, Burundi, Rwanda, Cambodia, Colombia, Darfur, the wars in Central America in the 1970s and 1980s, and Somalia in the early 1990s.

Even if religious factors do not play a significant role in most conflicts, including some of the most notorious of the past century, are conflicts with a religious dimension more intractable and more violent than other conflicts? Statistical studies differ on this question. Monica Toft found that religious civil wars were nearly twice as likely to recur as nonreligious civil wars, and religious civil wars were four times harder on noncombatants than civil wars in which religion is peripheral.[16] In a review of recent studies, Svensson found conflicting results. Some studies concluded that in international conflicts where religious identity defined the conflicting parties, there was a significant decrease in the likelihood of settlement. Others, however, concluded that the religious identity of the conflicting parties did not affect the likelihood of settlement or the duration of the post-settlement peace. Still others have found that ethnic civil wars fought over religion were less difficult to mediate than wars over secession and autonomy.[17] Svensson's own conclusion, based on the Uppsala Conflict Data Program, is that in civil conflicts differences in religious identities of the parties did not reduce the likelihood of a negotiated settlement, but conflicts in which religious claims were at stake did significantly decrease the chance of a negotiated settlement.[18]

These studies offer useful aggregate indicators of the incidence of and trends in the religious dimensions of conflicts, but they must be complemented with a much more sophisticated qualitative understanding of the role of religion.[19]

First, most of these quantitative studies do not attempt to measure the intensity of religious identity and beliefs. Nor do they offer insights into the complex interaction between religious identity and ethnic, national, racial, class, cultural, gender, and political identities. Amartya Sen reminds us, "The religious partitioning of the world produces a deeply misleading understanding of the people across the world and the diverse relations between them, and it also has the effect of magnifying one particular distinction between one person and another to the exclusion of all other important concerns."[20]

Second, it is important to avoid the monolithic, undifferentiated, and functionalist approach to religion that is so often associated with the secularist paradigm, and is sometimes reflected in statistical studies of religious conflict. In conflicts with a religious dimension, religious traditions are not equally implicated. Toft's study of civil wars distinguished among the major religious traditions. She found that when religion is a central factor in a conflict, Islam is the religion most likely to be involved. Gurr's earlier study of ethnic conflicts came to the same conclusion.[21]

These aggregate findings are useful in identifying global differences among major religious traditions and the incidence of conflict. They do not, however, purport to track or analyze differences within particular religious traditions. They also fail to disaggregate religious influences in particular conflicts, and therefore cannot account for the positive versus negative roles that religion plays in those conflicts. Statistical studies correctly identify religion as a dimension of the conflict in Iraq, for example, but they do not provide insight into the very different roles played by the followers of Shiite Grand Ayatollah Ali al-Sistani and the followers of his Shiite antagonist, Muqtada al-Sadr. Statistical studies also cannot adequately take into account nonreligious factors, such as long-standing clan rivalries, that explain why different Shiite groups fight each other in Iraq. In virtually every conflict where religion plays a role, it is a complex, variegated factor, with some religious elements playing negative roles, some positive, and some both.[22]

Northern Ireland, frequently described as a religious conflict, is a case in point. The strident sectarianism of the Reverend Ian Paisley and the Orange Order are one part of the religious collage, but so is the reconciling leadership of the Reverend John Dunlop, former moderator of the Presbyterian Church. That collage includes the "Catholic" Provisional IRA, whose motive force was never Catholicism and whose desired end was a socialist (not Catholic) Ireland, as well as the Catholic bishops, who are known for their condemnations of IRA violence.[23]

Another problem with the studies of religion and conflict is that they have mostly not included cases, such as Colombia, El Salvador, and northern Uganda, where religion might not be a factor in the conflict but plays an important role in peacebuilding.

If the role of religion in conflict is much more complex and variegated than the secularists acknowledge and statistical studies can map, then the relevant distinction is not between religious conflicts and other conflicts but between those religious actors who play a negative role in a conflict and those who play a positive one—between extremists and nonextremists.[24] The challenge, then, is to marginalize religious extremists, not religion. Especially where religious extremism is a central factor in a conflict, it is all the more important that there be authentic religious alternatives that can counter the extremists from within their own tradition. Promoting an uncompromising Western secularism as a solution to religious extremism can have the unintended effect of feeding extremism by further threatening traditional sources of personal, cultural, and religious identity. Contra the secularists, the best way to counter extremist religion is with more authentic religion, not less or weakened or privatized religion.[25]

From a sociological perspective, this distinction between extremist and nonextremist, or authentic and inauthentic religion, is problematic, because there is no objective way to distinguish among such actors, all of whom might be motivated by or pressing what they believe to be "authentic" religious claims. From a strategic peacebuilding perspective, however, this distinction is crucial. It reminds us that an adequate understanding of the role of religion in conflict requires an understanding of the internal dynamics of the ongoing development of doctrine, norms, and religious practices within diverse religious traditions—and a willingness to make subjective judgments about which doctrines, norms, and practices contribute to peacebuilding and which do not. Both Osama bin Laden and Ayatollah al-Sistani claim to represent "authentic" interpretations of Islam. That does not mean that both interpretations are equally legitimate or have equal saliency within lived Islam. Although it would be naive to expect universal assent to any one interpretation of Islam, it is possible to sort out these competing interpretations through theological and moral argumentation, just as it is possible to distinguish between legitimate and illegitimate interpretations of constitutional law or legitimate and illegitimate governments.

Strategic peacebuilding insists that we go much deeper than quantitative measures of religion's role in conflict, that we avoid treating religion as an easily categorizable monolith, and that we understand both the negative and positive roles of religion in conflict and peacebuilding. Strategic peacebuilding gives priority to qualitative analyses that take seriously pluralism within and among religious traditions as well as the complex qualitative factors that contribute to either conflict or peace in particular cases. Strategic peacebuilding makes a normative judgment that a political scientist or sociologist of religion might not be willing to make: that an interpretation of a religious tradition or certain religious practices that promote violence and injustice are "inauthentic," whereas those that are a force for peace and justice are "authentic."[26]

The Complexity of Religious Peacebuilding

To avoid some of the weaknesses of the secularist critique of religion's role in conflict, it is essential that religious peacebuilding be evaluated on its own terms and in all its complexity.

Defining Religion and Strategic Peacebuilding

Because there is little agreement in the literature on terminology or definitions, let me briefly define my terms. Religion, according to Appleby, can be defined simply as "the human response to a reality perceived as sacred."[27] Religious actors, in turn, can be defined as "people who have been formed by a religious community and who are acting with the intent to uphold, extend, or defend its values and precepts."[28] Religious peacebuilding includes, therefore, the beliefs, norms, and rituals that pertain to peacebuilding, as well as a range of actors, from religious institutions, faith-based private voluntary organizations that are not formally part of a religious institution, and individuals and groups for whom religion is a significant motivation for their peacebuilding. For example, Catholic peacebuilding requires an analysis of a billion-strong, complex, and diverse community that consists of multiple actors, from the pope and bishops to countless priests, women religious and lay people; from more than a hundred national episcopal conferences to thousands of dioceses and well over a hundred thousand parishes; from vast social service, health care, social action, and educational systems to a multiplicity of lay organizations and movements.[29]

Peacebuilding can be defined quite broadly as everything implied by a robust, positive understanding of a just peace. Alternatively, it can be defined more narrowly as an approach to healing broken societies, or, even more narrowly, as a set of nonviolent methods of dealing with conflict, from mediation and interfaith dialogue to relationship building and reconciliation programs. As Lederach and Appleby point out in chapter 1, strategic peacebuilding encompasses the broader definition:

> [It] nurtures constructive human relationships. To be relevant, it must do so strategically, at every level of society and across the potentially polarizing lines of ethnicity, class, religion, and race. . . . It focuses on transforming inhumane social patterns, flawed structural conditions, and open violent conflict that weaken the conditions necessary for a flourishing human community.[30]

Faith-based peacebuilding intervenes in these various stages of conflict through a broad array of roles and activities at the local, national, and international levels. Adapting typologies proposed by Lederach and Sampson, David Steele groups these roles into four types: observation and witness (e.g., fact finding, monitoring of cease-fires, accompaniment of victims), education and formation (e.g., conflict resolution training, education on peace and justice issues, faith formation in vocation of peacebuilding), advocacy and empowerment (e.g., mass protests, efforts to change specific public policies, incorporating peacebuilding in development programs), and conciliation and mediation (e.g., participation in truth and reconciliation commissions, facilitating peace processes, interfaith dialogues).[31] Because it involves multiple stages of conflict and multiple roles and activities, peacebuilding also involves multiple time horizons: before ceasefires and regime changes, during the conflict itself, the immediate aftermath, and the often decades-long process of reconstruction and reconciliation after the violence ends.[32]

Evaluating Religious Peacebuilding on Its Own Terms

Analyzing peacebuilding, broadly defined, in conflict situations with multiple security, political, economic, and cultural dimensions is a challenge. Adding religion to the mix further complicates the task. First, and most obvious, is the fact that there are countless religious traditions, and these traditions, themselves, are by no means monolithic. They differ remarkably in size, organizational structure, geographic reach, and the sophistication, content, and style of their teaching and action on social, political, economic, and other issues related to peacebuilding.

Second, in some respects it is valid to use standard metrics applied to political actors or transnational social movements to analyze religious peacebuilding. In other respects, it is not valid. Religious entities work on peacebuilding programs and issues, but their essential mission and identity are not defined in terms of those issues and programs, as is the case with secular nongovernmental organizations (NGOs). Religious bodies often have millions of members, but they are not membership organizations like Amnesty International or MoveOn. Religious bodies have rich intellectual traditions, but they are not think-tanks like the U.S. Institute of Peace or the International Crisis Group. Religious peacebuilding often involves distinctively religious and spiritual resources—such as ritual, prayer, and spiritual healing—that are not part of a secular NGO's peacebuilding portfolio and cannot be analyzed and measured with standard tools of sociology and political science.

The most important distinction between religious and other civil society actors is the mission and self-understanding of religious bodies *qua* religious bodies. Religious peacebuilding, whether done by individuals or institutions, is motivated and shaped by deeply held religious beliefs and has a stature and credibility that is derived, in large part, from religious identity. Therefore, any analysis of religious peacebuilding must go beyond a functionalist approach that focuses primarily on its political efficacy and understand it in the context of larger issues of religious identity and mission. Theological and pastoral traditions and practices might exclude or circumscribe certain ways of doing peacebuilding that are common to political actors and social action groups. Religious leaders and institutions often have a definite political impact—mediating conflicts, opposing authoritarian regimes, and advocating for specific public policies. They are sometimes reluctant, however, to engage in certain kinds of peacebuilding that are perceived as too "political" and thus beyond their competence, in the theological and ordinary sense of that word. When they get involved, they might want to engage at a general level appropriate to their role as pastors and teachers, to avoid being dismissed for inappropriately mixing religion and politics.

Restrictions on clerics holding public office, supporting political candidates or parties, or other forms of direct political engagement are not uncommon. In June 2007, for example, the Filipino government invited Fr. Elisio "Jun" Mercado, a Catholic priest who is respected by the Moro Islamic Liberation Front (MILF) in Mindanao, to be its chief negotiator in the peace talks with the MILF. After initially accepting the appointment, Fr. Mercado ultimately decided to forgo this formal role in the negotiations in part because it was seen as incompatible with his role as a priest.

For students of international relations and peace studies, the Sant'Egidio community, a lay Catholic community headquartered in Rome that is credited with helping negotiate an end to the Mozambique war, is an example of track-two diplomacy and the role of civil society in promoting peace. For students of the Catholic Church, Sant'Egidio is also an example of the proper relationship between lay and clerical roles. Similarly, a Catholic bishops' conference might be reluctant to become formally involved in mediating a conflict, even though it has the capacity and credibility to do so, because of its understanding of the institutional Church's role vis-à-vis the political order and a bishops' role vis-à-vis the Catholic laity. It might first choose to encourage lay Catholics to undertake that role, and only do so itself if it becomes clear that no other entity is available. Even then, the bishops might see their "substitute political role" as an exceptional case. If one does not understand theology, it is easy to misinterpret the bishops' reluctance to get involved in mediation as indifference or a failure of will. Strategic approaches to religious peacebuilding take into account these theological nuances that are too often missed or ignored by outsiders who see religion in purely instrumental terms and analyze it as they would a political institution.

Finally, as important as it might be in a particular conflict situation, religion is just one actor and one factor in a much wider project of strategic peacebuilding. As with the studies cited earlier, it is difficult to disaggregate religion from other factors in peacebuilding. As Appleby points out, one needs a "multilayered view" of religious peacemaking that avoids sharp distinction between the "religious" and the "secular."[33] Religious peacebuilders rarely act alone. Successful religious peacebuilding usually involves collaboration with other civil society actors, governments, and international institutions.

Religious Peacebuilding as a Function of the Nature of a Conflict

The nature of the conflict will have an important impact on whether religious bodies can play a constructive peacebuilding role and the nature of that role. In the conflict following the break-up of Yugoslavia, there are three different accounts of the role of religion. The *religious war* account contends that specifically religious divisions gave the conflict in the former Yugoslavia a dimension not unlike the religious wars Europe has known all too well over the centuries. The *ethnoreligious war* account of the conflict does not emphasize religion per se but religion's contribution to the rise of chauvinistic forms of nationalism. The *manipulation of religion* account of the war acknowledges that religious fears and symbols were manipulated and abused by cynical ultranationalists for their own ends, but downplays the role of religious differences or religious nationalism in fomenting conflict. According to this account, the conflict was over competing and mostly incompatible claims of self-determination that arose out of the failure of the Yugoslav idea.

The assessment of the role of the Serbian Orthodox, Roman Catholic, and Muslim communities in this conflict is, in large part, a function of which account of the war one adopts. The first account focuses on religious doctrines and practices that encouraged sectarianism and religious violence. Strategic peacebuilding, then, reexamines those doctrines and practices, and pursues inter-religious dialogue about divisive doctrines and practices, as well as areas of common ground.

Because the second account of the war defines the issue as religious nationalism, not religious violence, the relationship between religion and the political order and religion and national identity becomes most salient. In the face of religious nationalism, effective religious peacebuilding is less about finding common ground on religious issues per se and more about retrieving theological and moral teaching on the appropriate relationship between religion and politics and between religion and national identity. The peacebuilding challenge for religious leaders is to promote a civic form of national identity that distinguishes between the virtue of patriotism and the idolatry of chauvinistic nationalism, upholds the religious freedom of minorities, and embraces religious pluralism as an important part of a healthy democracy. Religious peacebuilding would also include intra- and interfaith efforts to oppose a partition of Bosnia-Herzegovina along religious, ethnic, and national lines that solidifies and, in effect, rewards "ethnic cleansing."

Like the second account of the war, the third leads to an examination of a political theology and ethics. The war's barbarity and intractability, according to this view, were not attributable to "ancient" religious-cultural hatreds but to the failure of politics to counter chaos, war-lordism, and cycles of violence in the wake of the implosion of Yugoslavia. Even more than the second account of the war, the third highlights a lacunae in Roman Catholic, Serbian Orthodox, and Islamic social ethics. In varying degrees, each lacks ethics that can constructively contribute to debates over secessionist self-determination and minority rights. Muslim and Catholic support for Bosnian secession, for example, reflected in part a desire to participate in the democratic transformation that was sweeping Eastern Europe and a realistic evaluation of the futility of remaining in a failed Yugoslav state dominated by Slobodan Milosevic's brand of Serbian nationalism, a futility confirmed by the ensuing war. No doubt the conflicting positions on self-determination hindered the ability of religious leaders in the former Yugoslavia to be reconcilers. But these differences, in part, reflected legitimate moral and religious concerns about nurturing and protecting human rights and the spiritual and cultural values of their respective societies. Reconciliation, therefore, requires not just addressing religious violence or religious nationalism but also a just resolution of competing claims of self-determination.

In short, an adequate analysis of strategic religious peacebuilding takes seriously the complexity of religion and religious actors; the multifaceted, sometimes distinctive religious strategies for peacebuilding; and the extent to which these strategies arise out of an accurate assessment of the nature of a particular conflict. Further elaboration of the religious resources for peacebuilding is needed, however.

The Power and Virtue of Strategic Peacebuilding

Madeleine Albright makes the controversial claim that faith-based organizations "have more resources, more skilled personnel, a longer attention span, more experience, more dedication, and more success in fostering reconciliation than any government."[34] To understand this statement, it is useful to provide a schematic of the rather unique mix of ideals, institutions, and people that together constitute a robust set of religious resources for strategic peace-building.[35]

Religious Resources for Peacebuilding

It is difficult to generalize about the endless number of religious beliefs and ideas that play a role in fomenting conflict or promoting peacebuilding. In assessing commonalities among a dozen prominent religious peacebuilders, David Little concludes that they all share a "hermeneutics of peace, namely, an interpretive framework that begins with the conviction that the pursuit of justice and peace by peaceful means is a sacred priority in each of the traditions represented."[36] A hermeneutics of peace acknowledges that religious beliefs sometimes inspire sectarianism and violence but also self-sacrificial work for justice and peace. Commands to treat all people as children of God and to be peacemakers are no less powerful than teachings that encourage religious exclusivity and sanction religious violence. Religious traditions also often contain core precepts that contribute to peacebuilding that are generally not found in conventional political discourse, such as forgiveness, love of enemy, and solidarity with the poor and oppressed. Moreover, although religious absolutes are generally seen as conflict-producing because they leave no room for compromise, in fact, few wars are fought today over these absolutes. Wars are usually fought over political power, territory, access to resources, and ideology. Although religion sometimes is used to reify these goods,[37] at least as often, religion opposes as idolatry an uncompromising or absolutist approach to the conflicts over the (nonreligious) issues that fuel most wars.

Ideas alone have little social relevance unless they shape the actions of institutions and individuals. In many poor, war-torn countries and failed or failing states, religious bodies are often the most important civil society institutions. In Latin America and Africa, many of the schools, hospitals, social services, relief and development, and human rights programs are sponsored by religious institutions. The experience of these institutions can give religious bodies special expertise that cuts across many aspects of peacebuilding. Because religious bodies are deeply rooted in society and the daily lives of ordinary people, they can bring greater credibility and deeper relationships to their engagement in peacebuilding than most NGOs. Religious institutions also have the advantage of being able to influence not just public policies but also cultural mores and the beliefs and practices of individuals.

The indigenous nature of much religious peacebuilding is strengthened by the fact that many religious institutions are relatively unique transnational actors. They are deeply rooted in local communities yet also have a global reach that can surpass that of governments, international institutions, or multinational companies. Their global reach enables them to bridge the global divide between zones of conflict and poverty and zones of peace and prosperity. Their indigenous character enables them to provide early warning of simmering conflicts and can help outsiders better understand and respond to the dynamics of a particular conflict. Catholic Relief Services and World Vision, which serve tens of millions of people in more than a hundred countries, are only two of numerous large faith-based relief and development agencies that have integrated peacebuilding into their work in war-torn areas. Hundreds of thousands of missionaries also provide unique connections between countries in conflict and wealthier, powerful countries like the United States. Religious bodies in these powerful countries often give their religious counterparts from places like Sudan and El Salvador direct access to the leaders of international institutions and governments who can play a constructive role in helping resolve local conflicts.

Finally, because, at root, religious bodies are communities of people, religion has an ability to reach, educate, inspire, and mobilize the masses. Some of the most dramatic examples of religious "people power" are the Catholic Church's role in the mass protests that helped bring down the Marcos regime in the Philippines, the Evangelical Lutheran Church's role in providing safe space for organizing the protests that brought down the communist government in East Germany, and the Serbian Orthodox Church's role in toppling the regime of Milosevic in Serbia. In many ways, though, these and other mass mobilizations are exceptional cases. More typical are advocacy efforts, such as the landmines and debt relief campaigns, that rely heavily on religious institutions and faith-based NGOs to reach millions of people through their congregations and schools.

People power is also about individuals. Religious leaders at the local, national, and international level often have a moral credibility that political, governmental, media, and corporate leaders lack. This moral credibility allows them to be effective advocates for peaceful social change, to mediate between conflicting parties, and to provide new visions for the future in societies torn by conflict. Finally, countless peacebuilders are lay people—some famous, most not—whose peacebuilding arises out of their religious beliefs. In fact, over the past twenty-five years, almost half the Nobel Peace Prize laureates have been religious leaders or lay people whose work was inspired by their faith.

Integrating Ideas, Institutions, and People

Religious peacebuilding is strategic when it effectively integrates these diverse religious resources. Integrating ideas, institutions, and people power is comparable to what Appleby calls "the saturation model." According to Appleby: "Nonviolent religious militancy becomes politically effective over the long term only when it spans a spectrum of actors at different levels of society, all of whom are working in collaboration for the nonviolent resolution of conflict and the building of stable political structures and social relations."[38] Similarly, Douglas Johnston and Brian Cox conclude that effective faith-based diplomacy requires four attributes:

1. A well-established and pervasive influence in the community.
2. A reputation as an apolitical force for change based on a respected set of values.

3. Unique leverage for reconciling conflicting parties, including an ability to rehumanize relationships.
4. The capability to mobilize community, national, and international support for a peace process.[39]

Their first attribute is about faith-based people power, the second and third mostly involve faith-based values, and the fourth, faith-based institutions. Put another way, the effectiveness of religious peacebuilding depends on integrating theology, ethics, and praxis; integrating the peacebuilding work of different parts of religious institutions; and integrating peacebuilding policy and process. Let me briefly elaborate on each.

It is banal to say, but a religious body is an effective peacebuilder when there is continuity between what it preaches and what it practices. My contention that religious peacebuilding must be analyzed on its own terms, not solely by the standard metrics for assessing political actors, interest groups, or NGOs, assumes that peacebuilding is integrated into the life and mission of religious bodies. Peacebuilding must be an authentic means to fulfill one's religious mission; religion cannot be simply a means to pursue peacebuilding. Instrumentalizing religion, even for the worthwhile objective of peacebuilding, will undermine religion as well as the effectiveness of religious peacebuilding.

Rooting peacebuilding in mission and integrating it into the life of the religious body has practical consequences. Stand-alone peacebuilding programs, although necessary and important, are not necessarily best able to use the full panoply of religious resources. Stand-alone programs must be complemented by efforts to make peacebuilding an integral part of religious formation of its leaders and its members, its prayer and rituals, its pastoral strategies, and its charitable work. A Catholic trauma healing program in Rwanda, for example, will be rooted in the Church's sacramental tradition, especially reconciliation and the eucharist, as well as in the Church's experience in pastoral counseling. A Muslim program to reintegrate refugees in Iraq will not be based on the narrowly defined humanitarian needs and short-term time frame of a government grant but on the broader spiritual and social needs and the long-term horizon of the mosque, which will be dealing with the consequences of the war not only for today's refugees but also for their children and grandchildren.

Integrating peacebuilding and mission can be challenging. Religious traditions that emphasize an individual's personal relationship with God might not have a strong theological basis for claims that peacebuilding at the societal level is integral to the faith. In other traditions, peacebuilding is considered integral, but there is often a considerable gap between official teaching and the integration of that teaching into the daily life of that community.

Not surprisingly, the impact of religion in a particular conflict depends, in large part, on the intensity of religious affiliation. One reason extreme nationalists were able to manipulate religion during the Balkan wars of the 1990s is that five decades of communism had severely weakened religion, resulting in low levels of religious literacy and practice.[40] Dowd suggests that low levels of meaningful religious affiliation are one reason the Catholic Church in Rwanda was ineffective in preventing the genocide.[41] Mennonites, Quakers, and other historic "peace churches" have had a disproportionate role in faith-based peacebuilding training and conflict resolution around the world because the vocation of peacebuilding has become an integral part of the life of those communities.

Religious peacebuilding is often effective in the short term in places where religious leaders retain a high degree of influence and respect in society at large. Paradoxically, religious bodies might become more effective peacebuilders over the long term if the task of peacebuilding was not so often confined to those in clerical roles. In some countries, the leading role of clerics is often a function of the relatively low levels of education of ordinary believers as well as the traditional role that religious leaders have played in society. Peacebuilding will be more deeply integrated into the lived religion of the whole faith community as the peacebuilding role and capacity of lay leaders and ordinary believers becomes more important. The role of nonclerics is especially important for peacebuilding with a political dimension for which religious leaders might not be well suited.

Closely connected to the integration of teaching and practice is institutional integration. Religious bodies are the envy of the Central Intelligence Agency and MoveOn only when they are integrated vertically and horizontally. The Roman Catholic Church is probably the most vertically integrated religious body; its hierarchical structure has clearly defined leaders and institutions at all levels of a pyramidal structure and clear lines of teaching and organizational authority (though it is quite decentralized in its operations).[42] Many religious institutions are much less vertically integrated but still have the capacity, through their identifiable religious leaders and national and international structures, to operate at levels beyond the local community. As Lederach has pointed out, strategic peacebuilding resists the temptation to give priority to peacebuilding at one level of the hierarchical pyramid or for peacebuilding at one level to operate in isolation from the other levels.[43] In Northern Ireland, Catholics and Protestants collaborated rather effectively at the leadership level and through a proliferation of ecumenical "grassroots" peace and reconciliation groups, such as the Corrymeela Community. This remarkable ecumenical collaboration would have been even more effective if there was not such a dearth of ecumenical engagement at the parish and congregation level.

The political science term for horizontal integration—transnational actor—has its theological correlates in such concepts as solidarity and the Body of Christ. Religious institutions vary considerably in the extent to which horizontal collaboration among coreligionists around the world is valued and practiced. The most effective religious peacebuilding occurs where a high value is placed on being in solidarity and maintaining unity with those suffering from conflict, and these values are institutionalized through regional and international structures and meetings, congregation-twinning, missionary and aid programs, and ad hoc engagement around issues of peace and justice.

Vertical and horizontal integration are critical in enabling religious leaders to meet a common challenge: maintaining a proper balance between the deeply embedded ties to cultural, ethnic and national identities that give religion its influence in particular conflict situations, and the cosmopolitan or universal elements that give religion its moral credibility and transnational reach. What Lederach and Appleby say about strategic peacebuilders generally applies especially to religious peacebuilders: "Practitioners specialize in the dynamics of peacebuilding within the boundaries and on the terms set by local communities, but they recognize that local communities today always already exist within national and global contexts."[44]

Religious individuals and institutions are especially effective peacebuilders because they are inculturated—they are deeply rooted in their own communities, representing a complex web of relationships that often cut across economic, political, and ethnic divisions. They also often enjoy a moral credibility that is unmatched by other local actors. Especially in times of war and repression, local religious leaders and institutions share in their community's suffering (unlike many international institutions and international NGOs) and are often prominent defenders of their community's rights and legitimate aspirations.[45] In Poland and Tibet, for example, religion has been a protector of national and cultural values and rights in the face of repression and aggression. In Guatemala, Colombia, Mozambique, northern Uganda, and other conflicts, religious leaders have used their local influence to facilitate or mediate peace processes.

These characteristics of indigenous religious peacebuilders are not without challenges. Precisely because they are so deeply entrenched in their own communities, they must resist taking refuge in a comfortable ethical and pastoral parochialism at the expense of the cosmopolitan ethic and universal religious vision that can be religion's most important contribution to peacebuilding. Perhaps the greatest sin of omission of religious actors who are deeply rooted in communities embroiled in conflict is their failure to condemn, in unambiguous terms, violence and human rights abuses committed by their own religious, ethnic, or national group. Because of their condemnations of IRA violence, the Catholic bishops in Northern Ireland were severely criticized, particularly by many Catholics, for not being "prophetic" in their witness on behalf of a beleaguered Catholic community. At the same time, the Catholic bishops in Croatia were strongly criticized for being too nationalistic in rallying international support for a victimized Croatian Catholic community.

It is easy, and in some respects appropriate, to applaud the former and condemn the latter. But a fair analysis would have to take into account the extreme conditions under which religious leaders operate, the moral dilemmas they face, and the failures of moral courage and vision to which religious leaders and ordinary believers are not immune. Despite doctrines on the equal dignity of all people and the centrality of peacebuilding, it is not easy for religion to counter the dehumanization and scapegoating of the enemy during conflict, to overcome the tendency to give the benefit of the doubt to one's own group or nation, and to engage in the prophetic self-criticism that could undermine national unity, give the enemy a propaganda bonanza, and risk one's own and other lives. For these and other reasons, religious leaders can easily come to see their pastoral role as being chaplains to their own community, even at the expense of their role as religious leaders.

Religious leaders become effective peacebuilders only when they are able to rise above this ethical and pastoral parochialism, while not abandoning the religious inculturation that can make them such a force for peace in the local context. Most (if not all) religious traditions contain within them rich resources for overcoming parochialism and fostering a more universal vision. Concepts of transcendence, charity, justice, reconciliation, and human dignity are consistent with and reinforce the pluralist goal of engendering unity while respecting diversity. The fact that most religious bodies are transnational actors, closely aligned with coreligionists around the world, also serves as a brake on any tendencies to become too nationalistic and see the world exclusively from the prism of their own particular ethnic or national group.

Finally, the integration of principles and practices and vertical and horizontal institutional integration should correspond to an integration of different types of peacebuilding. Strategic peacebuilding requires a link between the various roles assumed by religious peacebuilders: observation and witness, education and formation, advocacy and empowerment, and conciliation and mediation. The Acholi Religious Leaders' Peace Initiative in northern Uganda, started in 1997 by Anglican, Roman Catholic, Muslim, and Orthodox leaders, is a good example of the effectiveness of this kind of integration. The religious leaders' peacebuilding work grew out of their humanitarian aid programs in the camps for the displaced. They used their influence to play a key role in facilitating the peace process between the Ugandan government and the Lord's Resistance Army. As a complement to their work on the peace process, they worked with their religious counterparts in the United States and other key countries, first, to bring greater attention to what was, in the 1990s, a mostly ignored conflict, and later to urge the United States and the United Nations to play a constructive role in the peace process by (among other things) supporting indigenous alternatives to the indictments handed down by the International Criminal Court. They did not, however, work only at the elite level. They also formed local and later district-level peace committees to educate their own people about peacebuilding, address land issues, organize peace rallies and prayers, mediate local conflicts, and develop programs of trauma healing.[46]

The Acholi Religious Leaders Peace Initiative is an example of the strategic value of integrating religious resources for peace. Most important were the common religious principles and moral credibility that allowed them to be strong witnesses for peace. Also essential were the variety, reach, and strength of their religious institutions in the zone of conflict and their institutional ties to their counterparts around the world. Finally, they had the capacity to address the needs of and mobilize ordinary Acholis to be a force for peace and reconciliation amid one of the world's most brutal and intractable conflicts.

Three Challenges for Religious Peacebuilding

This chapter has argued that a strategic approach to religious peacebuilding rejects the prevailing secularist paradigm that sees religion as mostly a source of conflict and division; takes seriously the complexity of religion and religious actors, the multifaceted, sometimes distinctive religious strategies for peacebuilding and the extent to which these strategies are a function of the nature of a conflict; and integrates the complex of ideas, institutions, and individuals that can serve as a potent source of religious peacebuilding. I now address three key issues raised by religious peacebuilding: (1) the public nature of religious peacebuilding, (2) the role of principled nonviolence in religious peacebuilding and (3) the relative importance of ecumenical and inter-religious peacebuilding compared to single-identity peacebuilding.

A Strong Public Role for Religion

If the secularists are mistaken in their assumption that the antidote to religious conflict is to marginalize and privatize religion, then strategic religious peacebuilding cannot be limited to motivating individuals to be peacebuilders and transforming interpersonal relationships; it must be tied to a strong public role for religion. The role of religion in postconflict situations is a case in point. Many religious traditions are well equipped to address the moral dimensions of the use of force before and during a violent conflict. Most also have a rich theological, spiritual, and pastoral tradition on personal reconciliation with God and neighbor. But few have well-developed teaching or pastoral practices related to the political or communal dimensions of reconciliation after a war is over. Northern Ireland is not atypical. During two decades of conflict, the four largest churches developed a clear and mostly constructive approach to the complex political and religious dynamics of the conflict. But after the Good Friday Agreement in 1998, they were somewhat at a loss in dealing with postconflict issues, such as amnesty for paramilitaries and long-term pastoral strategies for healing and reconciliation. The growing theological and ethical literature on the political dimensions of forgiveness is beginning to fill this gap.[47] The point is that effective religious peacebuilding depends on a sophisticated public theology and social ethic that justifies and gives substance to religious engagement in the social, economic, cultural, and political dimensions of peacebuilding.

The complexity and variety of perspectives on the theology and ethics underlying a public role for religion can only be hinted at here. As a general rule, those religious traditions that historically have been most concerned with personal religious experience or posit a sharp distinction between the religious community and the wider social order have not developed the kind of sophisticated public theology and social ethic necessary for strategic peacebuilding. Christian Anabaptists (traditional peace churches) are on one side of the spectrum. They emphasize the need for a distinctive community of believers that can model nonviolent, just behavior. For the most part, they do not believe it is possible or part of their religious mission to seek to influence the public order. On the other end of the spectrum is political Islam, which seeks to create a public order that reflects, safeguards, and promotes Islamic religious and moral teaching. So-called mainline Christian denominations tend toward a middle ground in which religious and moral values can help shape and inform the social, political, and economic realms, but these sectors retain some degree of autonomy from the religious realm.

This spectrum of views on the public role of religion is reflected in three large and complex sets of issues that are central to an understanding of the essential public dimension of religious peacebuilding: religion–state relationships, religion and politics, and religion and culture.

Religion–state relationships can have a major impact on whether religion is a source of conflict or peace. I briefly examine four types of religion–state relationships and their relationship to peacebuilding:

1. the atheist state, which is intolerant of religion;
2. the state religion, where one religion has a monopoly in society and relies on the state for both special privileges and to restrict or deny the rights of minority religions;
3. church–state separation, which privileges religious pluralism by ensuring a secular state that is neutral toward religion; and
4. the preferred religion(s) model, where the state gives preference to one or more religions, but state and religion are separate and no effort is made to restrict minority religions.[48]

The first two types of religion–state relationships are most problematic for religious peacebuilding. Where religion is severely circumscribed by atheist states, so is religious peacebuilding. The Catholic Church in Poland could play the role it did in the peaceful demise of communism because it was the principal social institution in Poland that was independent of the government and capable of pursuing an alternative vision of Poland's social, political, and economic future. In the former Yugoslavia, religious peacebuilders were handicapped in their efforts to counter religious nationalism in part because the public role of religion had been systematically circumscribed and undermined under communism. State religions can sometimes parlay their privileged position into a peacebuilding role, but more often a religious monopoly is a source of conflict, as with the Khartoum government's efforts to impose sharia law in southern Sudan. Paradoxically, in the long run, the direct religious role in government and politics can weaken the public role of religion given the risks of religion being politicized or coopted by government, either of which can undermine its public credibility.

If the atheist state and state religion models have serious negative connotations for religious peacebuilding, it does not necessarily follow that religious peacebuilding thrives best in liberal democracies with strict church–state separation. In the United States, church–state separation has arguably contributed to the peacebuilding role of religion. Church–state separation has not prevented and might have contributed to the strong role religion plays in public life. Religious opposition to U.S. policies that undermine the peace process in Colombia and faith-based advocacy campaigns for peace in Darfur and northern Uganda are fruits of the flourishing of public religion in the context of strict church–state separation. What works in the United States, however, does not necessarily work in countries with very different histories, cultures, political systems, and demographics. The temptation to try to remake the world in the U.S. image of church–state separation is a formula not for peacebuilding but conflict. In many cultures, the U.S. model is seen as the camel's nose of Western secularism and a threat to religion.

Although it can suffer from some of the problems associated with the state religion model, the preferred religion(s) model can sometimes contribute to effective religious peacebuilding. This model often coincides with and reinforces a situation in which one or more religious traditions have the public influence necessary to mobilize the masses against a repressive government or bridge divisions between conflicting parties in a civil war. Yet because there is not a state religion and the rights of minority religions are protected, the risk that religion will be politically coopted or become a source of conflict is diminished.

The religion–state issue is related to but distinct from the larger issue of religion and politics. Whatever the formal religion–state relationship, peacebuilding requires political engagement; therefore, religious peacebuilding is about religion and politics. (I define *politics* broadly to include engagement on issues of public policy, not just partisan politics.) For many religious peacebuilders, the challenge is to have a political impact without becoming politicized. Some are most comfortable in a public role where they serve as a social conscience, criticizing the actions of warring parties, addressing the moral dimensions of policy issues, and offering a vision of a more peaceful, just, and reconciled society. Not infrequently, religious peacebuilders assume a more overtly political role when they identify with one party in a conflict or take on roles usually reserved for governmental actors. In several prominent cases, notably the Democratic Republic of the Congo, Poland, East Germany, Serbia, and the Philippines, religious leaders have assumed political roles in mediating between the government and rebels or calling for a change of regimes. In Guatemala, South Africa, and Peru, religious leaders have played prominent roles in truth and reconciliation commissions. For some, such roles are perfectly compatible with their public theology and their conception of proper religious leadership. Others might avoid such roles as an illegitimate mixing of religion and politics. Still others might justify what they consider a substitute political position only in exceptional cases when there is a dearth of other credible leaders to fill the peacebuilding role. A strategic approach to religious peacebuilding will carefully assess the wide variety of normative perspectives among religious peacebuilders on religion and politics, not just the potential political effectiveness of their interventions. In my own judgment, when religious peacebuilders move from a temporary political role to a more permanent political role, they risk losing their moral legitimacy and, over time, become less effective as peace-builders. The work of religious peacebuilders will and ought to have political implications to be effective, but the religious peacebuilders undermine their constructive role when they become political actors as such.

The attention given to the important issues of religion and state and religion and politics can sometimes obscure the public role of religion in influencing the cultural dynamics of peacebuilding. According to Lederach and Appleby,

> Promoting reconciliation and healing as the sine qua non of peacebuild-ing is predicated on a hard-won awareness that violent conflict creates deep disruption in relationships that then need radical healing—the kind of healing that restores the soul, the psyche, and the moral im-agination. Such healing, it is recognized, draws on profound rational, psychological, and transrational resources, especially the spiritual dimension of humanity. Its preferred modalities are therefore symbolic, cultural, and religious—the deepest personal and social spheres, which directly and indirectly shape the national and political spheres.[49]

Etzioni calls this challenge of developing a "moral culture," the "soft under-belly of security" in countries where authoritarian regimes are failing, have collapsed, or have been replaced.[50] He recognizes that in contrast to Western secular approaches that emphasize the establishment of liberal democracies as the source of peace and stability, "religion is one source, in many cases a main source, and in some cases the major or exclusive source, of moral culture" in countries trying to escape violence and instability.[51] Etzioni's "soft underbelly of security" applies not just in cases of authoritarian regimes but in many conflicts, particularly long-standing civil wars. It is common for religious leaders in countries riven by conflict to see their main challenge as addressing the cultural casualties of war. In Colombia, the Catholic Church has a formal role in the official peace process (what might be seen as a substitute political role), but it is clear that it must also help cultivate civil society efforts to counter the culture of violence that has developed over decades of conflict and help the long process of creating a culture of peace, without which the peace process cannot succeed. Of course, the Church in Colombia could not play either role if it were not a major public force in Colombia.

In sum, a robust religious contribution to peacebuilding requires a robust public role for religion. That role must arise out of a sophisticated public theology and social ethic and can be understood only in light of the variety of religious perspectives on the complex set of issues related to the relationship between religion and state, religion and politics, and religion and culture.

The Role of Nonviolence in Religious Peacebuilding

The secularist critics of religion and some critics of the secularists contend that religiously motivated and justified violence is a serious (if not the principal) challenge for religious peacebuilding. If that is correct, a signal contribution that religion can make to peacebuilding is to reconsider its teachings on war and peace and embrace nonviolence.

According to Etzioni, a critic of the secularist paradigm, the problem with Samuel Huntington's "clash of civilizations" thesis is that it "obscures that crucially important differences run *through* each 'civilization,' between those who believe in the use of violence to advance their cause and those who seek to rely on persuasion, between Warriors and Preachers."[52] Etzioni defines *warriors* as those who use religion to justify terrorism or violent coercion against nonbelievers; *preachers* are those who might pursue illiberal political objectives but do so through persuasion, not coercion. He rejects Bernard Lewis's contention that the solution to Islamic violence is to secularize and modernize Muslim nations. Rather, he argues that "illiberal Moderate Muslims," those who do not support Western secular conceptions of human rights, democracy, and religion and politics, are nevertheless "our political allies" in opposing those who advocate violence, terrorism, and unjust war.[53] Etzioni is strategic in that he avoids monolithic and reductionist approaches to religious violence that fail to acknowledge the diversity of views within and among religious traditions on the use of force and political theology, and the complex relationship between the two. But his analysis of religious violence needs nuancing.

Religious traditions have taken three distinct approaches to the ethics of force: holy war, just war, and pacifism, or principled nonviolence. Etzioni's warriors represent the first approach. In holy war, there are no limits to the use of force because it is necessary to defend and promote ultimate religious ends. The principal contemporary forms of holy war are extremist forms of Islam, personified by Osama bin Laden,[54] and extremist forms of nationalism, in which preserving or promoting ethnic or national identity justify total war and indiscriminate violence. Etzioni's preachers fall under either the just war or pacifist approaches. Most contemporary forms of the just war tradition reject holy war, and many share with pacifism a strong presumption against the use of force. Just war traditions recognize, however, that the limited use of force may sometimes be justified to achieve limited goals, such as defending the innocent against aggression. The pacifist tradition, exemplified by the traditional peace churches in Christianity, considers nonviolence to be an exceptionless norm.

Etzioni's focus on warriors versus preachers is helpful to a point, but it needs further nuance on the role of violence and some modification on the role of political theology. Obviously, religious peacebuilding has to be about finding nonviolent ways to resolve conflict, but it need not be grounded in principled nonviolence. The first task of religious peacebuilders is to delegitimate holy war and abuses of the just war tradition. Perhaps paradoxically, those best positioned to do so are not pacifists but those who preach a restrictive interpretation of just war. My own Christian tradition has a long and less-than-proud record of holy war. The refinement and narrowing of the just war tradition, not the emergence of pacifism, ultimately delegitimated holy war within mainstream Christianity.[55] Just war norms continue to be used, even by pacifists, to counter the religious and moral appeals of terrorists and contemporary holy warriors. In Northern Ireland, one of the most important contributions of Catholic and

Protestant leaders to peacebuilding was to appeal to just war norms to condemn IRA and Loyalist paramilitary violence.[56]

Properly used, the just war tradition can serve not only to delegitimate religious violence but also as a valuable form of violence prevention and conflict mitigation. Religious leaders are often in the forefront in using just war categories to oppose their own government's resort to military force and condemn the indiscriminate and disproportionate uses of force, which so often fuel cycles of violence. The just war tradition also helps counter the widely held realist view that morality has little or nothing to do with issues of national security and war. Furthermore, a restrictive just war interpretation allows religious leaders to challenge holy war and the permissive abuses of the just war tradition while not being dismissed as morally irrelevant in the face of genocide, ethnic cleansing, and blatant aggression. A theology, ethics, and praxis of nonviolent peacebuilding has a lot to learn from the tradition of nonviolence, especially the seriousness with which it pursues alternatives to war. An ethic of peacebuilding, however, is not an alternative to the just war tradition but a necessary complement to it. An ethic of peacebuilding is grounded, as Marc Gopin suggests, in the recognition that pacifists are not alone in wanting to strengthen the capacity of religious peacebuilders to effectively engage in conflict resolution strategies as an alternative to the use of force.[57] For these reasons, religious peacebuilding must be attentive to a nuanced understanding of religious teachings on the ethics of war and how they interact with an ethics of peacebuilding.

But what of Etzioni's view that illiberal religious moderates are not a significant problem for peacebuilders? Etzioni rightly rejects the secularist argument that the solution to religious violence is to secularize and modernize highly religious societies. But he does not give enough weight to the role of political theology in fomenting conflict. It matters a great deal whether religious traditions are "illiberal" or not; exclusivist political theologies are not "moderate" simply because they might reject violence. Efforts to delegitimate religious warriors must be tied to an effort to delegitimate the political theologies and nationalist ideologies that undergird their holy wars and abuses of the just war tradition.

One of the toughest peacebuilding challenges in places like Sri Lanka and Israel-Palestine is not religious violence but religious nationalism. The link between religion and nationalism might seem less terrifying, but it is arguably a much greater source of injustice and violence than religious militants preaching holy war. Religion plays a peacebuilding role when it embraces inclusivist forms of civic nationalism and legitimate expressions of patriotism while condemning chauvinist and exclusivist forms of religious nationalism. In Bosnia, the problem was not that some religious leaders appealed to just war norms to justify the use of force to stop ethnic cleansing. Rather, the problem was finding religious resources that could delegitimate the chauvinist forms of nationalism that fueled the ethnic cleansing.

Similarly, religious terrorism is based on a belief that faith demands or sanctions violence. According to Philpott, however,

Near the center of virtually every religious terrorist group's beliefs also lies a political theology. They believe that one or more regimes is illegitimate for having defiled and failed to promote authentic faith, and should be replaced by one where political authority is tightly meshed with religious authority, which actively promotes right religion, and that thereby subordinates other religious communities.[58]

He finds that 93 percent of all religious terrorist groups hold an "integrationist political theology. They have taken up the gun to replace corrupted, secularized orders with ones where political authority is rightly oriented."[59] If Philpott is correct that a particular form of political theology, particularly Islamic revivalism, is behind most religious terrorism, then the solution lies not just in condemning religious justifications of terrorism but, more so, in the efforts of more responsible voices within Islam to counter this political theology.

Religious peacebuilders need not resolve the historic debate between pacifism and just war. These traditions address the important but narrow question of the ethics of the use of force; they cannot address the wider range of issues that must be part of religious peacebuilding. The task for religious peacebuilding is not to embrace principled nonviolence but to use insights from both the pacifist and just war traditions to delegitimate unjustifiable violence, especially holy war.[60] The emphasis in both traditions on the moral imperative of finding alternatives to the use of military force point to the need to deepen the theological, ethical, and practical bases for strengthening the capacity to prevent and resolve conflicts through nonviolent means. Perhaps most important is the need to go beyond the categories of just war and pacifism to delegitimate the political theologies and ideologies that fuel violence. More Mahatma Gandhis are always needed, but even more needed are more Reinhold Niebuhrs.[61]

The Significance of Inter-Religious and Ecumenical Peacebuilding

Inter-religious and ecumenical peacebuilding has increased significantly in response to the terrorist attacks of September 11, 2001, and the identity conflicts of the 1990s. Organizations like the World Conference on Religions for Peace, the Appeal of Conscience Foundation, and the Sant'Egidio Community; the peacebuilding programs of the World Council of Churches and other inter-religious and ecumenical bodies at the international, national, and local levels; the inter-religious peacebuilding programs of the major faith-based relief and development agencies; the religious peacebuilding program of the U.S. Institute of Peace and the Tony Blair Faith Foundation; and a host of inter-religious NGOs are examples of these collaborative efforts.[62]

Inter-religious peacebuilding usually has one or more of five purposes: (1) deepening relationships, (2) improving understanding, (3) finding common ground on beliefs and issues, (4) promoting common action, and (5) encouraging complementary action. Each goal is worthy in itself, but a strategic approach to inter-religious peacebuilding defines the purpose of a particular initiative in light of the nature of the conflict, the theory of change underlying the engagement, and the actors involved.

As with peacebuilding generally, the purposes of inter-religious peacebuilding must be defined in light of the *nature of the conflict*. Inter-religious peacebuilding often suffers from a paradox: the more religion is central to a conflict, the greater the need for inter-religious peacebuilding; the less religion is central to the conflict, the greater the likelihood that inter-religious peacebuilding will bear fruit.

Because many agree with the secularist assumption that religious differences lead to conflict, many also assume that a main purpose of inter-religious peacebuilding is to find common ground on ethical and theological beliefs. Interestingly, in practice, the formal inter-religious dialogues that seek to resolve long-standing differences on such issues often take place on separate tracks from those dialogues that relate to particular conflicts. Major inter-religious initiatives on peace in the Middle East, for example, would not have been possible without the relationships of trust that have developed between Jews and Christians through formal theological dialogues, but the initiatives themselves have usually been undertaken outside of these formal theological dialogues. This separation between dialogue around doctrine and dialogue around peacebuilding is due in part to a desire not to allow political conflicts to sidetrack doctrinal dialogues and in part to a conviction that the long-term process of resolving doctrinal differences will have little impact on conflicts that, while having a religious dimension, are not about religious beliefs and differences.

Reinforcing commonalities in religious beliefs is an important purpose to the extent that agreement on the sacredness of human life, the obligation to seek the common good of all, and the rejection of religious violence provide a deep foundation for inter-religious peacebuilding. But making this a central purpose of inter-religious engagement can be futile and even counterproductive. It can be futile because, as Appleby points out, "it is not apparent that even broad concepts such as forgiveness and reconciliation are universal beyond their most generalized usage. . . . Religions, in short, have not arrived at a universal set of values or priorities in pursuing peace."[63] Religious traditions hold different world-views, and even within religious traditions and individual denominations, there are vast differences in approaches to conflict. It is not necessary to discover or agree on a global theology and ethic of peacebuilding for religion to be effective in peacebuilding. Efforts to do so take an enormous amount of time and resources and usually produce a least-common-denominator approach to religious peacebuilding whose impact is minimal, in part because it emasculates the richness and distinctiveness of existing traditions, thereby reducing the ability of religious concepts to motivate and inspire people to be peacebuilders. For Catholics, the sacrament of reconciliation can be a powerful motivation for seeking communal forgiveness and healing, whereas an effort by diverse religious traditions to come to agreement on the role of forgiveness in a conflict might be a source of unnecessary division over doctrinal nuances and differences over how forgiveness would apply in the case at hand. As a result, such efforts often result in watered-down statements that lack the capacity to move ordinary believers. The time and resources spent trying to find common ground on theological issues is often better spent pursuing collaborative or complementary action on carefully selected issues that relate more directly to the conflict.

Efforts to find common ground can be especially counterproductive in identity conflicts where a community's religious and communal identity and even survival are threatened. In those cases, efforts to deemphasize what is distinctive in one's own religious tradition can exacerbate the problem of what Gopin calls "negative identity," the tendency to define one's religion in opposition to the "other." The solution is not to downplay religious identity but to find those elements within that identity that can contribute to peacebuilding. As Gopin notes, seeking common commitments might work with more moderate segments of religious groups, but such efforts will not work with religious extremists until well after the conflict has abated.[64] He continues, "especially during a crisis, it is vital that we elicit that which is most unique and most sacred as a source of prosocial practice and social change, if we truly want to move the *entire* religious culture to a new and lasting commitment to peacemaking."[65]

Clearly, when religion and religious identity are being used or manipulated to deepen communal divisions and conflict, inter-religious dialogue is essential to overcome mistrust and misunderstandings, deepen relationships that can bridge the communal divide, and take at least symbolic common actions to counter the extremists who preach religious conflict. Particularly in conflicts with a religious dimension, however, the purpose and benefit of inter-religious engagement might not necessarily be in common action but in what the coming together allows one to do alone within one's community. As an instrument of peacebuilding, inter-religious collaboration often has limited direct impact; complementary action (not collaborative action) is often more effective. The trust needed for inter-religious collaboration is often undermined by a gap between inter-religious statements for peace and what the signatories say to their own communities. Effective inter-religious dialogue enables participants to go back and work within their communities to help them break out of myths of unique victimization, counter stereotypes and prejudices, and promote better understanding and respect for the hopes, fears, and legitimate grievances of the other community. A major test for inter-religious dialogue amid identity conflicts is whether it enhances the ability of moderate religious leaders, who are usually the participants in these dialogues, to draw on their improved understanding of the "enemy" and what is distinctive in their own tradition to more effectively counter the extremists in their own community.

In Mindanao in the southern Philippines, the Bishops-Ulema Dialogue was established in 1996 to bring together Catholic and Muslim leaders to support the formal peace process between the government and Muslim rebels. After more than a decade of dialogue, mostly about very general areas of common ground on religious beliefs, both sides have concluded that the next challenge is to do much more sustained education and dialogue within their own communities, who remain mired in myths and misconceptions about the other community.

In Northern Ireland, dialogue between Catholic and Presbyterian leaders from the United States and Northern Ireland led to a level of trust that resulted in a groundbreaking joint statement and initiative on fair employment. Equally important, however, was the impact of the ecumenical relationships on the work of the individual religious bodies. The U.S. Catholic bishops would routinely send their draft statements on Northern Ireland to their Presbyterian counterparts in the United States and Northern Ireland to ensure that the bishops did not inadvertently misinterpret the situation or further inflame the sectarian divide. Likewise, the U.S. Presbyterian Church would send its draft statements to Catholic leaders for review.

Unfortunately, in part because of the focus on inter-religious dialogue where religion is a dimension of a conflict, not enough attention is paid to some of the most effective cases of inter-religious peacebuilding, cases where religion plays a central role in society but is not central to the conflict. In these cases, inter-religious peacebuilding can be effective for the simple reason that it is easier to find common ground on issues at stake in the conflict and religious actors can more easily bring what David Little calls an "empathetic detachment." Empathetic detachment requires a reputation for moral engagement and concern combined with an ability to transcend narrow partisanships. "Prominent religious identity," Little suggests, "provides a badge of trustworthiness and impartiality that can be of great benefit in either formal or informal negotiations."[66] Between 1999 and 2002, the Inter-religious Council of Sierra Leone, for example, facilitated a peace agreement between the rebels and the government because the religious leaders, working together, were able to use the trust and moral credibility they enjoyed to build bridges between conflicting parties.[67] The work of the Acholi religious leaders in brokering peace in northern Uganda is another example of the power of united efforts at peacebuilding where religion is not a factor in the conflict.

Linking the purposes of inter-religious peacebuilding to an assessment of the nature of the conflict is closely related to the theories of change that underlie these initiatives.[68] Reina Neufeldt identifies four theories of change that are usually at work in inter-religious engagement. Affective theories focus on (1) changing the hearts and minds of participants about the conflict and each other, and (2) building and deepening relationships across deeply divided societies by providing a safe space for those from conflicting sides to come together. The more ambitious social and political purposes include (3) promoting cultural change by overcoming sectarian stereotypes and building a culture of peace, and (4) promoting structural or policy changes by, for example, mediating in a peace process, advocating for disarmament, or promoting democratization in response to repressive governmental policies.[69]

Effective inter-religious peacebuilding closely ties purposes of inter-religious engagement to realistic theories of change. Each of the purposes of inter-religious peacebuilding could be linked to one or more of these theories of change. As already mentioned, in Northern Ireland, one purpose of such dialogue was to strengthen and improve understanding among the moderates in each community so that they could address sectarianism more effectively by working within their own community. Another purpose was to deepen relationships of trust so that religious leaders could respond to crises in ways that would reduce the risk of escalation. In Macedonia, the purpose of inter-religious efforts was to establish parent–teacher groups that included Muslims, Orthodox, and Catholics based on the theory that such common action around issues not related to the conflict would change hearts and minds and build bridges across religious and ethnic divides. In northern Uganda, united advocacy on amnesty, the International Criminal Court indictments, and other policy issues was a key element of the religious leaders' efforts to promote the peace process.

With the exception of some elements of the fourth strategy—for example, responding to crises, mediating in peace processes, and pursuing specific policy initiatives—these strategies for change are long term and difficult to measure and thus easily dismissed as irrelevant. Gopin argues, however, that conflict resolution strategies, which tend to be crisis-driven and problem-focused, limit the creative potential of religion. "By contrast," he maintains, "eliciting long-term strategies of coexistence well before a crisis, in a way that draws out the religious tendency across many cultures to dream and conceive of better realities and work toward them, positively engages religious traditions when they are not driven into extreme positions by the passions of conflict and the suffering of their constituencies."[70] Given the long-term nature of the strategies for change, effective inter-religious peacebuilding must be based on long-term, sustained engagement across the timeline of conflict, from before violence erupts to well after it is over.[71]

The nature and effectiveness of inter-religious peacebuilding is also a function of who is involved—elites, mid-level, or grassroots; insider only or also outsider. Inter-religious peacebuilding often involves religious leaders, but in many places there is also a proliferation of mid-level and grassroots inter-religious peacebuilding. Given the role of religious leaders in their communities, inter-religious dialogue is likely to be most successful when it is part of a larger, multilevel process that has been modeled and encouraged by religious leaders.[72] Unfortunately, too often, inter-religious engagement occurs at the leadership level or in ad hoc grassroots initiatives with little connection or coherence between them.

Inter-religious engagement can be impeded by difficulties in finding dialogue partners when, for example, hierarchical Christian communities seek to engage with decentralized Muslim communities or there are significant power imbalances (e.g., the Muslim and Christian communities in Iraq), which usually leaves little incentive for the dominant religious group to engage.

Most inter-religious dialogues involve moderates. This is partly making a virtue of necessity—extremists are likely to see dialogue as entailing illegitimate compromise or risking their own status—and partly a well-established strategy—moderates gain a voice and legitimacy that will help them marginalize the extremists. Engaging moderates enhances prospects for effective common or complementary action and avoids giving legitimacy to those who misuse religion to foment division and violence. But it also limits the effectiveness of dialogue because those most responsible for the violence are not engaged.[73] Sometimes, however, the engagement by moderates can build the trust necessary to allow them, together or alone, to reach out to the extremists within their own community without being accused by the other side of legitimating extremism.

The effectiveness of inter-religious peacebuilding can be enhanced when outsiders (those not from the area of conflict) contribute to the dialogue of insiders (those from the area of conflict). The Presbyterian and Catholic leaders in the United States worked with their counterparts in Northern Ireland on a twelve-year transatlantic ecumenical initiative—the Inter-Church Committee on Northern Ireland—that opened up possibilities for collaboration that did not exist when the ecumenical collaboration was limited to Northern Ireland.[74] Through ecumenical speaking tours and other visits to the United States, this initiative helped counteract the Presbyterian sense of siege by giving Presbyterian leaders a voice in the United States they had not had before, especially among Catholic elites who had influence over U.S. policy. The involvement of U.S. religious leaders also provided the necessary impetus for the four main churches in Ireland to undertake controversial initiatives, such as a common initiative on the neuralgic issue of fair employment.

Inter-religious peacebuilding can be effective if its purposes are clear; they are related to the nature of the conflict; they are linked to realistic, mostly long-term strategies for change; they involve sustained engagement by religious leaders at all levels; and they are supported by coreligionists from outside the area of conflict. A caution is in order, however. Inter-religious peacebuilding is essential and can be extremely effective, but too much emphasis has been placed on it to the exclusion of single-identity peacebuilding, or peacebuilding within one's own community.

Inter-religious peacebuilding faces obstacles that single-identity peacebuilding does not. Inter-religious peacebuilding requires significant time and resources that might better be used mobilizing one's community for peace. As Gopin points out, it is easier to convince someone to engage in peacebuilding from within one's community than it is to engage in authentic dialogue with one's adversary.[75] Moreover, given the dynamics of conflicts with a religious dimension, participation in inter-religious initiatives during times of crisis can undermine one's credibility with those within one's community who are most susceptible to the appeals of extremists.

Because it is prone to a least-common-denominator approach, inter-religious peacebuilding also lacks some of the power of single-identity peacebuilding. In some of the world's most devastating and long-standing conflicts, such as Colombia and the Democratic Republic of the Congo, religion plays a key role in peacebuilding, but inter-religious peacebuilding is largely irrelevant simply because of the religious demographics of the country. The remarkable political and social transformations in Poland, East Germany, the Philippines, and Serbia were influenced by a single dominant religion, often with close ties to national identity. Peacebuilding within one's community can draw on the full complement of a tradition's rituals, beliefs, norms, spirituality, and communal identity, which is not possible even in the most effective inter-religious peace-building. Extremists within a religious tradition will most likely be marginal-ized, not because the moderates are engaged in inter-religious initiatives but because they can appeal to this rich set of religious resources to convince their coreligionists that extremism is antithetical to their tradition. In short, inter-religious peacebuilding is sometimes essential and effective, but it is often not the most essential and effective form of religious peacebuilding.

Conclusion: Religious Peacebuilding and Policy

Jeff Stein, the national security editor at *Congressional Quarterly*, asked mem-bers of Congress and the Bush administration who specialize in counterter-rorism if they could explain the basic differences between Shiite and Sunni Muslims, the two principal antagonists in Iraq and elsewhere. The FBI's chief of national security incorrectly thought that Iran and Hezbollah were Sunni. In what he described as typical of most American counterterrorism officials, two chairpersons of different House Intelligence subcommittees dealing with ter-rorism also did not know the difference between the two Islamic traditions.[76] Not surprisingly, in U.S. planning for postwar Iraq, especially the Pentagon's planning, relatively little attention was given the role of religion.[77] In fact, under the Coalition Provisional Authority (CPA), the only Iraqi ministry with-out a shadow minister (i.e., a CPA overseer of the Iraqi minister) was religious affairs. The CPA was also slow to recognize the significant peacebuilding role of Grand Ayatollah Ali al-Sistani and how the complex intra-Muslim divisions in Iraq might contribute to conflict.

These anecdotes are symptomatic of a general incompetence with respect to the role of religion in international affairs on the part of many foreign policy elites, an incompetence rationalized by a secularist perspective, which, even after 9/11, does not place a premium on developing a sophisticated understand-ing of this role. Students of religion and U.S. foreign policy can resonate with Albright's complaint that although she had abundant expertise at her disposal on virtually any foreign policy issue, she had almost no one to turn to on mat-ters of religion.[78]

An extensive report on U.S. government engagement with religion by the Center for Strategic and International Studies concluded that despite a signif-icant increase in attention to religion since 9/11, major obstacles remain to effective U.S. engagement with religion.

- U.S. government officials are often reluctant to address the issue of religion, whether in response to a secular U.S. legal and political tradition, in the context of America's Judeo-Christian image overseas, or simply because religion is perceived as too complicated or sensitive.
- Current U.S. government frameworks for approaching religion are narrow, often approaching religions as problematic or monolithic forces, overemphasizing a terrorism-focused analysis of Islam and

sometimes marginalizing religion as a peripheral humanitarian or cultural issue.
- Institutional capacity to understand and approach religion is limited due to legal limitations, lack of religious expertise or training, minimal influence for religion-related initiatives, and a government primarily structured to engage with other official state actors.[79]

This report recommends a variety of ways the United States could address these obstacles to effective engagement with religion. The first task is to enhance the institutional competence on religion throughout the U.S. foreign policy apparatus. It would be helpful, for example, to expand the mission of the State Department's Office for International Religious Freedom and the Commission on International Religious Freedom to include not just religious freedom issues but also the less understood issue of religion, conflict, and peacebuilding. Much more important, however, would be to develop expertise on religion throughout the State Department, intelligence agencies, the Defense Department, and other relevant agencies. Religion cannot continue to be assigned to low-level cultural affairs officers at embassies who often have no expertise in religion and whose portfolio is far too broad to develop any.[80] The United Nations would also benefit from a similar institutionalization of expertise in religion by establishing a subcommission on religion as part of the new Peacebuilding Commission or by ensuring that it has experts in religion on the Peacebuilding Commission and its peacekeeping missions.

The second task is to increase engagement with a wide range of religious actors while also reconsidering the nature of that engagement. Concerns about engaging with or supporting terrorists have severely limited the ability of the U.S. government and, to a lesser extent, development organizations involved in religious peacebuilding from working with any but "moderate" religious actors in areas of conflict. Strengthening the moderates and marginalizing the extremists is a reasonable strategy for change, but effective peacebuilding cannot be limited to that single strategy. It is also important to engage with a wide range of religious traditions, not just dominant groups, and to engage at multiple levels (though it is appropriate for a government to give priority to religious leaders given their often crucial role and so as not to appear to be undermining those leaders).

The nature of engagement with religious actors is also important. The tendency of policy makers to be concerned with religious entities mostly when they play a political role in crisis situations limits the ability for effective engagement in long-term, culture-changing peacebuilding which is the forte of religious peacebuilding. Governments often place unrealistic expectations on religious leaders because they seek short-term political impact during a crisis. In conflicts with a religious dimension, governments often try to convene religious leaders or otherwise encourage religious peacebuilding under governmental auspices. With some notable exceptions, these initiatives are misguided. Governments should be wary of interfering in the internal dynamics of religious bodies or attempting to coordinate or promote religious peacebuilding. In most cases, direct and visible governmental involvement with a religious peacebuilding initiative is not needed (often the religious groups are doing much more than the government knows or acknowledges), nor is it helpful. Governments rarely have the knowledge, credibility, or neutrality needed to intervene, and governmental involvement can undermine the independence and credibility of religious bodies. More appropriate and helpful are government efforts to include experts in religion and, in exceptional cases, religious leaders indirectly in negotiating and implementing peace processes. Because religious leaders usually are deeply rooted in their communities and might have a broader, more long-term vision than political leaders, their input into the process can help ensure that a peace agreement will take into account issues crucial to a sustainable peace.[81]

The third, and by far most important, task is to reconsider the substantive approach to religion. Despite rhetoric about Islam being a religion of peace, the emphasis of U.S. policy on the "war of ideas" between the West and Islamic extremism risks framing the challenge much as bin Laden and other religious extremists do—as a war of Islam against the West and the West against Islam.[82] The almost exclusive focus on extremism has inhibited the development of a sophisticated understanding of Islam and has also diverted attention and resources from the role of other religious traditions in conflicts. The preoccupation with Islamic extremism arises from legitimate concerns about a grave threat, but it also reflects the predisposition among policy elites to see religion mostly as a problem to be dealt with, rather than a force for peace. The United States and other nations recognize the critical role of religious entities in relief and development and have long engaged with these efforts; a similar appreciation is needed of the positive peacebuilding role of these same religious actors. When religion is taken seriously by policy makers, it is usually treated in instrumentalist ways. It needs to be considered on its own terms, not simply as one of a host of NGOs or potential political allies in promoting the government's agenda in a particular conflict. It is a daunting task that will require resources that do not yet exist within the policy-making apparatus; religious peacebuilding has to be considered not just from a political science or conflict resolution perspective but also from a more robust and holistic theological, sociological, and cultural perspective.[83]

The final substantive issue that has to be addressed more forthrightly is the impact that U.S. policies have on the capacity of religious actors to build peace. The U.S. intervention in Iraq has fed Islamic extremism and deepened divisions within Islam and between Islam and Christianity—just as many religious leaders predicted it would. It is also difficult to exaggerate how U.S. support for dictatorial regimes throughout the Middle East and its failure to pursue vigorously an equitable peace between Israelis and Palestinians have diminished the peacebuilding capacity of moderate religious actors and strengthened the hand of religious extremists. The cultural impact of U.S. policies is also critical. Even public diplomacy programs on religion tend not to listen to and learn from religious actors but promote Western, secular approaches to religion and democratization that are seen as threats by even moderate religious actors in some cultures.[84] If the United States continues to be seen as the principal engine of Western secularization, individualism, and materialism, bin Laden and his supporters will have little trouble recruiting sympathizers from the many who see such efforts at secularization as further proof of America's anti-Islamic neocolonialism.

NOTES

1. Madeleine Albright, *The Mighty and the Almighty: Reflections on America, God, and World Affairs* (New York: HarperCollins, 2006), p. 8.

2. The secularist paradigm draws on the literature analyzing the dynamics of secularization, but goes beyond this analysis to assert the normative value of secularization. For a particularly polemical example of the ideology of secularism, see, e.g., Christopher Hitchens, *God Is Not Great: How Religion Poisons Everything* (New York: Twelve Books, 2007).

3. Zbigniew Brzezinski, "The Illusion of Control," in Powers, G., Christiansen, D., and Hennemeyer, R., eds., *Peacemaking: Moral and Policy Choices for a New World* (Washington, D.C.: U.S. Conference of Catholic Bishops, 1994), pp. 26, 31. Reprinted from Zbigniew Brzezinski, *Out of Control* (New York: Macmillan, 1993).

4. Ibid., p. 31.

5. See Joseph Nye, Jr., *Soft Power: The Means to Success in World Politics* (New York: Public Affairs, 2004), pp. 5–17; Stanley Hoffmann, "The Case for Leadership," *Foreign Policy* (Winter 1990–1991): 25–30.

6. Samuel Huntington, *The Clash of Civilizations and the Remaking of World Order.* (New York: Simon & Schuster, 1996): p. 66. See also Samuel Huntington, "If Not Civilization, What?" *Foreign Affairs* 72 (November/December 1993): 192. Samuel Huntington, "The Clash of Civilizations?" *Foreign Affairs* 72 (Summer 1993): 49.

7. Brzezinski, "The Illusion of Control," pp. 26, 31.

8. R. Scott Appleby, *The Ambivalence of the Sacred: Religion, Violence, and Reconciliation* (Lanham, Md.: Rowan & Littlefield, 2000): pp. 5–7.

9. Some excellent examples of this literature include Mark Rogers, Tom Bamat, and Julie Ideh, eds., *Pursuing Just Peace: An Overview and Case Studies for Faith-Based Peacebuilders* (Baltimore, Md.: Catholic Relief Services, 2008); David Little, *Peacemakers in Action: Profiles of Religion in Conflict Resolution* (New York: Cambridge University Press, 2007); Tsjeard Bouta, S. Ayse Kadayifci-Orellana, Mohammed Abu-Nimer, *Faith-Based Peace-Building: Mapping and Analysis of Christian, Muslim and Multi-Faith Actors* (Washington, D.C.: Netherlands Institute of International Relations in cooperation with Salam Institute for Peace and Justice, 2005); Harold Coward and Gordon Smith, eds., *Religion and Peacebuilding* (Albany: State University of New York Press, 2004); Douglas Johnston, ed., *Faith-Based Diplomacy: Trumping Realpolitik* (Oxford: Oxford University Press, 2003); Mary Ann Cejka and Thomas Bamat, eds., *Artisans of Peace: Grassroots Peacemaking among Christian Communities* (Maryknoll, N.Y.: Orbis Books, 2003); David Smock, ed., *Interfaith Dialogue and Peacebuilding* (Washington, D.C.: U.S. Institute of Peace, 2002); Marc Gopin, *Between Eden and Armageddon: The Future of World Religions, Violence, and Peacemaking* (Oxford: Oxford University Press, 2000).

10. Appleby, *The Ambivalence of the Sacred*, pp. 76–78.

11. Henry Kissinger, "Bosnia: Reasons for Care," *Washington Post*, December 10, 1995, p. C9.

12. Isak Svensson, "Fighting with Faith: Religion and Conflict Resolution in Civil Wars," *Journal of Conflict Resolution* 51 (2007): 932–934.

13. Ibid., pp. 938–939. See also Monica Duffy Toft, "Religion, Civil War, and International Order," BCSIA Discussion Paper 2006–03, Kennedy School of Government, Harvard University, July 2006. Toft finds that since 1940, "most civil wars are fought over issues not involving religion, except perhaps peripherally: *religious civil wars are rare.*" Monica Duffy Toft, "Getting Religion: The Puzzling Case of Islam and Civil War," *International Security* 3 (Spring 2007): 97–131. On the other hand, Toft found that there has been an increase in the relative number of religious civil wars over the years, with religious civil wars making up a disproportionate number of the ongoing wars after 2000 (eight of seventeen as of 2000).

14. Only 8 of 49 militant sects (out of 233 communal groups) in the early 1990s were defined solely or mainly by their religious beliefs. Ted Robert Gurr, *Minorities at Risk: A Global View of Ethnopolitical Conflicts* (Washington, D.C.: U.S. Institute of Peace, 1993), p. 317.

15. According to Philpott, citing Bruce Hoffman, *Inside Terrorism* (New York: Colombia University Press, 1998), in 1968, none of the world's 11 terrorist groups were religious; by 1980, 2 of 64 terrorist groups were religious; by 1995, 26 of 56 (46 percent) of all terrorist groups were religious. Today, based on the Terrorism Knowledge Base, Philpott finds that 95 of 262 (36 percent) of known terrorist groups are identifiably religious. The knowledge base is presented by the National Memorial Institute for the Prevention of Terrorism and can be found at http://www.tkb.org/Home.jsp. Daniel Philpott, "Explaining the Political Ambivalence of Religion," *American Political Science Review* 101 (August 2007): 520.

16. Ten of the forty-four (23 percent) religious civil wars recurred, compared with only eleven of ninety (12 percent) of the nonreligious civil wars. There were 28,974 versus 7,666 average deaths per year for central and peripheral religious involvement, respectively. Toft, "Getting Religion," p. 116.

17. Svensson, "Fighting with Faith," pp. 930–949.

18. Ibid., pp. 938–942.

19. See ibid., p. 932.

20. Amartya Sen, *Identity and Violence: The Illusion of Destiny* (New York: Norton, 2006), p. 76.

21. Ted Robert Gurr, *Minorities at Risk: A Global View of Ethnopolitical Conflicts* (Washington, D.C.: U.S. Institute of Peace, 1993).

22. For a detailed evaluation of efforts to quantify religion in conflict and other situations, see Jonathan Fox, *A World Survey of Religion and the State* (Cambridge: Cambridge University Press, 2008), pp. 32–61.

23. On the views and strategy of the IRA, see Padraig O'Malley, *The Uncivil Wars: Ireland Today* (Belfast: Blackstaff Press, 1983), pp. 258–313.

24. No one term adequately describes the distinction that needs to be made. Appleby rightly notes in *The Ambivalence of the Sacred*, for example, that the problem is not religious militancy, because religious militants include both bin Laden and Martin Luther King Jr., suicide bombers, and saintly advocates of nonviolence. The phrase "religious extremism" is not an entirely adequate alternative, but I use it to distinguish between those religious actors who seek a just peace in conflict situations and those who foment violence, division and sectarianism.

25. On the question of religion, there is a significant gap between the views of the policy elites in Washington, London, Paris, Berlin, Moscow, and Tokyo and the

views of ordinary people around the world. In fall 2003, the Zogby polling firm and the University of Rochester released what they called the first ever worldwide poll on religious beliefs, which found that people care about religion far more than politics, that a clear majority associated violence within their own country with politics not religion, and that a majority says that their country would be better if it were more religious. Poll results are summarized at http://www.zogbyworldwide.com/news/ReadNews1.cfm.

26. Pope Benedict XVI made this distinction in his message for the twentieth anniversary of the Inter-religious Meeting of Prayer for Peace, initiated by his predecessor, John Paul II, at Assisi in October 1986: "demonstrations of violence cannot be attributed to religion as such but to the cultural limitations with which it is lived and develops in time. . . . In fact, attestations of the close bond that exists between the relationship with God and the ethics of love are recorded in all great religious traditions." David Little warns that those who claim that "good [or authentic] religion brings peace" oversimplify, but notes that one lesson from a study of religious peacebuilders is that "proper religion exhibits a preference for pursuing peace by peaceful means (nonviolence over violence) and for combining the promotion of peace with the promotion of justice." D. Little, "Religion, Violent Conflict, and Peacemaking," in Little, *Peacemakers in Action*, p. 429, 437.

27. Appleby, *The Ambivalence of the Sacred*, p. 8.

28. Ibid., p. 9.

29. *Catholic Almanac* (Huntington, Ind.: Our Sunday Visitor, 2009).

30. See Appleby and Lederach, chapter 1 in this volume.

31. David Steele, "An Introductory Overview of Faith-Based Peacebuilding," in Mark Rogers, Tom Bamat, and Julie Ideh (eds.), *Pursuing Just Peace: An Overview and Case Studies for Faith-Based Peacebuilders* (Baltimore, Md.: Catholic Relief Services, 2008), pp. 22–32.

32. Ibid.

33. Appleby, *The Ambivalence of the Sacred*, pp. 7–8.

34. Albright, *The Mighty and the Almighty*, p. 77.

35. I borrow this formulation from J. Bryan Hehir, "Responsibilities and Temptations of Power: A Catholic View," *Journal of Law and Religion* 8:1 & 2 (1990), p. 75.

36. Little, "Religion, Violent Conflict, and Peacemaking," p. 438.

37. Philpott shows that radical Islamic revivalist groups, while small in number, foment conflict by sacralizing such conflicts. Philpott, "Explaining the Political Ambivalence of Religion," pp. 515–516.

38. Appleby, *The Ambivalence of the Sacred*, p. 122.

39. Douglas Johnston and Brian Cox, "Faith-Based Diplomacy and Preventive Engagement," in Douglas Johnston, ed., *Faith-Based Diplomacy* (Oxford: Oxford University Press, 2003): p. 14.

40. Lenard Cohen reviews surveys on religious affiliation in "Bosnia's 'Tribal Gods': The Role of Religion in Nationalist Politics," in Paul Mojzes, ed., The *Religion and the War in Bosnia* (Atlanta: Scholars Press, 1998), pp. 43–54.

41. Dowd suggests that the low level of meaningful religious affiliation in Rwanda was, in part, a function of the fact that most Rwandans were Catholic, so Catholic identity meant less than if Rwanda had been a more religiously plural country. According to Dowd, there is "an inverse relationship between the extent to which membership is inclusive and the meaningfulness of membership. The more exclusive membership is, the more meaningful membership is." Robert Dowd,

"Religious Pluralism and Peace: Lessons from Sub-Saharan Africa in Comparative Perspective," Paper presented at the Annual Meeting of American Political Science Association, Chicago, September 2–5, 2004. Dowd might be correct in his assertion, but factors other than religious pluralism must be at work. Otherwise, it is difficult to explain the role of the Catholic Church in Poland, the Philippines, El Salvador, Colombia, and other religiously homogenous countries in mobilizing the masses in opposition to repressive governments.

42. Timothy A. Byrnes, *Transnational Catholicism in Postcommunist Europe* (Lanham, Md.: Rowman and Littlefield, 2001).

43. John Paul Lederach, *Building Peace: Sustainable Reconciliation in Divided Societies* (Washington, D.C.: U.S. Institute of Peace Press, 1997), p. 39.

44. Lederach and Appleby, chapter 1 of this volume.

45. Little, *Peacemakers in Action*, pp. 4–6.

46. Kelsie Thompson, "Uganda: Alliances for Peace: The Acholi Religious Leaders Peace Initiative," in Mark Rogers, Tom Bamat, and Julie Ideh (eds.), *Pursuing Just Peace: An Overview and Case Studies for Faith-Based Peacebuilders* (Baltimore, Md.: Catholic Relief Services, 2008), pp. 133–144.

47. See, e.g., William Bole, Drew Christiansen, S.J., and Robert Hennemeyer, *Forgiveness in International Politics: An Alternative Road to Peace* (Washington, D.C.: U.S. Conference of Catholic Bishops, 2004); Raymond Helmick and Rodney Petersen, eds., *Forgiveness and Reconciliation: Religion, Public Policy, and Conflict Transformation* (Philadelphia: Templeton Foundation Press, 2001); Donald Shriver, *An Ethic for Enemies: Forgiveness in Politics* (Oxford: Oxford University Press, 1998).

48. For a highly nuanced analysis of the wide variety of religion–state relationships around the world, see Fox, *A World Survey of Religion and the State*.

49. Lederach and Appleby, chapter 1 of this book.

50. Amitai Etzioni, *Security First: For a Muscular, Moral Foreign Policy* (New Haven: Yale University Press, 2007), p. 152.

51. Ibid., p. 163.

52. Ibid., p. 151.

53. Ibid.

54. According to Philpott, 91 percent of all religious terrorist groups are radical Islamic revivalists. Philpott, "Explaining the Political Ambivalence of Religion," p. 521.

55. For historical studies of religious and ethical approaches to war and peace, see, e.g., Roland Bainton, *Christian Attitudes toward War and Peace: A Historical Survey and Critical Re-evaluation* (Nashville: Abingdon Press, 1960); James Turner Johnson, *Just War Tradition and the Restraint of War: A Moral and Historical Inquiry* (Princeton, N.J.: Princeton University Press, 1981).

56. David Little points out that the Rev. Dr. Roy Magee, the Presbyterian minister who helped convince Loyalist paramilitaries to give up their violence, is not a pacifist, nor are several of the other religious peacebuilders he examines. Little, "Religion, Violent Conflict, and Peacemaking," pp. 436–437.

57. Gopin, *Between Eden and Armageddon*, pp. 30–31.

58. Philpott, "Explaining the Political Ambivalence of Religion," p. 520.

59. Ibid.

60. On the limited role of the just war tradition in peacebuilding, see Gopin, *Between Eden and Armageddon*, pp. 35–37.

61. Reinhold Niebuhr was a twentieth-century American theologian generally known as a "realist."

62. For an excellent review of the plethora of major inter-religious dialogues since 9/11, see John J. DeGioia, *Islam and the West: Annual Report on the State of Dialogue* (World Economic Forum, January 2008), pp. 56–69.

63. Appleby, *The Ambivalence of the Sacred*, p. 141.

64. Gopin, *Between Eden and Armageddon*, p. 63.

65. Ibid., p. 64.

66. Little, *Peacemakers in Action*, p. 440.

67. Ibid., pp. 278–298, 440–441.

68. For a general discussion of peacebuilding and theories of change, see John Paul Lederach, Reina Neufeldt, and Hal Culbertson, *Reflective Peacebuilding: A Planning, Monitoring, and Learning Tool Kit* (Notre Dame, Ind.: Joan B. Kroc Institute for International Peace Studies, University of Notre Dame, 2007)

69. I am drawing on an excellent analysis of theories of change in inter-religious peacebuilding; see Reina Neufeldt, "Interfaith Dialogue: Assessing the State of Theory, Practice and Impact," unpublished manuscript, 2008.

70. Gopin, *Between Eden and Armageddon*, p. 62.

71. "We are all familiar with what I have privately dubbed 'the dialogue of drones,' a polite—but tedious—exchange of theological generalities and self-serving slogans. . . . But that process takes time; it involves repeated meetings, sometimes over months and years, and it requires secluded spaces. Fruitful dialogue is not a quick fix and it does not happen in a fishbowl." Jane Dammen McAuliffe, "Context and Continuity Is Crucial," in *World Economic Forum Report on West-Islam Dialogue*, p. 61.

72. Gopin, *Between Eden and Armageddon*, pp. 42–43.

73. Thomas Banchoff, "The Circle of Dialogue," in N. Tranchet and D. Rienstra, eds., *Islam and the West: Annual Report on the State of Dialogue* (Geneva: World Economic Forum, 2008), p. 67.

74. Josiah H. Beeman and Robert Mahony, "The Institutional Churches and the Process of Reconciliation in Northern Ireland: Recent Progress in Presbyterian—Roman Catholic Relations," in Dermot Keogh and Michael H. Haltzell, eds., *Northern Ireland and the Politics of Reconciliation* (Cambridge: Cambridge University Press, 1993), pp. 150–159.

75. Gopin, *Between Eden and Armageddon*, p. 48.

76. Jeff Stein, "Can You Tell a Sunni from a Shiite?" *New York Times*, October 17, 2006, p. A23.

77. Liora Danan, "Mixed Blessings: U.S. Government Engagement with Religion in Conflict-Prone Settings," A Report of the Post-Conflict Reconstruction Project, Center for Strategic and International Studies, July 2007, p. 6.

78. Albright, *The Mighty and the Almighty*, p. 75.

79. Danan, "Mixed Blessings," p. 3.

80. Many of the recommendations for improving the U.S. government's capacity to address religious freedom issues would also be relevant to religion and conflict issues. See *Final Report of the Advisory Committee on Religious Freedom Abroad to the Secretary of State and to the President of the United States*, May 17, 1999.

81. Little, *Peacemakers in Action*, pp. 20–21.

82. Danan, "Mixed Blessings," p. 43.

83. Ibid.

84. See ibid., pp. 14–17.

Conclusion: Strategic Peacebuilding beyond the Liberal Peace

Oliver P. Richmond

The concept and theories of strategic peacebuilding developed in this study are indicative of a much needed and radical attempt to reframe the liberal peacebuilding project of the post–Cold War world. This project was derived from the "UN revolution" and the "age of peacebuilding" that Philpott refers to in the introduction to this volume. It is now clear that what appeared to be the loose "peacebuilding consensus" of the 1990s faces many challenges.[1]

This volume represents the latest stage of this ongoing project. Boutros-Ghali's groundbreaking policy statement, *Agenda for Peace,* was followed by the lesser known "agenda" on democratization and development,[2] documents such as the Carnegie Report, the Brahimi Report, "The Responsibility to Protect," the High Level Panel Report, and expert panels on peace operations, conflict resolution, and peacebuilding.[3] The dominant impulse, at least until the war on terror diverted attention and resources, has been to draw together the wide-ranging responses that have emerged across institutions and disciplines to try to produce one universal blueprint for peace, one that can now be called a liberal peace for the post–Cold War world.[4] I have described this elsewhere as the product of a third generation of thinking about peace and conflict.[5] This represents a rational and secular post-Enlightenment project in which democratization, development, the rule of law, and human rights form the basis for building a postconflict state, guided by external experts and conditions.[6] The state is based on the liberal norms of a mixture of legal regulation and freedoms, as well as on self-determination and sovereignty. This liberal project has become key to the production of international order, but it is also subject to internal inconsistencies and criticisms, external resistance, and increasingly obvious shortcomings.

Clearly, there are different interpretations of the liberal peacebuilding project, from those of a conservative nature (focusing on security matters and institutions) to those that incorporate many of the attributes of more emancipatory thinking (focusing on civil society and issues related to social justice).[7] They all share assumptions about the state, sovereignty, territoriality, governance, democracy, self-determination, human rights, rule of law, and development. The relative emphasis on these components depends on which version of liberal peacebuilding is being pursued. As I argue elsewhere, mainstream thinking on peacebuilding has generally come to agree on an "orthodox" form of the liberal peace, which is somewhere between its conservative and emancipatory gradations.[8]

The model of the 1990s quickly proved to be inadequate, and even worse, sometimes ethically inconsistent, particularly given the UN withdrawal from Rwanda during the genocide, the failure to instill a liberal state through "peace enforcement" in Somalia, and the failure to combat ethnic cleansing in Bosnia and Kosovo. The dominant peacebuilding actors (e.g., the UN system, the international financial institutions, nongovernmental organizations, and major donors) tried to escape this predicament by a combination of humanitarian intervention, prioritization of military security, efforts to create liberal states, and, after the terrorists attacks of 2001, regime change (as the precursor for liberal statebuilding). The goal of creating a liberal state meant that almost any intervention, using almost any method—whether coercive, conditional, or consensual—became automatically legitimate in the view of some prominent U.S. and U.K. policy makers. This liberal and "positive" peace was all the justification that many policy makers required, even though it focused primarily on installing often alien institutions on people, culture, and society.

As a result, in the Middle East, Cyprus, Sri Lanka, the Balkans, and many other locations, peace processes began to undermine themselves by reinforcing state-centric models and ultimately confirming ethnonationalism and territoriality (despite a concerted move in the 1990s to go "beyond Westphalia").[9] As peacebuilding came to merge with statebuilding, local actors renewed their competition for control of the new state. This appropriation of liberal agendas for peacebuilding, without concern for the everyday needs of the population and with too great a reliance on force and discourses of securitization,[10] meant that the liberal goal of emancipation and a just peace was often lost. Instead, the focus returned to far more limited conflict management approaches.

The broad consensus on a liberal peace remains to a certain degree, though it has had limited outcomes so far and many reverses. Its proponents claim that their priorities of security and institutionalism represent realism and pragmatism. They are concerned that the peace agenda may already be overextended. Its critics—including myself—argue that in practice such approaches represent limitations that weaken the very project of peacebuilding and its contemporary associated dogmas.[11] Such tensions are clear in the strategic vision of peacebuilding that this volume represents and begins to address in its quest for a *justpeace*. It has ably outlined the liberal arguments for and about peacebuilding but goes further and suggests a new stage in the development of peacebuilding.

In this conclusion, I outline the range of peacebuilding issues discussed in this volume. The overall thesis is that strategic peacebuilding is an alternative to the (now fading) more securitized post-9/11 strategy. Through a reflexive engagement with liberal peacebuilding, the challenge is to return to inclusive peace processes and a more robust conception of sustainable peace. In the next section, I examine how strategic peacebuilding challenges the liberal peace which has become the predominant focus of peacebuilding. Finally, I offer some thoughts on how the liberal peace might be improved on, drawing to a large degree on research I have recently conducted on what I call "liberal peace transitions" in five cases.[12]

Overview of Issues

The critical and strategic agenda for peacebuilding that emerges in this volume is developed in increasing detail as this book progresses. The volume begins with a conceptual discussion, followed by a discussion of institutional forms of peacebuilding from above and below. Lederach and Appleby develop a concept of strategic peacebuilding to which the subsequent chapters refer. They attempt to conceptualize a broad horizontal, vertical, and temporal dynamic that takes into account the interrelationship between theory, policy, and practice; introduces diversity into policy debates; and prepares the ground for an ethical and strategic critique of actual peacebuilding. It moves beyond the more usual evaluation based on issues of efficiency and coordination.

In the following conceptual chapter, Peter Wallensteen optimistically points out that the number of conflicts has significantly declined from the high of the immediate post–Cold War environment. He attributes this decline in part to the development of peacebuilding practices, institutions, and theory during this period. Although states are obviously necessary for peacebuilding, he is critical of the tendency to equate peacebuilding with statebuilding; engagement with a wider set of issues and actors is also essential. For example, the reconciliation between and within France and Germany after World War II was achieved by addressing issues of human dignity and security for communities as they arose in everyday political, social, economic, and cultural life. Incorporating a wide range of issues increases the complexity of peacebuilding, which many policy makers (and some academics) take to be implausible. But as Wallensteen argues, embracing the theoretical, methodological, ontological, and practical complexities of peacebuilding helps peace be more self-sustaining. A more self-sustaining peace also entails engaging with local peacebuilders and regional contexts while avoiding stifling international engagement as well as market solutions that, at least in the difficult and lengthy transitional period, might not meet urgent needs for jobs and activities that build a common future. Wallensteen offers valuable and wide-ranging insight into peacebuilding and its evolution, representing and concurring with much innovative research into an agenda for *justpeace* over the past few years.

Hal Culbertson raises the problem of learning and evaluation in the following chapter. Especially since 1990, peacebuilding practices have tended to be broader in scope and increasingly focused on efficiency and integration. Yet the philosophy underlying liberal peacebuilding, which provides the parameters of this broadening, has not been subject to much reflection. As Culbertson points out, this is partly because this would involve questioning the universal applicability of the blueprint itself. An evaluation process that reflects diverse contexts and addresses failures is necessary if peacebuilding is to develop legitimacy internationally and at the local level. In my view, peacebuilding practice has been a singular failure in developing legitimacy, mainly because it has become so indebted and subservient to a liberal, Western, and developed-world paradigm of peace that is more a technology of governance than a response to local realities.[13] Culbertson's emphasis on developing reflective capacities at the micro level of peacebuilding projects is vital if they are to contribute to a *justpeace* that has both emancipatory qualities and everyday relevance.

Philpott's chapter on an ethics for political reconciliation opens up an area that rarely appears in policy and academic literature, which has focused on developing a managerial approach to peacebuilding in the context of the Weberian state.[14] Disciplinary, cold, and lacking in empathy, such literature often focuses on the international dimensions of a state-centric peace, which gives primacy to security rather than reconciliation at all levels. Philpott shows how this approach overlooks colossal injustice and suffering.

Unfortunately, many actors have already evolved standard operating procedures that have avoided reconciliation—not consciously, perhaps, but as a result of far too much faith in the liberal state and a far too parsimonious an approach to researching and constructing reconciliation as the basis for peace. The key elements of political reconciliation—acknowledgment, reparations, accountability, forgiveness, apology, and just political and economic institutions—provide a more comprehensive approach to the ethics of peacebuilding. Nonsecular, non-Western models of state and authority and cultural and religious practices are very difficult to build into a liberal state model and therefore generate an internal tension within the current peacebuilding paradigm.

Philpott argues that religious and cultural traditions are crucial to reconciliation, taking it far beyond the liberal project into a terrain more likely to connect populations and leaders and to develop a sustainable ethics of peace. The question then becomes how to actualize these practices to create a locally acceptable social contract. Philpott rightly notes that this requires a much more thorough engagement with questions of social justice. If as much effort had been put into this area as has been devoted to governance, institutions, and security over the past twenty years, the track record of the peacebuilding project might have been far better. Perhaps it might not have reached the heights of reconciliation and reconstruction in Europe after World War II, but the basis for such an achievement might now be present.

Some of these issues are also raised in Simon Chesterman's chapter on the role of international institutions in peacebuilding. He asks the provocative and important question: whose strategy, whose peace? This gets at why reconciliation, for example, is generally a low priority in the liberal agenda. In my view, much of what has developed so far has attempted rather unreflectively to transfer to conflict zones a "one-size-fits-all" package, based in a Western ideology and experience that leaves little room for local adjustment. The priority is peace between states rather than pursuing more ambitious forms of conflict resolution and transformation within and between societies.

Chesterman shows how this tendency has led to approaches to transitional administration that aim to replace divided or collapsed states with more stable forms of statehood, mainly determined by external agendas and ideologies rather than an equitable and transparent processes of negotiation between locals and internationals. International practitioners determine the language of issues raised in such conversations through their own expectations, processes, and institutional frameworks, creating local peacebuilding industries that are mimicked but not necessarily internalized. Chesterman provides an excellent account of the need for a far better understanding of local political dynamics and their sustainability and legitimacy. He argues for channeling political resources through institutions rather than individuals, through civilians rather than the military, and through democratic processes. Great care is needed on the part of internationals to avoid any semblance of a colonial relationship with local actors. If he is correct in saying "states cannot be made from the outside," a radical revision is required of the peacebuilding project. I would go a step further and encourage an examination of polities other than states and the sorts of capacities they require to rebuild a local social contract in a regional context. Many of the problems that Chesterman points to represent a failure of current models of peacebuilding to build social contracts between states, international peacebuilders, politicians, and local communities. Local communities are the most ignored, yet most crucial constituencies of peacebuilding.

The preceding chapters have grappled with the normative aspects of peacebuilding. In particular, they reach for a shared ethics that is plausible at both the local and international level. Nicholas Sambanis reverts to a more classical methodology but shares many of the same concerns in engaging with a notion of sustainable peace. He offers a "peacebuilding triangle," developed with Michael Doyle, that shows the relationship among the depth of the conflict, remaining local capacity, and the requirements for international assistance. He asks a fascinating question: what is the standard of peace required? He answers: a "participatory peace." A participatory peace focuses on local engagement and the social contract, and the capacity to survive after international actors have left. He offers a complex and convincing explanation for failed peace agreements as well as prescriptions for greater success, include more attention to local capacity building, greater UN engagement, more foreign assistance, and more multidimensional hybrid engagements. In addition, he argues that democracy needs to be rooted not just within a nation-state but also in a broader regional context.

This argument about increased participation and hybridity runs into difficulty with his assertion that integrated missions might have to rely on stronger security interventions and delays in political liberalization. Peace operations might reduce local government capacity, especially in terms of political economy, in the short term, with the longer term goal of a more participatory peace. As Iraq and Afghanistan have unequivocally shown, however, this approach will anger the participants in a peace process in the short term and make it less likely that they will participate in good faith or that a *justpeace* will be achieved. Indeed, it runs the risk of undermining the legitimacy of peacebuilding because it involves internationals supplanting local input into statebuilding. At least in the short term, they lose the two elements of a *justpeace*—self-determination and self-government. Perhaps if Iraq and Afghanistan had been run under the auspices of the UN, such a bargain could have been made and accepted by locals as legitimate. But even then, history shows this is unlikely. Even "participation" is often not seen as enough for local actors, elites and grassroots alike, who have often invested blood and resources in a struggle for self-governance. Before any international intervention that might legitimately defer local governance and place it in the hands of international actors, there must be a consensus that has both broad international *and* local legitimacy.

The following chapter adds a further dimension to the discussion of strategic peacebuilding in that it seeks to find a balance between excluding and sanctioning terrorists and developing a viable peace process based on democracy, the rule of law, and human rights. Given that the era of the war on terror has generally been a substitute for the promising peace processes of the 1990s, this is a difficult balance to find. Clearly, as George Lopez and David Cortright show, such strategies have to be considered where parties to a peace process cannot be persuaded to renounce actual or structural violence. They argue that this balance is more achievable with a targeted approach to sanctions, as has emerged within the UN system since the mid-1990s. Targeted sanctions can be a substitute for military intervention, particularly in the context of arms embargoes.

Sanctions must be used with caution. They should not be indiscriminate, nor should they be expanded without great care for they may further radicalize extremists or predatory elites (state and nonstate). Moreover, they can place the peacebuilding process at risk by excluding the most difficult actors (or spoilers). In cases such as Northern Ireland in the 1990s, these are the very actors with whom it is most important to open lines of communication. Yet those targeted are often engaged in behavior that is generally considered to undermine peace. Given this paradox, sanctions are a strategy to be applied with great sensitivity. Indeed, as recent UN actions have shown,[15] it is important to maintain a sharp separation between counterterrorism strategies and peacebuilding. In many peace processes where this has not occurred, such as in the Middle East, Kashmir, and Sri Lanka, state counterterrorism strategies have obstructed the peace processes at various phases. It has proven very difficult to persuade the UN that this is not the case (see, for example, the quiet marginalization of the Counter-Terrorism Committee in the UN system). As the authors point out, however, involving the UN adds more nuance to such strategies while avoiding what Mark Duffield would call the securitization of peacebuilding and development through the adoption of a "hard" security agenda.[16]

Robert Johansen examines the contribution of international judicial processes in his chapter, which aims at overturning the widely held assumption that peace and justice are mutually exclusive. Clearly, importing external standards of justice into conflict zones can have an impact on accommodations reached between disputants. This is often most noticeable in investigating human rights abuses and atrocities committed during a conflict. As Johansen points out, since the International Criminal Court has made it plausible that political leaders will later be held responsible for war crimes, a compromise peace agreement might not be in their interest. To deal with this dilemma, he proposes a "rule-utilitarian ethic" aimed at achieving the lowest possible loss of life in both the short and long run. In this ethics, legal justice is one element in a wider peacebuilding framework, not the dominant element. Peacebuilding and justice do not require an either/or choice but share common goals of strengthening human rights and the rule of law as part of a *justpeace* ethic. Peacebuilding should take into account the political and normative utilities of justice, which requires an account of political interests in their local context as well as in the context of international norms. Where there is a tension between processes of justice and an overall goal of peace, Johansen argues that "truth telling" should be encouraged as a foundation for a broad reconciliation process that does not favor certain groups (especially those implicated in violence or crime) and does not allow justice to be a cover for vengeance. Thus, peace and justice are always integral to each other. Separating them probably will lead to a "virtual peace" that likely favors those who had defied international and local norms or are intent on usurping control of state structures. Peacebuilding must show how the rule of law operates fairly to provide justice for perpetrators and victims; it must strengthen the rule of law in ways that are relevant and legitimate both at the international and local levels.

Such sentiments are mirrored in the following chapter, which examines the place of human rights in peacebuilding. Naomi Roht-Arriaza argues for an ecological model of peacebuilding driven by human rights and humanitarian law frameworks operative at the local, national, and global levels. Justice mechanisms rooted in local communities are especially vital. But as Roht-Arriaza illustrates, there are problems with the assumption that the local milieu, often one of the drivers of conflict, is the source of unambiguous conflict resolution. Yet coopting and formalizing justice in a local context using Western standards also runs the risk of alienating the very communities who need and want to be part of a new, democratic, and pluralistic polity. Narrow versions of justice that are disconnected from broader social and political issues need to be avoided.

Larissa Fast's chapter on humanitarian operations looks at whether humanitarian action by outsiders might be integrated into strategic peacebuilding. She argues that the need to maintain a moral response to human suffering must take priority over integrated approaches to peacebuilding. This means, quite rightly, that humanitarian assistance is more important than the political or institutional aspects of peacebuilding. Humanitarian assistance does not build peace or deal with the roots of conflict but instead focuses on specific and isolated issues, beginning with avoiding harm. An integrated approach compromises the capacity of humanitarian agencies to operate because it requires them to become involved in the structures of political conditionality. A separate space is required. Although humanitarian assistance is vital to the project of peacebuilding, it must be able to focus on need alone, even where rights are still problematic. This neutral, needs-based goal is important, even if lack of neutrality and bias are inevitable given an intervener's expectations, culture, biases, and, in many cases, lack of local knowledge.

Jackie Smith's fascinating chapter focuses on the problems raised by the often unthinking adoption of neoliberal economic strategies, which have had serious unintended consequences across a whole range of cases. I would go further than Smith and argue that such impulses are now built into the institutional structures of liberal peacebuilding because they rest on an inherent perception that peacebuilders possess expert knowledge and locals do not. An automatic devaluing and distancing from the local context results.[17] This propagates a hierarchy that neoliberalism and liberal institutionalism confirms in economic, political, and sometimes even class terms.[18] Smith shows how peacebuilding, like the conflict it treats, is globally embedded and reproduces the power relationships and inequality of global political and economic systems. This is a crucial insight, which gets to the heart of why liberal peacebuilding has not reproduced a liberal and local social contract and instead has often led to predatory states and benefited their elites. Much of this stems from the marketization strategies that ignore social welfare and force postconflict developing economies to compete in a wider milieu that consigns people to poverty in the crucial peacebuilding transition. It is exacerbated by an unwillingness of internationals to engage with local culture, customs, institutions, and processes. As a result the "postconflict individual" who aspires to be an active citizen generally finds that the state she has worked so hard for fails to provide her with basic resources, recognition, or a stake in the development of peace. Peacebuilding, then, should not reflect existing inequalities and promote an elitist class system, protected by emerging security forces whose energies would better be devoted to protecting ordinary citizens.

Peacebuilding needs to be delinked from globalization, Smith argues. Postconflict situations should be treated as special transitional cases, as with Europe after World War II.[19] This requires a global (not just local) democracy. Smith's chapter might be accused of idealism by some in more realist, positivist, liberal institutionalist, or neoliberal quarters. But the practice of the past twenty years illustrates clearly that what she offers is actually a necessary and pragmatic strategy for promoting democratic states and polities founded on a social contract that benefits the most needy and vulnerable.

The following chapter turns to a discussion of civic friendship and how to overcome hatred through forgiveness, particularly in the context of contemporary Belfast. This fascinating chapter shows the possibilities inherent in the creative humanistic turn opened up by the critique of security and institutionally oriented peacebuilding. Robert Enright, Jeanette Knutson Enright, and Anthony Holter argue that any strategic notion of peacebuilding must develop civic friendship through forgiveness. Indeed, in places like Bosnia and East Timor, they argue, new conflict dynamics have emerged as unintended consequences of liberal peacebuilding. Perhaps indicative of the liberal bias of Western academics and policy makers, the authors acknowledge that theirs is a long-term strategy, almost as if this was a failing! Of course, long-term strategies need no apology. Any strategic version of peacebuilding must always have an eye on the long term—on generations and life spans. Otherwise, it runs the risk of being self-defeating. Witness East Timor, where the failure to address long-term problems of social welfare, custom, and new identity conflicts led to the near collapse of the peace after it had earlier been widely lauded as a major success by the UN, World Bank, and others. The authors show how educational institutions can contribute to peacebuilding if they are able to transcend societal divisions. Education addresses the roots of conflict and how they are transmitted across generations. The educational system is often both a part of this transmission and an obvious site in which to prevent it. Yet institutional peacebuilders normally ignore it because of their mistaken belief that peace starts mainly in political, economic, or security—not social or cultural—institutions. A sustainable *justpeace* requires a forgiveness that is rooted in society, culture, and attitudes, as well as institutions.

Gerard Powers contends that religion, a critical element of culture and sometimes a political force as well, has generally been overlooked in conflict and peacebuilding situations, even though it is increasingly recognized as central to the modern world. He shows how the "prevailing secularist paradigm" has led many policy makers and academics to underestimate the impact of religion, especially its positive role in peacebuilding. He describes the essential public nature of religious peacebuilding and the potential and limits of ecumenical and inter-religious peacebuilding. A strategic approach to peacebuilding that takes religion seriously has major implications not just for U.S. foreign policy but also for other peacebuilding actors who share the prevailing secular approach to peacebuilding.

Implications for the Evolution of Peacebuilding

The liberal paradigm of peacebuilding has offered significant advantages, as Doyle, Sambanis, Paris, and many others have documented.[20] It has represented a step forward compared to earlier conflict management approaches and incorporates many of the goals of earlier versions of conflict resolution and peacebuilding.[21] This volume has shown that there is now a need to consolidate the wisdom of liberal peacebuilding and move beyond this dominant paradigm to approach the goal of sustainable and locally owned forms of peace now endorsed by the UN system and other actors. There is a growing consensus on the failure so far of liberal peacebuilding to achieve this goal.[22]

Some contributors to this volume suggest that this framework can be salvaged and improved. Others suggest that more radical thought is required to go beyond this paradigm of peacebuilding.[23] This difference in approach reflects the fact that even postliberal peacebuilding faces intellectual tensions similar to those faced by liberal peacebuilding. Such tensions are inevitable. So much has been invested in the liberal project—the culmination of at least 100 years of developing liberal institutions and the social contract within states and several hundred years of liberal philosophy—that it would be very difficult to move into a radically new agenda that was not, in some way, indebted to the liberal project. What is distinctive about this volume is that it approaches these tensions through a much broader pluralism of method, ontology, and practice than ever proposed before in the quest for a self-sustaining, locally rooted *justpeace*.

Another dimension of this volume's contribution to the "multiplicity of peacebuilding" is worth noting—the need for peacebuilding to respond theoretically and reflexively to its own failings. Such a response means modifying and simultaneously reinventing peacebuilding through the many institutions that have grown up around it. Only through this wider methodological, ontological, and epistemological reflection might a *justpeace*—that is, a postliberal, emancipatory, empathetic, or caring peace[24]—be achieved.

Several other key issues emerge in the context of the necessarily broad yet strategic discussion included in this volume. The first relates to the discussion that began before 9/11, but was then interrupted, on the shift from notions of absolute sovereignty toward a post-Westphalian approach to politics. Peacebuilding has generally adopted the state as its vehicle, but in many conflicts—Bosnia, for instance—the state is the source or root of contention. Many of the authors in this volume consider the state as a key to successful peacebuilding, but they must ask what type of state is envisaged by all stakeholders, with an emphasis on the views of the least powerful. It should not be assumed that the state represents a preexisting package of tried and tested values, norms, institutions, and processes, simply to be transferred through peacebuilding.

As Lederach and Appleby suggest, peacebuilding should focus on the creation and nurturing of multilevel and constructive human relationships, rather than merely instrumental and technical responses to conflict. A strategic peacebuilding approach offers an engagement with the shifting and complex, geopolitical, economic, and cultural realities via a range of agencies, actors, and institutions, formal and informal, across an interdisciplinary and interdependent spectrum of knowledge and issues—all aimed directly at dealing with root causes of conflict. This calls for a fourth generation of conflict resolution or transformation activities, not a return to conflict management.[25] Ultimately, it engages reflexively with the most as well as the least marginalized people in postviolence situations. This requires a normative position and an engagement with difference rather than a reliance on universal blueprints. Strategic peacebuilding offers the opportunity to connect the localized conditions and contexts of specific conflicts with the international and institutional designs of peace that are still being developed.

Beyond the Liberal Peacebuilding Agenda?

Given the relatively uneven record of the embryonic efforts in peacebuilding over the past two decades, I argue that a maximalist case for peacebuilding, rather than a reductionist and parsimonious version, is the most "strategic" option currently available. A plausible and pragmatic paradigm for peacebuilding promotes a "culture" of peacebuilding across the life cycle of a conflict, rather than lazily equating it with the construction of liberal or neoliberal states. Peacebuilding begins and ends with the local, Lederach and Appleby argue, but within an international context. Here I might add that the "local" should be as local as it possibly can be and not merely representative of local elites.

As I elaborate elsewhere, what emerges from this discussion is not just a better concept of liberal peace, but a postliberal peace in which the liberal and the local combine to form a *liberal-local hybrid*.[26] This implies a far better understanding of the dynamics of the relationship between the liberal and the local and of the interface between the two in everyday life. This liberal–local interface, and the nature of peace it suggests, requires extensive and ongoing contextual consultation and research to develop these ideas so that they are ready to be negotiated, accepted, rejected, and constructed when and where that becomes necessary. For example, when internationals engage in conflict zones, they might ask of disputants at all levels what type of peace could be envisaged, what type of reconciliation might be achieved, and what is needed to understand, engage, and support everyday life. Security, institution-building, democratization, the rule of law, human rights, marketization, and development might be constructed from these informed perspectives. This inclusive conversation between local disputants and internationals could uncover a consensual ethic of discourse and praxis by which a postliberal peace might be achieved.

The need for this international–local conversation was evident when I visited Bosnia Herzegovina in March 2008. The Office of the High Representative (OHR), the linchpin of the post–Dayton era peace, was demoralized and in turmoil. Its representatives felt that they had lost their leverage over local politics (with the peacekeeping troops long gone, and the bluff called on their "Bonn powers" by local politicians). After years of working to ensure that Bosnia stayed peaceful and "became liberal," they could no longer exert coercive influence. A representative of the OHR argued that it probably was time the office closed and passed the baton to the European Union. The EU argued that it was up to local politicians and constituencies to make the reforms necessary to join the EU and that the EU could not relax its rules to allow the country to move more quickly toward accession, even if this would make the local peace more sustainable. The Organization for Security and Cooperation in Europe and the United Nations Development Programme representatives in turn argued that the EU might have to relax its entry rules, given that this was the only hope for a sustainable peace once the OHR closed. The latter in turn acknowledged that closing the OHR was risky: war had been mentioned in the media for the first time since Dayton, and everyone's eyes were on what the Republika Sprska's position would be in the light of Kosovo's Unilateral Declaration of Independence.[27] The OHR has created an either/or situation: either wield power to build peace or leave and risk conflict. This is not the only option, however. It can develop other strategies to ensure peace in Bosnia and remain committed to peacebuilding in a strategic sense, rather than remain imprisoned within its mandates, which clearly no longer reflect the realities in Bosnia. One might argue that passing responsibility to the EU would partly reflect the current situation, but despite more than a decade of involvement by these institutions, peace has become neither self-sustaining nor locally owned.

Consistent with Lederach and Appleby's approach to peacebuilding, eliciting local cultural and social resources for constructing peace would be far more strategic and pragmatic. Indeed, local actors in Bosnia's peacebuilding sector have long recognized this.[28] International commentators have also recognized the risks of an organization like OHR, which may undermine local capacity to promote democracy and human rights while simultaneously seeking to improve it.[29] An elicitive approach offers a pathway out of the unintended consequences of such dogmatic liberal prescriptions.

It is interesting to note that in two other peacebuilding contexts in which I conducted fieldwork in late 2008, I found that such sophistications had recently been adopted by international peacebuilders, including formerly resistant institutions like the World Bank. After the collapse of the peace in Timor-Leste in 2006, there is now an ongoing and elicitive attempt to redevelop a liberal state that incorporates local customs as well as an embryonic welfare system to provide disincentives for violent behavior. In the Solomon Islands, a mixed international and local team is working on major constitutional reforms that would produce a hybrid-liberal and custom-based constitution. In both cases, there has been a clear recognition that the liberal state and liberal peacebuilding alone cannot provide a framework for peace.[30] Thus the liberal-local hybrid is already emerging. So far, such work is in its infancy, but it does appear to represent a logical response to the weaknesses of previous approaches to peacebuilding.

Peacebuilding, like ethics, is an "ongoing historical practice"[31] that needs to be incorporated into any renewed "agenda for peace." As with the search for a sustainable peace in Bosnia, Timor-Leste, or the Solomon Islands, this is a reason not to announce the failure of peacebuilding after so much effort but to try even harder for its renewal and success. Success should now be defined as a locally sustainable *justpeace*[32] and not merely a grand narrative of geopolitical practices, institutions, or markets that mainly benefit local and international political, economic, and peacebuilding elites.

Weberian states are primarily concerned with security through power and territorial governance; liberal states are primarily concerned with the "good life" through checks and balances in particular territories; and neoliberal states focus, in addition, on the role of the free market in distributing scarce resources. Strategic peacebuilding broadens the processes and the goals of peacebuilding beyond the liberal paradigm, meaning that the attainment of a *justpeace* requires more than merely a state apparatus for security or a market apparatus to redistribute resources. It requires greater levels of democracy to engage with the machinery of checks and balances, and it also requires communication and mediation with and between international liberal prescriptions and the often nonliberal local context.

A strategic version of peacebuilding may well, on the surface, be taken to offer retrogressive hints of methodological reductionism, one in which the

Weberian, liberal, or neoliberal state remains the basis of the imagined polity. Linking the term *strategic* to a reformed version of peacebuilding carries its own baggage. *Strategic* implies "hard" security. Although security is a precondition for any polity or state recovering from conflict, it is only one of several. The choice of the phrase "strategic peacebuilding" is in itself strategic. It engages with a language that policy makers and officials comprehend and deploy themselves but brings to it a far wider range of issues and connections. In effect, strategic peacebuilding tries to develop wide-ranging responses to the problems raised by using the Weberian, liberal, and neoliberal state as a toolkit for conflict resolution, and so it offers a window into a postliberal peace that may be more locally and contextually sensitive. Ultimately, strategic peacebuilding as developed in this volume illustrates the pragmatism of localized, sensitized, multidimensional, and multilevel peacebuilding that moves far beyond what has so far proven to be a rather self-defeating approach based more narrowly on security and institutions.

Conclusion

The evolution, reform, and refinements of peacebuilding discussed in this chapter retain the normal tools of peacebuilding—democratization, human rights and the rule of law, marketization and development, secularity, and a balance of powers. In addition, it advocates a localized, culturally and socially just, representative, and participatory political system, a process of politics that respects local culture, provides for social welfare, and is open to religious influences. Underlying all the contributions to this volume is the assumption that an integrated, multidimensional approach is required to produce a rapid peace dividend, one that will persuade disputants that peace is better for them than war. An integrated approach would be in my view much more strategic (and effective) than previous approaches because it does not privilege parsimonious versions of security—that is, state or elite security, as opposed to human security[33]—before and above all else. Nor does it, by implication at least, privilege one-size-fits-all liberal peace packages, imported and controlled mainly from afar, over the needs or rights of locals or customary and indigenous processes. Nor would it rest on restrictive time lines or budgets tailored solely to the requirements of donors. A *justpeace* requires a negotiation between these levels and issues of peacebuilding and an outcome that is both locally "authentic" and consistent with the most rigorous international norms pertaining to needs, rights, and institutions.

This volume provides a survey of the state of the art of peacebuilding, and contained within many of the chapters are strong indications of a far more reflexive approach involving alternatives to the liberal peace and a media that allows scholars and policy makers to escape the "rigor" of their own reductionist technology of governance. A positive *justpeace* requires an engagement with as broad, representative, and participatory a representation of everyday life in postconflict zones as possible if it is to be empathetic, emancipatory, elicitive of recognition and care, and hence sustainable.

Any attempt to develop a strategic paradigm of peacebuilding must remember that its roots lie in the lives and the consent of real people and societies who have the capacity to make choices within their own context and aspire to such agency. To maintain its integrity, any approach to peacebuilding on their behalf must be able to offer a form of peace that is rhetorically defensible across the range of platforms with which this book has shown that strategic peacebuilding engages. Far from pursuing a utopian agenda, this volume offers a realistic and pragmatic terrain into which peacebuilding must move as it begins to respond to the problems that have emerged with the liberal peace paradigm of the post–Cold War world. A *justpeace* is the challenge for the next phase or generation of peacebuilding.

NOTES

1. See Oliver P. Richmond, "UN Peace Operations and the Dilemmas of the Peacebuilding Consensus," in *International Peacekeeping*, vol. 10, no. 4, 2004.

2. Boutros Boutros-Ghali, *An Agenda for Peace: Preventative Diplomacy, Peacemaking and Peacekeeping*, New York: United Nations, 1992; Boutros Boutros-Ghali, "An Agenda for Development: Report of the Secretary-General," A/48/935, May 6, 1994; Boutros Boutros-Ghali, "Supplement to an Agenda for Peace" A/50/60, S.1995/1, January 3, 1995; Boutros Boutros-Ghali, "An Agenda for Democratization," A/50/332 AND A/51/512, December 17, 1996.

3. In particular, see *Report of the Secretary-General's High Level Panel on Threats, Challenges, and Change*, United Nations, 2004; International Commission on Intervention and State Sovereignty, "The Responsibility to Protect," Ottawa: International Development Research Centre, 2001.

4. See my *Transformation of Peace*, London: Palgrave, 2005/2007, esp. conclusion. See also Kofi Annan, "Democracy as an International Issue," *Global Governance*, vol. 8, no. 2, April–June 2002, pp. 134–142; A. Bellamy and P. Williams, "Peace Operations and Global Order," *International Peacekeeping*, vol. 10, no. 4, 2004; D. Chandler, *From Kosovo to Kabul: Human Rights and International Intervention*, London: Pluto, 2002; J. Chopra, and Tanja Hohe, "Participatory Intervention," *Global Governance*, vol. 10, 2004; Mark Duffield, *Global Governance and the New Wars*, London: Zed Books, 2001; Roland Paris, *At War's End*, Cambridge: Cambridge University Press, 2004; M. Pugh, "Peacekeeping and Critical Theory," *Conference Presentation at BISA*, LSE, London, December 16–18, 2002.

5. Oliver P. Richmond, *Maintaining Order, Making Peace*, London: Palgrave, 2002, chapter 5.

6. Paris's book, *At War's End*, is perhaps the apogee of this development, in that his "institutionalization before liberalization" concept depends on a coercive external importation of the "privileged" processes of peacebuilding.

7. See my argument in *Transformation of Peace*, p. 216.

8. Ibid., p. 219.

9. Gene M. Lyons and Michael Mastunduno, *Beyond Westphalia*, Baltimore, Md.: Johns Hopkins University Press, 1995.

10. Barry Buzan, O. Waever, and J. de Wilde, *Security: A New Framework for Analysis*, Boulder, Colo.: Lynne Rienner, 1998.

11. For supporters and critics of the liberal peace, see, among others, Michael Doyle, "Kant, Liberal Legacies, and Foreign Affairs," *Philosophy and Public Affairs*,

vol. 12, 1983; Michael Doyle and Nicolas Sambanis, *Making War and Building Peace*, Princeton, N.J.: Princeton University Press, 2006; Charles T. Call and Elizabeth M. Cousens, "Ending Wars and Building Peace: International Responses to War-Torn Societies," *International Studies Perspectives*, vol. 9, 2008; Stephen D. Krasner, "Sharing Sovereignty. New Institutions for Collapsed and Failing States," *International Security*, vol. 29, no. 2, 2004; Paris, *At War's End*; J. Snyder, *From Voting to Violence*, London: Norton, 2000; David Rieff, *A Bed for the Night*, London: Vintage, 2002; Michael Mandelbaum, *The Ideas that Conquered the World*, New York: Public Affairs, 2002; Michael Pugh, "The Political Economy of Peacebuilding: A Critical Theory Perspective," *International Journal of Peace Studies*, vol. 10, no. 2, 2005; David Chandler, *Bosnia: Faking Democracy after Dayton*, London: Pluto Press, 1999; Duffield, *Global Governance and the New Wars*; Roland Paris, "International Peacebuilding and the 'Mission Civilisatrice,'" *Review of International Studies*, vol. 28, no. 4, 2002; Roger Mac Guinty, "Indigenous Peace-Making versus the Liberal Peace," *Cooperation and Conflict*, vol. 43, no. 2, 2008: 139–65; Beate Jahn, "The Tragedy of Liberal Diplomacy: Democratization, Intervention and Statebuilding (Part II)," *Journal of Intervention and Statebuilding*, vol. 1, no. 2, 2007; Neil Cooper, "Review Article: On the Crisis of the Liberal Peace," *Conflict, Security and Development*, vol. 7, no. 4, 2007.

12. Oliver P. Richmond and Jason Franks, *Liberal Peace Transitions: Between Peacebuilding and Statebuilding*, Edinburgh: Edinburgh University Press, 2009.

13. Michel Foucault, "Governmentality," in *The Foucault Effect: Studies in Governmentality*, edited by Graham Burchell, Colin Gordon, and Peter Miller. Chicago: Chicago University Press, 1997, pp. 87–104.

14. Ibid.

15. Recent meetings at the UN in New York at which I was present indicated that there is significant internal tension in the UN system between peacebuilding and development projects and the Counter-Terrorism Committee.

16. Mark Duffield, *Development, Security and Unending War*, Cambridge: Polity Press, 2007.

17. Oliver P. Richmond, "The Romanticisation of the Local: Welfare, Culture and Peacebuilding," *International Spectator*, vol. 44, no. 1, 2009: 149–69.

18. David Harvey, *Neoliberalism*, New York: Oxford University Press, 2005.

19. Karl Polyani, *The Great Transformation*, New York: Rinehart, 1944.

20. Paris, *At War's End*; Doyle and Sambanis, *Making War and Building Peace*.

21. It is generally taken that conflict management represents limited attempts to focus mainly on security matters, whereas conflict resolution deals with underlying and social causes. See for example, John Burton, *World Society*, Cambridge: Cambridge University Press, 1972.

22. For my own empirical and theoretical discussion of the achievements of the liberal peace, see my *Liberal Peace Transitions* (with Jason Franks). See, among many others, Chandler, *From Kosovo to Kabul*; Mac Guinty, "Indigenous Peace-Making versus the Liberal Peace," pp. 139–163; M. Pugh and N. Cooper, with J. Goodhand, *War Economies in a Regional Context: Challenges of Transformation*, Boulder, Colo.: Lynne Rienner, 2004; Michael Pugh, Neil Cooper, and Mandy Turner (eds.), *Whose Peace? Critical Perspectives on the Political Economy of Peacebuilding*, London: Palgrave, 2008; Snyder, *From Voting to Violence*, p. 43; Annan, "Democracy as an International Issue," p. 136; Chopra and Hohe, "Participatory Intervention," p. 292; Rieff, *A Bed for the Night*, p. 10; Paris, "International Peacebuilding and the 'Mission Civilisatrice,'" p. 638.

23. See among others Christine Sylvester, "Bare Life as Development/Post-Colonial Problematic," *Geographical Journal*, vol. 172, no. 1, 2006, p. 67.

24. See Oliver P. Richmond, *Peace in IR*, London: Routledge, 2008.

25. See Richmond, *Maintaining Order, Making Peace*, esp. conclusion.

26. Oliver P. Richmond, "Eirenism and a Post-Liberal Peace," forthcoming in *Review of International Studies*, 2009. The term *liberal* is used here in its philosophical sense.

27. Fieldwork and personal interviews in Bosnia Herzogovina, March 10–16, 2008; Timor-Leste, November 2008; Solomon Islands, December 2008.

28. See *Liberal Peace Transitions*, chapter 2. See also the discussion at a project workshop in Sarajevo in March 2007, where local discussants were extremely critical of liberal peacebuilding in Bosnia.

29. Chandler, *Bosnia: Faking Democracy after Dayton.*

30. Volker Boege, M. Anne Brown, Kevin P. Clements, and Anna Nolan, "States Emerging from Hybrid Political Orders—Pacific Experiences," The Australian Centre for Peace and Conflict Studies Occasional Papers Series, no. 11, September 2008.

31. R. B. J. Walker, *Inside/Outside: International Relations as Political Theory*, Cambridge: Cambridge University Press, 1992, p. ix.

32. See Oliver P. Richmond, "Reclaiming Peace in International Relations," *Millennium: Journal of International Studies*, 2008; "A Post-Liberal, Everyday Ethic of Peace?" Article for PRIO project on the Ethics of the Liberal Peace, 2009.

33. Shahrbanou Tadjbakhsh and Anuradha Chenoy, *Human Security: Concepts and Implications*, London: Routledge, 2006.

Index

Achieving TABE® Success in Reading

Level E

Wright Group

Executive Editor: Linda Kwil
Production Manager: Genevieve Kelley
Marketing Manager: Sean Klunder
Cover Designer: Vickie Tripp

 **Wright Group**

ISBN: 0-07-704463-0

Send all inquiries to:
Wright Group/McGraw-Hill
130 E. Randolph, Suite 400
Chicago, IL 60601

Manufactured in the United States of America.

6 7 8 9 MAL 13 12 11 10

The *McGraw·Hill* Companies

Table of Contents

To the Reader

If reading has never been easy for you, Contemporary's *Achieving TABE Success in Reading* will help. Each selection in this reader will let you practice reading. The article or story will grab your interest and keep you reading to the end. When you finish reading, you will answer questions to

- check your understanding of the story
- apply reading skills to help your understanding of the story

You may answer these questions alone or with your classmates. You might write the answers or you might use the questions to have a discussion. Suggested answers to the questions are at the back of this book.

Your teacher may ask you to read a selection after a lesson in the workbook that ends with a Read On note. Or you may read these selections any time you wish.

Achieving TABE Success in Reading will build your confidence in your ability to read by letting you practice on short, interesting stories.

A Home in the North

Why is a snow house the right kind of house for the Arctic?

1 It is 50 degrees below zero. You are dressed all in fur, but the wind is in your face. Now your skin stings. You know that you are getting frostbite on your nose. Your dogs are pulling the sled well. You can ride on the sled if you want. But when you get cold, you run beside it.

2 You have been traveling across the flat land of the Arctic [Ark'•tik] for six days. All around you is nothing but ice and snow. You are tired. The dogs are tired.

3 Suddenly your dogs begin to bark. In the distance, more dogs are barking. You can't see anything but more ice and snow. But you know you are almost home.

4 The dogs run even faster. They run toward three big bumps in the snow. Now your family is crawling out of the bumps to meet you. You have come home to your snow house.

Building a Shelter

5 The Arctic is a huge place with few people in it. It is flat, and no trees can grow there. It is bitterly cold in the winter. The wind blows so hard that it feels even colder. The snow house works well in this land.

6 The Eskimo [Es'•kih•moh] people use the word *igloo* [ihg'•loo] to mean any kind of house. A snow house is called an *igluivigag* [ihg•loo'•ee•vih•gahg]. In the central part of the Arctic, Eskimo families built snow houses to live in for the winter. In other parts, Eskimos made snow houses only when they were traveling. The rest of the winter they lived in houses made from sod and stones. In the summer, they made tents out of animal skins.

7 A snow house was made out of snow that had been packed hard by the wind. An Eskimo would use a long snow knife made out of bone to cut blocks of the hard snow. The blocks were about three feet long and a foot and a half wide. The blocks were only four to six inches thick. Even though the Arctic is very cold, there is not

much snow. Cold air is very dry—too dry for snow. So blocks could not be very thick.

8   The blocks were cut out of the place where the snow house would be built. This way the floor was sunk down into the snow, out of the wind. The blocks were piled up in a circle. For each layer, they were placed closer and closer in, until they met in the middle for a domed roof.

9   More blocks were cut from a trench leading out from the dome. With the blocks covering it, this would be a sunken tunnel. The tunnel led up to the snow house, keeping the wind out. Sometimes a wider space in the tunnel would be built as a storeroom.

10   A snow house could be made very quickly. Two men could build one in an hour or two. Speed could be important if you were outside with a storm coming!

11   A hole was cut in the roof of the snow house to let the stale air out. Fresh air would come in through the tunnel. The snow house was heated only with stone lamps. These were little bowls filled with burning seal oil. The snow house really wasn't very warm inside, but it felt warmer just to be out of the wind!

12   On one side of the snow house was a platform made of snow. This was covered with animal skins. The family used the platform as a

seat and as a bed at night. They also built racks to hang up cooking pots and wet clothes.

Close Ties

13 The family cooked over the stone lamps. Most of their food was meat, and it was eaten raw. In fact, *Eskimo* is an American Indian word that means "a person who eats raw meat." Raw meat gave the Eskimos the energy needed to live in this cold land.

14 Sometimes the married children of a family would build other snow houses near the first one. All might be connected by one tunnel.

15 In the long winters, when the sun never comes up, the village people might build a big snow house. There they all gathered to play games, tell stories, or sing songs. They enjoyed being together.

Changing Times

16 Now times have changed. Most Eskimos live in modern frame houses. Instead of dog sleds, they use snowmobiles. Instead of hunting and fishing in the cold, they work at jobs indoors. Today about 100,000 Eskimos live in the Arctic. They call themselves the *Inuit* [Ih'•noo•wuht]. This name means "the people." They live in a world caught between the old ways and the new.

Questions

1. How long did it take to build a snow house for Eskimos who traveled?

2. What does the word *Eskimo* mean?

3. How do people in the Arctic live today?

Antonym/Synonym Search

1. Look for antonyms for the following words: *hot, slower, small, summer, wet, long, soft, thin, down, slowly.*

2. Find the sentences that use antonyms to tell about the air in the snow house.

3. Use a pair of antonyms to tell how the way Eskimos live today is different from the way they lived in the past.

4. Look for synonyms for the following words: *weary, start, enormous, arched, fast, uncooked.*

5. Rewrite the first paragraph in "Building a Shelter" substituting synonyms for as many words as you can.

What Is Color?

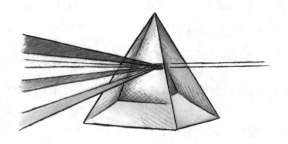

How do we see color?
To see color, we first must have light.

1   Our world is full of color. Most people can see colors, but animals cannot. They see the world in shades of black and white.

2   To see color, we first must have light. A flower that is bright yellow in the daytime looks gray or black at night.

Roy G. Biv[1]

3   White light contains all the colors of the rainbow. We see rainbows in the sky when it rains while the sun shines. The sun's rays pass through raindrops. Each raindrop is a prism[2] that splits the sun's rays into a rainbow.

---

[1] Roy G. Biv: a way to remember in order the colors of the rainbow—red, orange, yellow, green, blue, indigo, and violet
[2] prism: a transparent object with three sides that bends a light ray into a rainbow of color

4   When a ray of light goes through a prism, it bends the light ray. Blue light is bent more. Red light is bent less. In this way, the prism splits the ray of light and spreads out the colors. The rainbow of colors is called a spectrum [spek'•trum].

How It Works

5 Light has colors in it. But how does this help us see the colors of things around us? Imagine you are looking at a colored picture on the page of a book. Light comes from the sun or from an electric lamp. It hits the colors on the page. Some of the light is reflected. It bounces off the page and into your eyes. The parts of the picture that are red reflect red light into your eyes. The blue parts of the picture reflect blue light. And so on.

6   When light passes into the eye, it goes to the back of the eye to the retina [reht'•nuh]. The retina has two kinds of cells. Some are shaped like tiny rods. The rods respond to light but not to colors. The other cells, called cones, do respond to color. The rods and cones together form an image on the retina. This image is sent to the brain. Then you can see the picture on the page.

7   The rods in the retina respond even to very dim light. This is why we can see the shapes of things even when it is dark. But the cones do

not work in dim light. This is why, in dim light, we can't see color.

Color Families

8 The colors of the spectrum are grouped into three families. These are red, yellow, and blue. They are called primary colors. All other colors are made from them.

9   Every color has an opposite. It's called a complementary [kom•pleh•ment'•uh•ree] color. As an example, yellow is the complementary color to blue. Blue green is the complementary color to red.

10   If we look at one color and then look at a different color, our eyes have to change. Most of the time, we don't even notice. Sometimes, though, we can be surprised.

11   For example, stare at a brightly colored picture for about 30 seconds. Then move your eyes quickly to a blank piece of white paper. You will see an afterimage—an image with the same shape as the original image but different colors. The afterimage will stay on your retina for a few moments because your eyes can't change that fast. Where the picture was yellow, you will see blue. Where the picture was blue green, you will see red. And you will see white where the picture was black.

12   Knowing how we see color takes away some of its mystery, but, luckily, none of its beauty.

Questions

1. How does a prism work?

2. How does light help us see the colors of things around us?

3. Which cells in the retina respond to color?

4. Why can we see shapes of things in dim light but not colors of things?

Using Context Clues

1. Which colors are primary colors?

2. What are complementary colors?

3. What is an afterimage?

Who Wears the Pants?

When did people start wearing pants and why?

1 During the Ice Age, the first people wore only animal hides. Then the earth grew warmer, and the ice melted. Cloth was invented about 10,000 years ago. Men would just wrap a piece of cloth around their middles. This was called a loincloth. Today, men still wear loincloths in countries where it is hot, such as India.

2 People learned to sew cloth into clothes. Men began to wear robes, or tunics [too'•niks]. Then, about 3,000 years ago, a tribe from Persia [Pur'•zhah] made war on other tribes. The Persian men were great horsemen. And they wore pants. It just isn't easy to ride a horse in a skirt!

3 In countries with warm weather, men went on wearing robes. But in colder parts of the

world, men wore pants. The Vikings wrapped ties in a crisscross around their legs on top of the pants.

Fancy Pants

4 Men did not always wear long pants. Until about 1800, men wore short pants and stockings when they dressed up. That way, everyone could admire their good-looking legs. The men would look in the mirror to decide which of their legs was better looking. When they went to a party, they would stand with that leg in front of the other. We still tell people to put their best foot forward.

5 Sometimes men had special pants to wear just to parties. These pants were very tight. The men couldn't sit down all evening!

What's Good for the Goose . . .

6 When did women start wearing pants? Through most of history, men fought in wars. The sports they played often were warlike, too. Women stayed at home. At last, around 1850, women began to be active in sports. But what could they wear? The style at the time was long, full skirts that got in the way.

7 A woman named Amelia Bloomer had an idea. She said women should wear loose pants that came down to the knee. Everyone laughed

at her. Then the bicycle was invented. Women found that their skirts got caught in the gears. So, by 1890, pants for women were very popular. And they were called bloomers!

8   Women still wore pants only for sports. Then movie stars began wearing pants in films. But it was World War II, in the 1940s, that really got women into pants for good.

9   During the war, it was hard for women to buy stockings. So they wore pants to cover their bare legs. Many women also worked in factories while the men were away at war. Pants just made more sense for that kind of work.

10   Women were still not wearing pants when they dressed up. They could not wear pants to a fancy restaurant. Nor could they wear them to work in a bank or as teachers. But women kept wearing pants. A matching jacket gave pants a more formal look. By the 1970s, people were used to seeing women in pantsuits.

A Choice for All

11   Today no one is surprised at seeing women in pants. Everyone wears them. But people are not used to seeing men in skirts. The men of Scotland sometimes wear skirts called kilts. In Scotland's early days, men did not wear kilts. They wore shirts and pants with crisscross ties on the legs.

12   Poor people in that country wrapped themselves in warm plaid [plad] blankets. Scotland is famous for its plaid wool cloth. A plaid pattern has colored stripes going in two different directions. Rich people, too, wore plaid blankets as they hunted or farmed. In the 1600s, people started to cut the blanket into pieces of cloth. Each piece was two feet wide and six feet long. A belt held the cloth in place.

13   By the 1700s, they folded the cloth into pleats. Men from the Highlands wore these pleated skirts, or kilts, to show which part of Scotland they came from. They wore the kilt with a shirt, jacket, and knee socks. Another piece of plaid cloth was draped over the shoulder. This is what proud men of Scotland still wear on special days. Scottish men wear kilts to show that Scotland is still alive and proud.

Questions

1. Why did men start wearing pants?

2. When did women first wear pants? Why?

3. How did World War II affect what women wore?

4. What is a plaid?

5. Why do men in Scotland wear kilts?

Spelling Word Alert

1. Find the sentences that use the following words: *piece, sew, wear, great, bare, sense, two.* Write a homophone for each.

2. Find a word with a silent letter that names a part of the body. Find another word with a silent letter that tells what you do to a gift before you give it.

3. Find the sentences with the words *admire* and *decide.* Add *-ing* to the words.

Egypt's Wonders

Have you ever wondered why the pyramids were built? Or why the kings of Egypt were made into mummies?

1 What if you were a king? What if you believed that you could live forever if your body were kept safe after you died? What would you do? You'd build a very safe place for your body.

2 That's just what the kings of Egypt did more than 4,000 years ago. Each one had a huge pyramid [peer'•ah•mid] built as a tomb. The body was placed in a secret room inside the pyramid. Two million blocks of stone protected the body.

3 The largest pyramid of all still stands in Egypt next to the Nile River. It was built just for King Khufu [Koo'•foo]. The base is square. It covers enough ground for ten football fields. The pyramid is 481 feet high. It is made of two

million stone blocks. Each block weighs about 2½ tons. But the men who built King Khufu's pyramid, known as the Great Pyramid, had no power tools. Each block was cut and moved into place by hand!

Hard Labor

4   Thousands of men worked year round to cut and smooth the blocks. They used tools made of copper, stone, and wood. Then a work crew of 50,000 farmers was brought in to move the stones.

5   The farmers worked on the pyramid from July to November each year. During this time, their fields were flooded with water from the Nile River. Work gangs of 25 men moved one stone at a time. Their only pay was food and clothing.

6   Most of the blocks were cut near the building site. But some were cut across the river, and others were cut hundreds of miles away. These had to be brought down the Nile River by boat.

7   Workers made the site level. They cut a trench in the rock all the way around the site. The trench was then filled with water. The rest of the site was cut down or filled in to match the level of the water.

8   The work gangs dragged in the big stone blocks. They laid a long row of logs in the sand

so that the blocks would not sink. Each block was placed on a wooden sled. A team of 20 men pulled the sled over the logs. The workers slid the blocks into place. Each block had to fit just right, or the whole pyramid would be weak. The first layer of blocks was done.

9   The workers continued. They built a ramp of stones and mud to drag the blocks up to the next layer.

Sky High

10 The ramp went up and around, layer after layer. In all, the pyramid had more than 120 layers, each smaller than the one before it. The sides were four triangles that came together to one point at the top. This shape made you look high up toward the sky and the sun.

11   At the very top, a huge capstone was put in place. Then white casing stones were placed over the blocks to make the outside of the pyramid smooth. The snug fit of these stones made the pyramid look as if it had been cut from one huge stone.

A Look Inside

12 Deep inside the pyramid, secret rooms were built. The walls were painted with beautiful pictures and writing that told about the king's life. When the king died, his body would rest

in one of these rooms. Other rooms would store his gold, treasures, and the everyday things he might need in the afterlife.

13   Long hallways inside the tomb led to the secret rooms. Painted on these walls, too, were many beautiful pictures. Perhaps, in the afterlife, the king would not need light to see them.

14   What was it like for the workers to walk through these long passages, in the dark and under millions of tons of stone? The work had taken 25 years to finish. Thousands of workers had been killed by the heavy blocks.

Careful Preparation

15   After death, the king's body had to be preserved so that his soul could live forever. First, special workers took out the brain through the nose with small hooks. Then they took out the lungs and stomach through a cut in the left side of the body. They put these into jars to preserve them.

16   Next, the body was dried in salt and then washed. It was wrapped in layers of cloth. Gold and jewels were placed within the wrappings. In the dry air of Egypt, the preserved body, called a "mummy," would keep year after year.

A Long Journey

17 When the mummy was ready, priests carried it into the pyramid. In a long ceremony [seh'•reh•moh•nee], they placed the mummy in the tomb. Besides the king's treasures, the rooms were filled with food, clothing, furniture, and weapons. Even games were placed in these rooms, in case the king became bored. Forever is a long time!

18 Then the hallways were sealed. Workers put the last casing stones into place on the outside of the pyramid. This way, no one would know where the entrance was.

19 But the people did find the entrance to the tomb. Over the years, robbers broke into the pyramids and stole the gold and jewels. Sometimes they destroyed the mummies, too. But the pyramids were built so well that they still stand.

20 Perhaps King Khufu didn't live forever. But his pyramid has kept his name alive for almost 5,000 years.

Questions

1. What were the pyramids built for?

2. Why did the farmers work only from July to November of each year?

3. Why was the king's body preserved?

4. Why did people later want to enter the pyramid?

Noting Details

1. How tall is King Khufu's pyramid?

2. What is another name for King Khufu's pyramid?

3. How did the workers get the big stone blocks up to each layer of the pyramid?

4. How many layers were there in the pyramid?

5. What was on the walls of the secret rooms in the pyramid?

6. What was the last step in preserving the body of the king?

A Good Cup of Coffee

Why do we feel more alert when we drink coffee?

1 What do you drink when you feel tired or when you just want to take a break? Many people like a cup of hot coffee.

2 Coffee comes from beans. They grow on trees with green shiny leaves. Coffee trees grow only where it is warm all year round. They also need lots of rain. Coffee trees grow high in the mountains. The best trees are in South America and Africa.

Where It Comes From

3 Coffee trees grow on plantations. Workers prune the trees so that they stay under 15 feet tall. This makes it easy to pick the beans.

4   The beans start as pretty, white flowers. When the flowers drop, bunches of green coffee berries start to grow. Each berry has two beans in it. The berries turn red as they ripen. It takes from 6 to 14 months for them to get ripe. On some plantations, all the berries are picked at once. But for the very best coffee, workers pick only the ripe berries.

Green Gold

5 Picking the berries is the first step. The berries go through many more steps before they can be made into coffee. The berries are spread out in the sun to dry. Next, workers rake them to be sure they all get dry. Then they put the berries into a machine to rub off the outer hulls. The beans remain, but they are still green. The workers call them green gold.

6   The coffee beans are shipped to other countries. They still are not ready to be made into coffee. They are roasted until they turn brown. Then the beans are put through big rollers that grind them. Most coffee that we drink does not come from just one kind of bean. It is made from a blend of beans from different kinds of trees. Some people work as trained tasters. They sip the coffees to see how they should be blended. Then the coffee is packed

in airtight containers. It is finally ready to go to the stores.

Look Alive!

7 Why do people drink coffee when they are tired? Coffee contains a drug called caffeine [ka•feen′]. By itself, caffeine is white, like sugar. Caffeine stimulates the body's nervous system. This makes a person feel more alert. It also helps the brain work a little faster.

8   Caffeine also stimulates the heart and the stomach. This is bad for some people. It keeps some coffee drinkers awake at night. For these reasons, many people drink decaffeinated [dee•kaf′•fi•nay•tud] coffee. This brew has had much of the caffeine removed.

9   While they are still green, coffee beans are treated with a chemical. This chemical joins itself to the caffeine. Then the chemical is steamed out, taking the caffeine with it. Like regular coffee beans, these beans are dried, roasted, and ground. Both kinds of beans can also be used to make instant coffee.

How It Began

10 We drink billions of cups of coffee each year. People in the United States drink one-third of all the coffee in the world! How did it all start?

Coffee trees first grew in Africa. People there chewed the berries to stay awake. Then they found that they could grind the beans to make a drink. Coffee became very popular. Trees were planted in many other places.

11   There were no coffee trees in North America or South America. Around 1700, a young French soldier brought one tree from a garden in France. He carried it to North America on a sailing ship. It was a long, hard trip. The people on the ship began to run out of drinking water. But the young soldier shared his water with the tree, and he kept it alive. When he got to North America, he planted the tree. Almost all the coffee trees in this part of the world come from that one tree!

A Popular Custom

12   Throughout history, thousands of lively talks about art and politics have taken place in coffeehouses. And they are popular places today for the same reasons. Important decisions have been made over cups of coffee. There are even songs about coffee. Its good taste and smell has placed coffee among the most popular of all hot drinks. Whether taken black, creamed, weak, or strong, it seems that coffee is here to stay.

Questions

1. Where are the best coffee trees in the world?

2. How long does it take for coffee berries to ripen?

3. How is caffeine taken out of coffee?

4. How did coffee first come to North America?

Identifying Sequence

1. What is the first thing that is done to the coffee berries after they have been picked?

2. When are the coffee beans roasted?

3. What is the last thing that is done to the coffee before it is shipped to stores?

The Trail of Tears

What made the Trail of Tears such a tragic event in American history?

1 It was a sad sight. Thousands of men, women, and children trudged across the land. Soldiers forced them on with gun butts. Many fell dead from hunger and cold. The Native American Cherokee people will never forget or forgive this Trail of Tears.

Quiet Lives

2 The Cherokees once lived in the Great Smoky Mountains of Tennessee. For hundreds of years, they lived quiet lives high in the mountains. The Cherokees hunted in the woods and fished in the streams.

3 When white people settled the land, Cherokee life changed. To try to save what land was left, the Cherokees began to live as

the settlers did. Like their white neighbors, they became farmers.

4   In 1828, gold was found in the Smokies. The discovery brought heartbreak to the Cherokee Nation. White men wanted the gold. To get it, they wanted the Cherokees to move away. The settlers also wanted the Cherokee land for farming. They hoped to set up their own farms with fields these Native Americans had cleared.

5   In 1830, the United States government stepped in—to side with the settlers! The government said that the Cherokees would have to relocate. They would have to move west to Oklahoma Territory and set up new farms there.

6   The Cherokees did not want to move away. The Smokies had always been their home. The Cherokees asked President Andrew Jackson to help them, but he said no.

Troops Arrive

7   In 1838, United States troops came to the Smokies. They began to round up the Cherokees. Only 1,000 Cherokee people got away. They hid deep in the mountains. The rest of the Cherokees were caught.

8   Soldiers dragged men from their fields. They pulled women and children from their homes. The troops showed no kindness to the

frightened Cherokees. The soldiers shouted at them in English. It was a language many Cherokees did not understand.

9   Soldiers forced the Cherokees into stockades and split up their families. Some children wound up in camps far from their parents. The soldiers did not care. They had orders to move the Cherokee people.

A Long, Hard March

10   When the camps were filled, the long march began. Armed soldiers put the Cherokees into 17 large groups and pushed them west. About 15,000 Cherokees set out.

11   The march was grim from the start. The Cherokees were herded onward like cattle. Some were shoved into wagons. A few rode on horses. Most of the people had to walk. They did not have enough blankets or warm clothes. Many did not even have shoes.

12   Children cried as they waved good-bye to their mountain homes. Men and women also cried. As one Cherokee said, ". . . all look[ed] sad like when friends die."

13   Oklahoma was a thousand miles away. To get there, the Cherokees had to tramp through mud and dust. They slogged through rain, sleet, and snow. John Burnett was a soldier on the march. He later wrote about that time. "The

sufferings of the Cherokee[s] were awful," he said. "The trail of the exiles was a trail of death. They had to sleep in the wagons and on the grounds without fire. And I have known as many as 22 of them to die in one night. . . ."

Death on the Trail

14 Some people died from the cold. They shivered and shook but could not get warm. At last, their bodies ran out of heat. Others, too tired to keep going, died from exhaustion [eg•zaus'•chun]. Still others died from disease; they were too weak to fight off sickness.

15   Hunger was always a problem. The marchers had only the food they could carry with them. Their grain sacks got wet and were soon filled with bugs. No one had enough to eat. They all grew weak. Many Cherokees starved to death.

Cruel Treatment

16 The soldiers saw the pain and death they were causing. Yet they kept the groups of Cherokees moving anyway. It was hard for old people to keep up the pace. The heartless soldiers whipped them to make them move faster.

17   Mothers with young children struggled along. Burnett told of one woman with three small children. She set out ". . . with a baby

strapped on her back and leading a child with each hand." As Burnett told it, "the task was too great for that frail mother. . . . She sank and died with her baby on her back and her other two children clinging to her hands."

18   There was no time to give the dead funerals or burial. The soldiers forced the groups to keep moving. Bodies of the dead were thrown into ditches dug along the trail.

19   After about six months, the march ended. The Cherokees had reached Oklahoma. By then, 4,000 people had died. More than one-fourth of those who set out died on the Trail of Tears.

A Different Life

20   The Cherokees looked at their new land. It was not at all like their old home. The land was flat, dry, and hot. The Cherokees had to start new lives. But they never forgot the horrors of the long march. They named it the "Trail Where We Cried." Today it is called the Trail of Tears. The trail still marks a sad chapter in United States history.

Questions

1. Where was the Cherokees' original home?

2. Who was the president at the time of the march?

3. What problems did the Cherokees face during the march?

4. What happened to the marchers who died on the way to Oklahoma?

5. About how long did it take the Cherokees to march to Oklahoma?

Recognizing Stated Concepts

1. How did the discovery of gold in the Smoky Mountains affect the Cherokees?

2. How did the United States government settle the dispute between the settlers and the Cherokees?

3. Why was hunger always a problem on the march?

Ellis Island

Why was Ellis Island called "The Island of Tears"?

1   Why does Ellis Island have a special place in American history? Ellis Island was the country's first immigration [im•mih•gray′•shun] port of entry. It lies about a half-mile north of the Statue of Liberty. From 1892 to 1954, about 15 million people came through its gates. Today, more than 100 million Americans have an ancestor who passed through Ellis Island.

2   Most immigrants arrived by ship from Europe. Their life in the old country was hard. It wasn't easy to find work. They were tired of unfair treatment. Some wanted to escape army service. Others had family members who had left for America earlier. Their families' letters had told of jobs and good living conditions.

There was a chance for a better life. Some even believed the streets were paved with gold!

Journey to America

3 Try to imagine a family ready to leave their homeland. They had filled out the necessary forms. Their relatives in the United States had sent tickets and money. Everything they could take was packed. They would need clothing, bedding, and food for the journey.

4 Their ocean voyage could take as long as three weeks. The luckier ones traveled as first class passengers. But many came by way of steerage class. For those people, life on board was full of hardships. They slept and ate in close quarters. But finally, the ship arrived at New York. The people were greeted by a welcome sight: the Statue of Liberty.

5 What was it like when they got off the ship? The travelers were tired but very excited. They wanted to meet their family and see the land of their dreams. But they weren't allowed to enter the city yet. First they boarded a ferry for Ellis Island. What they faced next was not always pleasant.

Island of Tears

6 In the main building, noise surrounded them. There was shouting and pushing. And so

many languages were spoken! Guards called out the numbers of the tags the immigrants wore on their coats. They joined a long, slow-moving line.

7   Papers were checked and questions asked. "What's your name?" "Do you have a job skill?" "Who sent you tickets?" "Can you read and write?" "Do you want to harm the government?"

8   Then came the part feared most: the health station. That's where doctors checked over the newcomers. If the doctors found a heart problem or eye disease, they could send the person back to where he or she came from. Nothing could be worse than that!

9   If one family member failed the health check, what about the rest? Should the whole family go back? Should one parent or an older child go back with the sick person? Such heartbreak is why Ellis Island was often called "The Island of Tears." Only about 250,000 (2 percent) of the immigrants at Ellis Island were deported [dee•por'•ted].

10   What relief for a family who passed through the lines with no problems! Finally, they were able to board another ferry. It would take them to the land of promise. But there was more to do. They had to change the money of their

country into U.S. dollars. Many had to buy train tickets to go on to another city.

11   Not all immigrants came through Ellis Island. Some came through Philadelphia [Fil•a•del'•fee•a], San Francisco, Boston, Galveston, and other ports. But those cities never matched the large numbers that came through New York.

A Closed Door

12   After World War I, some laws changed. The United States let fewer immigrants enter the country. And those who could come were checked before they left the old country. Another rule was that adult immigrants had to take reading and writing tests. The tests were in their own language or in English. If they failed the tests, the people were sent back to their native land. These new rules marked the end of Ellis Island's being a major immigration center.

13   During World Wars I and II, Ellis Island had other uses. The U.S. Army, Navy, and Coast Guard needed the buildings for way stations and a hospital. Ellis Island was also for aliens [ay'•lee•ehns], or people thought to be enemies. The government held them there and then forced them to return to their

native country. At the end of 1954, Ellis Island was closed.

Courage Remembered

14   In 1965, Ellis Island became part of the Statue of Liberty National Monument. Many visitors at the statue wanted to see Ellis Island, too. They had heard stories about it from their grandparents. It opened to the public in 1976. It closed again in 1984 to be restored.

15   Six years later, Ellis Island reopened as a museum and a memorial. Tens of thousands of people have visited. They view films and exhibits. Some exhibits have old photos of the immigrants. Others have items the immigrants brought from their countries. There are displays that visitors can operate. One has a computer people can use to find names of family members. As they walk through the halls, many hope to capture the spirit of their ancestors. And they think about how lucky they are.

Questions

1. About how many Americans have ancestors that came through Ellis Island?

2. Why did people want to come to the United States?

3. What was the immigrants' greatest fear?

4. What is Ellis Island used for today?

Signs and Map Skills

1. Draw pictures of the signs the immigrants might have seen after they arrived on Ellis Island.

2. Use a map to locate the U.S. cities that were the major ports of entry for the immigrants, according to the article. Give the coordinates for each city.

3. Use a map to locate Europe and the body of water that the immigrants crossed to get to Ellis Island.

Building a Budget

Do you know where your money really goes?

1 Does every person need a budget? Before you answer this question, consider a few more. Are you always running out of money? Do you pay your bills late? Will you need to buy a car someday? Will you need more schooling? If you answered "yes" to any of those questions, you probably need a budget.

2 What is a budget? It's a spending plan. The main parts of the plan are income and expenses. The money we earn is income. The things we spend money on are expenses. For a budget to work, expenses cannot be more than income.

Starting Out

3 Before you start a budget, you need to know your net income. That's the amount of money

you actually get. For example, your salary may be $300 a week. But your paycheck is less than that. Items such as taxes and insurance are taken out, or deducted. If you have a paycheck, study it to see what was taken out.

4   Knowing your net income is pretty easy. The hard part is figuring out what your expenses are. It helps to write a list. Put the necessary costs first. List food, rent or mortgage [more'•ghedj] payments, electricity, gas, and telephone. Then add bus or train fare, car payments, clothing costs, and school and book fees. Also add any other expenses.

5   You may find it helpful to list these costs on a chart. Use headings like "Food," "Clothing," "Rent," and "Transportation." You might list movies, concerts, and rental tapes under "Entertainment." What you spend in restaurants can go under "Food" or "Entertainment." List things wherever they make sense to you.

Getting It Together

6   How will you get information about your spending? Some of it will be easy to figure out. Other costs may be harder to gather. You get receipts for most things you buy. Save those receipts. If you have a charge account, the statements can help you. Now is the time to

begin your record keeping. At the end of each day, write down what you have spent.

7   Keep track of your expenses for a month. This will give you a good idea of where the money goes. You may be quite surprised. Eating in restaurants and buying snacks may be costing you a lot. A few items of new clothing might add up to hundreds of dollars. But that doesn't mean you should stop eating out or shopping. It may mean only that you have to spend more carefully.

8   Some expenses, like car insurance, come only once or twice a year. You may want to figure out what it comes to for each month. That will help you plan a monthly budget.

9   Keeping records may sound like a lot of work. It is, but it's time well spent. And it's not a chore you must do forever. Once you see where your money goes, you can control your spending.

Looking Ahead

10 This is a good time to think about the future, too. Perhaps you're planning to buy a car or a house. You may need money for future schooling or vacations. These things are costly. You need to put money away to pay for them.

11   Have you heard the old saying "Save for a rainy day"? It's not really about weather. It's

about being prepared. Something might happen—good or bad—for which you haven't planned. That's a reason to have savings. Try to save some money from each paycheck. Put it in a savings bank or other safe place.

Belt Tightening

12 What if you find that you spend more than you earn? Then you had better look hard at your spending. Look for ways to cut back. Use food expenses as an example. Maybe you can eat in restaurants less often. Maybe you can cook meals from scratch instead of buying prepared foods. Try to become a more careful shopper. Watch for special sales. Perhaps an item costs less one week. Buying enough for a month will save you money.

13 Budgeting isn't easy. It's hard to change your spending habits. But remember, the money you *don't* spend can be put to good use. You can spend it on that "rainy day" and on a wonderful future!

Questions

1. Why is a budget important?

2. What are the two main parts of a budget?

3. How does income differ from net income?

4. What are some ways to figure out how much money you spend every month?

Making Graphs

1. Create a monthly budget for yourself. Write down the necessary costs: food, rent or mortgage, electricity, gas, and telephone. Then add other expenses you have. Subtract these expenses from your total monthly income. Decide if you can spend less on some expenses to save more money.

2. Show your monthly budget on a bar graph. Make bars that show what you spend on rent, food, clothing, transportation, entertainment, and other items.

Armchair Shopping

Is the ease of buying through the mail worth the risks?

1 When you got to the mailbox, it's there. Sometimes it's in a plain envelope. Or the envelope may be big and shiny. It may even come as a full-color catalog. The nice term for it is "direct mail." The other term is "junk mail."

Toss or Read?

2 Some people toss all their junk mail right into the trash. Most people, though, don't do that. They pick and choose. They throw out much of this mail after a quick glance. It holds no interest for them. But other pieces look intriguing [in•treeg'•eng]. These are the ones that people open and read.

3   That's the whole idea of direct mail. Direct mailers want you to open their letters. They want you to read what they write and then buy something. Sometimes that seems like a pretty good idea. After all, if the item is something you want, why not buy it?

How Handy!

4 Direct-mail buying has two things going for it. First, it's convenient [kun•veen'•yunt]. You can stay home and be an armchair shopper. All you have to do is write a check and lick a stamp. Or you can make a toll-free call with your credit card in hand.

5   Second, direct-mail firms give you a lot of choices. They offer a wider span of merchandise than stores do. Direct-mail firms that sell clothing or shoes carry all sizes. Many times, local shops don't have the room to store all their goods in every odd size.

The Downside

6 There are also reasons *not* to buy through the mail. Three big problems come to mind. First, you can't inspect what you are buying. That is important when you buy clothing. With good direct-mail companies, this may not be a problem. They show good pictures in their catalogs and describe each item with care.

Still, you can't feel the fabric with your own hands before you buy.

7   Second, costs for shipping and handling can add up. When you buy through the mail, you pay all shipping costs. These fees can sometimes be pretty steep. Some firms add on a charge for what they call insurance. That is a false fee. By law, all mail-order firms must get a product to you in perfect shape. An insurance charge is, in fact, nothing more than a price hike.

8   Third, you have to wait to get what you buy. The law says that a firm must get goods to you within 30 days. But that law does not apply if the seller states a later date in print. A company can then take from five to eight weeks to get an order to you. If the seller doesn't make the deadline stated, you have a choice. You can wait for the order even longer. Or you can get your money back.

9   With good mail-order firms, these are not big problems. They deliver the product quickly, and their goods are top of the line. These firms will also return your money if you don't like the product. Some of the best direct-mail firms are ones that sell clothing, outdoor gear, and hard-to-find tools.

Protect Yourself

10 How can you protect yourself when you buy through the mail? Here are some tips:

11 **1.** Read with care what the catalog says. Photos may look nice, but they can mislead you. If an item sounds too good to be true, it is!

12 **2.** Find out what the company's return policy is. Who pays for shipping costs if you return an item? Many times, *you* will! But you don't need to pay for the company's mistakes. It would be the company's mistake if, for instance, you got a shirt in a size you didn't order. The same is true if an item's color doesn't match the catalog color. Maybe the stitching on an item is poorly done. That is the company's fault. On the other hand, who is at fault if you return an item because you changed your mind?

13 **3.** Know the facts. If you place an order by phone, note the date and time. Write the name of the person who takes your order. Also jot down any order number the phone clerk gives you. Keep the catalog. Mark the pages and circle the items you order.

14 **4.** Protect yourself when you pay for mail-order goods. The best way is to pay by credit card. That way, if something goes wrong, it is easy to cancel your debt. You might pay by check. Most of the time, that's fine. But what if you have a complaint about an item you get? What if the firm goes bankrupt? In both cases, the company can cash your check but not make good on your order. The worst way to pay is to send cash through the mail. Not only do you risk losing the cash—but most direct-mail firms won't take it.

Mountain of Mail

15 How many catalogs do you really want? The more items you order by mail, the more catalogs you will get. The reason is that direct-mail firms sell your name to other firms. You may get catalogs from firms you've never heard of. That's because your name has been sold to those companies.

16 You can put a stop to all of the junk mail. You can write to the Direct Marketing Association [uh•so•see•a′•shun] in New York City. Ask them to take your name off their list. Then, *presto*, no more catalogs—*if* that's what you want.

17   Most people like to get catalogs. They like the convenience of shopping by mail. Maybe you do, too. But use common sense when you buy this way. You can then enjoy the pluses of armchair shopping and avoid most of the minuses.

Questions

1. Why do some people call direct mail "junk mail"?
2. Name two good reasons for buying through the mail.
3. What are the risks of buying through the mail?
4. Why is paying by credit card the best way to buy through the mail?
5. How can you stop junk mail, such as unwanted catalogs?

Using Forms, Consumer Materials, and Dictionary

1. Identify and write what abbreviations such as *COD, F.O.B., H/C, est., min., lbs., item no., qty.,* and *exp. date* stand for in a direct-mail catalog.
2. Use a dictionary to find the correct meaning of *intriguing* (paragraph 2), *convenient* (paragraph 4), and *merchandise* (paragraph 5).
3. Fill out a mail-order form, making sure you have filled in all information. Ask another person to check your order.
4. Figure out the shipping and handling costs for your order. Compare the costs of different shipping options.

The Fabulous Miss Bly

Why would a newspaper reporter want to stay at a home for the mentally ill?

1   In 1890, New York held a parade in honor of Elizabeth Cochrane [Kock'•run]. Was she a movie star? An astronaut [as'•tro•naht]? A visiting princess? No. She was a newspaper reporter. She was about 23 years old. And she had just circled the globe in 72 days.

2   In those days, many young women had hard, dull jobs. Their pay was low. Almost all good jobs went to men. After all, people said, a woman's place is in the home. In 1885, the *Pittsburgh Dispatch* printed an editorial about working women. It said that women could not do a good job outside the home.

Look Out, World!

3   Elizabeth Cochrane read the article. She was young and eager for adventure. The article made her angry. She wrote to the *Dispatch*. Women, she said, could do many jobs well. It was wrong to waste their talents. The paper printed her letter. Then Cochrane asked for a job as a reporter. The editor liked her letter. So he gave her a try.

4   Cochrane wrote under another name. She chose Nellie Bly. "Nellie Bly" is the name of a song by Stephen Foster, an American songwriter who lived in the 1800s.

Travel to Mexico

5   Nellie Bly's first reports told about the hard lives of other working women. She wrote about the slums of Pittsburgh. She wrote about divorce. She got readers excited about her topics.

6   The *Dispatch* saw how popular Bly's work was. So in 1887 the paper sent her to Mexico. For six months, Bly traveled around Mexico. She wrote reports about all that she saw.

7   In those days, few people saw other countries. There were no movies or TV shows about far-off lands. So almost everything in Bly's reports was new to her readers. They were eager to learn about Mexico. Later, Bly

published her reports in a book called *Six Months in Mexico.*

Bly Tells All

8   Soon after Bly came home to Pittsburgh, she moved to New York. She had a new job with a larger paper. She then worked for the *New York World.*

9   Bly's first big topic in New York was insane asylums [uh•sy'•lums]. Most often, the city asylums made little news. People with mental illnesses were just "put away" and forgotten. But how well were patients treated? Bly wanted to find out.

10   Bly knew that visitors are always shown the best things. She wanted to see the worst things, too. So she pretended to be insane. She was sent to a New York asylum as a patient.

11   Inside, Bly learned that patients were often mistreated. Many were dirty and hungry. They were left for long times without care. Instead of getting better, patients got worse.

12   Two weeks later, Bly was out of the asylum. But the outcome of her daring stunt lasted for years. Her reports about asylums were first printed in the *World.* Later, they came out as a book called *Ten Days in a Madhouse.* Readers were shocked by what she wrote. They cried

for changes. Because of Bly, life got better for patients in New York asylums.

The Biggest Trip of All

13   Nellie Bly had proved she was a great reporter. But she still wanted adventure. A book gave her the idea for her greatest success. *Around the World in Eighty Days* was a popular book in 1889. It tells the tale of Phileas [Fil'•ee•us] Fogg, a noted English gentleman. On a bet, he travels around the world in just 80 days. Few people believed the trip was possible. Bly thought she could make the trip even faster.

14   At first, the *World* would not let her try. The idea was crazy. No one could go around the world in so few days! And for a woman, there would be added danger. But Bly kept asking. Finally, her boss told her to go ahead. He knew Bly loved adventure. Besides, the trip could make both her and the paper famous.

15   Bly packed a single bag. Then she set off. On November 14, 1889, at 9:40 A.M., her ship left New Jersey. Bly first landed in England. Then she went on to France. There she met Jules Verne, the writer of *Around the World in Eighty Days*. After Verne wished her good luck, Bly left for Hong Kong.

A Race Against Time

16 Nellie Bly traveled by ship, train, horse, handcart, and burro. Wherever she went, she wrote. She kept an exact record of what she saw and did. Bly planned to share her adventures with others. She wanted her readers to feel as if they had traveled along with her.

17 When Bly's ship from Hong Kong reached San Francisco, she was famous. The *World* sent a train to meet her. It would bring her to New Jersey as fast as it could. Even so, crowds met the train at each stop. Everyone wanted to see the young world traveler.

18 At last, the train reached New Jersey. Bly jumped from it on January 25, 1890, at 3:31 P.M. She had circled Earth in exactly 72 days, 6 hours, and 11 minutes. The waiting crowd cheered. A few days later, New York greeted her. Fireworks went off. Brass bands played. A parade marched down Broadway.

19 Of course, Bly reported on her trip in the *World*. She also wrote *Nellie Bly's Book: Around the World in Seventy-Two Days*. This was her most popular book.

Other Adventures

20 Nellie Bly kept up her writing until 1895. Then she married Robert Seaman, a very rich man.

After he died, she ran his business. But her gift was for news, not business. By 1920, she was writing again.

21   Nellie Bly died in 1922. By then, planes carried people over land and seas. Bly's speed record was broken. Yet Bly's boldness is still a model. And her spirit of adventure will never age.

Questions

1. What was Nellie Bly's real name?

2. What was the first newspaper Bly worked for?

3. What were some topics of Bly's first newspaper reports?

4. What gave Bly the idea for her trip around the world?

5. Why did New York City hold a parade in Bly's honor?

Identifying Character

1. Why was Nellie Bly angry when she read the article in the *Pittsburgh Dispatch?*

2. How and why did Nellie Bly enter the New York insane asylum as a patient? What does that stunt tell you about her?

3. What three words would you use to describe Nellie Bly?

4. Why did Nellie Bly want to travel around the world?

All Kinds of Cats

Why were cats once burned alive?

1 To some people, a cat means beauty and grace. To others, a cat means mystery or power. Cats have held a special place in people's lives for thousands of years.

Traits in Common

2 Except for size, all cats are much the same. All are very strong for their size and move in much the same way. They can be fast and mean. Most can fish. All cats can swim. Some don't really like water unless there is no other way to escape.

3 Most cats can climb. All have good sight, hearing, and smell. All have pads on their feet with sharp claws under them. They kill quickly, so they are great hunters.

An Old Family

4 No one knows when the first cat lived. But the most famous cat of long ago is the saber-toothed tiger. During the Ice Age, this cat moved into all parts of the world. It died out many, many years ago.

5   Cats were part of every family in Egypt 5,000 years ago. They were pets, but they also killed the mice and rats that ate stored grain. People even got their cats to fish and hunt for them. The people of Egypt saw their cats as gods. When a cat died, its owner made it a mummy. In the 1800s, a graveyard just for cats was found in Egypt with mummies of 300,000 cats.

6   People of the Middle Ages were afraid of cats. They believed that cats held the power of black magic. So they began to kill them. They burned them alive in the center of town. Over time, there weren't enough cats left to kill mice and rats. Rat bites made people very sick. Many people died because there were not enough cats.

Close to Home

7 By the 1700s, cats were again friends and mice killers. Today there are about 30 million pet cats in the United States.

8   A little more than 100 years ago, there were no cat breeds. Then people began mating the cats they liked best. A certain color, ear shape, or

leg size was passed down over the years. These became breeds such as Siamese [Sy•uh•meez'], Persian [Per'•zhun], and Manx [Manks]. Clubs around the world help people keep the breeds pure and also start new breeds.

Tigers

9 The biggest wild cat in the world is the tiger. Tigers live in China and other parts of Asia. They are found in no other parts of the world, except in zoos.

10   There are different kinds of tigers, but all have black stripes on a yellow or orange body. The tiger's tail has black rings. A male tiger may weigh as much as 500 pounds and be 10 feet long. Three feet of his length is his tail.

11   Tigers are big, strong, and fierce. They like to hide in the jungle or in thick brush along a river. Tigers can swim better than any other cat. They may walk around during the day to see what's in the area. Then at night they go hunting. Tigers will kill cows, horses, sheep, and goats. They will kill almost any kind of wild animal. But tigers won't go after elephants or bears for fear of getting killed first.

Lions

12 Lions and tigers act much the same. Their bones look alike. They are about the same size.

When a lion and a tiger mate, their offspring is called a liger. Lions and tigers are different in that the lion has no stripes. Also, the male lion has a mane. Most lions stay with their mates for life.

13   Lions also hunt at night, in pairs or groups. The team goes out looking for a zebra, giraffe, or other animal. The female lion hides near a water hole. The male lion scares the animal with his loud roar. The female then jumps on it and bites deeply into its neck. The male keeps up the loud roar. When the animal is dead, he joins the female to feed.

14   Lions and tigers kill people only if they can't go after animals. That can happen if their teeth or claws are broken. It can happen also when they are too old and slow to hunt wild animals.

Other Family Members

15 A leopard may be as long as a lion or tiger. But it has spots and weighs less than 200 pounds. The leopard climbs trees. It jumps long and high. It lives in Asia and Africa.

16   The hunting leopard of India is the cheetah. It can run at speeds of up to 70 miles per hour. That is faster than any other land animal.

17   The jaguar is the leopard's cousin. It is the biggest cat in Central or South America. The

jaguar is six or seven feet long. Not many jaguars are left. They are in danger of dying out.

18   A smaller leopard cousin is the ocelot [ah'•suh•laht]. It weighs 25 to 35 pounds and has both stripes and spots. Some are still found in both the United States and Mexico.

19   Big or small, each kind of cat is important to other living things. The largest tiger helps balance life in the wild. The smallest house cat can brighten the life of a person. Whatever their role, cats are special in our lives and our world.

Questions

1. What was the most famous cat of the Ice Age?

2. How did the people of ancient Egypt feel about cats?

3. What was the effect of burning cats during the Middle Ages?

4. Outside of zoos, where do tigers live?

5. What is a liger?

Comparing and Contrasting/ Identifying Main Idea

1. In what ways are all cats alike?

2. Which cat is the best swimmer?

3. Which cats hunt in pairs or groups?

4. Which cat is the fastest?

5. What is the main idea of this article?

The Great Depression

How did President Franklin Delano Roosevelt make sure that people would have some money for their old age?

1 Today, many of us wish we had more money. But in the 1930s, nearly everyone was in deep money trouble. During the worst times, 14 million people were out of work. Those who did have jobs were paid only pennies. Those terrible years were called the Great Depression.

Trouble Brewing

2 The trouble started in the 1920s. Most of those years, everything seemed to be fine. But things were not as good as they seemed. Farmers were not getting fair prices for crops. Coal mining, railroad, and clothing businesses were having a hard time. And too many people were getting bank loans they could not pay off.

3   Then, in 1929, prices of stock in American business began to drop. A stock once worth $100 might end up being worth only $3. On October 29, 1929, the stock market "crashed" to an all-time low. It was called Black Tuesday. Anyone who owned stocks lost a great deal of money. Suddenly, many rich people were poor.

Hard Times

4 That was the start of the Great Depression. Many companies went out of business. Millions of workers lost their jobs. When people went to get their money, they found the banks were closed. There was no welfare, unemployment checks, or social security. Millions of people went broke. The same thing was happening in other countries, too.

From Bad to Worse

5 President Herbert Hoover promised that better times were "just around the corner." He didn't think the government should step in. But over the next three years, wages fell for those who still had jobs. Prices also fell, but low prices didn't help. Most people were lucky to pay for food and rent. Some families ate "cracker soup" for dinner. Others sorted through garbage for food.

6   Many families lost their homes. They built shacks out of boxes, tin, and old car parts. They

slept under newspapers. Soup kitchens and bread lines were set up. Some children stopped going to school because they didn't have clothes to wear. Men out of work stood on the street selling apples for five cents. Others begged in the street. Many people who had lost hope killed themselves.

7   The weather made matters even worse. In 1930, there was little rain. The land from South Dakota to Texas to Illinois—called the Dust Bowl—became as dry as sand. Then, in 1931 and 1932, dust storms blew whole farms away. Sand got into food and water. People stayed indoors. They stuffed cloth and paper into any holes in their houses so the wind could not get in.

8   A few years later, there was too much rain. Eleven large rivers flooded. In Ohio, 500,000 homes were washed away. Towns along the great rivers were washed out.

The New Deal

9   Herbert Hoover ran for president again in 1932. But he lost to Franklin Delano Roosevelt. President Roosevelt believed that the government should step in to end the depression. His plan was called the New Deal. It started a number of new programs.

10   Roosevelt and Congress put new government controls on banks and the stock

market. They sent out $500 million to help the poorest people. They set up jobs for people to plant trees and build dams and power plants. To drive up farm prices, they paid farmers to plant less. To help people keep their homes and farms, they gave government loans. They worked with companies to hire more workers.

More Programs

11 Then the Works Progress Administration, or WPA, began. Under this new program, people built schools, hospitals, bridges, roads, airports, and government buildings. It also paid people to paint, sculpt, write, dance, and make music. Even today, many post offices, schools, and parks have works by WPA artists.

12   In 1935, Social Security began. Workers paid a tax so they would have money in their old age. Social Security paid women and children who had lost a working man in the family. It also started a state welfare program and an unemployment plan. People who were out of work would get some money until they found another job.

13   President Roosevelt helped the country make it through the Great Depression. Not everyone liked what he did. Yet Roosevelt was the only president to win the office of president four times.

Chasing Away the Blues

14 Movies filled with music and dance helped people to smile through the worst of the 1930s. Hollywood came into its own and radio became a big hit. People heard Bing Crosby sing. They enjoyed listening to radio shows such as "The Shadow" and "The Lone Ranger." They laughed with Bob Hope or listened to new music by Benny Goodman, the "King of Swing." But the most famous song of the depression was "Brother, Can You Spare a Dime?"

Coming Back

15 Slowly, America crawled out of the Great Depression. But Roosevelt's programs alone could not end this awful time. When World War II broke out, America needed its factories and farms again. Men went off to fight, and women went to work. The war got America back on its feet.

16   The country has been up and down since the Great Depression. But the laws passed under Roosevelt helped make sure that it can never happen again.

Questions

1. What year did the stock market crash?

2. Who was the president at the time?

3. What was the New Deal?

4. What is Social Security, and when did it start?

5. How many times did Roosevelt win the presidency?

Identifying Cause and Effect/Drawing Conclusions

1. What were some of the causes of the Great Depression?

2. What were some of the effects of the Great Depression?

3. Why were parts of the United States called the Dust Bowl in 1930s?

4. Why was Herbert Hoover defeated by Franklin Roosevelt in the 1932 presidential election?

5. Besides the New Deal, what helped end the Great Depression? How?

Electric Cars

Are you getting choked up over gas fumes? Perhaps it's time for another kind of car.

1 Try to think of life without cars. It's not easy. But our cars make us sick. Their exhaust pollutes the air. Dirty air is hard to breathe. On some days in large cities, the air is thick and gray. Polluted air drifts all over. It even rises high above Earth. Many scientists feel that it can change the weather. Everyone is hurt by pollution.

2 Each day there are more cars, buses, and trucks. Each day they cause more pollution. We can't get rid of our vehicles. But we can change them. Their gasoline engines are the problem. Vehicles could be powered some other way. A likely form of energy is electricity. Today, researchers are trying to build a useful electric car.

3   The electric car is not a new idea. The first electrics were made about 100 years ago. In fact, three kinds of engines were used on early cars.

Early Electrics

4 Around 1900, thousands of cars ran on electric batteries. They were silent, so they never scared horses. They were clean. They were easy to start. Almost every woman driver chose an electric car.

5   But electric cars were slow. Their top speed was 20 or 30 miles per hour. Going uphill, top speed fell to 4 or 5 miles per hour. Even worse, they couldn't go far. After about 30 miles, the batteries had to be recharged.

Some Progress

6 Other cars had steam engines. A steam-powered car was almost as clean as an electric. And it was much faster. Racing steamers reached speeds of over 100 miles per hour. With normal use, steamers ran at 30 miles per hour for more than 150 miles.

7   Cars with gasoline engines also went fast. And they had a wider range. Refueling took only minutes. As long as a car could get fuel, its range had almost no limits.

8   But these gasoline-powered cars had drawbacks. There were many moving parts

that could break. They often did. A driver had to fix many things on, in, and under the car. Driving one of these cars could be dirty. Worst of all, the engine had to be cranked before the car would start. Only a strong person could do that.

9   Then, in 1912, the self-starter came into use. Now an electric battery, not a crank, would start a gas-powered car. Suddenly, these cars were as easy to start as electrics. They were already as fast as steamers. Both the electric car and the steamer began to lose ground. Within 20 years, no one made them anymore.

Modern Electrics

10 In the 1960s, attention turned once more to the electric car. What could increase its speed and range?

11   Some researchers looked at the lead-acid battery. They tried new designs. They tried different materials. Some batteries they made were better than those of today. But the strongest ones cost too much.

12   Other researchers worked on a slightly different power source. It is called a fuel cell. A fuel cell could be twice as strong as a lead-acid battery. But, even today, it is too heavy and costly.

13 Recharging was also studied. Drivers wouldn't mind stopping so often for a recharging if it took only minutes. Still another idea was to design a lighter car. Then a regular battery could push it faster and farther.

14 Today, many designs are being tested. Large and small companies and even people on their own are building electrics. Reports say that work is moving ahead.

Road Tests

15 One owner tried to drive cross-country in his modern electric car in 1991. Noel Perrin later wrote about his trip in *Solo: Life with an Electric Car.* Perrin was happy with his car's speed on flat land. The car could go 50 miles per hour easily. It went up to 60 miles between charges. For short bursts, the car could even reach 60 miles per hour.

16 But going up a steep hill, the car could barely reach 30 miles per hour. Worse, it ran out of power very quickly.

17 Each time Perrin stopped to recharge, he had big problems. There were no charging stations along the highways. So Perrin had to plug his car into regular outlets. At best, recharging took four hours. Sometimes it took

twice that time. That meant that Perrin could travel only about 100 miles a day.

18   The same year, someone else drove an electric car for 24 hours straight under special conditions. Recharging was much quicker. This car went more than 600 miles.

19   In 1992, an electric vehicle did even better with a new charging station. A small electric truck was driven around a race track. Every 60 miles or so, it pulled into the station. A computer controlled the recharging. Each time, the job took less than 20 minutes. The truck traveled 831.8 miles in 24 hours, a new world record.

Planning Ahead

20   Could we have fast charging stations—or electricity pumps—along the roads? These would give electric cars the range they need. But such pumps would cause new problems.

21   Electric power companies have more than enough energy at night. Electric cars that are recharged at night could use that energy. But suppose that they needed to recharge during the day. Then they would need to stop at electricity pumps. The power companies would have to put out more energy. So the power companies would do more polluting,

since coal is used to make electricity. That wouldn't help.

22   In short, there is little chance that your next car will be an electric. But new technology has created a gasoline-electric hybrid car. Your next car might be a pollution-free hybrid.

Questions

1. About what year did cars first run on electric batteries?

2. How fast could the first electrics go?

3. What new addition to gas-powered cars made them more popular than electric- or steam-powered cars?

4. Name two things that made Noel Perrin unhappy with his electric car.

5. What was the 1992 world record for distance traveled in 24 hours?

Making Predictions

1. Predict what your life would be like without a car. What changes would you have to make? Would your life be easier or more difficult?

2. Imagine that electric cars become popular. Predict how fueling stations would operate. Would people have to use less electricity elsewhere to have enough for their cars? Would the cost of electricity increase or decrease?

3. In the near future, widespread use of electric cars seems unlikely. What do you think will happen if gas-powered cars continue to be used? Write a letter to the editor predicting the effect on the environment and offer a solution.

Pride of the Giants

Why did Chief Meyers quit his studies— all expenses paid—at one of the best schools in the country?

1 John "Chief" Meyers was a major league baseball player about 90 years ago. He was proud to be in baseball. He was just as proud of his Native American heritage.

2 The Cahuillas [Kah•hoo•ee'•yuz] were one of the tribes of the Mission Indians of southern California. They lived high in the peaks of the San Jacinto [Juh•seen'•toe] Mountains. John Tortes Meyers was born in a Cahuilla village in 1880. His people were known as a proud and independent tribe. It is no wonder that Meyers grew up to be that way, too.

Following a Dream

3 When Meyers was about 11, the family moved to the city of Riverside. He attended public schools there. When he finished high school, college was far from his mind. His heart was set on playing baseball.

4   Meyers's skills were so good that several semiprofessional [seh•mi•proh•feh'•shun•ul] teams hired him as a catcher. Meyers made no secret of his Native American background. He was aware of the prejudice against minorities in those days. But he had pride in his heritage. Soon he got the nickname of "Chief."

Help from Abroad

5 In 1904, Chief Meyers's life took an interesting turn. His baseball team was playing in Albuquerque [Al'•buh•ker•kee], New Mexico. That's where he met an all-American football player named Ralph Glaze. Glaze was a student at Dartmouth College in New Hampshire.

6   Glaze told Meyers about a scholarship at Dartmouth. Who had set up the scholarship? An earl in England! In the 1700s, the school was known as Moor's Indian Charity School. The teachers were English missionaries [mih'•shun•air•eez]. The Earl of Dartmouth heard about the school. He sent money for a

special scholarship fund. The scholarship could go only to a Native American who was a good enough student to study there. The school was later renamed for the earl.

7   Meyers put in for the scholarship and was accepted. He could not play baseball for the school because he was not an amateur [am'•uh•cher]. When school was out for the summer, he played for Harrisburg, Pennsylvania, in the Tri-State League. He had planned to return to Dartmouth at the end of the summer. But he was called home to the bedside of his sick mother. When her health improved, it was too late for him to return to school. He regretted that for the rest of his life.

Play Ball

8 The best thing Chief Meyers could pursue was another career in baseball. At first, he played for minor league teams in Montana and Minnesota. In 1908, he joined the National League's New York Giants.

9   At that time, John McGraw was the team's manager. Meyers greatly admired him. He felt that McGraw had changed the public's feeling toward baseball players. In the early part of the century, players were not always treated with respect. As an example, they weren't allowed in the better hotels for out-of-town games. But

McGraw didn't go along with that. He paid for his players to stay at the best hotels.

Hail to the Chief

10 Chief Meyers also had great respect for umpire Bill Klem and Giants pitcher Christy Mathewson. By 1910, Meyers became the team's regular catcher. His highest batting average was .358 in 1912. The team won pennants in 1911, 1912, and 1913.

11   In 1916, Meyers was traded to the Brooklyn Robins (later renamed the Dodgers). Meyers retired the following year. His lifetime batting average was .291. His top salary was about $6,000 a year.

It's All in the Game

12 The subject of salary came up in an interview when Chief Meyers was in his 80s. Meyers said that today's players are businessmen. "They've got agents and outside interests and all that sort of thing. We played for money, too. Naturally. That's how we made our living. But mostly we played just for the love of it. . . . Most of us would have paid *them* just to let us play. We loved baseball."

13   In that same interview, Meyers compared himself to an old warrior chief of the great Six Nations. The chief had said, "I am like an old

hemlock. My head is still high, but the winds of close to 100 winters have whistled through my branches, and I have been witness to many wondrous and many tragic things. My eyes perceive the present, but my roots are imbedded deeply in the grandeur of the past." Chief Meyers died in 1971 at the age of 90.

Questions

1. Where does the Cahuilla tribe come from?

2. Why was John Meyers nicknamed "Chief"?

3. What year did Meyers join the New York Giants?

4. Why did Meyers admire the Giants' manager, John McGraw?

5. What position did Meyers play most often with the Giants?

Fact vs. Opinion

1. Do you think that the nickname "Chief" showed respect or disrespect for John Meyers? Why?

2. Do you think professional athletes are overpaid today? Write a paragraph defending your opinion.

3. "John 'Chief' Meyers was a credit to the game of baseball." Use facts from the article to support this opinion.

Life Beneath a Blanket of Snow

How does snow act as a blanket for animals?

1 Flake by flake, snow covers the ground in winter in cold areas. This blanket can last for weeks or months. It's hard for rabbits, birds, and deer to find food in the snow. But other animals need the snow to protect them.

2 Fresh snow looks smooth and clean. Underneath, the ground is the same as it was in the fall. There are fallen trees and leaves on the forest floor. There are rock piles under the cliffs and tall grass in the fields. Short grass covers the lawns. When snow falls, it does not fill in every space. It bends the grass. It flows around trees and rocks. It isn't a solid block. Under it are spaces and tunnels.

3   Under the snow, it is warmer and brighter than you might think. In summer, the sun warms the soil, which stores up this heat. In winter, the heat rises toward the cold air. If there were no snow, all the heat would escape. The ground would be frozen solid. But snow acts as a blanket. It keeps the ground much warmer than the temperature that we feel in the air.

Animals Under the Snow

4   Some animals, like the fox, may dig into the snow to make a warm shelter from a storm. But many small animals live under the snow all winter long.

5   The largest of these animals is the red squirrel. It is about one foot long and weighs less than seven ounces. Most of the year, red squirrels live in trees. But when it gets cold, red squirrels build tunnels under the snow. They eat pine cones they have stored during the fall.

6   Meadow voles [volz], which are like mice, need snow to stay alive. Most of the year they live in burrows under the surface of the ground. When it is freezing cold and there is no snow on the ground, meadow voles are in danger. The ground begins to freeze. Their burrows can't protect them from the weather.

7   Once it snows, life becomes easier for meadow voles. The snow blanket keeps the ground warm. And the bottom layer of snow becomes loose and easy to tunnel through. Meadow voles build nests under the snow.

8   Because they are small, meadow voles must eat often to keep up their body heat. They dig tunnels near their nests and eat all the plants they find on the way. When the snow melts, you can tell where their tunnels were. There are narrow trails of very short grass.

Sharing Warmth

9   Meadow voles have many relatives. Some of these are prairie voles, pine voles, deer mice, and shrews. In warm weather, these animals keep to themselves. But in winter, they share their nests with others of their kind. Sleeping together keeps all the animals warmer. The animals take turns leaving the nest to feed. This way, the nest is always warm when they return.

10   There are drawbacks to these shared nests. It is easy for sickness to spread from one animal to another. And predators [pred'•uh•torz] are more likely to find the nests because of their strong smell.

The Hunters

11 There are many predators of these small animals. They include foxes, coyotes, owls, hawks, weasels, and house cats. These predators may hear or smell a vole moving under the snow. But they will have a hard time catching one.

12 The long, thin weasel [wee'•zul] is the best hunter. It can easily dig through snow and travel along tunnels. Often a weasel will take over a nest. It will eat the animals inside and line the walls with their fur. When the snow melts, you can see these fur-lined nests. They tell the tale of life and death under the snow.

13 Shrews also hunt under the snow. They are not good diggers, so they use tunnels made by other animals. Shrews need a lot of food, so they hunt for insects. Shrews sniff to find their prey. They also use their whiskers to feel prey and their ears to hear it moving.

Insect and Plants

14 Snow fleas are closely tied to winter. They are found in the northeastern part of the United States. These little blue insects live in the leaves on the forest floor. On warm days, they come to the surface of the snow. There may be enough of them to form a dark patch on the snow.

15   Snow fleas are also known as springtails because they can jump. When the temperature drops, they go back under the snow. Snow fleas are proof of life under the snow.

16   Plants get a head start on spring under the snow. Light can get through the snow and make the ground warm and moist. This lets plants live and grow. Some plants, like wild onions, push through the snow. Other plants, like snow buttercups or glacier [glay'•sher] lilies, even bloom above the snow.

17   As spring arrives, the snow melts. The plants and animals that live safely under the snow must get ready for the new season. There will be many challenges ahead. But when winter returns, the snow will again provide a blanket to protect them.

Questions

1. Which is the largest animal that lives under the snow?

2. Why do meadow voles eat often?

3. What are some drawbacks of shared nests?

4. Which animal is the best hunter of animals that live under the snow?

5. How do shrews find their prey?

6. Why are springtails a good name for snow fleas?

Applying Passage Elements

1. Why isn't the ground frozen solid in the winter?

2. How does sharing a nest below ground help meadow voles and their relatives?

3. How does light help plants under the snow?

Answer Key

A Home in the North

Page 9: Questions

1. A snow house could be built in an hour or two.
2. *Eskimo* means "a person who eats raw meat."
3. Today people in the Arctic live in modern frame homes, use snowmobiles, and have indoor jobs.

Page 9: Antonym/Synonym Search

1. Possible answers: hot–cold; slower–faster; small–big; summer–winter; wet–dry; long–short; soft–hard; thin–fat; down–up; slowly–quickly
2. A hole was cut in the roof of the snow house to let the stale air out. Fresh air would come in through the tunnel.
3. Answers will vary.
4. Possible answers: weary–tired; start–begin; enormous–huge; arched–curved; fast–quick; uncooked–raw
5. Answers will vary.

What Is Color?

Page 13: Questions

1. A prism works by bending a ray of light and spreading out the colors.
2. Light hits the colors of an object. Some of this light is reflected off the object and into our eyes.
3. Cones respond to color.
4. The cones in our eyes do not work in dim light.

Page 13: Using Context Clues

1. Red, yellow, and blue are primary colors.
2. Complementary colors are opposites. Yellow is complementary to blue. Blue green is complementary to red.
3. An afterimage is an image with the same shape as an original image, but with different colors.

Who Wears the Pants?

Page 18: Questions

1. Men started wearing pants to ride horses easier and to keep warm.
2. Women started wearing pants by 1890 to make riding bicycles and playing sports easier.
3. It was hard for women to buy stockings during the war, so they wore pants to cover their bare legs.
4. Plaid is a pattern that has colored stripes going in two different directions.
5. Men in Scotland wear kilts to show which part of Scotland they come from.

Page 18: Spelling Word Alert

1. piece–peace; sew–so; wear–where; great–grate; bare–bear; sense–cents; two–too
2. *Knee* has a silent letter (k) and names a part of the body. Before you give a gift, you *wrap* it; *wrap* has a silent letter (w).
3. Lines 6–7: That way, everyone could *admire* their good-looking legs. *admiring*

Lines 7–9: The men would look in the mirror to *decide* which of their legs was better looking. *deciding*

Egypt's Wonders

Page 24: Questions
1. Each pyramid was built as a tomb.
2. Farmers worked from July to November while their fields were flooded from the Nile River.
3. The king's body was preserved so his soul could live forever.
4. People wanted to enter the tombs to steal gold and jewels that were entombed with the mummies.

Page 24: Noting Details
1. King Khufu's pyramid is 481 feet high.
2. King Khufu's pyramid is also called the Great Pyramid.
3. The workers built a ramp of stones and mud to get blocks up to each layer of the pyramid.
4. The pyramid had more than 120 layers.
5. The walls of the secret rooms had beautiful pictures and writings that told about the king's life.
6. The king's body was wrapped in layers of cloth.

A Good Cup of Coffee

Page 29: Questions
1. The best coffee trees are in South America and Africa.
2. Coffee berries ripen in 6 to 14 months.

3. Coffee beans are treated with a chemical and then the caffeine is steamed out.
4. A young French soldier brought one coffee tree with him on a sailing ship around 1700.

Page 29: Identifying Sequence
1. After coffee berries are picked, they are spread out in the sun to dry.
2. Coffee berries are roasted after they are shipped to other countries.
3. Before coffee is shipped to stores, it is packed in air tight containers.

The Trail of Tears

Page 35: Questions
1. The Cherokee's original home was the Great Smoky Mountains in Tennessee.
2. Andrew Jackson was president at the time of the march.
3. The Cherokees faced a lack of warm clothes and shoes, bad weather, disease, and hunger.
4. Those who died were thrown into ditches dug along the trail.
5. It took about six months to march to Oaklahoma.

Page 35: Recognizing Stated Concepts
1. White men wanted the gold and the Cherokees had to give up their land.
2. The U.S. government told the Cherokees that they had to relocate to the Oaklahoma Territory.
3. The Cherokees had only the food they could carry; their

grain sacks would get wet and would soon be filled with bugs.

Ellis Island

Page 41: Questions

1. More than 100 million Americans have ancestors who came through Ellis Island.
2. People came to the U.S. to find work, to avoid army service in their home country, and to avoid unfair treatment at home.
3. The immigrants' greatest fear was the health station on Ellis Island.
4. Today Ellis Island is a museum and memorial.

Page 41: Signs and Map Skills

1–3 Answers will vary.

Building a Budget

Page 46: Questions

1. A budget helps you keep track of your money.
2. Income and expenses are the two main parts of a budget.
3. Income is money you earn. Net income is the amount of money you actually get after taxes and insurance are deducted.
4. To figure out how much you spend each month, you could make a list, save receipts, and keep track of expenses.

Page 46: Making Graphs

1–2 Answers will vary.

Armchair Shopping

Page 53: Questions

1. "Junk mail" holds holds no interest for them.

2. If you buy through the mail, you can shop from home and you have a wider variety of choices.
3. If you buy through the mail, you can't inspect what you are buying, you have to pay shipping costs, and you have to wait for what you buy.
4. If you use a credit card and something goes wrong with the order, it is easy to cancel your debt.
5. You can stop junk mail by writing to the Direct Marketing Association to ask them to remove your name from their list.

Page 53: Using Forms and Consumer Materials

1. COD–cash on delivery; F.O.B.–freight on board; H/C–handling charge; est.–estimate; min.–minimum; lbs.–pounds; item no.–item number; qty.–quantity; exp. date–expiration date
2. *intriguing*–fascinating, interesting; *convenient*–handy, easy; *merchandise*–materials to be sold **3–4** Answers will vary.

The Fabulous Miss Bly

Page 60: Questions

1. Nellie Bly's real name was Elizabeth Cochrane.
2. *Pittsburgh Dispatch* was the first newspaper she worked for.
3. Bly reported on working women, slums, and divorce.
4. Bly's idea for the trip around the world came from the book *Around the World in Eighty Days*.

5. New York held a parade because Bly made the trip around the world in record time.

Page 60: Identifying Character
1. Bly felt that women could do many jobs well outside the home.
2. Bly entered the insane asylum to report on the conditions of an asylum. She pretended that she was insane. This showed that Bly was a brave and caring person.
3. Answers will vary.
4. Bly wanted to travel around the world because she loved adventure and wanted to make her paper and herself famous.

All Kinds of Cats

Page 66: Questions
1. The saber-toothed tiger was the most famous cat of the Ice Age.
2. The people of ancient Egypt loved and honored their cats like gods.
3. During the Middle Ages, the lack of cats available to kill rats and mice led to the plague that killed millions of people.
4. Tigers live in China and other parts of Asia.
5. A liger is a cross between a lion and a tiger.

Page 66: Comparing and Contrasting/Identifying Main Idea
1. Answers will vary.
2. The tiger is the best swimmer.
3. Lions hunt in groups or pairs.
4. The cheetah is the fastest cat.

5. There are many different kinds of cats in our world.

The Great Depression

Page 72: Questions
1. The stock market crashed in 1929.
2. Herbert Hoover was president during the Great Depression.
3. The New Deal was a plan to help end the depression.
4. Social Security started in 1935. It provides benefits and payments to people when they retire.
5. Roosevelt won the presidency four times.

Page 72: Identifying Cause and Effect/Drawing Conclusions
1. Causes of the Great Depression: farmers were not getting fair prices; mining, railroads, and businesses were having a hard time; too many people were getting bank loans they could not pay off; stock prices dropped.
2. Effects of the Great Depression: rich people became poor; companies went out of business; workers lost their jobs; banks closed; people went broke, lost their homes, and didn't have enough to eat.
3. Some parts of the U.S. were called the Dust Bowl because there was little rain that year.
4. Roosevelt defeated Hoover in 1932 because Hoover didn't feel that the government should take over and end the depression and Roosevelt did.

5. Besides the New Deal, the WPA and Social Security helped end the Great Depression. Answers will vary.

Electric Cars

Page 78: Questions
1. Cars ran on electric batteries around 1900.
2. The first electric cars could go 20 or 30 miles per hour.
3. The self-starter made gas-powered cars more popular.
4. Noel Perrin's car could barely reach 30 miles per hour going up a hill, and it ran out of power quickly.
5. The 1992 world record was 831.8 miles in 24 hours.

Page 79: Making Predictions
1–3 Answers will vary.

Pride of the Giants

Page 85: Questions
1. The Cahuilla tribe came from southern California.
2. John Meyers was called "Chief" because of his Native American background.
3. Meyers joined the New York Giants in 1908.
4. McGraw changed the public's feelings toward baseball players and also treated his players with respect.
5. Meyers was usually the Giants' catcher.

Page 85: Fact vs. Opinion
1–3 Answers will vary.

Life Beneath a Blanket of Snow

Page 91: Questions
1. The largest animal living under the snow is the red squirrel.
2. Meadow voles must eat often to keep up their body heat.
3. Because of shared nests, sickness can spread from one animal to another and predators can find the nest easier because of the strong smell.
4. The best hunter under the snow is the weasel.
5. Shrews sniff and use their whiskers and ears to find their prey.
6. Snow fleas are called springtails because they can jump.

Page 91: Applying Passage Elements
1. Snow acts as a blanket to keep the ground warm during the winter.
2. Meadow voles and their relatives keep each other warm when sleeping. They keep the nest warm when the animals take turns leaving the nest to feed.
3. Light can get through the snow and make the ground warm and moist. This lets plants live and grow.